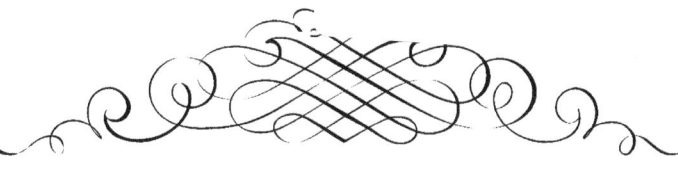

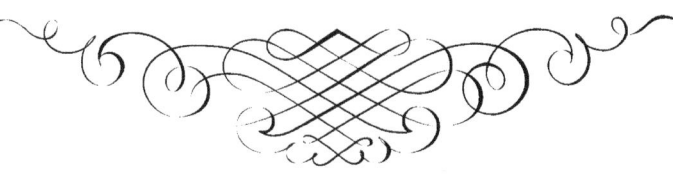

ISBN 978-0-332-56525-5
PIBN 11240988

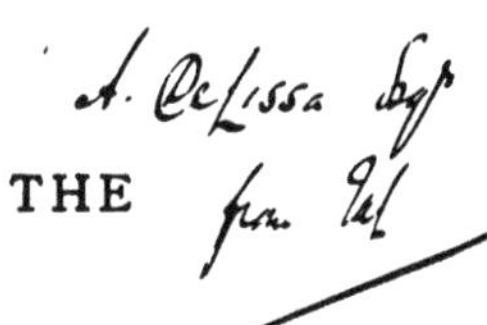

THE

WEALTH AND PROGRESS

OF

NEW SOUTH WALES

1890-91.

BY

T. A. COGHLAN, A.M., Inst. C.E.,
GOVERNMENT STATISTICIAN.

FIFTH ISSUE.

Sydney:
GEORGE STEPHEN CHAPMAN, ACTING GOVERNMENT PRINTER, PHILLIP-STREET.
E. A. PETHERICK & CO., 333, GEORGE-STREET
AND AT
MELBOURNE, ADELAIDE, AND LONDON.

1891.

855 66—91

PREFACE TO THE FIFTH ISSUE.

THE matter contained in former issues of this work has been enlarged, so that the present volume deals with nearly every subject in regard to which statistics have hitherto been obtained. Under the provisions of the Industrial Census an inquiry is in progress concerning the cost of production in various industries, the displacement of labour by machinery, the employment of women and children, and other kindred topics. This inquiry, however, has not been sufficiently advanced to enable an extended reference being made to these subjects, but it is hoped that much interesting information will be available for the next edition.

It has been thought desirable to limit, except in special cases, the period covered by the tables to ten years. Should more detailed figures be required than are given in the text, these will be found in the "Statistical Register." The necessity of comparing the progress of New South Wales with that of the other Colonies, except on the most important points, is obviated by the publication of "The Seven Colonies of Australasia," which deals with the Colonies as a whole, as well as with their individual resources.

In preparing a work of this kind a difficulty is always experienced in making the information it contains interesting to persons outside the Colony who are not concerned about the details of local affairs, and at the same time to those living in the Colony who require such details. It is believed that in the present instance the difficulty has been fairly met. Every care has been taken to correct such errors as may have passed through previous editions, and to keep this issue free from them. If, however, any such should be discovered, it would be deemed a favour if their nature and position were pointed out.

Sydney, 24th November, 1891.

CONTENTS.

PART I.

Historical Sketch.

THE Columbus of Australia was undoubtedly Don Pedro Fernandez de Quiros, a Spanish nobleman and navigator, who sailed in 1606 from Lima, in Peru, for the express purpose of discovering a southern continent, in the existence of which he had repeatedly expressed his confident belief. Like Columbus, he failed to sight the main land, but having succeeded in reaching a coast that stretched for a great distance north and south, he mistook it for the continent in search of which he had come, and named the land Australia del Espiritu Santo. This was one of the islands of the New Hebrides group, still known as Espiritu Santo. Sickness and discontent led to a mutiny on De Quiros' vessel, the sailors insisting so vehemently on returning to Peru, that the Admiral was forced to abandon the further prosecution of his discoveries. In company with De Quiros was Luiz Vaez de Torres, in command of another ship, named the Almirante, who after parting company with De Quiros, discovered that Espiritu Santo was only an island. Torres, being afterwards forced to bear up for the Philippines for the purpose of refitting, discovered and sailed through the strait which now bears his name, and even sighted Cape York, which he supposed to be only another of the many small islands abounding in the neighbourhood. Expedition of De Quiros.

Prior to the expedition from Lima, it is possible this continent was visited by navigators, the records of whose voyages have not been transmitted to us. The chart of Marco Polo would favour the supposition that the existence of a great south land was known to the Chinese; and, though the claims of De Gonneville to have discovered Australia as early as 1504 are not tenable, charts bearing the date of 1542 exist whereon is marked an extensive territory to which the name of Great Java was given, and which might have been intended to represent the north-west coast of Australia. But however valid these claims may be the merit of the Spaniard is no wise lessened. It is certain that previous Earliest charts navigators endeavoured to conceal their discoveries, and no really authentic records remain to show how far those discoveries extended.

ch
overers.

About the time of De Quiros' voyage the Dutch sent out an expedition from Bantam in a small vessel called the Duyfhen, which discovered the Gulf of Carpentaria. Some of the crew landed, and are believed to have been the first Europeans who trod the shore of Australia. Being attacked by the natives they were forced to abandon any attempt to explore the country; and after naming the place Cape Keerweer, or Turn-again, they departed, apparently in total ignorance of the fact that they had landed on the northern shore of a great continent. Other Dutch adventurers discovered, during the following twenty years, various parts of the coast. Dirk Hartog, in 1616, landed on the island now bearing his name. Jan Carstens, in command of the yachts Pera and Arnhem, in 1623 sailed along the northern shores, for a long time called Arnhem's land. About the same time another Dutchman, Captain Edel, explored the greater part of the western coast. In 1622 a Dutch vessel, the Leeuwin, coasted along the south-west shore, from the cape which has been named after her, to King George's Sound; and in 1627 Peter Nuyts discovered the Great Australian Bight. Other Dutch explorers were Pelsart, who was shipwrecked on Houtman's Abrolhos in 1629, and Tasman, the discoverer of Tasmania and New Zealand.

pier's
dition.

Dampier, an English buccaneer and discoverer, also explored the west coast, from Shark Bay to Dampier's Archipelago, and the north-west coast, as far as Roebuck Bay, a distance of about nine hundred miles. This was in 1699, and he appears to have landed in several places. On his return he published an account of what he had seen. He described the country as sterile in the extreme, and almost devoid of animals, the only one of any importance somewhat resembling a racoon, a strange creature, which used only its hind legs, and, instead of walking, advanced by great bounds, or leaps, of twelve or fifteen feet at a time. This is the first notice of the kangaroo which has reached us. Dampier also describes the aboriginal inhabitants of the north-west coast in terms the reverse of favourable, which, however, apply equally to the natives of New South Wales as first seen by Captain Cook. The mention of this last distinguished man brings the narrative to the period when the real history of New South Wales, and therewith that of Australia, begins.

Voyage of Captain Cook.

The great voyage of James Cook, in 1769-70, was primarily undertaken for the purpose of observing the transit of Venus, but his instructions also mention among its objects the making of further geographical discoveries. The ship in which Cook sailed was a small vessel of 320 tons, carrying twenty-two guns. Originally built for service as a collier, she was selected for the use of the expedition on account of her unusually strong construction. This craft had been chosen by Cook himself, and was renamed the Endeavour, in allusion to the great work which her commander was setting out to achieve. Mr. Green was to conduct the astronomical observations, and Sir Joseph Banks and Dr. Solander were appointed botanists to the expedition. After successfully observing the Transit from the island of Tahiti, or Otaheite, as Cook wrote it, the Endeavour's head was turned south, and then north-west, beating about the Pacific in search of the eastern coast of the great continent, whose western shores had been so long known to the Dutch. After circumnavigating, and minutely surveying New Zealand, Cook stood due west, and in three weeks sighted the cliffs of New Holland, as Australia was then called.

The Endeavour.

Cook anchors in Botany Bay.

The first important point observed was Cape Howe, which was so named by Cook. After passing and naming Mount Dromedary, the Pigeon House, Point Upright, and Cape St. George, on the 28th April, 1770, Botany Bay was discovered, which, as it apppeared to offer a suitable anchorage, the Endeavour entered, and dropped anchor. The ship brought-to opposite a group of natives, who were cooking over a fire. Cook and his crew, unacquainted with the character of the Australian aborigines, were not a little astonished that these natives took no notice of them or their proceedings

Even the splash of the anchor in the water and the noise of the cable running out through the hawse-hole in no way disturbed them at their occupation, or caused them to evince the slightest curiosity. But as the captain of the Endeavour ordered out the pinnace and prepared to land, the natives threw off their nonchalance; for on the boat approaching the shore two men, each armed with a bundle of spears, presented themselves on a projecting rock and made threatening signs to the strangers. It is interesting to note that the ingenious "wommera," or throwing stick, which is peculiar to Australia, was first observed on this occasion. As these men were evidently determined to oppose any attempt at landing, a musket was discharged between them, in the hope that they would be frightened by the noise, but it produced no effect beyond causing one of them to drop his bundle of spears, of which, however, he immediately re-possessed himself, and the two natives still preserved the same menacing attitude. One of them at last cast a stone towards the boat, which earned him a charge of small shot in the leg. Nothing daunted, the two men ran back into the bush, and presently returned furnished with shields made of bark, with which to protect themselves from the firearms of the crew. The intrepidity of these men is certainly worthy of passing notice. Unlike the American Indians, who supposed Columbus and his crew to be supernatural beings, and their ships in some way endowed with life, and who were thrown into convulsions of terror by the first discharge of firearms which they witnessed, these Australians were neither excited to wonder by the ship nor overawed by the superior number and unknown weapons of the strangers. Cook examined the bay in the pinnace, and landed several times; but by no endeavour could he induce the natives to hold any friendly communication with him. The well-known circumstance of the great variety of new plants here obtained, from which Botany Bay derives its name, should not be passed over. Before quitting the bay the ceremony was performed of hoisting the Union Jack, first on the south shore and then near the north head, thus taking formal possession of the territory for the British Crown.

Encounter with the Aborigines.

After leaving Botany Bay Cook sailed northward. He saw and named Port Jackson, but, for some unexplained reason, forebore to enter the finest natural harbour in Australia. Broken Bay was also seen, but the vessel did not come to an anchor till Moreton Bay was reached. Still sailing northward, and taking notes, as he proceeded, for a rough chart of the coast, Cook passed over 1,300 miles without the occurrence of any event worthy of being chronicled, till suddenly one night at 11 o'clock the water was found to shoal, without any sign of breakers or land. While Cook was speculating on the cause of this phenomenon, and was in the act of ordering out the boats to take soundings, the Endeavour struck heavily, and fell over so much that the guns, spare cables, and other heavy gear had to be at once thrown overboard to lighten the ship. As day broke, attempts were made to float the vessel off with the morning tide; but these were unsuccessful. The water was rising so rapidly in the hold that with four pumps constantly going the crew could hardly keep it in check. At length one of the midshipmen suggested the device of "fothering," which he had seen practised in the West Indies. This consists in passing a sail, attached to cords, under the vessel's keel, in such a manner that the suction of the leak may draw the canvas into the aperture, and thus partially stop the vent. This was performed with great success, and the vessel was floated off with the evening tide. The land was soon after made, near the mouth of a small river, which Cook called after the ship, the "Endeavour River." A headland close by he named Cape Tribulation. The ship was steered into the river, and there careened and thoroughly repaired. Cook afterwards completed the survey of the east coast, to which he gave the name of New South Wales, and returned by way of Torres Straits and the Indian Ocean.

Port Jackson seen and named.

The Endeavour in danger.

The favourable reports brought to England by the Endeavour on her return, and the graphic account of his voyage published by Cook, together with the fact that Great Britain had just lost her North American Colonies, by their successful rebellion, turned all eyes to Australia, or New Holland, as it continued to be called. The difficulty of disposing of their criminal population was only

Return of the Endeavour.

one of the causes which determined the Government of the day to found the colony of New South Wales; for it will become evident, as the narrative proceeds, that all concerned felt they were engaged in founding a new home in the Southern Hemisphere for the British people, and that visions of even greater progress than has yet been attained filled the minds, not only of Viscount Sydney and Governor Phillip, but also of many reflecting persons in the Colony itself. The truth of this view is amply demonstrated by the testimony of several contemporary writers; but it is nowhere more strongly emphasized than in the lines entitled "The Visit of Hope to Sydney Cove," the author of which was Darwin, whose "Botanic Garden" is well known. The lines have been often quoted; but they contain so distinct a prophecy of the greatness to which the Colony has attained that they may be appropriately introduced:

Darwin's prophetic lines.

Where Sydney Cove her lucid bosom swells,
Courts her young navies and the storm repels;
High on a rock amid the troubled air
Hope stood sublime and waved her golden hair,
Calmed with her rosy smile the tossing deep,
And with sweet accents charmed the winds to sleep;
To each wild plain she stretched her snowy hand,
High waving wood and sea-encircled strand.
'Hear me,' she cried, 'ye rising realms! Record
'Time's opening scene and Truth's unerring word.
'*There* shall broad streets their stately walls extend,
'The circus widen and the crescent bend;
'*There*, ray'd from cities o'er the cultured land,
'Shall bright canals, and solid roads expand,
'*There* the proud arch, Colossus-like, bestride
'Yon glittering stream, and bound the chafing tide;
'Embellished villas crown the landscape scene,
'Farms wave with gold and orchards blush between.
'*There* shall tall spires, and dome-capped towers ascend,
'And piers and quays their massy structure blend;
'While with each breeze approaching vessels glide,
'And northern treasures dance on every tide.'
Then ceased the nymph—tumultuous echoes roar—
And joy's loud voice was heard from shore to shore—
Her graceful steps descending pressed the plain,
And Peace and Art and Labour joined her train.

Such words as these could not have been inspired by the prospect of the "big gaol growing still bigger," which some foreign writers assert was all the Colony was ever expected to become. On the contrary they mark the prescience of those who, one hundred years ago, saw clearly what a great enterprise was being then initiated.

It was in the early part of 1787 that Viscount Sydney, Secretary of State for the Colonies, determined to plant a colony in New South Wales, and by May of that year the "First Fleet" had been assembled. It consisted of the 20-gun frigate Sirius; the armed tender Supply; three store ships—the Golden Grove, Fishburn, and Borrowdale; and six transports—the Alexander, Scarborough, Lady Penrhyn, Prince of Wales, Friendship, and Charlotte. The largest of these vessels measured only 450 tons, and the smallest was no more than 270 tons. On board of the six transports were packed no fewer than 564 men and 192 women, all prisoners who had been sentenced to expatriation. There were also carried 168 marines and 10 officers, commissioned and non-commissioned. These, with 5 medical men, a few mechanics, and 40 women, wives of marines, together with 13 children, the offspring of the convicts, made up the total number of persons despatched to found the Colony. Captain Phillip, R.N., was placed in command of the expedition, and also bore a commission as Governor and Captain-General of New South Wales. Second in command was Captain John Hunter, of the Sirius, and Mr. David Collins accompanied the expedition as Judge Advocate.

Viscount Sydney determines to found the Colony.

The fleet sailed at the end of May, 1787, and after calling at Rio Janeiro, arrived in Botany Bay in the beginning of January, 1788. A cursory examination convinced Captain Phillip that a more unsuitable site for a new settlement could hardly have been chosen than the shores of this bay. Despite the profusion of new plants which had so delighted Banks and Solander, the neighbourhood of Botany Bay is by no means fertile. The scarcity of good water was a further disadvantage, while the bay itself was so shallow as to forbid the ships approaching the shore, which would

Sailing and arrival of the "First Fleet."

have necessitated the erection of piers and jetties of great length. It was besides exposed to the full swell of the Pacific, being destitute of bays, creeks, or coves of any kind. The Governor accordingly determined to explore the coast in search of a more suitable site for the settlement. After proceeding with three of the boats about nine miles, he found himself abreast of the entrance of Port Jackson, which Cook had supposed to be a mere shallow indentation of the land, fit for nothing but a landing-place for boats. Undeterred by this opinion, Phillip rounded the South Head and soon saw opening before him the whole expanse of one of the finest harbours in the world. For miles to the west stretched the peaceful waters of Port Jackson, which must have delighted the minds of the explorers, disheartened as they had been by the appearance and surroundings of Botany Bay. In place of the stunted scrub which formed the greater part of the vegetation of that locality, Port Jackson was found to be surrounded by a thick forest of noble trees, which extended to the water's edge, and promised an abundant supply of timber for building. In place of the open roadstead at Botany a countless succession of bays and inlets opened on the astonished gaze of the hardy navigators as they proceeded up the harbour. Deep water was found to extend to the very base of the rocks, thus obviating any necessity for expensive wharves, the construction of which must have occupied the little community for many months, to the neglect of more immediately pressing wants.

Discovery of Port Jackson.

Sydney Cove selected for settlement.

The Governor's choice of the site of the present metropolis of Australasia was determined by the fact that an apparently perennial stream of the purest water was found discharging itself into a beautiful sandy cove, about six miles from the entrance, which was named Sydney Cove, in honour of the statesman under whose auspices the enterprise had been undertaken. Before finally deciding on this site, Captain Phillip spent three days in exploring the various bays, but was confirmed in his original choice by the fact that no such stream of water had been found elsewhere, though in other respects numerous positions equally eligible presented themselves.

La Pérouse's Expedition.

Returning immediately to Botany, preparations were made for bringing the colony round to Sydney Cove, when as the fleet were standing out of the bay an interesting incident occurred. Two strange vessels evidently making for the entrance were discerned in the offing. Captain Phillip went out in the Supply to meet the strangers, who proved to be a French exploring party under the command of Jean François Galaup, Comte de la Pérouse, their vessels being the frigates Astrolabe and Boussole. After an interchange of courtesies, the French were left to refresh and refit in Botany Bay. They stayed there till March, 1788, and buried one of their company on shore—Father le Receveur, of the Order of St. Francis, the naturalist of the expedition, who died of wounds received in an encounter with the natives of the South Seas. His tomb is still extant at La Pérouse, near the north head of Botany Bay, where also a monument was placed, in the year 1825, to the memory of the commander of the expedition, who was shipwrecked and whose crew were murdered on the Santa Cruz Islands. The monument was erected by Messrs. De Bougainville and Ducampier, commanding the French war vessels, Thétis and Espérance, then lying in Port Jackson.

Foundation of the Colony.

On Captain Phillip's arrival in Sydney Harbour, on the memorable 26th January, 1788, the ships anchored in the Cove, and preparations were at once made for landing the colonists. The clearing of the ground in the vicinity, and along the banks of the little stream, was commenced, and when a sufficient space had thus been obtained a flagstaff was erected, and the Union Jack run up. After the firing of three volleys by the marines, the Governor read his commission, and addressed words of counsel, warning, and encouragement to the prisoners, the ceremony closing with general festivity. Arduous labour succeeded this scene, for it was well understood that unless the settlers could raise supplies for themselves, the existence of the Colony would be precarious, as the store of provisions in their possession was calculated to last only a very short time.

Farming first attempted.

Accordingly ground was cleared at the head of Farm Cove, adjoining the settlement, and an attempt made to raise wheat, but time has shown that the soil in the immediate neighbourhood of Sydney is not suited to the cultivation of this cereal, and even if a good crop had been obtained the colonists must have starved while it was maturing. No food worth mentioning was procured from the land, and the little community was on the brink of starvation, when a ship arrived with another batch of colonists, but without stores. This brought matters to a climax, whereupon Governor Phillip sent the Sirius to the Capo Colony, and the Supply to Batavia, to procure provisions, which, however, could only be obtained in insufficient quantity, so that in a few weeks after the return of these vessels the state of affairs became as bad as before, and starvation again stared the Colony in the face. Under these circumstances, everyone, including the Governor himself, was placed on short allowance, and even the sheep and cattle which had been reserved for breeding purposes were killed for food. In this aspect of affairs the Governor bethought himself of Norfolk Island, whither, shortly after his arrival, he had sent Lieutenant Philip Gidley King, of the Sirius, to establish a branch colony. A detachment of 200 convicts, with a guard of 70 marines, was, therefore, despatched to the island. On arrival they found that King and his men had cleared a considerable portion of land, and had succeeded in raising an abundant crop. But the Sirius, in which the new detachment sailed, was wrecked on a reef off the island, so that no supplies were procured thence at that time.

The "Second Fleet."

When the prospects of the settlement at Sydney Cove had reached their gloomiest, the "Second Fleet," consisting of three store-ships, arrived, and snatched the Colony from the very brink of destruction by famine. This tided over the difficulty, and so great a privation of food was never again experienced. Fresh difficulties, however, beset the settlers by the arrival of some shiploads of immigrants, most of whom were in a sick and dying condition. Of 1,700 men and women who had been embarked,

200 died on the voyage, and several hundred more were found to be *in extremis* on arrival. In the midst of these horrors the Governor's responsibilities were further increased by the attempts of some of the prisoners to escape from the Colony. Some took to the bush, others stole boats and put to sea, intending to reach the Dutch settlements in the Indian Ocean. Daring as this latter attempt may appear, it was in one instance successful; two men and a woman, in an open boat, succeeded in reaching Timor, where they were imprisoned and sent back to Sydney on the first opportunity. Numerous efforts were made to escape from the settlement by land, the ignorance of the convicts being such that many imagined they could walk overland to China, and not a few perished in the bush while making the attempt. Escape of prisoners.

Governor Phillip's health gave way under the care and anxieties of his office, and in 1792 he returned to England, where in reward for his exertions in founding the Colony he received a pension, and died at an advanced age. Major Grose and Captain Paterson, officers in charge of the military, administered the Government till the arrival of his successor. In 1795, Captain Hunter, who after the loss of the Sirius had gone to England, arrived as the second Governor. With the arrival of Governor Hunter affairs took a new turn. He brought out a number of free settlers, mostly farming men; and some fine alluvial land having been discovered on the banks of the Hawkesbury, farming was successfully started, and in a short time more than 6,000 acres were under crops of wheat and maize. The attempts to introduce cattle were for a time unsuccessful, but in 1796 a herd of 60 head was discovered at the "Cowpastures," near Camden. These were the descendants of some cattle which had strayed from the settlement several years before. Though their quality was found to have deteriorated, they proved a very welcome addition to the live stock of the settlement. In 1800, when Captain Hunter left the Colony, the population was over 6,000; attempts had been made to penetrate into the interior, but without success; the Hunter River and its coal mines

Departure of Phillip.

Farming enterprise initiated.

had been discovered, and the mines were being worked by a detachment of prisoners; the city of Newcastle had been founded, and the New South Wales Corps, a military body enlisted for service in the colony (the first detachments of which had arrived in 1790), formed an efficient garrison, and guard over the more refractory prisoners. During Governor Hunter's term of office Bass and Flinders minutely examined the coast to the south of Sydney, in a small boat only 9 feet over all; and the former discovered the strait which bears his name, thus proving Tasmania to be an island, and not the southern extremity of the continent, as previously supposed.

Newcastle founded.

Governor King.

The next Governor was Philip Gidley King, previously mentioned as the Lieutenant of the Sirius, who was despatched by Phillip to found a settlement on Norfolk Island. Though all fears of famine had now disappeared, Governor King soon found himself involved in difficulties of a scarcely less distressing nature. To explain these it will be necessary to describe the constitution of the New South Wales Corps. This body had been specially raised for service in the Colony, the officers of the King's regiments not unnaturally objecting to be sent to such a far distant settlement, where they knew that they would find no intellectual occupation, and where their sole work would consist in acting as a prison guard, or, at most, in making a few raids, in alleged reprisals for the misdeeds of the illused, and often sorely provoked, aborigines. As a military guard of some sort was necessary, this corps was raised, and a few enterprising spirits—many of whom had never served before—were induced to accept commissions, with the view of obtaining grants of land and making their fortunes in the Colony. Unfortunately, the readiest means to this end was found in the import trade, and as rum was in great request, the officers of the New South Wales Corps became importers of that spirit in large quantities, and even set up private stills, in defiance of a Government order to the contrary. As an instance of the enormous profits made in this trade, it may be mentioned

Traffic in spirits.

that the retail price of rum, on the arrival of Governor King, was £2 per gallon, 7s. 6d. to 10s. being the utmost cost to the importer. To put a stop to this state of things—in which the officials and rulers of the Colony were really doing their best to debase those committed to their charge—a clause was inserted in the instructions of the new Governor, as follows:—"You are to order and direct that no spirits be landed from any vessel coming to Port Jackson without your consent." In consequence of this order, King proceeded to act promptly, and when he left the Colony in 1806, he had sent away no less than 69,484 gallons of spirits, and 31,293 gallons of wine. The quantity which he allowed to be landed was sold, by his order, at various prices, the maximum not exceeding 10s. per gallon. It may be easily imagined what a storm such vigorous proceedings caused among the importers, and how embittered the officers of the New South Wales Corps became against the Government.

Suppression of the "Rum currency."

During King's time a serious mutiny occurred among the prisoners. The more tractable of the convicts were "assigned" as servants to the settlers, and engaged in working the farms and squattages, but the more desperate characters, made desperate in many instances by the treatment they received, were worked on the roads, in chain-gangs. A party of over 300 of these chain-gang men was employed at Castlehill, on the road between Parramatta and Windsor. These men, taking advantage of the small number of their guard, abandoned their work, managed to remove their irons, seized some firearms, and marched towards the Hawkesbury, expecting to be reinforced by the men employed in that neighbourhood. Major Johnston, second in command of the New South Wales Corps, pursued them, however, with only twenty men, and on coming up with them, charged with such precipitation that the mutineers were fain to lay down their arms and beg for mercy. Three or four of the ringleaders were afterwards hanged, and the rest were permitted to return to their duty on undertaking to be of good conduct for the future.

The Castlehill Revolt.

Initiation of wool-growing.

An event of the utmost importance to the Colony also took place under the administration of Governor King. This was the initiation of wool-growing. John Macarthur, who had held a commission as captain in the New South Wales Corps, procured, by great trouble and perseverance, some Spanish merinos, and having obtained a grant of 10,000 acres of land across the Cowpasture River, which estate he named "Camden," commenced the growth of wool on a large scale. In a short time his enterprise showed every sign of a successful issue, to the great benefit of the Colony generally, and his own personal advantage. In spite of these evident signs of material progress Governor King was so worn out with the conflicts caused by his endeavours to suppress the rum traffic, and in such constant collision with the officers of the New South Wales Corps on that account, that he seized the first opportunity of leaving the Colony, and was succeeded in the Government in 1806, by William Bligh, a post-captain in the navy.

Governor Bligh.

Governor Bligh was a distinguished naval officer. His wonderful voyage after the Mutiny of the Bounty had caused the Imperial Government to entertain a high opinion of his conduct, as well as his courage and determination. His services were numerous, and he had been publicly thanked by Lord Nelson, after the bombardment of Copenhagen, for the gallantry and skill which he displayed on that occasion. Hence he was selected as a fit man to crush the clique of officers engaged in the rum traffic, and to purify official life in the Colony. King had been only partially successful in this direction, and the British Government gave the strictest injunctions to Captain Bligh to stop the trade in spirits. Accordingly in February, 1807, he issued the following general order:—"His Excellency the Governor laments to find by his late visit through the Colony that the most calamitous evils have been produced by persons bartering, or paying, spirits for grain of all kinds, and the necessaries of life in general, and to labourers for their hire; such proceedings depressing the industrious and depriving the settlers of their comforts. In order, therefore, to remedy these grievous complaints, and to relieve the inhabitants, who have suffered by the traffic, he feels it his duty to put a total stop to this barter in future, and to prohibit the exchange of spirits or other liquors as payment for grain, animal food, wearing apparel, or any other commodity whatsoever, to all descriptions of persons in the Colony and its dependencies."

This order is in itself sufficient to indicate to what fearful lengths the "rum currency" had been carried. Naturally it would have been expected that all respectable people, the military and ex-military especially, would have joined the Governor heart and soul in his efforts to put a stop to the traffic, and induce a more healthy state of things. Such, however, was not the case; and the struggle in respect to the illicit trade continued throughout the whole period of Bligh's governorship.

Embittered relations between the Governor and settlers.

Other matters embittered the relations between the Governor and the colonists, and in these Bligh was not so obviously in the right as in his attempt to put down the contraband traffic in spirits. The contest reached its climax on the arrest of John Macarthur, whose efforts to promote the growth of wool have been alluded to. That gentleman had become specially obnoxious to the Governor; and as he was also the chief trader in the community, he was selected as a scapegoat for the sins of the rest. Matters were brought to a crisis in the following manner, though the immediate circumstances of his prosecution had no direct connection with the barter of spirits. Mr. Macarthur had been part owner of a vessel that traded to Tahiti for salt pork and other articles, for the supply of the Colony. At a time when this vessel was lying in Port Jackson, he received a summons from Mr. Atkins, the Judge Advocate—that is, Chief Justice—to appear before him to answer to a complaint on the part of the crew of his vessel of withholding from them their wages, in consequence of which they alleged that they had been compelled to break through the port regulations, by coming ashore without special order. Macarthur returned an answer in writing, explanatory of his conduct in the matter, but did not obey the summons by appearing in person. This was construed to be an act of contumacy, which some attributed to a feeling of personal resentment towards the Governor, engendered by the action of the latter against the "rum currency."

Arrest of Macarthur.

A warrant was accordingly issued for Macarthur's apprehension, and on the 25th January, 1808, he was brought before the Judge Advocate and a military jury of six, consisting of officers of the New South Wales Corps—such being at the time the composition of the Supreme Court of the Colony. Mr. Macarthur objected to the Judge Advocate sitting on his trial, on the ground that he bore him personal ill-feeling, for which assertion it would appear that there was some foundation, especially as Atkins's adviser throughout the whole proceedings was one George Crossley, a transported attorney, who is believed to have been an enemy of Macarthur. Be this as it may, the Judge Advocate refused to abdicate his position, and the Governor declined to supersede him, for which, indeed, he had no authority, Atkins having been appointed by the British Government.

Conduct of the military officers.

At this juncture the Governor summoned the six officers to his presence, to explain their conduct in supporting Macarthur's protest and refusing to sit with the Judge Advocate, but they declined to obey. The Governor also sent several times during the next day to Major Johnston, the Commandant, at his residence at Annandale, asking him to confer with him as to the conduct of his subordinates. That officer, however, declined to come to town, on the plea of ill-health. This was an evident subterfuge, for between 6 and 7 p.m. on the same day (the Anniversary of the foundation of the Colony) he suddenly made his appearance in the Barrack Square, where, if we may believe his statement, he found everything in a state of ferment and confusion, and himself beset with the clamours of a number of the leading inhabitants, civil as well as military, calling upon him to put the Governor under arrest. He accordingly marched at the head of his regiment, with drums beating and colours flying, to Government House, and Governor Bligh was put in close confinement in his own residence. Johnston thereupon assumed the Government, his first act being to suspend the Judge Advocate, the Commissary, the Provost-marshal, the Chaplain, and other principal officials, and to appoint others to act in their place.

Deposition of Bligh.

Major Johnston continued to administer the Government till his Lieutenant-Colonel (Foveaux) superseded him, as the senior officer in the Colony, and eventually Colonel Paterson came from Tasmania and assumed the direction of affairs. Both these officers approved Johnston's proceedings, but the latter set Bligh at liberty after a detention of twelve months, on condition of his proceeding straight to England, in a vessel which was then ready to sail. Bligh promised to do so, but called at Tasmania on his way, where the military authorities attempted to detain him, but he escaped their hands.

News of the affair had meanwhile reached England, and the Government was very much concerned at the proceedings of the military, and had despatched Lieutenant-General Macquarie to the Colony as Governor. His instructions were to reinstate Governor Bligh for twenty-four hours, to assume the government himself, and to send Johnston home under close arrest. Bligh could not be reinstated, as he had left Sydney; so Macquarie's first act was to arrest Major Johnston, who was subsequently tried by court-martial in England and sentenced to be cashiered, the leniency of the sentence being such as to call forth special remark from the Prince Regent, in a minute appended to the proceedings, distinctly stating that it was not to be drawn into a precedent. Johnston afterwards returned to the Colony, and died at his estate at Annandale.

Johnston tried by Court-martial.

With the arrival of Governor Macquarie, the colony entered on a stage of decided progress. The final abolition of the traffic in rum was followed by a marked improvement in the morals of the population. Schools were established, and the children, who had

Arrival of Macquarie.

hitherto grown up in total ignorance, were taught to read and write, and instructed in useful handicrafts. An impetus was given to exploration, and the dwellings of the settlers in the bush were much improved by the efforts of the Governor during the annual tours which he made through the Colony. Churches and public buildings were erected, asylums founded, and a better tone was given to society generally by the exertions of this philanthropic governor, ably seconded by the endeavours of his high-minded wife, who laboured to improve the condition of her sex and the children in the Colony. Among the many beneficial works undertaken by Macquarie, by far the most important was the road over the Mountains, via Lapstone Hill and Mount Victoria, to Bathurst. After many attempts to penetrate the Coast Range, it had been at last successfully crossed in 1813 by Blaxland, Wentworth, and Lawson, names memorable in the annals of the Colony. An account of the expedition will be found in another place.

Schools and Churches opened.

Macquarie's policy.

Another distinguishing feature in Governor Macquarie's policy, which was almost as beneficial as his efforts to instruct the population in religion and morality, and to open up the country, was the favour with which he treated the "emancipists," that is, those convicts who had become free by serving out their sentences. When it is remembered that the majority of those transported had been guilty of petty offences only, or of acts which in these days would scarcely be deemed offences at all, the Governor's determination to give every encouragement in the way of official recognition to emancipists must be strongly commended. To transport a person for a petty offence, to ostracise him for the rest of his life, and to extend the social ignominy to his children was in the highest degree unjust; and Governor Macquarie, as a humane man, set his face against the custom. In religious matters he showed a largeness of mind, in advance of public opinion, by removing, as far as lay in his power, the religious disabilities under which a large section of the colonists laboured. In 1821, after a longer term of office than has been allotted to any Governor either before or since,

"L. Macquarie, Esq.," as he modestly styles himself in the inscriptions on the public buildings he erected—discarding the prestige attaching to his military rank—left the Colony, to the regret of the entire population, and was succeeded by Sir Thomas Brisbane. Governor Brisbane.

The new Governor trod in the steps of his predecessor. He carried on the work of exploration, and in 1823 despatched Mr. Oxley, Surveyor-General, to survey Moreton Bay, Port Curtis, and other parts of the north-eastern coast-line. Oxley discovered a river debouching into Moreton Bay, which he named after the Governor, and a town was founded on its banks, also named Brisbane, which has become the capital of the Colony of Queensland. The Murray and Murrumbidgee Rivers were discovered soon afterwards by Hovell and Hume, who had formed an exploring party under the auspices of the Governor. The immigration of free settlers was much encouraged by Sir Thomas Brisbane, the result being the arrival of numbers of young men, many possessing capital, who became squatters, and soon wrought an important change in the Colony, by causing the costly Government farms to be broken up. As a consequence the wants of the community were more cheaply and better supplied by private enterprise. Censorship of the press, which had been strictly enforced up to this time, was abolished by Governor Brisbane, by proclamation dated 15th October, 1824. Trial by jury was introduced about the same period, by which the privilege of being tried by his peers was extended to every man; the assessors to the judge before that time having been chosen exclusively from officers in the army. Sir Francis Forbes, the first Chief Justice, was mainly instrumental in introducing this great and salutary change in the administration of the law. The first normally constituted jury sat at the November Quarter Sessions of 1824. An Act had also been passed by the Imperial Parliament, in 1823, which conferred another most important privilege on the Colony. It was provided that the Governor should nominate a Legislative Council of seven members, by whose advice he was to be guided. Previously to the appointment of

Free immigration encouraged.

Trial by Jury introduced.

this Council the Governor had been virtually absolute in power, the only check upon him being the public opinion of the colonists and the authority of the British Government, as represented by the Secretary of State for the Colonies. This Council of Seven was really the nucleus around which have gathered our present Constitution, and the liberties we now possess. It was the first step, in which, says the proverb, all the difficulty consists; and yet it was only after much agitation that even this modicum of justice was conceded.

Governor Darling.

The next Governor was Sir Ralph Darling, who, finding the Colony in the state of progress above described, by a series of blunders nearly succeeded in marring the beneficial result of the efforts of his predecessors. Arriving in Sydney in 1825, he soon became involved in very serious disputes with the colonists and the press. In order to meet the criticisims of the latter, a number of Acts were passed by the Council, which had the effect of stifling obnoxious comments for the time. One good result which sprang indirectly from these arbitrary acts was the enlargement, in 1828, of the Legislative Council from seven to fifteen members. The "Bushranging Act" was passed by this Council to put down a prevalent nuisance—the gangs of escaped prisoners who infested the principal roads and robbed allcomers without distinction.

Exploration.

The work of exploration made some progress in Governor Darling's time, the famous journeys of Captain Charles Sturt having been undertaken under his sanction. Other explorers were Allan Cunningham, Hume, and George Macleay, son of Alexander Macleay, the Colonial Secretary of that day.

French settlements suspected.

It was strongly suspected at this time that the French had an idea of forming settlements in Australia. French ships constantly appeared off the coast, ostensibly fitted out for the purpose of making geographical discoveries, but really, it was believed, to found a colony in any Australian territory which they might find unoccupied. To frustrate this suspected design, Darling despatched two expeditions, in 1826, to King George's Sound and to Western Port, in which neighbourhood it was surmised the French were hovering. To show that there was some ground for these fears, chimerical as they may now appear, it will be sufficient to quote the Governor's instructions to the officers in charge of the expeditions. He says:—"Should you find the French already in occupation, you will, notwithstanding, land the troops, and signify to the Frenchmen that their continuance with any view of establishing themselves, or colonization, will be considered an unjustifiable intrusion on his Britannic Majesty's possessions." No Frenchmen, however, were found at either of the places named, and settlements were therefore promptly formed at Western Port, King George's Sound, and Swan River, in Western Australia. When Governor Darling left the Colony in 1831, much progress had been achieved, in spite of the newspaper war, and his personal unpopularity, the population having reached over 51,000 for the whole of New South Wales, while the value of the total exports was £500,000.

New settlements formed.

The unpopularity of Governor Darling gave a factitious advantage to his successor, Sir Richard Bourke, even before his sterling qualities had become known. Sir Richard Bourke may be said to have been the real founder of our present free institutions, as, under his rule, the foundations of the Constitution we now enjoy were well and firmly laid, on the solid basis of full and equal rights to all, whatever their sect or belief, and whether emancipist or originally free. Immigrants began to arrive in large numbers, under a policy of assisted immigration, which was then first commenced. The first vote in aid of immigration was made by the Legislative Council at Bourke's suggestion, and the British Government doubled the amount given by the Colony. Under that system the first batches of immigrants to arrive were fifty young women from an orphan school in Cork, and fifty-nine mechanics from Scotland, whom the Rev. Dr. Lang introduced to aid him in building the Australian College.

Governor Bourke.

Assisted Immigration initiated.

Establishment of Religious Equality.

But the great achievement of Sir Richard Bourke's reign was the establishment of religious equality, and the breaking up of the monopoly of Government aid enjoyed by one communion. For his services in the cause of liberty, in this and other instances, a movement was set on foot after his departure—which took place in 1837, twelve months after the passing of the Church Act—to erect a statue of him in Sydney. Mr. Westmacott was commissioned to design a figure of Sir Richard in bronze, which, together with a granite pedestal, arrived in Sydney in 1842. It was erected where it now stands, at the Macquarie-street entrance to the Domain, opposite to the Public Library, and was unveiled on the 11th April, 1842. A general holiday was proclaimed on the occasion, and the assemblage was the most numerous which had up to that time gathered, for any purpose, in the metropolis. The succeeding Governor, Sir George Gipps, delivered a speech, laudatory of his predecessor, in whose steps he said he was resolved to tread. This was the first statue ever set up in Australia. It was no more than a fitting tribute to the virtues of the Governor, and serves even now as a reminder of the new order of things which he introduced.

Governor Gipps.

Free grants of land abolished.

Free grants of land were abolished at this time. All land in the settled districts was put up to auction at an upset price of 5s. per acre, except in the Port Phillip district, where £1 per acre was fixed as the lowest price, on account of the fitness of the land for agriculture. Beyond the settled districts the runs of the squatters, whose boundaries had hitherto been undefined, were marked out, and a small rent charged, in return for a partial fixity of tenure, the squatters having previously been liable to be turned out at any time.

Sir Thomas Mitchell's explorations.

The famous expeditions of Sir Thomas Mitchell, who had succeeded Oxley as Surveyor-General, were undertaken during Bourke's tenure of office. The first was to the north, as far as Liverpool Plains; in the second, the country between the Bogan and the Macquarie was surveyed; and in the third, the course of the Darling was traced, from its source to its junction with the

Murray. In the fourth, Mitchell discovered the rich lands of Victoria, which so enraptured him that he named the country Australia Felix.

Transportation abolished.

The reign of Sir George Gipps was marked by the abolition of transportation. The system of assigning convicts as servants to the settlers had ceased in 1838, and transportation itself was abolished by an Order in Council in 1840, though an attempt was made to revive it nine years later, an account of which will be given in due course. For many years previous to its abolition, the system of transportation was viewed with great disfavour by the colonists, and a powerful league was formed as early as 1830, to bring about its cessation. During the fifty-three years when New South Wales was open to receive British prisoners, the number of convicts sent to Sydney was 83,290, of whom 70,928 were males and 12,362 females. At the census of March, 1841, there were in the colony 18,248 persons, 14,718 males and 3,530 females, originally bond, but free by servitude or emancipation—and 24,489 persons, 21,367 males and 3,122 females, whose period of servitude had not expired. It would therefore appear that out of the total number of convicts sent to the Colony, 42,737 remained at the abolition of the system of transportation, while 40,553 had either been removed by death or had left the settlement.

Legislative Council established

The great event of Governor Gipps's time was undoubtedly the introduction of a new Constitution, by the establishment of a Legislative Council composed of thirty-six members, twelve nominated by the Crown, and the remainder elected by those who were placed on the electoral roll, a small property qualification being required. The new Council met on 1st August, 1843.

Commercial crisis.

A great commercial crisis followed soon after the introduction of the new Constitution, so that the subject of paramount importance which engaged the attention of the Legislature was the financial condition of the Colony. The cessation of transportation had, of course, caused the withdrawal of large sums of British money, which used to be spent on public works and in maintaining the prison establishments, and the military necessary to guard them; and much distress was also caused by an unwise interference on the part of the Imperial Government with the land laws. The price of sheep fell in the most alarming manner, 1s. per head being a common price. Mr. O'Brien, who occupied a run in the Yass District, at length hit upon the happy idea of boiling down sheep for tallow, for which at the time there was a good market in Europe; and the price of sheep was thus raised to 3s. or 4s. a head, five shillings' or six shillings' worth of tallow being obtainable by the process of boiling-down. The meat-canning industry was started at the same time by Mr. Sizar Elliott, of Charlotte-place, Sydney, but was not financially a success, although the preserved meats, it is said, were of excellent quality.

Boiling-down introduced.

The Legislative Council, imagining that the very existence of the Colony was threatened by the prevailing state of things, sought to "avert ruin"—to use their own expression—by "pledging the public credit," but the Governor refused the Royal assent to the Bill passed for that purpose. It was then proposed to issue Treasury Bills, but the Council would not entertain the idea. The failure of the Bank of Australia, the liability of whose shareholders was unlimited, brought affairs to a crisis, and it was proposed to relieve the shareholders of their liability by a Bill empowering the bank to dispose of its assets by a public lottery. No attempt was made to defend lotteries in general, but it was contended that if the goods of proprietors of the bank were seized under executions, the bailiff would be seen in possession of one house in ten in Sydney, and that the result would be a panic, which would annihilate the value of property. Under pressure of such an argument as this the "Lottery Bill" passed, but was disallowed by the British authorities. The necessity of the case was so urgent, however, that the lottery took place, and was successfully completed before the law officers of the Crown could interfere to prevent it. Desperate diseases require desperate remedies, and the lottery was, no doubt, in the main beneficial.

The Bank of Australia Lottery.

Separation of Port Phillip.

The first agitation for the formation of the Port Phillip district, into a separate colony, took place towards the close of Governor Gipps's administration, and the claims of the trans-Murray residents to govern themselves were ably advocated by Dr. Lang, one of the six members returned by the district since known as the Colony of Victoria. The entire population of what is now New South Wales, Victoria, and Queensland did not, at that period, exceed 150,000, of which the Port Phillip district contributed only 30,000. Their distance from the seat of Government, nevertheless, justified the demand of the Victorians for separation, which was conceded in 1851, to their great permanent benefit. A few years subsequently, on the 1st December, 1859, New South Wales was again dismembered, losing its northern province, which was constituted a separate colony, under the name of Queensland.

Governor Fitzroy.

Sir George Gipps was succeeded as Governor by Sir Charles Augustus Fitzroy, in whose tenure of office occurred several of the most important events in the history of Australia. These; in the order of their happening, were the final abolition of transportation in 1849; the separation of Victoria in 1851; the discovery of gold in the same year, and the establishment of Responsible Government in 1855–6.

Attempt to revive transportation.

Prisoners had ceased to be sent to New South Wales in 1840, but owing to the great depression of trade which prevailed during the rule of Governor Gipps, station properties, in 1849, so depreciated in value as to threaten ruin to their holders. Many of the squatters thought that a revival of the system of assigned servants would be beneficial to their interests, and, as it happened, the Imperial Government wished at that time to possess once more a large penal colony. Two powerful interests therefore were allied in an effort to re-establish transportation, and the system of assigned servants. To meet this threatening combination, a number of public meetings were held in Sydney under the auspices of the Anti-transportation League, and an overwhelming expression of popular opinion, most vehemently adverse to the scheme, was

Attempt to revive transportation.

given; nevertheless the British Government, under the advice of Sir Charles Fitzroy, persisted in their endeavours to force prisoners upon the unwilling inhabitants of the Colony. Several ship-loads of convicts were accordingly sent out, and an attempt was made to land them in the first instance at the new settlement at Port Phillip, now the City of Melbourne. The settlers there, however, would not tolerate the proceeding, whereupon the ships were compelled to leave for Sydney and Moreton Bay, now Brisbane. One of the vessels, named the Hashemy, cast anchor in Port Jackson, and there immediately ensued a serious contest between the inhabitants and the Executive. Immediately on the fact becoming publicly known that the Hashemy was off the Heads with convicts on board, the people of the metropolis were lashed into a fever of excitement, and a great public meeting was forthwith convened to consider what steps should be taken in this pressing emergency, as it then was universally considered.

Landing of convicts forbidden.

The result was that the Government saw fit to forbid the landing of the prisoners at that time, not caring to face the obloquy and public indignation which the adoption of any other course would certainly have brought upon them. As, however, the Hashemy could not be sent back, and as her prisoners could not permanently remain on board, a compromise was entered into. The prisoners were removed from the ship, and a large batch sent to Moreton Bay, in order that the settlers in that district might have an opportunity of hiring them. The remainder were allowed to be assigned to various persons in the Colony, though it was stipulated that the men should not be landed in Sydney, nor employed in the county of Cumberland.

The Legislative Council afterwards proceeded to take action in the matter, and a resolution was proposed, to the effect "that an address be presented to Her Majesty, praying that the Order in Council which declared New South Wales a Colony to which convicts might be sent be at once revoked." The adjournment of the Council was, however, agreed to before the motion could be put. In consequence of this partial shelving of the question an

Anti-transportation meetings

overwhelming public meeting was held, which petitioned the Council to use its utmost endeavours to prevent the revival of transportation in any form. The petition in a short time was signed by over 35,000 persons (more than two-thirds of the population of the metropolis). There was no resisting this manifestation of public opinion, and the pro-transportation members temporarily withdrew from the Council, whereupon the motion just stated was carried unanimously, and the address to the Queen was accordingly transmitted. The Order in Council was revoked, and transportation to New South Wales was thus, after many years of fruitful agitation, absolutely and finally abolished. The discovery of gold, which shortly followed, gave a new impetus to Australian society, and by developing the industry and wealth of the country rendered a return to the "prison times" for ever impossible.

Final abolition of transportation.

Discovery of gold.

The discovery of gold, in 1851, was by far the most important incident which had yet occurred in the annals of the country. An account of that remarkable event will be found in its proper place, but a few remarks are here called for as to the historical bearing of the great discovery. For many years previous to 1851 it was known that small quantities of gold had been found in the Bathurst district, and a colonist offered, during the administration of Sir George Gipps, to conduct the Government surveyors to a spot where he said gold existed in payable quantities. The project was, however, discouraged. The Colony was enjoying at the time a period of great prosperity, the depression of previous years having been successfully tided over; and it was probably thought unadvisable by the authorities to disturb the settled industries of the Colony, by the incitement to speculation which the gold fever would generate.

Gold fever

A few years passed away, and the recollection of the supposed gold discoveries was still fresh in men's minds. The prosperous days with which Governor Gipps's administration closed gave place to less fortunate times. Wages were low and work scarce, when suddenly the tale of the gold discovery was on every tongue.

The first nuggets.

In the early part of 1851 nuggets began to arrive in Sydney. They had been found in the vicinity of Bathurst, and their inspection by the public raised a wave of excitement, which affected all classes. It is not surprising that the possibility of amassing a fortune in a few months—which seemed indisputable from the presence of so many specimens of gold—should have induced hundreds of people of all ranks to abandon their employments, and set out for Bathurst. Nor could news of such a nature be confined within the Colony, and before many months had elapsed, the presence of gold in Australia was known all over the world. Then followed a mighty rush, from every quarter of the globe, of the most enterprising spirits, and those physically the most capable of enduring the unknown hardships before them, a circumstance on which Australians in the future will have occasion to congratulate themselves, for the splendid physique of the early colonists, already manifested in their sons and daughters, must undoubtedly become the inheritance of succeeding generations.

Effects of the discovery of gold.

The effect produced on society by this most fortunate discovery, was unpleasant enough at first. Stations throughout the Colony were left without hands, and all ordinary occupations were threatened with extinction, in consequence of the general exodus to the gold-fields. The squatters even petitioned the Government asking that martial law might be proclaimed, and all gold-digging peremptorily prohibited, in order that the regular industrial pursuits of the country should not be interfered with. The Governor however, refused to accede to this manifestly absurd request. So great a change in the circumstances of the country as that wrought within so short a time by the gold discovery, could not fail to affect many persons prejudicially. But after a few years, affairs resumed their normal course, and gold-mining found its level as one of the ordinary industries of the country. The great and permanent benefit which resulted from the influx of an enterprising population, the increase of wealth, and the consequent development of many other industries cannot be overrated. Nothing, since the introduction of wool-growing, has tended to develop its resources and to make so widely known the great advantages which Australia offers to the overcrowded populations of the Old World, as the discovery of gold in 1851. Since that era the country's progress has been by leaps and bounds, and Australia, which was before regarded merely as a far off dependency of Great Britain, now takes a place amongst the nations of the world, and is in a fair way of realizing the prophetic visions of future greatness which inspired its founders.

The series of events which led to the introduction of Responsible Government still remains to be touched upon. With a narrative of these, and an account of the actual inauguration of representative institutions—that is, with the political occurrences of 1855—this narrative will fitly close. All occurrences since that period have been treated as far as possible as matters of statistics, and will be found in their places in other parts of this volume. Events preceding Responsible Government.

For several years before the discovery of gold there had been growing up among the colonists a strong desire for a larger measure of self-government. The position of the Colony as a Crown dependency was a galling one, especially when the population became so largely increased through the outbreak of the gold-diggings. It was felt that the old system, which might have sufficed for the government of the people when their numbers were few was quite unsuitable for so large a community as New South Wales had now become. Hence the agitation that had already been commenced in favor of a free Constitution was continued with ever-increasing force. Desire for self-government.

In 1851 an Act was passed by the Imperial Parliament (13 and 14 Vict., No. 59) in accordance with which the dependency of Victoria was erected into a separate Colony, and a Constitution was to be conferred upon New South Wales. Accordingly, in 1852, a Select Committee of the Legislative Council was appointed to prepare a Constitution for the Colony in pursuance of the powers conferred by the Act above cited. The first result of the labours of the Committee was that a remonstrance was sent to the Secretary Victoria erected into a separate Colony.

of State for the Colonies, directed not so much against the old form of government, as against the amendment of the Constitution, which it was proposed to introduce. Subsequently, after much correspondence, and the receipt of a despatch from the Secretary for the Colonies, Sir John Pakington, practically conceding all that the colonists demanded, a Committee of the Legislative Council was appointed to draft the new Constitution. It consisted of the following gentlemen:—Messrs. Wentworth, Deas-Thomson, James Macarthur, Cowper, Martin, Macleay, Thurlow, Murray, and Dr. Douglas.

Framing of the Constitution Act.

The Committee, in their report, stated that they desired to have a form of government in perfect accordance with the British Constitution, and that a conservative element ought to be constantly present in the Constitution; and for this reason they declared they did not feel inclined to hazard the experiment of an Upper House based on the general elective franchise. To provide for this Upper House, the Committee gravely made the following recommendations. They proposed that an hereditary nobility should be created, leaving the Crown to decide whether or not to give the first holder of a title a seat for life, and that the aristocracy, to be thus established, should, in the future, elect a certain number of their order to form the higher branch of the Legislature. The question of federation was also noticed in the report:—"One of the most prominent legislative measures required by the Colony, and the colonies of the Australian group generally, is the establishment at once of a General Assembly, to make laws in relation to those intercolonial questions that have arisen, or may hereafter arise, among them. The questions which would claim the exercise of such a jurisdiction appear to be (1) Intercolonial tariffs and the coasting trade; (2) Railways, roads, canals, and other such works running through any two of the colonies; (3) Beacons and lighthouses on the coast; (4) Intercolonial gold regulations; (5) Postage between the said colonies; (6) A general court of appeal from the courts of such colonies; (7) A power to legislate on all other subjects which may be submitted to them by addresses from the Legislative Councils and Assemblies of the colonies, and to appropriate to any of the above mentioned objects the necessary sums of money, to be raised by a percentage on the revenues of all the colonies interested."

This report, when it was made public, caused a good deal of commotion in the metropolis, and at a public meeting held at the Royal Hotel, the following energetic protest against part of the scheme was adopted:—"That this meeting views with surprise, and strong feelings of opposition, the scheme proposed for the political constitution of the Colony, especially in respect to the establishment of an Upper House of Crown nominees, and a certain unprecedented order of colonial nobility;" and a further resolution decided that "a larger meeting should be held, in order to record a protest against a measure so repugnant to the feelings of British subjects, and fraught with so much danger to the political rights of the people." A more numerous meeting was accordingly held, the principal speakers at which were Mr. (now Sir Henry) Parkes, Messrs. Robert Johnson, Montefiore, Deniehy, Mort, Piddington, Flood, and Archdeacon McEncroe. Hereditary nobility proposal.

In spite of these meetings the Council proceeded to debate the Report as it stood. After a great deal of opposition to the retention of the "aristocratic" clause, and after the holding of more public meetings, the "Constitution Act," the basis of the rights we now enjoy, was finally passed on the 21st December, 1853. This Act established two Legislative Chambers. The first was to consist of not less than twenty-one natural-born or naturalized subjects, four-fifths of whom were to be persons not holding any office of profit under the Crown, who were to be nominated by the Governor in the name of the Queen. The first members were to hold their seats for five years, at the expiration of which period all appointments were to be made for life. The President was to be appointed by the Crown. The Legislative Assembly was to consist of fifty-four members, the qualification for the franchise being fixed as follows:—All inhabitants of full age, The new Constitution adopted.

being native-born or naturalized subjects of the British Crown, and not having been convicted of any crime—or, if convicted, pardoned—and having paid all rates and taxes for which they were liable, were placed in the condition precedent required for either voting or being elected to the Assembly, but they were required, in addition, to be qualified in the following respects:—As the owner of a freehold estate of £100; as householders, lodging occupiers, or leaseholders for three years at £10 per annum. To these were added boarders at £40 per annum, persons receiving £100 a year salary, and pasture-license holders for one year. Ministers of religion were declared incapable of being elected to the Legislature. Subsequent alterations to the Constitution Act removed that restriction, and made the principle of universal manhood suffrage the basis of the electoral system of the Colony, though non-resident property holders are still entitled to the franchise under certain conditions. A full account of the parliamentary system will be found under the chapter of this work treating of the constitution of the Colony.

Inauguration of Responsible Government.

Before the constitution could become operative it was necessary that the sanction of the British Parliament should be obtained, and for this purpose Wentworth, whose name has become identified with the establishment of responsible government, and E. Deas-Thomson, were authorized by the Council to proceed to England in order to do what lay in their power to facilitate the passage of the necessary measure. Accordingly, about the middle of the year 1855 an Act was passed by the Imperial Parliament empowering the Queen to assent to the Bill drawn up by the Council, and on the 19th December, the new Constitution was formally inaugurated by the new Governor-General, Sir William Denison, who had just succeeded Fitzroy, being sworn in afresh under a Commission from the Queen, which revoked his former credentials and appointed him "Governor-in-Chief" of New South Wales. The writs for the first parliament were issued on the 22nd May of the following year.

The succession of Governors from the foundation of the Colony to the present time is given in the following table:— **Succession of Governors.**

Names.	From	To
Captain A. Phillip, R.N.	26 Jan., 1788	10 Dec., 1792.
Captain F. Grose (Lieutenant-Governor) ...	11 Dec., 1792	12 Dec., 1794.
Captain Paterson, New South Wales Corps (Lieutenant-Governor).	13 Dec., 1794	1 Sept., 1795.
Captain Hunter, R.N.	7 Sept., 1795	27 Sept., 1800.
Captain P. G. King, R.N.	28 Sept., 1800	12 Aug., 1806.
Captain W. Bligh, R.N.	13 Aug., 1806	26 Jan., 1808.
During Governor Bligh's suspension the Government was successively administered by—		
Lieutenant-Colonel G. Johnston .... Lieutenant-Colonel Foveaux.................. Colonel William Paterson................. ...	26 Jan., 1808	28 Dec., 1809.
Major-General L. Macquarie	1 Jan., 1810	1 Dec., 1821.
Major-General Sir T. Brisbane, K.C.B.......	1 Dec., 1821	1 Dec., 1825.
Colonel Stewart, 3rd Regiment (Acting Governor).	6 Dec., 1825	18 Dec., 1825.
Lieutenant-General R. Darling	19 Dec., 1825	21 Oct., 1831.
Colonel Lindsay, C.B. (Acting-Governor)...	22 Oct., 1831	2 Dec., 1831.
Major-General Sir Richard Bourke, K.C.B.	3 Dec., 1831	5 Dec., 1837.
Lieutenant-Colonel K. Snodgrass (Acting Governor).	6 Dec., 1837	23 Feb., 1838.
Sir George Gipps	24 Feb., 1838	11 July, 1846.
Sir Maurice O'Connell (Acting Governor) ..	12 July, 1846	2 Aug., 1846.
Sir Charles A. Fitzroy.........................	3 Aug., 1846	17 Jan., 1855.
Sir William Thomas Denison, K.C.B.	20 Jan., 1855	22 Jan., 1861.
Lieutenant-Colonel John F. Kempt (Administrator).	23 Jan., 1861	21 Mar., 1861.
The Right Honorable Sir John Young, K.C.B., G.C.M.G. — Administrator	22 Mar., 1861	15 May, 1861.
The Right Honorable Sir John Young, K.C.B., G.C.M.G. — Governor-in-Chief...	16 May, 1861	24 Dec., 1867.
Sir Trevor Chute, K.C.B. (Administrator)...	25 Dec., 1867	7 Jan., 1868.
Right Honorable the Earl of Belmore, P.C.	8 Jan., 1868	22 Feb., 1872.
Sir Alfred Stephen, Knt., C.B. (Administrator).	23 Feb., 1872	2 June, 1872.
Sir Hercules George Robert Robinson, G.C.M.G., Governor-in-Chief.	3 June, 1872	19 Mar., 1879.
Sir Alfred Stephen, K.C.M.G., C.B. (Lieutenant-Governor).	20 Mar., 1879	3 Aug., 1879.
The Right Honorable Lord Augustus William Frederick Spencer Loftus, P.C., G.C.B.	4 Aug., 1879	9 Nov., 1885.
Sir Alfred Stephen, G.C.M.G., C.B. (Lieutenant-Governor).	10 Nov., 1885	11 Dec., 1885.
The Right Honorable Charles Robert, Baron Carrington, P.C., G.C.M.G.	12 Dec., 1885	1 Nov., 1890.
Sir Alfred Stephen, G.C.M.G., C.B. (Lieutenant-Governor).	3 Nov., 1890	15 Jan., 1891.
The Right Honorable Victor Albert George, Earl of Jersey, P.C., G.C.M.G.	15 Jan., 1891	(still in office.)

PART II.

Limits and Area.

Boundaries of the Colony.

THE Colony of New South Wales lies almost entirely between the 29th and 36th parallels of south latitude, and between the 141st and 153rd meridians east of Greenwich. It is bounded on the east by the Pacific Ocean, to which it presents a coast-line extending over 700 miles, from Point Danger at its north-eastern extremity to Cape Howe at the south-east. From the point last mentioned, which is also the north-east limit of the Colony of Victoria, it is bounded by an imaginary line, running in a north-westerly direction to the source of the Indi, a stream rising at the foot of Forest Hill, a few miles south of the Pilot Mountain, one of the most conspicuous peaks of the Australian Alps. The southern boundary of the Colony follows the course of the Indi, and afterwards of the Murray, into which the first-named stream ultimately merges, as far as the 141st meridian of east longitude. The intersection of the Murray with this meridian forms a common point of the three Colonies of New South Wales, Victoria, and South Australia.

On the west, the Colony is separated from South Australia by the line of the 141st meridian, as far as its intersection with the 29th parallel of south latitude, at which point New South Wales, South Australia, and Queensland touch. Commencing at this point, the northern boundary of the Colony follows the 29th degree of latitude, till it is crossed by the Macintyre River, one of the upper branches of the Darling, not far from the 149th meridian. Thence it follows the course of the Macintyre upward, to the junction of its tributary, the Dumaresq; leaving the Macintyre it follows the tributary stream till it meets a spur extending from the main Dividing Range to the junction of Tenterfield Creek and the Dumaresq. The boundary runs along this spur until it joins the main range, thence, almost parallel to the coast, it follows the Dividing Range to Wilson's Peak, where the Macpherson Range branches eastward. Following the last-named range, the northern boundary reaches the coast at Point Danger.

Area.

The area comprised within these limits is estimated at 310,700 square miles, or 198,848,000 acres, being a little over two-and-a-half times that of Great Britain and Ireland. Excluding the surface covered by rivers and lakes, the area would be 195,882,150 acres or about 306,066 square miles.

Length and breadth.

The length of the Colony, from Point Danger on the north to Cape Howe on the south, is 680 miles. From east to west, along the 29th parallel, the breadth is 760 miles, while diagonally from the south-west corner, where the Murray passes into South Australia, to Point Danger, the length reaches 850 miles.

PART III.

Physical Configuration.

THE surface of New South Wales is divided naturally into three distinct zones, each widely differing in general character and physical aspect, and clearly defined by the Main Dividing Range, which traverses the country from north to south. The table-land, which forms the summit of this range, comprises one of the zones above mentioned, and marks the division between the coastal region, forming the eastern watershed, and the great plain district of the interior.

MOUNTAINS, TABLE-LAND, ETC.

Dividing Range. The Main Dividing Range runs almost parallel to the coast, at no great distance from it. On the eastern edge of the table-land the mountains rise abruptly to a height which averages between 2,000 and 3,000 feet, while on the western side they slope gradually towards the great central plain. The geographical centre of the whole mountain system of South-Eastern Australia lies in the south-eastern portion of New South Wales, close to the confines of Victoria. Here some of the peaks rise to a height of over 7,000 feet above the level of the sea. Mount Kosciusko and Mount Townsend, two of the highest peaks of the Australian Alps, attain an elevation of 7,171 feet and 7,256 feet respectively.

Central Plateau. The central plateau, which these heights dominate, becomes subdivided into several branches, marking the watershed of three distinct river systems. The eastern watershed extends throughout the whole length of New South Wales and Queensland, and drains into the Pacific Ocean. The western watershed, embracing a portion of the three eastern colonies, is drained by the river system of the Murray and Darling into the Southern Ocean. In the southern watershed the Snowy River has its source, its upper basin being entirely in New South Wales, although its waters flow through Victoria and enter the sea near Bass' Straits.

The south-eastern portion of the Colony has the appearance of having been convulsed by some great physical disturbance. The mountains are rugged, and their slopes abrupt, as is also the case in other portions of the Dividing Range, particularly in the Blue Mountains and the eastern parts of New England; but the width and altitude of the table-land are greatest in this portion of the Colony. The average height of the Snowy and Muniong Ranges, which belong to this district, reaches 5,000 feet; the width of the plateau, in the direction of east and west, may be set down as 100 miles. The altitude of the Monaro district averages 2,000 feet above the sea level; but as the table-land runs northward it decreases greatly in height and in width, until it narrows to only a few miles, with an elevation of scarcely 1,500 feet. The south-eastern portion of the Colony.

The table-land rises again at the Blue Mountains, where the principal summits attain a considerable elevation, Mount Beemarang reaching 4,100 feet. The general level of the plateau itself will be best understood when it is remembered that the great western railway of the colony traverses a district in these mountains, of which the Clarence siding, Mount Victoria, Mount Wilson, and Blackheath are stations, situated at an elevation of over 3,000 feet. The dividing chain again decreases gradually in its spread northward of the Blue Mountains, until, as a comparatively narrow chain, it divides the waters of the Goulburn and the Hunter, on the eastern slope, from those of the Namoi and the Castlereagh, on the western. The mass once more widens out in the Liverpool Ranges, where Mount Oxley stands conspicuous, at a height of 4,500 feet, whilst, still further north Ben Lomond, Blue Mountains.

reaches 5,000 feet, and the table-land maintains an average altitude of 3,000 feet, giving to this district, although situated at no great distance from the tropics, the climate and aspect of much higher latitudes.

Mountain scenery

Narrow valleys and deep gorges everywhere break the continuity of the Dividing Range. Such is especially the case in the Blue Mountains, where the scenery is of striking and characteristic grandeur. The table-land everywhere presents one strange peculiarity. The level land suddenly terminates, and many hundred feet below, as far as the eye can reach, wooded valleys extend, whose undulating floors are walled in by sandstone cliffs, of height so enormous as to be without parallel elsewhere in the world. At the bottom of these valleys small rivulets and tiny streams, fed by waterfalls from the table-land, trace their way, under an ever verdant dome of graceful tree-ferns and giant eucalypti.

The mountain scenery of this part of New South Wales produces on the traveller an entirely new impression. There are no snow-capped peaks upon which the rising and setting sun produces strange and magnificent colour effects; nor does any peculiar shape of the summits strike the imagination, as in the Alps and Pyrenees of the Old World. On the contrary, from the plains the New South Wales mountains look rather insignificant. But gazing from the edges of the high table-land into the deep valleys below, the mind is awed by the realization of the magnificent scale on which Nature has worked in these solitudes. In many places the cliffs rise 2,000 feet perpendicularly from the valley beneath, and the hills at their feet, formed by the accumulation of débris from their sides and from the plateau above, appear as slight undulations. The valleys and sides of the gorges, wherever there is soil, are clothed with dense vegetation, and over all is the mantle of blue haze, which makes the whole effect most striking, and has given to the range visible from Sydney its appropriate name.

Coast Ranges.

The main range throws off many spurs towards the sea on the eastern slope. These divide the waters of the numerous rivers which flow into the Pacific Ocean. Almost everywhere between the coast range and the sea the country is hilly and serrated, more particularly in the southern portion of the Colony. In the Illawarra district, 50 miles to the south of Sydney, the mountains skirt the very edge of the coast, presenting towards the ocean a perpendicular face of cliffs nearly 1,000 feet in height. Further north there are wider valleys, and greater stretches of country available for tillage and pasture.

The western slope is entirely different. Numerous ramifications of the general mountain system are thrown off, but all slope gently towards the great central plain of the interior. So gentle, indeed, is the declivity, that the dividing lines of the various watersheds as they extend westward, are scarcely visible, being only indicated by a succession of low ridges and isolated elevations.

Western Mountain system.

In the extreme west of the Colony, verging on South Australia, another mountain system exists, forming the western edge of an immense depression, through which the largest rivers of the Australian continent hold their devious course. The Great Barrier and the Grey Ranges are part of this system. They consist of low hills, hardly rising to the dignity of mountains, culminating in a few solitary peaks, such as Mount Arrowsmith and Mount Lyell, which attain an elevation of only 2,000 feet above sea level.

Traces have been found of the existence at some earlier period of a range of primary rocks, extending from Orange to Cobar and Wilcannia, forming the watershed between the Lachlan and part of the basin of the Darling. The range no longer exists as a landmark, for, owing to denudation, it has almost entirely disappeared.

Mountains below limit of perpetual snow.

The whole mountain system of New South Wales lies below the limit of perpetual snow. On the south-eastern slopes of the Snowy Ranges, however, and on the summits of the high peaks of the Australian Alps, snow sometimes lingers throughout the year.

LAKES OF THE MOUNTAIN REGION.

On the summit of the Main Dividing Range, and within a few miles of the inland towns of Goulburn, Queanbeyan, and Braidwood, two of the principal lakes of the Colony are situated. Lake George is 16 miles in length and 6 miles in width, draining a basin whose area is about 490 square miles. The lake is situated at an elevation of 2,200 feet above the sea, and the scenery around it is very beautiful. This lake exhibits the phenomenon of a large drainage area without a visible outlet; for though it receives many small water-courses no stream leaves it. Lake Bathurst, a few miles eastward of Lake George, is another depression on the summit of the Dividing Range, and covers in ordinary seasons an area of about 15 square miles. It is similar in character to Lake George, having no outlet to the sea. Both lakes, in periods of great drought, shrink considerably in area; but Lake George in most seasons is a fine sheet of water, and now that the railway to Cooma skirts its shores, the attractiveness of its scenery makes it a favourite resort of tourists.

Lake George.

Lake Bathurst.

THE COASTAL REGION.

Rivers of New South Wales.

Rivers.—The main range already described, traversing the country from north to south, gives rise to numerous rivers flowing into the South Pacific. Compared with the western rivers those of the eastern slope appear insignificant enough. But compared with the principal rivers either of England or France, their relative size and importance are at once manifest.

The Tweed and Brunswick.

In the extreme north of the Colony, the Tweed and Brunswick Rivers flow through a rich country, of semi-tropical aspect. Their courses are short, and bar entrances render them navigable only for small craft.

The Richmond.

A few miles south of the Brunswick, the Richmond descends from the heights of the Macpherson Range, on the slope of Mount Lindsay, one of the highest peaks of the northern table-land. The river has three branches, and is navigable on the main arm as far as Casino, 62 miles, and on Wilson's Creek to Lismore, 60 miles from the sea. The Richmond drains an area of about 2,400 square miles of country, rugged in its upper basin, and heavily timbered, and in its lower course, flowing through rich alluvial land, where the produce of semi-tropical climes grows luxuriantly.

Immediately south of the last-named stream is the Clarence—the largest river on the eastern watershed. It takes its rise in a spur of the Main Dividing Range, and runs in a south-easterly direction for 240 miles, carrying a considerable body of water through one of the richest districts of the Colony, and emptying itself into the Pacific at Shoal Bay. The upper part of its basin is very rugged, so much so that its principal tributaries, the Mitchell, Nymboi, Timbarra, and Orara Rivers, rising in the New England table-land, between Armidale and Tenterfield, all flow in an opposite direction to the course of the main stream, generally trending to the north-east, and even, in the case of the Orara, to the north-west. The Lower Clarence is a magnificent stream, averaging half a mile in width from its mouth upwards, for nearly 50 miles, and is navigable for 67 miles, as far as Copmanhurst. Ocean-going steamers of large tonnage ascend the river as far as Grafton, 42 miles from the sea. The area of country drained by the Clarence is over 8,000 square miles, or nearly half as large again as the basin of the Thames, whose course is about as long as the Clarence, but navigable for only 60 miles. The Clarence.

Two short rivers, the Bellinger and the Nambuccra, both navigable for some distance by small craft, enter the Pacific between the Clarence and Trial Bay. The Bellinger. The Nambuccra.

Into Trial Bay, the Macleay, one of the principal rivers of the coast, discharges after a course of 200 miles from its source near Ben Lomond. With its principal feeders, the Gyra and the Apsley, the Macleay drains an area of 4,800 square miles of country, the upper part of which, especially that portion through which the Apsley flows, is extremely rugged and precipitous. Series of The Macleay.

waterfalls, some of which have a perpendicular descent of over 200 feet, mark the course of this stream as it runs through narrow gorges, whose sides rise in places to a height of about 2,000 feet. In its lower course the valley widens very considerably into magnificent alluvial plains, fast becoming the home of a numerous and thriving population. The Macleay is navigable for more than 30 miles, as far as the town of Greenhills, a few miles above Kempsey. The country through which it flows is for the most part thickly timbered.

The Hastings. The Hastings is the next stream met with, emptying itself into the sea at Port Macquarie. The country which it drains is rich, undulating, and densely wooded, and the area within its watershed is 1,400 square miles. Its chief arm is formed by the Wilson and Maria Rivers, on the left bank, the latter joining the main stream at Port Macquarie.

The Manning. The Manning rises in the Main Dividing Range, and flows almost due east through a prosperous district, rapidly becoming settled. The valley through which it flows is densely wooded, and the agricultural land on both sides of the river is unsurpassed for fertility. The Manning has a length of 100 miles, and, like most of the rivers of the seaboard, its course lies through undulating country, broken in the upper portion, but widening out as it nears the sea. Its chief tributary is the Barrington, on the right bank; on the left it receives the Barnard River, the Dawson, the Lansdowne, and other small streams. The river is navigable for ocean-going vessels as far as Wingham, about 20 miles from its mouth.

Before reaching the Hunter, several small streams are met with, amongst which may be mentioned the Woliomba and Maclean, falling into Wallis Lake, the Myall, which empties into Myall Lake, and the Karuah, which reaches the ocean at Port Stephens.

The Hunter. The Hunter is one of the chief rivers of the Colony, and has its source in the Liverpool Range. It flows first in a southerly

a until its confluence with the Goulburn, thence it takes
erly course, and reaches the sea at Port Hunter, on the
f which is situated the City of Newcastle. The Hunter
numerous tributaries. The chief of these, in addition to
lburn, already mentioned, are the Wollombi, the Paterson,
Williams. With its tributaries, the Hunter drains a
extending over 11,000 square miles, an area more than
large as the basin of the Thames. The river is navigable
n-going vessels as far as Morpeth, 34 miles from the sea,
he Paterson and the Williams are both navigable, the one
tance of 18 miles, and the other for 20 miles. The upper
of the main river and its branches are through hilly, if not
nous, districts, but its lower course is mainly through rich,
lluvial flats. Through its lower course the river drains the
nd most important coal-field of Australia, whose emporium
astle, the second city of the Colony in shipping and
ce. The length of the Hunter is over 200 miles.

gh less important from a commercial point of view than the , the Hawkesbury, which reaches the sea at Broken Bay, the less one of the finest rivers of the eastern seaboard. rmed by the united waters of many streams, each of cone local importance. Its chief tributaries come from the nd or gorges of the Blue Mountains, but the principal of the river itself rises in the main range, further south. ge forming the watershed between the Hawkesbury and eams flowing eastward leaves the main range near Lake st, runs north-easterly, and terminates at the sea near I. The Hawkesbury.

r the name of the Wollondilly, the Hawkesbury has its Wollondilly. set many miles from Goulburn. Flowing past that town eds in a northerly direction until it receives the waters of t River, which come from the Blue Mountains, after passough wild gorges, wherein may be found some of the most cent scenery in Australia. From the junction of the Cox

River the stream is known as the Warragamba, which name it retains until its junction with the Nepean. This river rises in the coast range overlooking Wollongong, and together with its tributary streams, the Cataract and Cordeaux, forms the source of the water-works from which Sydney now draws its supply. Though smaller than the Warragamba, the Nepean gives its name to the united waters of the two streams. After receiving the Nepean the river flows along the foot of the Blue Mountains, through a rich valley highly cultivated. From the Blue Mountains two streams add their waters to it, the Grose and the Colo, and from the junction of the last named the river is called the Hawkesbury. From the Colo junction the river still runs northward until it is joined by the Macdonald, an important stream, navigable for some distance above its confluence with the Hawkesbury. The Macdonald comes from the north, and joins the river on the left bank. The Hawkesbury, after turning to the east, holds its course through broken country, the scenery of which has been pronounced equal to any other river scenery in the world, and finally reaches the sea at Broken Bay. The course of the Hawkesbury extends over 330 miles, and the drainage area may be set down as 8,000 square miles. Navigation is possible as far as Windsor, 70 miles from the mouth, and a little dredging would enable sea-going vessels to reach this town.

The Hawkesbury.

In the neighbourhood of Sydney some small streams fall into Botany Bay. Two of these, the Woronora and George's Rivers, have their sources on the eastern slope of the ranges in which the Nepean, Cordeaux, and Cataract rise, and after rapid courses unite their waters before falling into the bay.

Rivers south of Sydney.

Generally speaking, the rivers south of Sydney are of less importance than those to the north, as the width of the coastal strip narrows considerably. The Shoalhaven, nevertheless, merits more than passing notice. It rises in the coastal range and follows the direction of the coast, flowing northerly through deep gullies, marked by magnificent scenery peculiarly Australian. Turning to the east, it enters the alluvial plains, which are counted t the richest and most productive in the country. The ven is 260 miles in length, but is navigable only for a few .nd drains a district 3,300 miles in area. Further south, narrow belt between the ranges and the sea, flow the Clyde, , Tuross, and Bega Rivers. They all pass through rich, ing, agricultural country, and each has an average length 60 to 70 miles. The Towamba River, at the extreme f the Colony, empties itself into the Pacific at Twofold Bay.

physical aspect of all the eastern rivers is much the same, per courses being amidst broken and mountainous districts, ir lower waters flowing through undulating country with uvial flats along their banks, for the most part highly culti- Where not cultivated, the country is densely covered with some of which attains a magnificent growth, yielding the ardwood, and, in the north, cedar and pine. Eastern rivers.

gh belonging to another river system, the upper basin of owy River is situated in New South Wales. This river the snow-fed streams rising on the southern slopes of the Range; its principal tributaries being the Bombala and cumbene. The Snowy River and its tributaries water a rable portion of the highest table-land of the Colony, the mountain ranges of which are found large tracts of land, where the produce of colder climes may be grown to on. After leaving New South Wales, the Snowy has a nd tortuous course, and finally enters the sea between Cape nd Bass Straits, in the Colony of Victoria. The area of rshed in New South Wales is about 2,800 square miles. The Snowy River.

HARBOURS AND PORTS.

a coast so extensive as that of New South Wales, it would ral to expect many harbours and bays affording outlets for duce of the country. Such is the case. Besides harbours nercial importance, there are others, which afford shelter Natural harbours.

for vessels in stress of weather, and a refuge in time of danger. Fortunately, however, harbours of refuge are not often required. The coast of the Colony is singularly free from cyclones, hurricanes, and like visitations. Gales are certainly not unknown, nor are casualties infrequently recorded; but the coast is very safe, and disasters are in many cases to be attributed to causes which ordinary prudence would have avoided.

Byron Bay.

Inside Cape Byron, in the north of the Colony, the bay of the same name offers shelter to vessels trading to Queensland, in all but north-east weather. A large pier has been constructed, by which the produce of the neighbouring districts of the Brunswick and Tweed may be shipped, when an entrance to these rivers is impracticable.

Shoal Bay.

At Shoal Bay, the entrance to the Clarence, the anchorage is safe and commodious, and when the works designed for improving the river entrance are completed, it promises to be one of the best ports on the coast.

Trial Bay.

Trial Bay, at the mouth of the Macleay, affords ample shelter and safe anchorage. The Government have erected a large prison on the hill overlooking the Bay, and are now utilizing the prisoners' labour in constructing a breakwater, with the view of making Trial Bay not only a harbour of refuge, but a shipping port. When this design is accomplished, there is every reason to suppose that it will become one of the most frequented places on the coast, as the resources of the Macleay District are great and rapidly developing.

Port Macquarie. Port Stephens.

Port Macquarie, at the mouth of the Hastings, and the harbour at Forster, near Cape Hawke, afford good anchorage. Port Stephens, a little further south, offers at all times the most safe and commodious harbour desirable. As a natural port it is hardly inferior to Port Jackson, and the scenery of its shores is very beautiful. At present, Port Stephens is little used, owing to its proximity to Newcastle, and the sparseness of the population in its immediate district.

Twenty miles further south is Port Hunter, at the mouth of the river of that name. When first used, the harbour was inconvenient and somewhat dangerous; but this has been altered entirely by the breakwaters and training walls which have been constructed. Newcastle harbour is now safe and roomy, with shipping facilities equal, if not superior, to those found in any other Australian port. Magnificent wharves line its shores, provided with hydraulic and steam cranes of the most modern type. The length of wharf frontage at Newcastle is two miles, the trade is large and increasing, and the city ranks third amongst Australasian seaports. The importance of Newcastle is mainly due to the existence of immense coal deposits in its neighbourhood, which supply not only all the Australian Colonies, but the China seas, and the Pacific slopes of the United States, and the countries bordering on the Spanish main. Latterly, too, large shipments of wool have been made direct to English ports, Newcastle having direct communication by railway with the northern districts of the Colony. Port Hunter

A few miles further south is Lake Macquarie, in the centre of the coal-field of the Newcastle district, and covering an area of 44 square miles. The great drawback to the lake as a shipping port has been the shallowness of its entrance; but extensive dykes and training walls are being constructed, which have already increased the draught of water in the channel, and with some further improvements Lake Macquarie will become an important shipping place. Lake Macquarie.

Broken Bay, 15 miles north of Port Jackson, forms the mouth of the River Hawkesbury. It has a bold entrance, and on Barrenjoey, the southern headland, is erected a fine lighthouse. The bay has three branches, Brisbane Water being the northern, the Hawkesbury mouth the centre, and Pittwater the southern arm. The first-named opens out into a series of lakes, and the town of Gosford, standing at the head of one of them—the Broadwater—is the centre of an important district. The scenery at and around Broken Bay is characteristically Australian, and Broken Bay in natural beauty rivals even Sydney Harbour. South of Broken Bay the coast-line is a succession of high cliffs and sandy beaches.

Port Jackson. The entrance of Port Jackson lies between perpendicular cliffs of sandstone several hundred feet high, and only 74 chains, or nearly 1 mile, apart. Sydney Harbour has been too often described to require further description here. It holds the first place amongst the harbours of the world for convenience of entrance, depth of water, and natural shipping facilities. Its natural beauties are the charm of all who visit its shores, and in the quiet waters of its numerous bays and coves the navies of the world might securely rest. The area of water surface of the harbour proper is 15 square miles, and the shore-line is 165 miles in circuit. At the South Head is erected a splendid light-house, fitted with an electric arc light, the power of which is scarcely exceeded on any coast. On the shores of Port Jackson stands Sydney, the capital of New South Wales and the mother city of the Australias. The city and its suburbs occupy 137 square miles, and have within their boundaries about 386,400 people.

Botany Bay. Botany Bay, the first port entered by Captain Cook, the discoverer of this territory, lies a few miles south of Sydney. It covers an area of 24 square miles, and receives the waters of several small rivers. The bay has very little trade, by reason of its proximity to Sydney, but it is frequented by craft in search of shelter during stress of weather.

Wollongong and Kiama. Wollongong, Kiama, and Ulladulla are small harbours which have been snatched, as it were, from the sea, and are important shipping places.

Jervis Bay. About 80 miles to the south of Sydney the coast is broken by an important inlet called Jervis Bay. Its entrance is 2 miles wide, and on its bosom safe anchorage may be found in any part. It is surrounded by rich agricultural and mineral country, as yet, unexploited. Nature has been so bountiful to the country as a whole, that particular districts, undoubtedly rich, must remain for undeveloped, through want of labour and capital to open , and ports which would in older countries be prized for ivenience and capacity, here remain unused, save as refuges y weather.

ıan's Bay, at the entrance to the Clyde, is an inlet of some nce, and coastal steamers also load produce at the mouths [oruya, Tuross, and Bega Rivers. Bateman's Bay.

dd Bay is a magnificent sheet of water, near the southern the Colony. Formerly it was the seat of a large whaling ɔw no more. It is well sheltered, and a fine jetty affords ipping facilities. Its trade is chiefly with the neighbour- ıies, in produce and live stock, the bay being the nearest ı the sea coast for the rich district of Monaro. A railway ed to connect the port with the table-land and the metro- d Twofold Bay promises to become a considerable shipping the near future. On its shores is situated the town of Twofold Bay

es the ports and harbours, properly so called, which have ɔve enumerated, there are several lakes, or arms of the sea, ill, with the development of the resources of the country, ports of shipment. From Cape Hawke to Port Stephens of lakes extends, communicating with the latter through ll River, and covering a large area. The most extensive lis Lake, Myall Lake, and the Broadwater. The country bout is richly timbered, but its resources are still unde- Between Lake Macquarie and Broken Bay is Tuggerah lso an extensive sheet of water. Near Wollongong is awarra, of considerable area, but shallow, and towards the ' the colony are Coila and Tuross Lakes, into which the River discharges. Coastal Lakes.

ISLANDS.

lands of any note belong geographically to New South The Broughton Islands, lying a few miles northward of Islands.

the Heads of Port Stephens, are the largest in extent. Solitary Island, situated near the northern part of the coast, between the Bellinger and Clarence Rivers, and Montague Island, 18 miles south-east of the Moruya River estuary, have been selected as the sites for light-houses, but are not otherwise important. Norfolk Island, having an area of 8,607 acres, and also Lord Howe Island, belong politically, but not geographically, to New South Wales. The last-named island has an area of 3,220 acres.

Norfolk Island.

WESTERN WATERSHED.

The Western Watershed.

The western watershed of the Colony is in physical features and geographical character the antithesis of the eastern. Instead of a narrow strip of country shut in by the sea and mountains, intersected by numerous short rivers with a rapid flow, the western watershed forms a vast basin through which the quiet waters of a few great rivers have their long, though uncertain, courses. The rivers of the western region of the Colony all belong to the fluvial system of the Murray, which carries to the Southern Ocean, through the colony of South Australia, the drainage of a watershed immense in extent, embracing the northern portion of Victoria, and the western and larger part of New South Wales, and reaching almost to the centre of Queensland.

The Murray.

The Murray, or Hume, the southern branch of this vast river system, rises in the Snowy Mountains, from which its three principal sources, the Hume, the Tooma, and the Indi descend. The first two of these streams rise on the northern and western slopes of Mount Kosciusko; the Indi, which is really the main river, has a longer course, rising in a gully near the Pilot Mountain, at an elevation of 5,000 feet above the sea. From the confluence of these rivers, the Murray rapidly descends towards the plains below Albury, where it is only 490 feet above sea level, and has still a course of 1,439 miles to run. From Albury downwards the river receives many tributaries on both banks, those from New South Wales being the most important. Above Albury the tributaries

: the most part mountain torrents, carrying to the main the melted snows of the Australian Alps. In its lower however, the Murray is augmented, through the Murrumand Darling, by the waters of secondary systems as im-as its own.

re being joined by the Murrumbidgee, the Murray receives, series of ana-branches, the drainage of a large portion of ntry lying between the two main streams. The Billabong runs almost through the centre of the plain spreading n the Murray and Murrumbidgee; in the middle of its it communicates with the latter river, through Colombo nko Creeks, whilst on the south it feeds the Murray by nnel of the Edward River. The Edward is itself an im-stream. It forms with the Wakool and Tuppal Creeks, ny other smaller and less important watercourses, a fluvial interlacing the whole country from Tocumwal to the Mur-gee junction, which has been justly named Riverina. The l and Wakool are together navigable for over 400 miles, as he important town of Deniliquin. From its furthest source foot of the Pilot Mountain to the town of Albury the r has a length of 280 miles. Thence to the Darling River n its course is 852 miles, and from that point to the sea, Lake Alexandrina, it is 587 miles in length. The river has total course of 1,719 miles, of which 1,132 are within the of New South Wales. The river has been navigated as the Ournie gold-field, about 150 miles above Albury, and iles from its mouth.

Ana-branches.

The Edward.

Murrumbidgee has its source at the foot of a hill overlooking laman Plains, at a height of nearly 5,000 feet above the sea. se first shapes itself southward, but near the town of Cooma a sharp curve and runs in a northerly direction until it as. Here it curves again, trending to the west in a line to the Murray, but turning south-west on receiving the , it finally joins the main river after a course of 1,350 miles.

The Murrumbidgee.

Murrumbidgee Basin.

The area drained by the Murrumbidgee is estimated at 15,400 square miles. In the upper part of its course it receives from both sides numerous rivers and creeks, the most important of which are the Umaralla, Molonglo, and Yass Rivers on its right, and the Goodradigbee, and Tumut Rivers on its left bank. All these rivers flow through mountainous country over a series of plateaux, which from the Coolaman and Coorangorambula Plains to the plains round Gundagai and Wagga successively diminish in height from 5,000 feet to 720 feet and 607 feet above the sea.

The upper valleys.

The upper valleys, both of the Murrumbidgee and the Murray, are of similar physical aspect. Both rivers are snow-fed, the Murray to a greater extent than its tributaries, owing to the higher elevation of the mountains and plateaux from which it descends. In the lower basins they are also similar in character, and the plains which they drain are amongst the most fertile in the Colony. With an intelligent system of water conservation and irrigation the lower valleys of these rivers would support a large population of agriculturists on land hitherto devoted entirely to sheep pasturing.

The Lachlan.

The chief tributary of the Murrumbidgee is the Lachlan, rising in the main Dividing Range, where also its principal feeders have their source. These are the Boorowa, Crookwell, Abercrombie, and Belubula, all rapid streams, occasionally swollen by melting snow from the table-land. After receiving the Boorowa the Lachlan flows to the Murrumbidgee, through 500 miles of plain country, without receiving any tributary of permanent character. The water-courses which carry off the surplus water from the rich plains on either side of the river, only reach it in time of flood. The total length of the river is 700 miles, and its basin has an area of 13,500 square miles. The country drained by the Lachlan is similar in most respects to that of the Murray and Murrumbidgee, and with regular rainfall or irrigation, the light red soil and sandy loam of its lower valley would yield abundant returns to the farmer. The lines of demarcation between the Lachlan ıd that of the Murrumbidgee on the south, and the on the north-west, are hardly perceptible on the ground, the country through which these great rivers flow.

The Darling.

l the tributaries of the Murray, the Darling drains the ırea, extending as it does over the greater portion of the district of New South Wales, and embracing nearly all ı Queensland. From its confluence with the Murray at ›rth up to its junction with the Culgoa a few miles above the Darling receives only two tributaries, the Paroo and rrego, both intermittent, though of vast size in times of For over 1,000 miles this great river holds its solitary course, ›, feeding the thirsty plains of the south with water falling ındred miles distant on the downs of Queensland. The f the river is tortuous in the extreme; in many places a neck of land, a mile or two across, separates parts of the miles distant, if the stream were followed. The Darling the phenomenon, not uncommon in Australian rivers, of nuch higher than the plain behind, indeed the river bed ıough from 30 to 40 feet beneath the bank, is in some at little below the general level of the country. Successive ave added to the height of the banks, and have raised the he stream correspondingly.

The Upper Darling.

Darling has no source under that name, which applies only part of the river as far as the Bogan junction. Above this takes the name of the Barwon, until its confluence with rdir, then it is known as the Macintyre, and afterwards the anch receives the name of the Dumaresq. The last-named ıas its source in the Dividing Range, on the summit of the nd at the extreme north-east of the Colony, not far from ıd of the Richmond. The Dumaresq, Macintyre, and form, however, what might be really called the Upper ; and this appellation would be geographically accurate. iety of names, by which not only the Darling, but many ustralian rivers are known, is due to the fact that they were discovered in sections, the identity of which was not established until years afterwards, and the sectional names have survived.

Tributaries of the Darling.

The Darling receives, in its upper course, many tributaries, which drain the southern portion of Queensland, but these rivers only flow for a short part of their courses in New South Wales. Chief among them are the Mooni, Narran, Bokhara, Culgoa, Warrego, and Paroo. The principal affluents of the Darling within the boundaries of New South Wales are on the left bank. The Gwydir, Namoi, Castlereagh, Macquarie, and Bogan are the most important. These streams are all of considerable length and similar in character, their upper valleys are on the table-lands, and their lower courses lie through alluvial plains and good pastoral country. The Darling is navigable, in times of freshets, as far as the township of Walgett, 1,758 miles from its confluence with the Murray, thence to the sea the distance is 587 miles, making a total length of navigable water from Walgett to the sea of 2,345 miles, and it therefore ranks high amongst the rivers of the world, as estimated by navigable length. Unfortunately, however, its upper course is open only during part of the year.

Length of navigable water.

If the fluvial system of the Murray and Darling, and their principal tributaries, be considered in the light of the facilities it affords for water carriage, its value will appear not inconsiderable. The Darling River may be made available for navigation for 1,758 miles, from Wentworth to Walgett, the Murrumbidgee and Lachlan combined have 900 miles, and the Murray, from Ournie gold-field to the point where it enters the territory of South Australia, has a length of 1,120 miles. If to this be added the navigable length of the Wakool and Edward, the total distance of river which could be navigated reaches nearly 4,200 miles, in the western district alone, a length nearly twice that of the railways of the Colony.

LAKES OF THE WESTERN DISTRICT.

Western Lakes.

Here and there along the course of the western rivers are found lakes sometimes of considerable dimensions. These lakes are in reality shallow depressions, receiving water from the overflow of the rivers in times of flood, and in return feeding them when the floods have subsided. Lake Urana is the most important in the Murray and Murrumbidgee basin, and Lakes Cowal, Cudgellico, and Waljeers, in that of the Lachlan. Along the Darling are Lakes Poopelloe and Gunyulka on the left bank and Laidley's Ponds and Lakes Pammaroo, Jandoo, and Cawndilla on the right, near Menindie. On the South Australian frontier are Lake Victoria, formed by the overflow of the Murray, and others of less importance. The area of these lakes is undefined, as they vary in size according to the rainfall, sometimes covering vast extents of country, and at others being reduced to the proportions of mere waterholes, whilst in seasons of great drought they are absolutely dry.

PART IV.

Climate.

IT is accepted as an ascertained fact that the temperature of lands in the southern hemisphere is lower than that of countries situated in corresponding latitudes north of the equator; to this general law New South Wales is no exception. The researches of the Government Astronomer of the Colony conclusively confirm this, and show, from the records of temperature extending over many years, that the climate of New South Wales is one of the most temperate and uniform anywhere experienced. Just as the country is divided naturally into three distinct geographical regions, so it is separated into the same climatic divisions, each of which has its characteristic features.

Coastal Region. The coastal region extends from 28° to 37° south latitude, and if the temperature accorded with that of similar latitudes in the northern hemisphere, Casino and Grafton would resemble the country bordering on the Gulf of Suez, in the Red Sea; Delhi, in India; Ningpo, in China, and New Orleans, in the United States. Such, however, is not the case. Casino has a mean temperature of 67°, only 1° more than that of Messina, in Sicily, which lies more than 9° further from the equator. Eden, which is situated at the extreme south of the Colony, in latitude 37°, has a mean temperature of 60°, which is practically the same as that of Nice and Rome, places respectively 460 and 330 miles further removed from the equator. Not only is the climate of the coastal region more mild in regard to average temperature than the corresponding latitudes in the northern hemisphere, but the range is not as great. This is a very important factor in estimating the healthiness of a country.

As regards Sydney, situated as it is midway between the extreme points of the Colony, in latitude 33° 51′ south, the same truth is apparent. Its mean temperature is 63°, and corresponds with that of Barcelona, the great maritime city of Spain, of Toulon in France, the former being in latitude 44° 22′, and latter 43° 7′ N. At Sydney, the mean summer temperature lightly under 71°, and that of winter 54·5°. The range is thus 5° Fahrenheit. At Naples, where the mean temperature for the r is about the same as at Sydney, the summer temperature reaches ean of 74·5°, and the mean of winter is 47·5°, with a range of 27°. s the summer is warmer, and the winter much colder, than at lney. The greatest temperature in the shade ever experienced Sydney was 106·9°, the lowest winter was 36·8°, giving a range 70°. At Naples the range has been as great as 81°, the winter imum falling sometimes below the freezing point.

Temperature of Sydney.

Taking the coast generally, the difference between the mean imer and mean winter temperature may be set down as averag not more than 24°, a range so small that it will be rarely nd elsewhere. The famed resorts on the Mediterranean seard bear no comparison with the Pacific slope of New South les, either for natural salubrity, or for the comparative mildness the summer and winter, while the epidemics and pestilences ich have devastated those regions of ancient civilization have er made their appearance on these shores.

Climate of the Coast.

Passing from the coast to the table-land, a distinct climatic ion is entered. On the high southern plateau, at an elevation 4,640 feet, stands the town of Kiandra, having a mean summer perature of 54·5°, and a winter temperature of 33°, correspond- with that of Dunfermline, in Scotland, in latitude 56° 5′ N., ile Kiandra is in 35° 50′ S. Cooma, in the centre of the Monaro ins, at an elevation of 2,640 feet above sea-level, enjoys a nmer as mild as either London or Paris, while its winters are less severe. On the New England table-land, the climate of midale, and other towns, may be considered as nearly perfect can be found. The yearly average temperature is scarcely 57° ile the summer only reaches 69°, and the winter falls to 46°, a ge of temperature approximating closely to the famous health orts in the south of France.

Climate of table-land.

Western Districts.

The climatic conditions of the western districts of the Colony are entirely different from those of the other two regions, and have been often cited as disagreeable. Compared with the equable temperature of the coastal district, or table-land, there may appear some justification for such reputation, but only by comparison. The climate of the great plains, in spite of the heat of part of the summer, is very healthy, and an inspection of the returns of death-rates, both of children and grown persons, given elsewhere, amply bears out this view. The town of Bourke may be taken as an example. Seated in the midst of the great plain of the interior, it illustrates peculiarly well the defects, as well as excellences, of the climate of the whole region. Bourke has exactly the same latitude as Cairo, yet its summer temperature is 5° and its mean 6·5° less than the Egyptian city. New Orleans also lies on the same parallel, but the American city is 4° hotter in summer. As regards winter temperature, Bourke leaves little to be desired. The mean winter reading of the thermometer is 52·3°, and accompanied as this is by clear skies and an absence of snow, the season is both refreshing and enjoyable. The great heat experienced on occasional days in summer, when the thermometer reads considerably over 100° in the shade, is not accompanied by that moisture in the air which at the sea-coast would make a less degree of heat almost unbearable.

Dryness of climate.

It is fortunate for the country that dryness is one of its characteristics; otherwise, instead of being the abode of health, the interior of the Colony would, with abundant rains, have become an impenetrable jungle, the lurking-place of those malarial fevers which devastate so many fair regions of the Old World and America. New South Wales may therefore be compared favourably with any part of the world; and, taking into consideration the comparatively low latitudes in which it is situated, it offers a most remarkable variety of temperate climates. From Kiandra, on the highest part of the great Dividing Range, to Bourke, on the great interior plain, the climate may be compared with that of the ope extending from Edinburgh to Messina, but more resembling that of Southern France and Italy. It may regarded as peculiarly fitted for the habitation of ropean race, embracing, as it does, within its limits, conditions under which the most advanced races of ave prospered. The following tables, showing the orological conditions in certain places, fairly repre- e Colony :— Climate adapted to European race.

Rainfall, and other Meteorological Conditions of certain Stations in New South Wales.

South latitude.	Mean temperature.	Mean summer temperature.	Mean winter temperature.	Mean daily range of thermometer in shade.	Highest reading of thermometer in shade.	Lowest reading of thermometer in shade.	Mean annual rainfall.
			Table-land.				
° ′	°	°	°	°	°	°	in.
35·52	45·0	54·5	33·1	25·4	96·2	-8·0	62·1
36·50	50·8	62·8	41·5	26·6	98·4	20·9	29·4
36·12	52·2	64·6	41·6	...	107·5	15·0	18·5
35·20	53·6	67·2	41·9	16·7	109·0	20·0	23·8
33·36	54·2	65·4	42·3	20·1	105·1	21·8	35·1
33·16	55·2	67·7	42·3	16·9	99·5	22·2	41·1
34·45	55·3	68·3	44·8	25·8	109·0	18·0	26·2
34·32	56·3	66·9	43·6	15·9	108·7	26·8	48·8
30·34	56·9	69·0	45·9	24·8	100·0	11·2	35·5
33·24	57·2	70·8	45·0	30·3	112·5	3·0	25·0
29·60	57·5	67·3	46·4	22·3	104·0	16·0	30·9
29·45	59·5	73·2	46·1	23·9	105·0	20·0	30·9
32·35	59·8	74·8	47·9	19·4	114·0	21·6	28·0
33·27	60·8	74·7	48·7	21·0	110·0	24·0	20·9
32·00	61·0	74·7	47·4	25·6	112·2	22·2	25·9
			Coastal District.				
37·00	60·3	67·7	51·1	13·9	106·0	36·0	44·6
34·25	62·1	70·0	53·6	14·9	101·9	34·8	38·4
33·51	62·2	70·7	54·5	14·0	106·9	36·8	49·2
32·47	62·5	73·1	51·4	21·5	112·0	24·0	34·9
31·25	62·7	72·4	55·8	15·7	101·3	32·4	63·2
32·56	62·8	72·3	52·6	26·1	113·9	21·5	34·5
29·46	62·9	71·9	54·7	17·9	120·0	31·3	50·0
28·43	63·3	75·6	56·3	27·8	118·0	21·0	38·2
			Western District.				
35·32	59·9	73·2	48·5	30·6	121·0	16·0	16·7
35·00	62·2	74·4	46·7	19·7	111·0	20·0	26·1
32·18	62·6	73·3	48·0	25·1	112·9	17·0	20·1
34·00	64·4	77·8	52·1	23·3	119·0	27·2	13·7
30·00	65·6	80·3	52·3	20·9	120·0	30·0	18·5

Average Meteorological Conditions of Sydney for each Month from 1859 to 1890.

	Jan.	Feb.	Mar.	April.	May.	June.	July.	Aug.	Sept.	Oct.	Nov.	Dec.	Yearly Mean.
Average reading of standard barometer at 32° Fahrenheit and mean sea-level at 9 a.m.	30·066	29·989	9·110	30·198	30·232	30·023	30·170	30·081	30·060	29·842	29·950	29·982	30·053
Average hourly reading of self-registering electric barograph, corrected to 32° Fahrenheit	29·770	29·802	29·801	29·947	29·920	29·920	29·951	983	29·884	29·835	29·800	29·748	29·855
Mean temperature (in shade)	71·5	70·9	69·3	64·8	58·4	54·3	52·5	55·0	58·8	63·3	66·5	69·8	62·9
Average reading of maximum thermometer (in shade)	78·0	77·3	75·6	71·1	65·0	60·7	59·2	62·7	66·5	71·1	73·9	77·0	70·0
Average reading of minimum thermometer (in shade)	65·2	65·0	63·4	58·7	52·2	48·3	45·9	47·4	51·2	55·9	59·5	62·9	56·3
Mean temperature of sea water	70·1	70·1	70·3	68·1	62·9	58·4	57·0	57·7	60·9	64·8	68·1	70·9	64·9
Greatest monthly rainfall, inches	10·68	18·56	18·70	25·43	20·85	16·30	11·95	12·77	14·06	24·69	11·13	7·80	Mx. 25·43
Least monthly rainfall, inches	0·42	0·40	0·42	0·06	0·18	0·27	06	0·04	0·08	0·07	0·14	0·39	Min. 0·04
Average monthly rainfall, inches	3·47	5·36	4·46	6·24	5·48	5·19	4·35	2·97	3·06	2·95	3·20	2·51	Total 49·23
Average number of days' rain	13	14	14	13	16	12	12	11	12	13	12	12	Ttal 54
Average monthly evaporation	4·613	3·501	2·914	2·278	1·687	1 32	1·530	1·787	2·359	3·246	3·959	4 34	Tot. 33·979
Average monthly ozone	4·5	4·6	4·9	5·1	4·7	5·6	5·2	5·0	5·4	5·4	5·1	4·7	5·0

The mean standard barometer at 9 a.m., corrected to 32° Fahrenheit and sea level, is .... 30·053
To compare this with the electric barograph subtract for altitude .... 0·166
For average difference between mean of 9 a.m. observation and barograph mean for the day subtract .... 0·032 = 0·198

True mean of the standard barometer in the Observatory at 32° Fahrenheit, for the year 1891, and mean of all hourly readings of the barograph .... 29·855

PART V.

Geological Formation.

THE geology of the Colony has been ably treated by various learned scientists, and this work is being continually added to by Mr. C. S. Wilkinson, the present eminent Government Geologist. To the Rev. W. B. Clarke we are indebted for the first systematic classification of the various sedimentary formations found in New South Wales. These were classified by him as follows :— Classification of rocks.

Palæozoic :	Silurian	
	Devonian	
	Carboniferous	
	Permian.	
Mesozoic :	Triassic	
	Jurassic	
	Cretaceous.	
Cainozoic :	Tertiary	Miocene
		Pliocene
	Post Tertiary	Post Pliocene
		Recent.

Palæozoic.—This formation extends throughout almost the whole eastern portion of the Colony, the rocks of the upper Silurian age principally occurring on the western watershed of the main Dividing Range, in the country where the Murrumbidgee, Lachlan, and Abercrombie Rivers rise. They appear on the eastern watershed, along part of the coast near Bateman's Bay, and, striking inland, are found in the basin of the Clyde, and the upper valley of the Shoalhaven. Palæozoic formation.

The upper Silurian rocks extend as far north as Mudgee, where they are overlaid by the Carboniferous strata of the Hunter Valley, and by the belt of volcanic rocks extending along the Liverpool Range. They reappear further north, in the upper valley of the Macleay River, on the east slope, and in the basin of the Namoi, on the west of the Dividing Range. The Silurian rocks consist of sandstone, slate, and limestone, and exhibit evidence of metamorphism, particularly in the country around Bathurst and Hill End.

Limestone.

Limestone beds, of considerable extent, are scattered throughout this formation. These are chiefly composed of crinoids and corals which outcrop prominently in the Wellington District, near Molong and Gulgong, at Tuena, and also in the Murrumbidgee District. In the limestone formations are found magnificent caves, such as the Wellington, Wombeyan, and Fish River or Jenolan Caves, the fame of which has spread even beyond the confines of Australia. The caves at Yarrangobilly, in the Kiandra district, are also said to be very attractive. Rocks of the Devonian age also exist near Rydal, where Mr. C. S. Wilkinson has measured a section of strata, showing a thickness of not less than 10,000 feet.

Carboniferous Deposits.

The carboniferous formations occupy the whole valley of the Hunter, and of its chief tributary, the Goulburn, on the east slope of the main range. They are also found on the opposite slope, in the upper valley of the Castlereagh, and along the edge of the great tertiary depression which the Upper Darling drains. They appear again on the south coast, at Bulli and Coal Cliff, extending southwards to Bateman's Bay, and embracing the basins of the small rivers between the Clyde and the Shoalhaven, as well as the lower valley of the last-named river. Cut off by the high coast range, the formation reappears at Marulan and Berrima, again in the valley of the Cox River, at Lithgow Valley, and at Capertee River, thus forming a distinct connection with the great series of the Hunter.

The lower coal measures are included in the upper carboniferous series, and contain many seams of workable coal, some of remarkable thickness. These are situated principally in the lower valley of the Hunter River, comprising amongst others the Greta, Anvil Creek, and West Maitland seams. These seams are over-topped and underlaid by conglomerate and sandstones, of great thickness, the strata of this age being estimated by Mr. Wilkinson to be 10,000 feet thick. The seams in the Newcastle coal-fields, as well as those in the Illawarra and coast districts above and below Jervis Bay, belong to the upper coal measures, in which also are included the Berrima and the Lithgow seams. They appear frequently, as in the case of the last named, at a great elevation above the sea, and owing to their almost horizontal strata are worked with great facility. The coal-bearing strata extend as far as the upper valley of the Castlereagh, thence northward, as already mentioned, along the edge of the great tertiary series, to Queensland, in which colony they reappear at a considerable elevation. Coal seams.

Mesozoic.—To this period belong the Hawkesbury and Wianamatta series, which overlay the carboniferous formation of that part of the country through which the Hawkesbury and its principal tributaries flow. It is in this formation that the wonderful gorges of the Blue Mountains, and the beautiful harbours of Port Jackson, Port Hacking, and Broken Bay occur. The rocks are of warm yellow sandstone, and the thickness of the strata is estimated at about 1,000 feet. Mesozoic formation.

The Wianamatta series extend round the metropolis and cover a space in the shape of an irregular triangle, the angular points of which rest at Picton on the south, Richmond on the north, and Sydney on the east. The beds are composed of fine sedimentary deposits of argillaceous shales, and are of comparatively little thickness. They appear to have been deposited in hollows worn by denudation out of the sandstone, on which they directly rest. The Wianamatta series.

To the Mesozoic period belongs also the basin of the Clarence River, the strata of which consist of sandstone, shales, and conglomerates, intersected by occasional coal seams. The extent of the series, distinctively known as the Clarence, is considerable, stretching as it does along the coast from the Tweed to Red Head, and inland some 50 miles.

Cretaceous formations.

The Cretaceous formations occupy the north-western part of the Colony, extending from the Darling westward, towards the north-west corner. Water-bearing strata have been reached at depths varying from 300 feet to 1,100 feet, and large quantities of water have been obtained. The existence of subterranean water throughout this extensive region has been practically demonstrated, and it remains for the settlers to avail themselves of the stores with which nature has charged her reservoirs in the ages that have long since been counted out.

Artesian water.

Since 1882 the Department of Mines has had at work in different parts of the Colony a number of diamond and other kinds of drills, and water augers. Bores have been put down, wells sunk, and artesian supplies obtained in the cretaceous formations of the counties of Killara, Landsborough, and Barrona, and lately at other points of the north-western portion of New South Wales, particularly in the vicinity of the townships of Bourke and Tibooburra. Several valuable supplies of subterranean water have been obtained in other parts of Australia, one of the most important discoveries being the artesian well at Barcaldine, in Queensland, one of the most arid districts on the continent. The water from this well is said to flow at the rate of 240,000 gallons per day. This supply was obtained at a depth of 690 feet, and, compared with the magnificent result, at the insignificant cost of £775.

Boring operations.

The boring operations conducted by the Mines Department during 1890 consisted of 7,857 feet bored by the diamond drill, and 497 feet with the water augers. The average cost per foot with the diamond drills was 14s. 6d., very nearly, as compared with 14s. 3¼d. in 1889. The persons who employ the drills are, as a rule, prospectors engaged in developing the mineral resources of the country, and in order that they should obtain the fullest benefit from the drills provided by the State, the charge made is only sufficient to cover the actual cost of working, and leave the barest margin of profit.

The Water Augers.

The work done by the water augers cost 32s. per foot. There were only two bores in operation during the year—one at the 106-mile, and the other at the 121-mile, on the Wanaaring to Milparinka road. The former has now reached 1,206 ft. 6 in., and the latter 1,112 ft. 8 in. deep.

There are already eight artesian springs utilized in the Colony, seven of which are west of the Darling, and one is near Jervis Bay. One of the bores, near Bourke, sunk to a depth of 144 feet, gives 60,000 gallons of water per day. Another, bored to 966 feet, gives a daily supply of 22,400 gallons.

Private enterprise in artesian well-boring.

Important discoveries of underground water have been made by private enterprise. In 1888 the Federal Company put down a bore at Kerribree Station, near Bourke, and at 1,073 feet obtained a yield of 473,000 gallons per day. Artesian water was found in 1889 at Dunlop Station at 880 feet, yielding 600,000 gallons per day—more than the flow of the Barcaldine Well in Queensland. It is impossible to over-value the effects of these discoveries in promoting settlement in the western regions of the Colony.

Cainozoic formation.

Cainozoic.—To this formation belongs the greater portion of the central and western districts of the Colony. It therefore embraces the valleys of the great western rivers, and their chief tributaries. The formation is, however, intersected by a broad belt, chiefly of Silurian rocks, extending across its centre, from the Bogan River towards the Great Barrier Range, on the further side of the Darling. Large patches of Devonian formation are also met with in the same region. Making these deductions, the tertiary formation covers more than one third of the whole Colony. The vast alluvial plains were formed during the Pliocene and Post Pliocene periods. The alluvial deposits are of variable thickness, sometimes shallow, but in the great plains, between the main rivers which intersect the country, the deposits are of very great depth.

IGNEOUS AND METAMORPHIC FORMATION.

The area occupied by this formation comprises one-eighth of the Colony—the principal rocks belonging to the series consisting of varieties of granite, porphyry, diorite, and serpentine. The granite formation occurs for the most part in the northern and southern masses of the great dividing chains, but is found out-cropping throughout the Silurian deposits, which cover so large a part of the centre of the Colony. Diorite and basalt occur principally in the country between the Macleay and Manning Rivers, and on both slopes of the Liverpool Range, between the upper waters of the Namoi and Macleay, and divide the upper Silurian and Carboniferous deposits of the eastern and western watersheds. Serpentine is found scattered in different parts of the Colony, chiefly at Gundagai, Bingera, Lucknow, and Port Macquarie. The granites, porphyries, and diorite rocks have been recognised as belonging to the Palæozoic age, whilst the volcanic rocks, basalts and others are contemporaneous with the tertiary series.

Granite formation.

PART VI.

Mines and Minerals.

THE progress of the Colony during the first sixty years of its history, viewed in the light of later events, seems painfully slow, and somewhat uncertain. Yet the earlier colonists must have been conscious of the vast heritage destined to become the fortune of Australia, for on no other supposition can their sacrifices and exertions be understood. To the nations of the old world this was practically an unknown land, and it was not till the story of the gold discoveries was noised abroad that the importance and possible future of Australia were in any way realised.

Gold-mining.

Gold-mining was but for a brief period the leading industry of these colonies, even in the wonderful years which succeeded the memorable discovery of Hargraves. Now, amongst the minerals obtained in New South Wales, it yields in importance to coal and silver, and is little above copper and tin; whilst compared with that of pastoral and agricultural produce the value of gold procured is inconsiderable. The discovery of gold, nevertheless, made Australia a nation, for the current of immigration which set southward on the presence of the precious metal becoming known has never ceased. Thousands of men in the prime of life, attracted to these shores by the hope of fortune easily acquired on the fields of the Turon and Bendigo, seeing patient industry everywhere rewarded, remained to share the general prosperity, and those who came to dig for gold readily turned their attention to their former, but less exciting, pursuits.

Immigration due to gold discovery.

New South Wale less affected by gold discovery than Victoria.

The settlement of New South Wales has not been affected by the gold discovery to the same extent as that of Victoria, yet the number of persons engaged in actual search for the precious metal was at one time considerable. This number has gradually decreased, as the fields have been despoiled of the treasures contained in their easily worked alluvial deposits. The abandonment of a gold-field is not, however, always a loss to the country. After the excitement has died out, the digger makes room for the agriculturist, and resources of a more permanent character are developed, in parts of the Colony, which, but for the prospector, would have been unknown, and, but for the farmer, would have remained a wilderness.

Modern system of gold-mining.

Gold-mining now requires the expenditure of capital for the erection of plant and gold-saving machinery; and the miner, whose stock-in-trade of gold-digging appliances consisted solely of a pick, a shovel, and a tin-dish, has had, in the great majority of instances, to seek other fields of labour. Still the mining industry of New South Wales is in a very flourishing condition, and maintains in employment a fair proportion of the people of the Colony. Many of the gold-miners have turned their attention to the silver, copper, and tin mines, and the coal and shale mines find occupation for large numbers. Every year the variety of minerals wrought shows an increase. At the end of 1890, 205,774 acres of Crown lands were held under lease to mine for various minerals, and 46,009 acres were held under application to lease. A large area of freehold lands and Crown lands was also held under miners' rights and mineral licenses. There were 174 permits to dig and search for gold, under section 45 of the Act of 1884, and 91 under section 7. There were no permits issued to search for minerals in conditional leaseholds, under section 98. There had been 172 applications for permits to search for gold and other minerals within conditional leases, under the Mining Act of 1889, of which number 164 were dealt with, and 100 were granted. The amount received as royalty on reserved mineral during the year was £5,606.

Number of persons engaged in mining

The following table gives the approximate number of persons actually engaged in the principal departments of mining during each of the past seven years:—

Persons engaged mining for—	1884.	1885.	1886.	1887.	1888.	1889.	1890.
Gold	6,548	5,911	6,767	6,060	8,278	10,192	12,589
Silver and silver lead........	45	929	1,297	1,670	4,215	6,587	6,044
Copper	1,746	1,000	622	503	1,214	542	702
Tin	2,850	3,395	2,814	3,188	3,499	1,234	2,345
Coal	6,227	7,097	7,847	7,996	9,301	10,277	10,469
Shale	116	324	100	120	258	138	189
Total	17,532	18,656	19,447	19,539	26,760	28,970	32,338

There were also 20 men engaged in mining for alum, 110 iron-miners at Lithgow, and 114 men mining for opals near Wilcannia, making a total of 32,582 miners at work in 1890, representing with their families a population of about 150,000 persons, directly dependent upon mining for a livelihood.

The summary hereunder shows the quantity and value of the products of the various minerals since their first discovery, as well as the quantity won in the year 1890. Quantity and value of mineral products of the Colony.

Mineral Production to end of 1890.

Minerals.	During the year 1890.		To the end of the year 1890.	
	Quantity.	Value.	Quantity.	Value.
	oz.	£	oz.	£
Gold*	127,761	460,285	10,220,117	38,075,172
Silver	496,553	95,410	4,211,549	846,965
	tons.		tons.	
Coal	3,060,876	1,279,089	49,526,709	23,891,629
Shale	56,010	104,103	612,692	1,338,552
Coke†	31,097	41,147	31,097	41,147
Tin	....	179,057	....	5,541,700
Copper........................	....	84,107	....	3,362,728
Iron‡	....	....	....	265,465
Antimony	1,026	20,240	5,132	93,741
Bismuth	2	306	168	36,142
Silver lead (Bullion)	41,320	2,667,144	107,232	6,835,541
Silver and silver lead Ores ...	89,719		164,319	
Lead (pig)	126	1,587	649	8,298
Oxide of iron	455	884	944	2,213
Sundry minerals§	....	70,544	....	116,746
Total Value	....	5,003,903	....	80,456,039

* The figures for 1890, included quartz and pyrites to the value of £1,822 exported, and computed as equal to 472 oz. of gold.
† Not distinguished previous to 1890.
‡ The figure for 1889 has been repeated, the iron manufactured at Eskbank being from old iron rails, and not from ore the produce of the Colony.
§ [illegible], limestone flux, alum, manganese ore, opals, and "sundry minerals" (so called in Mining Report).

It will be seen from the foregoing table that the Colony has produced various minerals of the total value of nearly eighty and a half millions sterling. The figures differ somewhat from those given by the Mines Department, but are correct.

METALLIC MINERALS.

Gold.

Gold.—Amongst the metallic minerals found in the Colony, gold occupies a foremost place, both on account of the quantity which has been, and is now being, raised, and of the influence which its discovery has had on the settlement of the country. The date of the discovery of gold in New South Wales was for a long time the theme of much controversy, and the question as to the original discoverer, long disputed. It is now agreed, however, that the existence of gold was known to the authorities during the early days, when the Colony was a convict settlement, but for obvious State reasons the matter remained secret. The first authentic record of the discovery of gold is contained in an extract from Assistant Surveyor James McBrian's Field-book, bearing date 16th February, 1823, in which the following note appears:—"At 8 chains 50 links to river, and marked gum-tree—at this place I found numerous particles of gold in the sand and in the hills convenient to the river." The river referred to is the Fish River, at about 15 miles from Bathurst, not far from the spot to which the first gold-rush was made twenty-eight years afterwards.

First mention of gold.

In 1839, Count Strzlecki found gold in the Vale of Clwydd, and communicated the discovery to Governor Gipps, but he was requested to keep the matter secret, lest the knowledge of the existence of gold should imperil the safety and discipline of the settlement. The Rev. W. B. Clarke also found gold in 1841 in the Macquarie Valley and the Vale of Clwydd, and expressed his belief that the precious metal would be found abundantly dispersed throughout the territory.

Actual discovery of payable gold.

But it was not until the year 1851 that payable deposits were proved to exist in New South Wales, and this important discovery was due to Mr. E. Hammond Hargraves, who, on his return some time previously from California, pointed out to the Government the localities in which he had found payable deposits of alluvial gold, viz., at Lewis Ponds and Summer Hill Creek, in the districts of Bathurst and Wellington. Prospecting operations followed in the neighbourhood, with the result of which every one is now familiar. A few weeks later rich deposits were discovered at Ballarat, Mount Alexander, and other gold-fields, in Victoria; and the world witnessed a gold rush from all parts of the earth to these colonies, similar to that which some years before had taken place to California. The probable effects of the movement were not clearly seen at the time, either here or in the United Kingdom, but the result has been the creation of states, whose future is surrounded with the brightest promise.

Native gold is the only true mineral species of gold which has, so far, been found in New South Wales, and was first met with in easily worked alluvial deposits. Alluvial diggings have always attracted the greater number of miners, as the precious metal is dug out without costly appliances. But, however rich they may be, these deposits are very soon worked out, for their area is generally of limited extent. In the alluvial deposits gold is found associated with a variety of minerals; it occurs in the shape of grains and nuggets, water-worn in appearance, and some of considerable size. Though New South Wales has not yielded nuggets of so extraordinary a size as those found in the neighbouring Colony of Victoria, some very splendid specimens of that gold formation have, nevertheless, been unearthed at various times. Alluvial gold.

Thus, in July, 1851, a mass of gold was found on the Turon River gold-fields which weighed 106 lb., or 1,272 oz. In November, 1858, at Burrandong, near Orange, another nugget was found which, when melted at the Sydney Mint, gave 1,182 oz. 6 dwt. of pure gold, of the value of £4,389 8s. 10d. A third nugget, called the Brennan, was sold in Sydney in 1851 for £1,156. In 1880 and 1882, several nuggets which were unearthed at Temora weighed Remarkable nuggets and their value.

from 59 to 139 oz., and in 1887 nuggets were found by fossickers in various parts of the country, four of which, weighing respectively 357 oz., 200 oz., 47 oz., and 32 oz., were obtained at Hargraves; and another, weighing 30 oz., at Limestone Creek. The Jubilee nugget, weighing 344 oz., was also discovered in that year at Maitland Bar, in the Mudgee District, and was worth about £1,236.

Further discoveries probable.

Although the alluvial deposits discovered in the early days have been practically abandoned, and are considered as worked out, there is ample evidence that the surface of the country has been merely scratched. The search for gold has been vigorously prosecuted for more than thirty-six years; but new gold-fields and fresh deposits are nevertheless being continually discovered in localities supposed to have been thoroughly examined. The gold formation is very widely diffused throughout the Colony, as may be gathered from the fact that the gold-fields of Albert, Delegate, and Ballina are between 600 and 700 miles distant from each other; and it has been estimated that the extent of country covered by formations in association with which gold always occurs, exceeds 70,000 square miles, whilst the precious metal has also been found in formations where its presence was never suspected. A considerable portion of this area, equal to nearly one-fourth of the whole surface of the Colony, has never been touched by the pick of the miner.

Want of appliances in early days.

It is well-known to the mining public that many mines which gave promise of handsome results were abandoned in the early days, simply because the appliances at hand were not sufficiently powerful or well directed to save the gold contained in the foreign matter with which it was found associated. At Wattle Flat, on the Turon River, and at many places on the older gold-fields, gold was found in deposits of iron pyrites, which have since proved to be in a very high degree payable; but these claims, when apparently exhausted, were abandoned some years ago, the miners lacking the necessary knowledge or skill to obtain from the pyrites the whole of the gold they contained. Improved methods of extraction have since been invented and a rich harvest awaits the skilled miner who shall bring to bear upon the development of this industry, modern knowledge, and appliances such as are being successfully employed in other countries.

Formation in which gold occurs.

Gold is also found in quartz-veins, occurring in older and metamorphic rocks, such as argillaceous slates, chloritic, and talcose schists, as well as granite, diorite, serpentine, and porphyry. Vein gold is associated more commonly with iron pyrites, though found with copper, lead, zinc, and silver ores, and occurring also in asbestos. But the extraction of gold from quartz-veins requires the erection of extensive machinery and gold-saving appliances, involving an outlay of capital such as the ordinary miner seldom possesses. Quartz-mining is generally carried on by companies, many of which regularly pay handsome dividends to their shareholders.

Richness of good veins.

Some idea of the exceeding richness of many of these gold veins may be gained from a few particulars relating to the yield from various mines at Hill End, which were recorded during 1873. In January of that year 1·02 cwt. of gold was raised at Beyers and Holtermann's mine from 10 tons of quartz, and a slab of vein stuff and gold from the same mine, weighing 630 lb., and estimated to contain £2,000 worth of gold, was also exhibited. Many other similar rich blocks were also shown. The Mint returns for the gold obtained in this mine during 1873 from 415 tons of vein stuff were 16,279·63 oz., value £63,234 12s. Krohman's Company, also at Hill End, raised during the same year 436 tons 2 cwt. of stone, for which the Mint returns were 24,079 oz. 8 dwt. of gold, value £93,616 11s. 9d. Very rich returns from a quartz-vein were being obtained in March, 1891, at Hill End.

Gold in coal measures.

Gold has been found in the Coal Measures, and Carboniferous strata. The Rev. W. B. Clarke detected it in the Hawkesbury sandstone formation, on the north side of Sydney Harbour, and he also mentions that it is distributed through the sand at the mouth of the Richmond River. Along the southern part of the coast of New South Wales gold has been found near the shore in the sand washed by the waves of the Pacific Ocean, whilst at Bermagui, and in the district extending between Moruya and Eden, important discoveries of the precious metal have also been made. It would be impossible to name every part of the colony in which gold is found, as it appears throughout the greater part of the territory, and there is ample evidence that deposits exist which will offer to the prospector or the miner a profitable field of employment for many years to come.

Weight and value of gold coined and exported.

The following table shows the quantity and value of the gold coined and exported yearly since 1851 :—

Year.	Weight.	Value.	Year.	Weight.	Value.
	oz.	£		oz.	£
1851	144,120·88	468,336	1872	424,100·23	1,634,821
1852	818,751·93	2,660,946	1873	360,849·97	1,389,705
1853	548,052·99	1,781,172	1874	270,710·12	1,038,844
1854	237,910·70	773,209	1875	229·385·55	881,480
1855	170,145·73	613,148	1876	155,166·37	581,689
1856	183,946·36	666,155	1877	122,619·24	463,130
1857	161,043·26	616,712	1878	117,977·88	423,184
1858	280,557·93	1,082,865	1879	107,640·38	399,187
1859	323,984·02	1,237,662	1880	116,750·52	434,641
1860	381,613·96	1,445,158	1881	145,532·05	550,111
1861	459,879·26	1,771,855	1882	129,233·28	491,594
1862	616,909·71	2,360,383	1883	122,256·58	452,611
1863	467,399·05	1,791,534	1884	105,933·43	390,229
1864	341,954·12	1,304,735	1885	100,667·16	366,388
1865	364,540·63	1,390,803	1886	98,446·27	355,600
1866	287,534·29	1,103,246	1887	108,101·46	386,771
1867	269,407·35	1,043,458	1888	85,295·49	308,821
1868	258,773·41	1,003,002	1889	118,947·54	431,138
1869	252,130·14	967,625	1890	127,288·89	458,453
1870	240,401·86	916,409			
1871	321,468·70	1,232,011	Total	10,177,438·69	37,668,721

Decline in gold production.

This table shows that the production of gold in New South Wales has, since the year 1872, considerably decreased. This decrease is explained by the fact that the rich alluvial deposits discovered in the early days have been exhausted, and that other resources of a more permanent nature are being developed. The latter offer steadier employment to the labouring classes, without, it is true, the chance of accumulating rapid fortunes, but with more security against loss.

Alluvial gold mining.

The principal seats of alluvial gold-mining are the Bathurst and Mudgee districts, and the country watered by the various feeders of the Upper Lachlan, and also in the Tumut and Adelong and Braidwood districts. In 1880, the Temora gold-fields, in the Murrumbidgee district, about 30 to 40 miles from the inland town of Wagga Wagga, were discovered, and were for some years in a flourishing condition. The district is now drifting from mining into an important agricultural settlement. In the north of the Colony, in the New England district; on the coast, in the county of Gloucester; and in the extreme north-west, at Mount Poole, Mount Browne, and Tibooburra, the gold-fields sustain a considerable population of miners. The system of hydraulic sluicing is adopted in only two or three mines in the New England district, and at Kiandra, on the southern tablelands, where extensive reservoirs have been formed, and the face of the rocks attacked in various places.

Quartz-mining.

The principal quartz-veins are situated near Bathurst, Armidale, Hill End, and Mudgee; the two last-mentioned gold districts had, up to the end of 1890, already yielded 1,115,991 oz., or over 34 tons of gold, valued at £4,330,501. The Geological Surveyor, who examined this field in 1886, reported that its resources were far from being exhausted. At Adelong, Tumut, Temora, Parkes, [illegible], and near Gundagai, reefs are also profitably worked, as well as on the south coast of the Colony and in the north-western district. A promising gold-field was opened up at Peak Hills, about 45 miles from Dubbo, towards the end of 1889, and another at Pambula, near Twofold Bay, during 1890.

Revival of quartz mining in 1887 and 1888.

Much enterprise has been shown during the last few years in the search for gold; and quartz-reefs have been opened up in many parts with profitable results. Old workings, which had been abandoned years ago under a prevailing idea that they were valuable only on the surface, and which had scarcely, in any instance, been tested to a greater depth than 200 feet, have been reopened with very encouraging results. This is principally the case at Hill End, Ironbarks, and at Lewis Ponds, the latter district having proved as rich in silver as in gold deposits. In the country surrounding the great copper-mines of Cobar, Nymagee, and Mount Hope, between the Bogan and the Darling Rivers, reefs have been recently discovered; the prospects thoroughly justifying the outlay of capital for the development of these mines, some of which were successfully floated in 1888 in the Melbourne market, considerable sums being spent in the erection of machinery for the treatment of the quartz, the results of which are only now beginning to appear. From the extreme west of the Colony the reports of the mining wardens are equally encouraging while in the Tumut and Adelong, and other southern mining districts, much enterprise is being exhibited in the search for the precious metal. In the New England District the gold-reefs of Hillgrove in the neighbourhood of Armidale continue to attract considerable attention. A large population has already settled in that district, and several important discoveries have been made. It appears to have been proved that these veins greatly resemble in character the reefs found in Victoria. They are in reality true fissure veins, and the permanency of the lodes seems to be established beyond doubt.

Decline of alluvial mining.

An important feature of the gold-mining industry of late years is that the number of persons employed in alluvial mining and the revenue derived from this source, have diminished considerably, whilst quartz-mining is more and more becoming a permanent industry, the returns from that source being greater in the last three years than for a long period.

The gold found in New South Wales is never absolutely pure, always containing traces of other metals, such as copper, iron, and bismuth, and often a fair percentage of silver. To the presence of the latter its light-yellow colour is due. New South Wales gold is generally lighter in colour than Victorian gold, but of a deeper yellow than that found in the fields of Southern Queensland; its specific gravity averages about 17·5. Composition, colour, and specific gravity.

The authority to dig for gold costs only 10s. a year, and entitles its possessor not only to take up ground for mining, but also to occupy, in a mining township, a ¼ acre, or, outside a town, 1 acre of land for a business site. Authority to dig.

In 1890, 1,263 applications were made for auriferous land, comprising an area of 10,255 acres. The steam-engines employed in quartz-mining numbered 143, with an aggregate of 1,969 horse-power. There were also 58 crushing-machines, and 688 stamp-heads. In alluvial gold and tin mining there were employed 26 steam-engines, whose aggregate horse-power equalled 351. The value of the machinery employed in gold-mining is estimated at £459,246. During the year 1890 the number of persons more or less regularly employed, in various parts of the Colony, in gold-mining was 12,589, of whom 11,882 were Europeans and 707 Chinese. There were 6,285 persons engaged in quartz-mining, and 6,304 in the alluvial diggings. Extent of mining enterprise.

The quantity of gold, the produce of New South Wales, received at the Sydney Mint for coinage during 1890 amounted to 119,564 oz., of the gross value of £435,983, the average price being £3 12s. 11d. per ounce. Gold sent to Sydney Mint.

The figures for 1890 show an increase of 5,078 oz. when compared with those of the previous year, which is very satisfactory on the whole. It must always be borne in mind that Coinage of gold in Sydney.

the results of quartz-mining are, in few cases, immediately seen. Much patient labour and the expenditure of a large amount of capital must take place before payable gold is obtained, and the leases taken up two years ago are only now beginning to show a return for the time, labour, and money which have been bestowed upon them. The average weight of gold obtained by each miner in 1890 was 10 oz. 3 dwt., valued at £36 11s. 3d. It must not be supposed, however, that these men were employed during the whole year for so small a wage. Many of the miners follow other pursuits during a portion of the year; besides which, there were several new fields, from which as yet very little returns have been made, and a large number of men were engaged in prospecting.

Yield from quartz.

The following table shows the average yield of gold obtained from certain parcels of quartz crushed in several of the mining districts:—

District.	Quantity.			Average per ton			Yield of Gold.		
	Tons	cwt.	qr.	oz.	dwt.	gr.	oz.	dwt.	gr.
Bathurst	8,428	0	0	0	6	18	2,855	6	11
Tambaroora and Turon	2,502	0	0	0	10	9	1,298	5	0
Lachlan	3,768	0	0	0	18	5	3,579	0	0
Southern	1,730	11	0	0	17	16	1,538	0	18
Adelong and Tumut	12,321	0	0	0	8	12	5,253	12	14
Peel and Uralla	13,810	0	0	1	6	2	18,150	14	0
Hunter and Macleay	415	0	0	1	1	13	447	4	9
Clarence and Richmond	282	10	0	1	7	17	380	13	9
Mudgee	2,522	0	0	0	13	12	1,704	2	9
Cobar	1,023	0	0	0	13	19	704	10	0
	46,802	1	0	0	15	8	36,911	8	13

Yield of alluvium.

Owing to the reluctance shown by miners to disclose the result of their labours, it has been found possible to obtain a return of the treatment of alluvium in 1890 only from the Lachlan district. The yield, though good, is not so high as the average for 1889, though there is nothing to show whether the figures here given indicate the general average of the Colony or not. The statement embraces such a very small proportion of the total quantity treated, as to be of comparatively little value for statistical purposes, and is only given because fuller details are wanting :—

District.	Quantity.	Average per ton.	Yield of Gold.
	Tons.	oz. dwt. gr.	oz. dwt. gr.
Lachlan	11,761	0 9 11	5,717 10 0

The number of fatal accidents in gold-mines during 1890 was not quite so large as in the previous year. Five men lost their lives in auriferous quartz-mining, two in alluvial workings, and nine were injured in quartz-mines. Accidents in gold mines.

From the date of the first discovery of payable gold, in 1851, to the end of the year 1890, the quantity of gold produced in the Australasian colonies represents a total value of £341,906,358, extracted in the short space of forty years. The share of each colony in the production of this wealth is given hereunder :— Total production of gold in Australasia.

Production of Gold in Australia to end of 1890.

Colony.	Value.	Proportion raised in each Colony.
	£	per cent.
New South Wales	38,075,172	11·14
Victoria	227,357,436	66·50
Queensland	26,034,662	7·61
South Australia	1,169,768	0·34
Western Australia	605,535	0·18
Tasmania	2,238,156	0·65
New Zealand	46,425,629	13·58
Australasia	341,906,358	100·00

By far the largest proportion of this amount was produced by the Colony of Victoria, amounting in fact to two-thirds of the whole. New Zealand is the next largest producer, New South Wales coming third.

Silver.

Silver.—Up to the year 1882 the quantity of silver raised in New South Wales was very small, but in that and the following years extensive discoveries of this metal, associated principally with lead and copper ore, were made in various parts of the Colony, notably at Boorook, in the New England district, and, later on, at Sunny Corner, near Bathurst, and at Silverton, on the Barrier Range, in the western district. Unfortunately smelting operations in the latter district were retarded, owing to the serious drought which prevailed during the two years following the discovery of the lodes. In 1883 and 1884, however, the principal difficulties were surmounted; smelting furnaces were erected on the most modern principle, both at Sunny Corner and at Silverton, and extensive shipments of the metal were made.

The Broken Hill silver mines.

The field of Silverton has since proved to be of immense value. Discoveries have been made along the Barrier Range at Broken Hill, Umberumberka, The Pinnacle, and many other points; and the fame of the Silverton mines has spread over the whole world. The yield of minerals in this district in 1890 showed a total value of £2,785,398, while the machinery employed is valued at £406,885.

Barrier Ranges and Broken Hill silver-lead mines.

The argentiferous lead ores of the Barrier Ranges and Broken Hill districts of New South Wales have, more than any other, attracted attention. This rich silver-field, which was discovered in 1883 by Charles Rasp, a boundary-rider on Mount Gipps Run, extends over 2,500 square miles of country, and has developed into one of the principal mining centres of the world. It is situated beyond the river Darling, and on the confines of the neighbouring Colony of South Australia. In the Barrier Range district the lodes occur in Silurian metamorphic micaceous schists, intruded by granite, porphyry, and diorite, and traversed by numerous quartz-reefs, some of which are gold-bearing. The Broken Hill lode is the largest as yet discovered. It varies in width from 10 feet to 200 feet, and may be traced for several miles, the country having been taken up all along the line of the lode, and subdivided into numerous leases, held by mining companies and syndicates.

The Broken Hill Proprietary Company hold the premier position. They have erected on their lease a complete smelting plant on the latest and most approved principles, and have enlisted the services of competent managers, whose experience has been gained in the celebrated silver-mining centres of the United States. From the commencement of mining operations in 1885 to the beginning of June, 1891, the Company treated 656,000 tons of silver and silver lead ores, producing 25,750,000 oz. of silver and 107,038 tons of lead, valued in the London market at £5,913,292. They have paid dividends to the amount of £2,728,000, and bonuses amounting to £592,000, besides the nominal value of shares from the several "Blocks," amounting to about £1,744,000, or a total return from the mine of £5,064,000. The sum spent in the erection and construction of plant, from the opening of the property, was £382,429. During the year 2,545 men were employed, of whom 1,412 were engaged under ground. The mine wage-sheet for the half-year ended on June 30, 1891, was £117,696, and smelting wages and salaries came to £43,165. The gross profit for the half-year was £625,948. Broken Hill Proprietary Company.

Besides the mines at Broken Hill, there are very valuable workings at Silverton and Thackaringa in the same district; the value of silver and ore exported during 1890 from the Barrier country, was silver lead bullion, £1,844,262, and silver lead ore, £774,500, making a total value of over two millions and a half. As a natural consequence of the success of these mines, numbers of miners were attracted to the district, and the population, which in 1883 consisted of only a few station hands, had risen to an estimated total of 25,500 souls at the end of 1890. The proximity of Silverton and the Barrier district to the Colony of South Australia could not fail to attract the attention of the business people at Adelaide, who were not slow to realise the advantages which they would obtain by attracting towards their Silverton and Thackaringa.

capital the traffic of a region of such immense wealth. The railway system of South Australia was immediately extended to the border, and in the Colony of New South Wales a tramway was laid down, thus connecting the town of Silverton, and the mines of Broken Hill, with the railway to Adelaide and Port Pirie, in the latter instance reducing the land carriage by some 70 to 80 miles.

Valuable silver discoveries.

The success of the Barrier Ranges Mines gave rise throughout New South Wales to a veritable silver fever, and parties of miners were soon abroad in all directions searching for the precious mineral. Their energy was in many instances rewarded by the discovery of payable lodes. Thus at Lewis Ponds, Tuena, Mount Costigan, and many other places between Goulburn and Orange, huge deposits of silver-bearing ore have been discovered.

Sunny Corner.

The Sunny Corner Company, which had paid handsome dividends in 1886, and yielded £160,000 worth of silver, suffered a temporary check in 1887, but has since recovered to some extent. In the Tumut and Monaro districts numerous argentiferous lodes were found, and great excitement was the consequence. The discovery of silver lodes, said to be of great richness, at White Rock, near Fairfield, in the New England district, followed by that of auriferous and argentiferous deposits in the neighbourhood, brought up the excitement to fever heat, and considerable sums of money were asked for these mines, which were offered to the public at prices that may, without exaggeration, be termed fabulous. The closing months of 1887, and the early part of 1888, witnessed all over Australia an extravagant silver mania, which has since considerably subsided, to the detriment of many who were induced to invest their capital in speculative properties. Numerous companies were formed, whose shares, notwithstanding the fact that work had not in many instances been carried out beyond the initiatory and prospecting stage, became a medium of speculation which could not but end in disaster. But this refers principally to undeveloped mines, and properties whose value it is difficult to ascertain. Old and fairly established mines continued to prosper, notwithstanding the depression in the share market, and the result

Silver mania.

was a very large increase in the production of silver and silver ores in New South Wales. In most cases great difficulty is experienced in reducing refractory ores, and it is found more profitable to ship the ore to the Continent of Europe in a concentrated state, which fact explains the anomaly exhibited by the figures showing the value of silver produced in 1887, 1888, 1889, and 1890, as compared with the production of 1886.

The quantity and value of silver and silver lead ore exported to the end of 1890 from New South Wales is shown in the following table:— Silver and silver lead ore exported.

Year.	Silver.		Silver lead Ore.			Total Value.
	Quantity.	Value.	Quantity.		Value.	
			Ore.	Metal.		
Up to	oz.	£	Tons cwt.	Tons cwt.	£	£
1881	728,779	178,405	191 13	....	5,025	183,430
1882	38,618	9,024	11 19	....	360	9,384
1883	77,065	16,488	126 4	....	2,075	18,563
1884	93,660	19,780	9,167 11	....	241,940	261,720
1885	794,174	159,187	2,096 16	190 8	107,626	266,813
1886	1,015,433	197,544	4,802 2	....	294,485	492,029
1887	177,308	32,465	12,529 3	....	541,962	574,410
1888	375,064	66,668	11,739 7	18,102 5	1,075,737	1,142,405
1889	416,895	72,001	46,965 9	34,579 17	1,899,197	1,971,198
1890	696,336	95,410	89,715 15	41,319 18	2,667,144	2,762,554
Total......	4,413,549	846,965	177,358 19	94,192 8	6,835,541	7,682,506

It will be seen that the production of silver has, during the past few years, considerably increased, until that of last year exceeded the largest annual production of gold, even in the palmiest days of the diggings. Since the important discoveries of silver deposits were made sufficient time has hardly elapsed to enable all the principal mines to be properly developed; and it may be confidently expected that, as new deposits are opened, and the mines first discovered are brought into full working order, the exports of this metal will rapidly increase. The number of miners engaged in Increase in production of silver.

silver and lead mines in 1890 was 6,044, and the average value of mineral won, per miner engaged, amounted to £457 1s. 5d.

Accidents in silver-mines.

The total number of accidents which took place in the silver-mines of New South Wales during the course of the year 1890 was only twenty-one, nine persons losing their lives, and twelve others being injured. Such a small proportion of casualties when compared to the number of persons engaged in silver-mining, where the elements of danger are great, must be taken as reflecting considerable credit on the management of the mines.

Tin.

Tin.—This mineral occurs principally in the granite and basaltic country in the extreme north of the Colony, near Tenterfield and Vegetable Creek (now called Emmaville), and in other districts of New England. Tin has also been discovered in the Barrier Ranges, at Poolamacca; near Bombala, in the Monarc district, and in the Valley of the Lachlan, but none of these deposits have as yet been worked to any extent. The deposits occur in the shape of stream and lode tin, and are worked by European and Chinese miners. Although this mineral was discovered by the Rev. W. B. Clarke as far back as the year 1853 the opening of the tin-fields of New South Wales only took place in the year 1872, and since that date, to the year 1882, the output from the mines, and the export of tin, increased in a remarkable ratio, as illustrated in the following statement:—

Output of tin mines.

Year.	Ingots and Ore. Value.
1872 to 1876	£1,032,483
1877	248,906
1878	214,613
1879	256,732
1880	354,252
1881	568,795
1882	541,413
1883	448,887
1884	281,188
1885	308,760
1886	277,545
1887	311,889
1888	309,510
1889	207,670
1890	179,057
Total	£5,541,700

Tin has, it will be seen, contributed in a very considerable degree to the general development of the natural wealth of the Colony, and in point of value its aggregate production stands in the third place next to gold and coal; for the years 1881-82 its yearly production was even in excess of that of gold. The production of this metal is now one of the settled industries of the country, and, as the supply is practically unlimited, the quantity raised depends almost entirely upon the price realised. The figures given, though differing from those published by the Department of Mines, are correct. Importance of tin to the Colony.

In 1881, when the tin-mining industry was at its greatest height and prosperity, the value of the mineral exported had increased to £568,795 from £249,779 in 1876. In 1882 the production of the former year was nearly maintained, but after that time, owing to protracted dry seasons, which in many cases prevented mining operations, combined with the comparatively low price which the metal brought, the value of the output decreased considerably. Since then, however, the principal causes of the falling-off in value having been removed, a more satisfactory price induced a revival. The value of the tin produced in 1890, it will be seen, was less than that of any year recorded in the table. The decrease was largely owing to the fact of the shallow deposits of stream tin being to a great extent exhausted, while the deep deposits and the tin lodes have as yet scarcely been touched. Nearly all the tin hitherto produced has been from alluvial deposits. The principal lode worked up to present time is the Ottery Mine, near Emmaville. For a period of some months in 1887 the tin market was controlled by a French syndicate, and the price of the metal, which was quoted at £116 per ton in January, 1887, ran up to £166 at the end of the year, fluctuating between the latter price and £170, until February, 1888, when the syndicate, unable to hold any longer, collapsed, and the metal fel. rapidly to nearly as low a level as it ever reached within the last twenty years. During the latter months of 1888 the tin market Value of tin exported.

again improved, and the price obtained during that year attained an average even above that of 1887, though lower prices ruled in 1889. In June, 1891, Australian tin was quoted in the London market at £94 5s. per ton, at which figure the rich deposits of New England and the western districts should, if worked on economical principles, handsomely reward industrious proprietors. Within the nineteen years that have elapsed since the opening of the tin-fields the value of the tin exported from New South Wales amounted to £5,541,700.

Chinese and Europeans in alluvial tin-mines.

In the alluvial tin-fields of Tingha and Emmaville the number of Chinese engaged in this industry greatly exceeded the Europeans. In 1890 the Chinese numbered 1,050, whilst the Europeans working alluvial tin drifts numbered only 800. The total number of miners employed in tin mining in the New England district in 1890 was 2,345. No accidents occurred in tin mines in 1890.

Copper.

Copper.—The principal deposits of this mineral are found in the central part of the Colony, between the Macquarie, the Bogan, and the Darling Rivers. Deposits have also been found in the New England and Southern district, as well as at Broken Hill, showing that the mineral is widely diffused throughout the Colony. The very low price of copper within the last few years has deterred many from embarking in operations which showed every promise of success, and some of the mines which had been worked for many years were closed. Still, in spite of the low price of the metal, there is little doubt that, with the adoption of the more modern methods of smelting, such as are now in almost general use in the principal centres of copper production—in Spain, France, England, the United States, and Chili—the rich mines of New South Wales could be made to show handsome results. Another difficulty, common to other branches of the mining industry, lies in the great distance of some of the chief copper-mines from the port of shipment, and the consequent large cost of land-carriage.

The prospect of an improvement in the price of this metal did not appear very encouraging at the opening of the season of 1887, and the English quotations continued to exhibit a tendency to maintain the low prices ruling in 1887, and even to further decrease; but towards the middle of that year a French syndicate entered into arrangements with the principal producers of copper, and succeeded in controlling the market for this metal. The prices, in consequence, rose to a much more satisfactory level. The operations of the syndicate, however, were of only short duration, and, owing to the large accumulation of unsaleable stock, prices fell unprecedently low. In 1872 copper realized as much as £108 per ton, whilst in December, 1886, the lowest price on record was touched, and only £38 7s. 6d. could be obtained for Chili bars. During the years 1884–1886, the price of the metal fluctuated between £58 7s. 6d., the highest quotation for January, 1884, and £38 7s. 6d., the lowest for December, 1886, the average prices for each of the successive years showing the following unsatisfactory state of the market:— Price of copper.

	£	s.	d.
Average for 1884	54	7	6
" 1885	44	0	0
" 1886	40	5	0

At the end of 1887, however, copper had risen to £74 per ton, and in August, 1888, it was selling at £81 5s. per ton, a price which is certainly satisfactory, and much nearer the statistical value of the metal than the prices realised during the three years above quoted. The operations of the French syndicate raised the price of copper but for a comparatively short period, and when, eventually, its failure took place, it had the effect of causing the abrupt cessation of the contracts entered into with some of the principal colonial mines. The average price for copper sold in Sydney by independent companies reached £71 7s. for the year 1888, thus accounting for the enhanced estimated value of the total Operations of the French Syndicate.

export of this metal during that year. The copper market in Europe has remained much disturbed since the failure above alluded to. In June, 1891, copper was quoted in London at £52 per ton, cash quotation.

Future of copper-mining.

With a reduction in the cost of production and of carriage the copper lodes of New South Wales, which contain ores of a very much higher percentage than those of many well-known mines worked at a profit in other parts of the world, should return satisfactory results, notwithstanding the position of affairs at the present time.

Principal copper-mines.

The more important mines are those of Cobar and Nymagee situated in the Central Division, and within 80 miles of each other. The former employed over 500 men and boys, but is now idle; the deepest shaft is 566 feet, and the width of the lode from 2 to 50 feet. From the date of the commencement of operations in 1876, that company treated 205,005 tons of ore, giving a return equal to 22,943 tons of refined metal, an average production of 11·2 per cent. of copper per ton of ore, and the sum of £154,000 has been paid in dividends to the shareholders. Nymagee employs a complement of 250 persons, and its ores contain an average proportion of copper equal to 11·42 per cent. Since its formation, in 1883, this mine has paid large dividends. The yield for 1890 of this mine was 7,865 tons of sulphide ore, which when melted yielded 794 tons of copper, valued at £43,868. The refined Nymagee copper is superior to that of Cobar, and commands a higher price in the market. A depth of 734 feet has been reached in sinking through the lode. The New Mount Hope and the Great Central copper-mines are also said to be rich in payable ores. The first mentioned employed 56 men and 6 boys in 1889, and raised 1,143 tons of ore, equal to 318 tons of copper, valued at £15,900. The total yield of the Cobar district during 1890 is estimated at 1,162 tons of copper, valued at £62,268. The Burraga Mine yielded during 1889, 476 tons of copper, valued at £36,625; and during 1890, 420 tons, worth £24,150. The deepest shaft is 300 feet, and the lode is said to be 15 feet wide.

It only requires a small advance in the price of the metal to cause great activity in the copper-mines of New South Wales.

The following table shows the quantity and value of copper, the produce of the Colony, exported during each year, from 1859 to 1890. The figures, though different from those in the Annual Report of the Mines Department, are correct:— Produce of copper.

Year.	Ingots and Ore—Value.	Year.	Ingots and Ore—Value.
	£		£
1859 to 1876	406,071	1884	362,287
1877	127,396	1885	170,993
1878	209,030	1886	122,990
1879	210,623	1887	115,444
1880	268,700	1888	247,304
1881	257,884	1889	122,444
1882	182,473	1890	84,107
1883	472,982	Total	£3,362,728

The total number of miners engaged in copper-mining in 1890 was 702. There were no accidents recorded in copper-mines during the year.

Iron.—Iron is widely diffused throughout the Colony of New South Wales, and occurs principally in the form of magnetite, brown hematite or goethite, limonite, and bog iron. Deposits of chrome iron are also found. Magnetite is the richest of all the ores of iron, sometimes containing a little over 72 per cent. of available metallic iron, though it is not often found reaching this very high percentage. These ores are widely distributed throughout the Colony. The results of a number of analyses made from deposits at Brown's Creek, in the County of Bathurst, and at Wallerawang, where veins were opened out a few years ago, show that the samples of

Iron.

Maximum richness of magnetic ores of iron.

Analysis of magnetite from Wallerawang mines.

ore yielded from 40·89 to 56·85 per cent. of metallic iron. At Wallerawang a variety of garnet, containing a large percentage of metal, occurs in conjunction with the ore in the veins, which is described as "extremely well adapted for reduction in the blast furnace." Brown hematite or goethite occurs in very extensive deposits in the Blue Mountain Ranges, the principal centres, so far explored, being situated at Mittagong, Picton, and Berrima, at Lithgow Valley, Wallerawang, and in the Rylstone and Mudgee Districts. The result of a number of analyses of this kind of ore denotes that it is very rich in metallic iron, containing a percentage of 42·69 to 64·48 per cent., and in the majority of cases over 55 per cent. of metal. A sample of hematite from the Maitland district contained 60·83 per cent of metallic iron. The value of these deposits is enhanced by their almost invariable occurrence in proximity to limestone and coal-beds. It is fortunate, also, that the main lines of railway pass through the regions where the deposits are most easily worked.

Brown hematite or goethite.

Richness of English and Colonial clay-bands.

Limonite—a variety of brown hematite—principally occurs at Lithgow, Eskbank, and Bowenfels in the Blue Mountains, in several parts of the Hunter River coal-field, and at Bulli in the Illawarra district. This ore is usually found very rich in metal, and contains an average of over 50 per cent. of iron, while the English clay bands, which are mostly carbonates, only contain about 30 per cent. of metallic substance. It occurs in lenticular layers of no great extent, in the Coal Measures. *Bog Iron Ore*, which is impure *limonite*, is principally found at Mittagong; and assays of this ore gave a percentage of metal equal to an average of over 45 per cent.

Bog iron ore.

No other colony of the group possesses deposits of iron ore approaching in extent or richness those of New South Wales; it is therefore possible that at some future time this Colony will become the great seat of the iron industry of Australia. As illustrating the present extent of the supply required, the following table has been compiled; the figures given include the values of all

Australasian imports of iron and iron manufactures.

description of iron, machinery, or iron manufactures, except cutlery and implements, to end of 1889:—

Value of Iron and Iron Manufactures imported into the various Colonies.

Colony.	1886.	1887.	1888.	1889.	Total for Four Years.
	£	£	£	£	£
New South Wales	1,465,401	1,221,332	2,041,091	2,141,857	6,869,611
Victoria	1,147,863	1,374,859	1,902,946	2,392,768	6,818,436
Queensland	645,285	568,403	918,829	746,877	2,879,394
South Australia ..	307,783	345,707	475,657	319,291	1,448,438
Tasmania	245,516	193,598	203,228	227,870	870,212
New Zealand......	861,928	873,060	697,784	901,801	3,334,573
Totals	4,673,776	4,576,959	6,239,465	6,730,464	22,220,664

The average yearly import for the four years covered by the above statement amounts to £1,717,403 for New South Wales, and £5,555,166 for Australasia; and the quantity of pig iron required to produce the material represented by these values was approximately 150,000 tons and 480,000 tons per annum, for New South Wales and the whole group of colonies respectively. In a report, dated January, 1891, by Mr. C. S. Wilkinson, Government Geologist, on some of the iron ore deposits of the Colony where they occur convenient to coal and limestone, it is stated that they contain in sight 12,944,000 tons of ore, estimated to yield 1,853,000 tons of metallic iron.

The only works for the manufacture of iron from the ore are situated at Eskbank, near Lithgow, where the metal treated is red siliceous ore, averaging 22 per cent., and brown hematite, yielding 53 per cent. metallic iron. Abundance of coal and limestone are Iron manufactories in N. S. Wales.

found in the neighbourhood. This establishment, however, has for some time abandoned the manufacture of pig iron, for which it was originally built. The principal work now carried on is the rerolling of old rails, the manufacture of iron bars, rods, and nails, and of ordinary castings. A successful attempt has been made at Mittagong to make gas-pipes, &c., from iron smelted from the ore, and taken direct to the mould, without first making it into pig iron. Some years ago the iron smelting works at Fitzroy, Mittagong, were established, but after producing a considerable quantity of pig-iron the operations were discontinued.

Chromite.

Chromite is found in the northern portion of New South Wales, in the Clarence and Tamworth districts, and also near Young. It is usually associated with serpentine, but so far very little has been done to develop these valuable deposits.

Antimony.

Antimony.—Deposits of antimony occur in the Colony in various places, chiefly in the Armidale, Bathurst, and Rylstone districts. The principal centre of this industry is at Hillgrove, near Armidale, where the Eleanor Mine, one of the richest in the Colony, is situated. The ore is also worked for gold. The results of a number of analyses, made by the authorities of the Geological Museum, show a per centage of metal ranging from 39·90 to 69·97 per cent. of metal; but notwithstanding these encouraging assays the price of this metal has not been sufficiently high to tempt Colonial producers. A considerable quantity of antimony was raised some years ago at the Carangula mines, in the Macleay district. Lodes have been opened and partly worked near Nambucca, Drake, Gulgong, and Razorback. Up to the end of 1890 the value of antimony (metal and ore) exported from the Colony was £93,741. As soon as a practicable method of separating the gold from the antimony ores is introduced, it is expected the output will be largely increased.

Manganese.

Manganese.—Deposits of manganese ore have been discovered during the past few years in various parts of New South Wales.

Pyrolusite, in the form of black oxide and manganese dioxide, occurs principally in the Bathurst districts and Bendemeer. Some of the specimens analysed have yielded a very high percentage of metal, but the demand for manganese in the Colony is very trifling, and until a foreign market is found, or local manufactories spring up requiring the metal, the rich deposits of this ore will remain comparatively untouched. The ore is found extensively in conjunction with iron in coal and limestone country, and often contains a small percentage of cobalt.

Bismuth.

Bismuth is found associated with molybdenum and gold, in quartz-veins in the neighbourhood of Glen Innes, whence the quantity raised has been chiefly obtained. The principal mine is at Kingsgate, where this mineral occurs in a granitic formation, associated with molybdenum, mispickel, and tin. This mine was closed at the end of 1889, there being no demand for the mineral. The largest mass of native bismuth yet discovered in New South Wales weighed more than 30 lb. The value of metal exported up to the end of 1890 was £36,142. Deposits of *Cobalt* have been found at Bungonia, and near Carcoar, but the market for this metal is small, and no attempt has yet been made to produce it on any large scale.

Cobalt.

Mercury.

Mercury in the form of *Cinnabar* has been discovered on the Cudgegong River, near Rylestone, and it also occurs at Bingara and Solferino, but the deposits have not been much worked. In all cases it was associated with gold and other minerals.

Platinum and Iridosmine.

Platinum and the allied compound metal *Iridosmine* have been found in New South Wales, but so far in inconsiderable quantities, the latter occurring commonly with gold or tin in alluvial drifts. It is believed, however, that the beach deposits at Ballina and other places on the northern coast could be profitably worked for platinum. This metal has also been discovered in the Parkes district, and in lodes near Broken Hill, and Orange.

Graphite. *Graphite* has been discovered at Undercliff, in the New England district, from a lode 6 ft. wide. It is of inferior quality.

Tellurium. Another of the noble metals, *Tellurium*, has been discovered at Bingara and other parts of the northern districts, though at present only in such minute quantities as would not repay the cost of working. It has been found at Captain's Flat, in association with bismuth.

NON-METALLIC MINERALS.

Coal. *Coal.*—The carboniferous formations extend over a considerable portion of the colony, and workable coal-seams have been discovered in many places. At present, however, the coal-mining industry is confined to those centres, which, from their close proximity to ports of shipment, or to the railway lines, afford ready means for the disposal of the commodity when raised.

Discovery of coal. Coal was first discovered in the Colony in the year 1797 near Mount Keira, in the Illawarra district, by a man named Clark, who was supercargo of the "Sydney Cove," and had been wrecked upon the coast. Later in the same year Lieutenant Shortland discovered the River Hunter, with the coal-beds situated near its mouth. A.A. Co.'s monopoly. In 1826 the Australian Agricultural Company obtained a grant of 1,000,000 acres of land, together with the sole right, conferred upon them by charter, of working the coal-seams which were known to exist in the Newcastle district. Several mines were opened up, and profitably worked for a number of years; but it was not until the expiration, in 1847, of the monopoly enjoyed by the company, that the coal-mining industry showed signs of extensive development.

Output of coal. In the year named the yearly output of coal had only reached the total of 40,732 tons, of the value of £13,750. Six years afterwards the production had been doubled, and the output of this mineral has rapidly increased, year by year, until coal-mining has now become one of the staple industries of the Colony. Newcastle is singularly well fitted by situation to become the port of supply for all the countries of the southern seas. Every week coal-laden vessels leave its wharves, not only for the Australian colonies, but for China, India, the Pacific Slope of North and South America, Mauritius, the Cape of Good Hope, and other lands. Every provision has been made by the Government for shipping coal, and over two miles of wharves, furnished with cranes and shoots capable of loading 16,200 tons per day, line its shores. The markets of the Colonies are also supplied with quantities of excellent coal from the seams worked in the Illawarra district.

From the 40,732 tons extracted in 1847 under the monopoly of the Australian Agricultural Company, the quantity raised under public competition and enterprise had in 1889 expanded to the large figure of 3,655,632 tons, valued at £1,632,849. The output for 1890, however, showed a decrease of 594,756 tons, valued at £353,760. This serious decline was owing to the strike, which commenced in August, and lasted until November, causing the collieries to be closed for a considerable period. Up to the end of 1890 the total quantity of coal extracted from the New South Wales mines, from their opening in the earlier years of the century, amounted to 49,526,709 tons, valued at £23,891,629. Total quantity obtained.

The deposits found in the Blue Mountains, near the line of railway which runs along their crest, at Katoomba, Lithgow, Wallerawang, and elsewhere, supply a portion of the requirements of the city, and other industrial centres in its neighbourhood, as well as part of the western district of the Colony. Coal is also mined at Berrima and other places in that district, whence a large quantity of the coal consumed in the southern districts of the Colony is obtained. The area over which coal is distributed is very great, and has been computed at 23,950 square miles; besides this it is known to underlie the Hawkesbury sandstone in and around Sydney, having been discovered at various places, by boring. It has been found near Liverpool at a depth of 2,600 feet. Coal

Mountain coal.

Coal area.

has also been found in the Clarence series, though it has not yet been worked commercially. Three seams were recently proved at Coraki, on the Richmond River. The quantity of coal in the coal measures down to a depth of 4,000 feet, and excluding seams less than 30 inches, is estimated by the Government Geologist at 78,198 million tons;—this estimate allows for one-third loss in working.

Coal-mines registered in New South Wales.

The number of coal-mines registered in New South Wales during 1890 was 94, as compared with 99 in the previous year. These gave employment to 10,469 persons, of whom 8,311 were employed underground, and 2,158 above ground. The average quantity of coal extracted per miner was 368 tons, as against an average of 438 tons for the previous year. In 1882 the weight per miner stood at 578 tons; but the yield has since gradually declined, and the average for 1890 was less than that of any of the preceding ten years, owing to the collieries standing idle for several months during the year on account of the general strike.

Coal raised in New South Wales.

Amount of Coal raised in New South Wales, and number of Coal-miners employed.

Year.	Number of persons employed in and about mines.	Number of persons employed underground.	Quantity of coal raised.		
			Total.	Per person employed in and about mines.	Per person employed underground.
			Tons.	Tons.	Tons.
1881	4,098	3,419	1,769,597	431	517
1882	4,587	3,649	2,109,282	459	578
1883	5,481	4,407	2,521,537	460	572
1884	6,227	5,050	2,749,109	441	544
1885	7,097	5,627	2,878,864	405	511
1886	7,847	6,346	2,830,175	360	446
1887	7,998	6,539	2,922,497	365	447
1888	9,301	7,622	3,203,444	344	420
1889	10,277	8,349	3,655,632	356	438
1890	10,469	8,311	3,060,876	292	368
Average for 10 years.	7,338	5,932	2,770,101	377	467

The total weight of coal won in the Colony in 1890 was 3,060,876 tons as against 3,655,632 tons in 1889, as shown in the previous table, being a decrease of 16·3 per cent. It is not satisfactory to note that in consequence of the strike the Colony lost the benefit arising from the hewing and handling of 594,756 tons of coal, in addition to the serious disturbance of trade which always follows these untoward events. One effect of the strike was to cause the development of the coal-mines of Japan, where coal, some of which is said to be as fine as any in the world, is produced at a price which seems likely to drive Australian coal entirely out of the Eastern market, and probably out of that of the Pacific also.

Effects of the late strike.

From the preceding table it would appear that every miner working underground extracts annually an average of 467 tons, which, calculated at the mean price of coal at the pit's mouth, is equivalent to £210 3s. This production is certainly very large, and compares favourably with the results exhibited by the principal coal-raising countries of the world, as will be evident from the following figures given by Mulhall :—

Output per miner.

Country.	Tons of coal raised per miner.	Value at the pit's mouth per ton.			Total value of coal raised per miner.		
		£	s.	d.	£	s.	d.
New South Wales	467	0	9	0	210	3	0
Great Britain	330	0	6	0	111	0	0
United States	347	0	8	4	139	0	0
Germany	336	0	5	3	78	0	0
France	196	0	9	0	88	0	0
Belgium	168	0	7	6	63	0	0
Austria	270	0	5	0	57	0	0

Earnings of Miners.

In the absence of information as to the average amount of wages paid to coal-miners in other countries an exact comparison is not possible, but it is abundantly clear, that whatever may be the drawbacks to a miner's lot in the Australian Colonies in no other country is it so satisfactory. The foregoing table proves this, for on the improbable supposition that the miner everywhere receives in wages the same proportion of the value of the coal as in New South Wales, that is, about 40 per cent. of the selling price at the pit's mouth, the average earnings in each country would be :—

Country.	Coal per miner.	Wages per ton of coal.			Earnings of miner per annum.		
	tons.	£	s.	d.	£	s.	d.
New South Wales	467	0	3	7	83	13	5
Great Britain	330	0	2	5	39	17	6
United States	347	0	3	4	57	16	8
Germany	336	0	2	1	35	0	0
France	196	0	3	7	35	2	4
Belgium	168	0	3	0	25	4	0
Austria	270	0	2	0	27	0	0

Northern District.

Coal-mining in the Northern Districts.

In the Northern or Hunter River District the number of collieries under official inspection in 1890 was 66, employing a complement of 7,874 persons, 6,345 of whom were miners and wheelers. The quantity of coal raised amounted to 2,120,046 tons, or 69·3 per cent. of the whole production of New South Wales, showing a decrease of 504,301 tons compared with the output of 1889, caused by the strike.

The table following shows the growth of the coal industry within the last ten years in the Hunter District. It will be seen that the quantity of mineral raised and the number of persons employed have steadily increased prior to 1890 :—

Northern District Coal-mines.

Year.	Number of persons employed in and about mines.	Number of persons employed underground.	Quantity of coal raised.		
			Total.	Per person employed in and about mines.	Per person employed under-ground.
			tons.	tons.	tons.
1881	3,234	2,744	1,352,472	418	492
1882	3,475	2,830	1,569,517	452	554
1883	4,184	3,436	1,899,700	454	552
1884	4,735	3,927	2,055,343	434	523
1885	5,380	4,400	2,113,373	393	480
1886	6,133	5,044	2,178,116	355	432
1887	6,287	5,217	2,243,792	356	430
1888	6,873	5,736	2,067,042	300	360
1889	7,559	6,216	2,624,347	347	422
1890	7,874	6,345	2,120,046	269	334

SOUTHERN DISTRICT.

In the Southern Districts there were in 1890 fourteen collieries under official inspection, giving employment to 1,959 persons, of whom 1,434 were at work underground. These numbers exhibit a decrease of 106 persons employed in and about the mines, and 164 underground workers over those so engaged in 1889. There is, moreover, a decrease of 103,974 tons in the production. The total quantity raised in 1888 was 796,806 tons, which was more than double the output of the previous year. This large increase was, no doubt, owing to the cessation of work in the northern mines for about three months during the strike. The yield of 1889 was 701,572 tons. In 1890, however, the strike, which as already stated was sufficiently disastrous in the Northern district, was still more bitter and lasting in the South, the effect being the decrease in production just noted. Coal-mining in Southern Districts.

The history of coal production in this region may be gathered from the following table :—

Southern District Coal-mines.

Year.	Number of persons employed in and about mines.	Number of persons employed underground.	Quantity of coal raised.		
			Total.	Per person employed in and about mines.	Per person employed underground[1]
			tons.	tons.	tons.
1881	654	499	253,283	387	507
1882	878	633	342,126	389	540
1883	998	736	389,419	390	529
1884	1,097	820	419,942	382	512
1885	1,348	918	453,728	336	494
1886	1,298	947	370,830	286	390
1887	1,313	982	376,658	287	383
1888	1,676	1,244	796,806	475	640
1889	2,065	1,598	701,572	339	439
1890	1,959	1,434	597,598	305	417

WESTERN DISTRICT.

Coal-mining in Western Districts.

In the Western Districts there were in 1890 a total of 14 collieries registered, giving employment to 636 persons, of whom 532 were at work underground. From the subsequent table it will be seen, that, the output was in excess of all former years during the decade, not even excepting 1888, when the demand for Western coal was larger than usual, owing to the scarcity caused by the strike in the Northern Collieries. The average quantity of coal raised per miner is much greater in the Western collieries than elsewhere in the Colony. This is due to a variety of causes, but chiefly to the greater thickness of the seams and the more brittle character of the coal, and to the circumstance that the coal-beds are almost horizontal and generally at small depths; in some cases the mouths of the pits are on a level with the surface of the ground. The facility for working coal is therefore much greater in these mines than in those at Newcastle. But though the out-put is greater per miner than in the other coal regions, the price for hewing is lower, so that the earnings of the individual miner do not differ greatly wherever the mine is situated.

The following table shows the growth of coal production in the Western region during the last ten years. The progress has been very regular and in keeping with the advance of settlement in the portion of the colony extending from the Blue Mountains to the Darling, in which the Western collieries have a monopoly of the coal trade. Situated as these mines are in close proximity to the principal iron-fields of New South Wales, their future prospects will be greatly assured should the manufacture of iron from the ore become an established industry in this part of the Colony :— Coal production in the Western Districts.

Western District Coal-mines.

Year.	Number of Persons employed in and about Mines.	Number of Persons employed underground.	Quantity of Coal raised.		
			Total.	Per Person employed in and about Mines.	Per Person employed underground.
			Tons.	Tons.	Tons.
1881	210	176	163,842	780	930
1882	234	186	197,639	844	1,062
1883	299	235	232,418	777	989
1884	396	303	273,824	693	904
1885	369	309	311,763	845	1,009
1886	416	355	281,229	676	792
1887	398	340	302,137	759	888
1888	752	642	339,594	451	529
1889	653	535	329,713	505	616
1890	636	532	343,232	540	645

Accidents in coal-mines were, fortunately, less frequent in 1890 than in the preceding year, and far less than those of 1887, when the loss of life was especially large, owing to the disastrous explosion in the Bulli Mine, whereby eighty-one persons lost their lives. In England, during 1889, the latest year for which returns are available, there were 1,064 lives lost in the coal-mines, or 1·89 of every thousand persons employed, or at the rate of 166,234 tons of coal raised for every life lost. The number of accidents, with the proportion of miners to each fatal and non-fatal case, in New South Wales, is given herewith, as well as the quantity of coal raised to each life lost. Accidents in coal-mines.

Accidents in Coal Mines.

Year.	Accidents.		Number of miners employed to each person.		Number of tons of coal raised to each person.	
	Injured.	Killed.	Injured.	Killed.	Injured.	Killed.
1882	33	12	139	382	63,917	175,773
1883	34	15	161	365	74,160	168,102
1884	34	14	183	445	80,858	196,364
1885	40	11	177	645	71,971	261,714
1886	43	29	182	270	65,818	97,592
1887	45	94	178	85	64,944	31,095
1888	43	15	216	620	74,500	213,563
1889	57	41	180	251	64,134	89,162
1890	36	13	291	805	85,024	235,452

Bulli Explosion.

Owing to the number of lives lost at Bulli in 1887 the average for this Colony appears considerably higher than for Great Britain, although the circumstances surrounding mining in New South Wales would warrant the expectation of a much lighter average.

The following table shows the value of coal raised in the Colony from the earliest times. It will be seen that the total value to the close of 1890 was £23,891,629:—

Value of coal raised.

Coal raised in the Colony, and average price per Ton.

Year.	Quantity.	Average per ton.	Value.
	Tons.	s. d.	£
Prior to 1829	50,000	10 0	25,000
1829	780	10 1	394
1830	4,000	9 0	1,800
1831	5,000	8 0	2,000
1832	7,143	7 0	2,502
1833	6,812	7 7	2,575
1834	8,490	8 10	3,750
1835	12,392	8 10	5,483
1836	12,646	9 1	5,747
1837	16,083	9 9	7,828
1838	17,220	9 9	8,399
1839	21,283	9 10	10,441
1840	30,256	10 11	16,498
1841	34,841	12 0	20,905
1842	39,900	12 0	23,940
1843	25,862	12 7	16,222
1844	23,118	10 8	12,363
1845	22,324	7 10	8,769

	Tons.	s.	d.	£
1846	38,965	7	0	13,714
1847	40,732	6	9	13,750
1848	45,447	6	3	14,275
1849	48,516	6	0	14,647
1850	71,216	6	7	23,375
1851	67,610	7	7	25,546
1852	67,404	10	11	36,885
1853	96,809	16	2	78,059
1854	116,642	20	6	119,380
1855	137,076	13	0	89,082
1856	189,960	12	4	117,906
1857	210,434	14	1	148,158
1858	216,397	15	0	162,162
1859	306,213	13	3	204,371
1860	368,862	12	3	226,493
1861	342,067	12	10	218,820
1862	476,522	12	10	305,234
1863	433,889	10	11	236,230
1864	549,012	9	11	270,171
1865	585,525	9	4	274,303
1866	774,238	8	4	324,049
1867	770,012	8	11	342,655
1868	954,231	8	9	417,809
1869	919,774	7	6	346,146
1870	868,564	7	4	316,836
1871	898,784	7	0	316,340
1872	1,012,426	7	10	396,198
1873	1,192,862	11	2	665,747
1874	1,304,612	12	1	790,224
1875	1,329,729	12	4	819,430
1876	1,319,918	12	2	803,300
1877	1,444,271	11	11	858,908
1878	1,575,497	11	8	920,936
1879	1,583,381	12	0	950,879
1880	1,466,180	8	5	615,336
1881	1,769,597	6	10	603,248
1882	2,109,282	9	0	948,965
1883	2,521,457	9	6	1,201,942
1884	2,749,109	9	6	1,303,077
1885	2,878,863	9	4	1,340,213
1886	2,820,175	9	3	1,303,164
1887	2,922,497	9	3	1,346,440
1888	3,203,444	9	1	1,455,198
1889	3,655,632	8	11	1,632,849
1890	3,060,876	8	4	1,279,089
Total.....	49,526,709	9	8	23,891,629

to a large extent arisen, in the past, from uncertainty in the markets. This uncertainty no longer exists, for the local markets and those of the other Australian Colonies, demand a large share of the coal raised. The proportion of the total taken by Australasia increases every year, and operates in the direction of steadying the price, by removing the principal cause of fluctuation. The highest average price obtained during any year was in 1854, the first of the Crimean war, and the third after the gold rush, when the price per ton was not less than 20s. 6d. In 1872 the output reached 1,000,000 tons, ten years later it had increased to 2,000,000, and in 1889 to 3,655,632 tons.

Local consumption.

The Colony was its own chief customer during 1890, when out of a total production above stated, of 3,060,876 tons, the consumption amounted to 1,239,002 tons, or over 40 per cent. Victoria came next, with 778,803 tons, or 43 per cent. of a total export of 1,821,874 tons. The quantity of coal required for local consumption denotes a satisfactory increase during most years, as the following statement shows:—

Year.	Tons of Coal.	Year.	Tons of Coal.
1877	528,544	1884	1,058,346
1878	569,077	1885	1,122,507
1879	585,332	1886	1,094,310
1880	712,824	1887	1,132,055
1881	739,753	1888	1,279,572
1882	847,737	1889	1,267,930
1883	1,009,012	1890	1,239,002

Consumption per head.

The annual consumption per head increased from 15 cwt. in 1876 to 24½ cwt. in 1888, but declined to 22½ cwt. in 1890. The larger use of steam for railway locomotives, for manufacturing, and other purposes, as well as the multiplication of gas-works, accounts for a great portion of the increase, but it must also be borne in mind that there is a large and increasing demand for bunker coal for ocean-going steamers, which appears not as an export, but as required for home consumption. The amount of coal taken by the steamers during 1890 was little short of 200,000 tons.

The quantity of coal supplied to the customers of the Colony abroad shows also a large increase during this period:— Export of coal.

Year.	Tons.	Year.	Tons.
1877	915,727	1884	1,690,763
1878	1,006,420	1885	1,756,356
1879	998,049	1886	1,735,865
1880	753,356	1887	1,790,442
1881	1,029,844	1888	1,923,872
1882	1,261,545	1889	2,387,702
1883	1,512,445	1890	1,821,874

There was a decrease in the export trade of 565,828 tons, while the home consumption showed a decrease of 28,928 tons. There were 31,097 tons of coke manufactured during the year, valued at £41,147. Of the quantity mentioned 15,886 tons of coke came from the collieries in the northern districts, and 15,211 tons from the southern mines.

The chief customers of New South Wales for coal during the years 1889-90 will be found in the following table, from which it will be seen how wide is the circle which relies upon the Colony for the supply of one of the chief necessaries of civilized life:— Countries to which New South Wales coal is principally exported.

Countries to which Coal was exported during the years 1889 and 1890.

Country or Port.	1889.		1890.	
	Quantity.	Value.	Quantity.	Value.
	Tons.	£	Tons.	£
Victoria	857,578	488,344	778,803	415,824
United States	407,601	226,956	182,602	102,205
Chili	153,183	85,585	173,906	96,139
New Zealand	160,637	85,347	161,118	86,453
South Australia	190,412	92,756	131,205	65,614
Singapore	66,580	37,575	51,660	31,243
Hongkong	102,702	56,248	53,370	29,140
Tasmania	65,251	31,913	56,863	28,743
Java	86,057	49,408	35,531	19,595
India	67,266	37,207	31,172	16,904
Philippine Islands	49,426	27,675	29,543	16,275
Sandwich Islands	28,096	15,518	26,509	14,734
Peru	25,263	14,153	24,272	13,348
Western Australia	15,180	8,428	15,302	7,982
New Caledonia	14,428	8,470	10,061	7,563
Fiji	13,859	7,480	10,636	5,645
South Sea Islands	7,369	4,232	9,129	4,941
Mauritius	15,497	8,393	7,238	4,028

Countries to which Coal was exported—*continued.*

Country or Port.	1889.		1890.	
	Quantity.	Value.	Quantity.	Value.
Ceylon	3,938	2,121	6,700	3,900
Queensland	7,311	3,932	6,253	3,492
Great Britain	480	264	3,000	3,375
Mexico	10,025	5,534	5,564	3,055
Guam	3,328	1,832	3,115	2,482
Penang	2,414	1,410	3,720	2,046
Siam	725	399	1,213	667
China	19,505	10,285	1,031	585
Sumatra	5,449	2,996	966	531
New Britain	....	....	920	487
Tahiti	....	....	380	175
Marshall Islands	....	....	2	2
Celebes	3,740	2,056	....	....
Kaiser Wilhelm's Land	1,979	1,421	....	....
Japan	1,003	552	....	....
Cochin China	933	513	....	....
Natal	487	268	....	....
Total	2,387,702	1,319,271	1,821,874	987,173

Wealth of Colony in coal.

The wealth of the Colony of New South Wales in coal is enormous, and the further development of the industry may be regarded as almost a certainty. As the great Australian Continent is only in the early period of the development of its immense resources, the coal-mining industry of New South Wales may also be said to be in its infancy. It is, however, a very vigorous infancy, giving promise of a great future.

Coal as a heat producer.

New South Wales coal, especially that obtained in the northern mines, compares favourably as a heat producer with the best foreign coal. It has the advantage of a greater specific gravity to the extent of 5·4 per cent., and it contains less sulphur. The tabular comparison on next page gives a clear view of the properties of the principal Australian coals, as contrasted with the mean of British coals. The average of English, Welsh, and Scotch mines will be found after the analysis of Northern District coals, and it will be seen that there is practically little difference between the British and Hunter River coal.

Analysis of Northern District Coals, New South Wales.

Locality.	Specific Gravity.	Composition per cent. exclusive of water only.						Water per cent.	Coke per cent.	Water at 212° converted into steam by 1 lb coal.
		Carbon.	Hydrogen.	Oxygen.	Nitrogen.	Sulphur.	Ash.			lb.
Wallsend	1·333	79·96	6·26	7·08	·68	1·25	4·77	2·75	61·86	13·20
Waratah	1·303	81·06	5·81	6·52	1·23	1·14	4·24	2·21	59·97	14·30
A. A. Co., Newcastle	1·297	78·76	6·34	7·28	·79	1·36	5·47	2·20	62·87	12·92
Greta	1·287	78·41	6·60	9·34	1·43	1·44	2·78	2·25	57·13	13·21
Russell's Mine	1·274	77·37	6·48	10·46	1·51	1·43	2·75	1·85	52·65	13·21
Anvil Creek	1·323	77·15	5·91	6·07	1·46	1·48	7·93	1·74	55·70	12·65
Cardiff Mine	1·286	82·25	4·38	6·95	1·03	·35	5·04	1·85	54·43	.....
Mean	1·300	79·28	5·97	7·67	1·16	1·21	4·71	2·122	57·80	13·25
British Coals (mean)	1·279	80·40	5·19	7·87	1·21	1·25	4·05	0·63 to 9·13	61·00	14·82

Analysis of Western District Coals.

Locality.	Specific gravity.	Composition per cent. exclusive of water only.						Water per cent.	Coke per cent.	Carbolic intensity calculated.	Water at 212° converted into steam by 1 lb. coal.
		Carbon.	Hydrogen.	Oxygen.	Nitrogen.	Sulphur.	Ash.				lb.
Eskbank	1·335	72·30	5·43	6·65	·85	1·60	13·17	2·00	62·88	74·26	12·65
Bowenfels	1·399	70·72	5·65	9·65	·93	1·38	11·67	2·36	......	72·45	12·65
Lithgow	1·329	69·41	6·10	11·70	1·03	1·44	10·32	1·95	62·46	72·06	12·10
Vale of Clwydd	1·323	69·86	5·82	11·89	1·02	1·40	10·07	2·10	63·18	71·38	12·10
Mean	1·346	70·57	5·75	9·97	·96	1·45	11·31	2·10	62·84	72·54	12·37

Analysis of Southern District Coals.

Locality.	Specific gravity.	Composition per cent. exclusive of water only.						Water per cent.	Coke per cent.	Carbolic intensity calculated.	Water at 212° converted into steam by 1 lb. coal.
		Carbon.	Hydrogen	Oxygen.	Nitrogen.	Sulphur.	Ash.				lb.
Nattai	......	91·24	3·60	0·59	......	trace.	4·56	3·28	92·37	85·90	undetermined.
Mt. Kembla	1·363	80·67	5·30	1·58	·70	·87	10·88	1·50	......	82·70	13·21
Mt. Keira	1·379	78·82	5·17	3·87	1·33	1·00	9·81	1·15	74·35	79·83	12·92
Berrima	1·364	69·92	4·55	13·09	·56	1·30	10·58	1·70	64·24	66·53	11·82
Bulli	1·471	76·35	4·75	5·04	......	·55	13·31	1·03	74·78	......	12·21
Mean	1·394	79·40	4·67	4·83	·52	·74	9·82	1·73	76·43	78· 7	12·54

KEROSENE SHALE.

This mineral is found in various parts of the Colony, but principally at Hartley, Katoomba, Megalong, Bathgate, near Wallerawang, Joadja Creek, Berrima, Mount Kembla, Burragorang, and Greta, and also at Colley Creek, near Murrurundi, and lately in the Capertee District, and in the valley of the Wolgan River. The shale occurs in saucer-shaped deposits, varying in thickness from a few inches to 6 feet. It is a species of cannel-coal, similar to the Boghead mineral of Scotland, but yielding a much larger percentage of volatile hydro-carbon than the Scotch mineral. The richest quality yields upwards of 150 gallons of crude oil per ton, or 18,000 cubic feet of gas, with an illuminating power of thirty-eight or forty-eight sperm candles. The specific gravity is 1·06, amount of sulphur 0·49 per cent., and yield of tar 40 gallons per ton. It is found advantageous for mixing with ordinary coal for the manufacture of gas, and is largely exported to Great Britain, America, and other foreign countries, as well as the neighbouring colonies, for gas purposes. On analysis the following result was obtained from average specimens :— Shale deposits.

Volatile Hydro-carbons, including moisture......	82·50	per cent.
Fixed Carbon............	6·50	,,
Ash............	11·00	,,

Though analyses of this mineral have proved that payable seams occur in many places, only two companies have as yet systematically worked kerosene shale in the Colony—the New South Wales Shale and Oil Company, at Hartley, and the Australian Oil and Mineral Company, at Joadja Creek. These companies not only raise shale for export, but also manufacture from it petroleum oil and other products. The quantity and value of kerosene shale raised since the opening of the mines in 1865 amounts to 612,692 tons, of the value of £1,338,552, as shown in the following table. Quantity and value of shale raised.

Kerosene Shale raised in New South Wales.

Year.	Quantity	Average price per ton.	Total value.	Year.	Quantity.	Average price per ton.	Total value.
	Tons.	£ s. d.	£		Tons.	£ s. d.	£
1865	570	4 2 5	2,350	1879	32,519	2 1 2	66,931
1866	2,770	2 18 10	8,150	1880	19,201	2 6 7	44,725
1867	4,079	3 14 9	15,249	1881	27,894	1 9 3	40,748
1868	16,952	2 17 7	48,816	1882	48,065	1 15 0	84,114
1869	7,500	2 10 0	18,750	1883	49,250	1 16 11	90,861
1870	8,580	3 4 3	27,570	1884	31,618	2 5 8	72,176
1871	14,700	2 6 4	34,050	1885	27,462	2 9 0	67,239
1872	11,040	2 12 0	28,700	1886	43,563	2 5 11	99,976
1873	17,850	2 16 7	50,475	1887	40,010	2 3 10	87,761
1874	12,100	2 5 1	27,300	1888	34,869	2 2 3	73,612
1875	6,197	2 10 0	15,500	1889	40,561	1 18 3	77,667
1876	15,998	3 0 0	47,994	1890	56,010	1 17 2	104,103
1877	18,963	2 9 1	46,524				
1878	24,371	2 6 11	57,211	Total	612,692	2 3 8	1,338,552

Yearly output of shale compared.

Compared with the years 1882 and 1883, the production of the two years 1884 and 1885 exhibits a considerable decrease, somewhat compensated for by the higher price obtained for the shale. The year 1886, however, shows a renewal of activity in the production of this mineral, though a tendency to decrease was again observable in 1888. A satisfactory advance is observable in the figures of 1889 and 1890. The cause of the irregularity in the quantity of shale mined will probably be found in the uncertainty of the demand for export, although the quantity required for local consumption has also greatly varied. During the ten years, 1881–90, the total export was 224,425 tons, while the amount required for home consumption was 174,877 tons.

DIAMONDS AND GEM-STONES.

The existence of diamonds and other gem-stones in the territory of New South Wales has been known for many years, but no attempt was made to work the deposits until the year 1872. In the course of the following year several deposits of diamantiferous wash were discovered in the country near Inverell, in the New England district.

Number of diamonds found

The number of diamonds found in the Colony to the end of 1887 is estimated at 50,000, the largest being one of 5⅝ carats, or 16·2 grains. The diamonds occur in old tertiary river drifts, and in the more recent drifts derived from them. The deposits, which occur in the Inverell, Bingara, Mittagong, Cudgegong, and Narrabri districts, are extensive, and have not yet been thoroughly prospected. The New South Wales diamonds are harder and much whiter than the South African diamonds, and are classified on a par with the best Brazilian gems. During the year 1889 the Malacca Company, near Tingha, found diamonds weighing 2,195⅝ carats, valued at £878 5s. Other gem-stones, including the sapphire, emerald, oriental emerald, ruby, opal, amethyst, garnet, chrysolite, topaz, cairngorm, onyx, zircon, &c., have been found in the gold and tin-bearing drifts and river gravels in numerous localities throughout the Colony. An emerald mine, in which the emerald occurs in a granitic lode, was opened near Emmaville in 1890. Precious opal is now being mined in the cretaceous formation near Wilcannia. It also occurs in basalt near the Abercrombie River, and in sandstone, near Lismore.

Distribution of gems.

MICA.

Mica.

Mica is known to exist in many parts of New South Wales, but has never yet been worked, although there is a considerable demand for the article, especially if in blocks of fairly large size that could easily be split into thin plates. It is to be met with in the numerous granitic areas that occur in various parts of the Colony, especially in the coarsely-crystalline granitic formations in the Silverton District, and elsewhere in the Barrier Ranges.

MARBLE, BUILDING STONES, FIRE-CLAYS, AND SLATES.

Marble limestone.

The Colony possesses a most abundant supply of all the various kinds of stone, and other materials, for the building and adornment of its cities. Marble limestone is found in great masses near Wallerawang, Bathurst, Molong, Marulan, Tamworth, and Kempsey, localities which are all within convenient distance of the great arteries of communication, and it is obtainable in all its different varieties. Marble quarries have been opened at Cow Flat, Marulan, Wallerawang, Orange, and Tamworth, but only those of Cow Flat and Marulan are being worked.

Granite.

Granite is found near Goulburn, Moruya, Montague Island, and Trial Bay, as well as at many other places throughout the Colony. Most of the granite hitherto used in Sydney has been obtained from Moruya, a port about 180 miles south of Sydney.

Building stone.

The Hawkesbury formation, over which the City of Sydney is built, provides the city with an inexhaustible supply of sandstone, of the highest quality for building purposes. This material is admirably adapted for architectural effect, being of a pleasant colour, fine grain, and very easily worked. The beauty of Sydney street architecture is due in no inconsiderable degree to the free use of this excellent sandstone.

Bluestone.

Bluestone, which is extensively used as road metal and for the ballasting of the railway lines, is obtained at Kiama, Prospect, Pennant Hills, and Bowral. This stone has not yet been used to any extent for building purposes.

Fire-clays.

The Coal Measures also contain numerous beds of fire-clays, and in every part of the Colony excellent clays, well adapted for brick-making purposes, are extensively worked. Slates are found in several districts, but are principally quarried at Gundagai, and in the surrounding district, as well as near Bathurst and Goulburn. It will be seen, therefore, that the Colony has no need to import building material of any description, as it possesses a supply amply sufficient to provide for its own wants and those of its neighbours. Building materials.

ASBESTOS.

Asbestos has been found in veins in serpentine in the Gundagai, Bathurst, and Barrier Range districts, in the latter in considerable quantities. Asbestos.

ALUM.

Alum-stone occurs as a large deposit at Bulladelah, about 35 miles from Port Stephens. It yields up to 80 per cent. of alum, and a quantity of the stone is to be exported to the alum works, near Liverpool, in England. Alum.

PART VII.

Flora.

THE surface of New South Wales presents a vegetation characterized by little variation in form and colour. The dense foliage and varieties of tints with which the old world is familiar are alike wanting in Australia, where the dull evergreen leaves alter little with the changes of the seasons. What the flora of the country lacks in picturesqueness it, however, makes up in usefulness. The task of collecting, describing, and classifying the Australian flora has been undertaken by several eminent scientists, amongst whom are Bentham, Müeller, and Hooker. The "Flora Australiensis" of the first-named botanists, Hooker's "Flora of Tasmania," the "Census of Australian Plants," and the "Eucalyptographia" of Baron von Müeller, are works of standard value. In dealing, however, with the description of the varied specimens of plant life found in Australia there remained the task of describing those species whose properties rendered them capable of application to industrial life. To Mr. J. H. Maiden, of the Sydney Technological Museum, the Colony is indebted for an excellent classification of those varieties which properly belong to Australian economic botany. The number of specimens so far described in each class will be found below, and it will probably appear to many as a revelation that the country should possess resources so varied and elements of wealth so promising, and at the same time so singularly neglected.

Australian economic botany.

Classification of Australian plants of economic value :—

Classification of Plants.	Number of varieties.
1. Human food and food adjuncts	212
2. Forage plants—	
a. Grasses	156
b. Exclusive of grasses, and including plants injurious to stock	92
3. Drugs	123
4. Gums, resins, and kinos—	
a. Gums	40
b. Resins	21
c. Kinos	39
5. Oils—	
a. Volatile or essential	47
b. Expressed or fixed	10
6. Perfumes	14
7. Dyes	35
8. Tans	87
9. Timbers	630
10. Fibres	67
11. Miscellaneous	36
Total	1,613

It does not come within the scope of this volume to deal at length with a subject so comprehensive as economic botany; it may, however, be pointed out that beyond some of the timber trees and a very limited number of oils and tans, few of the resources of the Colony disclosed in the foregoing list have received any practical application.

Forests extend over almost the whole area of the Colony, excepting portions of the Monaro, the Lachlan, and the Murrumbidgee districts, where extensive treeless plains occur, clothed with salt-bush, scrub, or varieties of natural grasses. The country covered by timber may be divided into three classes—open, brush, and scrub forests. Open forests cover the greatest portion of the surface of the Colony, and are found in every formation. The varieties of trees met with are chiefly species of the Eucalyptus tribe, and Melaleuca, Callistemon, and other genera of the order Myrtaceae. Forests.

lence of ypti.

The prevalence of the eucalypti, and the large extent covered by the forests, give the country a rather monotonous aspect. But the park-like appearance of the open forests and the beauty of the many flowering shrubs win admiration, in spite of the sameness of the trees; while even the dull, greyish blue of the foliage of the gum-trees, when relieved by the yellow blossoms of the wattle, the graceful myall, or the beautiful and shapely kurrajong, is not without its attractiveness. The trees are for the most part straight and cylindrical in the trunk, and when full grown, their first branch is at a considerable height from the ground. The roots of the eucalyptus lie at no great distance from the surface soil, an adaptation of nature to the peculiar climatic conditions of the country. The finest specimens of most of the timber trees, those yielding the most valuable timber, are found on ridges and hill sides, in places frequently too rough and stony for cultivation. This circumstance is in many ways fortunate for the Colony. In the course of settlement, when the rich plains are denuded of their trees, and when scarcity will make timber more appreciated than it is at present, land not adapted for agricultural settlement will still be available for the cultivation of the finest trees. It would be impossible, in the limits of this volume, to enumerate all the trees which are of commercial value; but a list of the best known varieties will not be without interest.

varieties ber trees.

On the river flats immense specimens of flooded gum (*E. rostrata*) and apple-trees (*Angophora subvelutina*) mark the course of the streams. The flooded gum grows to a height of 100 feet, and its wood is most useful for heavy work, and for structures liable to attack by the white ant. The apple-tree has more spread than the majority of indigenous trees, its wood is strong, heavy, and durable. The distribution of the species is very extensive.

On the ridges and mountain sides other varieties of trees predominate. The box reaches 180 feet in height, with a thickness of 6 feet, and the timber is used chiefly for firewood, for which purpose it has no superior. The bastard box, supposed to be a cross between the box and grey gum, is widely distributed over the Colony. The quality of the timber varies greatly, according to the place of growth; some varieties are surpassed amongst hard woods by nothing except ironbark.

Ironbark *(E. leucoxylon* and *E. paniculata)* is a tree of moderate size, usually when full grown from 60 to 80 feet in height, though the white ironbark attains a height of 150 feet. The timber is heavy, and renowned for its great strength, fine specimens bearing a tensile strain nearly twice as great as the best oak. The timber is used most extensively for wharves and bridges, as also for house-work. Ironbark is very widely distributed, and frequently grows to perfection on the poorest soil. The ironbark and box are slow growing trees, as compared with many other varieties of eucalyptus, such as the blue gum, which latter attains a great height in a very few years. Ironbark.

The blue gum *(E. globulus)*, one of the finest of the eucalyptus tribe, is only met with in portions of the southern table-land, but the blue gum *(E. goniocalyx)*, also called flooded gum, grows extensively in the coastal districts. It attains a moderate height, but is rather thicker in the trunk than most varieties of gum trees, sometimes reaching 7 feet in diameter. The timber is greatly in demand, owing to its comparative lightness, and is easily worked, being used for all purposes to which hardwood is applied. Blue gum.

The spotted gum grows in all the coast districts, and in some portions of the interior, generally where the soil is poor. This is one of the handsomest of the forest trees, and attains a height of 100 feet. The quality of the wood varies greatly, according to the habitat and the character of the soil; when good, it is considered specially adapted for ship-building. Spotted gum.

Stringybark. Stringybark, so called from its peculiar fibrous bark, grows chiefly on the northern table-lands. It is a large tree, and its wood is of great and general utility. The bark is extensively used for roofing, and forms a very useful paper-making material.

The messmate *(E. obliqua)*, also called stringybark, is one of the largest of Australian trees, being frequently met with more than 250 feet in height. It grows in the south-eastern portion of the Colony. The bark is used for roofing, being similar in character to that of the tree just described; it would also form an excellent paper-making material.

Blood-wood. The blood-wood is a large tree, growing in the coastal districts of the Colony. The timber is used chiefly for fencing purposes, and for railway sleepers.

Grey gum. The grey gum *(E. tereticornis)* grows to a height of 150 feet, and is extensively distributed over the whole of the coastal districts. It yields excellent timber, hardly inferior to ironbark. There are several varieties of this tree, some of which produce wood of remarkable beauty, and of great durability.

Tallow-wood. The tallow-wood is a very large tree, growing extensively in the forests north of Sydney. Its wood is more easily wrought than most of the hardwoods, and has great strength and durability, being employed largely for floors, and other building purposes, and for the decking of ships.

Mountain ash. The mountain ash, or white-top, is found both on the table-lands and in the coast districts. Its timber is in demand for coopers' work, and for rough carpentry. The tree grows to about 150 feet in height.

Turpentine tree. The turpentine tree *(Syncarpia laurifolia)* is found mainly in the district lying between the Shoalhaven and the Macleay. It grows to magnificent proportions, sometimes reaching a height of

200 feet, with a diameter of 6 feet. The timber is largely used for piling, and other work in sea-water, as it resists the attack of the teredo better than any other New South Wales timber.

BRUSH FORESTS.

Features of brush forests.

The brush forests cover a considerable extent of country along the coast. The trees found in them differ entirely from those of the open forests, and there is no lack of variety either in the character of the trees or the colour of their foliage. Tall graceful fern trees, sometimes attaining a height of 60 feet, beautiful varieties of palms, cabbage-trees, and Moreton Bay figs of enormous proportions, are prominent features of the brush, though these are perhaps more ornamental than useful. There are, however, found in the brush forests timber trees of the greatest value.

Red and white cedar.

The red and white cedar (*Cedrela toona* and *Melia composita*) were once abundant in the northern forests, but at present most of the full grown trees are met with only on the high ridges. The red cedar is a magnificent timber tree, often attaining a height of 150 feet, with a girth of over 30 feet. Its timber is of great value, being light, easily wrought, durable, splendidly grained, and well adapted for furniture and cabinet-making. The white cedar is a pretty tree growing to a height of 80 feet, with a diameter of 3 feet. Its timber is soft and easily worked, but is deficient in tensile strength and durability, and therefore in no great demand.

Silky oak.

The silky oak grows to the height of almost 100 feet, under favourable circumstances, and yields a wood highly prized for staves.

Tulip-wood.

The tulip-wood is a tall tree with beautifully marked timber of various shades, and susceptible of a fine polish.

Ash.

The ash, or pigeon berry-tree, grows to a great height, sometimes reaching 130 feet, with a diameter of 5 feet. Its timber is light and tough, and in good demand.

Colonial pine. The colonial pine (*Araucaria Cunninghamii*) is one of the finest trees of Australia, sometimes reaching a height of 200 feet, with a trunk 5 feet thick. Its timber is extensively used, being cheaper than any imported pine; it is white in colour and easily wrought.

Beech. Native beech is also a tree of noble proportions, reaching 150 feet in height. Its timber is greatly in demand, being superior to most native timber when exposed, as it neither shrinks nor warps. In colour the wood is white or silvery, with a fine close grain.

Besides the varieties mentioned above, there are in the brush forests many other trees, yielding timber of large size and of great value, but the abundance of timber of other descriptions more readily accessible, has hitherto satisfied the local demand, and the resources of these forests have been almost entirely overlooked.

Great variety of timber in brush forests. The character of the vegetation of the brush forests alters considerably according to the latitude. The trees of the Araucaria and Flindersia tribes, as well as the principal varieties of cedar, find a home chiefly in the northern parts of the Colony, while many of the trees growing in the south have no representatives in the northern forests. The soil of the brush lands is wonderfully fertile, consisting as it does of decomposed volcanic rocks, enriched by the accumulation of decayed vegetable matter, and when cleared it yields an abundant return.

SCRUB FORESTS.

The scrub forests are found in the poor soils, principally in the Lachlan and Darling districts. The chief species represented are the pine, the acacia, and the eucalyptus, but although some of the trees are of great beauty, they have little commercial value. The most uninviting portion of the Colony is covered with scrub, and the mallee districts, clothed as they are with stunted timber—a variety of the eucalyptus—impress the traveller more unfavourably than would even a barren waste.

Dividing the timber trees of New South Wales into the natural divisions of hardwoods, softwoods, and pinewoods, the largest portion, both as to the variety of trees and the area covered by the forests, comes under the first-mentioned class. All the trees already referred to as growing in the open forests are hardwoods; and besides those described there are many others, of recognized commercial value, which are extensively used.

Australian hardwood trees are remarkable for the great size of the beams which may be obtained from them, as well as for the extreme toughness and durability of their wood. In a subsequent table the mean strength of various timbers is given, from which it will be seen that the grey ironbark has a resistance to breaking equal to 17,900 lb. per square inch, as compared with a mean of 11,800 lb. for English oak, and 15,500 for teak. None of the other timbers has so high a resistance to breaking as this description of ironbark, but nearly all the varieties have a greater strength than oak. As already pointed out, the quality of the wood is materially influenced by the soil on which the trees grow, and the resistance to breaking shown in the subsequent table is the average of various samples, the range in some woods being considerable. The absence of branches for the greater portion of the height enables the timber to be obtained to the best advantage; and as full-grown trees of most varieties are rarely less than 100 feet high, with corresponding girth, the quantity of timber obtainable is very large. Hardwoods.

The softwoods of the Colony are found chiefly in the brush forests of the coast district, and rival those of any other part of the world. Some of the least known of the brush forest trees have wood grained and marked most beautifully, which is capable of receiving the highest polish, while others are fragrantly perfumed. These woods are adapted to the finest description of cabinet-making, and it is strange that their merits should have so long escaped attention. Amongst the chief varieties of woods of this class may Softwoods. Beauty of brush timber be mentioned the red cedar, now unfortunately disappearing, the beautiful wood of which, somewhat resembling mahogany, is admirably adapted for the finer kinds of cabinet-makers' work. Some of the cedar trees grow to immense size, as much as 2,500 cubic feet of valuable timber having been obtained from one tree. In addition to the cedar may be mentioned rosewood, tulipwood, yellowwood, white maple, white beech, myall, marblewood, mock orange, and many others. Besides their use for cabinet-making, many of the brush timbers are of great utility for the rougher kinds of carpentry, while some, both hard and soft woods, are admirably adapted for coachbuilders' and coopers' work.

Pinewoods.

The chief description of pine growing in New South Wales is the Moreton Bay white pine, found in the coast districts, as far south as the Bellinger. It is soft, light, and easily wrought, and suitable for all the interior wood-work of houses, as well as for cabinet-making. The red or black pine is extensively distributed over the Liverpool Plains, and in the Lachlan and Darling River districts, as well as around Berrima. It is beautifully marked in the grain, takes a fine polish, and has an agreeable fragrance. There are numerous other varieties of pine, but these resemble in their main features the trees already described.

Colonial deal is an excellent timber, and is obtained in very large scantling, the tree frequently reaching 120 feet in height. It is soft, close-grained, easily wrought, and remarkably free from knots. Its use, therefore, is extensive for cabinet-makers' work and house fittings.

Importation of timber very large.

Notwithstanding the great resources of the Colony as a timber-growing country, the importation of wood is very considerable. In 1890 the quantity amounted to 6,820,000 feet of dressed timber, valued at £65,000, and 50,333,000 feet of undressed, valued at £340,000; besides which there were sundries to the value of £4,800, the total value of timber imported being £409,800.

Importation of timber.

The importation of timber is chiefly from South Australia, New Zealand, the United States, Scandinavia, the Canadian Dominion, and the United Kingdom.

During 1890 the Colony received 1,511,716 feet of dressed and 15,522,623 feet undressed timber from South Australia; and 396,530 feet dressed and 14,323,378 feet undressed from New Zealand; over 56 per cent. of all the timber imported thus coming from those two Colonies. From the United States the Colony imported 434,869 feet dressed and 10,014,483 feet undressed timber—not much more than half the quantity imported from the States in the previous year. From Scandinavia New South Wales received about 4½ million feet of timber, and over 3 million each from Canada and the United Kingdom. Over 2½ million feet came from the Colony of Victoria.

The export of colonial hardwood is relatively small as compared with the timber imported. During the year 1890, 399,232 feet of dressed timber, valued at £2,797, and 20,819,819 feet of rough or undressed, valued at £80,984, also sundries to the value of £287, or a total value of £84,068, were exported. Exportation of timber.

During the nine years which closed with 1890 the exports of New South Wales timber were:— Exports.

Year.	Dressed Timber.	Undressed Timber.
	Feet of 1 in. thick.	Feet of 1 in. thick.
1882	132,894	5,771,868
1883	218,517	8,611,237
1884	320,093	14,239,211
1885	203,930	9,777,797
1886	133,973	13,255,804
1887	179,572	15,541,220
1888	255,889	32,519,134
1889	206,469	24,306,206
1890	393,232	20,819,819

It will be seen that the quantity exported varied greatly; this is entirely due to the fluctuation in the amount taken by Victoria. From the year 1884 large public works were executed in that colony, requiring considerable quantities of hardwood

wood, which was more readily procurable from New South Wales.

Intercolonial exportation.

Out of a total export of 14,239,211 feet of undressed timber in 1884, Victoria took 11,170,536; in the following year out of 9,777,797 feet 6,696,653 feet went to Victoria; during 1886, 10,553,955 feet were taken by that colony, out of a total export of 13,255,804 feet. In 1887 Victoria took 11,165,833 feet, the total export being 15,541,220; in 1888, 26,465,056 feet out of a total of 32,519,134 feet of undressed timber exported; in 1889, out of 24,306,206 feet she took 20,463,678 feet, and in 1890, 18,956,376 feet out of a total export of 20,819,819 feet.

No necessity to import timber.

As already pointed out, although the Colony is endowed with great wealth of timber, not only of hardwood but of softwood and pine, the imports very largely exceed the exports. The imports, however, are chiefly pine and softwood. The pine grown in the Colony is in some respects inferior to both oregon and kauri, hence the large importation of these timbers, but the softwoods of the country will bear favourable comparison with those of any part of the world, both for durability and beauty. They are easily wrought and well adapted for the finer kind of carpentry and cabinet-work, and it is only because they are so little known that the softwoods of the brush forests have not been more extensively used.

Strength of N. S. W. timber.

The specific gravity and resistance to breaking of various New South Wales timbers, and of some of the best known European and other varieties, are shown in the following table. With regard to the New South Wales timbers it should be mentioned that the tests were made with picked specimens, so that the results are perhaps considerably higher than would be obtained in actual practice. The modulus of rupture is eighteen times the load which is required to break a bar 1 in. square, supported at two points 1 foot apart, and loaded in the middle between the points of support, or

$$s = \frac{3 W l}{2 b d^2}$$

when W = load applied at middle of beam between supports; b = breadth, d = depth, l = length of beam, and s = co-efficient of rupture or breaking stress per square inch.

Specific Gravity and Strength of New South Wales Timber, as compared with European and other Varieties of Timber.

New South Wales timber trees.	Specific gravity.	Resistance to breaking or modulus of rupture. = S	European and other Foreign timber trees.	Specific gravity.	Resistance to breaking or modulus of rupture. = S
		lb. per sq. inch.			lb. per sq. inch.
Hardwoods—					
Spotted gum	·995	13,300	Ash	·753	13,000
Grey gum	·917	13,100	Beech	·690	10,500
Flooded gum	1·178	14,800	Birch	·711	11,700
Red gum	·995	6,900	Bullet-tree	1·046	19,000
Woollybutt	1·022	12,700	Chestnut	·535	10,660
Blackbutt	1·067	13,700	Ebony	1·193	27,000
White ironbark	1·177	16,900	Elm	·544	7,900
Grey ironbark	1·182	17,900	Fir, Red pine	·48 to ·70	8,300
Red ironbark	1·224	16,300	,, Spruce	·48 to ·70	11,100
Forest oak	1·208	15,500	,, Larch	·50 to ·56	7,500
Turpentine	1·109	11,700	Greenheart	1·001	22,000
Stringybark	1·141	13,900	Kauri pine (New Zealand)	·579	11,000
Blackwood	1·129	10,300	Lance wood	·675 to 1·01	17,350
Tallowwood	1·233	15,260	Lignum vitæ	·65 to 1·33	12,000
Australian teak	1·006	14,400	Mahogany (Honduras)	·56	11,500
Mahogany	1·201	14,500	,, (Spanish)	·85	7,600
Forest mahogany	1·156	13,800	Oak (British)	·69 to ·99	11,800
Swamp mahogany	1·216	12,100	,, (Dantzic)	·69 to ·99	8,700
White beech	1·008	15,600	,, (American)	·99	10,600
Mountain ash	1·065	11,500	Sycamore	·59	9,600
Rosewood	1·189	10,600	Teak (Indian)	·66 to ·88	15,500
Pine	·868	8,800	Willow	·40	6,600

FOREST CONSERVATION.

Destruction of timber.

The necessity of preserving the timber resources of the Colony, and preventing the ruthless destruction of the best species of brush and hardwood, hitherto carried on by settlers and timber-getters, principally in the Clarence River district, and in the eucalyptus forests on the Murray, decided the Government, in 1871, to establish a certain number of forest reserves throughout the country, in which permission to cut timber should be granted upon payment of a fixed fee. It soon became apparent that stringent regulations alone could put a stop to the reckless operations of the licensed timber-getters, but it was not until September, 1878, that such regulations were issued. These appeared not a day too soon, as the best species of cedar, which abounded in the Clarence River districts, had been exploited to such a wasteful extent that the supply of this magnificent timber threatened to give out. Cutting down indiscriminately trees of all sizes, and clearing the lower lands of their best timber, the cedar-cutters, after disposing of all that could be cheaply transported, or easily floated down the rivers in time of flood, left a considerable surplus of felled timber on the ground to lie and rot. They then travelled further north, to carry on the same depredations along the rivers of the neighbouring Colony of Queensland. The same system had been pursued in the gum forests of the Murray. Considerable quantities of excellent timber were destroyed in the forest reserves of that part of the Colony, to the detriment of the district, which was deprived of its natural wealth, and to the injury of the Colony at large, which suffered the loss of much of its best timber without receiving an equivalent in revenue.

Forest Conservation Branch formed.

In 1875 the office of Forest Ranger was first created, and this led to the formation of a Forest Conservation Branch attached to the Department of Mines, which was established in March, 1882. During the year 1889, however, the Forest Conservation Branch was placed under the administration of the Colonial Secretary. In the year 1882 the Colony was subdivided into of districts. These are frequently inspected by forest whose duty is to report on the existing state of pro- serves, control the operations of licensed timber-getters, royalties on the various kinds of timber, upon which may be levied, and report upon applications to ringbark Crown lands, whether comprised in State forests, reserves, rise. The forest rangers and assistants employed by the nt have the supervision of twenty-one State forests with an ,724 acres. The timber reserves throughout the Colony 945, and cover an area of 5,459,937 acres, so that the of land devoted to the conservation of timber in New ales amounts to 5,557,611 acres. In April, 1890, Mr. own, of South Australia, was appointed Director-General s of New South Wales. Forest rangers

reserves subject to royalty, the quantity of timber cut amounted to 10,978,967 superficial feet. In 1889 the of timber cut measured 16,225,207 superficial feet, in to which there were 1,072 trees felled for piles and other Timber obtained from reserves.

revenue derived from the issue of timber licenses, from permits, and other dues, amounted in 1890 to £15,437 revenue received from the forest reserves of the Crown coming into force of the regulations proclaimed on the September, 1878, in each of the following years was— Revenue from timber licenses.

	£
1879	7,310
1880	8,328
1881	10,156
1882	12,327
1883	16,301
1884	17,565
1885	13,144
1886	13,934
1887	13,629
1888	19,019
1889	16,521
1890	15,437

or a total for 12 years of £163,671 which, before the introduction of the present system, would have been a loss to the country, without taking into consideration the much greater loss caused by the indiscriminate felling carried on in former years. Under the present regulations care is taken to preserve from destruction all timber below a certain girth, measured at a height of 5 feet from the ground, according to a careful classification of the various timbers at present in demand. Trees not named in this list may be cut at the minimum girth that may be endorsed on the license, or as specified in writing by the forest ranger in charge of the reserve.

Girth of timber which may be felled.

The prescribed girth is set forth hereunder:

Hardwoods.

Timber.	Girth. ft.	in.	Timber.	Girth ft.	in.
Blackbutt	7	6	Blood-wood	7	0
Tallow-wood	7	6	Mountain ash	6	0
Red gum or flooded gum	7	6	Mahogany (forest)	6	0
Gray gum	7	0	*Ironbark (red, gray, and broad-leaved)	7	6
Woollybutt	6	6	Peppermint or red-wood	5	6
Brush or white box	6	6	Swamp mahogany	5	6
Turpentine	7	0	*Stringybark	5	0
Blue gum	6	6	Blackwood	4	0
Spotted gum	6	6	Yellow and white box	4	0
Messmate	7	0			

Softwoods, &c.

Timber.	ft.	in.	Timber.	ft.	in.
Red cedar	9	0	Black, red, or white pine (Frenela)	3	0
Hoop or Moreton Bay pine	7	6	Swamp oak	3	0
White beech (Gmelina)	7	0	Forest oak	2	3
Silky oak	6	0			
Rosewood	6	0			

* West of Great Dividing Range, 4½ feet for ironbark, 4 feet for stringybark.

State nursery and cultivation of trees.

The operations of the Forest Conservation Branch are not solely limited to the preservation of native trees. It is also charged with the creation of a State nursery, the site for which was selected at Wyong, in the beautiful district of Brisbane Water, where the acclimatization of valuable foreign timber trees, and the conservation of such of the best indigenous species as might be otherwise likely to disappear, are attended to.

The formation of plantations in various parts of the Colony, and along railway lines, also forms part of a programme which is yearly becoming enlarged. In the forest reserves of Orara and Dorrigo, in the north-eastern district of the Colony, cedar planting has been carried on for some years, under departmental supervision, and up to the end of 1888, 24,978 trees and root-cuttings of cedar trees, and self-sown seedlings, had been counted in the latter reserve. Plantations of the American *Catalpa speciosa* were also made on the Railway Reserve at Cootamundra, where there are about 2,713 catalpa, black walnut, and other trees planted on the 6¼ acres cleared, and wattle plantations have been formed along the southern railway line from Minto to Burradoo. The total number of cedar trees planted to the end of 1889 was about 30,000, in addition to which a great many plants have been raised from seed.

Plantations in forest reserves.

The Forest Conservation Branch has collected a large number of varieties of indigenous timber trees, which were placed on view at the London Colonial and Indian Exhibition; and a second collection consisting of several hundred specimens of different kinds of colonial timber is now exhibited in the Geological Museum attached to the Department of Mines.

Reserves for the preservation of timber are divided into two classes, viz., State Forests and Timber Reserves, and the latter are subdivided into three sub-classes, A, B, and C, according to their importance, and the particular quality and value of the timber which they contain.

State forests and timber reserves.

Licenses are issued to cut timber on reserves in class A at a fixed fee of £6 per annum, or 10s. per month, and without royalty; on reserves in class B the fee demanded amounts to £9, or 15s. per month; on reserves in class C general permits to cut timber for saw-mills are issued at a rate of £6 per annum, to which is added the payment of a royalty, which differs according to the

Timber licenses and permits.

value of the timber felled, and is based on the following classification:—

Saw-mill timber	placed in the	1st class,	1s. 6d.	per 100	superficial feet.
"	"	2nd "	1s. 3d.	"	"
		3rd "	1s.	"	"
		4th "	9d.	"	"
		5th "	6d.	"	"
"	"	6th "	3d.	"	"

Timber-cutting on Crown lands. Licenses are also issued to cut and remove timber on ordinary Crown lands—excepting State forests, timber reserves, reserves for public recreation, or sites for towns and villages, or permanently dedicated for any public purpose; also lands within 1½ chain of any navigable river, or held under conditional lease, measured for sale, within an enclosure of less than 200 acres, or within half a mile of a head station. The fee in this case is fixed at £3 per annum, or 15s. per quarter, or 5s. for any current month, and the license enables the holder to cut and remove any kind of timber, except cedar. The license fee for cutting cedar, and for shipping wattle bark, is fixed at £6 per annum, and no cedar-tree of less girth than 9 feet, measured at 5 feet from the ground, may be felled without special authority.

Permits to cut and strip bark. Permits are issued for cutting mining props, and for thinning out timber, in order to improve the growth of the trees remaining; for cutting and removing from a reserve a specified number and kind of trees; and also for stripping wattle-bark, or the bark of other trees for tanning purposes.

Penalties. Infringements of the timber regulations are punishable by fine, not exceeding £5 for the first offence, £10 for the second, and £20 for the third, irrespective of the value of the timber and material destroyed, for which also the offender may be held responsible.

PART VIII.

Fauna.

THE fauna of New South Wales is characterised by the absence of the forms of animal life familiar to the Old World, and the presence of genera and species peculiar to the Australian Continent.

MAMMALIA.

The order of mammalia is represented in this Colony by the oldest animal known, the marsupial, which is extinct in all other parts of the world except North America. The Macropidæ include several kinds of kangaroos and wallabies, the characteristics of which are too well known to need more than passing reference. The progress of settlement has driven these animals from the more densely populated parts of the Colony, but in the country districts they are still numerous enough to cause very considerable damage to the natural grasses. So serious has been the injury thus wrought, that the State and run-holders pay a small sum per head for the destruction of these animals. The number of kangaroos and wallabies, as estimated by Inspectors of Stock, existing in the Colony in 1890, was about 3,669,000, besides which it is estimated that there were 3,135,000 native dogs, and 7,880 wild pigs—the latter of course being the descendants of imported animals. Number of kangaroos, &c.

The genus Paramelidæ is represented by the wombat, and several kinds of rats and rabbit-rats, which latter burrow underground like their European prototype. They abound particularly in the western districts.

The Phalangystæ, which embrace several varieties of opossums, are found in all parts of New South Wales. Some of the speci- Phalangystæ.

mens of this family are very handsome, and their thick soft furs afford a valuable article of commerce.

Dingo. The dingo, or native dog (*Canis Dingo*), is found in all parts of the Australian mainland. It will inbreed with the domestic dog, and crosses are common throughout the settlements. The dingo does not bark, and, according to Dr. Geo. Bennett, it is allied to the wild dog of India, and may probably have been introduced by the Malays some centuries ago. Great destruction has been wrought amongst the flocks of the settlers by these animals, and a price is paid for every native dog destroyed.

Native Cats. There are two varieties of native cats (*Dasyurus Maculatus* and *D. Viverrinus*), both very handsomely marked. They are nocturnal animals, incapable of domestication, and prey upon birds and small mammals.

Echidnæ. The Echidnæ are represented by several varieties of spiny ant-eaters, somewhat resembling the English hedgehog. The favourite food of these animals is the various kinds of ants, which are found all over the country. The female Echidna carries its young in a pouch, which is only visible during the breeding season.

Flying foxes. Flying foxes, and numerous varieties of bats, are also indigenous to New South Wales, and make great depredations among the fruit-trees.

Platypus. Of all the animals found in the Colony the most curious and interesting is, perhaps, the *Ornithorhynchus paradoxus*, or Duck-billed platypus, called by the aborigines the Mallangong or Tambreet. This animal is a mammal, and has now been authoritatively shown to be also oviparous. The eggs brought forth are membranous, so that the platypus must be classed amongst the Reptilia.

Most of the animals above mentioned appear to be more destructive than useful, and if we except the trade in opossum and native-cat furs, and kangaroo skins, the commercial value of the indigenous mammals is very small. They are being gradually displaced, as civilisation advances, by the more useful animals of the Old World, for which the climate of New South Wales seems especially adapted, and which now form the principal source of the wealth of its inhabitants. The acclimatisation of the more useful European species is quickly followed by the destruction of indigenous animals, and the wilds of the interior of the Colony, which erstwhile were the abode of the kangaroo and dingo, are now the home of vast flocks.

Destruction of native animals.

Geological research has brought to light the remains of numerous extinct species of gigantic mammalia. The largest of these prehistoric animals was the *Diprotodon*, a marsupial quadruped, which, according to Professor Owen, was as large as the rhinoceros or hippopotamus. Fossil remains of another large marsupial, the *Nototherium*, somewhat resembling a tapir, and of a marsupial lion (*Thylacoleo*) have also been discovered. Bones of gigantic kangaroos (*Macropus titan*) have been frequently met with, as well as those of a species of wombat larger than that actually in existence.

Extinct species.

The remains of animals belonging to two distinct genera, representatives of which still exist in Tasmania, the *Thylacinus*, or pouched hyena, and the *Sarcophilus*, more commonly known as the Tasmanian devil, have also been found in the fossilised state.

BIRDS.

All the more important families of birds are represented in the fauna of New South Wales, which contains also a number of families peculiar to the Colony. Few countries can boast of a greater variety of beautiful birds. The parrot family is represented by a large number of species, including the love bird (*Melopsittacus undulatus*), the green parrot, and many kinds of lories, all gorgeously clothed; and amongst the larger species, the

Variety of birds.

white and black cockatoo, yellow and pink-crested, and the grey pink-crested gallahs. The family of honey-eaters (*Meliphagidæ*) is also represented by numerous and very beautiful varieties.

Amongst the larger kinds of birds found in the Colony are the *Megapodidæ*, which includes the brush turkey. These exist in great numbers in the western parts of the Colony, and their flesh is highly prized. In the western districts are also found the emu, the largest of Australian birds, and the native companion, a large water bird, somewhat like the crane in appearance.

Emu.

Lyre bird.

In the more thickly-timbered parts of the brush forests, the home of the stately tree-fern, is found the lyre-bird (*Menura superba*) a species of pheasant, whose tail forms a most graceful ornament. Here also abound the satin-bird, species of regent-birds, and the rifle-bird, all famed for the beauty of their plumage.

Aquatic birds.

Amongst water-birds are several species of cranes, and enormous numbers of wild fowl of all descriptions, as well as black swans. The latter is essentially an Australian bird, and may be met with in all parts of the Colony. The great kingfisher, or laughing-jackass, so named from its extraordinary cry, is one of the most useful of birds, owing to the readiness with which it destroys snakes. Magpies and mocking-birds may be included amongst those denizens of the forest which more prominently attract the attention of travellers. There are also several species of owls, and other night-birds, and the eagle family has not a few representatives.

The kingfisher.

The pigeon tribe.

The pigeon tribe is found in large numbers, especially in the great primæval forests of the coast districts. In the cedar brushes of the Liverpool Range white-headed fruit pigeons are very numerous; and in the brush forests of the Clarence, the Richmond, the Macleay, and Illawarra, the top-knot and large-tailed pigeons, and the Wonga Wonga (*Leucosarcia picata*), so prized for its large size and the whiteness and delicacy of its flesh, are very plentiful. The bronze-winged pigeon is common to almost all parts of the Colony. Several varieties of these birds are remarkable for their beautiful plumage, their size, and the excellence of their flesh. One of the finest varieties, the partridge bronze-winged pigeon, is found almost exclusively in the plains of the interior. Doves are also numerous, and most of the species are extremely delicate and beautiful. The little turtle-dove of the Murray River *(Geopelia cuneatra)* is the prettiest specimen of this family.

Other varieties.

Besides the varieties of birds mentioned above there are others, of perhaps less note, but numerous, and frequently very beautiful. They are all admirably described and depicted in the celebrated work of Dr. Gould, which occupies a high rank amongst the scientific publications of the century.

FISHES.

Fishing industry neglected.

The seas which wash the shores of New South Wales abound with fish, but none of the resources of the Colony has been so much neglected as the fishing industry. All the best fishing-grounds lie within a moderate distance of Sydney, and, as recently pointed out by the Fisheries Commission, it is not necessary, in order to obtain the fish most adapted for food, to despatch large smacks or fishing vessels, victualled and equipped for a cruise of several months, to fishing grounds distant hundreds of miles from home. The coast of the Colony presents many natural features peculiarly favourable to the existence of a very large supply of the best food fishes. In the quiet waters of its numerous bays and estuaries, and in the vast lakes and lagoons communicating with the sea, are found shelter and sustenance, as well as excellent breeding-grounds. The principal fishes found on the coast are not migratory, and as a consequence may nearly always be procured in the market.

Classification of fishes.

Sixty different families of fishes comprising 348 species are found in New South Wales waters. According to the classification of the late Rev. J. S. Tenison-Woods, S. J., these are as follows:—

Name of family.	No. of species.	Name of family.	No. of species.
Percidæ	50	Ophiocephalidæ	1
Squamipinnes	4	Trachypteridæ	1
Nandidæ	2	Pomacentridæ	4
Mullidæ	3	Labridæ	18
Sparidæ	14	Gadopsidæ	1
Cirrhitidæ	6	Gadidæ	4
Scorpænidæ	11	Pleuronectidæ	9
Teuthididæ	2	Siluridæ	5
Berycidæ	3	Scopelidæ	6
Kurtidæ	2	Salmonidæ	1
Polynemidæ	2	Galaxidæ	7
Sciænidæ	2	Scombresocidæ	6
Xiphiidæ	1	Clupeidæ	12
Trichiuridæ	1	Chirocentridæ	1
Acronuridæ	1	Symbrachidæ	1
Carangidæ	15	Murænidæ	11
Cyttidæ	1	Syngnathidæ	6
Coryphænidæ	2	Sclerodermi	21
Scombridæ	10	Gymnodontes	12
Trachinidæ	5	Carcharidæ	8
Batrachidæ	1	Lamnidæ	1
Pediculati	4	Scyllidæ	3
Cottidæ	7	Cestraciontidæ	2
Cataphracti	1	Spinacidæ	1
Gobiidæ	15	Rhinidæ	1
Blenniidæ	17	Pristiophoridæ	1
Sphyrænidæ	3	Rhinobatidæ	2
Atherinidæ	4	Trygonidæ	3
Mugilidæ	7	Torpedinidæ	1
Fistularidæ	1	Raiidæ	1

The edible fishes comprise 105 different species; amongst the best known may be mentioned:

The schnapper.

The schnapper *(Pagrus unicolor)*, the most valuable of all Australian fishes, is found along the whole extent of the coast, and is very abundant. It is a deep-water fish, found generally near rocky points or reefs running out into the sea. The schnappers "school," as it is termed, during the summer months, and are then most plentiful. The young fish, known as red bream, frequents the harbours and estuaries of the coast, but is never found in shallow water. The schnapper is caught by the hook, which it takes freely, as it will attack almost any bait. It sometimes attains a very large size, weighing as much as 30 lb.

The nannigai is a deep-water fish, caught with the hook, and ranks high in public estimation as an edible fish. The supply is not large, as the fish is not specially sought after, being chiefly obtained by fishermen in search of schnapper. The nannigai is scientifically interesting as one of the oldest forms of bony-fishes now surviving. Nannigai.

The black rock-cod is considered one of the best of Australian fish, and is also a deep-water fish, never captured by the net. It is found more abundantly in the warmer waters of the north of the Colony, where, as a rule, it attains larger proportions than to the southward of Sydney. It grows to a great size, specimens from 35 to 40 lb. being not uncommon. Rock-cod.

A fish of great size and beauty, known in Australia as the salmon, is found off the coast in prodigious quantities. It has no affinity whatever to the true salmon, and is inferior as an article of food. Salmon.

The flathead, a fine fish, of which there are several varieties, is captured both by the hook and net. It is of excellent quality and ranks high amongst New South Wales fishes. Flathead.

There are four species of whiting found in these waters. The common sand-whiting and the trumpeter-whiting are both very abundant, but the other two species are more rare. The sand-whiting is perhaps the fish most in demand in the metropolitan markets, where it is to be obtained all the year round. Whiting.

The jew-fish is the largest edible fish found on the New South Wales coast, attaining sometimes a length of 5 feet. It is found at all seasons, but most frequently during summer. The teraglin is of the same family as the jew-fish, though it does not reach an equal size. The air bladder is large and of excellent quality, being of great value for the making of isinglass. Jew-fish.

The mackerel is obtained in enormous quantities off the coast, and sometimes even in the harbours. It is a good fish when eaten fresh, but it decomposes rapidly.

Mullets.

The family of *Mugilidæ*, or mullets, is well represented in Australian waters. The sea mullet is a large fish, often attaining a length of 2 feet, and a weight of 8 lb. It is regarded by some authorities as unsurpassed in richness and delicacy of flavour by any fish in the world; and it visits these shores in countless numbers in the season when it is in the best condition. While young the fish keeps entirely to the creeks and lakes, where it increases in size very rapidly, but when full-grown it seeks the open waters.

Gar-fish.

There are four species of gar-fish found on the New South Wales coast. The Sydney gar-fish is very abundant, especially towards the end of summer, making its appearance in shoals, sometimes of enormous size. The river gar-fish is even of better quality than the last mentioned, but is not so plentiful as formerly. The other species are seldom met with. There are numerous other varieties of fishes found in the waters of New South Wales, many of which are very valuable as articles of food, but for the most part are neither so numerous nor so easily obtained as those referred to.

Destructive fishes.

Destructive fishes are by no means rare; the shark family being largely represented, not only in the deep-sea, off the coast, but even in the harbours. The shark is not, however, absolutely valueless. The fins find a ready sale in the Chinese markets; the skin also has some commercial value, while from the liver is extracted a large quantity of valuable oil, equal in every respect to cod-liver oil.

Neglect of fisheries.

As already pointed out, the fisheries of New South Wales have been much neglected, and, as a further instance of this, it may be mentioned that although during the winter season immense shoals of herrings visit these coasts, no attempt is made to take and preserve them. The Rev. J. E. Tenison-Woods, Sir William Macleay, and the members of the Fisheries Commission, have strongly directed attention to the value of this fish. It is quite as abundant as the herring of Scotland, and superior in flavour; and, preserved like sardines, it would no doubt rival that delicacy. There is ample evidence that the application of a little capital, and intelligent management, would make the herring fishery a very profitable industry.

In Sydney the supply of fresh-water fish is very limited, although the rivers of the Colony produce some most excellent specimens. The rivers Murray, Murrumbidgee, Lachlan, and Darling are the most plentifully stocked, the Murray cod *(Oligorus Mitchelli)* being perhaps the most highly esteemed of their fishes. Another fish of the same species is the *Oligorus Macquariensis*, which is to be met with in the upper branches of the Clarence. Both these specimens of Murray cod have been found weighing as much as 100 lb. The silver perch and several kinds of the Percidæ family, so highly prized for their delicacy, are plentiful in the rivers. In the Richmond River the cat-fish *(Copidoglanis Tandanus)* is very common, whilst herrings and mullet are caught in almost all the eastern rivers of the Colony. Fresh-water fish.

Little systematic attempt has yet been made to acclimatize European varieties of edible fishes, although success would most probably attend any efforts in this direction, every difficulty having been overcome in Victoria, New Zealand, and Tasmania. Some five or six thousand trout ova, presented by the Geelong Acclimatisation Society, have been distributed in various localities, including the Prospect Reservoir. Fish acclimatisation.

Among the Crustaceæ, which abound on the coast and in the water-courses of the interior, the lobster and several varieties of salt and fresh-water crayfish are most noticeable. The prawn (*Penæus esculentus*) is very abundant in all the shallow bays and harbours. Crustacea.

Oysters are excellent and were very plentiful. The oyster-beds of Port Jackson, Port Stephens, the Hawkesbury, and the Shoalhaven, however, have been greatly injured, and the markets of the metropolis are supplied chiefly from the Clarence, the Richmond, and other northern rivers. Before the appointment of the Royal Commission of Fisheries, in 1880, these molluscs were threatened with extinction in the near future. The Commission has effected some improvement, but has been checked in its operations by defective legislation, and the improvidence of Oysters.

the lessees of the oyster-beds, who strip the beds without any regard to future supply. There is but little doubt that the establishment of "parcs" like those which may be seen along the coasts of France and Belgium, where oyster culture is conducted on scientific principles, would be remunerative, as the demand for this delicacy is great and continually increasing.

Oyster culture.

Remarkable fishes.

Several varieties of fishes which have long disappeared from other parts of the world are still represented in New South Wales. Amongst these are the cestracion, or Port Jackson shark, whose teeth resemble those of the fossil acrodis found in the mesozoic deposits, and the ceratodus, an existing ganoid, otherwise exclusively represented in the trias formation, its anatomy showing a connecting link between a lizard and a fish. Amongst other remarkable fishes found in these waters, several may be enumerated. The frog fish, belonging to the order Pediculati, has fins adapted for walking on the ground rather than for swimming, and is found floating in-shore amongst marine plants, from which it is with difficulty distinguished, owing to its great resemblance to them in point of colour. The hopping fish, a variety of gobii, or sea-gudgeon, has its fins developed into legs, so that the animal is able to leap along the mud flats which it frequents. The eyes of this fish are curiously placed at the top of its head, and are capable of being thrust far out of their sockets, and of moving independently of one another. The Hippocampus, or sea-horse, so named from a resemblance in the shape of the head and fore part of the body to that of the horse, is a very singular fish, but the phyllopteryx is perhaps, the most remarkable fish of Australia, if not of the world. It is like the ghost of a sea-horse, with its winding-sheet all in ribbons around it. Its tattered cerements are in shape and colour like the sea-weed it frequents, so that it hides and feeds with safety. The dugong (*Halicore Australis*) was formerly met with at the mouths of the Richmond, Tweed, and Brunswick Rivers, but is now seldom seen south of the Brisbane River, in Queensland. It resembles the porpoise in shape and size, but has no dorsal fin. The skin is heavy and thick, and is said to make excellent leather.

Dugong. The habits of this animal are those of a graminivorous ruminant, its stomach being exactly like that of an ox; it frequents the flats and shallows along the margin of the shore, and feeds upon the grass which is found thereon. Like the whale family, it suckles its young, is warm-blooded, and therefore is incorrectly described as a fish. The dugong attains a large size, sometimes measuring 14 feet long and 10 feet in girth. An animal of such dimensions would weigh about 300 lb.

The Fish Market. During 1890 the Fish Market, Woolloomooloo, was supplied with 63,967 baskets fish, including 2,083½ dozen schnapper, 55½ dozen salmon (*arripis solar*), 398¼ dozen king-fish, 88¾ dozen jew-fish, 539 dozen teraglin, 172½ dozen nannigai, 5 dozen groper, and 2,951 dozen cray-fish, besides 4,636 baskets prawns. The amount realised at the market for the fish referred to was £38,695. 6,092 bags of oysters were taken from the tidal waters of the Colony in 1890, and 12,099 bags were imported, chiefly from Queensland and New Zealand. 40,076 lb. weight of Murray River cod were exported during the year. Considerable quantities of prawns arrive in Sydney by coasting steamers, which never go into the Fish Market, and are not included above.

REPTILES.

The snake and lizard families number many varieties, which are distributed over all parts of the country. These reptiles, however have generally disappeared from the settled portions of the Colony, having been deprived of the means of subsistence which the condition of the country in its natural state afforded them. Several species of snakes are venomous, particularly the death-adder, the black snake, the brown, and the tiger snake, but accidents due to snake bite are now of rare occurrence. Most reptiles retreat at the approach of man, and there is comparatively little danger to be apprehended from their presence. Lizards are common, very beautifully marked, and some species, particularly the iguanas, attain a considerable size. Venomous snakes.

Although the rivers of the Colony of Queensland are the abode of several species of alligators, those of New South Wales are entirely free from the presence of these dangerous saurians.

PART IX.

Commerce and Shipping.

THE commerce of New South Wales is exceeded in value by that of no other colony or dependency of Great Britain, India alone excepted. India, with a population about 250 times larger, has a trade hardly four times as great as this Colony, while the Dominion, whose population numbers five times that of New South Wales, does not equal it in the value of its commerce. Thus in the year 1889 the trade of these countries was:—

Country.	Imports.	Exports.	Total trade.
	£	£	£
India	83,285,427	98,833,879	182,119,306
Canada	23,676,356	18,326,541	42,002,897
New South Wales	22,863,057	23,294,934	46,157,991

SHIPPING.

Early shipping records.

Prior to the year 1825 the records of the shipping trade of the Colony are very meagre; in the year mentioned, however, the shipping amounted to 85 vessels inwards, aggregating a tonnage of 24,559; and 75 vessels outwards, with a total tonnage of 22,688. Twenty-five years afterwards, just before the separation of Port Phillip, the figures stood thus: 976 vessels inwards, with a tonnage of 234,215 tons, and 1,014 vessels outwards, with a tonnage of 263,849 tons. In 1851, the year of the separation of Victoria from the parent Colony, the trade fell to 553 vessels inwards, measuring 153,002 tons, and 503 vessels outwards of 139,020 tons.

Separation of Queensland caused no decline in trade.

The separation of Queensland caused no decline in the trade of the Colony, as shown by the returns. Possibly the classing of northern boats as foreign traders, instead of as coasters, would be the cause of even an apparent increase, for in 1860, the year following the separation, the shipping amounted to 1,424 vessels inwards, with a tonnage of 427,835 tons, and 1,438 vessels out-f 431,484 tons, a considerable advance on the figures of rious year. From 1860 to the present time trade has ncreased, and at a greater ratio than the population, so 1890 the tonnage, inwards, amounted to 2,413,247 tons, outward tonnage to 2,348,625, or 4,761,872 tons in all.

ate of increase has been fairly constant, though checked ally by the occurrence of bad seasons here, or failure of the European markets. The following table shows the and tonnage of shipping arriving and departing from sth Wales, at intervals of five years, from the date of the records to the year 1890. A marked falling off is shown gures for 1890, a circumstance attributable to the mari- ike which was so unfortunate a feature of the industrial ns of that year :— *Increase of shipping.*

ssels Entered and Cleared in New South Wales.

ear.	Inwards.		Outwards.	
	Number.	Tonnage.	Number.	Tonnage.
[illegible]	85	24,559	75	22,688
[illegible]	157	31,225	147	28,822
[illegible]	260	63,019	269	66,964
[illegible]	709	178,958	665	163,704
[illegible]	597	105,352	614	103,961
[illegible]	976	234,215	1,014	263,849
[illegible]	1,152	353,323	1,185	362,482
[illegible]	1,424	427,835	1,438	431,484
[illegible]	1,912	635,888	2,120	690,294
[illegible]	1,858	689,820	2,066	771,942
[illegible]	2,376	1,109,066	2,294	1,059,101
[illegible]	2,108	1,242,458	2,043	1,190,321
[illegible]	2,601	2,088,307	2,583	2,044,770
[illegible]	3,254	2,632,081	3,229	2,689,098
[illegible]	2,889	2,413,247	2,777	2,348,625

lready stated, the trade of New South Wales greatly that of any other colony of the Australian group. stands next; after which in their order come South ia, New Zealand, Queensland, Tasmania, and Western ia. Of the total shipping of Australasia in 1890 about [illegible] entered and cleared in New South Wales ports. *Shipping of New South Wales compared with other colonies.*

Trade of Colony in British hands

The trade of the Colony is, to a very large extent, in British hands, though there has been a noticeable increase in foreign shipping since 1881. In 1872 the British shipping entered and cleared amounted to 1,400,672 tons, while in 1890 it was 4,156,963 tons, showing an increase of 2,756,291 tons. The foreign shipping amounted to 187,368 tons in 1872, and 604,909 in 1890, being an increase of 417,541 tons.

French and German mail steamers.

The advent of the French line of Messageries Maritimes, and of the German Lloyd's steamships, has tended to increase the amount of the foreign trade of the Colony; but notwithstanding this, the tonnage under the British flag was in 1890 not less than 87·3 per cent. of the whole. The annexed table shows the respective amounts of each class since 1872:—

British and Foreign Vessels Entered and Cleared in New South Wales.

Year	British.	Foreign.	Total.
	Tons.	Tons.	Tons.
1872	1,400,672	187,368	1,588,040
1873	1,619,019	143,459	1,762,478
1874	1,820,146	170,748	1,990,894
1875	2,001,641	166,546	2,168,187
1876	1,969,457	158,268	2,127,725
1877	2,022,728	215,253	2,237,981
1878	2,203,491	256,012	2,459,504
1879	2,292,733	247,991	2,540,724
1880	2,259,924	172,855	2,432,779
1881	2,563,999	222,501	2,786,500
1882	2,977,756	318,909	3,296,665
1883	3,532,955	473,282	4,006,237
1884	4,185,549	475,409	4,660,958
1885	3,615,582	517,495	4,133,077
1886	3,746,725	511,879	4,258,604
1887	3,836,527	486,231	4,322,758
1888	4,141,551	623,868	4,765,419
1889	4,659,798	661,381	5,321,179
1890	4,156,963	604,909	4,761,872

Larger portion of tonnage owned in colonies.

Of the total tonnage set down as British, the larger portion is owned in the colonies. In 1876 out of 1,969,457 tons of shipping entered and cleared under the British flag, 1,293,813 tons, or about 66 per cent., were Australian; in 1881, out of 2,563,999 tons entered and cleared, 1,543,431 tons, or 60 per cent., represented colonial shipping; while in 1890 the colonial shipping amounted to 2,579,172 tons, out of a total of 4,156,963 tons, or 62·04 per cent. The amount of British and British-colonial shipping entered and cleared from New South Wales ports during each year since 1880 is shown below:— British shipping.

Tonnage of British Vessels trading to New South Wales.

Year.	Shipping belonging—		Total, inwards and outwards.
	To Great Britain.	To British possessions.	
	Tons.	Tons.	Tons.
1880	760,688	1,499,236	2,259,924
1881	1,020,568	1,543,431	2,563,999
1882	1,301,347	1,676,409	2,977,756
1883	1,429,725	2,103,230	3,532,955
1884	1,716,255	2,469,294	4,185,549
1885	1,520,091	2,095,491	3,615,582
1886	1,503,921	2,242,804	3,746,725
1887	1,599,191	2,237,336	3,836,527
1888	1,717,549	2,424,002	4,141,551
1889	1,842,727	2,817,071	4,659,798
1890	1,577,172	2,579,791	4,156,963

Compared with the figures just given, the tonnage of the foreign vessels trading with New South Wales will appear very small. Taking the year 1890, for which the inward and outward tonnage for the principal nationalities are given below, Germany stands first, then America, after which comes France. Scandinavia is the only other nation whose carrying trade with the Colony is important. Tonnage of foreign vessels

Foreign vessels Entered and Cleared in New South Wales during 1890:—

	Tonnage.
Germany	229,413
U.S. America	173,770
France	137,466
Norway and Sweden	20,678
Holland	12,124
Other nations	31,453
Total	604,909

[illegible] of the steam [illegible]

[illegible] was [illegible] being [illegible] relative [illegible] sailing [illegible]

		Tons
[illegible]	[illegible]	[illegible]
[illegible]	[illegible]	[illegible]
[illegible]	[illegible]	[illegible]
[illegible]	[illegible]	[illegible]
[illegible]	[illegible]	1,500,9[illegible]
[illegible]	[illegible]	1,602,801
[illegible]	[illegible]74,814	1,167,058

[illegible] Wales trade to ship- [illegible] age coming to [illegible] leaving without cargo. [illegible] in ballast come from [illegible] delivered a general cargo there, and, being unable to obtain return freight, go to Newcastle for a cargo of coal. The largest amount of tonnage in any one year since 1877 entered in ballast was in 1889, when it reached 704,267 tons, and the largest cleared was 66,846 tons in 1890. The tonnage entered and cleared for each year is given herewith:—

Tonnage Entered and Cleared in Ballast.

Year.	Entered.	Cleared.	Year.	Entered.	Cleared.
	Tons.	Tons.		Tons.	Tons.
1877	295,569	8,393	1884	395,990	60,457
1878	354,917	13,115	1885	345,366	53,381
1879	337,696	19,892	1886	353,969	40,635
1880	217,763	16,219	1887	507,177	36,434
1881	271,343	5,179	1888	628,732	41,736
1882	325,480	23,338	1889	704,267	65,898
1883	384,645	27,855	1890	544,264	66,846

Notwithstanding the fact that between one-fourth and one-fifth of the tonnage arriving in the Colony is in ballast, as against one-thirty-fifth of the clearances, the average value of freights inward is higher than of those outward. Thus in 1890 the average value of the cargoes imported was £7 8s. 5d. per ton of vessels inward, or, if an allowance be made for ships in ballast, the value per ton was £9 11s. 8d. The mean value of goods exported per ton of shipping outward was £5 19s. 5d., and allowing for vessels leaving in ballast, £6 2s. 11d.; in the former case 19·56 per cent. and in the latter 35·88 per cent. lower than the value of tonnage imported. Value of imports per ton.

New South Wales exports have, generally speaking, a high value per ton, and the lower value of the exports per ton than the imports is due to the large amount of coal exported, the quantity for 1890 being 1,821,874 tons weight, or 1,237,000 tons measurement, out of a total of 2,348,625 tons. The value of the exports of the Colony per ton exceeds that of the imports in the case of Great Britain, Victoria, and France alone. In every other case, as will be seen from the following statement, the import value per ton is much higher than the export:— Value of exports per ton.

Value per Ton Measurement of Imports and Exports of New South Wales, 1889.

Country.	Value of imports per ton.	Value of exports per ton.	Country.	Value of imports per ton.	Value of exports per ton.
	£ s. d.	£ s. d.		£ s. d.	£ s. d.
United Kingdom ..	22 12 7	24 10 10	Belgium.........	79 11 1	78 12 2
Victoria	1 5 4	1 14 7	France	3 16 3	8 7 11
Queensland......	12 3 6	5 8 2	Germany	8 19 2	6 10 5
South Australia	2 10 9	1 10 3	United States..	13 6 11	8 4 6
Tasmania	2 18 11	1 18 6	Other Foreign countries.	6 0 4	1 15 3
New Zealand ...	6 7 7	1 11 8			
Other British Possessions...	4 16 3	4 4 8	Average.........	7 8 5	5 19 4

Trade with various countries compared.

The following table shows the total amount of shipping of some of the principal nations of the world, and of New South Wales, with the rate of tonnage per head of the population:—

Shipping of Various Countries and the Tonnage per Head of Population, 1888.

Country.	Tonnage.	Per Head of Population.	Country.	Tonnage.	Per Head of Population.
United Kingdom ..	68,519,145	1·91	Italy	13,070,253	0·46
France............	28,491,665	0·75	Spain	22,323,708	1·27
Germany.........	18,876,166	0·40	United States.	26,208,356	0·52
Norway	4,775,281	2·40	Arg'ntine Republic	9,205,196	3·07
Sweden	10,004,865	2·11	Canada (1889)	9,296,601	1·83
Netherlands ...	10,181,333	2·54	New South Wales (1890)	4,761,372	4·32
Russia (in Europe).	14,784,098	0·16			

Tonnage of exports to Great Britain.

Of the tonnage of New South Wales exports, Great Britain took only 11·49 per cent., though in value the exports were 47·24 per cent. of the total. The exports by sea to Victoria and the other Australasian Colonies amounted to 57·86 per cent. of the whole, while in value they reached only 23·12 per cent. As regards the other British possessions, the tonnage of vessels carrying goods from New South Wales to their ports amounted to 6·96 per cent. of the whole, but the value reached only 4·94 per cent.

Value of British commerce.

In the case of Foreign Countries, the tonnage amounted in 1890 to 23·49 per cent. and the value to 24·70 per cent., the great increase over last year's figures being due to the considerable expansion of the direct trade in wool with European continental countries. The following table shows the tonnage inward and outward from Great Britain and the Colonies, and to the United States, as well as the value of the cargoes; but it must be borne in mind that the tonnage figures represent the nominal tonnage of the vessels carrying the goods, and not the actual weight of the goods themselves, which latter information it is impossible to obtain :—

Tonnage of Vessels and Value of Cargoes during 1890.

Country.	Inwards.				Outwards.			
	Tonnage.		Value.		Tonnage.		Value.	
	Total.	Per cent.	Total.	Per cent.	Total.	Per cent.	Total.	Per cent.
	Tons.		£		Tons.		£	
United Kingdom	381,246	15·80	8,628,007	48·18	269,886	11·49	6,623,431	47·24
Victoria........	874,789	36·25	1,110,732	6·20	664,457	28·29	1,149,549	8·20
Queensland	273,004	11·31	3,323,630	18·56	250,114	10·65	1,352,748	9·65
South Australia	186,887	7·74	474,500	2·65	151,189	6·44	228,469	1·63
Tasmania	146,904	6·09	432,615	2·42	111,987	4·77	215,674	1·54
New Zealand ..	147,065	6·09	932,073	5·20	185,728	7·91	294,118	2·10
Other British possessions.	137,967	5·72	664,155	3·71	163,464	6·96	692,012	4·94
Belgium	1,644	0·07	130,819	0·73	12,782	0·54	1,011,846	7·22
France	29,287	1·21	117,871	0·66	27,859	1·19	233,924	1·67
Germany	71,365	2·96	639,475	3·57	62,003	2·64	404,280	2·88
United States ..	64,375	2·67	859,102	4·80	158,108	6·73	1,300,375	9·27
Other foreign countries.	98,792	4·09	594,684	3·32	291,119	12·39	513,140	3·66
Total	2,413,247	100·00	17,907,668	100·00	2,348,625	100·00	14,019,561	100·00

The average tonnage of vessels trading with the Colony has gradually increased since 1845; previously to that year transports formed so large a portion of the total tonnage as to swell the average considerably. The average tonnage per ship at each decennial period since 1825 was as follows :— Average tonnage of vessels trading with N. S. Wales.

Year.	Average tonnage of vessels.	Year.	Average tonnage of vessels.
1825	295	1865	329
1835	246	1875	463
1845	173	1885	797
1855	306	1890	840

Tonnage of British, Foreign and Colonial vessels.

The tonnage for the last ten years has been separated into British, Foreign, and Colonial, and the average for each year will be found below. It will be seen that during this period the average tonnage of British vessels trading here has increased 47 per cent., of foreign vessels 71 per cent., and Colonial about 20 per cent.

Year.	Average tonnage of vessels.			Year.	Average tonnage of vessels.		
	British.	Foreign.	Colonial.		British.	Foreign.	Colonial.
	Tons.	Tons.	Tons.		Tons.	Tons.	Tons.
1881	1,105	780	498	1886	1,329	986	600
1882	1,067	787	533	1887	1,385	1,108	549
1883	1,060	982	594	1888	1,516	1,194	576
1884	1,146	973	611	1889	1,534	1,123	600
1885	1,312	997	602	1890	1,624	1,330	600

Decrease in hands required per ton.

The natural corollary to the increase in the size of ships and the improvements to the rigging and fittings is the decrease in the number of hands required per ton, though the actual number of hands employed per vessel has increased. Intercolonial vessels in 1890 carried an average of 22 men to every vessel, or 1 man to every 28·6 tons. British vessels carried in 1890 an average complement of 24·3 men, or 1 man to every 52 tons, while foreign ships carried an average crew of 49 men, or 1 man to every 29·3 tons. In 1876 British ships carried 1 man to every 25 tons, intercolonial vessels 1 man to every 22½ tons, and foreign vessels 1 man to 35 tons, the decrease in the tonnage per sailor in foreign vessels being due to the finer class of ships that began to trade here in 1883, which are fitted in the most modern fashion, and manned accordingly:—

Average crews carried.

Year.	Average crews of vessels.			Year.	Average crews of vessels.		
	British.	Foreign.	Colonial.		British.	Foreign.	Colonial.
1880	44	25	21	1886	45	39	23
1881	40	23	22	1887	48	49	22
1882	35	18	22	1888	45	44	23
1883	37	38	24	1889	46	40	22
1884	41	36	25	1890	52	49	22
1885	44	36	24				

The relative importance of the various ports of Australia may be ascertained by an inspection of the following table, from which the rank of Sydney becomes evident. Melbourne takes the first place; but, as hereafter pointed out, its trade, for purposes of comparison, should be reduced by a large amount to allow for the circumstance that the great ocean steamers whose terminal port is Sydney are counted as twice entering and twice clearing at Port Phillip; but even with this allowance the shipping of Melbourne probably exceeds that of Sydney. Port Adelaide comes next after Sydney, exceeding in tonnage both Newcastle and Brisbane. It should be noted in respect to Queensland ports, that the tonnage of vessels is recorded at every port of call, and on this account the towns north of Brisbane also appear more important than they really are. Comparison of Australian ports.

Tonnage Entered and Cleared at principal Australasian Ports.

Port.	Entered.	Cleared.	Port.	Entered.	Cleared.
	Tons.	Tons.		Tons.	Tons.
Sydney	1,644,899	1,356,632	Port Pirie ...	80,394	121,707
Newcastle ...	625,396	842,180	Albany	431,817	388,725
Melbourne ...	2,061,826	2,045,156	Hobart	273,494	272,863
Brisbane	416,814	415,350	Launceston ..	149,785	148,616
Townsville ..	269,178	269,039	Wellington ..	141,890	142,977
Port Adelaide.	866,458	833,971	Auckland ...	185,444	176,660

The progress of the shipping trade of Sydney has been very uniform, the increase being at an average rate of about 8 per cent. per annum. The vessels registered as entering the port of Sydney considerably exceed in tonnage those clearing. To account for this difference it is only necessary to state that vessels leaving Sydney for Newcastle for the purpose of shipping coal are reckoned as departures from Newcastle, and not from Sydney. For this reason Increase of Sydney trade.

the clearances of Newcastle uniformly exceed the arrivals, as will be noticed in the subsequent table. The practice of clearing vessels at both ports at one time obtained, but has been abandoned for many years, and vessels are now cleared at the port which they last leave. The following statement shows the shipping entered and cleared at both Sydney and Newcastle for twenty years. It will be seen that the tonnage of the first-named port has increased twofold during every ten years.

Tonnage of Vessels Entered and Cleared at Sydney and Newcastle.

Year.	Sydney.		Newcastle.	
	Entered.	Cleared.	Entered.	Cleared.
	Tons.	Tons.	Tons.	Tons.
1871	409,063	394,289	277,959	376,378
1872	418,164	360,735	342,514	427,845
1873	474,203	367,351	389,121	498,468
1874	499,326	422,693	510,291	543,693
1875	590,700	468,423	510,902	573,626
1876	635,269	502,866	433,423	535,738
1877	662,217	511,623	469,349	577,676
1878	712,303	511,801	542,745	665,885
1879	759,980	581,694	492,163	651,501
1880	827,738	641,996	400,598	516,480
1881	955,531	655,161	481,695	645,543
1882	1,101,756	844,677	559,228	737,772
1883	1,260,595	1,115,411	656,916	926,956
1884	1,554,118	1,277,843	708,449	1,066,462
1885	1,608,169	1,283,888	452,946	722,865
1886	1,638,802	1,399,545	416,518	686,179
1887	1,483,045	1,303,488	566,702	780,588
1888	1,692,268	1,424,429	633,119	815,516
1889	1,759,658	1,432,340	744,113	1,126,892
1890	1,644,589	1,356,632	625,398	842,180

Trade of Sydney compared with British ports.

The comparative importance of the trade of Sydney may be seen from viewing it in connection with the trade of the chief cities of Great Britain. It will be observed that in absolute tonnage Sydney was surpassed by five English ports—London, Liverpool, Cardiff, Newcastle, and Hull; though in point of value, the trade of Sydney exceeded that of any port in Great Britain, London, Liverpool, and Hull excepted. Thirteen of the most important ports of Great Britain are shown in the following table. The figures are in every instance those for 1890.

Tonnage of principal Ports of Great Britain and of Sydney.

Port.	Inwards.	Outwards.
London	7,708,705	5,772,062
Liverpool	5,782,351	5,159,450
Cardiff	3,173,699	5,641,511
Tyne Ports (Newcastle, North Shields, and South Shields).	3,401,216	5,010,098
Hull	1,997,138	1,655,996
Sydney	1,644,589	1,356,632
Glasgow	1,121,700	1,697,662
Newport	920,560	1,316,430
Sunderland	725,859	956,266
Southampton	888,352	813,133
Dover	789,846	767,724
Middlesbrough	833,562	623,967
Swansea	565,644	858,215
Bristol	556,971	221,180

No other seaport of the Colony can be compared with either Sydney or Newcastle, though for some time Wollongong has maintained a trade of some consequence, especially in coal; and of late years the importance of Eden, Twofold Bay, has steadily increased.

Murray and Darling trade.

The trade borne by the Rivers Murray and Darling varies greatly from year to year, according as they are favourable or otherwise for navigation. The Murray River is navigable during the greater part of each year, but the same cannot be said of the Darling, which as a rule can only be used by shipping during the period from March to September, when its volume is augmented by the flood waters from the interior of Queensland. For the period over which the records extend both rivers have been navigable, and the tonnage at Wentworth on the Darling, at its confluence with the Murray, and at Moama and other Murray River ports, is given in the following table:—

Riverina trade.

Trade at Riverina ports.

Year.	Tonnage Inwards at—	
	Wentworth.	Moama and other Murray Ports.
1886	25,366	17,432
1887	35,392	30,470
1888	22,427	28,339
1889	38,335	29,279
1890	42,637	30,140

Number of vessels registered.

During the year 1890, 981 steamers and sailing vessels, representing 111,063 tons net, stood registered in the books of the Custom House, as belonging to the port of Sydney. Of these 439 were steamers, collectively of 48,905 tons net and of 17,516 nominal horse-power. There were 59 sailing vessels registered at Newcastle (8,001 tons net), and 55 steamers of 2,650 nominal horse-power, and 4,368 net tons. The total tonnage registered in the Colony was 123,432, of which 53,273 was steam tonnage, with 20,166 nominal horse-power.

The total tonnage registered in New South Wales during the last twelve years was :—

Vessels Registered in New South Wales.

Year.	Sailing vessels.			Steamers.			Total.	Total tons.	Total men.
	No.	Tons.	Men.	No.	Tons.	Men.			
1879	54	5,870	281	36	3,561	291	90	9,431	725
1880	54	7,003	325	20	2,159	168	74	9,162	493
1881	51	10,300	328	23	2,713	115	74	13,013	443
1882	87	14,246	511	41	7,764	509	128	22,010	1,020
1883	83	10,566	420	72	9,406	575	155	19,972	995
1884	77	10,850	507	84	11,484	707	161	22,334	1,214
1885	49	4,876	280	50	6,387	394	99	11,263	674
1886	45	5,969	166	47	3,489	235	92	9,458	401
1887	39	9,138	258	36	10,303	603	75	19,441	861
1888	25	5,101	164	25	2,357	237	50	7,458	401
1889	18	1,038	53	20	2,381	144	38	3,419	197
1890	28	6,234	191	21	4,027	278	49	10,261	469

No reliable data have as yet been procurable as to the number and tonnage of vessels built abroad for the New South Wales local trade, but that number must be considerable, and forms an import of large value altogether lost sight of in the Customs returns. Some idea, however, of the large number of vessels imported may be gathered from the tonnage registered, which will be found in the following table. In estimating the value of the vessels imported, approximate figures can alone be given. The value per ton of the British mercantile fleet averages about £30 for steamers and £15 for sailing vessels, but in this Colony the Import of vessels.

figures would be somewhat lower, and for the purpose of the estimate which follows, the average value of steam tonnage has been taken at £25, and sailing vessels at £12 10s.:—

Foreign Tonnage Registered in New South Wales.

Year.	Sailing.	Steam.	Value.	Year.	Sailing.	Steam.	Value.
	Tons.	Tons.	£		Tons.	Tons.	£
1877	4,469	2,616	121,262	1884	8,332	6,339	262,625
1878	5,329	3,732	159,912	1885	4,076	3,395	135,825
1879	4,332	2,764	123,250	1886	4,630	852	79,175
1880	5,065	1,298	95,762	1887	8,502	9,525	356,900
1881	9,558	1,948	168,175	1888	4,797	1,963	109,137
1882	12,788	4,488	272,050	1889	834	1,718	42,950
1883	8,681	4,038	209,462	1890	5,820	3,330	156,000

Shipbuilding record.

The building of steam vessels has become of more importance than that of sailing ships, the tonnage during the last ten years being 22,715 of steam tonnage, and 10,280 tons of sailing, respectively. Schooners and ketches are the principal classes of sailing vessels built in the Colony, the general tonnage of each class averaging somewhat under 100 tons burden. The general tendency to supplant sailing vessels by steamers, and the substitution ot iron for wood for the frames and hulls of vessels, have given a check to the wooden ship-building industry, which at one time promised to grow to important dimensions. Every kind of timber suitable for the construction of ships is found on the rivers of the coast districts of the Colony, but, as the demand for this description of vessel has not increased, little advantage can be taken of the resources of the Colony in this respect.

Tendency to supplant sail by steam.

Vessels built in the Colony.

The years 1883 and 1884 were marked by great activity in the construction both of sailing and steam vessels, 50 sailing and 52 steam vessels, valued at about £157,762, having been built in 1883, whilst 39 sailing vessels and 64 steamers, valued at £160,100, were built in the subsequent year. Trade has not been so active since, and the industry shows a tendency to die out, as in 1888 it had fallen lower than in any of the preceding years and there has been little improvement since, the value of sailing vessels built during 1890 being only £4,925, and of steamers £17,425, in all £22,350. The number of vessels built during each year since 1876 is given in the table annexed :—

Vessels Built in New South Wales.

Year.	Sailing vessels.		Steamers.		Total vessels.	Total tonnage.
	No.	Tons.	No.	Tons.		
1876	38	2,066	22	1,399	60	3,465
1877	34	1,995	27	2,515	61	4,510
1878	23	1,782	26	1,660	49	3,442
1879	31	1,538	19	797	50	2,335
1880	29	1,938	12	861	41	2,799
1881	14	742	15	765	29	1,507
1882	41	1,458	24	3,276	65	4,734
1883	50	1,885	52	5,368	102	7,253
1884	39	2,518	64	5,145	103	7,663
1885	29	800	36	2,992	65	3,792
1886	27	1,339	40	2,637	67	3,976
1887	14	636	16	778	30	1,414
1888	9	304	11	394	20	698
1889	9	204	14	663	23	867
1890	9	394	6	697	15	1,091

Dock accommodation in Sydney.

The accommodation provided both by the Government and by private enterprise for the fitting and repairing of ships, is equal to the requirements of the trade of the Colony. At Sydney there are three graving docks, four floating docks, and five patent slips. At Newcastle there is one patent slip, and on the Clarence River a floating dock, besides which there are other docking and building yards in different parts of the Colony for the convenience of coasters and small craft. The principal docks and slips in Sydney, as well as their leading dimensions and size of vessel they will carry, are shown in the following table:—

Docks and Slips in Sydney Harbour.

Name of Dock.	Where situated.	Length of Keel.	Breadth	Draught of vessel taken.	Lifting power of patent slip or dock.
Graving docks—		ft.	ft.	ft. in.	tons.
Fitzroy (Government)..	Cockatoo Island ...	475	59	20 0	...
Sutherland „ ...	„ ...	635	84	32 0	...
Mort's	Balmain	410	68	20 0	...
Floating docks—					
Anderson's	Johnston's Bay ...	100	23	7 0	150
Anderson and Goodall	„ ...	320	57	27 0	1,400
Rountree's	Waterview Bay ...	164	42	12 0	600
Atlas Company's*	Woolwich	300	73	25 0	2,000
Patent slips—					
Bayle's	Balmain	...	...	...	..
Davy and Sands'	Pyrmont	180	...	...	600
Mort's No. 1	Balmain	250	...	...	1,500
„ „ 2	„	200	...	...	1,600
„ „ 3	„	...	...	...	40

* Pontoon Depositing Dock.

New graving dock.

All the necessary tools and appliances for the repairing of ships are found in the dockyards. The new graving dock recently completed by the Government is the largest single dock in the world, and capable of receiving vessels drawing 32 feet of water. For natural facilities for shipping Sydney stands unrivalled. The water deepens abruptly from the shores, so that the largest vessels may be berthed alongside the wharves and quays. The wharfage is chiefly in private hands, and powerful shipping appliances and roomy stores are found at all the important wharves. The Government still holds the shores of Sydney Cove, along the margin of which magnificent echelon wharves have been constructed. The south and west sides of Darling Harbour also belong to the Government, and two jetties capable of accommodating the largest ships have been constructed, communicating directly with the railway, which has been carried to the water's edge. The total wharf frontage amounts to about 6 miles.

Wharfage, Sydney.

Newcastle is also a well-equipped port, where vessels of 4,000 tons can be safely berthed; and every modern steam and hydraulic appliance for loading coal is found on its wharves. The Government owns nearly all the wharfage, which extends over a length of about 10,500 feet. The Government shipping appliances include seven steam cranes of 15 tons, and twelve hydraulic cranes, two of 25 tons, six of 15 tons, and four of 9 tons, as well as a number of shoots. There are also two slips owned by private individuals, capable of taking up vessels of 300 and 1,200 tons respectively. Staiths, cranes, and other coal-shipping appliances have been erected at Wollongong, Bulli, Coal Cliff, and other ports. Private as well as Government wharfs are found at all the chief centres of population along the rivers of the Colony, and all ports with a trade of any importance have their jetties and shipping facilities. Equipment of the Port of Newcastle. Private wharfs.

The coast of New South Wales is free from any source of danger to vessels navigating it, and where reasonable precautions were taken wrecks have been very rare. The majority of losses have been amongst vessels under 100 tons burthen. During the year 1890 there were sixteen wrecks within the jurisdiction of New South Wales, with a total of 4,303 tons, valued with cargo at £145,350. No less than 31 lives were lost, out of 185 passengers and crew all told. Only two of the vessels lost were of any size—the "Riverina" steamer, 1,810 tons, wrecked near Ram Head, during thick weather, but all the passengers and crew were saved; and the "Alberta," steam collier, wrecked on Sutherland Reef, in fine weather, but during the night; in this case also all on board were saved. Three vessels—the "Kent," schooner, "Summer Rose," schooner, and "Sussex," schooner—were known to be off the Richmond River Heads during the heavy gale at the end of January, but were never heard of again, and the crews were all lost. On April 13 the dredge "Clarence," valued at £16,000, was swept out to sea by the heavy flood current in the Clarence River, and was seen to founder soon afterwards. The crew, fortunately, were not on board. Two vessels were sunk by Vessels wrecked during 1889.

collisions during the year—the "Colonist," which was sunk by the s.s. "Adelaide," off Bradley's Head; and the "Royal Shepherd," which came into collision with the steamer "Hesketh," near the South Head of Port Jackson.

Vessels lost since 1880.

The following statement shows the number of vessels, which were lost on the coast of New South Wales during the years 1880–90:—

Vessels Wrecked off New South Wales.

Year.	Under 50 tons.	50 to 100.	100 to 200.	200 to 300.	300 to 400.	400 to 500.	Over 500 tons.	Total.	Lives lost.
1880	7	2	3	...	...	...	2	14	*
1881	6	1	1	3	1	...	1	13	*
1882	5	4	2	1	1	1	1	15	*
1883	2	6	3	1	...	...	...	12	*
1884	6	3	1	...	...	...	1	11	*
1885	3	4	1	1	1	...	1	11	*
1886	6	5	7	1	1	...	3	23	111
1887	4	5	2	1	...	...	1	13	2
1888	6	2	3	1	1	1	1	15	8
1889	4	8	5	2	...	...	1	20	4
1890	3	6	2	1	1	...	3	16	31

*Not ascertained.

Average tonnage in port.

In the port of Sydney, in the year 1890, there was a daily average of 34,707 tons of sailing vessels, and 35,191 tons of steamers, or 69,898 tons in all, ranging from 116,037 on November 22nd to 39,154 tons on May 26th and 27th. At Newcastle the daily average was 34,611 tons, varying from 98,429 tons on November 19th and 20th, to 15,079 tons on August 4th.

The following table shows the average daily tonnage, sailing and steam (exclusive of coasters), in Port Jackson during each month of the year 1890 :— Tonnage in Port Jackson.

1890.	Tonnage.		
	Sailing.	Steam.	Total.
January	33,317	31,107	64,424
February	28,829	29,874	58,703
March	31,963	38,431	70,394
April	29,159	39,009	68,168
May	25,783	27,880	53,663
June	26,616	24,809	51,425
July	26,872	26,066	52,938
August	37,449	25,012	62,461
September	45,383	33,164	78,547
October	42,685	44,370	87,055
November	48,940	47,489	96,429
December	43,114	47,140	90,254
Average	34,707	35,191	69,898

In the case of the port of Newcastle the total average daily tonnage for every month in the year, taking sailing vessels and steamers together, was as follows :— Tonnage in Port Hunter.

Month.	Tonnage.	Month.	Tonnage.
January	16,690	July	20,969
February	19,876	August	20,590
March	26,041	September	34,020
April	19,385	October	53,886
May	19,682	November	85,985
June	20,840	December	77,117
Average for the year, 34,611 tons.			

These figures are somewhat below the average of previous years, owing to the disturbing effects of the great strike. Thus, in 1889, the average tonnage of shipping in Sydney was 73,110 tons, and at Newcastle 35,835 tons. The value of shipping afloat in Sydney Harbour varies, of course, with the season; but on one day—November 22nd—the estimated value was £2,900,000; and at Newcastle, on the 20th of the same month, the estimated value of the shipping was £1,750,000.

IMPORTS AND EXPORTS.

The value of goods imported into, and exported from, New South Wales, has increased during the sixty-five years over which the records extend, from £400,000 in 1825 to £44,660,941 in 1890. The yearly values have been somewhat uncertain in their increase, the imports from 1840 to 1852 being especially erratic; but of late years the progress of the Colony, as evidenced by its trade, has been remarkably steady. The gross value from year to year of the exports, for the reasons hereafter pointed out, forms the surer index of the progress of a country circumstanced like New South Wales, and the result of a rise or fall in the value of the staple commodities, or of a depression in production, may be readily traced in the corresponding rise or fall in the export values. The amount of the trade of the Colony, in decennial periods since 1825, is as follows:—

Exports an index of production.

Imports and Exports of New South Wales.

Year.	Imports.	Exports.	Total Trade.
	£	£	£
1825	300,000	100,000	400,000
1835	1,114,805	682,193	1,796,998
1845	1,233,854	1,555,986	2,789,840
1855	4,668,519	2,884,130	7,552,649
1865	10,635,507	9,563,818	20,199,325
1875	13,735,133	13,797,397	27,532,530
1885	23,737,461	16,750,107	40,487,568
1890	22,615,004	22,045,937	44,660,941

The following table shows the total value of the Imports and Exports of the Colony of New South Wales, from and to each Country, during the year 1890:—

Countries and Ports.	Total Imports therefrom.	Exports thereto.		
		Domestic Produce or Manufacture.	Other Produce or Manufacture.	Total.
	£	£	£	£
United Kingdom	6,628,007	5,618,229	1,005,202	6,623,431
AUSTRALASIAN COLONIES.				
Victoria	2,097,259	4,983,027	403,526	5,386,553
Queensland..................	5,482,452	432,003	1,238,462	1,670,465
South Australia	2,036,492	3,516,943	183,181	3,700,124
Western Australia	830	9,837	7,974	17,811
Tasmania.............	432,615	82,902	132,772	215,674
New Zealand	932,073	142,071	152,042	294,113
Total Australian Colonies	10,981,721	9,166,783	2,117,957	11,284,740
OTHER BRITISH POSSESSIONS.				
Canadian Dominion	18,784	10	....	10
Cape Colony	55	310	704	1,014
Ceylon	42,702	3,969	111	4,080
Fiji	99,853	26,278	72,673	98,951
Gibraltar	57	... .	180	180
Hong Kong.....	271,730	31,735	223,315	255,050
India..	195,368	128,274	125,006	253,280
Malta	400	....	10	10
Mauritius	5,059	25,697	118	25,815
New Guinea	....	103	25	128
Norfolk Island	1,169	84	728	812
Penang.........................	....	2,046	32	2,078
Seychelle Islands	....	365	159	524
Singapore	27,148	31,433	836	32,269
Total other British Possessions.	663,325	250,304	423,897	674,201
FOREIGN STATES.				
Austria	225	....	....	....
Belgium	130,819	1,008,008	3,838	1,011,846
Brazil..........................	450	....	....	....
Chili	....	107,076	490	107,566
China	241,840	807	230	1,037
Denmark......................	292	....	....	....
Egypt	8,998	....	5	5
France.........................	117,871	228,236	5,688	233,924
Germany......................	639,475	392,007	12,273	404,280
Greece.........................	10,392	....	....	....

Countries and Ports.	Total Imports therefrom.	Exports thereto.		
		Domestic Produce or Manufacture.	Other Produce or Manufacture.	Total.
FOREIGN STATES—*contd.*	£	£	£	£
Guam	....	2,482	....	2,482
Italy...........................	23,961	24,290	208	24,498
Japan	22,040	6,467	689	7,156
Java...........................	122,152	20,861	10,648	31,509
Kaiser Wilhelm's Land..	429	....	1,086	1,086
Macao	1,130	....	....	....
Mexico........................	....	3,144	....	3,144
Netherlands	190	18,661	188	18,849
New Caledonia	83,920	42,229	151,160	193,389
Norway	20,891	....	....	....
Peru...........................	....	13,348	....	13,348
Philippine Islands.........	4,414	16,385	25	16,410
Pondicherry	....	....	140	140
Sandwich Islands	313	15,168	2,959	18,127
Siam...........................	....	667	....	667
South Sea Islands..	40,214	16,313	50,401	66,714
Spain	....	6,232	22	6,254
Sumatra	....	730	29	759
Sweden	9,852	....	....	....
Turkey........................	2,981	....	....	....
United States..............	859,102	274,298	1,026,077	1,300,375
Total, Foreign States..	2,341,951	2,197,409	1,266,156	3,463,565
General Total......	22,615,004	17,232,725	4,813,212	22,045,937

The following table shows the import and export business done at the different ports of the Colony :—

Imports and Exports by sea

Imports and Exports by Sea at each Port of the Colony, 1890.

Port.	Imports.	Exports.			Total Trade.
		New South Wales Produce.	British and Foreign Produce.	Total.	
	£	£	£	£	£
Ballina	1,206	1,674	......	1,674	2,880
Bateman's Bay..	......	1,739	......	1,739	1,739
Eden	303	23,182	......	23,182	23,485
Grafton	17,994	19,000	......	19,000	36,994
Nambucca	......	1,335	......	1,335	1,335
Newcastle	93,550	1,763,758	4,621	1,768,379	1,861,929
Sydney	17,792,986	7,556,308	4,621,745	12,178,053	29,971,039
Tweed River......	1,624	237	240	477	2,101
Wollongong	......	25,722	......	25,722	25,722
Total...... £	17,907,663	9,392,955	4,626,606	14,019,561	31,927,224

Overland Trade. The amount of overland trade at the different border stations is shown below; a peculiar feature connected with the figures is the circumstance that the value of domestic produce exported overland is greater than that from the port of Sydney, and equal to nearly 46 per cent. of the total of the Colony:—

Imports and Exports Overland at each Station of the Colony, 1890.

Name of Station.	Imports.	Exports.			Total Trade.
		New South Wales Produce.	British and Foreign Produce.	Total.	
Albury	468,979	1,389,721	43,854	1,433,575	1,902,554
Barringun	1,116,142	67,654	22,243	89,897	1,206,039
Boggabilla	682,329	74,440	216	74,656	756,985
Bourke	....	18	15,213	15,231	15,231
Corowa	74,727	504,364	8,296	512,660	587,387
Euston	8,131	50,587	5,316	55,903	64,034
Howlong	13,251	36,523	146	36,669	49,920
Moama	315,875	925,681	6,821	932,502	1,248,377
Mulwala	26,120	20,806	......	20,806	46,926
*Silverton	123,318	213,092	38,845	251,937	375,255
Swan Hill	22,404	987,245	......	987,245	1,009,649
Tocumwal	25,392	84,059	455	84,514	109,906
Wallangarra	256,981	124,092	10,716	134,808	391,789
Wentworth	237,021	634,503	3,648	638,151	875,172
Wilcannia	....	....	252	252	252
†Willyama	1,336,671	2,726,985	30,585	2,757,570	4,094,241
Total	4,707,341	7,839,770	186,606	8,026,376	12,733,717

* From 1st July, 1890, to 31st December, 1890.
† Includes Thackaringa returns up to 30th June, 1890, after which date that station was abolished.

IMPORTS.

Increase in value of imports. During 1890 the gross value of goods imported into the Colony amounted to £22,615,004, or at the rate of £20 10s. 6d. per head; the imports for home consumption were valued at £17,801,792, or £16 3s. 2d. per head of the mean population during the year, thus showing a decrease on the previous year of 18s. 3d. per head of gross imports, and an increase of 4s. 6d. per head of not imports. As the imports, generally speaking, represent the money return or value in kind of the exports of the previous season, the increase is due to an advance in the value of the exports of 1888. The value of the imports, distinguishing the amount required for home consumption, is given in the annexed table for the twenty years 1871–1890 :—

Value of Imports per Inhabitant.

Year.	Imports for home consumption.	Total imports per head.	Year.	Imports for home consumption.	Total imports per head.
	£ s. d.	£ s. d.		£ s. d.	£ s. d.
1871	17 10 6	21 10 3	1881	17 6 0	22 19 8
1872	13 12 2	18 3 5	1882	21 5 3	26 17 8
1873	15 12 10	20 2 7	1883	20 5 11	25 13 7
1874	17 15 9	21 12 8	1884	21 2 3	26 4 6
1875	19 14 10	23 9 11	1885	20 10 10	25 12 0
1876	19 0 11	22 16 9	1886	17 14 4	21 19 8
1877	19 15 5	23 12 4	1887	14 16 4	19 1 7
1878	19 10 11	22 19 3	1888	15 6 2	20 9 11
1879	17 3 1	21 0 0	1889	15 18 8	21 8 9
1880	14 9 4	19 10 7	1890	16 3 2	20 10 6

Classification of imports.

For the purpose of more readily understanding the nature of the imports they have been classified under certain leading heads, and during 1890 the value of each class of imports was :—

Nature of Principal Imports.	Total Imports.	Imported for home consumption.
	£	£
Food and beverages, including breadstuffs	3,494,154	2,976,090
Wines, fermented and spirituous liquors	1,143,754	974,769
Live stock	2,354,310	2,288,373
Animal and vegetable products, including wool	1,971,575	1,511,197
Clothing and textile fabrics	4,437,789	4,029,164
Minerals and metals, raw or partly worked up. .	1,822.077	1,423,047
Coal and coke	256,601	256,601
Specie and precious metals	2,672,702	503,376
Articles of education, art, amusement	1,100,499	912,095
Manufactured articles not elsewhere included ..	3,276,273	2,905,312
Articles, unclassified by Customs	85,270	21,768
Total value .... £	22,615,004	17,801,792

During 1890, therefore, the Colony imported food and drink to the value of £3,950,859, or at the rate of £3 11s. 8d. for each inhabitant, and manufactured goods to the amount of £7,846,571, or at the rate of £7 2s. 5d. per head, both together representing £10 14s. 1d. per head, out of a total of £16 3s. 2d. The three principal items of the balance are live stock, animal, and vegetable products, and minerals and metals, raw or partly worked up. Of the animal and vegetable products, as also of the precious metals, a large portion is worked up in the Colony for its own consumption, but the greater portion of the gold imported is treated at the Mint, and re-exported in the shape of coin. The value per head of some of the principal articles imported is given below:— Rate of imports per head.

Value per head of principal articles imported for home consumption —1886-90.

Articles.	1886.		1887.		1888.		1889.		1890.	
	s.	d.	s.	d.	s.	d.	s.	d.	s.	d.
Apparel—wearing	25	5	18	7	21	4	20	1	19	1
Beer	8	0	6	8	6	9	7	6	6	3
Boots and Shoes	10	4	9	0	9	4	9	8	8	8
Drapery	52	11	37	4	45	9	37	8	37	1
Flour	12	1	9	9	9	5	11	6	6	11
Grain and Pulse	9	4	5	9	10	1	16	3	6	4
Hardware	11	1	5	4	6	4	7	7	10	2
Iron and Steel	16	3	11	8	10	1	14	3	16	3
Live Stock	12	11	22	2	13	7	24	8	41	6
Machinery	5	8	5	10	5	9	7	1	7	9
Paper, Books, &c	7	10	6	2	7	0	5	10	6	2
Spirits	9	0	8	0	6	11	8	3	7	4
Sugar	11	10	7	5	8	2	15	0	12	6
Tea	5	8	7	1	7	3	6	7	6	7
Timber	8	11	7	2	9	7	7	7	7	1

The import of drapery stands first in the list of values, and if wearing apparel be added to it the value of these goods would represent a sum of £2 16s. 2d. per head during 1890, the greatest amount for any one year having been in 1882, when the value imported reached almost £5 for every inhabitant. The value per Drapery and apparel.

head of iron and steel, machinery and hardware combined, was £1 14s. 2d.; wine and liquors, 15s. 3d.; flour, 6s. 11d.; grain and pulse, 6s. 4d.; boots and shoes, 8s. 8d.; sugar, 12s. 6d.; tea, 6s. 7d. None of the other values reach such large figures as those mentioned above except those for live stock and timber, the former of which was exceptionally large during 1890, though many other articles form individually very important imports. Two things are plain from a consideration of this table—the great purchasing power of the people, and the very large scope that exists for the production of goods which are now imported, and for the extension of manufactures within the Colony. This will, perhaps, be seen more clearly from an inspection of the gross values of some of the principal articles imported during the year 1890, as given in the following table:—

Scope for manufactures proved by large imports.

Values of the Principal Imported Articles.

Article	Value	Article	Value
Apparel, wearing	£1,027,382	Jewellery	£56,834
Arms and ammunition	130,573	Leather	91,001
Beer	365,771	Malt	113,470
Boots and shoes	552,235	Matches	44,355
Butter	32,381	Milk, condensed	62,393
Candles	77,249	Musical instruments	111,671
Chaff and hay	144,599	Paints, paperhanging, lampware	104,044
Cement	102,222	Paper, books, stationery, etc.	530,804
Cutlery and grindery	93,553	Pickles, sauces, and oilmen's stores	86,188
Drapery	2,196,065	Potatoes and vegetables	238,530
Drugs and apothecaries' ware	217,822	Saddlery and harness and saddlers' ware	
Fancy goods and toys	124,498	Silver plate and ware	106,526
Fish, preserved	123,795	Spirits	84,241
Flour	534,595	Sugar	467,992
Fruit, bottled, dried, and green	336,222	Tea	779,419
Furniture and upholstery	162,204	Timber	401,218
Glass and glassware	112,464	Tobacco and cigars	220,595
Grain and pulse	372,050	Watches and clocks	55,298
Hardware	621,350	Wine	98,956
Iron and iron manufactures and machinery	1,658,190		
Jams and jellies	79,507		

The value of the imports into New South Wales for the past ten years is shown in the following table:— Value of imports since 1880.

Value of Imports into New South Wales from Great Britain, British Colonies and Possessions, and Foreign States, 1880–89.

Year.	Great Britain.	Australasian Colonies.	Other British Possessions.	Foreign States.	Total.
	£	£	£	£	£
1881	8,986,838	6,229,916	580,877	1,789,381	17,587,012
1882	11,155,917	7,289,823	821,425	2,200,734	21,467,899
1883	10,624,081	8,054,390	704,581	2,139,789	21,522,841
1884	11,423,047	8,507,199	1,012,008	2,218,662	23,160,916
1885	11,885,597	8,595,429	818,689	2,437,746	23,737,461
1886	10,445,980	8,082,198	624,893	2,160,056	21,313,127
1887	7,998,568	9,016,575	549,805	1,606,369	19,171,317
1888	9,212,981	9,085,567	736,224	2,194,505	21,229,277
1889	8,736,478	10,647,312	814,718	2,664,540	22,863,057
1890	8,628,007	10,981,721	663,325	2,341,951	22,615,004

EXPORTS.

The export trade of New South Wales, like the import, is larger than that of any other Australian colony, both in regard to the total value and the value per head of population. Compared with the imports generally, the exports, for the reasons which will hereafter appear, usually fall considerably short—in 1890 by £569,067; but compared with those of other colonies, the extent of the New South Wales exports of home produce is very satis- New South Wales exports larger than other colonies.

factory. For the year 1890 the export trade of domestic produce of the Australasian Colonies was:—

	£
New South Wales	17,232,725
Victoria	10,291,821
Queensland	8,412,244
South Australia	4,410,062
Western Australia	669,681
Tasmania	1,430,806
New Zealand	9,428,761

Large re-export trade of certain colonies.

There is a defect in the figures, as far, at least, as two of these colonies are concerned. Victoria and South Australia have each a large re-export trade, especially in raw produce, and it frequently happens that credit is taken for the produce of other colonies in the returns showing the export of home produce. New South Wales was formerly over-credited with the gold received from Queensland for coinage, and is still, to some extent, with regard to tin and copper from Queensland and South Australia. To what extent the Customs value of home produce is overstated in Victoria and South Australia is unknown, but much of the New South Wales produce passing through Victoria for shipment to England is exported as Victorian produce, especially the wool, of which large quantities shipped from Victoria as home produce is really the production of New South Wales. How far this system obtains in other directions it is impossible to say.

Preponderance of domestic products in exports.

Dividing the exports of New South Wales into two classes—those which are the produce and manufacture of the Colony, and those imported from other countries,—the preponderance of home produce exported is very marked. The figures for the ten years that closed with 1890, which are given herewith, show a large increase in home produce exported, reaching £15,751,818 in 1883, falling, however, in the subsequent years, until in 1886 the amount reached only £11,583,229. The figures for 1887 show a gain of £2,657,133, while those of 1889 and 1890 are the highest on record, viz., £17,423,311 and £17,232,725 respectively. The decline between 1883 and 1886 is to a great extent due to the fall in the price of wool, and to the losses sustained by reason of the dry season of 1885–6. The exports of produce other than that of the Colony have also shown a decline since 1883, a circumstance to a large extent to be ascribed to the same causes, the decline being very noticeable in the value of wool and tin re-exported:—

Domestic and Foreign Produce Exported.

Year.	Domestic produce exported.	Other produce exported.	Total exports.
	£	£	£
1881	11,955,277	4,352,528	16,307,805
1882	13,189,951	4,487,404	17,677,355
1883	15,751,818	4,510,455	20,262,273
1884	14,063,227	4,514,063	18,577,290
1885	12,059,280	4,690,827	16,750,107
1886	11,583,229	4,134,708	15,717,937
1887	14,240,362	4,281,438	18,521,750
1888	15,544,875	5,375,255	20,920,130
1889	17,423,311	5,871,623	23,294,934
1890	17,232,725	4,813,212	22,045,937

This table shows that the value of New South Wales produce exported in 1889 exceeded that of any of the previous years, while that of 1890 was somewhat less, yet the value per head is less, as will be seen by the following figures, than most of the years since 1871. A considerable improvement is visible over the figures of the five previous years, which are, however, much below those

Value of export trade declined, per head.

of the perhaps abnormal year 1883. In that year the exports of domestic produce amounted to £18 15s. 10d. per head, decreasing in 1886 to £11 19s., or 36 per cent. The figures for 1889 show a marked improvement, being £16 6s. 9d., or £2 9s. 1d. less than those of 1883. Greater part of the decrease may be attributed to the fall in wool, coal, and copper. The value of exports per head for each year since 1871 was as follows:—

Value of Exports of New South Wales per head.

Year.	Domestic produce exported.	Other produce exported.	Year.	Domestic produce exported.	Other produce exported.
	£ s. d.	£ s. d.		£ s. d.	£ s. d.
1871	18 3 4	3 19 9	1881	15 12 7	5 13 9
1872	15 6 9	4 11 3	1882	16 10 4	5 12 4
1873	18 13 9	4 9 9	1883	18 15 10	5 7 8
1874	18 2 5	3 16 11	1884	15 18 6	5 2 3
1875	19 16 11	3 15 1	1885	13 0 1	5 1 2
1876	17 16 6	3 15 10	1886	11 19 0	4 5 3
1877	17 11 0	3 16 11	1887	14 3 5	4 5 2
1878	16 11 0	3 8 4	1888	14 16 4	5 3 9
1879	15 13 4	3 6 11	1889	16 6 9	5 10 1
1880	16 11 0	5 1 3	1890	15 12 9	4 7 4

Price-level of domestic exports.

The total value of the exports of the Colony is greatly affected by the prices obtained for certain leading lines of raw produce, of which wool and coal are the most important. In the following table the price-level of exports is given for twenty years, beginning with 1871. In order to ascertain the price-level, all the principal articles of domestic produce exported have been taken, and the prices of 1871 and 1890 have been applied to the quantities of each of the other years, and the result compared with the actual total of such year. The value of the articles included in this table amounted in 1890 from 90 to 95 per cent. of the total exports, excluding coin. It is considered that this system enables a truer estimate of the relative prices to be obtained than that of selecting the prices of certain articles without giving due weight to the quantities of such articles exported :— Price-level.

Year.	Price-level.		Year.	Price-level.	
	1871 prices = 1,000.	1890 prices = 1,000.		1871 prices = 1,000.	1890 prices = 1,000.
1871	1,000	1,433	1881	834	1,195
1872	910	1,305	1882	854	1,224
1873	965	1,383	1883	860	1,233
1874	967	1,386	1884	852	1,222
1875	954	1,367	1885	749	1,074
1876	903	1,295	1886	719	1,030
1877	828	1,186	1887	736	1,055
1878	825	1,182	1888	710	1,018
1879	856	1,227	1889	715	1,025
1880	840	1,203	1890	698	1,000

The years comprised in the foregoing table divide themselves into three periods—from 1871 to 1876, the average level of prices, if 1890 prices be taken as 1,000, was 1,361; in 1877 prices fell, and for the next 8 years averaged about 1,209; in 1885 prices again experienced a heavy fall, and have since remained at a low level—the figures for the past year being actually the lowest touched during at least twenty years.

Wool and coal have contributed to much of the wealth of the colony, and the fluctuation in their prices has had a very marked effect on the condition of trade; the price-level of these commodities has been computed for the period which is covered by the Prices of Wool and Coal.

general table just given. It will be seen that the fluctuations in the value of both wool and coal have been more marked than those in the value of the general exports, but the same tendency to fall is clearly enough discernable.

Value of Exports of Wool and Coal.

Year.	Wool. Actual value.	Wool. At 1890 prices.	Wool. Price-level. 1890 Price = 1000.	Coal. Actual value.	Coal. At 1890 prices.	Coal. Price-level. 1890 Price = 1000.
1871	4,748,160	2,902,323	1,636	256,690	306,376	838
1872	3,342,900	2,382,192	1,403	307,861	362,554	849
1873	4,248,259	2,919,305	1,455	526,069	418,690	1,256
1874	5,010,125	3,497,845	1,432	632,247	473,020	1,337
1875	5,651,643	4,019,621	1,406	671,483	502,295	1,337
1876	5,565,173	4,123,294	1,350	625,211	470,765	1,328
1877	5,256,002	4,088,232	1,286	648,977	496,183	1,308
1878	5,723,316	4.689,663	1,220	708,406	545,324	1,299
1879	6,491,198	4,988,232	1,301	694,707	540,789	1,285
1880	8,040,625	6,104,486	1,317	425,299	408,202	1,042
1881	7,149,767	5,448,209	1,312	417,530	559,762	746
1882	7,433,091	5,747,289	1,293	647,033	683,563	947
1883	9,598,761	7,303,093	1,314	829,662	819,513	1,012
1884	8,953,100	6,795,057	1,318	931,045	916,133	1,016
1885	7,246,642	6,530,195	1,110	966,663	951,675	1,016
1886	7,028,596	6,825,467	1,030	947,002	940,572	1,007
1887	8,911,155	8,414,044	1,059	960,539	970,144	990
1888	9,069,770	8,959,426	1,015	1,064,472	1,042,443	1,021
1889	10,620,636	9,935,124	1,069	1,279,271	1,293,767	989
1890	8,991,396	8,991,396	1,000	987,173	987,173	1,000

Price-level of imports.

It is impossible to establish any general price-level for imports, but taking the export prices of Great Britain as indicating the price-level of imports into Australia, it would appear that prior to 1879 the values of the imports were better sustained than the exports; but since the date mentioned the price-level of imports has fallen proportionately more than the exports, so that local produce had, during these years, an advantage in the exchange for British goods; compared with the export prices, the advantage of exchange was greatest on the side of the imports in 1872, 1873, 1874, and 1877, and greatest in favour of the exports in 1883, 1884, and 1887.

The chief articles of export are wool, coal, live-stock, tin, silver, silver-lead ore, copper, skins, and tallow. Other articles have also been exported to considerable value in times past, but their importance has disappeared, or is lost in comparison with that of the products just named. Amongst such may be mentioned grain, leather, preserved meats, and sugar. Preserved meats are still exported in fairly large quantities, but in no instance is the export per head so large as formerly, while in the case of sugar it has wholly ceased. Chief articles of export.

WOOL.

Wool is the staple export of the Colony, and comprises considerably more than half the value of the total exports. The quantities and values of the wool exported during each year since 1880 are given in the next table, and from the figures it will be readily seen how greatly the Colony depends for its prosperity upon the produce of its flocks. The weights given represent the actual exports, washed and greasy wool being taken together:— Wool the staple export.

New South Wales Wool Exported.

Year.	Weight.	Value.	Year.	Weight.	Value.
	lb.	£		lb.	£
1880	154,871,832	8,040,625	1886	173,985,640	7,028,596
1881	139,601,506	7,149,787	1887	216,450,342	8,911,155
1882	146,221,182	7,433,091	1888	235,848,944	9,089,776
1883	[illegible],161,710	9,[illegible],761	1889	261,853,484	10,620,636
1884	172,[illegible]	8,953,100	1890	236,322,828	8,991,396
1885	168,151,[illegible]	7,946,642			

Re-export of wool.

Besides the wool grown in the Colony there has been a large re-export of other wool, chiefly from Queensland. In 1885 the export of foreign wool amounted to slightly more than 10,000,000 lb. weight, valued at £431,605; since then the quantity has fallen very largely. The exports, as returned by the Customs, are given herewith; but the quantities fall short of the actual amount, as not a little wool, the produce of other places, was exported in past years as New South Wales wool, on the same principle, probably, that leads to the shipment from Melbourne, as the produce of Victoria, of nearly 40,000,000 lb. weight of wool grown in New South Wales:—

Wool Exported—not the produce of the Colony.

Year.	Weight.	Value.	Year.	Weight.	Value.
	lb.	£		lb.	£
1880	7,614,490	431,605	1886	4,664,971	173,380
1881	7,582,181	396,909	1887	7,844,867	288,916
1882	7,130,162	381,005	1888	7,407,309	268,739
1883	8,878,422	340,613	1889	4,375,545	164,434
1884	9,030,215	537,483	1890	7,415,438	241,276
1885	10,221,766	429,399			

Severe seasons have affected wool trade.

The severe seasons experienced during the past few years have very materially interfered with the production, and consequently with the exportation, of wool; but the splendid season of 1886–7 was attended with a considerable increase in this staple export, and this improvement has been continued. A falling off in the quantity exported during 1890 is exhibited in the table on the preceding page, but this is due not to the non-production of the wool, but to the inability of the growers to get their produce to market during the strike to which reference has already been made. There was formerly a disposition to export washed wool; the tendency is now, however, towards the export of wool in grease, except where the conditions as to carriage, &c., are exceptional.

The other animal products—tallow, skins, leather, and such-like —form together an export of considerable value, though, owing to the large local demand, it is not probable that there will be any material increase in the quantity of these articles exported. Other exports.

Coal, also, forms one of the staple exports of New South Wales, having been exported to the value of £987,170 in 1890. The development of the coal trade of the Colony has been traced in the chapter on Mines and Minerals, and it will be seen that this product has been subject to less fluctuation than any other item of export. Coal.

The export of silver and silver-lead ore has become important since 1884, the figures for the past year amounting to £2,762,554. The export of locally produced copper and tin revived somewhat during 1888, but fell off very considerably since. Copper was exported to the value of £173,311, and tin to the extent of £329,841. These figures are from the returns of the Customs Department, but the amounts are swollen by imports of ore from other Australasian Colonies, particularly from Queensland and South Australia, sent to be refined in this Colony. The actual local production of copper and tin during 1890 may be set down as £84,107 and £179,057 respectively. The trade in these metals is still very much below that of 1884 and previous years. Silver.

Gold Bullion and specie form one of the most important exports of the Colony. The export during each year since 1871 was— Bullion and specie.

Year	£	Year	£
1871	2,329,426	1881	1,957,842
1872	2,394,037	1882	1,733,024
1873	2,936,467	1883	1,703,116
1874	1,953,942	1884	947,513
1875	2,106,074	1885	1,461,478
1876	1,661,772	1886	1,619,278
1877	1,895,030	1887	1,318,917
1878	1,810,670	1888	2,122,337
1879	806,687	1889	3,211,747
1880	863,012	1890	2,289,022

Taken by itself, the foregoing statement might seem to favour the opinion sometimes hazarded that the Colony is being denuded of its gold. Such is not the case. The gold shipped is chiefly the produce of other colonies, sent to Sydney to be minted; for out of the large sum exported during 1890 only about £137,169 was New South Wales produce. In another part of this volume it has been pointed out that the amount of coin in the Colony is yearly increased, so that the circulation in 1890 was fully twice that of 1878.

Exports of domestic produce.

Divided into the classes adopted for the imports, the exports of home produce in 1890 appear as follows:—

	£
Food and beverages, including breadstuffs	465,099
Wine, fermented and spirituous liquor	22,344
Live stock	2,155,649
Animal and vegetable products, including wool	9,872,194
Clothing and textile fabrics	11,271
Minerals and metals, raw or partly worked up, not including coal, coin, and bullion	645,800
Coal and coke	1,005,659
Specie and precious metals, including silver ore	2,901,545
Articles of education, art, and amusement	61,106
Manufactured articles not included elsewhere	69,099
Unclassified	22,959
Total	17,232,725

Raw materials largest export

By far the larger portion of the exports consists of raw materials. As an export manufacturing country New South Wales has not yet achieved any position; and, though its manufactures are not without their importance, as will hereafter appear, its own markets furnish so wide a scope for manufacturing industry as to make it improbable that there will be any great development of export trade in home manufactures in the immediate future. So many channels have been presented for the successful employment of capital that little attention has been bestowed upon the possibility of New South Wales supplying other countries with its own manufactures; but as these outlets of capital are closed, the vast possibilities of the country in other directions will doubtless be recognised. The following table has been prepared with the view of showing the relative importance, and the value per head of population, of each of the principal articles exported. The preponderance of raw material, and raw material advanced one stage towards the finished manufacture, will be apparent:—

Chief articles exported.

Value per Head of Principal Articles Exported, declared to be the Produce of New South Wales, 1886–90.

Articles.	1886.		1887.		1888.		1889.		1890.	
	s.	d.	s.	d.	s.	d.	s.	d.	s.	d.
Boots and Shoes	0	6	0	8	0	6	0	3	0	2
Coal	19	4	18	9	20	0	23	2	17	3
Copper	3	5	3	5	5	2	3	10	3	0
Flour	0	5	0	5	0	10	1	4	0	11
Fruit	2	3	2	11	2	5	2	7	2	9
Grain and pulse	1	1	1	6	1	6	1	6	0	8
Leather	2	1	1	9	2	2	2	10	2	2
Live stock	23	0	28	11	35	2	19	11	37	7
Provisions	1	7	3	10	2	5	1	10	3	0
Silver and silver ore	8	8	11	3	21	5	35	8	52	10
Skins	6	2	5	8	5	10	6	11	4	6
Tallow	3	0	4	9	3	8	3	7	3	2
Timber	1	3	1	8	2	3	1	10	1	7
Tin	9	6	10	3	10	11	7	6	6	4
Wool	143	5	174	4	170	10	192	5	156	11

Home produce exported.

The values of some of the principal articles of home produce exported, during 1890, including those mentioned above, were as follows:—

Export of Domestic Produce.

	£		£
Boots and shoes	8,488	Provisions (meat)...... ..	159,358
Coal	987,173	Shale (kerosene)	103,608
Copper	173,311	Silver and ore	2,762,554
Flour	54,638	Skins	294,634
Fruit	137,400	Tallow	266,507
Gold	137,169	Timber	84,068
Grain	37,874	Tin	329,841
Leather	126,456	Wool	8,991,396
Live stock	2,155,649		

Trade in live stock.

The number and value of the live stock exported have varied considerably from year to year, being affected greatly by the seasons experienced both in this and the neighbouring colonies.

Import and export of horses.

The export of horses has increased both in number and value; and the same may be said as regards the imports, though it should be borne in mind that the figures in respect to horses are to some extent misleading, as the number of thoroughbred racing animals passing backwards and forwards between Sydney and Melbourne, which are entered as exports and imports, gives more importance to the trade than its magnitude really warrants.

Export and import of cattle and sheep.

The export of cattle in 1890 amounted to 146,427 head, valued at £770,521, being nearly double the export of the previous year, while the import, 517,384, valued at £1,866,303, showed a still larger increase. The export of sheep for the year, 2,973,232, worth £1,180,016, was more than twice that of 1889, but the imports had declined from 832,565 to 598,077 in number, and in value from £416,935 to £331,904.

Returns of stock misleading.

But, as in the case of horses, the figures for the export and import of other live stock are to a certain extent misleading, inasmuch as the returns are swollen by the inclusion of stock sent from one colony to another, in the hope of obtaining better pasturage, or for fattening or breeding purposes. The general tendency of the trade, however, can be gathered from the table below. The total trade in live stock during 1890 was:—

Trade in live stock.

Trade in Live Stock.

Live stock.	Imported.		Exported.	
	Number.	Value.	Number.	Value.
		£		£
Horses	5,707	149,119	4,711	193,141
Horned cattle	517,384	1,866,303	155,138	822,635
Sheep	598,077	331,904	2,987,902	1,191,998
Pigs	4,795	3,149	6,044	11,867
Other stock	....	3,835	....	1,945
Total	....	2,354,310	....	2,221,586

RE-EXPORT TRADE.

The re-export trade of the Colony has increased considerably during the past decade, but has now reached a point beyond which it is not likely to advance for some years. The shipping facilities of Sydney have hitherto attracted to the port a large amount of trade from New Zealand, Queensland, and the South Seas, for transhipment to Europe; but the establishment of direct communication between these colonies and Europe has checked to some extent the expansion of the re-export trade, though it is not probable that it will fall below its present dimensions. The re-export overland trade is comparatively limited, amounting in 1890 to £186,606, out of a total £4,813,212.

Re-export trade considerable.

Overland trade in foreign produce.

The total value of the re-exports of the Colony during each of the past ten years was as follows:—

Value of re-exports.

Year.	Seaward.	Overland.	Total.
	£	£	£
1881	4,291,972	60,556	4,352,528
1882	4,409,153	78,251	4,487,404
1883	4,415,527	94,928	4,510,455
1884	4,380,036	134,027	4,514,063
1885	4,525,883	164,944	4,690,827
1886	3,999,328	135,380	4,134,708
1887	4,120,184	161,254	4,281,438
1888	4,822,269	552,986	5,375,255
1889	5,499,370	372,253	5,871,623
1890	4,626,606	186,606	4,813,212

Re-export trade has kept pace with increase of population.

It will be seen that the amount of re-exports has kept pace fairly with the increase of population, the greatest decline being during 1886, which was due in all probability to the depression in trade experienced almost everywhere during that year. A slight revival took place in 1887, which was continued through the two following years, though the ratio per head of population is still below that of 1881-2. The subsequent table, giving the value per head of foreign produce exported since 1873, will illustrate its comparative importance during each year.

Value per Head of Foreign Produce Exported.

Year.	Value.	Year.	Value.	Year.	Value.
	£ s. d.		£ s. d.		£ s. d.
1873	4 9 9	1879	3 6 11	1885	5 1 2
1874	3 16 11	1880	5 1 3	1886	4 5 3
1875	3 15 1	1881	5 13 9	1887	4 5 2
1876	3 15 10	1882	5 12 4	1888	5 3 9
1877	3 16 11	1883	5 7 8	1889	5 10 1
1878	3 8 4	1884	5 2 3	1890	4 7 4

Value per head of re-exports.

The following table shows the value per head of the principal articles re-exported during the last five years :—

Value per Head of Principal Articles Exported of British and Foreign Produce and Manufacture—1886-90.

Articles.	1886.	1887.	1888.	1889.	1890.
	s. d.	s. d.	s. d.	s. d.	s. d.
Apparel—wearing	0 8	0 4	0 7	0 4	0 8
Boots and shoes	1 7	1 7	1 2	1 3	1 3
Coin	32 6	25 2	39 4	37 3	37 10
Copra	1 3	0 6	0 9	0 9	1 0
Copper	2 2	1 3	2 6	1 8	1 0
Drapery	6 7	6 0	6 8	5 3	4 3
Flour	1 3	3 9	2 8	2 3	2 7
Hardware	1 7	1 9	1 9	1 3	1 0
Live stock	1 7	1 1	2 2	1 0	1 2
Machinery	1 1	1 1	1 4	1 6	1 4
Paper, books, &c.	1 0	1 0	1 1	1 0	1 0
Spirits	1 2	1 6	1 3	1 0	1 1
Sugar	2 2	2 1	0 9	1 7	1 6
Tea	0 9	0 6	0 6	0 8	0 8
Tobacco	1 2	1 3	1 3	1 4	1 2

Amongst raw materials the principal articles re-exported are copper, tin, and wool; the manufactured articles are chiefly drapery, apparel, hardware, iron and steel, books and stationery, boots, beer and spirits, and also large quantities of provisions. Grouped under the several heads already adopted for the imports and exports, the value of the trade for the year 1890 will be found below:— Principal re-exports.

Re-export Trade.

	£
Food and beverages, including breadstuffs	518,064
Wines, fermented and spirituous liquors	168,985
Live stock	65,937
Animal and vegetable products, including wool	460,378
Clothing and textile fabrics	408,625
Minerals and metals, raw or partly worked up, excluding coin and bullion	399,030
Specie and precious metals	2,169,326
Articles of education, art, and amusement	188,404
Manufactured articles not elsewhere included	370,961
Articles unclassified by Customs	63,502
Total	4,813,212

The benefit derived by the Colony from its re-export trade is indirect and can hardly be estimated. The freights earned by New South Wales vessels carrying such produce do not amount to a large sum, as the carriage is chiefly in other hands. Still the trade is valuable, the probable sum accruing to the Colony from this source being about 5 per cent. on the total value of the trade. Indirect benefit of re-exports.

OVERLAND TRADE.

As the major portion of the goods exported overland simply passes through the border colonies of Victoria and South Australia, to Great Britain, the diversion of the trade along the railways of the Colony to its ports, must be looked upon as a distinct gain. It was believed that the extension of the trunk railways to the centres of the pastoral industry would have the effect of permanently Overland trade affected by railway.

Effect of railways on trade.

diverting a no inconsiderable amount of trade from Victoria and South Australia, but it will be seen from figures in another part of this volume that such diversion has only been partial. The condition of the Darling and other western rivers exercises a marked influence on the overland trade, especially in wool; and it is found that when the rivers are not easily navigable a larger proportion of this staple reaches the sea-board than is the case in other seasons. A marked increase will be noticed in 1889 and 1890. This was largely due to the requirements of the population of the Broken Hill silver-field, whose nearest market is by rail to Adelaide :—

Overland Trade.

Year.	Imports.	Exports.	Total.
	£	£	£
1881	1,708,648	4,022,461	5,731,109
1882	1,912,409	4,995,645	6,906,054
1883	2,320,495	4,307,623	6,628,118
1884	2,186,553	4,830,770	7,017,323
1885	2,611,130	3,405,073	6,016,203
1886	2,039,168	4,251,800	6,290,968
1887	3,166,573	5,231,454	8,398,027
1888	3,040,010	5,559,681	8,599,691
1889	3,150,698	6,919,491	10,070,189
1890	4,707,341	8,026,376	12,733,717

TRADE OF AUSTRALASIAN COLONIES.

Trade larger than any other colony.

The trade of New South Wales is larger, both in the gross amount and the value per head, than that of any of the other Colonies of Australasia. The total trade of each colony for the past twelve years is given in the following table; and though the latter part of the poriod was one of severe depression, the magnitude of the trade, not only of this Colony but of the rest of the group, is very suggestive. In gross amount the trade of Victoria ranks second, and the other Colonies in the following order :— South Australia, New Zealand, Queensland, Tasmania, and Western Australia.

Trade of Australasian Colonies.—Total Imports and Exports in each Colony.

Year.	Total Value.			
	New South Wales.	Victoria.	Queensland.	South Australia.
	£	£	£	£
1881	33,894,817	32,970,624	7,603,991	9,631,821
1882	39,145,254	34,941,660	9,852,915	12,067,678
1883	41,785,114	34,142,709	11,500,959	11,193,516
1884	41,738,206	35,252,098	11,055,840	12,373,057
1885	40,487,568	33,596,362	11,665,894	11,184,658
1886	37,031,064	30,325,896	11,037,197	9,341,760
1887	37,693,067	30,373,206	12,275,556	10,427,073
1888	42,149,407	37,825,897	12,773,100	12,397,736
1889	46,157,991	37,137,494	13,788,871	14,378,376
1890	44,660,941 *	36,220,237	13,621,212	17,090,051

Year.	Total Value.			
	Western Australia.	Tasmania.	New Zealand.	Australasia.
	£	£	£	£
1881	907,601	2,986,720	13,517,911	101,513,485
1882	1,091,810	3,258,261	15,267,278	115,624,856
1883	963,856	3,564,236	15,070,037	118,229,427
1884	926,860	3,131,975	14,755,555	119,233,591
1885	1,097,063	3,071,179	14,209,860	115,402,604
1886	1,388,406	3,088,107	13,431,804	105,644,234
1887	1,271,010	3,046,188	13,111,684	108,197,874
1888	1,466,596	2,943,929	13,709,225	123,265,890
1889	1,579,519	3,070,892	15,636,362	131,749,505
1890	1,546,260	3,384,504	16,072,245	132,595,450

BRITISH TRADE.

British trade holds first position

The British trade holds the first position in regard to value, being larger, in most years, than even the intercolonial trade of the Colony; and if to the value of goods coming directly from Great Britain were added that of goods passing through the neighbouring colonies, but destined for, or coming from, England, the proportion of British trade would be still higher. For, though the nominal trade between Great Britain and New South Wales amounted in 1890 to the large sum of £15,251,438, out of a total trade of £44,660,941, it is probable that the actual value of this trade was little short of £20,000,000. The amount of trade as set down in the subsequent table is, therefore, much below the truth, especially in regard to exports, as the larger part of the produce exported to Victoria and South Australia overland is in reality destined for British ports. The seaward trade alone can be given, and this will be found in the following table, for each year since and including 1870:—

Trade with Great Britain.

Year.	Imports.	Exports.	Total British trade.
	£	£	£
1870	3,200,706	2,492,640	5,693,346
1871	3,252,617	4,378,281	7,630,898
1872	3,728,457	4,926,728	8,655,185
1873	5,137,139	6,657,559	11,794,698
1874	4,888,725	5,737,066	10,625,791
1875	6,062,226	6,374,503	12,436,729
1876	5,763,533	5,918,187	11,681,720
1877	6,471,780	6,018,926	12,490,706
1878	6,658,628	5,516,437	12,175,065
1879	6,749,519	5,148,609	11,898,128
1880	6,536,661	7,525,637	14,062,298
1881	8,986,838	7,561,114	16,547,952
1882	11,155,917	7,309,691	18,465,608
1883	10,624,081	9,884,207	20,508,288
1884	11,423,047	7,683,880	19,106,927
1885	11,885,597	7,293,133	19,178,730
1886	10,445,980	6,026,954	16,472,934
1887	7,998,568	6,966,056	14,964,624
1888	9,212,981	8,476,669	17,689,650
1889	8,736,478	8,964,625	17,701,103
1890	8,628,007	6,623,431	15,251,438

INTERCOLONIAL TRADE.

Next in importance to the British trade stands the intercolonial, the value of which amounted in the year 1890 to £10,981,721 imports, and £11,284,740 exports, or a total trade of £22,266,461. A large part of this trade, however, must be credited to the United Kingdom, as the natural outlet for the produce of the Southern and Western districts, by way of Victoria and South Australia. Value of intercolonial trade.

Year.	Imports.	Exports.	Total trade.
	£	£	£
1881	6,229,916	6,981,456	13,211,372
1882	7,289,823	8,425,903	15,715,726
1883	8,054,390	7,943,332	15,997,722
1884	8,507,199	8,708,323	17,215,522
1885	8,595,429	6,936,139	15,531,568
1886	8,082,198	7,705,863	15,788,061
1887	9,016,575	8,993,324	18,009,899
1888	9,085,567	9,614,615	18,700,182
1889	10,647,312	10,741,045	21,388,357
1890	10,981,721	11,284,740	22,266,461

The trade of the other Australasian colonies with New South Wales showed an increase during 1890 of £878,104, and of £6,478,400 since 1886. The reason of this advance will be found in the increased value of the wool clip, and the diversion of part of the trade of the Western districts of the Colony from New South Wales seaports to those of the neighbouring colonies. As already Trade with other colonies during 1886–1888.

pointed out, a great proportion of the intercolonial export trade, especially that which is sent overland, represents produce of this colony ultimately destined for European markets, though credited to the colony to which it is sent in the first instance. Similarly with the import trade, the large part of the increase comprises goods originally coming from Great Britain, but purchased in the Melbourne and Adelaide markets. The total value of the intercolonial trade as already stated, amounted during 1890 to £22,266,461, a sum much larger than in any former year.

TRADE WITH VICTORIA.

Value of trade with Victoria.

Victoria comes first amongst the colonies of the group, as regards the value of its trade with New South Wales; but the value of goods which it sends to this Colony has sensibly declined during late years. It is estimated that prior to the extension of the railway system of this Colony into the Riverine districts, nearly one-fourth of its territory, comprising some of the richest districts in the Colony, traded almost exclusively with Victoria. This has now been, to a great extent, diverted along New South Wales lines to Sydney; and the trade, instead of increasing with the settlement of these districts, has remained almost stationary.

Large range of articles imported from Victoria.

The import trade of the Colony from Victoria covers a large range of articles, and in this respect differs from the export, which is mainly comprised in three leading items of raw produce—wool, stock, and coal. Dividing the imports from Victoria into two classes, viz., Victorian and other produce, the chief imports under the former class are agricultural implements, butter, breadstuffs, fruit, oats, hay and other fodder, and vegetables; while under the second head come drapery and apparel, drugs, hardware, iron, jewellery, machinery, stationery, and other manufactured articles. Victorian produce, properly so called, comes chiefly to Sydney; the other articles are taken by the southern and western portions of the Colony, which have for many years looked to Victoria as a market whence such supplies are to be derived. The following are the values of the principal items of import from Victoria during the last five years:— Imports from Victoria.

Principal Imports from Victoria.

Description of Goods.	1886.	1887.	1888.	1889.	1890.
	£	£	£	£	£
Agricultural implements	26,005	53,229	32,474	36,110	33,060
Bags and sacks	11,773	12,922	9,146	7,469	10,005
Beer (in wood and bottle)	11,717	20,309	17,562	17,814	14,833
Biscuits	6,133	3,289	2,122	1,930	1,355
Boots and shoes	28,662	30,772	54,939	25,123	24,180
Butter	35,331	7,986	18,795	8,542	4,555
Candles	4,678	5,668	9,290	5,578	4,250
Cheese	6,304	1,285	2,671	3,828	1,067
Cordage and ropes	6,394	6,248	4,953	4,523	4,821
Drapery and apparel	396,850	366,072	339,167	313,006	302,067
Drugs & Apothecaries' wares	19,038	22,711	24,720	27,275	26,576
Earthenware and China	7,625	9,787	7,209	6,344	6,667
Flour	384,037	364,107	284,928	247,006	217,763
Fruit—					
Green	27,265	14,914	19,628	16,163	12,860
Dried	21,326	17,803	6,733	9,272	14,588
Furniture and upholstery	22,120	14,860	19,152	20,091	18,679
Gold (coin, bars, and dust)	303,312	274,628	125,461	4,178	4,800
Grain and Pulse—					
Wheat	57,729	34,050	15,515	90,764	11,294
Oats	14,201	17,264	103,173	7,090	6,395
Others	33,109	24,694	17,782	7,472	6,724
Hardware	39,248	39,234	38,464	36,326	40,619
Hay and chaff	183,319	59,492	107,795	116,224	77,041
Hops	3,721	10,398	4,562	3,590	10,568
Iron and steel goods	30,649	41,769	66,604	80,362	86,899
Jams and jellies	8,979	4,019	4,344	3,877	6,635
Jewellery	19,365	7,917	16,600	13,080	11,743
Leather	15,202	17,255	16,137	13,260	15,411
Live stock	225,746	542,588	517,249	335,061	286,824
Machinery	30,537	41,318	52,209	70,378	56,654
Malt	2,937	4,220	3,319	2,008	2,123
Musical instruments	13,347	13,529	14,038	15,912	8,950
Oatmeal	14,025	8,845	17,346	22,134	17,190
Oils	11,428	17,834	12,551	12,349	19,038
Paper, books, stationery, &c.	59,293	56,611	55,666	64,263	64,181
Potatoes	166,986	71,812	97,627	65,854	29,625
Saddlery and harness	7,714	9,872	7,940	8,459	8,343
Soap	7,961	7,777	11,061	12,974	16,487
Spirits	30,075	31,221	23,754	27,593	28,650
Sugar (raw)	36,118	56,104	53,538	62,962	57,019
Tea	93,463	121,731	92,977	83,183	98,690
Timber	18,634	11,951	12,920	13,333	20,647
Tobacco, cigars, &c.	15,151	22,249	20,489	24,581	21,839
Toys	9,132	11,569	17,822	13,235	9,608
Vegetables (green) and onions	35,275	32,633	36,667	26,711	34,817
Wines	7,004	7,780	6,372	6,217	7,642
Woolpacks	9,646	22,713	13,958	16,449	15,052

Wool export.

The chief export to Victoria is wool, forwarded to Melbourne for shipment to London and other European ports. A large quantity of this wool is shipped to Europe as the produce of Victoria, on account of the fact that better prices are generally obtained for "Port Phillip" wool. The value of wool exported to Victoria during the last twelve years was:—

	£		£
1879	2,709,736	1885	1,868,019
1880	3,224,289	1886	1,931,278
1881	2.783,989	1887	2,451,552
1882	2,396,528	1888	2,187,759
1883	2,502,205	1889	2,952,107
1884	2,229,873	1890	2,521,898

The decrease shown since 1880 is chiefly owing to the decline in the market value of the staple, though also partly to the extension of the railways, which has diverted much of the traffic from the old routes.

Export of stock.

Live stock of all kinds forms a large portion of the exports to Victoria, though the imports, especially of sheep, have also been of importance. Victoria has already reached the point where the demand for meat exceeds the cast of stock; and is, therefore, dependent upon the other colonies, especially New South Wales, for the supply of the deficiency, the amount of which is little short of one-fourth of the whole consumption. The sheep exported are almost entirely New South Wales produce; the cattle, however, are generally bred in Queensland, but fattened for market on runs in New South Wales.

Export of coal.

Coal is next in importance as an export of this Colony to Victoria, the value during 1890 being £415,824. The only other produce worthy of special note are skins and timber, the former being sent to Victoria for re-export. The following table gives the trade of each year since 1870; but as no records were kept during certain years in which border duties were not collected, the totals for such years are necessarily only approximate. The figures since 1874 are, however, fairly exact.

Trade with Victoria.

Year.	Imports.	Exports.	Total.
	£	£	£
1870	1,153,695	2,583,552	3,737,247
1871	1,698,236	4,577,559	6,275,795
1872	1,188,781	2,858,191	4,046,972
1873*	....	3,366,963	....
1874	1,349,062	3,614,456	4,963,518
1875	2,066,156	4,269,770	6,335,926
1876	2,376,777	4,043,566	6,420,343
1877	2,531,449	3,898,129	6,429,578
1878	2,897,503	3,694,434	6,591,937
1879	2,234,381	4,177,871	6,412,252
1880	2,187,119	4,578,867	6,765,986
1881	2,414,590	4,052,694	6,467,284
1882	2,770,245	3,781,421	6,551,666
1883	3,012,268	4,170,599	7,182,867
1884	3,064,816	4,170,497	7,235,313
1885	3,309,696	3,450,796	6,760,492
1886	2,789,700	3,697,343	6,487,043
1887	2,894,681	4,773,815	7,668,496
1888	2,472,621	5,455,196	7,927,817
1889	2,419,038	5,385,300	7,804,338
1890	2,097,259	5,386,553	7,483,812

* No Returns of the overland trade for this year.

The following table shows the value of the principal articles exported to Victoria during five years:— Exports to Victoria.

Principal Exports to Victoria.

Description of Goods.	1886.	1887.	1888.	1889.	1890.
	£	£	£	£	£
Coal	336,979	379,206	406,744	488,344	415,824
Coin—Gold	45,000	......	......	200,000	30,028
Copper	4,658	12,590	7,257	7,735	4,121
Flour	17,043	10,463	11,969	5,854	11,060
Fruit (fresh)	55,861	73,760	60,014	71,069	94,538
Grain and Pulse—					
Wheat	17,159	14,991	18,667	21,709	22,026
Others	17,102	5,203	5,339	45,572	1,321
Kerosene shale	12,942	13,703	12,708	12,595	21,439
Live stock	696,028	1,112,720	1,636,580	918,487	1,660,588
Periodicals, books, paper, stationery, &c.	1,783	28,190	20,710	53,866	49,468
Skins	66,777	70,334	81,043	59,126	49,872
Timber	42,224	54,081	83,138	89,524	82,663
Wool	1,981,878	2,451,562	2,187,759	2,962,107	2,521,898

Overland trade with Victoria.

The greater portion of the exports to Victoria, as well as nearly half the imports, are borderwise. The value of the imports overland, however, fell greatly, from the causes already specified, during the year 1886, when they reached only £874,680, and for the past five years averaged about one million. The exports, on the contrary, show a decided tendency to increase. The value in each year since 1870 was:—

Overland Trade with Victoria.

Year.	Imports.	Exports.	Total.
	£	£	£
1870	448,308	1,811,848	2,260,156
1871	491,632	3,027,714	3,519,346
1872	464,185	2,123,622	2,587,807
1873*	....	2,758,116	....
1874	452,086	2,812,477	3,264,563
1875	945,049	3,546,674	4,491,723
1876	1,246,880	3,294,795	4,541,675
1877	1,360,171	2,869,945	4,230,116
1878	1,357,715	2,661,639	4,018,754
1879	933,999	3,394,764	4,328,763
1880	963,620	3,824,310	4,787,930
1881	1,210,931	3,229,664	4,440,595
1882	1,217,120	2,867,810	4,084,930
1883	1,266,330	2,955,808	4,222,138
1884	1,331,908	3,118,389	4,450,297
1885	1,555,139	2,450,444	4,005,583
1886	874,680	2,537,549	3,412,229
1887	1,418,212	3,421,254	4,839,466
1888	1,005,497	4,029,349	5,034,846
1889	1,106,864	3,681,588	4,788,452
1890	986,527	4,237,004	5,223,531

* No returns of the overland trade for this year.

TRADE WITH QUEENSLAND.

Trade with Queensland.

Queensland ranks next to Victoria in regard to the value of its trade with New South Wales, which in some respects is even more important than that of the southern colony. The estimated value of the imports and exports since 1880 is given herewith. It is possible that the amounts are somewhat understated, as there is a good deal of trade in stock which does not come under the cognisance of the Customs officers. Though New South Wales and Queensland have a common boundary of 900 miles, the overland trade, except in live stock, is not large. If, however, the value of stock be added, the figures reach a very large total, as will be seen from the table on page 195:—

Trade with Queensland.

Year.	Imports.	Exports.	Total trade.
	£	£	£
1880	2,224,421	1,362,262	3,586,683
1881	2,169,105	1,959,925	4,129,030
1882	2,149,766	3,012,782	5,162,548
1883	2,951,558	2,314,087	5,265,645
1884	2,983,178	2,387,085	5,370,263
1885	2,913,588	2,174,266	5,087,854
1886	2,908,017	1,829,586	4,737,603
1887	3,517,745	2,026,598	5,544,343
1888	3,477,603	1,973,968	5,451,571
1889	4,667,700	1,747,853	6,415,553
1890	5,482,452	1,670,465	7,152,917

The imports from Queensland are chiefly comprised under a few items—gold, live stock, sugar, wool, and tin. Large quantities of gold are sent from Queensland to be minted at Sydney, there being no Mint in the northern Colony. The value of wool imported during 1890 was £265,217, being entirely for re-export. Stock was imported to the value of £1,965,861 of which £1,780,389 represented cattle, the very favorable season enabling a larger number of stock to be introduced into New South Wales, and depastured near the market for which they are ultimately destined. Below will be found the value of the principal imports during the last five years:— Imports from Queensland.

Description of Goods.	1885.	1886.	1887.	1889.	1890.
	£	£	£	£	£
Boots and shoes........	1,889	10,596	2,020	2,957	5,351
Drapery, apparel, &c.	9,690	11,946	10,800	18,603	9,720
Fruit (fresh)............	20,332	22,411	15,921	24,968	15,412
Gold (bars and dust)..	1,265,972	1,534,236	1,736,343	2,774,531	2,308,776
Live stock..............	386,367	556,172	479,366	832,519	1,965,861
Meat (preserved).......	635	11,998	47,551	4,286	10,512
Skins....	113,103	106,304	110,404	109,487	87,104
Sugar (raw).............	241,772	268,469	211,153	321,071	487,961
Tallow...........	21,328	41,990	42,223	32,282	45,461
Wool	276,714	305,549	203,880	320,730	265,217
Tin (ingots and ore)...	144,580	206,606	183,314	137,715	146,424

Exports to Queensland

The exports have varied greatly in value from year to year through causes similar to those affecting the imports; they comprise a large number of items, mainly, however, the produce of foreign countries. The values of the chief articles, exported from New South Wales to Queensland, have been as follows in the years named:—

Description of Goods.	1886.	1887.	1888.	1889.	1890.
	£	£	£	£	£
Boots and shoes	11,776	23,993	18,976	38,467	38,156
Butter	1,684	7,509	7,903	11,744	5,352
Coal	12,151	10,625	4,098	3,932	3,492
Coin (gold)	397,000	259,500	278,000	312,000	334,000
Flour	1,618	7,855	28,729	176,816	158,292
Fruit (fresh)	36,514	44,039	46,786	70,226	47,829
Grain and pulse—					
Maize	20,136	50,426	45,332	30,952	4,652
All others	1,653	5,575	7,921	35,114	17,792
Iron and steel	1,536	3,829	13,538	47,899	56,418
Live stock	119,449	216,568	63,695	131,743	251,249
Timber	4,650	19,495	26,942	14,250	3,408
Tin	18,949	20,002	16,625	15,259	14,490
Wool	10,890	3,872	734	5,280	2,000
Hay	3,214	4,085	7,940	12 301	3,296

Fluctuations in overland trade.

The most remarkable year in the series given on page 193 was 1882, when the export trade reached £3,012,782, the overland export trade amounting to £1,206,408. Of this sum £1,149,835 represents the value of stock exported, viz., 3,035 horses, valued at £25,525; 29,404 cattle, valued at £302,590; and 1,645,657 sheep, of the value of £821,720. During 1886 the value of stock exported was very much less than in previous years, amounting to only £119,449; while, in 1890, the value rose to £251,249. The fluctuation in the value of stock exported will account for the variation in the amounts shown in the following table:—

Overland Trade with Queensland.

Year.	Imports.	Exports.	Year.	Imports.	Exports.
	£	£		£	£
1877	257,867	394,592	1884	493,680	424,940
1878	345,691	229,255	1885	669,739	337,023
1879	312,118	118,112	1886	722,454	317,846
1880	231,161	245,651	1887	1,035,123	297,009
1881	261,948	494,793	1888	879,589	170,530
1882	282,726	1,206,496	1889	951,739	506,247
1883	648,843	569,263	1890	2,158,822	317,717

TRADE WITH SOUTH AUSTRALIA.

Trade with South Australia.

The trade with South Australia is perhaps more variable than with any other Colony, depending, as it does, so largely on the state of the Murray and Darling Rivers. Since 1886 a new field for the expansion of South Australian trade has been found in the requirements of the population of Broken Hill silver fields. The additional trade has proved of enormous advantage to that Colony, as the Barrier district of New South Wales may be looked upon as commercially a province of South Australia. The total imports and exports during each year since and including 1871 are annexed:—

Trade with South Australia.

Year.	Imports.	Exports.	Year.	Imports.	Exports.
	£	£		£	£
1871	729,826	490,646	1881	692,781	454,764
1872	658,903	442,016	1882	1,017,685	1,085,194
1873	596,527	630,537	1883	841,109	969,083
1874	574,421	657,768	1884	1,002,174	1,502,366
1875	987,923	654,232	1885	890,335	810,953
1876	1,166,706	670,138	1886	828,174	1,585,830
1877	811,292	352,825	1887	1,259,758	1,740,517
1878	869,691	1,053,642	1888	1,831,436	1,661,446
1879	721,186	773,611	1889	1,858,621	2,999,664
1880	698,497	830,256	1890	2,036,492	3,700,124

Imports from South Australia.

The list of imports is a long one, but the principal articles were as follows :—

Description of Goods.	1886.	1887.	1888.	1889.	1890.
	£	£	£	£	£
Beer	11,850	18,855	45,552	36,761	30,395
Boots and shoes	14,483	21,002	16,788	28,125	38,726
Butter	3,561	7,171	25,545	20,750	20,802
Coke and coal	21,554	19,841	64,292	126,047	245,008
Copper (ore and ingots)	148,324	140,530	155,733	179,201	136,460
Drapery, wearing apparel, &c.	53,875	83,197	126,008	123,323	153,109
Dynamite, powder, arms, &c.	7,042	11,183	25,042	17,881	27,612
Eggs	2,044	7,982	20,978	14,120	25,180
Flour	172,299	308,805	296,199	305,180	251,881
Fruit (fresh)	2,485	4,178	12,592	15,102	17,163
,, (dried)	5,327	5,277	5,798	6,532	9,335
Furniture and upholstery	4,877	5.385	27,551	11,321	15,480
Gold (coin, bars, and dust)	37,647	20,886	11,269	38,923	55,302
Grain and pulse—					
Wheat	853	11,338	98,097	122,772	6,321
Others	8,110	28,103	41,704	21,484	30,096
Hardware	14,470	27,080	38,479	22,140	32,262
Hay and chaff	22,800	45,144	102,782	139,647	45,883
Iron and steel	25,446	59,402	109,448	69,978	121,420
Jams and jellies	10,041	11,784	10,799	10,741	13,761
Live stock	32,708	27,641	18,318	49,365	31,932
Machinery	15,396	37,339	69,482	55,832	86,340
Potatoes	6,039	8,204	10,713	16,867	14,896
Paper, books, stationery, &c.	4,028	5,446	12,192	9,280	13,773
Spirits	25,972	35,378	29,901	28,310	32,198
Sugar (raw)	14,445	16,804	20,754	25,175	31,545
Tea	8,712	14,547	13,875	14,137	15,254
Timber	17,311	70,514	113,503	80,168	174,705
Tobacco, cigars, &c.	7,238	12,079	14,666	12,001	15,347
Vegetables and onions	1,388	3,316	8,687	10,825	11,774
Wines	6,912	6,785	13,190	9,396	9,842

The exports to South Australia are chiefly silver, lead, silver lead ore, and wool; the values of the principal items for the last five years are as follows:—

Description of Goods.	1886.	1887.	1888.	1889.	1890.
	£	£	£	£	£
Boots and shoes	7,409	7.468	3,439	17,686	14,685
Coal	73,063	62,715	51,370	92,756	65,614
Coin (gold)	39,000	17,000	41,000	5,000	3,000
Coke	4,557	5,098	18,410	13,505	4,490
Live stock	92,574	57,992	62,702	91,003	249,584
Silver (ingots, lead and ore)	372,064	530,462	1,001,749	1,847,178	2,633,338
Skins	4,766	10,583	16,253	20,002	23,512
Wool	857,940	872,896	244,388	784,802	569,576

The records of the overland trade cannot be procured with exactness beyond the year 1877, but the time which has elapsed since the year named is amply sufficient to illustrate the great variations in the value of the exports. The import trade is much more regular, and until the year 1887 showed no great tendency to increase. Since the year named there has been a large extension of trade, which now reaches a considerable figure. This expansion is due to the requirements of the newly-found silver-fields near the South Australian Border, and the imports from South Australia *viâ* Thackaringa, Silverton, and Willyama amounted to £1,356,619 during 1890. It is anticipated that the extensions of the railway system of this Colony to the banks of the Darling at Bourke and Wilcannia will eventually divert not a little of the traffic which has hitherto gone to Adelaide. The certainty of speedy delivery, and the less amount of handling to which goods will be subjected, will probably more than compensate for the additional expense of delivery at the ship's side:—

Overland trade with South Australia.

Overland Trade with South Australia.

Year.	Imports.	Exports.	Year.	Imports.	Exports.
	£	£		£	£
1877	253,838	210,414	1884	360,965	1,287,441
1878	387,205	954,754	1885	386,252	617,606
1879	289,304	636,171	1886	442,034	1,396,403
1880	243,374	698,581	1887	713,238	1,513,241
1881	235,769	298,004	1888	1,154,924	1,359,802
1882	412,563	921,427	1889	1,092,095	2,731,656
1883	404,322	782,552	1890	1,561,992	3,471,655

Victoria displacing South Australia in N.S.W. markets.

The prominence which Victoria has assumed of recent years as a wheat-growing country, acts detrimentally to the trade of South Australia, for much of the breadstuff consumed in New South Wales, which was formerly obtained from Adelaide, is now procured from Victoria. The falling-off in this staple commenced about the year 1878, and is coincident with the development of the Victorian trade in flour and wheat, as will be seen from the following table, showing the value of wheat and flour imported from each of these colonies :—

Wheat and Flour Imported from Victoria and South Australia.

Year.	Value of imports from South Australia.		Value of imports from Victoria.	
	Wheat.	Flour.	Wheat.	Flour.
	£	£	£	£
1870	76,397	123,958	20,758	33,966
1871	260,346	201,963	6,206	33,992
1872	105,523	205,042	7,833	7,715
1873	144,592	201,332	539	17,677
1874	141,675	230,251	1,423	4,160
1875	197,263	289,385	1,514	1,296
1876	187,444	295,371	902	2,188
1877	154,284	261,918	9,765	32,305
1878	116,089	251,246	34,401	153,126
1879	63,973	221,174	13,280	76,310
1880	42,340	263,546	43,249	126,142
1881	19,406	269,342	33,165	113,796
1882	62,117	321,127	23,680	194,823
1883	9,195	229,617	38,794	237,342
1884	36,460	299,274	23,907	216,546
1885	31,236	219,320	23,433	291,999
1886	853	172,299	57,729	384,687
1887	11,388	308,805	34,050	364,107
1888	98,097	296,199	103,173	284,928
1889	122,772	305,180	90,764	247,006
1890	6,321	251,881	11,294	217,763

TRADE WITH TASMANIA.

Trade with Tasmania.

The trade of New South Wales with Tasmania promises to develop into one of great importance, and its growth during the period comprised in the following table must therefore appear satisfactory. It will, however, be seen that the imports largely exceed the exports, though the latter were higher in 1890 than in any previous year. The chief imports are tin, entirely for the purpose of re-export; green fruit, potatoes, and other agricultural produce. The principal articles of import worthy of note are as follows:— Articles imported from Tasmania.

Description of Goods.	1886.	1887.	1888.	1889.	1890.
	£	£	£	£	£
Bark	29,550	27,254	25,284	19,111	21,795
Chaff and hay	10,746	30	8,775	31,737	16,024
Fruit (green).........	93,722	68,742	60,853	101,598	100,479
Jams and jellies ...	33.760	28,182	23,877	12,344	8,351
Gold (bars and dust)	....	21,986	303	....	....
Live Stock—Sheep.	15,590	20,382	32,544	41,065	48,075
Oats	15,127	1,587	631	6,735	8,953
Potatoes	61,344	68,815	23,844	148,363	76,784
Tin—Ingots	297,736	304,507	306,824	98,407	96,916

The export trade embraces a large number of articles, though coal is the only one which reaches any considerable amount. The value of coal exported to Tasmania in 1890 was £28,743. The other exports consist of manufactured articles, chiefly the produce of Great Britain. Articles exported to Tasmania.

Year.	Imports.	Exports.	Year.	Imports.	Exports.
	£	£		£	£
1871	107,002	23,049	1881	481,529	83,949
1872	163,018	54,993	1882	614,923	85,673
1873	128,770	36,044	1883	666,399	120,662
1874	145,865	52,127	1884	576,501	117,872
1875	167,870	44,274	1885	582,177	108,758
1876	207,075	53,484	1886	606,740	110,776
1877	374,393	57,168	1887	587,315	131,477
1878	286,343	75,453	1888	515,378	117,239
1879	166,064	82,842	1889	505,590	174,852
1880	263,105	81,484	1890	432,615	215,674

TRADE WITH NEW ZEALAND.

Trade with New Zealand. New Zealand gave promise at a former period of being one of the leading customers of this Colony, but, from various causes, both the imports and the exports fell away very considerably. The export trade shows no sign of recovery, while the value of the imports fluctuates with the character of the season in New South Wales, a bad season being always attended with large importations of New Zealand wheats, oats, and other produce.

Year.	Imports.	Exports.	Year.	Imports.	Exports.
	£	£		£	£
1871	881,501	285,463	1881	471,911	427,295
1872	326,369	228,930	1882	737,204	454,853
1873	196,368	279,153	1883	588,056	358,627
1874	233,981	273,910	1884	881,530	506,714
1875	135,480	362,764	1885	899,623	369,055
1876	258,441	480,241	1886	949,567	427,640
1877	223,482	489,856	1887	757,076	300,937
1878	245,907	588,419	1888	788,003	393,288
1879	285,063	639,051	1889	1,195,090	416,824
1880	460,735	525,174	1890	932,073	294,113

Chief imports. The imports consist chiefly of timber, agricultural and dairy produce. The value of the principal articles is given herewith ;—

Description of Goods.	1886.	1887.	1888.	1889.	1890.
	£	£	£	£	£
Butter	110,046	21,206	56,566	51,602	5,953
Cheese	30,350	3,638	11,998	18,029	643
Drapery, apparel, &c.	10,319	17,423	43,449	33,721	15,180
Flour	66,658	8,617	40,920	131,885	63,948
Gold, bars and dust	186,164	262,344	61,951	61,780	237,319
Grain and pulse—Wheat	86,608	3,476	87,155	270,818	40,615
Do Oats	109,780	143,604	118,307	125,824	130,588
Do Other	46,657	33,355	47,126	75,539	79,069
Gum	199	800	22,694	6,318	2,697
Live stock	49,578	16,364	8,195	9,639	5,772
Malt	15,139	8,681	2,107	9,085	21,896
Meat (preserved)	11,643	6,299	15,084	13,586	20,430
Do Bacon, &c.	21,207	25,590	13,553	19,552	23,068
Oatmeal	9,101	8,849	9,077	18,354	10,131
Potatoes	25,874	30,247	47,110	97,184	82,390
Timber	83,966	83,692	81,403	81,451	62,791

The value of the principal articles exported to New Zealand during each of the past five years was as follows :— Exports to New Zealand.

Description of Goods.	1886.	1887.	1888.	1889.	1890.
	£	£	£	£	£
Coal	90,187	81,478	74,841	85,347	86,453
Coin, gold	215,000	87,000	190,000	110,000	40,025
Fruit, fresh	14,304	19,114	15,007	15,897	10,088
Manures	9,390	11,554	5,801	13,962	10,883
Timber	8,367	5,927	7,844	9,022	9,064

TRADE WITH OTHER BRITISH POSSESSIONS.

Besides the Australasian Colonies and Great Britain, the only other British possessions whose trade with New South Wales is at all considerable are Fiji, Hongkong, and India. With the Fiji Islands the trade is valuable, and increasing. In 1876 the imports from these Islands were valued at £29,610, and the exports at £71,477, being a total of £101,087, while in 1890 the imports had risen in value to £99,853, and the exports to £98,951, the total trade thus being £198,804. The imports were highest in 1885, when they were valued at £192,450. The exports reached their highest total in 1883, when they amounted to £248,380; from that time there was a steady decline until 1887, when the lowest figure was reached. Since then the exports have slightly recovered, but the figures for 1890 are still not quite 40 per cent. of those for 1883.

The import trade from Hongkong consists principally of opium, tea, tobacco, sugar, and rice, but large quantities of China oil, flax, hemp, and matting, as well as Chinese fancy goods, are also imported. The export trade for 1890 is chiefly comprised in the following items:—Coin to the amount of £173,834; coal, £29,140; bêche-de-mer, £7,946; fungus, £11,640; copper, £914; lead, £285; and old metal, £18,682. Hongkong trade.

The Indian trade has grown up almost entirely since 1880, in which year it amounted to only £20,264, increasing to £422,137 India trade.

in 1884, though falling off greatly in the two following years, expanding again in 1887 to £321,067, but again declining in the following year. During 1889 a total of £306,498 was reached, increasing to £448,648 in 1890, the highest value yet attained. The figures given show the value of imports and exports during the last eleven years:—

Trade with India.

Year.	Imports.	Exports.	Total trade.
	£	£	£
1880	653	19,611	20,264
1881	27,871	142,053	169,924
1882	72,739	345,312	418,051
1883	108,154	310,608	418,762
1884	128,185	293,952	422,137
1885	117,206	122,066	239,274
1886	100,965	89,299	190,264
1887	147,559	173,508	321,067
1888	208,989	42,791	251,780
1889	169,619	136,879	306,498
1890	195,368	253,280	448,648

Goods chiefly imported from India.

Castor oil is an article very largely imported from India, the value of oil received during 1890 being £52,136. There is also a large trade in woolpacks, the importations amounting to £52,622; and in bags and sacks, of which goods to the amount of £38,342 were received. The only other articles imported during 1890 in any quantity were rice, £11,898, and tea, £14,487. There were no importations of grain and pulse during the year, except a small quantity of pease to the value of £552.

Export trade.

The outward trade with India is confined almost entirely to coin, coal, and copper; of coin the export was valued at £113,513, of coal £16,904, and copper £17,290—the three items mentioned comprising a value of £147,707, out of a total export trade during 1890 of £253,280. The great falling-off noticeable during some of the years since 1882 is due to the decline in the copper trade, and in the amount of gold coin exported, which, in the year 1882 was £242,358, and in 1883 £232,541, but in 1890 only £113,513.

TRADE WITH GREAT BRITAIN AND BRITISH POSSESSIONS.

To what extent the trade of the Colony follows the British flag may be gathered from the following figures, which show not only the value of the trade of New South Wales with Great Britain and her dependencies during the past fourteen years, but also the proportion which that trade bears to the whole :— Chief trade of Colony with Britain and dependencies.

Trade with Great Britain and British Possessions.

Year.	Imports from Great Britain and British possessions.	Percentage of total imports.	Exports to Great Britain and British possessions.	Percentage of total exports.
	£		£	
1877	13,621,916	91·70	12,999,571	96·59
1878	13,694,884	90·66	12,650,708	96·34
1879	13,032,949	89·86	12,573,104	95·71
1880	13,021,783	91·85	15,210,314	97·00
1881	15,797,631	89·82	15,008,960	92·05
1882	19,269,165	89·73	16,470,481	93·18
1883	19,263,052	90·03	18,670,373	92·15
1884	20,942,254	90·42	17,221,650	92·69
1885	21,299,715	89·74	14,794,052	88·33
1886	19,153,071	89·86	14,250,570	90·66
1887	17,584,948	91·62	16,465,109	89·00
1888	19,684,772	89·66	18,508,498	88·47
1889	22,196,596	88·34	20,281,259	87·06
1890	20,273,053	89·64	18,582,372	84·29

FOREIGN TRADE.

The value of the trade of the Colony with countries other than those under British dominion shows a large increase since 1880, as will be at once seen from the subjoined table. The import trade is marked by a fairly uniform growth, while the export trade, though less regular, showed proportionately a more considerable increase. During 1881 the value of imports advanced £635,101, and the exports £826,357, an increase due mainly to the peculiar development of trade with the United States; while the large expansion found in the subsequent years arose from the Uniform increase of foreign trade.

Foreign Import and Exports.

establishment of direct trade with France, Belgium, and Germany. The total value of imports shows a large decline in 1887, which is chiefly due to a falling-off in the United States trade, though a sensible decline may be also observed in the imports from other leading foreign States, however, the lost ground was more than recovered in 1889 and 1890.

Year.	Imports.	Exports.	Year.	Imports.	Exports.
	£	£		£	£
1877	1,230,862	458,329	1884	2,218,662	1,355,640
1878	1,409,761	483,697	1885	2,437,746	1,956,055
1879	1,470,877	558,827	1886	2,160,056	1,467,367
1880	1,154,280	472,488	1887	1,606,369	2,036,641
1881	1,789,381	1,298,845	1888	2,194,505	2,411,632
1882	2,200,734	1,206,874	1889	2,664,549	3,013,675
1883	2,139,789	1,591,900	1890	2,341,951	3,463,565

THE UNITED STATES.

United States largest foreign market.

The United States is the largest foreign market of the Colony, the value of both the imports and exports far exceeding that of any other country. The import trade has been marked by a fairly uniform rate of increase until 1886, since which year the value of trade has greatly fluctuated. The export trade also shows great variableness, and depends almost entirely on the demand for gold which prevails in the States. The peculiarity of the trade will be, perhaps, best exemplified in the following table:—

Trade with the United States.

Year.	Imports.	Exports.	Year.	Imports.	Exports.
	£	£		£	£
1877	481,565	108,273	1884	954,605	366,732
1878	622,261	128,805	1885	1,008,572	985,531
1879	546,630	211,206	1886	1,018,773	521,216
1880	387,056	172,648	1887	693,420	934,443
1881	587,865	866,962	1888	967,528	1,044,144
1882	886,171	676,598	1889	1,094,697	1,130,589
1883	922,574	872,983	1890	859,102	1,300,375

The imports comprise a large number of articles, amongst which the following are the most important, the values given being those for 1890 :— Class of goods imported from United States.

	£
Timber—undressed, dressed and worked up	87,781
Hardware	84,412
Tobacco, cigars, &c.	61,459
Beer	3,931
Carriages, and carriage materials	29,937
Kerosene	75,909
Fish (preserved)	40,229
Watches and clocks	16,192
Machinery	52,817
Leather	38,522
Furniture and upholstery	15,719
Agricultural implements	17,606

The other articles imported are mostly manufactured goods. In most years there has been a fairly large import of breadstuffs from the United States, and during 1886 the value of such imports was £96,216; in 1889 the value of flour imported reached £54,490, and wheat £142,397, but in 1890 the imports of grain and pulse of all kinds largely decreased, only amounting in the total to £10,350.

The exports to the United States are chiefly confined to a few articles of raw material, the produce of the Colony, the principal of which are gold, coal and shale, tin, wool, and marsupial skins. No other goods are exported in considerable quantities. During the year 1890 the amount of export of the articles mentioned above was— Exports to America.

	£
Gold, coin	991,940
Coal	102,205
Tin	74,384
Skins (chiefly marsupial)	47,391
Wool	33,326
Shale	7,379

For some years past there has been a considerable export of gold to America, the quantity sent away during 1885, 1889, and 1890 being especially large. This export practically commenced in 1880, and the value of the precious metal both coined and uncoined exported since the year named was :— Large export of gold to United States.

Gold Exported to America.

Year.	Value.	Year.	Value.
	£		£
1881	647,323	1886	229,137
1882	382,347	1887	651,612
1883	564,316	1888	578,488
1884	106,719	1889	751,220
1885	726,653	1890	1,016,940

The United States forms one of the natural markets for the wool of the Colony; but, owing to the tariff restrictions placed upon its importation, the trade in this commodity is extremely limited.

BELGIUM.

Trade with Belgium.

The direct trade between this Colony and Belgium began in 1881, and may, to a large extent, be attributable to the International Exhibition held in Sydney during 1879–80. In the year mentioned the combined imports and exports amounted to only £26,237, while in 1890 they had risen to £1,142,665, which cannot but be regarded as an enormous increase in so short a time. In point of value the Belgian trade of the Colony is larger than that of any other foreign country, the United States excepted; the port of Antwerp which receives the bulk of the trade is the distributing centre for the greater part of the wool destined for French and German markets.

Principal imports.

The goods imported from Belgium comprise a large number of articles. Iron in its various manufactures, and in bars, plate and wire, glassware, candles, drapery, cigars, cement, and starch are all imported to some extent, though the trade in each commodity is subject to considerable fluctuation.

Belgium a large purchaser of N.S.W. wool

The outward trade with Belgium is confined almost entirely to wool, though some tallow is also exported. During 1890 the amount of washed wool sent to Belgian ports was 2,600,984 lb., valued at £156,255, and 25,381,970 lb. of greasy wool of the value of £844,191, making a total of £1,000,446. Belgium is, therefore, next to Great Britain, the largest purchaser of New South Wales wool; for, though the export both to Victoria and South Australia exceeds that to Belgium, it is merely nominal, as very little of the wool is retained in these colonies for home use. The following table shows the import and export trade with Belgium since 1881:—

Trade with Belgium.

Year.	Imports.	Exports.
	£	£
1881	21,579	4,658
1882	39,951	21,659
1883	31,162	160,390
1884	74,904	326,488
1885	195,318	399,549
1886	173,831	424,938
1887	37,735	557,710
1888	64,766	723,286
1889	88,843	725,687
1890	130,819	1,011,846

FRANCE AND NEW CALEDONIA.

French trade.

The French trade has risen into importance since 1881, as will be seen by the subsequent table. The increase is due almost entirely to the establishment of direct communication between this Colony and the Republic by the Messageries Maritimes Company, but it has been accompanied by a corresponding falling off in the trade with New Caledonia, the chief dependency of France in the South Pacific. For though in 1881 the total value of French imports and exports amounted to only £65,833, as against £351,795 in 1890, those of New Caledonia fell during the corresponding period from £372,926 to £277,309.

Class of goods imported from France.

Wearing apparel and drapery form the largest class of imports from France; the imports of drapery and silk amounted in 1890 to £21,444; of apparel, £7,713; and of boots to £12,510. Next in importance are wines and spirits—the import of the former amounted to £18,538, and of the latter to £12,603. Oil to the value of £3,991; tobacco and cigars, £1,548; watches and clocks, £3,490, and toys, £5,120—are the only other goods largely imported. Large quantities of French goods are imported from Great Britain; but the indirect trade is now fast being superseded by direct trade, and the cost of commission and double handling thus saved to the Colony.

Wool chief export to France.

Wool forms the chief export to France. The value exported during 1890 was £135,152. Sheepskins to the value of £67,458 were also exported:—

Trade with France.

Year.	Imports.	Exports.
	£	£
1881	64,118	1,715
1882	96,176	9,744
1883	211,722	24,786
1884	218,755	183,890
1885	345,231	142,104
1886	216,193	149,509
1887	157,732	85,151
1888	154,856	120,723
1889	179,900	104,104
1890	117,871	233,924

New Caledonian trade.

As already pointed out, New Caledonia is an important market for the produce of the Colony, though its value has been considerably affected by the establishment of a regular communication between France and her dependency. The trade with New Caledonia reached its highest point in 1882, when produce was imported into New South Wales to the value of £273,370, and exported to the amount of £228,280. Since that year the imports and exports show a very considerable decline:—

Trade with New Caledonia.

Year.	Imports.	Exports.	Year.	Imports.	Exports.
	£	£		£	£
1881	188,745	184,181	1886	64,952	111,332
1882	273,370	228,280	1887	70,676	137,212
1883	152,096	212,528	1888	68,637	153,967
1884	107,509	210,552	1889	85,582	189,660
1885	82,181	153,094	1890	83,920	193,389

GERMANY.

Trade with Germany.

A large trade has been maintained with Germany since 1879. Direct communication was established in 1887 by the North German Lloyd's Company, of Bremen, and further extended by a line of German cargo boats trading between Hamburg and Sydney since 1888. This trade bids fair to develop into considerable dimensions, as will be seen from the following list, which shows the values of the principal articles imported from Germany during 1890. The only other articles besides these, of which the import was noteworthy, were paper and stationery, picture frames, starch, drugs, chemicals, and glassware :—

	£
Cement	15,602
Musical Instruments	66,769
Apparel, drapery, boots, &c.	114,046
Iron and iron manufactures, including hardware.	88,506
Spirits	45,554
Sewing machines	10,337
Tobacco, cigars, and cigarettes	36,371
Beer	15,236
Fancy goods and toys	21,146
Watches and clocks	1,312

Wool chief export to Germany.

The exports consisted almost entirely of wool, the value of which, in 1890, was £371,958, out of a total export of £404,280. This increase in the wool export during 1889 and 1890 is chiefly due to the greater facilities now existing for direct shipment.

Year.	Imports.	Exports.	Year.	Imports.	Exports.
	£	£		£	£
1879	32,436	4,775	1885	372,557	29,511
1880	47,169	......	1886	361,612	54,471
1881	124,910	11,993	1887	296,952	100,012
1882	180,951	11,661	1888	481,009	128,546
1883	213,709	7,947	1889	533,082	519,435
1884	337,881	43,979	1890	639,475	404,280

CHINA.

Trade with China.

The only other country whose trade with New South Wales reaches a large figure is China. The imports and exports credited to Hongkong, however, belong in reality to the country generally, and the diminution which is seen in the China trade since 1881, is to be attributed in no small degree to the transference of part of the trade from the ports of the Empire to Hongkong. Still, when allowance is made on this score, it will be found that the actual loss of trade is by no means inconsiderable. The main import from China is tea, which exhibits a falling off although no perceptible decline is observable in the consumption of the article; but the decline may be owing to a decrease in the quantity required for re-export, which denotes a loss to the Colony, and to the increased consumption of Indian teas, the imports of which are increasing every year. The direct export trade has never been large. The amounts shown as exported to China do not however represent the whole value of the trade, as a considerable portion is sent via Hong Kong, which is a distributing centre for the Empire.

Small direct export trade.

Year.	Imports.	Exports.	Year.	Imports.	Exports.
	£	£		£	£
1880	358,129	14,844	1886	195,930	16,462
1881	466,830	19,758	1887	251,722	14,510
1882	358,783	28,958	1888	309,934	7,651
1883	259,108	21,351	1889	257,353	11,587
1884	357,208	21,741	1890	241,840	1,037
1885	303,595	21,114			

TRADE WITH ALL COUNTRIES.

Total trade.

The amount of imports and exports of each country, in proportion to the total, during the eleven years which closed with 1890, is shown in the following tables. As already pointed out, the border colonies of Victoria and South Australia appear more advantageously than their importance warrants, owing to the large amount of trade merely passing through their territory for shipment to Great Britain, while the trade to the last named country, as shown on the table, is less than the truth, by the amount thus over-credited to Victoria and South Australia.

of the Imports from each of the Principal Countries.

	United Kingdom	Victoria.	Queensland.	South Australia.	New Zealand.	Other Colonies or Possessions.	Total British Possessions.
..	46·11	15·42	15·70	4·87	3·25	6·50	91·85
...	51·06	13·73	12·35	3·94	2·68	6·04	89·82
...	51·96	12·90	10·01	4·74	3·43	6·69	89·73
...	49·36	13·99	13·71	3·90	2·71	6·36	90·03
...	49·32	13·23	12·88	4·33	3·81	6·85	90·42
...	50·07	13·96	12·27	3·75	3·79	5·99	89·74
...	49·01	13·09	13·65	3·88	4·45	5·78	89·86
...	41·72	15·10	18·35	6·57	3·95	5·93	91·62
...	43·39	11·64	16·38	8·61	3·76	5·88	89·66
...	38·21	10·58	20·41	8·13	5·23	5·78	88·34
...	38·15	9·27	24·24	9·01	4·12	4·85	89·64

Foreign States.

	United States.	France.	Germany	Belgium.	China.	Other Foreign States.	Total Foreign States.
...	2·73	0·27	0·33	......	2·52	2·29	8·15
...	3·34	0·36	0·71	0·12	2·66	2·99	10·18
...	4·14	0·46	0·85	0·18	1·67	2·97	10·27
..	4·29	0·98	0·99	0·14	1·20	2·37	9·97
...	4·12	0·95	1·46	0·32	1·54	1·19	9·58
...	4·25	1·45	1·57	0·82	1·28	0·89	10·26
...	4·78	1·01	1·70	0·81	0·92	0·92	10·14
...	3·62	0·83	1·55	0·19	1·31	0·88	8·38
...	4·56	0·73	2·26	0·31	1·46	1·02	10·34
...	4·79	0·78	2·33	0·39	1·12	2·25	11·66
...	3·80	0·52	2·83	0·58	1·07	1·56	10·36

Exports—Percentage of Exports to each of the Principal Countries.

Year.	British Possessions.						
	United Kingdom	Victoria.	Queensland.	South Australia	New Zealand.	Other Colonies or Possessions.	Total British Possessions.
1880 ...	47·98	29·19	8·70	5·30	3·35	2·48	97·00
1881 ...	46·36	24·85	12·02	2·80	2·62	3·40	92·05
1882 ...	41·35	21·40	17·04	6·15	2·57	4·67	93·18
1883 ..	48·78	20·59	11·42	4·80	1·76	4·80	92·15
1884 ...	41·36	22·45	12·85	8·08	2·73	5·22	92·69
1885 ..	43·54	20·60	12·98	4·86	2·20	4·15	88·33
1886 ...	38·35	23·52	11·64	10·09	2·72	4·34	90·66
1887 ...	37·61	25·77	10·94	9·40	1·62	3·66	89·00
1888 ...	40·52	26·08	9·43	7·94	1·88	2·62	88·47
1889 ...	38·48	23·12	7·50	12·87	1·79	3·30	87·06
1890 ...	30·04	24·43	7·58	16·78	1·34	4·12	84·29

Year.	Foreign States.						
	United States.	France.	Germany	Belgium.	China.	Other Foreign States.	Total Foreign States.
1880 ...	1·10	...	...	...	0·09	1·81	3·00
1881 ...	5·31	0·01	0·07	0·03	0·12	2·41	7·95
1882 ...	3·83	0·05	0·06	0·12	0·16	2·60	6·82
1883 ...	4·30	0·12	0·04	0·80	0·10	2·49	7·85
1884 ...	1·98	1·00	0·23	1·75	0·12	2·23	7·31
1885 ...	5·88	0·85	0·17	2·40	0·12	2·25	11·67
1886 ...	3·32	0·95	0·35	2·71	0·08	1·93	9·34
1887 ...	5·05	0·46	0·54	3·01	0·08	1·86	11·00
1888 ...	4·99	0·58	0·61	3·46	0·04	1·85	11·53
1889 ...	4·85	0·45	2·23	3·11	0·05	2·25	12·94
1890 ...	5·90	1·06	1·83	4·59	0·01	2·32	15·71

Valuation of imports.

For Customs purposes imports are, as a general rule, set down at their value in the Colony. Such, too, is the plan followed in regard to exports. Taking into consideration the circumstances of the Colony, the system is a just one; for, assuming that goods imported have to be paid for in goods exported, the imports, if valued according to the ruling prices at the port of shipment, would be undervalued at the port of arrival by the amount of the freight and charges incurred. In order, therefore, to establish a fair comparison between the imports and exports, each must be taken at the value in the Colony. Under normal conditions the value of the trade inwards and outwards should be virtually equal. If the freight-earning vessels were owned in the Colony the excess would be on the side of the imports, but as comparatively little of the tonnage is owned in New South Wales the freight earned is small. On the contrary, a certain quantity of goods must be exported to pay for the carriage of the goods imported, and the amount of such represents the difference in the value of the goods purchased by the exports, as they leave the country where they are produced, and the value of the same goods landed in this Colony. Imports set down at Sydney value.

The imports of the Colony, taken over a series of years greatly exceed the exports. The causes of this excess are chiefly two—the flow of British money to the Colony for investment, and the proceeds of loans floated by the Government for the purpose of carrying out public works. Were these importations to cease, the exports of New South Wales would exceed the imports; for, not only would the Colony be required to send out the value of the goods imported, with their freight to its shores, but also the amount of interest payable on loans, the earnings of money sent here for investment, and the incomes derived by persons living abroad, from property held in the Colony. Imports exceed exports.

TARIFF.

The tariff in force in New South Wales is more simple in character than that of any other important country, except Great Britain. At the close of 1886 it comprised specific duties on 175 articles, with an *ad valorem* duty of 5 per cent. on the remainder—certain articles, about 100 in number, comprising chiefly food, raw material, and agricultural appliances, alone excepted. Since then, however, the tariff has been greatly modified, and now stands as follows:— The tariff.

Schedule of Customs and Excise Duties, for 1891.

Articles.		Rate of Duty.	
Bacon and Hams		℘ lb.,	2d.
Beer, ale, porter, spruce, or other beer, cider, and perry	In wood or jar	℘ gallon,	6d.
	In bottle	"	9d.
	For six reputed quarts or twelve reputed pints	"	9d.
	Excise	"	3d.
Biscuits, other than ship		℘ lb.,	1d.
Butter		"	1d.
Candles per lb., or reputed package of that weight, and so in proportion for any such reputed weight, and stearine		"	1d.
Cement		℘ barrel,	2s.
Cheese		℘ lb.,	2d.
Chicory, dandelion, and Taraxacum	Raw or kiln-dried	"	3d.
	Roasted, ground, or mixed with any other article	"	6d.
Chocolate—plain or mixed with any other article, and chocolate creams		"	4d.
Cigars		"	6s.
Cigarettes (including wrappers)		"	6s.
Cigars and cigarettes (Excise)		"	2s. 6d.
Corn flour and maizena		"	1d.
Cocoa	Raw, without allowance for husks or shells	"	3d.
	Prepared paste, or mixed with any other article (See "Chocolate")	"	4d.
Coffee	Raw	"	3d.
	Roasted, ground, or mixed with any other article	"	6d.
Confectionery (including cakes, comfits, liquorice, liquorice paste, lozenges of all kinds, cocoanut in sugar, sugar-candy, succades, and sweetmeats)		"	2d.
Essences, flavouring, and fruit, containing not more than 25 per cent. of proof spirit		℘ gallon,	4s.
Containing more than 25 per. cent. of proof spirit		"	14s.
Fish, dried, preserved, or salt		℘ lb.,	1d.
Fruits, dried and candied, exclusive of dates		"	2d.
Glucose	Liquid and syrup	℘ cwt.	3s. 4d.
	Solid	"	5s.
Iron	Galvanized, in bars, sheets, or corrugated	℘ ton,	40s.
	Iron and steel wire	"	20s.
	Galvanized, manufactures (except anchors)	"	60s.
Jams—per pound, or reputed package of that weight, and so in proportion for any such reputed weight		℘ lb.,	1d.
Milk, condensed or preserved		"	1d.
Naphtha and gasoline		℘ gallon,	6d.
Oils, except black, cocoa-nut, and sperm and palm.	Kerosene	"	6d.
	All other	"	6d.
	In bottle—		
	Reputed quarts	℘ doz.,	1s. 6d.
	Reputed pints	"	9d.
	Reputed half-pints and smaller sizes	"	6d.
Opium, and any preparation or solution thereof, not imported for use as a known medicine		℘ lb.,	20s.
Paints and Varnish	Paints and colours ground in oil	℘ cwt.,	3s.
	Varnish and lithographic varnishes	℘ gallon,	2s.

ıle of Customs and Excise Duties, for 1891—*continued.*

Articles.	Rate of Duty.	
nd shot { Sporting powder	⅌ lb.,	3d.
Blasting Powder	,,	1d.
Dynamite and Lithofracteur	,,	1d.
Shot...	⅌ cwt.,	5s.
, * jellies, and fruits boiled in pulp or partially rved other than by sulphurous acid	⅌ lb.,	1d.
....	⅌ ton,	60s.
ioca, and semolina	⅌ lb.,	1d.
....	⅌ ton,	20s.
ıs { If containing not more than 25 per cent. of proof spirit..	⅌ gallon,	4s.
ʟ If containing more than 25 per cent. of proof spirit	,,	14s.
On all kinds of spirits imported into the Colony, the strength of which can be ascertained by Sykes' Hydrometer. (No allowance beyond 16·5 shall be made for the under proof of any spirits of a less hydrometer strength than 16·5 under proof)		
Brandy	⅌ proof gall.,	14s.
Geneva	,,	14s.
Gin	,,	14s.
Liqueurs	,,	14s.
Rum	,,	14s.
Whisky	,,	14s.
Manufactured in the Colony (Excise)	,,	14s.
On all spirits and spirituous compounds imported into the Colony, the strength of which cannot be ascertained by Sykes' Hydrometer	⅌ liq. gallon,	14s.
Case Spirits—Reputed contents of two, three, or four gallons shall be charged—		
Two gallons and under as two gallons.		
Over two gallons and not exceeding three as three gallons.		
Over three gallons and not exceeding four as four gallons.		
Methylated	⅌ gallon,	4s.
Perfumed spirits, perfumed water, Florida water, and bay rum	⅌ liquid gall.	15s.
Refined	⅌ cwt.,	6s. 8d.
,, ex-refinery	,,	6s. 8d.
Raw..	,,	5s.
,, ex-refinery...	,,	5s.
Molasses and treacle	,,	3s. 4d.
,, ex-refinery	,,	3s. 4d.
....	⅌ lb.,	3d.
other than laths, building s, dyewoods, palings, un- sandalwood, staves, and n shooks). { Dressed	⅌ 100 ft.,	3s.
Rough and undressed	,,	1s. 6d.
Doors, sashes, and shutters	Each,	2s.

* Jellies included under jams.

Schedule of Customs and Excise Duties, for 1891—*continued.*

Articles.		Rate of Duty.
Tobacco	Delivered from ship's side, or from a Customs bond, for home consumption—Manufactured, unmanufactured, and snuff	℔ lb., 3s.
	Unmanufactured, entered to be manufactured in the Colony. At the time of removal from a Customs bond or from an importing ship to any licensed tobacco manufactory for manufacturing purposes only into tobacco, cigars, or cigarettes	,, 1s.
	Sheepwash	,, 3d.
	Excise	,, 1s. 3d.
Wines...	Sparkling—For six reputed quarts or twelve reputed pints	.... 10s.
	Other kinds	℔ gallon, 5s.
	Other kinds, for six reputed quarts or twelve reputed pints	.... 5s.

Customs Duties—Spirits.

The chief articles from which Customs revenue is derived are fermented and spirituous liquors, tobacco, tea, and sugar. The revenue from spirits stood at 10s. per gallon until 1879, when it was raised to 12s., and in 1887 the duty was fixed at 14s. per gallon for ordinary, 15s. for perfumed, and 4s. for methylated spirits. The revenue derived from imported spirits during the past twelve years was:—

Revenue from Imported Spirits.

Year.	Quantity on which duty was paid.	Duty.	Amount of duty collected.
	Gallons.		£
1878	1,089,191	10s.	544,596
1879	1,031,989	10s. and 12s.	521,273
1880	999,744	12s.	599,847
1881	1,103,101	12s.	661,861
1882	1,154,720	12s.	692,832
1883	1,194,650	12s.	716,790
1884	1,239,495	12s.	743,697
1885	1,204,790	12s.	722,873
1886	1,161,628	12s.	696,977
1887	1,121,101	12s., 14s., 15s.	759,608
1888	1,178,293	14s. and 15s.	806,938
1889	1,164,360	14s. and 15s.	804,426
1890	1,196,561	14s. and 15s.	827,314

Spirits subject to excise.

Colonial distilled spirits are subject to an excise equal to the duty on imported spirits. In 1884 the quantity subject to excise was 17,709 gallons, on which £10,625 was paid. In the following year the quantity fell to 14,242 gallons, and the amount of excise to £8,545. In 1886 the quantity fell still further, being only 9,733

, and the excise £5,846; but in 1887, notwithstanding the ed duty levied, the quantity subject to excise increased to gallons, and the amount of duty to £10,754, and a still advance to 17,111 gallons was made in 1888, the duty ting to £11,978. In 1890 the duty collected amounted to '4 on 33,105 gallons of spirit distilled.

Duty on wine.

wine is subject to an import duty of 5s. per gallon, and ng wine to 10s. per gallon. The import of the first named now than it was ten years ago, but owing to the increase duty in 1879 from 4s. to 5s. per gallon, the Customs has been fairly maintained. The amount of still wine ed during 1890 was 143,156 gallons, on which £35,789 as paid. The duty on sparkling wine was raised to 10s. lon in 1879, at which rate it now remains. The quantity kling wine on which duty amounting to £10,317 was col- was 20,634 gallons.

Australian wine checks import.

growing favour in which Australian wine is held will ly have the effect of checking any considerable importations ign wine, and no large increase in the amount of duty, that now received from such wine, can therefore be d. The quantity imported showed a fair increase up to the 1885; but the recent general depression having probably the amount of money available for luxuries of this kind, y paid has of late years somewhat fallen.

Beer imported.

import of ale and beer was larger during 1889 than in any s year. In 1890 there was a considerable decline. The ies of beer imported, on which duty was paid, being 80 gallons in wood, and 1,122,974 gallons in bottle, or a 2,242,054 gallons, paying duty to the amount of £71,601, rate of 6d. per gallon for beer in wood and 9d. for bottled. ise duty on beer brewed in the Colony is at the rate of 3d. lon. It was first collected for the second half-year of 1887, ounted to £63,565, the quantity on which duty was paid 5,085,217 gallons; in 1889 excise duty amounting to 40 was collected on 9,515,200 gallons, and in 1890

£120,245 on 9,619,600 gallons. As a set-off against the duty thus imposed, those levied on hops and malt have been removed.

Tobacco duty. The duties levied on tobacco imported into the Colony during 1886 were, on the manufactured article, 3s. per lb.; on tobacco for manufacturing purposes if delivered from Bond to any licensed Tobacco Manufactory, 1s. per lb.; on the leaf if delivered from Bond for Home Consumption, and not to any licensed Factory, 3s.; and on cigars and cigarettes, 6s. The excise on tobacco made in the Colony was 1s. per lb., and on cigars and cigarettes, 2s. 6d. The excise duty on manufactured tobacco was, however, increased during 1887, and now stands at 1s. 3d. The total amount of Import Duties collected on tobacco and cigars during 1890 was £245,136.

Excise on tobacco. Excise duties were first levied on tobacco manufactured in the Colony in 1884, and the amount collected since then has been:—

Year	Amount	Year	Amount
1884	£68,000	1888	£128,899
1885	106,658	1889	123,212
1886	102,212	1890	118,287
1887	127,545		

The excise derived from cigars and cigarettes has been trifling, exceeding £1,000 only in each of the last four years:—

Year	Amount	Year	Amount
1884	£490	1888	£1,038
1885	863	1889	1,150
1886	666	1890	2,806
1887	1,284		

During the last few years since the duty was increased the revenue derived from the imported leaf has steadily declined, its place being supplied by leaf grown in the Colony. To meet this falling off, the excise duty levied on colonial-made tobacco entered for home consumption was increased, as already stated, to 1s. 3d. per lb. If the American leaf, which is subject to a duty of 1s. per lb., were used exclusively in the manufacture of tobacco in the local factories, the actual duty paid on the finished product would have been, previous to the alteration in the tariff, 2s. per lb., and 2s. 3d. since the alteration, as against 3s. for the imported article. Such, however, is not the case—large quantities of

...leaf are used, and the absolute amount of duty paid tobacco made in the Colony, otherwise than cigars and tea, was 1s. 3¾d. in 1885, 1s. 3½d. in 1886, 1s. 5 1/10d. in 1s. 6½d. in 1888, 1s. 6 1/12d. in 1889, and 1s. 6 1/11d. in 1890.

duty on tea has remained at 3d. per lb., and the amount of e per head derived from the duty has varied very little from year. The revenue received from this source for the last ...was :— Revenue from tea.

Revenue from Tea.

	Amount.	Year.	Amount.
	£		£
	86,212	1886	105,979
	87,829	1887	106,815
	75,719	1888	100,617
	100,053	1889	106,954
	98,915	1890	106,986

ned sugar coming into the Colony is subject to a duty 8d. per cwt., but the Commissioners of Customs only loaf sugar under this heading. The quantity imported 1890 was 4,827 cwt., paying duty to the amount of £1,609. is levied on raw sugar, which includes all the ordinary of trade at the rate of 5s. per cwt., but notwithstanding ity, and the large area of the Colony adapted for sugar-g, the imports are considerable. Duty on sugar

Revenue from Raw Sugar.

Quantity.	Amount.	Year.	Quantity.	Amount.
Cwt.	£		Cwt.	£
187,548	46,887	1886	484,592	121,148
182,356	45,589	1887	520,192	130,048
203,496	50,874	1888	470,668	117,667
591,632	147,908	1889	642,880	160,720
554,064	138,516	1890	558,540	139,635

...fic duties are levied on other articles besides those just ned, as will be seen by the list already given; the articles yielded most revenue in 1890 being bacon and hams, ...6; butter, £3,436; candles, £14,587; cement, £16,778; £1,759; cocoa and chocolate, £9,413; confectionery, ...; fish, £17,472; galvanized iron, £20,324; galvanized Duties on other articles.

manufactures, £12,061; iron and steel wire, £14,775; jams and jellies, £15,254; condensed milk, £12,568; kerosene oil, £38,325; oils, £25,261; salt, £20,553; timber, £55,022; explosives, £8,583; fruits, dried and candied, £57,172; opium, £16,990; and rice, £15,947.

Customs revenue of various colonies.

Though more lightly taxed through the Customs, the revenue derived from this source is larger in New South Wales than in any of the other Australasian Colonies, with the exception of Victoria. During 1890, the revenue derived from the Custom-house, exclusive of excise, harbour dues, &c., in each Colony in Australasia was—

New South Wales...	£1,879,066	Western Australia ...	£178,231
Victoria	2,704,380	Tasmania	329,029
Queensland............	1,242,342	New Zealand	1,500,084
South Australia	675,145		

Customs Revenue collected at Sydney, Outports, and Inland Stations, during the year 1890-1.

Stations.	Amount.	Stations.	Amount.
	£		£
Sydney	1,855,057	Mulwala	2,164
Albury	29,468	Newcastle	124,783
Barringun	873	Richmond River	162
Boggabilla	101	Swan Hill Crossing	795
Bourke	23,500	Thackeringa and Silverton	7,129
Cobar	938	Tocumwal	2,134
Corowa	6,495	Tweed River	104
Deniliquin	11,397	Wallangarra	690
Eden	18	Wentworth	10,812
Euston	1,275	Wilcannia	15,939
Grafton	1,337	Willyama	75,888
Howlong	1,236	Wollongong	172
Kiama	1		
Moama	17,179		
Morpeth	25,064	£	2,214,711

The amounts shown on the next page, as collected by the Treasury, or as collected by the Customs Department, and paid direct into the Treasury, are not included in this table.

The amount of revenue collected by the Customs, including excise, during each of the last five years, is given in the next two pages.

…enue Collected by the Department of Customs.

…of Receipt and Rate of Duty.		1886. Amount collected.	1887. Amount collected.	1888. Amount collected.	1889. Amount collected.	1890.* Amount collected.
…ew Duties.		£	£	£	£	£
……	per gallon, 10s.	....	4,412	4,725	5,168	4,798
	„ 12s.	696,977	152,744	....	....	....
	„ 14s.	....	602,452	789,097	794,875	818,276
…ties..	„ 2s.	2,407	598	....	....	....
	„ 4s.	....	2,688	4,124	4,288	4,240
……	„ 5s.	32,280	35,396	39,157	37,300	35,789
…ng ….	„ 10s.	10,519	9,726	11,937	10,663	10,317
…wood..	„ 6d.	17,435	21,047	26,286	28,534	26,477
…bottle	„ 9d.	51,662	48,166	50,917	51,497	46,124
…nfactured per lb.,	2s.	56,802	75,603	89,662	107,364	118,130
…r ……	„ 3s.	1,826	1,052	544	809	618
…manufac-…ses only	„ 1s.	28,076	27,611	30,524	27,287	28,471
……	„ 6s.	67,058	63,799	68,336	73,961	75,287
……	„ 6s.	11,741	13,373	17,912	21,587	22,680
…d ……per cwt., 6s 8d.		1,648	1,840	1,377	1,014	1,349
……	„ 5s.	77,998	84,073	72,907	73,146	72,992
……	„ 3s. 4d.	1,895	1,455	909	1,030	965
…or Re-……	„ 6s. 8d.	13	37	127	260	360
…Refinery	„ 5s.	43,150	45,975	44,760	87,574	66,648
…finery..	„ 3s. 4d.	1,167	1,534	1,867	3,133	2,800
……	per lb., 3d.	105,979	106,815	100,617	108,964	106,996
……	„ 2d.	7,620	6,451	6,437	6,628	6,214
	„ 6d.	1,397	2,160	2,109	1,961	2,510
……	„ 2d.	1,848	2,479	255	1,480	1,249
	„ 6d.	2,324	2,038	1,863	1,166	841
……	„ 20s.	22,148	21,663	22,052	24,258	16,990
……	per ton, 60s.	17,583	18,478	19,061	17,480	15,947
……	per lb., 2d.	50,919	56,347	58,554	55,523	57,172
……	„ 1d.	1,244	731	....	....	....
……	per bushel, 6d.	3,190	....	....	....	....
	„ 9d.	11,459	5,888	....	....	....
……	per lb., 3d.	3,659	....	....	....	....
	„ 6d.	12,059	7,526	....	....	....
……	per gallon, 4s.	466	293	436	280	262
	„ 12s.	23	14	....	....	....
	„ 14s.	....	53	142	150	324
…on Samples ……		112	133	116	106	122
…Duties* ……		429,157	351,300	394,166	350,334	335,308
…uties* ……		277,227	226,743	3	....	....
…mport Duties……		2,065,578	2,002,717	1,871,097	1,897,925	1,879,086

* For Schedule of Customs Duties for 1890, see page 214.

Revenue Collected by the Department of Customs—*continued.*

Particulars of Receipt and Rate of Duty.	1886.	1887.	1888.	1889.	1890.*
	Amount collected.	Amount collected.	Amount collected.	Amount collected.	Amount collected.
EXCISE.	£	£	£	£	£
Colonial Distilled Spirits ⅌ gal., 12s.	5,846	1,685	....	....	....
Colonial Distilled Spirits ,, 14s.	....	9,068	11,978	16,691	23,174
Excise on Tobacco .... ⅌ lb., 1s.	102,212	26,627	....	....	....
Excise on Tobacco .... ,, 1s. 3d.	....	100,918	128,899	123,212	118,287
Excise on Cigars and Cigarettes .... ,, 2s. 6d.	668	1,284	1,038	1,150	2,806
Excise on Beer .... ⅌ gal., 3d.	....	63,565	116,253	118,940	120,245
Tobacco Factory License Fees......	1,180	1,306	1,375	1,377	1,376
Tobacco—Licenses to Sell	....	....	....	....	84
Distilleries and Refineries—License Fees †	89	75	82	95	104
TOTAL EXCISE.	109,995	204,528	259,625	261,465	266,076
MISCELLANEOUS COLLECTIONS.					
Tax on Chinese	12,840	17,980	4,710	100	300
Bonded Warehouse License Fees....	8,662	8,766	8,401	8,752	8,694
Rent of Goods in Queen's Warehouse	46	61	71	47	67
Pilotage	31,716	28,628	36,797	39,377	32,258
Harbour and Lights Rates..........	15,610	14,676	19,416	19,540	17,344
Removal Dues	4,703	4,297	5,465	6,457	3,973
Shipping Fees—Engaging and Discharging Seamen‡	3	2	8	9	6
Crown's Share of Seizures and Penalties‡	789	528	1,107	35	226
Surplus Proceeds, Sale of Overtime Goods‡	428	608	570	297	1,091
Surcharges ‡	36	83	32	11	8
Tonnage and Wharfage Rates	6,973	7,059	6,945	8,293	7,002
Fisheries Royalty..................	2,371	1,422	7	....	....
Proceeds of sale of Naphtha ‡	60	40	21	39	26
Sundries ‡	360	156	84	353	218
TOTAL MISCELLANEOUS COLLECTIONS	84,597	84,306	83,634	83,310	71,213
TOTAL CUSTOMS REVENUE.......£	2,250,170	2,291,551	2,214,356	2,242,700	2,216,375

* For Schedule of Customs Duties for 1890, see page 214. † Collected by Treasury.
‡ Collected by Customs Department and paid direct into the Treasury.

: the Federation Convention held in Sydney in March and , 1891, the possible adoption of a federal Customs tariff was ssed, together with the question of the loss of revenue which t result from the abolition of intercolonial duties. A series bles was compiled at the time, based on the Customs returns ch Colony for the year 1889, showing the amount of duty ted on Australasian produce and on produce not of Austral- origin. These figures, so far as they affect New South s, have been revised for the year 1890, and are given below:—

of which the Goods are the Produce.	Duty Collected on—		
	General Imports.	Intoxicants.	Total Imports for Home Consumption.
ia	£4,342	£1,313	£5,655
sland	111,208	8,331	119,539
Australia	5,975	6,264	12,239
nia	2,574	40	2,614
Zealand	16,216	98	16,314
Total	£140,315	£16,046	£156,361

uring 1890 no goods were received from Western Australia which duty was chargeable. Of the whole sum collected, ,539, or 76·4 per cent., was levied upon imports from Queens- mainly on sugar and spirits.

e duty collected on articles not of Australasian production ted into New South Wales for home consumption amounted g 1890 to £1,722,725, derived from the following sources:—

General imports	£528,231
Intoxicants	932,359
Tobacco	245,145
Opium	16,990
	£1,722,725

om the tables given in other parts of this chapter it will be that the Imports for home consumption during 1890 were d at £17,801,792; of this amount, £13,072,681 represents the value of Free Imports other than bullion, which latter was valued at £493,517; the dutiable goods other than intoxicants and narcotics were valued at £3,140,104, on which the duty paid was £668,546, equivalent to an *ad valorem* duty of 21·3 per cent. If, however, the whole of the General Imports be taken together, omitting only intoxicants, narcotics, and bullion, their value is £16,212,785, and the equivalent *ad valorem* duty about four and one-eighth per cent.

If goods produced in the other Colonies and imported into New South Wales be alone considered, the average *ad valorem* on goods subject to duty is 23·1 per cent., and for all goods other than intoxicants, tobacco, and bullion, 2·77 per cent.

The following figures are designed to illustrate the subject—distinction being drawn between goods the produce of Australasia, and other goods:—

Imports of Australasian Produce, 1890.

Articles.	Gross Imports.	For Home Consumption.	
		Value.	Duty Paid thereon.
	£	£	£
Free, except Coin and Bullion	5,221,506	4,454,931	......
Dutiable, except Intoxicants and Narcotics	667,961	607,813	140,315
Total	5,889,467	5,062,744	140,315
INTOXICANTS AND NARCOTICS—			
Wines, Spirits, Beers, &c.	22,421	21,794	16,046
Tobacco, &c.	......	......	......
Opium	......	......	......
Total	22,421	21,794	16,046
Coin and Bullion	2,620,005	485,304	......
Grand total	8,531,893	5,569,842	156,361

Imports of Extra-Australasian Produce, 1890.

Articles.	Gross Imports.	For Home Consumption.	
		Value.	Duty Paid thereon.
GENERAL IMPORTS.	£	£	£
pt Coin and Bullion	10,100,634	8,617,750	......
except Intoxicants and Nar-	2,782,882	2,532,291	528,231
Total	12,883,516	11,150,041	528,231
ICANTS AND NARCOTICS—			
irits, Beers, &c.	896,907	871,828	932,359
ke.	220,595	166,425	245,145
... ...	37,756	35,443	16,990
Total	1,155,258	1,073,696	1,194,494
Bullion	44,337	8,213	......
Grand total...	14,083,111	12,231,950	1,722,725

s of Australasian and Extra-Australasian Produce, 1890.

Articles.	Gross Imports.	Value.	Duty Paid thereon.
GENERAL IMPORTS.	£	£	£
pt Coin and Bullion	15,322,140	13,072,681	......
except Intoxicants and Nar-	3,450,843	3,140,104	668,546
Total	18,773,983	16,212,785	668,546
ICANTS AND NARCOTICS—			
pirits, Beers, &c.	919,328	893,622	948,405
&c.	220,595	166,425	245,145
... ...	37,756	35,443	16,990
Total	1,177,679	1,095,490	1,210,540
Bullion	2,664,342	493,517	......
Grand total...	22,615,004	17,801,792	1,879,086

FARES AND FREIGHTS.

ng at the extensive passenger traffic and shipping trade of uth Wales, it would naturally be expected that a liberal fares and freights would be in force, and this will be found actually to exist. In many instances, indeed, the intercolonial rates have been extremely low, owing to the keen competition among the various steamship companies. The following figures will give an idea of the average passenger rates during 1889:—

Colonial Fares.

New South Wales Port.—Bateman's Bay, £1 5s. first-class, 12s. 6d. second-class; Bellinger River, £2 and £1; Byron Bay, £2 10s.; Clarence River, £2 and £1; Eden, £1 10s. and 15s.; Gosford, 4s.; Kiama, 7s. 6d. and 4s.; Macleay River, £1 10s. and 15s.; Manning River, £1 10s. and 15s.; Nambucca River, £2 and £1; Newcastle, 6s. 6d. and 3s.; Port Macquarie, £1 10s. and 15s.; Richmond River, £2 5s. and £1 2s. 6d.; Shoalhaven, 15s. and 10s.; Ulladulla, £1 and 10s.; Wollongong, 5s. and 2s. 6d.

Intercolonial Fares.

Australasian Ports.—Adelaide, £3 10s. and £2; Albany (King George's Sound), £9 15s. and £6 10s.; Auckland, £8 and £4; Bowen, £8 and £5; Brisbane, £3 and £1 10s.; Bundaberg, £5 and £2 10s.; Cooktown, £10 10s. and £7; Hobart, £2 and £1; Maryborough, £4 10s. and £2 5s.; Melbourne, £2 5s. and £1 5s.; Mourilyan Harbour, £9 17s. 6d. and £6; Normanton, £16 and £10; Port Darwin, £18 and £9; Port Pirie, £3 10s. and £2; Rockhampton, £6 and £3 10s.; Thursday Island, £9 to £15; Townsville, £8 and £5; Wellington, £8 and £4.

Fares to Europe.

European Ports.—Bremen, £57 10s., £30, and £14; Brindisi, £55 to £65, and £30 to £35; Gibraltar, £55 to £65 and £30 to £37; London, £55 to £70, £30 to £37, and £17 17s.; Marseilles, £55 to £65, £30 to £40, and £20; Venice, £55 to £65, and £30 to £35.

Fares to Eastern Ports.

Eastern Ports.—Aden, £45, £30, and £15; Bombay, £40 and £25; Calcutta, £40 and £25; Colombo, £40 and £25; Hong Kong, £33 and £15; Japan, £41 2s. 6d. and £23 2s. 6d.; Java, £26 and £13; Penang, £42 and £24; Port Moresby, £22 10s. and £14; Shanghai, £39 and £20; Singapore, £40 and £22; Mauritius, £53, £35, and £17; Port Said, £55 to £63, £30 to £34, and £19 8s.; Reunion, £52, £35, and £17 12s.

cific Ports.—San Francisco, £40 and £20; Honolulu, £30 £16; Fiji, £12 10s. and £7 10s.; Noumea, £7 and £4. Fares to Ports in the Pacific.

res by Sailing Vessels are in nearly every instance a matter ivate arrangement between the Captain of the vessel and itending passenger, but the number of such passengers is ming smaller from year to year owing to the great decrease of ser fares. Fares to London are however given as £42 first and £25 second class, and to San Francisco as £30 first and £15 to £20 second class. Fares by Sailing Vessels.

e freights paid for the carriage of wool to London deter-, within certain limits, the freight of most other produce. The nt average cost of carriage of greasy wool to London is $\frac{7}{16}$d. b.; in 1834 the average was somewhat over 3d. Information iling freights is not available for early years, but since 1857, e following figures show, the freights on wool have been very and remarkably steady. The values are in every case for g ships, as the practice of shipping wool by steamers was) means general until very recent years:— Freights on Wool.

Freights on Pressed Greasy Wool per lb.

Year.	Freight.	Year.	Freight.	Year.	Freight.
[illegible]	[illegible]d.	1869	[illegible]d.	1880	[illegible]d.
[illegible]	[illegible]d.	1870	[illegible]d.	1881	[illegible]d.
[illegible]	[illegible]d.	1871	[illegible]d.	1882	[illegible]d.
[illegible]	[illegible]d.	1872	[illegible]d.	1883	[illegible]d.
1861	[illegible]d.	1873	[illegible]d.	1884	[illegible]d.
[illegible]	[illegible]d.	1874	[illegible]d.	1885	[illegible]d.
[illegible]	[illegible]d.	1875	[illegible]d.	1886	[illegible]d.
[illegible]	[illegible]d.	1876	[illegible]d.	1887	[illegible]d.
[illegible]	[illegible]d.	1877	[illegible]d.	1888	[illegible]d.
[illegible]	[illegible]d.	1878	[illegible]d.	1889	[illegible]d.
[illegible]	[illegible]d.	1879	[illegible]d.	1890	$\frac{7}{16}$d.
[illegible]	[illegible]d.				

e following table of freights calls for no particular comment, ices have remained fairly uniform for several years, except slightly affected by temporary causes:— General Freights.

FREIGHTS from Sydney to London per sailing and steam vessels.

Year.	Vessel.	Wool (Greasy).	Tallow.	Copra.	Leather.	Hides.	Preserved Meats.	Measurement Goods.
		per lb.	per ton (20 cwt.)	per ton (20 cwt.)	per ton (20 cwt).	per ton (20 cwt.)	per 40 c. feet.	per 40 c. feet.
1885	Sailing	From $\frac{1}{2}$d. to $\frac{5}{8}$d. Average, $\frac{9}{16}$d.	From 25/- to 40/- Average, 31/-	From 35/- to 40/- Average, 37/6	40/-	From 15/- to 20/- Average, 17/6	25/-	25/-
	Steam	From $\frac{3}{8}$d. to $\frac{1}{2}$d. Average, $\frac{7}{16}$d.	40/-	....	From 40/- to 45/- Average, 42/6	....	35/-	35/-
1886	Sailing	From $\frac{7}{16}$d. to $\frac{5}{8}$d. Average, $\frac{1}{2}$d.	From 20/- to 25/- Average, 23/-	From 25/- to 30/- Average, 28/-	From 30/- to 35/- Average, 33/-	15/-	25/-	25/-
	Steam	From $\frac{3}{8}$d. to $\frac{1}{2}$d. Average, $\frac{3}{8}$d.	30/-	....	From 30/- to 70/- Average, 50/-	17/6	From 30/- to 70/- Average, 44/-	From 30/- to 70/- Average, 44/-
1887	Sailing	From $\frac{5}{16}$d. to $\frac{3}{8}$d. Average, $\frac{3}{8}$d.	From 22/6 to 30/- Average, 26/-	From 25/- to 35/- Average, 30/6	From 30/- to 35/- Average, 33/-	From 15/- to 20/- Average, 16/6	25/-	25/-
	Steam	From $\frac{3}{8}$d. to $\frac{1}{2}$d. Average, $\frac{3}{8}$d.	From 30/- to 45/- Average, 36/6	....	From 40/- to 50/- Average, 45/-	....	....	From 25/- to 45/- Average, 35/-
1888	Sailing	From $\frac{5}{16}$ to $\frac{7}{16}$d. Average, $\frac{3}{8}$d.	From 25/- to 45/- Average, 37/-	From 47/6 to 50/- Average, 49/-	From 30/- to 45/- Average, 36/-	20/-	From 25/- to 30/- Average, 26/6	From 25/- to 30/- Average, 26/-
	Steam	From $\frac{1}{4}$d. to $\frac{3}{8}$d. Average, $\frac{3}{8}$d.	From 30/- to 52/6 Average, 42/6	....	From 35/- to 50/- Average, 42/6	....	30/-	60/-
1889	Sailing	From $\frac{5}{16}$ to $\frac{7}{16}$d. Average, $\frac{3}{8}$d.	From 25/- to 45/- Average, 33/6	From 32/6 to 50/- Average, 36/-	From 27/6 to 45/- Average, 36/6	From 15/- to 20/- Average, 16/-	22/6	From 20/- to 25/- Average, 22/6
	Steam	From $\frac{1}{4}$d. to $\frac{3}{8}$d. Average, $\frac{3}{8}$d.	From 25/- to 50/- Average, 37/6	50/-	From 40/- to 60/- Average, 50/-	....	....	....
1890	Sailing	From $\frac{3}{8}$d. to $\frac{1}{2}$d. Average, $\frac{7}{16}$d.	From 32/6 to 47/6 Average, 35/-	From 32/6 to 47/6 Average, 42/-	From 35/- to 45/- Average, 40/-	From 15/- to 25/- Average, 17/6	From 25/- to 30/- Average, 27/6	From 25/- to 35/- Average, 27/6
	Steam	From $\frac{1}{4}$d. to $\frac{3}{8}$d. Average, $\frac{3}{8}$d.	From 35/- to 50/- Average, 40/-	From 45/- to 50/- Average, 46/-	From 45/- to 60/- Average, 50/-	....	30/-	60/-

PART X.

Stock.

THE rapid settlement of the Colony has, in a great measure, been due to the fitness of its soil, vegetation, and climate, for the successful rearing of the principal species of stock which supply the wants of civilized men, and so largely contribute to the wealth of nations. For many years it was believed that a considerable part of Australia was quite unsuited for stock, and this opinion was fostered by the accounts of the earlier explorers, who reported that the interior of the continent was a vast desert. These apprehensions were soon dispelled, and the apparent difficulties offered to the successful rearing of stock disappeared before the energy of the colonists. One thing particularly favoured the settlers; though the number of native animals was very considerable, comprising chiefly marsupials of little commercial utility, there happily existed no large species of carnivora which could seriously interfere with the increase in the flocks.

Humble beginnings of stock breeding.

The beginnings of pastoral enterprise in the Colony were very humble. The whole stock of the community which accompanied Captain Phillip comprised only 1 bull, 4 cows, 1 calf, 1 stallion, 3 mares, 3 foals, 29 sheep, 12 pigs, and a few goats; and although the whole of the present flocks and herds of Australasia have not sprung from these animals alone, it will be seen on how small a scale the business of stock-raising was first attempted. No systematic record of the arrival of stock seems to have been kept in the early days of settlement, but it appears that in the period between Governor Phillip's landing and the year 1800 there were some slight importations, chiefly of sheep from India. In 1803 the number of sheep in the Colony was set down at 10,157. In 1825, thirty-seven years after the establishment of the Colony, there were in New South Wales 6,142 horses, 134,519 cattle, 237,622 sheep, and 39,006 pigs. In 1842 there were 56,585 horses, 897,219 cattle, 4,804,946 sheep, and 46,086 pigs. As soon as the produce of stock began to exceed the demand for food, the increase in number became very rapid, and, at the separation of Victoria, the stock of the Colony numbered 13,059,324 sheep, 1,738,965 cattle, 132,437 horses, and 61,631 pigs.

Separation of Victoria.

The severance of Victoria, then the fairest province of the mother Colony, involved a loss of 6,589,923 sheep, 390,923 cattle, 20,086 horses, and 7,372 pigs; so that in 1851 the flocks of New South Wales numbered 6,469,401 sheep, 1,348,042 cattle, 112,351 horses, and 54,259 pigs. After the separation of Queensland the numbers of each kind of live stock within the existing boundaries of the Colony were 6,119,163 sheep, 2,408,586 cattle, 251,497 horses, and 180,662 pigs; in the following year the numbers showed a considerable decline, both from the effects of the season, and from the large demand which arose for stock for the stations of the new Colony; and in 1861 the figures were, 5,615,054 sheep, 2,271,923 cattle, 233,220 horses, and 146,091 pigs. From the numbers just given, the sheep had, at the end of 1890, increased to 55,986,431, the cattle had declined to 1,909,009, the horses had increased to 444,163, and the pigs to 283,061.

Separation of Queensland.

SHEEP.

Land suited for pastoral pursuits.

The suitability of the land discovered in New South Wales for pastoral pursuits was undoubtedly the means of leading the infant Colony to take its first step on the path of commercial progress; and it is not a little surprising at this distance of time how steadily some of the settlers, in the face of the almost insurmountable difficulty of transport which existed a century ago, availed themselves of the opportunities at their disposal. The importation of valuable specimens of sheep from England or the Cape of Good Hope, prior to the introduction of steam, was at all times attended with great risk, and it frequently happened that many of these costly animals died during the tedious voyage. These enterprises were, however, on the whole successful, and thus the flocks and herds of the colonists surely, if at first slowly, increased and multiplied.

By the year 1795, Captain Macarthur, one of the first promoters of sheep-breeding in New South Wales, had accumulated a flock of 1,000, which were held in great estimation, and gradually increased in value, until, as recorded by an entry in his journal ten years later, the market price of a fat wether had risen to £5. Not satisfied with the natural increase of his flocks, Macarthur sought to improve the quality of his fleeces, by which means he could see opening before him the promise of great wealth, and the prospect of establishing important commercial relations with Great Britain. With these ends in view, he procured from the Cape of Good Hope, at great cost and trouble, a number of superior rams and ewes. A happy circumstance occurred which favoured his enterprise; for he had the good fortune to secure possession of three rams and five ewes of very fine Spanish breed, which had been presented by the King of Spain to the Dutch Government. These animals, out of a total of twenty-nine purchased at the Cape, arrived in Sydney in 1797, and were disposed of to various breeders. With the exception of Macarthur, however, those who had secured sheep of the superior breed made no attempt to follow up the advantage, being probably amply satisfied with the larger gains from the sale of an increased number of animals. Macarthur, on the other hand, thought little of present profits, and still less of breeding entirely for human consumption. He attentively watched the results of crossing his imported rams with the old stock, and by systematically selecting the finer ewes which were the offspring for further mingling with the sires, he gradually improved the strain, and in a few years obtained fleeces of very fine texture which met with the ready appreciation of English manufacturers.

Captain Macarthur promotes wool-growing.

Improvement of the flocks.

Prior to the present century the production of the finest wool had been confined chiefly to Spain, and woollen manufactures were necessarily carried on in England upon a somewhat limited scale, which was not likely to improve in face of certain restrictions the operatives endeavoured to place upon their em-

Spain formerly chief wool-grower.

ployers. These men, in support of their contention that the woollen trade could not be expanded, on account of the limited supply of the raw material, argued that fine wool was obtainable only in Spain; and it was at this favourable period that Macarthur arrived in England with specimens of the wool obtained from his finest sheep, conclusively proving the capabilities of Australia as a wool-producing country. In this way he opened up a small trade with English manufacturers, which, as Australasian wool rose in public estimation, gradually increased until it reached its present enormous dimensions. During his visit to England, Macarthur purchased an additional stock of ten rams and ewes of the noted Spanish breed, nearly equal in quality to those which in 1797 he had procured from the Cape of Good Hope. That these animals were the finest obtainable in Europe may be gathered from the fact they also had formed portion of a present from the King of Spain to George III. Thus did Macarthur, after his return to New South Wales, patiently continue for many years the process of selection, with such success, that in 1858, when his flock was finally dispersed, it was estimated that his superior ewes numbered fully 1,000. Victoria secured a considerable portion of Macarthur's flock, and the process of breeding proceeded simultaneously in that and other adjacent Colonies.

Trade opened up with Great Britain.

Importation of sheep.

Although the increase in the numbers of the finer sheep was satisfactory, the importation of superior stock was not discontinued, and the stock of the Colonies was augmented in 1823 and 1825 by the further introduction of Spanish sheep. Sheep-breeding was about this period commenced in the Mudgee district, and the climate of that region has produced a still more favourable result upon the quality of the fleeces than any other part of the Colony, and it is thence that the finest merinos are now procured. As might have been anticipated, the climate of Australia has in some respects changed the character of the Spanish fleece. The wool has become softer and more elastic, and while having diminished in density it has increased in length, so that the weight of the

Texture of wool.

...ce has only slightly altered. The quality of the wool has thus ... the whole improved under the beneficial influence of the climate, ...d if no further enhancement in its value can be reasonably hoped ..., there is at least every reason to believe that Australasian wool ...ll maintain its present high standard of excellence.

Number of sheep in New South Wales.

The following table, showing the numbers at the close of each ...ar since the separation of Queensland, illustrates the progress ...sheep-breeding :—

Progress of Sheep-breeding.

Year.	Number.	Year.	Number.	Year.	Number.
1860	6,119,163	1871	16,278,697	1881	36,591,946
1861	5,615,054	1872	17,566,048	1882	36,114,814
1862	6,145,651	1873	18,990,595	1883	37,915,510
1863	7,790,969	1874	22,797,416	1884	31,660,321
1864	8,271,520	1875	25,353,924	1885	37,820,906
1865	8,132,511	1876	25,269,755	1886	39,169,304
1866	11,562,155	1877	21,521,662	1887	46,965,152
1867	13,909,574	1878	25,479,484	1888	46,503,469
1868	15,080,625	1879	30,062,910	1889	50,106,768
1869	14,989,923	1880	35,398,121	1890	55,986,431
1870	16,308,585				

Annual Increase.

The ratio of annual increase for the whole period is 7·7 per cent. ...vided into three periods the ratios are—

1860–70 annual increase 10·3 per cent.
1870–80 „ „ 8·1 „
1880–90 „ „ 4·7 „

Natural law of increase.

The operation of the natural law regulating the increase of ...ecies, viz.—that the ratio of increase is inversely as the increase ... the number of individuals—is observable in these figures, and ... tendency of the rate of increase to decline as the numbers ...vance is clear enough.

Causes modifying rate of increase.

It is not possible to estimate the actual loss of sheep from drought and failure of grass, but an approximation can be made as to the number of stock in the Colony less than would have been the case had the seasons all been propitious. Thus the following table shows the expected increase of sheep after all causes of natural decrease are allowed for, the actual increase or decrease during each year, and the loss which may be attributable to the season. Under this last head are included not only the sheep which actually died, but also the expected increase from lambing which was not realized. Out of the seventeen years over which the information extends eight years only showed no loss, or loss so slight as to be inappreciable. On the other hand, five seasons of opposite character were experienced in which not only was there no increase, but an actual decrease, on the numbers of the previous year, ranging from 84,000 in 1876 to 6,255,000 in 1884. The loss on the year last named reached the enormous total of 8,138,000, a number larger even than the total of the flocks in some of the colonies of the group.

Effect of bad seasons.

Loss of Sheep through Drought and kindred causes.

Year.	Expected increase, allowing for all causes of natural decrease.	Actual increase or decrease.	Loss through Seasons.
1874	3,807,000	3,807,000	†
1875	2,556,000	2,556,000	†
1876	1,915,000	* 84,000	1,999,000
1877	1,802,000	* 3,748,000	5,550,000
1878	3,958,000	3,958,000	†
1879	4,583,000	4,583,000	†
1880	5,335,000	5,335 000	†
1881	2,947,000	1,194,000	1,753,000
1882	1,797,000	* 477,000	2,274,000
1883	3,193,000	1,801,000	1,392,000
1884	1,883,000	* 6,255,000	8,138,000
1885	6,160,000	6,160,000	†
1886	3,409,000	1,348,000	2,061,000
1887	7,796,000	7,796,000	†
1888	2,435,000	* 462,000	2,897,000
1889	5,339,000	3,603,000	1,736,000
1890	5,880,000	5,880,000	†

* Decrease during the year. † No loss, or, if any, very slight.

After allowing for the causes which naturally impede the increase of the flocks of the Colony, the demands of the slaughter-yard, the requirements of the neighbouring colonies, and the deaths occurring from other causes than drought, it will be found that the rate of increase in any year should be about 20 per cent., so that the flocks of the Colony would increase two-fold in about four years. Actual experience shows that such rate of increase has only approached once since the year 1861. During the period of five years from 1861 to 1866 there was a two-fold increase; the flocks of the Colony were again doubled in the eight years from 1866 to 1874 and in the thirteen years from 1874 to 1887. How many sheep could be sustained by the Colony under a system of artificial feeding and watering may hereafter become a question of national interest, but it is abundantly plain that even with a continuation of fair seasons it would be impossible, under the present mode of depasturing stock, for the Colony to support for any number of years an increase of sheep similar to the record of 1887, as in four years' time the flocks would number 100,000,000, a total nearly as large as that now found in all the colonies. Requirements of other colonies check increase.

The export and import of sheep during the ten years, 1881–1890, is shown in the following table :— Export and import of sheep.

Year.	Exported.	Imported.	Year.	Exported.	Imported.
1881	1,068,362	198,329	1886	1,247,514	288,225
1882	856,190	207,538	1887	1,218,504	864,313
1883	1,006,227	205,558	1888	2,327,406	254,018
1884	1,942,204	404,371	1889	1,217,325	832,565
1885	1,237,155	1,134,439	1890	2,987,902	598,077

The local demand for sheep for consumption was, until recent years, so small compared with the supply as not to appreciably Local demand formerly small.

affect the increase of the flocks of the Colony. Such, however, is not now the case, and the annual demand for slaughtering purposes is about 6 per cent. of the number of sheep depastured, and is, therefore, almost equal to half the annual cast. The question of the supply of sheep in the light of the possible demands of the future has been dealt with in previous issues of this work, and it will be seen that, enormous as are the numbers of stock in this and the neighbouring colonies, every year reduces the margin between the supply and demand.

Stock-carrying capacity of Colony.

The stock-carrying capabilities of the Colony are very difficult to estimate, as by far the greater portion of the country is yet in its natural state. Improvements, such as a better system of water conservation and irrigation, an intelligent extension of the salt-bush, cotton-bush, and other drought-resisting shrubs and natural grasses, and the cultivation of artificial fodder, are gradually being effected, and will indefinitely extend the capacity of the Colony for supporting stock of all descriptions.

Number of sheep in each colony.

The following table gives the number of sheep in the Australasian colonies, and shows the proportion owned by each colony:—

Colony.	No. of Sheep.	Proportion of each Colony to total Australasia.
New South Wales	55,986,431	49·1
Victoria	12,736,143	11·1
Queensland	18,007,234	15·8
South Australia	7,004,642	6·1
Western Australia	2,524,913	2·2
Tasmania	1,619,256	1·4
New Zealand	16,200,358	14·3
Total	114,078,977	100·00

It will be seen that New South Wales stands first of all the onies as a sheep-breeding country, both as regards the number its flocks, and the number of sheep depastured per unit of area. t whilst Victoria has nearly reached the limit of its natural abilities in this particular direction, a considerable proportion its area being now devoted to agriculture, New South Wales has ; yet approached these limits. In Queensland, as in South istralia, sheep-breeding does not absorb the attention of pastoral- i to the same extent that it does in New South Wales. The mer colony is more adapted to the breeding of cattle; whilst in southern and more settled districts of South Australia greater ention is paid to the cultivation of cereals, its northern terri- y, like that of Queensland, being more adapted by nature to breeding of cattle and horses. Western Australia is at present the early stage of its colonisation; much of its area is still known, and it is therefore impossible to estimate its future as heep-breeding country. It may, however, be surmised that the ithern portion of its immense territory will, in time to come, stocked with sheep, whilst the northern portion will probably found more suitable for the breeding of cattle and horses, on ount of its resemblance to portions of Queensland and the rthern territory of South Australia situated under the same itude. It was thought at one time that cattle-breeding would upy a position in New South Wales equal to that of sheep- eding, but experience has shown that the general climatic iditions are more favourable to sheep than to cattle, and the lony is probably destined to remain, as it now is, the great eep-breeding centre of Australia.

Colony stands first as sheep-breeder.

Certain colonies adapted for cattle.

The different degrees of success attending sheep farming in ferent parts of the country has long since directed attention to

Country not all fitted for sheep.

the fact that each part of Australia is not equally fitted for the production of fine wools. New South Wales may be divided climatically into four zones:—(1) The coast country extending from the seaboard to the main range, the breadth of which varies from 20 to 100 miles; (2) the table-land districts on the summit of the range; (3) the upper part of the western slopes; and (4) the interior, or "salt-bush country."

Seaboard not suited to merino.

The climate of the eastern seaboard for a considerable distance inland is too moist, and a large portion of it too poor, for the adequate sustenance of merinos, but it is probable that the coarser breeds of sheep would not deteriorate through the limited food supply and the rugged nature of the country. On the Hunter and other northern rivers, and in the southern coast districts, where the soil is very rich, dairy-farming and agriculture are the leading, and, no doubt, the most profitable, industries. Sheep-breeding is carried on to some extent in the regions towards the summit of the coast range; but, as in the case of the country near the sea, the soil as a rule is unfavourable to sheep. On crossing the coast range, however, the contrast between the aspect of the country just entered, and that left behind, is very striking. Here the grazing and wool-growing capabilities are at once apparent, and further to the westward a still greater improvement is visible.

Riverine country.

In the abundant pastures of the Riverine districts the wool is less fine than in the country immediately west of the table-lands, but the fleeces are generally sound and heavy. Further in the salt-bush country the wool suffers both in the weight of the fleece and in its quality; but the country is fattening, and the stock are generally more healthy than those nearer the sea. In the country on the further side of the Darling the great summer heat is adverse to the production of heavy fleeces; but even here a fair class of wool is produced, as the stock-owners are constantly introducing fresh blood, and so counteracting the tendency towards the degeneration of the breed of sheep which might otherwise ensue.

The importation of stud sheep from foreign countries, notably France, Germany, and America, which was continued for many years after the superfine quality of Australian wool had been established in the markets of the world, practically ceased even before importation was legally prohibited; for it had become apparent that the fleece, instead of showing signs of deterioration under the influence of the climate, had, on the whole, a tendency to improve. The introduction of sheep and cattle into New South Wales was forbidden for many years, owing entirely to the fear of the stock-owners that their herds would be contaminated by scab and other diseases prevalent in European flocks; but these restrictions were removed at the beginning of the year 1888, and 216 pure bred sheep, comprising 178 American merino, 23 German merino, and 16 English stud sheep arrived in 1890, in addition to 7,821 stud sheep from other parts of Australia. Importation of stud sheep.

It is now generally admitted that as far as the fleece is concerned the Australian merino has little to gain by any further admixture of European or American blood, but it is equally admitted that there is room for improvement in the physique of the animal. To produce a larger carcase, without interfering with the quality of the fleece, many experiments have been made, but without much success, and it has been found that the crossing of noted breeds of English rams with Australian ewes has invariably resulted, after a generation or two, in a deterioration of the merino. The breeding of sheep for consumption, and for the sake of the wool, has, therefore, developed naturally into two distinct fields of industry. It may here be mentioned that the carcass of the ordinary Australian merino when dressed averages about 46½ lb., whereas dressed carcases of the Lincoln or Leicester breed would average 57 to 60 lb. Superiority of Australian wool.

The various breeds of sheep in the Colony are the Merino, Lincoln, Leicester, Downs, and Romney Marsh, and crosses of Breeds of sheep.

the long-woolled breeds, principally with the merino. In 1890–91 the respective numbers of merino and long-woolled sheep and cross-breeds, stood thus :—

Merino	54,664,264
Long-woolled sheep	530,041
Cross-breeds	792,126
Total	55,986,431

Subdivided as per following table :—

MERINO.

Combing.

Sheep.	Rams.	Ewes.	Wethers.	Lambs.	Total.	
			Superfine.			
Pure and stud	61,867	776,751	270,223	406,913	1,505,754	
Ordinary	96,650	2,415,693	1,674,301	1,504,344	5,690,988	
						7,196,742
			Medium.			
Pure and stud	103,686	1,427,415	484,937	876,227	2,892,265	
Ordinary	178,225	6,959,915	3,503,608	4,237,840	14,879,588	
						17,771,853
			Strong.			
Pure and stud	51,106	1,192,789	571,934	716,722	2,532,551	
Ordinary	115,823	5,077,386	3,323,421	3,116,202	11,632,832	
						14,165,383
Total, *Combing*						39,133,978

Clothing.

Sheep.	Rams.	Ewes.	Wethers.	Lambs.	Total.	
			Superfine.			
Pure and stud	17,994	322,780	207,070	212,384	760,228	
Ordinary	33,646	848,171	626,731	507,601	2,016,149	
						2,776,377
			Medium.			
Pure and stud	34,423	534,942	253,325	349,861	1,172,551	
Ordinary	79,557	3,407,233	1,682,761	1,860,367	7,029,918	
						8,202,469
			Strong.			
Pure and stud	27,112	677,173	307,708	449,650	1,461,643	
Ordinary	45,247	1,273,371	1,008,205	767,974	3,089,797	
						4,551,440
Total, *Clothing*						15,530,286
Total number of MERINO SHEEP						54,664,264

LONG-WOOLLED SHEEP.

...p.	Rams.	Ewes.	Wethers.	Lambs.	Total.	
			Lincoln.			
...d stud	5,274	41,265	34,835	30,746	112,120	
...y	6,799	76,113	62,492	41,278	186,682	
Total					....	298,802
			Leicester.			
...d stud	2,800	25,880	19,401	17,043	65,124	
...y	5,003	42,501	50,415	30,345	128,264	
Total					....	195,388
			Downs.			
...d stud	881	5,260	4,424	3,905	14,470	
...y	769	8,778	7,119	6,483	23,149	
Total					....	37,619
			Romney Marsh.			
...d stud	15	27	......	30	72	
...y	39	21	......	40	160	
Total					....	232
Total number, LONG-WOOLLED SHEEP						530,041
			CROSSES—Long-woolled with Merino principally.			
....	4,982	269,916	332,278	184,950	792,126	
						792,126
Grand total						55,986,431

...sexes and classes of sheep were estimated as follows:—

Rams	871,898
Ewes	25,373,440
Wethers	14,420,188
Lambs	15,320,905
	55,986,431

...climate of New South Wales admits of stock of all kinds ...left in the open air, and there is no necessity for housing ...during the winter months. The sheep are either kept in

No necessity for housing stock.

paddocks or under the care of shepherds, though on some stations they are both shepherded and paddocked. During 1890 there were :—

Paddocked	54,188,395
Shepherded........................	1,181,127
Paddocked and shepherded............	616,909
	55,986,431

Paddocking system.

The advantages of the paddocking system have been stated as follows:—The country will carry one-third more sheep ; the wool will be longer and sounder, and the fleece as a whole one-third better ; the feed will be cleaner and less liable to grass-seed ; the lambing on the average of years will be better ; the sheep will increase in size, they will live longer and continue longer profitable ; they will be freer from foot-rot and other diseases ; the expense of working the station will be less than a quarter of what it would be if the sheep were shepherded ; and finally, the owner will be able to devote the principal part of his time to improving his sheep, instead of spending it in attempting to manage a number of shepherds and hut-keepers.

Percentage of lambing.

The following table shows the percentage of lambing under both systems for the last sixteen years :—

Year.	Paddocked.	Shepherded.	Total.	Year.	Paddocked.	Shepherded.	Total.
1875	73	68	72	1883	64	57	63
1876	61	54	60	1884	55	51	55
1877	56	50	55	1885	79	64	78
1878	83	74	82	1886	66	62	66
1879	78	72	77	1887	78	69	78
1880	81	72	80	1888	55	40	55
1881	63	49	62	1889	64	54	64
1882	59	51	58	1890	71	65	71

Lambs marked.

The number of ewes at the close of 1889 was 23,647,106 ; but allowing for deaths from natural causes, slaughtering, and export, the number at the time of lambing was probably not more than 22,000,000. A percentage of 71, as estimated by the Chief Inspector of Stock, would give a total of 15,928,200 lambs, while the number marked, as shown by the census returns, was 4,707,272. When due allowance is made for deaths between the ime of lambing and of marking, it will be found that the estimate f the Chief Inspector is very accurate.

The proportion of sheep shepherded to those paddocked is yearly rowing less. In 1880 one-tenth of the lambs born were from hepherded ewes; in 1885 the proportion was one-twentieth; and n 1890 one-sixtieth of the whole number.

Number of sheep at census of 1891.

At the census taken on April 5, 1891, the number of sheep in he Colony was found to be 54,113,158. These figures confirm he accuracy of the returns collected in December, 1890, by the tock Department, the decrease being due to the number of sheep laughtered for food consumption, and to the excess of animals xported over those imported during the period.

WOOL.

The wool clip

The amount of wool, the production of New South Wales, xported during the twelve years from 1879 to 1890 is shown elow, the quantities representing the weight of clip if the sheep rere shorn in the grease:—

Year.	Amount of Wool.	Year.	Amount of Wool.
	lb.		lb.
1879	149,293,186	1885	193,775,478
1880	181,766,451	1886	203,013,090
1881	161,740,362	1887	256,072,430
1882	171,019,915	1888	269,730,000
1883	216,681,214	1889	299,012,215
1884	201,899,941	1890	269,686,034

As the season for exporting wool does not wholly fall within he calendar year, the quantities of wool stated in the foregoing able for any year refer partly to that year, and partly to the revious one. The following table shows the total number of heep shorn, and distinguishes those whose fleece was washed pre-ious to shearing. It will be observed that there has been a arked tendency to shear in grease, owing no doubt to the fact that freights are now much lower than formerly. Besides, the price obtained for washed wool in excess of greasy is not commensurate with the cost of washing.

Number of Sheep shorn.

	Sheep.				Lambs.	
Year.	In Grease.	H.-W. and Spout.	Creek-washed.	Scoured.	In Grease.	Washed.
1880	25,298,211	1,015,556	6,164,859	2,660,141	Not reco	rded.
1881	29,485,675	398,800	2,415,714	739,592	3,129,995	155,939
1882	29,505,143	273,600	1,780,984	323,900	3,814,788	102,300
1883	30,075,145	317,375	2,156,874	149,468	4,833,437	83,241
1884	24,110,459	306,908	801,408	307,950	3,010,459	80,990
1885	28,324,595	38,000	642,424	267,250	4,113,383	42,584
1886	29,446,157	36,645	494,544	965,874	5,535,350	62,100
1887	31,082,201	90,000	647,945	554,687	8,135,458	123,745
1888	35,426,832	....	416,779	875,280	6,053,509	23,756
1889	36,553,856	80,000	475,254	1,446,105	6,790,889	74,698
1890	40,935,736	....	1,271,712	580,794	9,285,871	33,521

Weight of fleece

The average weight of fleece obtained since 1880 is given in the table herewith. The heavy fleece realized in late years from hot water and spout-washed sheep arose probably from the circumstance that the sheep so treated were few in number, and of a finer class than ordinary.

Average Weight of Fleeces.

	Sheep.				Lambs.	
Year.	In Grease.	H.-W. and Spout.	Creek-washed.	Scoured.	In Grease.	Washed.
	lb. oz.	lb. oz.	lb. oz.	lb. oz.	lb. oz.	lb. oz.
1880	5 7	2 14	3 3¾	2 9½	Not reco	rded.
1881	5 0	2 12¼	2 12½	2 8½	2 1	1 8 1/16
1882	5 0	3 0	2 14	2 9½	1 14½	1 4½
1883	5 2	3 0	3 0	2 12	1 14	1 6
1884	5 0	3 3	2 15	2 14	1 13	1 6
1885	5 7½	3 4	3 2	3 0	1 12	1 8
1886	5 5½	3 6	3 0½	2 14	1 9½	1 3½
1887	5 9	3 12	3 1½	2 14	1 12½	1 5
1888	5 6½	....	3 1½	2 9½	1 11	1 7
1889	5 13½	4 2	3 3	2 14	1 11½	1 9
1890	5 11¾	....	3 2	3 4½	1 14¼	1 7½

Much of the wool produced in New South Wales is sent to Melbourne and Adelaide for shipment to Europe, as will be seen from the following table. The weights given are on the assumption that all the wool was shipped in the grease :— Wool sent to other Colonies.

Quantity of New South Wales Wool Exported.

Year.	N.S. Wales ports.	Victorian ports.	S. Australian ports.	Queensland ports.	Total.
	lb.	lb.	lb.	lb.	lb.
1877	65,024,631	54,196,363	2,281,048	650,559	122,152,601
1878	68,949,633	55,496,732	16,785,661	328,114	141,560,140
1879	81,629,754	56,604,967	10,472,908	585,557	149,293,186
1880	100,506,949	65,892,226	11,927,018	440,258	178,766,451
1881	97,049,455	58,568,909	5,673,787	448,211	161,740,362
1882	96,927,768	52,259,856	21,257,679	574,612	171,019,915
1883	146,450,042	53,374,727	16,129,452	726,993	216,681,214
1884	133,570,339	46,239,608	21,658,427	431,567	201,899,941
1885	138,581,706	46,206,250	8,583,408	404,114	193,775,478
1886	128,299,245	50,229,330	24,170,392	314,123	203,013,090
1887	171,396,329	61,288,355	23,267,181	120,565	256,072,430
1888	201,630,000	61,541,000	6,540,000	28,000	269,739,000
1889	194,438,113	77,601,605	26,845,693	126,804	299,012,215
1890	178,055,996	73,227,045	18,347,889	55,104	269,686,034

The proportion of the total clip reaching New South Wales ports compared with what was despatched by way of Melbourne, Adelaide, and Brisbane was :—

Year.	Percentage shipped from New South Wales ports.	Percentage shipped from other ports.
1877	53·23	46·77
1878	48·71	51·29
1879	54·67	45·33
1880	56·22	43·78
1881	60·00	40·00
1882	56·67	43·33
1883	67·59	32·41
1884	66·15	33·85
1885	71·52	28·48
1886	63·14	36·86
1887	66·90	33·10
1888	74·75	25·25
1889	65·03	34·97
1890	66·02	33·98

Wool is put up at the stations in packs which weigh from 10 lb. to 12 lb. each. The bales are usually 4 ft. 6 in. or 5 ft. 3 in. in Weight and size of bales.

length, and 2 ft. 2 in. in breadth and depth, and weigh when packed about 450 lb. Before being shipped they are, however, "dumped" in a hydraulic press, and thus reduced to less than half their original length.

VALUE OF THE WOOL CLIP.

Wool the most important export.

The wool clip of Australasia is its most important item of production, and it may be said that the prosperity of the colonies in a large measure depends upon the state of the wool market.

The following table summarises the state of the export trade of New South Wales wool during the period 1860–1890, and illustrates the growth of that important industry during thirty-one years; whilst, at the same time, the fluctuations in the value of the clip may be easily followed. The weights given represent the actual exports, washed and greasy wool being taken together: —

Weight and Value of Wool Exported.

Year.	Quantity.	Value.	Year.	Quantity.	Value.
	lb.	£		lb.	£
1860	14,962,362	1,454,289	1876	100,736,380	5,565,173
1861	18,171,209	1,768,978	1877	102,150,246	5,256,088
1862	20,988,393	1,801,186	1878	111,833,017	5,723,316
1863	15,842,520	1,316,520	1879	123,710,450	6,491,198
1864	25,827,917	2,294,615	1880	154,871,832	8,040,625
1865	29,858,791	2,283,560	1881	139,601,506	7,149,787
1866	36,980,685	2,830,348	1882	146,221,182	7,433,091
1867	27,327,452	2,125,737	1883	188,161,710	9,598,761
1868	27,067,256	1,960,360	1884	173,986,303	8,953,100
1869	51,269,672	3,162,522	1885	168,151,659	7,246,642
1870	47,440,610	2,741,141	1886	173,985,640	7,028,596
1871	65,611,953	4,748,160	1887	216,450,342	8,911,155
1872	50,233,453	3,342,900	1888	235,848,944	9,089,776
1873	62,998,692	3,936,408	1889	261,853,484	10,620,636
1874	75,156,924	5,010,125	1890	236,322,828	8,991,396
1875	87,534,280	5,651,643			

Effect of price of wool on national prosperity.

An examination of the preceding figures at once shows how greatly the fluctuations in the value of the staple article of export affect the national prosperity. The exports for the years 1884 and 1886, for instance, which may be taken as practically equal in quantity, represented a value of £8,953,100 in the former year, whilst in the latter year the value was reduced to £7,028,596. In this particular case the figures exhibit a double loss—in the quantity, and in the value of the produce exported. In 1884 the export per capita was equivalent to 242·33 lb. of wool weighed in the grease. Had the quantity of wool exported in 1886 been in proportion to the increased population, the figures would have stood at 234,928,000 lb., instead of 203,013,000 lb. actually exported. Thus the loss suffered in quantity amounts to 31,915,000 lb. The actual difference in value of the two clips against 1886 amounts to £1,924,504; but if to this sum be added the value of the quantity which the Colony failed to export in that year, it will be found that the proceeds of the export of wool in 1886 were actually less by £3,129,445 than would have been realised had the prices and yield of 1884 been maintained. Again, comparing 1883 with 1889, there was a difference in quantity in favour of the latter year of 82,331,000 lb. of wool weighed in the grease, and had the prices of 1883 been obtained the value of the 1889 clip would have exceeded that of the former year by £3,647,184, whereas the excess was only £1,021,875. The transactions of 1889, though much more satisfactory than those of the preceding year, as regards quantity of clip, compare very unfavourably with 1883 in respect to the average price obtained. The general strike of 1890, so frequently alluded to in these pages, had a very marked effect on the wool industry. In some cases the sheep remained unshorn until long after the usual time, and in many others the wool did not leave the stations until after the close of the year, so that from these causes the clip of 1890, judged by the weight exported, was apparently less than that of the previous year, though the number of stock depastured was larger. Such being the case, it would be idle to institute any comparison between 1890 and former years, based on quantity of wool exported.

Fluctuation in value.

The preceding table also shows that, although during the period under examination the value of wool has greatly fluctuated from one year to another, the tendency to a settled diminution of price is unfortunately too clearly discernible. In order to further illustrate the fluctuations in the value of this staple in the London market during the last ten years, the classification into scoured and greasy wool has been adhered to, and the following table will give an accurate idea of the average value realised for these two classes of wool during the last period of ten years. The values given were those ruling at the five principal sales of each year.

Average Value per lb. of New South Wales Merino Wool in the London Market.

Sales.	1881.		1882.		1883.		1884.		1885.	
	Scoured.	Greasy.	Scoured.	Greasy.	Scoured.	Greasy.	Scoured.	Greasy.	Scoured.	Greasy.
	d.	d.	d.	d.	d.	d.	d.	d.	d.	d.
1st Series	18	11	18½	11	18	10	16½	9½	16	9
2nd ,, ...	18½	11½	19	11	18	10	16½	9½	15½	8½
3rd ,, ...	18½	11½	19	10½	17	9½	16½	9½	14½	7½
4th ,, ...	18	11	18½	10½	17½	9½	17	10	13½	8
5th ,, ...	18½	11	18½	10½	17½	10	16½	9½	13½	8

Sales.	1886.		1887.		1888.		1889.		1890.	
	Scoured.	Greasy.	Scoured.	Greasy.	Scoured.	Greasy.	Scoured.	Greasy.	Scoured.	Greasy.
	d.	d.	d.	d.	d.	d.	d.	d.	d.	d.
1st Series	13	7½	16	9¾	14	8	15½	8½	16	9½
2nd ,, ...	12	6½	15½	9¼	15	8½	16	9	15	8⅝
3rd ,, ...	14½	8½	15¼	9	16	8½	16½	9½	14	8¼
4th ,, ...	16½	10	14¾	8½	17½	9	17	10	16	9¼
5th ,, ...	14	8½	14¾	8¼	17½	9½	17¾	10½	14½	8½

During the period covered by the foregoing table scoured Sydney-shipped wool fluctuated between a maximum of 18½d. per lb. and a minimum of 12d.; and greasy wool realized from 6½d. to 14d. The maximum prices for both descriptions of wool were realized during 1882, when the sales opened at 18½d. and 11d. per lb. respectively. Prices were fairly well maintained till 1883, but they began to decline rapidly until the lowest market was reached in the early part of 1886, when scoured wool realized as little as 12d., and greasy 6½d. per lb. Since 1886 there has been a much better market for all kinds of wool, the average price of unwashed ranging between 8¼d. and 9¾d. in 1887, and 8½d. and 9¼d. in 1888. The sales in the early part of 1890 also showed an upward movement, the quotations at the close of June being 10d. per lb. for greasy, and 17d. for washed, wool, a very material advance on the figure of four years previously. As will be seen from the preceding table, these prices were not maintained to the end of the year, and although the first sales of 1891 showed a slight improvement, the June prices dropped again to the level of those of 1890. The state of the wool market may be pronounced satisfactory, when all the circumstances of the trade are taken into consideration, though a return to the extremely prosperous years of 1871 to 1875, when scoured Sydney-shipped wool obtained as much as 26½d., and greasy wool 15d. per lb., is very doubtful. With the present markets, however, there is no cause to view unfavourably the further extension of the production of wool in these colonies. In the ancient seats of wool growing, production is now stationary, and in some of the areas recently devoted to this industry, many causes, both climatic and otherwise, are likely to offer serious checks to its extension, while population and the consequent demand for wool is everywhere increasing. Nevertheless, it seems certain that unless fresh avenues are open to the wool industry in those countries where its use is comparatively unknown, it would be hopeless to expect a marked rise in the value of the article. The establishment of a market for Australian wool among the teeming populations of China and

Maximum price obtained in 1882.

Fluctuation of prices of wool.

China and Japan as a market for wool.

Japan, where the nature of the climate itself points out the value of wool as an article of clothing, is an object towards which the intelligent glance of the statesmen of Australia might well be directed.

Combing and clothing wool.

It is a moot question as to whether the climate of New South Wales is more adapted to the production of a combing than a clothing wool. Although the former is looked upon with most favour by wool growers, it is generally recognised that there are very large tracts of country, especially where the salt-bush predominates, on which it is difficult to raise a good combing wool, and where it will probably be found more profitable by wool growers to give greater attention to the cultivation of the clothing variety.

Coarse-woolled sheep.

The breeding of coarse-woolled sheep, for the metropolitan market, is confined chiefly to the districts along the coast. The stock raised for this purpose are principally of the Leicester and Lincoln breeds, the latter being perhaps the greater favourite as a producer of fat lambs. There is no doubt but that, cultivated solely as an article of food, the coarse-woolled sheep is quite as profitable as the merino.

Wool clip of Australasia.

The quantity and value of wool, the produce of each of the various colonies of Australasia, exported during the year 1890, will be found hereunder:—

Colony.	Quantity—Wool in Grease.	Value.
	lb.	£
New South Wales	269,686,034	8,991,396
Victoria	61,479,872	2,743,364
Queensland	64,996,642	2,524,742
South Australia	42,655,311	1,358,725
Western Australia	6,969,380	261,352
Tasmania	8,984,281	419,173
New Zealand	118,762,056	4,150,599
Total	573,533,576	20,449,351

The estimated value of the wool grown in each colony may appear anomalous, when the weight of the clip only is considered; it must be borne in mind, however, in comparing the weight and value of this staple, that there is a wide margin of difference in the average value of the wool grown in one colony and that grown in another. Value of clip.

The quantity of wool consumed by the manufacturing nations of the world amounted in 1889 to 2,040,000,000 lb. weighed in the grease. Of this quantity 913,000,000 lb., or less than half, was grown in the various countries engaged in manufacturing, and of the balance 605,000,000 lb., or about 53·7 per cent., was Australasian. The consumption of wool was thus distributed:— Consumption of wool.

	Home production.	Imports.	Total consumption.
	lb.	lb.	lb.
United Kingdom	133,000,000	337,000,000	470,000,000
Continental Europe	450,000,000	660,000,000	1,110,000,000
North America	330,000,000	130,000,000	460,000,000
Total	913,000,000	1,127,000,000	2,040,000,000

During recent years a considerable change has taken place in the markets available for the shipment of wool; the United Kingdom is no longer the first amongst wool-manufacturing countries, though its consumption of imported wool is still equal to 29·8 per cent. of the total wool imported. The relative positions of the Principal wool consuming countries.

United Kingdom, America, and continental Europe as wool consumers during several years may be gleaned from the following table:—

Year.	United Kingdom.	Continental Europe.	North America.	Grand Total.
	lb.	lb.	lb.	lb.
1880	370,000,000	882,000,000	381,000,000	1,633,000,000
1881	320,000,000	952,000,000	355,000,000	1,627,000,000
1882	357,000,000	969,000,000	385,000,000	1,711,000,000
1883	340,000,000	969,000,000	418,000,000	1,727,000,000
1884	381,000,000	1,017,000,000	422,000,000	1,820,000,000
1885	365,000,000	1,021,000,000	444,000,000	1,830,000,000
1886	418,000,000	1,033,000,000	460,000,000	1,911,000,000
1887	392,000,000	1,030,000,000	450,000,000	1,872,000,000
1888	434,000,000	1,056,000,000	460,000,000	1,950,000,000
1889	470,000,000	1,110,000,000	460,000,000	2,040,000,000

Wool-producing countries.

An exact estimate of the produce of the various countries of the world cannot be given, but sufficient information is obtainable from which the relative importance of the different producing areas may be determined for the year 1889–90.

Producing areas.	Sheep.
Europe	214,499,000
Asia	71,669,000
Africa	60,820,000
America	143,581,000
Australasia	101,268,000
Total	591,837,000

CATTLE.

Cattle breeding.

Though still a most important industry, cattle-rearing does not now occupy so prominent a place as formerly. In 1861 the value of the horned cattle depastured in the Colony was about £7,000,000, while that of the sheep was not more than half this sum. In 1890 the relative positions of the two classes of stock had entirely changed; for, while the cattle were valued at £10,510,000, the sheep were worth £19,595,000, notwithstanding that in the interval cattle had considerably risen in value, and sheep had depreciated. The number of cattle returned during each year since 1861 is shown in the subjoined table, and it will be noticed how great has been the decline in the totals since 1875:—

Number of cattle declining.

Year.	Number of cattle.	Year.	Number of cattle.
1861	2,271,923	1876	3,131,013
1862	2,620,383	1877	2,746,385
1863	2,032,522	1878	2,771,583
1864	1,924,119	1879	2,914,210
1865	1,961,905	1880	2,580,040
1866	1,771,809	1881	2,597,348
1867	1,728,427	1882	1,859,985
1868	1,761,411	1883	1,640,753
1869	1,795,904	1884	1,425,130
1870	2,195,096	1885	1,317,315
1871	2,014,888	1886	1,367,844
1872	2,287,660	1887	1,575,487
1873	2,794,327	1888	1,622,907
1874	2,856,699	1889	1,741,592
1875	3,134,086	1890	1,909,009

Substitution of sheep for cattle.

If the above figures be compared with the returns of sheep for the same period, it will be found that the change which has taken place in the class of stock has been most remarkable. It is very debatable whether the substitution of sheep for cattle will in the end prove advantageous to the State, though there does not appear to be any doubt that sheep-breeding is at present more profitable to the individual owner. The increase in the number of cattle depastured in the Colony during 1890 was 167,417; but since 1875 there has been a decrease of 1,225,077. It would seem from these figures that the lowest point in cattle-raising was reached in 1885, the result, no doubt, of continued bad seasons. Since then the improvement has been gradual, and even if small it may be taken as evidence of the disposition of the pastoralists in some parts of the Colony to revert to cattle breeding in place of sheep.

Loss from failure of water and grass.

An exact statement of the loss of cattle from disease and failure of water and grass can only be made for about eight years, and of these years three showed an actual decrease on the figures of the previous year, the years 1887 and 1889, being the only ones of the series which could be considered favourable to stock. Estimating at the low figure of £5 a head, the loss in 1883 was equal to £1,670,500, and in 1884 to £1,398,500. For the four years 1886 to 1889 stockholders enjoyed comparative immunity, but in the season of 1890 the losses were again considerable. In this instance, however, the deaths were attributable, not to failure of grass and water, but to disease possibly induced by the prevalence of the opposite condition of too much rain. The following statement shows the increase in the numbers of cattle which would have occurred had the seasons been favourable, and also the increase or decrease actually experienced :—

Loss of Horned Cattle through Disease, Drought, and kindred causes.

Year.	Expected Increase, allowing for all causes of natural decrease.	Actual Increase or Decrease.	Loss through Seasons.
	No.	No.	No.
1883	114,900	*219,200	334,100
1884	64,100	*215,600	279,700
1885	30,600	*107,80	138,400
1886	66,800	50,500	16,300
1887	207,600	207,600	†
1888	82,600	47,400	35,200
1889	118,700	118,700	†
1890	299,500	167,400	132,100

* Decrease during the year.
† No loss, or if any, very slight.

The principal breeds of cattle now in the Colony are the Durham or Shorthorns, Hereford, Devon, Ayrshire, Alderney, and crosses from these various breeds. At the close of the year 1889 the numbers of each breed, as far as could be ascertained, were :— Principal breeds of cattle in Colony.

Shorthorns—	Pure and stud	55,345	
	Ordinary	688,293	
			743,638
Hereford—	Pure and stud	31,543	
	Ordinary	210,226	
			241,769
Devon—	Pure and stud	12,166	
	Ordinary	64,438	
			76,604
Black-polled—	Pure and stud	1,180	
	Ordinary	1,311	
			2,491
Ayrshire—	Pure and stud	3,935	
	Ordinary	8,024	
			11,959
Others—	Pure and stud	1,645	
	Ordinary	2,047	
			3,692
Crosses—	First	7,635	
	Ordinary	821,221	
			828,856

The cross-breeds were estimated as follows :—

Shorthorn and Hereford	281,819
Shorthorn and Devon	105,774
Hereford and Devon	53,430
Shorthorn and black-polled	9,069
Ayrshire, &c., and shorthorn	24,223
Jersey and Shorthorn	2,471
Unrecognizable	352,070
	828,856

The number of fat cattle which will be available for market during the year 1891 is estimated to be about 342,238 head. This number is certainly very high, if the produce of the herds of the Colony be alone considered. The cattle trade with Queensland is, however, very considerable, especially in store cattle sent to this Colony for fattening; these serve to swell the nominal cast of the herds of the Colony to the figures given above. If the produce of the Colony alone be reckoned, the cast for the year 1890 was about 217,000 fat cattle, and the cast for 1891 will probably be 238,000 head. "Cast" of cattle.

Number of cattle at date of census.

At the census taken on April 5, 1891, the number of cattle in New South Wales was returned at 2,055,229, including 333,023 head of dairy stock. The increase of 46,220 head over the number returned in December, 1890, by the Stock Department is evidently due to the movements of stock from the breeding runs of Queensland to the New South Wales fattening stations. The number of calves branded during the year ended at the date of the census is returned at 393,618.

Calves branded.

Breed of cattle improving.

The breed of cattle throughout the Colony is steadily improving, a result due to the introduction of good stud stock, as well as the care exercised in selection. Cattle are for the most part kept in paddocks, and of the total number in the Colony 1,486,357 are paddocked, 252,254 are in open runs, and the remainder, 170,398, are depastured both ways.

Pure bred cattle imported.

During the year 1890, 1,497 pure bred cattle, 503 bulls and 994 cows, were imported, chiefly from the other colonies of the group. Importations from Europe and America were prohibited for many years, owing to the natural dread of the stock owners lest their herds should contract diseases which have devastated the cattle of other countries. The prohibition was removed in 1888, and cattle are now admitted after strict quarantine.

Cattle of the world.

Compared with the other countries of the world the importance of Australia is not so manifest in the case of cattle as in that of sheep. The following are the numbers of cattle estimated from the most recent returns available:—

Europe	104,166,000
Asia	70,850,000
Africa	8,203,000
America	117,249,000
Australasia	10,677,000
Total	311,145,000

SLAUGHTERING.

Slaughtering for food is permitted only in places licensed for the purpose, but such establishments are very numerous. In the metropolitan district there are 20, and in the country districts

1,465 slaughter-yards, employing respectively 298 and 3,344 men, in all 1,485 establishments, and 3,642 men. The quantity of meat consumed in the metropolitan district during the year is about 310 lb. per head, comprising 121 lb. mutton and 189 lb. beef, allowance being made for the output of the Riverstone Meat Works, which supply the metropolitan market. In the rest of the Colony the demand for beef also greatly predominates, the yearly quantity being 67 lb. mutton and 169 lb. beef, making a total of 236 lb. per head. In addition to the stock mentioned above, there were slaughtered 108,180 pigs. From the foregoing statement it will be seen that the average annual consumption of mutton for the whole Colony equals 85 lb., of beef 176 lb., and of pork 10 lb., making a total consumption of 271 lb. of meat. The following table shows the quantity of stock of each kind killed for food in 1890:— Slaughtering for food.

Stock.	Number slaughtered in 1890.		
	Metropolitan.	Country.	Total.
Sheep	771,693	1,242,362	2,014,055
Lambs	27,320	44,567	71,887
Bullocks	56,923	133,776	190,699
Cows	10,864	52,006	62,870
Calves	13,942	8,556	22,498
Pigs	49,062	59,118	108,180

The value of stock slaughtered can be determined with exactness only for the metropolitan market. Taking all stock sent to the Homebush saleyards, at Sydney, during 1890, for the purpose of slaughter, the price of sheep averaged 9s. 6d. to 10s. for wethers, and 7s. to 7s. 6d. for ewes. For bullocks the average price was Price of fat stock.

£7 5s. per head, and for cows about £2 10s. less. At the Abattoirs mutton sold for 1¾d. to 2d. per lb., the skin being worth 5s. Beef ranged from 2d. to 2½d. per lb., the heads and feet being worth from 15s. 6d. per set, fat 1¼d. per lb., and the hide 15s.

DAIRY FARMING.

Dairy farming a promising industry.

Dairy farming has made very rapid progress of late years, especially in the south coast districts, and promises to develop into a very important industry. The number of dairy cows during the early part of the year 1891 may be estimated as 333,023, thus distributed :—

Number of Dairy Cows.

District	Cows	District	Cows
Metropolitan District	4,319	Macquarie, East	2,562
Albury	947	Macquarie, West	2,822
Argyle	12,602	Maitland, East	1,396
Balranald	2,303	Maitland, West	178
Bogan	5,609	Molong	3,381
Boorowa	2,046	Monaro	8,894
Bourke	2,169	Morpeth	2,328
Braidwood	5,717	Mudgee	5,290
Camden	26,516	Murray	2,500
Carcoar	4,576	Murrumbidgee	7,610
Clarence	1,572	Namoi	3,660
Central Cumberland	4,072	Nepean	2,309
Durham	4,922	Newcastle	345
Eden	35,293	New England	7,228
Forbes	3,341	Northumberland	1,496
Glen Innes	4,411	Orange	2,873
Gloucester	3,364	Parramatta	95
Goulburn	231	Patrick's Plains	8,165
Grafton	4,812	Queanbeyan	3,871
Grenfell	4,289	Richmond	15,477
Gundagai	3,589	Shoalhaven	20,482
Gunnedah	3,031	Sturt	643
Gwydir	4,710	Tamworth	4,812
Hartley	2,574	Tenterfield	3,588
Hastings and Manning	5,732	Tumut	4,027
Hawkesbury	2,311	Wellington	2,727
Hume	4,417	Wentworth	537
Hunter	4,774	Wilcannia	518
Hunter, Upper	6,543	Wollombi	2,386
Illawarra	8,931	Yass Plains	4,334
Inverell	2,799	Young	3,933
Kiama	14,775		
Macleay	5,059		333,023

Constant attention to the peculiarities of the climate, and the wants of the colonists, as well as the judicious crossing of strains, have developed a breed of cows peculiar to Australia. This is especially the case in the coast districts immediately south of Sydney, though all well-known breeds of milkers are found in New South Wales. The milk yielded by the dairy cows of the Colony amounts to 119,888,000 gallons, of which the quantity consumed in making butter and cheese during the past year may be set down as 60,399,000 gallons, and the weight of the butter made 18,534,130 lb., and of cheese, 4,796,567 lb. The yield of milk averages for ordinary unselected Ayrshire cows 600 gallons annually, while some yield 1,300 gallons per annum; 360 gallons may be taken as a fair average all round. The quantity of milk required to make a given weight of butter varies considerably according to whether the milk is treated by a separator or in the old fashion. A great proportion of the butter now made is what is usually termed factory or separator-made, and the average quantity of milk used per lb. of butter produced is 2·6 gallons, or 26 lb. 2 oz. For ordinary hand-made butter the quantity required is about 3 gallons, thus showing a saving of about 13 per cent. by the former method, in addition to the extra value of the butter, the price during 1890 being from 2d. to 3d. per lb. higher in the Sydney markets for the factory-made than for the ordinary kind. No statistics respecting the manufacture of butter and cheese were collected prior to 1887, when the quantity made was 16,106,000 lb. and 5,780,000 lb. respectively. The number of hands employed at dairy farming in 1890 was approximately 10,000; of these 2,169 were employed in the various factories. The factories numbered 287, of which 138 employed steam and 149 hand or other power. The plant developed about 783 horse-power, and was valued at £48,918, and the buildings and land £2,136,658, making the total capital invested, exclusive of stock, £2,180,576. Notwithstanding the extent of this industry, and the resources of the Colony, butter and cheese are still largely imported, the quantity imported and exported varying greatly with the seasons.

Butter and cheese made.

Factory butter.

Hands employed.

The following table shows the trade in these commodities during the past ten years :—

Year.	Butter.		Cheese.	
	Imported.	Exported.	Imported.	Exported.
	lb.	lb.	lb.	lb.
1881	660,128	762,397	171,544	145,833
1882	1,654,016	437,856	331,944	163,378
1883	1,813,504	778,635	161,753	259,742
1884	2,791,936	621,264	725,177	247,337
1885	3,624,092	521,473	769,148	123,585
1886	3,129,392	286,944	1,229,334	85,815
1887	1,034,544	1,041,152	318,099	247,826
1888	2,258,704	764,960	691,148	300,375
1889	1,904,737	662,489	955,494	300,750
1890	838,703	1,120,044	212,801	288,902

Butter and cheese making districts.

A former table shows the number of dairy cows in each electoral district. The following are the districts in which the largest quantities of butter, cheese, and bacon are made :—

District.	Butter made.	Cheese made.	Bacon and Hams made.
	lb.	lb.	lb.
Argyle	726,277	36,737	132,599
Camden	1,875,778	14,959	275,004
Eden	2,513,119	3,813,288	583,929
Illawarra	333,559	....	13,720
Kiama	2,398,198	....	431,770
Monaro	191,166	222,074	149,725
Richmond	1,025,934	130,962	64,625
Shoalhaven	2,720,479	37,220	1,249,476
Other districts	6,749,620	541,327	4,529,123
	18,534,130	4,796,567	7,429,971

HORSES.

Horse-breeding.

Australasia is eminently fitted for the breeding of most descriptions of horses, and attention has long been directed to this industry. At an early period the stock of colonial bred horses was enriched by the importation of some excellent thoroughbred Arabians from India; and the high name which was acquired by the horses of

Excellence of native grasses.

Australia was largely due to this cause. The abundance of good pasture everywhere obtainable also contributed to this result. The native kangaroo-grass, especially when in seed, is full of saccharine matter, and young stock thrive excellently upon it. This abundance of natural provender allowed a large increase in the stock of the settlers, which would have been a great advantage, had it not been that the general cheapness of horses led to a neglect of the canons of breeding. In consequence of the discovery of gold, horses became very high priced. Under ordinary conditions this circumstance would have been favourable to the breed of horses, and such was the case in Victoria. In this Colony it was far otherwise. The best of the stock of New South Wales, including a large proportion of the most valuable breeding mares, was taken by Victoria, with the result that for twenty years after the gold rush the horses of the Colony greatly deteriorated. One class of stock only escaped. The thoroughbred racer was probably improved both by the importation of fresh stock from England, and by the judicious selection of mares. The period of deterioration ended about the year 1870, since which year there has been a perceptible improvement in all classes of horses. The number of horses in New South Wales shows little increase for the last sixteen years, as may be seen from the table following:—

Partial deterioration of stock.

Year.	Number of horses.	Year.	Number of horses.
1875	357,696	1883	326,964
1876	366,703	1884	337,172
1877	328,150	1885	344,697
1878	336,468	1886	361,663
1879	360,038	1887	390,609
1880	395,984	1888	411,368
1881	398,577	1889	430,777
1882	328,026	1890	444,163

Small annual increase of horses.

The annual increase in the number of horses has been not more than 1·45 per cent. during the whole period covered by the above table, while the increase of population has been at the rate of 4·13 per cent.

Classification of horses.

For purposes of classification the horses of the Colony have been divided into draught, light-harness, and saddle-horses, the numbers of each particular kind being as follows :—

Class.	Thoroughbred.	Ordinary.	Total.
Draught	21,094	123,069	144,163
Light-harness	15,494	98,443	113,937
Saddle	27,100	158,963	186,063
Total	63,688	380,475	444,163

Saddle and harness horses.

Endurance of colonial horses.

The Colony is specially adapted for the breeding of saddle and light-harness horses, and it is doubtful whether these particular breeds of Australasian horses are anywhere surpassed. The bush horse is hardy and swift, and capable of making very long and rapid journeys, when fed only on the ordinary herbage of the country ; and in times of drought, when the grass and water have become scanty, these animals often perform astonishing feats of endurance. Generally speaking, the breed of horses is improving, owing to the introduction of superior stud horses and the breeding from good mares. Where there has been a deterioration in the stock, this has been due to breeding from weedy mares for racing purposes and from the effect of the drought.

Horses for market in 1891.

The approximate number of animals fit for market during the present year will be :—

Draught-horses	23,875
Saddle ,,	34,835
Light-harness horses	24,262
Total	82,972

India and China markets.

Of these it is estimated that nearly 21,340 are suitable for the Indian and China markets. The total number leaving the Colony for markets outside Australia during 1890 was only 1,056. Although the demand for horses in India is considerable and Australia is a natural market from which supplies may be derived there is no one employed by the Indian Government to make himself acquainted with the resources of the various colonies, or to furnish information to intending shippers. The speculation of sending horses to India is one open to many risks, as, apart from the dangers of the voyage, there is always an uncertainty as to the stock being accepted. Owing, therefore, to the limited demand, it has not been found advantageous to breed horses for any but local requirements.

Foreign demand for horses limited.

The number of wild horses in the Colony during the year is estimated at 4,490, an increase of 260 on the number in the previous year.

Wild horses.

SWINE.

The breeding of swine has also been very much neglected in New South Wales, so that in 1890 the number of stock was 23,752 less than in 1880. Considering the importance which the industry has attained in other countries, it is a matter of surprise that more attention has not been paid to it in this Colony, where the conditions of farming in many parts, more especially in the coast districts, offer great facilities for the raising of this class of stock. The estimated value of swine in the Colony at the close of 1890 was £640,000, and the estimated return therefrom for the year was about £332,500. The following table shows the number of pigs in New South Wales for each year since 1862 :—

Swine-breeding neglected.

Value of annual cast.

Year.	Number of swine.	Year.	Number of swine.
1862	125,541	1877	191,677
1863	135,899	1878	220,320
1864	164,154	1879	256,026
1865	146,901	1880	308,205
1866	137,915	1881	213,916
1867	173,168	1882	154,815
1868	176,901	1883	189,050
1869	175,924	1884	211,656
1870	243,066	1885	208,697
1871	213,193	1886	209,576
1872	218,904	1887	264,111
1873	240,680	1888	248,583
1874	219,958	1889	238,585
1875	199,950	1890	284,453
1876	173,604		

The number of swine slaughtered during 1890 was 108,180, of which 49,062 were killed at the Metropolitan abattoirs. The weight of pork obtained was about 11,000,000 lb., of which 7,429,971 lb. were made into bacon and ham; the principal seat of the bacon-curing industry being the South Coast district.

PASTORAL PROPERTY.

Value of pastoral property.

Pastoral property and stock form the largest factor in the wealth, not only of New South Wales, but also of all the other principal colonies of Australasia, and the return derived therefrom is the largest source of the income of its inhabitants. The total capital value of pastoral property in the colony, including land, improvements, and plant, as well as stock, was estimated at the beginning of 1891, £137,667,000, of which £71,860,000 represent the value of land, £30,620,000 of improvements and plant, and £35,187,000 of stock.

Total Live Stock in Australasia.

The number of stock of all kinds in each colony at the close of the year 1890 was as follows:—

Colony.	Sheep.	Cattle.	Horses.	Swine.
	No.	No.	No.	No.
New South Wales	55,986,431	1,909,009	444,163	283,061
Victoria	12,736,143	1,782,978	436,459	282,457
Queensland	18,007,234	5,558,264	365,812	96,836
South Australia	7,004,642	359,938	187,686	116,277
Western Australia	2,524,913	130,970	44,384	28,985
Tasmania	1,619,256	162,440	31,165	81,716
New Zealand	16,200,358	773,028	187,382	369,992
Total	114,078,977	10,679,627	1,697,051	1,259,324

Relative importance of each colony.

New South Wales, therefore, ranked first as regards the number of sheep—55,986,431 out of a total of 114,078,977, or 49·1 per cent. being depastured within its limits. In regard to cattle, this Colony stood next to Queensland, having 1,909,009 head of cattle out of a total of 10,676,627, or 17·4 per cent. of the whole of the cattle of Australasia. As a horse-breeding country New South Wales came first, with 444,163, or 26·2 per cent. of the total horses of the colonies, Victoria coming second with 436,459 head. New Zealand has a larger number of swine than any other colony—its total being 369,992, or 29·4 per cent. New South Wales ranked second with 284,453, or 22·5 per cent.

Stock runs.

The number of sheep and cattle runs in the Colony during the year 1890 was 40,802, of which 33,605 were enclosed, and 7,197 were open or unenclosed; 21,775 of the enclosed runs were properly subdivided into paddocks, and 11,830 were only partially subdivided. The area comprised in these holdings was 185,000,000 acres, about 35,000,000 acres being freehold, and 150,000,000 acres leased from the State. The improvements effected on pastoral estates for fencing and for watering stock have been valued by the Chief Inspector of Stock at £72,982,086. Of this sum fencing absorbs £63,173,784, representing 1,478,818 miles at an average rate of £42 14s. per mile. The dams for watering stock number 30,580, which, at an average value of £99 7s., give a total value of £3,038,664. There were 30,953 excavated tanks, worth on an average £195 11s., or, in all, £6,053,034, while the number of wells sunk or bored number 3,599, the average value of each well being £199 2s., and the total of all wells being £716,604. These figures represent the first cost, the present value of all improvements being £30,400,000.

Dams and fencing.

Public Watering Places.

Public watering places are established on all the main stock routes of the Colony, the construction and maintenance of which are vested in the Department of Mines and Agriculture. These works consist of dams, wells, and artesian bores. At the present time 117 tanks, 21 dams and reservoirs, 35 wells, and 6 artesian bores are either in course of construction or have been contracted for. The tanks vary in size up to 5,000,000 gallons, and in depth from 15 to 20 feet. They are so constructed as to be fed during rainy weather by surface drains. The soil from the excavations is embanked around, to shelter the tanks from the wind, and so lessen the evaporation, and also, where the contour is favourable, to conserve water above the ground surface. The total storage capacity of the tanks and wells abovementioned may be set down at 700,000,000, and the wells, if regularly worked, will yield a total of 400,000 gallons per day. Stock are not allowed direct access to the tanks, but are admitted to troughs which are filled by means of service reservoirs, into which the water is raised by various methods—steam, horse, or wind-power, as the case may be. There have been erected 54 steam pumps, 73 pumps worked by horse-power, and one windmill, the remainder being open watering places, supplied by hand-power. From the wells the water is mostly drawn by whims and self-acting buckets.

The World's flocks.

The latest figures which have come to hand respecting the flocks and herds of the principal countries, refer to various years from 1882 to 1890, and are given herewith. The important part which these colonies are destined to play in the wool markets of the world will be better understood when the character of the wool produced in Australia is made an item of comparison, as well as the actual number of sheep depastured :—

	Cattle.	Horses.	Sheep.	Swine.
Europe	104,166,000	34,865,000	214,409,000	46,152,000
Asia	70,850,000	4,443,000	71,669,000	417,000
Africa	8,203,000	721,000	60,820,000	840,000
America	117,249,000	21,920,000	143,581,000	53,974,000
Australasia	10,677,000	1,697,000	114,079,000	1,259,000
Total	311,145,000	63,646,000	604,648,000	102,642,000

Pastoral resources of New South Wales in terms of sheep.

In order to give a more definite idea of the extent of the pastoral resources of New South Wales, the following table has been compiled, showing in five-year periods, from 1860, the amount of stock that has been actually depastured in the Colony. For the sake of convenience the numbers of cattle and horses are expressed in terms of sheep ; that is, allowance has been made at the rate of ten sheep for each head of large stock, so that the total shows what would have been the result had the cattle and horses been replaced by their equivalent of sheep. There is also shown the number of acres of land in the Colony to each sheep of the totals thus found, at the end of every five-year period, as well as the number of such sheep per head of the population at the same periods :—

Live Stock of the Colony expressed in terms of Sheep.

Year.	Sheep.	Cattle.	Horses.	Total.	Acres per Sheep.	Sheep per Head of Population.
1860	6,119,163	24,085,860	2,514,970	32,719,993	5·99	93·87
1865	8,132,511	19,619,050	2,825,870	30,577,431	6·40	74·73
1870	16,308,585	21,950,960	3,375,970	41,635,515	4·70	83·49
1875	25,353,924	31,340,860	3,576,960	60,271,744	3·35	101·42
1880	35,398,121	25,800,400	3,959,840	65,158,361	3·00	87·83
1885	37,820,906	13,173,150	3,446,970	54,441,026	3·60	57·44
1890	55,986,431	19, [illegible]90	1[illegible]30	79,518,151	2·46	78·72

DISEASES IN STOCK.

Diseases in sheep.

On the whole the stock of the Colony was tolerably free from disease during 1890, especially as regards sheep and horses. Scab in sheep has been unknown in this Colony for some considerable time, and indeed the whole of Australasia is at present exempt from this malady, with the exception of New Zealand and Western Australia, where it exists to a very slight extent. Foot-rot has been noticed in thirty-six districts of New South Wales, attributed to wet seasons, running on low rich pasture, and contagion. In nine districts the sheep were affected with fluke, through depasturing on low swampy ground, unsound country, and rank pasture. The sheep in thirty-seven districts, to the extent of about 18 per cent., were reported to have been infested with worms. The year was unusually free from epizootic diseases in horses. Anthrax was reported in two districts, and Australian stringhalt had appeared in two districts in the early part of the year, a disease considered by the Government Veterinary Surgeon to be due to the presence of intestinal parasites. Prurigo continued to give trouble in seventeen districts. At the end of the year a rather severe outbreak of influenza, vulgarily known as "pink-eye," took place, causing a good many losses. 1,734 horses are said to have died during the year from wire in chaff, and other accidents.

Disease in horses.

Diseases in cattle.

With regard to cattle, pleuro-pneumonia was reported from thirty-five districts, or 219 runs, while in twenty-eight districts the cattle were reported as free from that disease. In most of the infected districts the presence of the disease was attributed to the introduction of cattle from Queensland, and contact with travelling stock from that colony. Inoculation had proved successful in twenty-nine districts. Stock-owners generally were largely in favor of compulsory inoculation. Forty-seven cases of tuberculosis had been detected at the Homebush and Maitland cattle saleyards during 1889. Cumberland disease was reported to have killed

593 head, in six districts, during the year, being 89 less than in 1889. Symptomatic Anthrax, or "Blackleg," had carried off 430 head, in one district, being a decrease of 352. Cattle to the number of 1,291 are reported to have died of tubercular swellings in the throat, and 490 deaths are reported from ophthalmia. No disease whatever was reported amongst pigs.

NOXIOUS ANIMALS.

The only large carnivorous animal in Australia at all dangerous to stock is the dingo, or native dog; but animals which consume the pasturage, such as kangaroos, wallabies, and rabbits, are equally deemed noxious by the settlers. The rabbits are the greatest pest. At one period over 100 million acres were infested with them, and 25,280,000 were destroyed in one year, and their skins paid for by the Government. So serious had the evil become in 1883 that a special Act was passed to deal with the trouble, and raise funds for the purpose by assessment on the stock in the infested country. The compulsory clauses of this Act were, however, suspended in 1890, and the payment of subsidies has been discontinued. It is estimated that over a million has been spent in the destruction of rabbits, a portion of which was expended on wire fencing, which is considered the only effective method of dealing with the plague. One line of fencing extends from Narramine, on the Macquarie River, to Bourke, on the Darling River, a distance of 207 miles; thence to Barringun, a further length of 84 miles, at an average cost of £82 per mile. Another fence has been constructed from the Murray northward, along the western boundary of the Colony, a distance of nearly 346 miles. The cost of this line was £26,135, or an average of £75 12s. 9d. per mile. The wire-netting used was 17 gauge, $1\frac{1}{4}$ inch mesh, and 42 inches in width. Besides these 633 miles of fencing erected by the Government, there has been a large amount of rabbit-proof fencing put up by

Rabbit pest.

Wire fencing.

individual pastoralists to protect their runs. The following table shows the yearly expenditure on account of rabbit destruction, with the amount derived from assessment and that paid out of general revenue:—

Year.	Assessment. £	General Revenue. £	Total. £
1883	490	......	490
1884	69,406	......	69,406
1885	46,926	88,128	135,054
1886	40,200	127,434	167,634
1887	47,518	161,916	209,434
1888	41,308	90,897	132,205
1889	47,726	36,359	84,085
1890	49,764	8,381	58,145
Total	£343,338	£513,115	£856,453

Extirpation of noxious animals.

For the destruction of noxious animals other than rabbits the amount of assessment paid by stock-owners was £33,649, and the Government subsidy was £7,885; the amount actually expended was £39,664. The number of kangaroos destroyed during the year was 175,755; of wallabies, 506,137; kangaroo rats, 92,014; bandicoots, 997; paddamellons, 2,844; wild pigs, 5,292; hares, 397,439; native dogs, 9,955; opossums, 11,169; bilbees, 82; eagle-hawks, 2,429; crows, 9,149; emus, 383. The loss of stock from native dogs is reported to have been 79,898 sheep, valued at £29,098; while the loss from tame dogs is returned at 57,653 sheep, valued at £24,606.

Rewards paid.

The reward paid for scalps of noxious animals differs greatly, according to the locality, and is determined by the various Boards. The prices paid were as follows:—For kangaroos, from 1d. to 1s.; wallaroo, 1d. to 1s.; wallaby, from 1d. to 1s.; paddamellon, from 1d. to 3d.; hares, from 2d. to 1s.; kangaroo rats, 2d. to 6d.; native dogs, from 10s. to 60s.; pups, 5s. to 10s.; opossum, 1d.; wild pigs, 1s.; bilbees, 2s. 6d.; eagle-hawks, 2s. to 7s. 6d.; emus, 1d. to 1s.; crows, 2d. to 6d.

PART XI.

Law and Crime.

THE law of New South Wales permits proceedings against any person charged with crime to be initiated either by arrest or by summons. During 1890 there were 66,087 cases dealt with by the magistrates; in 38,568 of these the persons charged with offences were arrested, and in 22,795 cases they were summoned by the police; while in the remaining 4,724 cases proceedings were taken by private persons.

ARRESTS.

Out of 66,087 persons brought before the magistrates of the Colony 64,611 were dealt with summarily, and convictions recorded in 48,102 cases; while 16,509 cases were dismissed either on their merits, or for want of prosecution; in the remaining cases, 1,476 in number, the persons concerned were committed for trial in the higher Courts of the Colony. Dividing the offences into three subdivisions—those committed against the person, those against property, and offences against good order or government—the numbers of persons brought before the Magistrates' Courts, and the manner in which they were dealt with during 1890, were as follows:— Persons brought before magistrates.

Number of Persons dealt with by Magistrates.

Offences.	Total number of persons brought before the Magistrates' Courts.	Number of persons.			
		Discharged for want of prosecution or want of evidence.	Whose cases were dismissed on the merits.	Summarily convicted.	Committed for trial.
Against the person........	8,729	2,559	1,281	4,473	416
Against property	7,616	1,913	1,135	3,666	902
Other cases*	49,742	6,597	3,024	39,963	158
Total number of persons summoned or apprehended......	66,087	11,069	5,440	48,102	1,476

* Not including cases brought up for lunacy.

Civil actions are not included in this table, but it includes arrest or summonses for breaches of various Acts, and for other offences, which, from a moral point of view, are not to be reckoned as crimes, although they are such in the eyes of the law. The total number of summary convictions for all offences still shows a decrease, the number during 1890, being 48,102 as compared with 48,703 in the previous year, and 50,876 in 1888. These figures disclose the gratifying fact, that while the population has increased the number of offenders against the law continues to decrease. The following table gives the number of summary convictions before magistrates during the past twelve years:—

Summary convictions.

Summary Convictions before Magistrates.

Year.	Offences against the person.	Offences against property.	Other Offences.	Year.	Offences against the person.	Offences against property.	Other Offences.
1879	4,885	3,217	30,726	1885	5,159	3,649	50,537
1880	5,151	3,286	33,768	1886	5,187	3,676	53,405
1881	5,239	3,453	42,438	1887	4,667	3,876	45,071
1882	5,350	4,014	40,762	1888	4,779	4,669	41,428
1883	6,257	3,395	45,811	1889	4,658	3,931	40,114
1884	5,810	3,594	48,502	1890	4,473	3,666	39,963

Arrests by police.

Fewer arrests were made by the police in 1890 than in any year, except 1889, since 1880; and the percentage of arrests to the whole population, which was 5·23 in 1884, had dropped to 3·50:—

Arrests by Police.

Year.	Arrests.	Percentage to population.	Year.	Arrests.	Percentage to population.
1880	35,774	4·91	1886	48,854	5·04
1881	41,402	5·41	1887	44,094	4·39
1882	39,758	4·98	1888	42,579	4·11
1883	43,177	5·15	1889	38,345	3·56
1884	46,199	5·23	1890	38,568	3·50
1885	48,261	5·20			

The number of police in the Colony during the years 1884-90 was

Number of Police.

Year.	Metropolitan.	Country.	Total.
1884	423	947	1,370
1885	466	977	1,443
1886	476	986	1,462
1887	502	989	1,491
1888	518	995	1,513
1889	543	1,024	1,567
1890	594	1,057	1,651

Duties of Police.

The protection of life and property does not form the whole of the duty performed by the police in this Colony; on the contrary, a very large portion of their time is taken up with administrative duties, such as the collection of the electoral rolls, the agricultural and stock schedules, and returns of works and manufactories; in many instances, too, the police act as Clerks of Petty Sessions and Mining Wardens, and fill other offices having no direct connection with police duties. The test sometimes applied as to the law-abiding character of the population of the different colonies, as deduced from the apparent number of persons protected by one police officer, is entirely worthless unless the circumstances of the duties performed and the diverse areas of the colonies are made elements of such comparison. The numbers of police in the principal colonies, and the proportion to the civilian population, are however given in the following table for what they may be worth:—

Police in different Colonies.

Colony.	Number of Police.	Proportion of Inhabitants to one Police Officer.
New South Wales	1,651	667
Victoria	1,505	756
Queensland	898	471
South Australia	426	762
Western Australia	173	281
Tasmania	306	475
New Zealand	506	1,236

A comparison of cities is given on the next page, and it would appear that the Colonial capitals have proportionately less police supervision than many of the places enumerated in the list.

This however, of itself, argues nothing in favour of the law-abiding character of the population of the two cities named, but rather that a large number of police could with advantage be added to the force now employed for their protection :—

Cities.	Strength of Police.	Population to each Police Constable.	Cities.	Strength of Police.	Population to each Police Constable.
Sydney	594	651	Belfast	800	287
Melbourne	742	659	New York	3,174	472
Brisbane	177	519	Philadelphia	1,624	643
Adelaide	167	795	Chicago	1,050	810
Hobart	50	663	Brooklyn	777	975
Auckland	48	1,068	St. Louis	502	900
Wellington	44	755	Baltimore	575	765
London	14,081	389	Boston	780	540
Glasgow	1,093	503	San Francisco	404	790
Edinburgh	500	500	Cincinnati	388	909
Manchester	940	401			

Number of arrests.

The following table shows the number of arrests made by the police in the Metropolitan and Extra-Metropolitan police districts, and distinguishes at the same time the various classes of offences :—

Arrests for	Metropolitan.	Extra Metropolitan.	Total.
Offences against the person	1,711	1,275	2,986
Offences against property, with violence	529	419	948
Offences against property, without violence	2,163	1,996	4,159
Forgery, and offences against the Currency	65	75	140
Offences against good order	14,381	13,855	28,236
Offences not included in the foregoing	883	1,216	2,099
Total	19,732	18,836	38,568

Charges often of a trivial nature.

Although the total number of arrests may appear large, it must be remembered that many of the offences charged are of a very trivial character. For instance, during 1890 there were 2,338 arrests for lunacy and vagrancy, and 3,136 for breaches of various Acts. Under the heading of offences against good order, such as drunkenness, riotous and indecent behaviour, and obscene language there were 24,861 arrests, making a total of 30,335, or nearly 79 per cent. of the whole number of arrests for the year.

No less than 48 per cent. of the arrests were for drunkenness, either with or without disorderly conduct, and in the Metropolitan Police District, where the population is concentrated, and police supervision, therefore, more complete, quite one-half of the arrests made were for offences of this nature. Arrests for drunkenness.

The following table shows the number of arrests for this offence in the Metropolitan and Extra Metropolitan Police Districts :—

Arrests for	Metropolitan.	Extra Metropolitan.	Total.
Drunkenness only	7,304	6,461	13,765
Drunk and disorderly	2,547	2,249	4,796
Habitual drunkenness	43	50	93
Total................	9,894	8,760	18,654

The ages of persons arrested for various classes of offences during the year 1890 are given below. It will be seen that the most serious offences were charged against persons between the ages of 20 and 30, while those against good order, consisting chiefly of drunkenness, were committed by persons from 20 to 50 years :— Ages and offences of persons arrested.

Ages of Persons Arrested.

Offences.	Ages.							Total apprehensions.
	Under 15.	15 and under 20.	20 and under 30.	30 and under 40.	40 and under 50.	50 and under 60.	Over 60.	
Against the person	15	246	1,264	805	412	187	57	2,986
Against property, with violence....................	26	130	423	194	104	37	34	948
Against property, without violence....................	349	511	1,658	919	432	187	103	4,159
Forgery and offences against the currency ...	...	20	58	35	16	8	3	140
Against good order, including drunkenness ...	393	1,514	7,639	7,901	5,600	3,389	1,800	28,236
Not included in the preceding	35	133	659	619	371	195	87	2,099
Total	818	2,554	11,701	10,473	6,935	4,003	2,084	38,568

Ages of offenders.

The number of arrests of persons at each period of life was much the same as in 1889, with the exception of under 15 years, which showed a satisfactory diminution. The proportion of offences committed at the respective ages is given herewith. It will be seen that the percentage of offenders under 15 years though higher than in 1887 was lower than the rate for either 1888 or 1889 :—

Percentage of Arrests at various Ages to Total Arrests.

Year.	10 and under 15.	15 and under 20.	20 and under 30.	30 and under 40.	40 and under 50.	50 and under 60.	over 60.
1879	2·19	6·76	28·22	27·93	19·17	9·33	6·40
1880	2·12	6·94	29·24	26·90	18·69	9·77	6·34
1881	2·11	5·43	28·98	27·22	20·31	9·74	6·21
1882	1·93	4·83	27·82	26·58	20·79	10·69	7·36
1883	1·94	5·80	28·98	26·08	20·45	10·40	6·35
1884	1·68	5·81	29·51	26·02	20·35	10·61	6·01
1885	1·73	5·38	30·25	26·47	20·42	9·77	5·98
1886	1·64	5·90	29·98	26·13	20·54	10·28	5·53
1887	1·88	6·29	29·82	26·86	19·50	10·17	5·48
1888	2·40	6·51	29·70	26·07	19·39	10·55	5·48
1889	2·88	6·59	29·80	26·74	18·71	9·06	5·32
1890	2·12	6·62	30·34	27·16	17·98	10·38	5·40

Absence of serious crime amongst native-born population.

The native-born population of New South Wales probably numbers not less than 64 per cent. of the whole, while the persons arrested during 1890 who were born in the Colony numbered 12,885 out of a total of 38,568 arrests, or 33·4 per cent. In connection with this matter, however, it should be borne in mind that the great bulk of the population under 15 years are also native born. The native countries of all persons apprehended during 1890 will be found in the following table, as well as the offences for which the arrests were made :—

Birthplaces of Persons Apprehended, 1890.

Country.	Against the person.	Against property, with violence.	Against property without violence.	Forgery and offences against the currency.	Against good order, including drunkenness.	Not included above.	Total.
New South Wales	1,248	436	1,905	59	8,669	568	12,885
Other Australian Colonies	264	94	24	14	1,893	37	2,826
England	87	169	727	38	6,139	25	8,135
Ireland	54	128	516	15	6,935	98	8,446
Scotland	174	59	190	5	2,378	158	2,84
Other British possessions	48	11	73	2	379	50	63
France	16	7	27	2	167	12	231
Germany	44	9	56	1	82	48	59
China	57	5	57	1	142	63	325
Other Foreign Countries	144	30	184	3	1,182	140	1,683
Total	2,986	948	4,159	140	28,236	2,099	38,568

Nominal religious professions of prisoners.

The nominal religious profession of each person arrested is ascertained and entered in the charge-sheet. During 1890 the arrests of persons belonging to each of the various denominations were :—

Religions of Persons Apprehended, 1890.

Religion.	Against the person.	Against property, with violence.	Against property, without violence.	Forgery and offences against the currency.	Against good order, including drunkenness.	Not included above.	Total.
Church of England....	1,139	351	1,89	73	10,27	885	14,594
Presbyterians	255	77	76	5	2,90	182	3,585
Wesleyans...............	56	20	16	1	96	44	643
Independents	6	....	9	...	37	2	54
Baptists.....	8	4	19	1	86	6	124
Other Protestants......	55	20	70	2	91	59	697
Roman Catholics	1,273	442	1,587	55	13,05	760	17,132
Jews	22	9	33	....	56	14	134
Pagans	58	4	57	1	84	61	365
Other persuasions, or religion unknown, Freethinkers, &c....	114	21	123	2	94	86	1,240
Total........	2,986	948	4,159	140	28,236	2,099	38,568

Education of persons arrested.

The degree of education of those who were arrested has also been obtained as far as possible. Four grades of education were formerly adopted for classification purposes, but in consequence of the difficulty of defining the term "Superior Education," that classification has been abandoned. The number comprised in each class from 1877 to 1890 was:—

Degrees of Education of Persons Arrested.

Year.	Neither read nor write.	Read only.	Read and write.	Superior education.	Total arrests.
1877	3,842	1,269	23,238	*	28,349
1878	4,017	1,529	25,172	*	30,718
1879	3,493	1,230	27,984	153	32,860
1880	4,065	1,197	30,350	162	35,774
1881	4,034	1,123	36,083	162	41,402
1882	4,059	964	34,553	182	39,758
1883	3,859	1,058	38,071	189	43,177
1884	3,871	1,096	41,030	202	46,199
1885	3,925	937	43,185	214	48,261
1886	4,142	916	43,588	208	48,854
1887	3,873	709	39,295	217	44,094
1888	3,730	848	37,734	267	42,579
1889	3,256	642	34,239	208	38,345
1890	3,014	591	34,963	*	38,568

* Included in previous column.

Effect of education on crime.

A superficial glance at the figures would seem to show that the progress of education has not been attended with that decrease in crime, which the friends of education confidently expect to follow in its train. But it must always be remembered that although the proportion of persons arrested who can read and write has much increased of late years, such increase is merely a proof of the spread of education, even amongst those whose environment offers inducement to the commission of crime.

Education of Offenders.

The following table gives the percentage of persons arrested of each degree of education from 1877 to 1890 :—

Year.	Neither read nor write.	Read only.	Read and write.	Year.	Neither read nor write.	Read only.	Read and write
1877	13·55	4·47	81·98	1884	8·37	2·37	89·26
1878	13·07	4·97	81·96	1885	8·13	1·94	89·93
1879	10·62	3·74	85·64	1886	8·49	1·87	89·64
1880	11·36	3·34	85·30	1887	8·78	1·61	89·61
1881	9·74	2·71	87·55	1888	8·76	1·99	89·25
1882	10·20	2·42	87·38	1889	8·49	1·67	89·84
1883	8·93	2·45	88·62	1890	7·81	1·53	90·66

Effect of education on crime.

The best proof of the effect of the spread of education on crime is the notable decrease, which has for many years been observable, in the number of committals and convictions for serious offences. Although the direct effect of the spread of enlightenment cannot be otherwise gauged, there is ample evidence to warrant the assumption that education is doing its work as an active leaven for good throughout the community.

Drunkenness.

The question of the relative prevalence of drunkenness, as tested by the number of persons arrested for that offence in the different colonies, has received of late no little attention, and it has been made to appear that New South Wales in this regard holds a bad pre-eminence. The total arrests for drunkenness and the number per 1,000 of population in the different colonies, for the latest available years, were :—

Arrests for Drunkenness in Australian Colonies.

	Total Arrests.	Arrests, per 1,000 of population.
*New South Wales	18,654	16·9
Victoria	18,068	16·5
Queensland	6,160	16·3
*South Australia	2,382	7·4
Tasmania	1,107	7·0
New Zealand	5,219	8·5

* 1890. Other Colonies, 1889.

These figures show a somewhat unexpected result. During 1889 the arrests for drunkenness in New South Wales exhibited a very gratifying decrease as compared with those of the previous year, which reached a total of 21,129; and the figures for 1890 show only a very small increase upon those for 1889. The figures for all the other Colonies show a slight decline, compared with those of the previous year. But an argument founded solely on the number of arrests for drunkenness is misleading, for a great deal depends upon the state of the law and the manner in which it is administered. The extent of the area supervised must also be taken into consideration, for it is evident that the law will be less strictly enforced in the sparsely settled districts of Queensland, South Australia, and Western Australia, than in the more thickly populated parts of Australia. The quantity of intoxicants consumed per head of the community is, perhaps, a better guide, though not always a safe indication, unless the manners and customs of the people are also taken into consideration. But where the habits of communities are so similar as is the case in regard to the Australasian Colonies, the consumption per head is a tolerably fair test. The figures given in the accompanying table may be taken as correct, with some slight hesitation as regards those relating to the consumption of beer in those Colonies where no excise duty is enforced, as Victoria, Queensland, South Australia, and Western Australia. In Victoria, where the returns are furnished by the brewers, the figures are probably over stated, causing the consumption of beer per head to appear largely in excess of that of New South Wales and other Colonies, although the habits of the community are very similar. As the table stands the amount of

Deduction from number of arrests misleading.

Consumption of intoxicants.

alcohol consumed is greatest in Western Australia and Victoria, while in New South Wales it is about the same as the average for Australasia :—

Consumption of Intoxicants in the Australasian Colonies, 1889.

Colony.	Spirits.		Wine.		Beer, &c.		Equivalent in Alcohol (proof) per inhabitant.
	Total.	Per inhabitant.	Total.	Per inhabitant.	Total.	Per inhabitant.	
	galls.	galls.	galls.	galls.	galls.	galls.	galls.
New South Wales	1,159,280	1·07	916,630	0·82	12,029,000	10·39	2·73
Victoria	1,104,074	1·00	1,216,024	1·11	21,585,581	19·40	3·32
Queensland	462,944	1·16	225,807	0·57	3,911,531	9·35	2·60
South Australia	185,172	0·57	307,600	0·96	4,261,711	13·26	2·38
Western Australia	53,069	1·23	146,836	3·41	562,236	13·10	2·95
Tasmania	81,609	0·55	39,607	0·27	1,449,234	9·74	1·88
New Zealand............	370,383	0·60	107,818	0·17	4,676,558	7·62	1·64
Total and Means	3,416,621	0·91	2,969,821	0·79	48,475,786	12·94	2·82

These figures at once dispose of the theory so persistently put forward as to the excessive prevalence of drunkenness in New South Wales, and the more effectually when it is borne in mind that the number of males engaged in laborious work is far larger here than in any other colony.

Arrests for drunkenness in towns.

The persons arrested for drunkenness are chiefly residents in or near large towns, and it is only natural to expect that, with an increase in the number and population of the towns, there will be an increase in the arrests for drunkenness. The number of arrests during each year since 1880 is shown in the following table, and it will be satisfactory to note the great decrease in the percentage of females arrested. And as the proportion of males arrested has maintained a high percentage for many years, due possibly to the greater increase in the urban than in the rural population, and consequently the larger number of persons whose inebriety has come under the attention of the local police, it is very gratifying to find a considerable decrease in 1890, both of the total number

Female drunkards decreasing.

Decrease in intoxication.

and the percentage to the population. Much stress cannot, however, be laid on the falling off in the arrests, if there were not other evidence of the decrease of drunkenness; as a word of instruction from the Inspector-General of Police could, according to its tenor, increase or decrease the number of those apprehended on this charge. The decline in arrests apparently follows a marked decrease in the consumption of intoxicants, so that it may be fairly assumed that drunkenness is on the wane:—

Persons Arrested for Drunkenness, with percentage of Total Population.

Year.	Total arrests.	Males.	Females.	Percentage of total arrests to whole population.	Percentage of males arrested to total male population.	Percentage of females arrested to total female population.
1880	18,777	14,801	3,976	2·58	3·72	1·20
1881	22,560	18,200	4,360	2·95	4·34	1·26
1882	21,393	17,574	3,819	2·68	4·01	1·06
1883	23,178	19,244	3.934	2·77	4·18	1·04
1884	24,438	20,261	4,177	2·77	4·17	1·05
1885	26,291	21,944	4,347	2·84	4·29	1·04
1886	26,310	21,879	4,431	2·71	4·10	1·01
1887	22,706	19,229	3,477	2·26	3·49	0·76
1888	21,129	17,438	3,691	2·04	3·08	0·79
1889	18,355	14,887	3,468	1·72	2·56	0·71
1890	18,654	15,636	3,018	1·69	2·61	0·60

Consumption of spirits per head.

The quantity of spirits consumed per head of population in 1890 was only about 75 per cent. of the consumption nine years previously, and the decline has been fairly regular, as will be seen from the following table:—

Consumption of Spirits per Head.

Year.	Imported.	Colonial.	Total.	Year.	Imported.	Colonial.	Total.
	Gallons.	Gallons.	Gallons.		Gallons.	Gallons.	Gallons.
1881	1·45	·008	1·46	1886	1·19	·010	1·20
1882	1·45	·012	1·46	1887	1·10	·015	1·11
1883	1·43	·024	1·45	1888	1·08	·016	1·10
1884	1·41	·020	1·43	1889	1·06	·013	1·07
1885	1·29	·015	1·30	1890	1·06	·030	1·09

Consumption of intoxicants decreasing.

There has also been, in all probability, a falling off in the amount of beer and wine consumed, but the statistics which would illustrate this view are available for only a few years. The total amount of intoxicants consumed in the Colony can best be compared by reducing the various kinds of drink to the common level of proof spirit. The average consumption of spirit per inhabitant during the years 1883–90 was:—

Year.	Gallons.
1883	3·52
1884	3·53
1885	3·37
1886	3·23
1887	2·97
1888	2·88
1889	2·71
1890	2·73

Decrease in drunkenness.

If the number of persons who render themselves liable to arrest may be fairly assumed to be in direct proportion to the amount of intoxicants consumed, a decrease in consumption is necessarily a sign of increased sobriety.

Habitual drunkenness.

The offence of habitual drunkenness has declined perceptibly, as will be seen from the following table, showing the number of persons arrested, with percentage of arrests to total arrests for drunkenness, 1881–90.

Habitual Drunkenness.

Year.	Number.	Percentage of arrests to total arrests for drunkenness.	Year.	Number.	Percentage of arrests to total arrests for drunkenness.
1881	101	0·54	1886	113	0·43
1882	141	0·65	1887	119	0·52
1883	100	0·43	1888	80	0·38
1884	108	0·44	1889	101	0·55
1885	116	0·44	1890	93	0·49

TRIALS.

The following statement shows the character of the offences for which prisoners were tried during each year since 1882, and affords material for interesting study:—

Trials for Prominent Offences in Superior Courts, 1882–90.

Offences.	1882.	1883.	1884.	1885.	1886.	1887.	1888.	1889.	1890.
Murder	7	10	16	18	17	11	22	13	0
Attempted Murder	7	4	10	7	5	7	9	9	8
Manslaughter	19	10	21	12	25	7	22	16	25
Wounding Maliciously, unlawfully	92	77	61	42	102	67	87	48	119
Rape, and Attempts to commit	24	15	19	9	41	7	16	22	14
Indecent Assaults	27	15	42	36	33	40	47	38	35
Unnatural Offences	9	4	12	14	14	18	13	10	25
Arson	20	9	28	15	16	10	15	23	21
Robbery with Violence, including Garrotting	47	47	48	39	43	40	24	42	55
Larceny and receiving Stolen property	332	377	271	261	231	211	178	255	246
Stealing in a dwelling, including Burglary	136	80	113	120	130	151	186	167	91
Forgery and Uttering	92	62	88	92	128	96	114	107	90
Stealing from the Person	109	108	66	44	61	44	54	70	56
Obtaining Money, &c., under false pretences	112	88	106	68	72	96	70	87	94
Embezzlement	50	39	39	19	39	38	47	38	25
Horse-stealing	104	105	96	88	78	76	70	71	74
Cattle-stealing	19	25	15	33	24	26	22	25	26
Sheep-stealing	37	19	22	20	33	18	19	20	19
Perjury	24	19	14	3	8	7	21	15	10

Epidemics of crime.

An inspection of this table will show how curiously an epidemic of a particular kind of crime sometimes appears to set in. Thus, with regard to murder, during the years 1884, 1885, and 1886, the number of trials recorded was above the average, and at the periods beginning and ending the series they fell considerably below it. Attempts to murder show very little variation during the nine years, while cases of manslaughter have been above and below the average in alternate years. Rapes and attempts to rape also alternated in a somewhat similar manner, the highest number, 41, being followed by the lowest, 7. Cases of wounding decreased from the beginning of the term, but increased again towards the close, ending with the highest figures of the series. Larcenies declined steadily from 1882 to 1888, but since then have been on the increase. Stealing from the person was at its height during the early years in question, declining in the middle of the term, and rising again towards the close. Horse-stealing and sheep-stealing have shown a general tendency to decline, and cattle-stealing to increase, during the ten years. Perjury was at its highest level in 1882, falling rapidly until 1885, rising again until 1888, and showing an inclination to fall in the two subsequent years. Embezzlements during the period in question averaged 37 per annum, but fell below that average only in 1885 and 1890. In 1882 and 1888, on the contrary the cases recorded numbered as high as 50 and 47 respectively.

PUNISHMENTS.

Punishments inflicted by magistrates.

Of the 66,087 persons brought before the magistrates of the Colony during 1890, 48,102 were summarily convicted, and of these 4,388 were imprisoned without the option of a fine. In no case was the punishment of whipping inflicted. In the great majority of cases fines were inflicted, or imprisonment with the option of paying a fine instead. The nature of the punishments, with the offences for which they were awarded, are given in the following table, for the year 1890 :—

Number of Summary Convictions, Nature of Offences and of Punishments inflicted by Magistrates.

Punishment.	For offences against the person.	For offences against property.	For other offences.	Total number of punishments.
Fine, levy and distress	1,429	811	16,454	18,694
Fine or surety, or in default, imprisonment	2,231	858	19,498	22,587
Peremptory imprisonment ...	513	1,848	2,027	4,388
Bound over, with or without sureties..................	129	14	114	257
Other punishments.............	171	135	1,870	2,176
Total..................	4,473	3,666	39,963	48,102

The number of persons fined, with the alternative of imprisonment, was 22,587; and of these 15,643 availed themselves of the option of paying the fine. The remaining 6,944 suffered imprisonment, in addition to 4,388 sentenced to peremptory imprisonment, making a total of 11,332 persons imprisoned, out of 48,102 summarily dealt with by the magistrates, or 23·6 per cent. Adding 18,694, the number fined (levy and distress) to 15,643, the number who paid rather than be incarcerated, gives 34,337 as the total number of fines paid during the year. Cases in which fines were inflicted.

Omitting from consideration summons cases, and dealing only with arrests by the police, three facts are noticeable—that the percentage of arrests to the total population has fluctuated considerably during the past ten years, and was lower in 1890 than in any previous year; that the number of summary convictions Decrease in committals for trial.

onvictions icreasing.

obtained is now proportionately greater than formerly; and that the number of committals for trial to the superior courts shows a remarkable tendency to decrease. The following table gives the annual average for twelve years:—

Proportion of Convictions and Committals in Magistrates' Courts, compared with Arrests.

Year.	Arrests.	Summarily convicted.	Summarily acquitted or discharged.	Committals.
	Percentage of arrests to the whole population.	Percentage of summary convictions to total arrests.	Percentage of those acquitted or discharged to total arrests.	Percentage to total arrests.
1879	4·75	77·63	17·52	4·85
1880	4·91	76·04	18·36	4·70
1881	5·41	79·86	16·29	3·85
1882	4·98	78·94	17·07	3·99
1883	5·15	82·08	14·26	3·66
1884	5·23	80·99	15·59	3·42
1885	5·20	82·89	14·07	3·04
1886	5·04	82·24	14·79	2·97
1887	4·39	81·57	15·33	3·10
1888	4·11	79·89	16·77	3·34
1889	3·60	78·81	17·43	3·76
1890	3·50	80·36	16·04	3·60

ecrease in ommittals r trial.

The proportion of offences deemed of sufficient gravity to be tried by a jury has largely decreased during the past twenty-five years, and the proportion of prisoners convicted also shows a substantial reduction. This will be plainly seen from a consideration of the following table:—

Committals irrespective of year and Convictions in Superior Courts.

Year.	Committals for trials.	Convictions.	Proportion of population committed.	Proportion of population convicted.
			Per 10,000 of population.	Per 10,000 of population.
1870	1,037	601	21·1	12·2
1871	1,084	628	21·3	12·3
1872	1,073	643	20·3	12·2
1873	1,166	647	21·4	11·8
1874	1,311	700	23·2	12·4
1875	1,245	707	21·2	12·0
1876	1,391	822	23·0	13·6
1877	1,411	829	22·4	13·1
1878	1,740	959	26·4	14·5
1879	1,743	1,090	25·2	15·7
1880	1,717	1,148	23·6	15·8
1881	1,626	1,058	21·3	13·8
1882	1,724	1,065	21·6	13·3
1883	1,606	1,008	19·2	12·0
1884	1,550	928	17·5	10·5
1885	1,540	785	16·6	8·5
1886	1,594	957	16·4	9·9
1887	1,402	854	13·9	8·5
1888	1,561	915	15·1	8·8
1889	1,595	910	15·0	8·5
1890	1,554	955	14·1	8·7

It will be seen that the number of convictions obtained in 1890 averaged about 61·85 per cent., while for the past twelve years the proportion convicted or discharged, per hundred persons committed for trial, was as follows :— Convictions of persons committed.

Percentage of Convictions.

Year.	Percentage of committals.		Year.	Percentage of committals.	
	Convicted.	Acquitted or discharged.		Convicted.	Acquitted or discharged.
1879	62·54	37·46	1885	50·97	49·03
1880	66·86	33·14	1886	60·04	39·96
1881	65·07	34·93	1887	60·91	39·09
1882	61·77	38·23	1888	58·62	41·38
1883	62·76	37·24	1889	57·05	42·95
1884	59·87	40·13	1890	61·85	38·15

The convictions in the higher courts of New South Wales, taken over a series of years, greatly exceed, both in number and in proportion, those of any other Colony. So marked is this fact that muth Causes of apparent high rate of crime.

speculation has been indulged in as to the probable cause of the anomaly. It is admitted that the people of all the colonies are practically derived from the same stock, while their occupations and habits of life are fairly alike, and a theory has been hazarded that the high rate of crime in New South Wales is due to a blood taint derived from the original bond-population of this Colony. Such theory is manifestly absurd, as Tasmania, the colony which received proportionately the largest number of convicts, and whose population has been least diluted by immigration, has for many years had the most favourable record of convictions.

Gold-fields attracted criminal population.

Besides this, Victoria stands somewhat low on the list, and there is every testimony that the large gold-finds of that colony, in the years succeeding the final cessation of transportation, attracted the worst classes of all these settlements, especially those of New South Wales and Tasmania. There is, however, no evidence that such a population now exists anywhere in these colonies: it certainly does not exist in New South Wales. But, though the gratuitous theory above alluded to may be easily disposed of, the fact remains that the largest proportion of convictions in the higher courts occurs in New South Wales. Western Australia has been omitted from the comparison, as its sparse population and peculiar situation would warrant the anticipation of a large amount of crime of a kind not found in the older settled colonies :—

Convictions after Trial in Superior Courts in Australasia, 1889.

	Number.	Per ten thousand of population.
New South Wales	910	8·53
Victoria	651	5·95
Queensland	256	6·78
South Australia	78	2·46
Tasmania	42	3·00
New Zealand	235	3·85

Number of convictions.

In the foregoing table it will be observed that New South Wales has by far the largest number of convictions after trial in the Superior Courts than any of the other Colonies in the Group. It may be mentioned, however, that South Australia and Tasmania have no intermediate Courts like the Quarter Sessions of New South Wales, and the District Courts with criminal jurisdiction of some of the other Colonies, and many persons who would be committed to higher Courts in New South Wales are convicted in the Magisterial Courts of South Australia and Tasmania; nevertheless this would only slightly affect the result in those Colonies, and the fact remains that New South Wales stands in the unenviable position of having by far the largest number of convictions after trial in the Superior Courts of any of the Group.

There has been in New South Wales for many years a large population whose abode in any district is determined by the existence of a demand for unskilled labour, and it is from the ranks of this floating population that a large proportion of the persons convicted of crime is derived. All the colonies have, to a greater or less extent, this class of population; but in New South Wales it is numerically the largest. As these people settle down to regular employment in a fixed abode and acquire interests apart from the excitements of an unsettled life, crime will be found to diminish. The neighbouring colony of Victoria, where the decrease of convictions has steadily kept pace with the settlement of its population, may be cited as an example of this truth, the proportion of convictions being reduced in 1889 to about 5·95 per ten thousand, as compared with 10·1 in 1866. Criminals come from floating population.

The laws relating to crime are somewhat similar in all the colonies; but the administration of these laws may possibly be more rigorous in New South Wales than in any other colony. This has already been shown to be the case in regard to drunkenness, and offers an additional explanation of the large number of convictions obtained in New South Wales. It should also be remembered that in this Colony there is no Act to prevent the influx of criminals, such as they have, and enforce stringently, in some of the other Colonies. Strict administration of law in N. S. Wales. No law against influx of criminals.

Executions have been less numerous of late years than formerly, the dread penalty being carried out in only a small proportion of cases wherein the death sentence has been pronounced. The number of executions since 1824 is given herewith. In three Capital punishment.

Females executed.

years only have there been no executions. Four females have been hanged during the period in question :—

Number of Capital Convictions and Executions, 1825 to 1890.

Year.	Convictions.	Executions.	Year.	Convictions.	Executions.	Year.	Convictions.	Executions.
1825	54	9	1847	10	6	1869	6	......
1826	72	21	1848	6	5	1870	3	......
1827	93	29	1849	6	4	1871	11	3
1828	106	28	1850	5	4	1872	19	3
1829	112	52	1851	8	2	1873	10	4
1830	136	50	1852	10	5	1874	14	3
1831	143	32	1853	4	2	1875	8	2
1832	156	12	1854	11	6	1876	15	4
1833	135	31	1855	12	5*	1877	9	2
1834	148	44	1856	7	......	1878	12	1
1835	142	40	1857	9	4	1879	21	1
1836	79	26	1858	9	1	1880	21	4
1837	90	12	1859	10	7	1881	6	2
1838	130	19	1860	11	5*	1882	14	3
1839	53	22	1861	32	2	1883	9	1
1840	13	8	1862	18	6	1884	8	2
1841	27	18	1863	16	6	1885	11	3
1842	47	13	1864	5	2	1886	22	2
1843	22	8	1865	10	3	1887	4	4
1844	22	8*	1866	20	6	1888	17	2
1845	15	3	1867	19	4	1889	4	3*
1846	11	1	1868	13	5	1890	2	1

* One female.

The following is a return of offences for which persons were hanged during the last twenty years; also, the number of convictions for these offences. Convictions and executions.

Year.	Murder and Attempt at Murder.		Rape.		Attempts at Rape. (convictions.)
	Convictions.	Executions.	Convictions.	Executions.	
1871	9	3	2	......	2
1872	14	3	5	......	4
1873	9	4	1	......	3
1874	7	2	7	1	10
1875	7	1	1	1	4
1876	12	4	3	......	3
1877	4	2	5	......	......
1878	8	1	4	......	3
1879	16	......	5	1	3
1880	15	4	6	......	......
1881	3	1	3	1	6
1882	10	3	4	......	3
1883	8	1	1	......	3
1884	7	2	1	......	......
1885	9	3	2	......	......
1886	10	2	12	......	9
1887	3	......	1	4*	......
1888	15	2	2	......	......
1889	3	3	1	......	......
1890	2	1	1	......	1

* Mount Rennie case; convicted in 1886.

GAOLS.

There are in New South Wales 59 gaols of all kinds; of these 39 are distinguished as police gaols. There is accommodation for 1,729 prisoners in separate cells, and for 4,502 when more than one prisoner sleeps in a cell. On the 31st December, 1890, there were 2,425 prisoners in confinement, thus distributed:— Gaol accommodation.

Prisoners and Prison Accommodation.

Prisons.	Prisoners.	Accommodation—one prisoner per cell.	Accommodation—more than one prisoner per cell.
Gaols	2,239	1,524	3,731
Police Gaols	186	205	771
Total	2,425	1,729	4,502

Decrease of prisoners.

The total number of prisoners received into the various gaols throughout the Colony during the year 1890 was 15,788—a lesser number than in any of the eight previous years. Of these 6,248 were received at Darlinghurst Gaol, Sydney. As many were detained for only short periods the above total may appear large compared with the average number in confinement at any one time. The following table gives the number of prisoners received into gaol from 1882 to 1890, exclusive of debtors and those in transitu:—

Prisoners Received into Gaol.

Year.	Under sentence.		Trial, &c.		Total.		
	Males.	Females.	Males.	Females.	Males.	Females.	Total.
1882	10,326	3,918	2,762	407	13,088	4,325	17,413
1883	11,309	4,096	2,740	421	14,049	4,517	18,566
1884	12,836	4,161	2,988	413	15,824	4,574	20,398
1885	13,045	4,324	2,808	509	15,853	4,833	20,686
1886	12,650	4,382	3,003	539	15,653	4,921	20,574
1887	11,554	3,728	3,006	499	14,560	4,227	18,787
1888	10,519	3,712	3,364	455	13,883	4,167	18,050
1889	9,299	3,583	2,956	412	12,255	3,995	16,250
1890	9,203	3,084	3,104	397	12,307	3,481	15,788

Prisoners in confinement.

The average number of persons in confinement during the year has not been ascertained, but the number in detention at the close of each year is known, and the figures for the past fourteen years will be found herewith. Prisoners have been classified under two heads—those under sentence, and those awaiting trial. The respective numbers of each of these classes for the period named were:—

Prisoners in Confinement at the close of each year.

Year.	Total persons in confinement.	Male.	Female.	*Under sentence.			Awaiting trial.		
				Male.	Female.	Total.	Male.	Female.	Total.
1876	1,490	1,267	223	1,154	203	1,357	113	20	133
1877	1,521	1,293	228	1,137	209	1,346	156	19	175
1878	1,781	1,512	269	1,318	251	1,569	194	18	212
1879	1,951	1,641	310	1,465	291	1,756	176	19	195
1880	2,121	1,759	362	1,610	349	1,959	149	13	162
1881	2,075	1,753	322	1,611	309	1,920	142	13	155
1882	1,935	1,646	289	1,497	274	1,771	149	15	164
1883	2,168	1,826	342	1,684	330	2,014	142	12	154
1884	2,464	2,115	349	1,966	337	2,303	149	12	161
1885	2,559	2,222	337	2,084	328	2,412	138	9	147
1886	2,501	2,119	382	2,018	369	2,387	101	13	114
1887	2,380	2,053	327	1,919	316	2,235	134	11	145
1888	2,353	2,044	309	1,931	301	2,232	113	8	121
1889	2,370	2,048	322	1,932	313	2,245	116	9	125
1890	2,425	2,143	282	2,023	273	2,296	120	9	129

* Includes 4 debtors in 1890.

The prisoners under sentence may be divided into four classes according to the description of offence for which they were convicted, as in the following table:— Classification of offences.

Offences of Prisoners under Sentence at close of each year.

Year.	Felony.		Misdemeanours					
			Larceny.		Assault.		Other offences.	
	Male.	Female.	Male.	Female.	Male.	Female.	Male.	Female.
1876	708	34	160	21	78	4	208	144
1877	798	57	81	16	32	3	226	133
1878	855	51	127	22	50	4	286	174
1879	911	42	176	29	70	21	308	199
1880	950	34	189	31	106	8	365	276
1881	925	18	201	15	78	5	508	271
1882	844	25	168	18	89	3	396	228
1883	802	47	263	26	138	15	481	242
1884	949	33	295	29	140	6	582	269
1885	1,047	33	307	47	162	10	568	238
1886	1,070	40	296	32	121	11	531	286
1887	1,024	30	221	28	137	3	519	255
1888	967	27	295	25	146	10	494	239
1889	1,061	29	293	34	140	4	436	246
1890	1,073	27	289	23	141	10	517	212

Felons under arrest.

The number of felons detained under sentence was larger in 1886 and 1890 than in any other year of the series, and, although the figures of 1890 are very little above those of the previous year, it will be seen that a notable increase has taken place from 1883 to 1888. This advance does not denote an increase in crime—for, as already shown, serious crime is decreasing in the community—but points rather to longer sentences. The increase in the term served by prisoners is due to the Criminal Law Amendment Act, which came into force on the 1st day of July, 1883. By the provisions of that Act in very many cases a minimum sentence was imposed which the Judges had not power to reduce. More recently, however, an Amending Act has been passed, by which the Judges are enabled to exercise greater discretion in the way of leniency in cases where they are of opinion that the circumstances render it expedient that they should do so.

The following table shows the average time served by each prisoner sentenced for felony :—

Average Term of Imprisonment served by Prisoners under Sentence for Felony.

Year.	Average sentence.	Year.	Average sentence.
	Years.		Years.
1878	1·39	1885	1·72
1879	1·27	1886	1·48
1880	1·21	1887	1·60
1881	1·15	1888	1·43
1882	1·22	1889	1·21
1883	1·20	1890	1·34
1884	1·40		

Ages of prisoners in gaols.

As in the case of the arrests, the largest number of prisoners at any age-period are those whose ages range from 20 to 30 years; but, proportionately to the numbers of the population, the ages of middle life, namely, from 30 to 50 years, are most productive of criminals. The following table gives the number and ages of persons sentenced to labour or imprisonment, during the year 1890 : —

Ages of Persons sentenced to Imprisonment.

Ages.	Sentenced to Labour.			To Imprisonment.			To Death.	Total Prisoners Sentenced.		
	Males.	Females.	Total.	Males.	Females.	Total.	Males.	Males.	Females.	Total.
Under 10 years.	...	...	...	6	...	6	...	6	...	6
10 and under 15.	26	...	26	59	2	61	...	85	2	87
15 ,, 20.	259	120	379	349	118	467	...	608	238	846
20 ,, 25.	459	82	541	620	240	860	...	1,079	322	1,401
25 ,, 30.	789	132	921	1,035	433	1,468	...	1,824	565	2,389
30 ,, 35.	359	100	459	730	407	1,137	1	1,090	507	1,597
35 ,, 40.	337	105	442	586	369	955	...	923	474	1,397
40 ,, 45.	248	83	331	520	241	701	...	768	324	1,092
45 ,, 50.	225	49	274	454	182	636	...	679	231	910
50 and upwards.	425	75	500	1,037	281	1,318	*1	1,453	356	1,819
Totals ...	3,127	746	3,873	5,396	2,273	7,669	2	8,525	3,019	11,544

* Afterwards commuted to imprisonment for life.

Number of persons convicted.

Taking the returns from all the gaols, it will be found that 7,939 distinct persons were convicted during the year 1890, of whom 6,556 were males, and 1,383 were females. The following tables show the ages of these prisoners, in sexes, who were convicted once, twice, thrice, and four or more times during the year. The total number here given differs from that returned by the Comptroller-General of Prisons, the discrepancy being accounted for by the fact that the same prisoner sometimes serves sentences at different gaols, in which case he is likely to be counted as a distinct person in each gaol. In the figures given herewith the returns from all the gaols have been combined, and each person is credited with the total number of sentences received, whether served in one or several prisons :—

Distinct Persons convicted once, twice, thrice, and four or more times, during 1890.

Males.

Ages.	Convicted once.	Convicted twice.	Convicted three times.	Convicted four or more times.	Total convicted more than once.	Total number of distinct persons convicted.
Under 10 years	4	...	...	......	.. ...	4
10 and under 15 years ..	76	8	...	......	8	84
15 and under 20 years ...	416	53	16	5	74	490
20 and under 25 years ...	672	77	41	26	144	816
25 and under 30 years ..	1,179	158	47	33	238	1,417
30 and under 35 years ...	780	106	32	20	158	938
35 and under 40 years ...	606	87	28	14	129	735
40 and under 45 years ...	470	91	23	9	123	593
45 and under 50 years ...	380	61	16	22	99	479
50 years and upwards ...	777	136	45	42	223	1,000
Total	5,360	777	248	171	1,196	6,556

Females.

Ages.	Convicted once.	Convicted twice.	Convicted three times.	Convicted four or more times.	Total convicted more than once.	Total number of distinct persons convicted.
Under 10 years	...	...	...	......	......	......
10 and under 15 years ...	2	...	...	.....	......	2
15 and under 20 years ...	84	24	12	8	44	128
20 and under 25 years ...	115	36	17	22	75	190
25 and under 30 years ...	137	29	15	50	94	231
30 and under 35 years ...	117	28	18	45	91	208
35 and under 40 years ...	109	32	20	37	89	198
40 and under 45 years ..	79	31	15	26	72	151
45 and under 50 years ...	66	12	6	15	33	99
50 years and upwards ...	109	33	13	21	67	176
Total	818	225	116	224	565	1,383

These figures disclose some interesting facts. It is sad to see that four boys less than 10 years old had to be sent to gaol, as well as the large number of 84 between the ages of 10 and 15; but it is well known that the problem of dealing with juvenile offenders is one of the most serious and embarrassing that the magistrates have to cope with, especially as there is no Reformatory in the Colony to which boys of the criminal class can be sent. In the absence of such an institution, the magistrates, unwilling to subject boys of tender age to the contaminating influences of a gaol, generally ignore the criminal charges and send the lads on board the nautical school-ship "Vernon," as deserted or neglected children. This, though the lesser of two evils, is manifestly unfair to the class of children for whom the "Vernon" was primarily intended, and must largely increase the difficulties of its management. There is a Reformatory for Girls at Shaftesbury, near the South Head, but nevertheless two girls under the age of 15 were sent to prison. *Juvenile offenders.*

Of the 6,556 males convicted in 1890, 777 were sentenced twice in the year; 248 suffered three convictions; 171 were sent to gaol *Males convicted more than once.*

four or more times. The majority of the twice convicted prisoners were of ages between 25 and 50, but no less than 136 were over 50 years old. More than half the thrice convicted were also between 25 and 50, but strange to say 16 youths between the ages of 15 and 20 were among this class. Those convicted four or more times include 5 youths of less than 20 years; 118 of this class were between 25 and 50, and 42 were over 50.

Women convicted more than once.

Of the female offenders, 225 were convicted twice in the year, 116 three times, and 224 four or more times. No less than 24 of the twice convicted prisoners were between the ages of 15 and 20, 36 were between 20 and 25, and 132 were between 25 and 50, and 33 were upwards of 50. Twelve females of 15 and under 20 head the roll of those convicted three times, followed by seventeen of 20 and under 25. Between 25 and 50 there were 74 of this class, with 13 of over 50 years of age. The list of those convicted four or more times commences with eight of 15 and under 20, twenty-five between 20 and 25, 173 of ages from 25 to 50, and 21 of 50 and upwards.

Total number of prisoners.

The total number of distinct persons committed to gaol during 1890 as compiled from returns furnished by the Prisons Department was 7,939. Of this number 6,556 were males and 1,383 were females. Out of the 7,939 prisoners referred to, 2,897, or 36·49 per cent., were natives of New South Wales; 1,761, or 22·18 per cent., were natives of England and Wales; 1,368, or 17·23 per cent., came from Ireland; 538, or 6·78 per cent., from Scotland; 229, or 3·77 per cent., from Victoria; and 63, or about ·8 per cent., were Chinese,—the remainder being of various nationalities. As regards religion, 3,319, or 41·81 per cent., described themselves as belonging to the Church of England; 3,556, or 44·79 per cent., were Roman Catholics; 600, or 7·56 per cent., were Presbyterians; 152, or less than 2 per cent., were Wesleyans, and the remainder were distributed among a variety of denominations; 6,954 prisoners, or 5,779 males and 1,175 females, could read and write; 186, or 114 males and 72 females, could read only; while 799, or about 10 per cent. of the whole, could neither read nor write. Of this class there were 2 males under 10 years; 10 males between 10 and 15 years; 34 males and 6 females between

Birth-places of prisoners.

15 and 20; 71 males and 5 females between 20 and 25; 117 males and 12 females between 25 and 30; 160 males and 43 females between 30 and 40; 117 males and 33 females between 40 and 50, and 152 males and 37 females over 50 years of age.

Although the number of distinct persons committed to gaol was 7,939, the total number of committals was 11,544, many persons having been sent to gaol several times in the year. Of these 778 males and 62 females, or 840 persons in all, were imprisoned for offences against the person; 202 males and 38 females, or 240 persons, for offences against property with violence; 1,555 males and 147 females, or 1,702 persons, for offences against property without violence; 43 males and 2 females, or 45 persons, for offences against the currency; 3,409 males and 1,121 females for offences against good order; and 569 males and 13 females for offences not included in the preceding list.

Total number of committals to gaol.

During the year 2 males were received into gaol under sentence of death for murder; one of these was hanged, and in the other case the sentence was commuted into imprisonment for life; 5 men were sentenced for attempted murder, one of whom received a sentence of between 5 and 10 years; 3 men were punished for manslaughter, but in only one case was the sentence over 5 years. 38 men were imprisoned for wounding with intent; 10 of these were sentenced to terms of between 5 and 10 years, and 1 to a period over 10 years. In 24 cases the offenders were punished for crimes against women, and 20 cases were for unnatural offences. 3 men were imprisoned for garrotting, 1 for a period exceeding 5 years.

Offences against the person.

For assault and robbery 29 males were imprisoned for various terms ranging up to 10 years. 78 prisoners were punished for breaking and entering, the sentences ranging from 2 to over 10 years, and 3 prisoners convicted of burglary received terms of between 2 and 5 years. Of the 1,640 males incarcerated for offences against property without violence, two-thirds, or 1,095, were convicted of simple larceny, 23 for stealing from the person,

Offences against property with violence.

Offences against property without violence.

19 for stealing from a dwelling, 43 for stealing horses, cattle, or sheep, 41 for embezzlement, 146 for obtaining money, &c., under false pretences, 120 for receiving or being in possession of stolen property, 31 for fraudulently retaining property, and 47 for being unlawfully on premises. 39 males were imprisoned for forgery and uttering, of whom 3 were sentenced to over 10 years, and 1 to between 5 and 10 years; 5 men were sentenced for possessing or passing counterfeit coin, of whom 3 were imprisoned for periods between 2 and 5 years.

Forgery and offences against the currency.

Offences against good order.

Of the 5,025 males who were sent to gaol for offences against good order, 2,555, or more than half, were punished for drunkenness, with or without disorderly conduct, and 45 for habitual drunkenness; 432 were confined for riotous or indecent behaviour and 1,127 for obscene or abusive language; 495 males were sentenced under the Vagrancy Act. The offences not included in the preceding are mostly breaches of various Acts and by-laws, for which light penalties were imposed. There were also 4 cases of perjury, 1 of bribery, 1 of defamatory libel, 1 of misappropriation, 1 of conspiracy, and 1 under the Fugitive Offenders Act.

Other offences.

Female offenders.

Among the female offenders 2 were imprisoned for wounding with intent, 1 for child exposure, and 2 for bigamy. There were no less than 54 women imprisoned for maliciously injuring property, 1 for assault and robbery, and 4 for breaking and entering. 143 women were sent to gaol for simple larceny, 1 for forgery and uttering, and 2 for passing counterfeit coin. 2,698 females were imprisoned during the year for offences against good order, of which 1,577 cases were for drunkenness, with or without disorderly conduct, besides 28 of habitual drunkenness, 97 of riotous behaviour, 424 of obscene language. 54 women were sent to gaol for loitering, 78 for being common prostitutes, and 416 for breaches of the Vagrancy Act.

Criminal class.

It is impossible to determine the extent of the criminal class in the Colony, or even the number of habitual criminals. The number of prisoners sent to gaol more than once during the year has, however, been ascertained for many years, but the figures for the past two years can alone be looked upon as reliable. These are given in the following table, the number of offences committed by such prisoners being also inserted :—

Persons convicted more than once.

Year.	Prisoners sent to Gaol more than once.		Offences Committed.		Average number of Offences Committed.	
	Males.	Females.	Males.	Females.	Males.	Females.
1889	1,224	663	3,126	2,539	2·58	3·83
1890	1,196	565	3,165	2,201	2·65	3·90

The terms for which women are sentenced are much shorter than those of males, as their offences are much lighter. On the other hand there must, from the evidence of the above table, be a constant reappearance of the same faces before the Courts to account for so high an average of reconvictions. The proportion of habitual offenders, if those with previous convictions may be so termed, is remarkable, and will perhaps be better illustrated by the following table than even by the one just given :— Habitual offenders.

Year.	Percentage of prisoners with previous convictions sent to gaol.	Year.	Percentage of prisoners with previous convictions sent to gaol.
1879	19·54	1885	26·99
1880	19·39	1886	26·40
1881	29·44	1887	25·41
1882	33·38	1888	25·26
1883	28·31	1889	22·49
1884	28·17	1890	22·18

The numbers of persons sent to prison for serious offences from 1875 to 1890 are given in the following table; they are arranged in classes according to the terms of their imprisonment. Reconvictions

Reference has already been, at page 272, made to the diminution of crime in New South Wales during the past few years. Perhaps no better illustration of this fact can be given than is afforded by the following statement showing the number of distinct persons imprisoned in each year since 1879:—

Number of Distinct Persons Imprisoned.

Year.	Persons.	Year.	Persons.
1879	8,698	1885	12,429
1880	8,663	1886	11,474
1881	10,169	1887	9,046
1882	9,618	1888	10,096
1883	10,793	1889	8,827
1884	12,264	1890	7,939

Classification of Prisoners reconvicted, omitting Drunkards and Petty Offenders.

Year.	1st Class. Sentence, 5 years and upwards.			2nd Class. Sentence, less than 5 years.			3rd Class. Sentence, imprisonment only.		
	Second conviction.	Third conviction.	Fourth, or more.	Second conviction.	Third conviction.	Fourth, or more.	Second conviction.	Third conviction.	Fourth, or more.
1876	19	40	...	56	86	...	25	44	—
1877	12	30	...	83	91	...	[illegible]	22	...
1878	10	27	...	51	66	...	17	28	...
1879	4	22	...	50	65	...	24	51	...
1880	20	3	3	186	39	30	113	36	57
1881	8	3	4	107	54	63	98	43	[illegible]
1882	16	5	12	231	82	93	152	28	[illegible]
1883	53	4	9	257	50	64	75	20	[illegible]
1884	35	10	46	136	72	57	86	29	[illegible]
1885	20	19	29	133	81	72	101	38	[illegible]
1886	23	10	23	108	43	115	93	31	[illegible]
1887	18	6	28	113	52	74	79	13	[illegible]
1888	16	17	35	136	66	113	76	40	[illegible]
1889	18	14	54	266	104	97	119	54	[illegible]
1890	17	10	50	217	94	120	156	72	[illegible]

This table must be read with the qualification that previous to the year 1880 prisoners with four or more convictions are included with those convicted for the third time.

The chief punishment inflicted on refractory prisoners is solitary confinement. Formerly other modes of punishment were equally used, but of late years these have been to a large extent superseded. The number of punishments inflicted upon refractory prisoners is given as follows:— Refractory prisoners.

Refractory Prisoners.

Year.	Prisoners punished in gaols.			Percentage of total prisoners punished.
	Solitary confinement.	Other punishment.	Total.	
1877	501	395	896	8·23
1878	768	192	960	8·17
1879	1,061	284	1,345	10·16
1880	1,210	263	1,473	10·84
1881	1,225	332	1,557	9·85
1882	1,133	319	1,452	10·19
1883	1,249	268	1,517	9·84
1884	1,473	436	1,909	11·23
1885	1,435	399	1,834	10·56
1886	1,420	389	1,809	10·61
1887	1,445	416	1,861	12·18
1888	1,302	246	1,548	10·89
1889	1,195	331	1,526	11·85
1890	1,458	266	1,724	10·47

There were sixty-one persons imprisoned for debt during the year 1890. And as the time of detention as a rule only extended for short periods, the number of debtors in confinement at any one time was not large. The figures for the last fourteen years will be found in the following table:— Debtors.

Debtors in Confinement.

Year.	Male.	Female.	Total.	Year.	Male.	Female.	Total.
1877	42	...	42	1884	61	3	64
1878	49	2	51	1885	50	2	52
1879	46	2	48	1886	61	1	62
1880	46	1	47	1887	48	2	50
1881	52	...	52	1888	56	1	57
1882	44	1	45	1889	71	1	72
1883	27	1	28	1890	59	2	61

The following table gives the number of the prisoners employed in the several gaols at the end of 1890, and those engaged in the principal callings. In some of the gaols there are no means of finding suitable employment of a profitable or useful nature, otherwise the numbers shown could be very much increased; but it also must be considered that there are many prisoners whose services are not available for labour, such as those whose sentence does not carry hard labour, and those exempt from work on account of medical and other reasons. The net value of the labour done during 1890 amounted to £42,406.

Employment of prisoners.

The following table shows how the prisoners in the gaols of the Colony were employed at the end of the year:—

Carpenters and assistants	42
Painters	16
Blacksmiths and assistants	29
Tinsmiths	19
Masons	5
Stonecutters	28
Labourers	158
Brushmakers	10
Matmakers	71
Shoemakers	125
Tailors	135
Bookbinders	34
Writers	25
Washing...	70
School assistants	14
Hospital attendants	30
Barbers	18
Needlework	116
Other employments	754
Total employed	1,699

Deaths in gaols.

The death-rate in gaols is very light, when the neglected state in which many of the prisoners are received is considered, and moreover shows signs of decreasing. No common ground of comparison exists between the death-rate in gaols and that of the general population. In the following table the number of deaths is given from 1878 to 1890, together with the death-rates per

1,000 of all prisoners under sentence during each year, and this includes those whose term had not expired at the close of the previous year:—

Deaths and Death-rate in Gaol.

Year.	Deaths.			Death-rate per 1,000 persons under sentence. (Both sexes.)
	Male.	Female.	Total.	
1878	39	7	46	4·39
1879	36	7	43	4·10
1880	37	...	37	3·48
1881	53	7	60	4·88
1882	40	6	46	3·92
1883	30	5	35	2·75
1884	35	4	39	2·70
1885	39	11	50	4·01
1886	38	10	48	3·27
1887	30	8	38	3·13
1888	30	5	35	2·80
1889	32	3	35	3·13
1890	24	2	26	2·52

THE SUPREME COURT.

The chief legal tribunal of the Colony is the Supreme Court, which is at present composed of seven judges—that is, one Chief Justice, and six puisne Judges. Civil actions are usually tried by a jury of four persons, but either party to the suit, on cause shown, may apply to a Judge in Chambers to have the cause tried by a jury of twelve. Twice the number of jurors required to sit on the case are chosen by ballot, from a panel summoned by the Sheriff, and from that number each of the parties strikes out a fourth, the remainder thus selected by both parties forming the jury who are to try the case. This jury are constituted the judges of the facts of the case only, being bound to accept the dicta of the Judge on all points of law. From the court thus constituted an appeal lies to what is called the "Full Court," sitting *in Banco*, which is generally composed of at least three of the Judges. The Chief Justice, or in his absence the senior puisne Judge, presides over the

Judges of the Supreme Court.

The Full Court.

Full Court, which gives its decision by majority. The circumstances under which new trials are granted are:—Where the Judge has erroneously admitted or rejected material evidence; where he has wrongly directed the jury on a point of law; where the verdict of the jury is clearly against evidence; or where, from some other cause, there has evidently been a miscarriage of justice.

Appeal to Privy Council permitted.

Provision is made for appeals to the Privy Council, but any suitor wishing to carry his cause before the supreme tribunal of the Empire must first obtain leave so to do from the Supreme Court. The amount in dispute must be at least £500, or affect the construction of a New South Wales statute. In other cases application for leave to appeal must be made to the Privy Council itself.

Vice-Admiralty Court.

The Chief Justice has also an extensive jurisdiction as Commissary of the Vice-Admiralty Court, in which all cases arising out of collisions, &c., in Australian waters, are determined.

Equity Jurisdiction.

One of the puisne Judges also acts as judge of the Equity Court, from whose decrees an appeal lies to the Full Court, and thence to the Privy Council.

Bankruptcy.

Affairs in Bankruptcy are also dealt with by a puisne Judge, assisted by the Registrar.

Divorce Court.

Another puisne Judge presides over the Divorce Court, in which cases are usually tried without a jury, an appeal lying to the Supreme Court.

Ecclesiastical Jurisdiction.

The equity Judge also represents the ecclesiastical jurisdiction of the Supreme Court, and hears and decides all applications for the probate of wills, and for letters of administration, and also determines suits as to the validity, &c., of wills. Motions for rehearing cases, adjudicated in this court, are sometimes made before the Supreme Court or Privy Council. Barristers only have the right of audience before the Supreme Court.

The following table gives the number of civil suits decided in the Supreme and Circuit Courts in each year from 1876 to 1890, inclusive :— Civil suits.

Civil Suits.

Year.	Number of		Defended.	Undefended or settled.	Total amount for which judgment signed.
	Writs issued.	Causes entered for trial.			
					£
1876	2,530	293	208	85	106,257
1877	2,887	286	188	98	127,205
1878	3,280	319	199	120	278,126
1879	3,806	292	179	113	436,356
1880	3,312	350	202	148	202,254
1881	2,845	331	173	158	....
1882	3,161	414	250	164	169,520
1883	3,830	377	225	152	....
1884	4,547	493	271	222	370,648
1885	4,079	494	255	239	399,952
1886	5,649	503	255	248	410,275
1887	5,149	478	223	255	457,704
1888	4,636	583	306	277	393,976
1889	6,408	599	300	299	690,753
1890	5,951	589	460	129	751,825

The number of probates and letters of administration in connection with wills for each year, of the same period, is given in the next table :— Probates and letters of administration.

Probates and Administrations.

Year.	No. of probates and administrations—Wills annexed.	Amount sworn to.	No. of letters of administration.	Amount sworn to.	Total
		£		£	£
1876	511	1,677,972	415	223,189	1,901,161
1877	530	1,336,599	471	291,391	1,627,990
1878	573	1,735,064	514	281,367	2,016,431
1879	579	2,116,906	472	269,991	2,386,897
1880	667	1,323,823	506	210,816	1,534,639
1881	671	2,011,305	526	307,818	2,319,123
1882	810	3,586,554	589	581,528	4,168,082
1883	862	3,528,602	613	588,029	4,116,631
1884	933	3,642,709	648	605,543	4,248,252
1885	961	3,721,805	659	601,542	4,323,347
1886	1,026	4,726,918	706	768,628	5,495,546
1887	961	3,621,874	665	641,426	4,263,300
1888	996	3,652,963	667	638,295	4,291,258
1889	1,115	4,317,734	682	473,611	4,791,345
1890	1,131	6,605,545	680	922,577	7,578,122

CRIMINAL JURISDICTION.

Trial by jury.

A Judge of the Supreme Court presides over the Central Criminal Court of Gaol Delivery held at Darlinghurst. All prisoners are tried by a jury of twelve, chosen by ballot from the panel provided by the Sheriff. Every person charged with felony has a peremptory right of challenge extending to twenty jurors, and he can also further exercise his right of challenge on cause shown and allowed. No prisoner is permitted to give evidence, but he has a right to the services of counsel in conducting his defence. The verdict of the jury must be unanimous, for even if eleven jurors were agreed their verdict could not be accepted. If the jury cannot agree they may be locked up until they either give a unanimous verdict, or are discharged by the Court. If no verdict is returned the prisoner is liable to be tried over again by another jury.

Gaol deliveries.

In addition to the supreme, civil, and criminal sittings of the Court held in Sydney, each Judge goes on circuit once in each half-year, and holds Courts of Gaol Delivery and for hearing civil cases at certain circuit towns, viz. :—In the north—Maitland, Tamworth, Armidale, and Grafton; in the west—Mudgee, Bathurst, Dubbo, and Broken Hill; in the south—Goulburn, Yass, Wagga Wagga, Albury, Deniliquin, Young, and Hay.

DISTRICT COURTS.

Minor civil causes.

District Courts have been established for the trial of civil causes where the value in dispute does not exceed £200. They are presided over by Judges specially appointed for the purpose, who also perform the duties of Chairmen of Quarter Sessions for the trial of all prisoners except such as are charged with capital crimes. District Courts sit ten months during the year in the metropolis, and are held twice a year in all considerable country towns. The Judge is not ordinarily assisted by a jury, but in cases where the amount in dispute exceeds £20, either of the parties may, by giving notice to the Registrar of the Court, have a jury summoned. On questions of law an appeal lies to the Supreme Court.

On the trial of prisoners at Quarter Sessions, the Chairman, at the request of the prisoner's counsel, must reserve questions of law for the consideration of the Supreme Court, or he may so act *motu proprio*. Questions reserved for Supreme Court.

The number of suits in the District Courts of the Colony, and the mode in which they were tried, whether with or without jury, &c., is given in the following table for the judicial year terminating the last day of February, 1890 :— Suits in District Courts.

Suits in District Courts, 1889-90.

District.	Number of suits.		Settled.		Number of cases tried.		Result of the trials.	
	Commenced.	Total amount sued for.	Without hearing.	By arbitration.	By jury.	Without jury.	For plaintiffs.	For defendants.
		£						
Metropolitan and Hunter..	8,200	155,006	4,587	4	72	3,485	3,345	212
Southern	1,174	32,582	478	3	17	609	549	77
South-western.	996	34,958	410	...	23	535	497	61
Western	864	24,170	430	...	19	383	371	31
Northern	1,839	48,911	715	...	24	977	861	140
North-western.	402	16,065	179	...	19	189	181	27
Total	13,475	311,692	6,799	7	174	6,178	5,804	548

The costs of the above-mentioned suits in the Districts Courts amounted to £28,855.

BANKRUPTCY COURT.

The statutes relating to bankrupt debtors are administered by the Supreme Court, and the jurisdiction is exercised by a Judge thereof, called the Judge in Bankruptcy, who may on occasion delegate certain of the powers vested in him to the Registrar of Bankrupt Estates. When any person becomes embarrassed, and is unable to pay his debts, the law allows him to sequestrate his Bankrupt debtors.

estate for the benefit of his creditors, or these latter may, under certain specified circumstances, apply for a compulsory sequestration. An officer of the Court, termed an official assignee, is appointed by the Judge to manage each sequestrated estate. His duties are to realise the bankrupt's assets, and pay *pro rata* the debts proved, subject to the approval of the Judge. After each bankrupt's case has been investigated, and all dividends have been paid, the Judge may at his discretion grant a certificate relieving the bankrupt from all future liability. This certificate is granted in all cases where no blame has been found to attach to the applicant; but where the bankruptcy has been brought about by recklessness or fraud, it is often withheld for some time, and, in very bad cases, refused entirely. An appeal from the decision of the Judge may be made on the same terms and in similar mode as is provided in respect to an order, decision, or ruling of a Judge of the Supreme Court, and by the rules of Court the Judge from whose decision an appeal has been made may not sit to hear such appeal.

Sequestration of estates.

The number of bankrupts, and the amounts for which they failed, and other particulars will be found in the chapter of this volume relating to finance.

PART XII.

Constitution and Government.

THE record of New South Wales as a Crown Colony belongs more to history than to current statistics. It is therefore not proposed, in the following sketch, to deal with matters prior to the establishment of Responsible Government, though a brief narrative of the early history and settlement of the country will be found in the opening pages of this volume.

Present mode of government began in 1855.

The present form of government was inaugurated about thirty-five years ago, the "Act to confer a Constitution on New South Wales, and to grant a Civil List to Her Majesty," having received the Royal assent on the 16th July, 1855. This important statute was proclaimed in Sydney on the 24th of November of the same year, and at once came into operation, sweeping away entirely the former system, and constituting an elective representative Chamber, thus, by the granting of equal privileges, making the colonists of New South Wales the equals of their countrymen in other parts of the Empire. The ties which bound the Colony to the Empire were in no way loosened, for the Constitution Act simply conceded to the people of New South Wales the same rights which prevailed in the United Kingdom, namely, of taxing themselves, and of being governed by Ministers responsible to a Parliament elected by the people. The authority vested in the Sovereign remains the same as before, though the mode of its exercise is widely different. The Sovereign, previously to Responsible Government, exercised, through the Governor, almost despotic power. This official, in times past, united in himself the executive and legislative functions, and personal liberty and independence

The Sovereign.

were to no small degree in his power. With the establishment of Responsible Government, this state of things ceased, and the greatest measure of individual liberty is now found compatible with the full protection of public rights. The readiness with which the people of the Colony adapted themselves to the forms and practice of their new government was not a little remarkable, and fully justified their assumption of its privileges.

Laws enacted in Queen's name.

All laws are enacted in the name of the Queen, "by and with the advice of the Legislative Council and Legislative Assembly," the Governor, as the Royal Deputy, giving the assent of the Sovereign immediately to Acts of Parliament, or reserving them for the consideration of the Sovereign, if he thinks fit. In order that the Constitution may be clearly understood, it will be well to consider, under distinct heads, the several elements of which the Government and Legislature consist.

THE GOVERNOR.

appointed.

Previously to the year 1879 the Governor of the Colony was appointed by Letters Patent under the Great Seal; but in that year the practice was discontinued by the advice of Sir Alfred Stephen, given during the tenure of office of Sir Hercules Robinson. The change was first carried out in the appointment of Lord Augustus Loftus. The office of Governor is now constituted by permanent Letters Patent, and by a standing Commission, instead of as formerly by letters issued *pro hac vice* only. The Governor receives his appointment at present by Commission under the Royal sign manual and signet, which recites the Letters Patent of the 29th April, 1879, as well as the instructions issued (under sign manual and signet) in further declaration of the Queen's "will and pleasure." The original Letters Patent, thus recited and enforced, declare that the Governor is directed and empowered "to do and execute all things that belong to his office according to the tenor of the Letters Patent, and of such Commission as may be issued to him under our sign manual and signet, and according to such instructions as may from time to time be given to him under our sign manual and signet, or by our order in our Privy Council, or by us through one of our Principal Secretaries of State, and to such laws as are now or shall hereafter be in force in the Colony." By a custom which has now long prevailed no Governor is allowed to retain his office longer than six years. Should the Governor die or become incapable during his tenure of office, or be removed before the arrival of his successor, or should he have occasion to leave the Colony for any considerable period, the Government is to be administered (1) by the Lieutenant-Governor; or, if there be no Lieutenant-Governor, (2) by an Administrator to be appointed according to the provisions of the Letters Patent and instructions. The present Lieutenant-Governor is Sir Alfred Stephen, who was appointed by a Commission, dated 30th April, 1879; and the Administrator was appointed by a Commission of the same date, directed to the President of the Legislative Council for the time-being. Lieutenant Governor.

The Lieutenant-Governor, or, in his absence, the Administrator, is empowered by his Commission to execute the office of Governor during any temporary absence of the Governor from the Colony; but the Governor may not be absent, except in accordance with the terms of his instructions. He may not leave the Colony without the Queen's special leave, unless on a visit to the Governor of a neighbouring colony, for a period exceeding one month at a time, nor exceeding in the aggregate one month for every year of his service; but, on the other hand, the Governor may leave the Colony for any period not exceeding one month without its being reckoned as a departure, if he shall have previously informed the Executive Council in writing of his intention, and appointed a deputy to act for him till his return. This deputy must, in the first instance, be the Lieutenant-Governor; but if, from any cause, his services are not available, the Governor may appoint whom he pleases as his deputy. The Administrator.

The Governor's functions, according to the Letters Patent, Commission, and Instructions may be recapitulated as follows:—

The Governor is the custodian of the Great Seal, under which all Crown grants, &c., must pass.

Governor appoints Executive.

The Governor has the appointment of his own Council—the Executive. He is also to summon that Council, and is, ordinarily its President; but in his absence some other member may be nominated to preside. It is usual, however, to appoint some member of the Ministry permanent Vice-President, who presides in the absence of the Governor.

The Governor is the fountain of honour within the Colony, since to him belongs the power to appoint, in the Queen's name, all Judges, Justices of the Peace, Commissioners, and other "necessary officers and Ministers"; and he may remove, by virtue of his powers as Viceroy, from the exercise of his office any official so appointed.

Prerogative of mercy.

The Governor is also the depositary of the prerogative of mercy within the Colony, having it in his power to pardon, either absolutely or conditionally, any offender convicted in New South Wales. He can also remit fines, penalties, and forfeitures due to the Crown, but he cannot pardon or remit on the condition of the offender voluntarily leaving the Colony, unless the offence has been a political one only. In all capital cases the Governor is required by his instructions to obtain a report in writing from the Judge who tried the prisoner, which is to be considered at a meeting of the Executive Council, and the Judge himself may also be examined before the Council, although his recommendations need not necessarily be adopted. The Governor, however, is not empowered to reprieve any capitally sentenced prisoner, or pardon him absolutely "unless it shall appear to him expedient so to do upon receiving the advice of the Executive Council, but in all such cases he is to decide either to extend or to withhold the pardon or reprieve according to his own deliberate judgment, whether the members of the Executive Council concur therein or otherwise." If the Governor decides to act contrary to the advice of the Executive he must make a minute in the proceedings, stating, *in extenso*, his reasons for so acting.

The Governor is also vested with the authority of the Crown, enabling him to nominate the members of the Upper House of the Legislature, and to summon, prorogue to a future day, or dissolve "any legislative body" existing in the Colony.

Governor acts by advice of Executive.

His instructions, however, provide that in the exercise of the above powers the Governor is to act by the advice of the Executive Council in all cases, except those whose nature is such that in his opinion the public service "would sustain material prejudice," or in matters too trivial to submit to the Council, or "too urgent to admit of their advice being given;" but in all such urgent cases he must communicate to the Council as soon as practicable the measures taken by him, and his reasons for acting. It is expressly provided, however, that the Governor may, if he think fit, disregard the advice of the Executive and act in direct opposition to the declared will of his advisers, but in such cases he is required to make a full report of the whole circumstances for the information of the Secretary of State for the Colonies.

Governor Viceroy as regards Royal assent.

The Governor acts as Viceroy as regards giving the Royal assent or vetoing Acts passed by the Legislature, or reserving Bills for the special consideration of the Sovereign. The instructions deal at large with this matter, but it is usual in practice to be guided to a large extent by the advice of the law officers of the Crown. There are eight different classes of Bills, however, to which the Governor is bound to refuse the Royal assent. They are:—

(1.) Divorce Bills (that is, private bills divorcing particular persons).

(2.) Bills making any kind of grant, gratuity, or donation to the Governor.

(3.) Bills affecting the currency.

(4.) Bills imposing differential duties, which are not in accordance with the "Australian-Colonies Duties Act, 1873."

(5.) Bills apparently contrary to Imperial treaty obligations.

(6.) Bills interfering with the discipline or control of Her Majesty's land or sea forces employed in the Colony.

(7.) Bills of great importance, or extraordinary in their nature, whereby the Royal prerogative, or the rights and property of Her Majesty's subjects residing beyond the Colony, or the trade and shipping of the United Kingdom and its dependencies may be prejudiced.

(8.) Bills containing provisions to which the Royal assent has already been refused, or which have been once disallowed, unless they contain a clause suspending their operation until the Queen's pleasure has been signified, or unless the Governor is satisfied that there is urgent necessity for bringing any such Bill into immediate operation, in which case he is empowered to assent to the Bill on behalf of the Queen, if it is not repugnant to the law of England, or inconsistent with Imperial treaty obligations; and in every such case he is required to transmit the Bill to Her Majesty, together with his reasons for assenting to it.

Acts regulating Royal assent.

The following Acts of Parliament regulate the action of the Governor in assenting to Bills on behalf of the Queen, or reserving them for the consideration of the Sovereign :—5 and 6 Vic., secs. 31–32, cap. 76 ; 7 and 8 Vic., sec. 7, cap. 74 ; and 13 and 14 Vic., cap. 59, secs. 13, 32, and 33. The effect of these enactments is to deprive any reserved Bill of all force and legality until the Queen's assent thereto has been formally communicated to the Governor ; and power is given to Her Majesty to veto any Bill to which the Governor has assented on her behalf within two years after the receipt of such Bill by the Secretary of State for the Colonies, in which case the Bill is to be declared null and void by message of the Governor, and proclamation. Reserved Bills are to be laid before Her Majesty in Council, and the Queen may allow them or not within a period of two years from the day on which they were reserved by the Governor. The Queen's assent to reserved Bills may be transmitted by telegram.

By the Act 7 Vic., No. 16, all Acts of Parliament which become law are required to be registered by the Registrar-General within ten days of their so becoming law.

Summoning of Parliament, &c.

The above is a summary of the powers and duties of the Governor, as defined by his instructions and the Letters Patent, but additional duties have been imposed upon him by the Constitution and Electoral Act. In accordance with these enactments he must summon the Legislative Assembly, appoint the President of the Legislative Council; prorogue or dissolve Parliament; appoint his ministers *proprio motu;* also appoint, with the advice of the Executive, all public officers whose appointment is not vested in heads of departments; issue all warrants for the payment of money; issue the writs for general elections, and, in the absence of the Speaker, issue writs to fill vacancies occurring in the Assembly. He also appoints all returning-officers, and issues the writs for additional members provided for by the expansive clauses of the Electoral Act.

Dissolution of Parliament.

In summoning, proroguing, or dissolving Parliament, the Governor usually acts according to the advice tendered him by the Cabinet, but he is in no way bound to do so; and, as a matter of fact, has sometimes declined to be guided by his Ministers. This, however, has never happened except in respect to granting a dissolution. As to summoning or proroguing a difference of opinion is hardly likely to arise. The relations established between the Ministry and the representatives of the people are in accordance with the time-honoured precedents prevailing in Great Britain, which may be thus defined. The Cabinet must be chosen from—"(1) Members of the Legislature; (2) Holding the same political views, and chosen from the party possessing a majority in the

House of Commons; (3) Carrying out a concerted policy; (4) Under a common responsibility, to be signified by a collective resignation in the event of Parliamentary censure; and (5) acknowledging a common subordination to one Chief Minister."

Circumstances under which a Government must resign.

The Imperial rule as to the circumstances under which a Government is bound to resign, is as follows:—Censure, involving loss of office, rests entirely with the Lower House, or popular branch of the Legislature. Hence directly a Ministry fails to command a majority of the House of Commons it must give place to another. Want of confidence in a Cabinet may be shown in three ways: first, by a direct vote of censure, or a specific declaration of want of confidence; secondly, by a vote disapproving of some act of the Government; or thirdly, by the rejection of some important measure introduced by the Ministry. In any of these cases Ministers must either resign, or appeal to the country if they can get the Sovereign to sanction a new election.

These rules have been virtually adopted in New South Wales and the undoubted right of the Governor, as the depositary of the Royal prerogative, to refuse to grant a dissolution, if he thinks fit, has been more than once exercised. In March, 1877, Sir Hercules Robinson refused to grant a dissolution to Sir John Robertson, and in September of the same year he also declined to enable Sir Henry Parkes to go to the country. The reason alleged in each case was that the Assembly refused to make provision for the expenditure of the year. It will thus be seen that a grave responsibility is thrown upon the Governor in the exercise of the undoubted right of granting or refusing a dissolution of Parliament, and in the cases mentioned it can hardly be doubted that Sir Hercules Robinson acted within his powers. The Viceroy is the conservator of the rights and interests of the whole population, and it must be evident that grave evils would ensue should a dissolution take place before supplies had been granted.

Prerogative of mercy.

The exercise of the prerogative of mercy is such an important function of the Governor, and he is so liable on some occasions to have strong pressure brought to bear upon him in connection with it, that it will be well to quote at length a despatch of Lord Carnarvon, explaining the instructions on this point. Under date 4th May, 1875, he wrote :—

"It should be understood that no capital sentence may be either carried out, commuted, or remitted, without a consideration of the case by the Governor and his Ministers assembled in Executive Council. A minor sentence may be commuted or remitted by the Governor, after he has duly considered the advice, either of his Ministers collectively in Executive Council, or of the Ministers more immediately responsible for matters connected with the administration of justice; and whether such advice is or is not tendered in Executive Council, it would seem desirable that, whether also given orally or not, it should be given in writing."

Governor as Commander-in-Chief of military forces.

One exception to the rule that every exercise by the Governor of the Royal prerogative is subject, practically, to the control of the Legislature, occurs in connection with the exercise of his office as Commander-in-Chief of the land and sea forces. The Governor's powers in this regard are defined and regulated by the Military and Naval Forces Regulation Act of 1871, which, after providing for the raising and maintenance of a standing force, goes on to vest the supreme command in the "Governor," which title, in the interpretation clause, is defined to mean "the Governor with the advice of the Executive Council," *unless the context shall otherwise indicate.* Full powers with relation to the Volunteer Force are also bestowed on the Governor by the Volunteer Regulation Act of 1867, but in this, as in the former statute, "Governor" only means "the Governor with the advice of the Executive Council," *if this meaning is not inconsistent with the context or subject-matter.* It will at once be seen that these are both important limitations, as in certain imaginable contingencies the Governor is left free to act on his own responsibility. This places the Governor almost in the position of the Commander-in-Chief in England (when such an officer exists, which is very seldom, the control of the army usually being vested in Generals commanding-in-chief); that is, he has at times the absolute disposal of the armed force of the Colony. This power is peculiar to New South Wales, as in other British Colonies the Governor possesses no more power over the military than he does over any civil department of the service. The position of the Governor as Captain-General does not, however, give him power to take the direct command of Imperial troops, should any such be stationed in the Colony.

Martial Law.

As regards the far more important power of the Governor to proclaim martial law, different opinions are held. But there is no doubt, as the power has not been conferred by any statute in force in the Colony, that, if it exists, it must be a matter of prerogative. The necessity for proclaiming martial law has happily never occurred since the advent of Responsible Government.

THE EXECUTIVE.

The Cabinet.

The Executive Council is composed of the ten Ministers, namely: The Colonial Secretary, the Treasurer, the Attorney-General, the Secretary for Lands, the Secretary for Public Works, the Minister of Justice, the Minister of Public Instruction, the Secretary for Mines, and the Postmaster-General, with sometimes a Vice-President of the Executive Council, who is without a portfolio. These form the Cabinet, and, of course, are responsible to Parliament. The Ministry, as the advisers of the Governor, must also retain his confidence, but practically, this is seldom likely to be withdrawn, so long as they can command a working majority in the Assembly. The Governor may dissolve Parliament although the Ministry have not sustained a defeat, and in this case the continued existence of any Government would depend directly on the vote of the constituencies, but such a contingency can happen but seldom.

Ministers not usually appointed from Upper House.

It is rare for more than one Minister to be selected from the Upper House, although at the present time there are three, and it will thus be seen that the principle of the responsibility of members of the Government to Parliament is fully carried out. For every act of the Governor as Viceroy some Minister is responsible to Parliament; and even in matters of Imperial interest, where the final onus rests upon the Governor, he himself is responsible to the Imperial Government, whose members are under the control of the House of Commons, so that no loophole is left for the exercise of any arbitrary act. The Crown, except in two instances (appeals to the Privy Council and the bestowal of titles), acts towards the Executive through its representative, the Governor; and so long ago as the inception of Responsible Government, Earl Grey declared, in an official despatch, that he should make "a judicious use of the influence, rather than of the authority, of his office," which wise maxim has usually been followed. But in extreme cases, such as when his sanction is requested to any illegal proceeding, the Governor is bound, without question, to keep the law, though he may thereby be brought into hostile relations with the Cabinet. Sir Michael Hicks-Beach, in a communication to the Governor-General of Canada in 1879, clearly laid down the doctrine that the Governor of any British Colony "has an unquestionable constitutional right to dismiss his Ministers, if from any cause he feels it incumbent on him to do so." This does not militate against the doctrine of responsibility, for if the Ministry appointed by the Governor do not possess the confidence of Parliament, they cannot hold office, and hence the Governor will be forced to give way, or else persevere till he can select a Ministry which the Assembly will accept. The final control will thus be, as in every other case, with the representatives of the people. In matters of routine the Governor will necessarily act on the advice of his Ministers, and in most cases relating to the internal economy of the departments, he will adopt even the individual recommendations of the Ministers by whom they are severally controlled.

Ministers responsible to Parliament.

Dismissal of Ministers.

As regards matters of purely Imperial interest the Governor is responsible to the British authorities for their due conservation.

If, in consequence of his action on any such matter, he is involved in a dispute with his Ministers, he is bound to refer them to the Sovereign, should his action have been endorsed by the Colonial Office. If his conduct is not approved of in England he would most likely be recalled. It follows from this, that in no case can the Governor be held to be responsible directly to Parliament for his conduct. His Ministers are responsible, but personally he has only to render an account to the Crown itself, that is, to the Imperial Parliament.

Executive must be summoned by Governor.

The Executive Council cannot discharge any function unless duly summoned by the Governor, and at least two members, besides the Governor or presiding member, are present to form a quorum. Formal minutes are, of course, kept of all proceedings. The Executive Council, as at present constituted, is as follows :—

Premier and Colonial Secretary.	The Hon. George Richard Dibbs.
Colonial Treasurer	The Hon. John See.
Attorney-General	The Hon. Edmund Barton, Q.C.
Secretary for Lands	The Hon. Henry Copeland.
Secretary for Public Works......	The Hon. William John Lyne.
Minister of Public Instruction	The Hon. Francis Bathurst Suttor.
Minister of Justice	The Hon. Richard Edward O'Connor.
Postmaster-General	The Hon. John Kidd.
Secretary for Mines	The Hon. Thomas Michael Slattery.
Vice-President of the Executive Council and Representative of the Government in the Legislative Council (without portfolio)	The Hon. Sir Julian Salomons, Q.C.

Since the introduction of Responsible Government there have been twenty-seven Ministries, the average tenure of office being one year and four months. Nine Governments have been displaced by votes of censure, expressed or implied, and three resigned through having been defeated on important measures of policy; while two retired on having been saved from defeat only by the Speaker's casting vote, and three others through a motion for the adjournment of the House having been carried against them. Three Ministries were merged into the succeeding ones; five resigned without a direct vote having been carried against them, but in consequence of not possessing a working majority; and one Government fell to pieces through internal disagreements.

THE PARLIAMENT.

Relative power of the two Houses undefined

It seems a singular omission in the Constitution Act that no definition is given of the relative powers of the Legislative Council and Legislative Assembly. Such is the fact, but no inconvenience has arisen thereby, since by common consent it has been agreed that the precedents regulating the proceedings and relations, *inter se*, of the two Houses of the Imperial Parliament shall be followed, as far as applicable, in New South Wales. The Constitution Act provides that all money bills shall be introduced in the Lower House only. The important rule of the House of Commons, affirmed two hundred years ago and constantly enforced ever since, that "all aids and supplies, and aids to Her Majesty in Parliament are the sole gift of the Commons, and it is the undoubted right of the Commons to direct, limit, and appoint in such bills, the ends, purposes, considerations, conditions, limitations, and qualifications of such grants, which ought not to be changed or altered by the House of Lords," is also held to be in force as regards the Parliament of this Colony, and has always been recognized and acted upon.

Parliament cannot punish for contempt.

The two Houses, however, do not possess the most important of the privileges of the Imperial Parliament, namely, the right of punishing for contempt, although the Legislative Assembly has, on one occasion, punished one of its members, for conduct assumed to be dishonorable beyond its precincts, by expelling him. As regards disorderly conduct within the walls of the Chamber it has been held by the Supreme Court and affirmed by the Privy Council, that the Assembly only possesses the power of suspending a member for disorderly conduct for the period of the sitting at which such conduct took place. A member may be also removed from the House by order of the Speaker if he persists in obstruction or contemns the Standing Orders; but fortunately this course has seldom been rendered necessary.

Witnesses may be summoned.

Witnesses may be summoned to give evidence before either House, or before committees of the Council or Assembly, the necessary powers for compelling their attendance having been conferred by an Act passed in 1881. Any person disobeying a summons may be arrested on a Judge's warrant, and the maximum penalty for refusing to give evidence is imprisonment for one calendar month.

No limit to numbers of Council.

As regards the maximum number of members of the Legislative Council no limit is assigned by the Constitution Act, although the minimum number is fixed at twenty-one. It will be seen that this gives power to a Governor to quash any possible obstruction on the part of the Council to the will of the Government, and the Lower House by "swamping" the Council. Such a proceeding, however, can hardly be held to be allowable, except under extreme circumstances. As a matter of fact, an attempt to "swamp" the Council was made during one of the premierships of the late Sir Charles Cowper, but public opinion condemned the course most strongly, although the somewhat peculiar circumstances of the case were thought at the time to justify the Governor's action. The authorities in England severely rebuked the Governor (Sir John Young) for the course he had taken, and since then, "swamping" the Council has never been seriously entertained, nor is there much chance that it will ever again be attempted. The principle in fact has been affirmed, on the basis of an understanding entered into between Sir John Young and the leading statesmen of the day (of both sides of the House), that the members of the Legislative Council should be limited to a convenient number, and that no nominations should ever be made merely for the purpose of strengthening the party which happens to be in power. A deadlock between the two Houses is provided against by the universal feeling that the Assembly represents the will of the people, and in such case the Council would certainly have to give way to the deliberate will of the people's representatives. The Council is intended as a check to hasty legislation; and it doubtless acts as a useful "brake" to violent party feeling.

THE LEGISLATIVE COUNCIL.

Constitution of the Legislative Council.

As before stated, the members of the Upper House are nominated by the Governor, the minimum number composing the House being fixed at twenty-one. No limit as to numbers is fixed by the Constitution Act, but in accordance with the arrangement already described the number is practically kept down by the exclusion of all purely political appointments. As the number of members of the Assembly has been greatly increased in pursuance of the "expansion" clauses of the Act, the present number of members composing the Council (seventy-one) will not be considered an unfair proportion, as the increase is in about the same ratio as that of the Assembly. The members must be of full age, and either natural-born or duly naturalized subjects of the empire. Four-fifths of the members must be persons not holding any paid office under the Crown, but this is not held to include officers "in Her Majesty's sea and land forces on full or half pay, or retired officers on pensions." Though the appointment is for life, a member may resign his seat, and he also forfeits it by absence from two consecutive sessions without leave, by becoming naturalized in a foreign State, by becoming bankrupt, by becoming a public contractor, or defaulter, by being attainted of treason, or being convicted of felony, or any infamous crime. The Governor appoints and removes, if considered necessary, the President, who may speak in debate, but can only give a casting vote. An attendance of one-third of the members on the roll was necessary to constitute a quorum, but an Act has lately been carried to reduce the proportion to one-fourth. The Council must hold a sitting at least once in every year, and no greater interval than twelve months must elapse between session and session. The proceedings are regulated by standing orders, which are, in the main, similar to those of the Assembly, the latter being framed on the model of the rules obtaining in the House of Commons. No member may sit or vote till he has taken the oath of allegiance, or the affirmation prescribed in lieu of that oath.

Members may resign.

Quorum.

THE LEGISLATIVE ASSEMBLY.

The Lower House of Parliament is elected by manhood suffrage, the number of electorates being at present seventy-four, returning 141 members. The qualification of electors is derived either from actual residence in an electorate or ownership of a freehold or leasehold therein. The following are the rules applying to each of the two cases:—

Qualification of electors.

1. Any person claiming a right to have his name on the electoral roll in respect of residence must prove that at the time of the collection of the roll he resided in the electorate in question, and had done so for six months previously.

Property qualification.

2. Any person who claims in respect of property must show that at the time the electoral list was made up, and during the preceding six months:—

(*a.*) He is and has been holder of a freehold or leasehold estate of the clear value of £100, or

(*b.*) He is and has been in the receipt of rents and profits of the annual value of £10, arising from freehold or leasehold property, or

(*c.*) Occupies and has occupied a house, warehouse, office, shop, room, or building, either with or without land attached, of the annual value of £10, or

(*d.*) Holds and has held a Crown lease or license for pastoral purposes within the electoral district.

The six months occupation is not required to be of the same premises, provided he has occupied continuously several sets of premises of the required value he is entitled to vote.

A man must be possessed of one or other of the above qualifications to entitle him to vote in any electorate; but he can only have one vote in each electorate, no matter how many qualifications he has in that electorate. If he is qualified in several electorates he is entitled to have his name on the electoral roll in each. There is now before the Parliament a measure to carry out the "one man one vote" principle.

A person is disabled from voting by reason of the existence of any of the following disqualifications at the time of making out the electoral roll:— Disabilities.

1. Being of unsound mind.
2. Being in receipt of eleemosynary aid.
3. Having been convicted of treason, felony, or other infamous crime, unless he has either received a free or conditional pardon, or has served his sentence.
4. Being in the military or naval service on full pay. Membership in a volunteer or militia corps does not disqualify.
5. Being a police magistrate or member of the police force (including the Inspector-General).

The "expansion clauses" of the Act, as they are called, provide that when an electorate which has previously returned only one member has 3,000 names on its electoral roll, or when one which returns two members is possessed of 5,000 voters, or one which returns three has reached 8,000, such electorate, in each case, is entitled to return an additional member; but the Governor must first notify the fact by proclamation in the *Gazette*. "Expansion clauses" of Electoral Act.

Any natural born or duly naturalized subject of Her Majesty is capable of being elected a member of the Assembly, subject to the same disqualifications as for voters, with the following additional ones:— Qualification for member of Assembly.

1. He must not be a member of the Legislative Council.
2. He must not hold any office of profit under the Crown, either for a term of years or during pleasure.
3. He must not be in any way interested in any contract for the public service.

By the "Constitution Act Amendment Act of 1884" the disqualification of persons holding office of profit was declared not to apply to the Colonial Secretary or other member of the Ministry. The third disqualification also does not apply to any contract made by a company consisting of more than twenty Offices of profit.

persons. If any disqualified person should be elected the election is voided by the House, and should such person presume to sit or vote he is liable to a fine of £500.

Payment of Members.

By an Act, assented to on the 21st September, 1889, members of the Assembly are allowed the sum of £300 per annum to reimburse them for expenses incurred in the discharge of their Parliamentary duties.

Members must take oath of allegiance.

Before taking his seat each member must take the oath of allegiance in the prescribed form, or make an affirmation in lieu of it. A member may resign his seat at any time, and he is held to have vacated it under any of the following conditions:—Absence during a whole session without leave, naturalization in a foreign country, bankruptcy, being a defaulter, or convicted of treason, felony, or any other infamous crime.

Parliament triennial.

The Act 37 Vic., No. 7, provides that no Assembly can prolong its existence beyond the term of three years. One session, at least, must be held every year, and twelve months must not elapse between any two sessions. On meeting after a general election, the first business is to elect a Speaker, who has only a casting vote. Twenty of the members (exclusive of the Speaker) constitute a quorum.

Writs.

Writs for general elections must be made returnable not later than thirty-five clear days after the date of the proclamation dissolving the former Parliament. Writs for general elections, and also for vacancies occurring between a general election and the meeting of Parliament for the despatch of business, are issued by the Governor. For all other elections the writs are issued by the Speaker, unless absent from the Colony, or unless no Speaker has yet been elected, when the Governor signs these writs in like manner to the others.

Election is by ballot.

Election is by ballot, the names of those entitled to vote being compiled once a year and published for general information.

Meeting of first Parliament.

The first Parliament elected under the Constitution Act met on the 22nd May, 1856, just six months after the proclamation of the Constitution. Its duration, unless Parliament should be previously prorogued, was originally fixed at five years, but in 1874 an Act was passed establishing triennial Parliaments, which has ever since remained law. Since the inauguration of Responsible Government there have been fifteen appeals to the people, so that it will be seen the duration of each Assembly has not averaged even the shorter period of life to which its existence is now limited. The subjoined table gives the duration of each Parliament elected under Constitutional Government.

Duration of Parliaments.

Duration of Parliaments since the Establishment of Responsible Government.

Parliament.	Opened.	Dissolved.	Duration. Yr.	mth.	dy.	No. of Sessions.
First	22 May, 1856 ...	19 Dec., 1857 ...	1	6	27	2
Second	23 March, 1858 ...	11 April, 1859 ...	1	0	19	2
Third	30 Aug., 1859 ..	10 Nov., 1860 ...	1	2	11	2
Fourth	10 Jan., 1861 ...	10 Nov., 1864 ...	3	10	0	5
Fifth	26 Jan., 1865 ...	15 Nov., 1869 ..	4	9	22	6
Sixth	27 Jan., 1870 ...	3 Feb., 1872 ...	2	0	7	3
Seventh	30 April, 1872 ..	28 Nov., 1874 ...	2	6	29	4
Eighth	27 Jan., 1875 ...	12 Oct., 1877 ...	2	8	15	3
Ninth	27 Nov., 1877 ...	9 Nov., 1880 ..	2	11	13	3
Tenth	15 Dec., 1880 ..	23 Nov., 1882 ...	1	11	8	3
Eleventh	3 Jan., 1883 ...	7 Oct., 1885 ...	2	9	4	6
Twelfth	17 Nov., 1885 ...	26 Jan., 1887 ...	1	2	9	2
Thirteenth ..	8 March, 1887 ...	19 Jan., 1889 ...	1	10	11	3
Fourteenth ..	22 Feb., 1889 ...	6 June, 1891 ...	2	3	15	3
Fifteenth ...	14 July, 1891 ...	....	....			...
		Average	2	2	6	3 to 4

The amount of interest displayed by the electors in the exercise of their franchise is very considerable, though the proportion of votes recorded may not appear to sustain this view. At the general election of 1891 the total number of voters on the electoral rolls was 305,456, or 10 voters to every 36 persons in the community. In seven electorates, with 19,559 electors, returning seven members, there were no contests. The remaining 67 electorates, returning 134 members, comprised 285,897 electors, and of these only 184,091, or 64·39 per cent., recorded their votes.

Interest displayed in elections.

Large area of electorates.

Owing to the vast extent of some of the electoral districts many electors can only record their votes at considerable inconvenience to themselves, and to this cause, combined with the fact that the number of non-resident voters is very considerable, must be assigned the apparently low percentage of votes recorded.

Proportion of population eligible to vote.

The number of males of full age, compared with the total population, is very large, the proportion at the last census being 28·18 per cent. The number of persons entitled to vote under the system of universal suffrage which prevails amounts to nearly 27 per cent. of the total population, there having been 305,456 persons on the electoral roll for 1891-92. The average number of electors per member at the time of the last general election was 2,166, and the estimated population to each member was 8,044. The subjoined table gives the result of all the general elections which have taken place under Representative Government.

Parliamentary Elections.

Date of the issue of Writs.	No. of Parliament.	Voters on Roll.	Total number returned.	Members unopposed.	Votes on Roll in the Electorates where the contests took place.	Votes recorded.	Percentage of Votes recorded.	Informal Votes.	Percentage of Informal Votes.
22 May, 1856	First	44,526	54	*	*	*	*	*	*
23 March, 1858	Second	72,177	72	14	54,896	27,894	50·81	*	*
30 August, 1859....	Third	88,346	72	19	63,022	27,490	43·62	22	·08
10 January, 1861 ..	Fourth	106,189	72	19	75,676	28,340	37·45	29	·10
24 ,, 1865 .	Fifth	119,872	72	15	90,736	44,311	48·84	31	·07
27 ,, 1870 ..	Sixth	128,734	72	11	108,080	56,331	52·12	102	·18
30 April, 1872......	Seventh ..	151,798	72	8	125,488	60,004	47·82	80	·13
27 January, 1875 ..	Eighth	160,848	72	10	104,575	57,651	55·13	334	·58
27 November, 1877..	Ninth	160,945	73	16	120,698	62,172	51·51	*	
18 December, 1880..	Tenth	188,500	108	14	140,848	90,657	64·36	1,785	1·97
3 January, 1883 ..	Eleventh ..	196,289	113	17	166,260	96,842	58·26	2,022	2·07
17 November, 1885..	Twelfth ..	232,190	122	8	203,669	124,378	61·07	2,564	2·06
27 January, 1887 ..	Thirteenth.	256,406	124	17	226,228	131,082	57·93	2,275	1·73
19 ,, 1889 ..	Fourteenth	280,160	137	13	257,768	154,924	60·10	2,641	1·70
8 June, 1891......	Fifteenth..	305,456	141	7	285,897	184,091	64·39	3,642	2·02

* Unrecorded.

The Federation Question.

At the present crisis of affairs a notice of the constitution and Government of the Colony would be incomplete without some reference to the question of Australian Federation, which is now more prominently before the public than it has been at any previous stage of Colonial history. It has already been shown, in the initial chapter of this work, that the question was not overlooked by the framers of the first free Australian Constitution, who proposed the establishment of a General Assembly "to make laws in relation to those intercolonial questions that have arisen, or may hereafter arise," and who, in fact, sketched out a tolerably comprehensive federation scheme. Unfortunately, however, that proposition was included with another for the creation of hereditary nobility, and in the storm of opposition and ridicule with which the latter idea was greeted, the former sank out of sight. From time to time since Responsible Government came into being the evil of want of union among the Australian Colonies has been forcibly apparent, and the idea of federation has gradually become more and more popular among the people. Some years ago the movement took such shape that, as the result of an intercolonial conference, the matter came before the Imperial Parliament, and a measure was passed, permitting the formation of a Federal Council, to which any colony that felt inclined to join could send delegates. The first meeting of that Federal Council was held at Hobart, in January, 1886. The Colonies represented were Victoria, Queensland, Tasmania, Western Australia, and Fiji. New South Wales, South Australia, and New Zealand declined to join, but South Australia sent representatives to a subsequent meeting. The Council has held four meetings, at which several matters of intercolonial interest were discussed; but, as from its very inherent constitution, it was only a deliberative body, having no executive functions whatever, it possessed no control of funds or other means to put its legislation into force. The advocates of Federation were therefore dissatisfied with the position the question was in, and agitation was instituted with a view of bringing about a more satisfactory state of things.

Federal Council.

An important step towards the federation of the Australasian Colonies was taken in February, 1890, when a Conference, con-

Federation Conference.

sisting of representatives of each of the seven Colonies of Australasia, was held in the Parliament House, Melbourne. The Conference met on February 6, and there were thirteen members present, being two representatives from each of the Colonies, except Western Australia which sent only one, Sir Henry Parkes, Premier and Colonial Secretary, and Mr. W. McMillan, Colonial Treasurer, representing New South Wales. Mr. Duncan Gillies, Premier of Victoria, was elected President of the Conference. The members held seven meetings, and discussed the question before them at considerable length. At the last meeting the Conference adopted an address to the Queen, expressing their loyalty and attachment, and enclosing certain resolutions as the result of the Conference, which affirmed the desirableness of an early union, under the Crown, of the Australian Colonies, on principles just to the several Colonies; that the remoter Australasian Colonies should be entitled to admission upon terms to be afterwards agreed upon; and that steps should be taken for the appointment of Delegates to a National Australasian Convention, to consider and report upon an adequate scheme for a Federal Constitution.

Address to the Queen.

National Australasian Convention.

In accordance with the terms of that resolution Delegates were appointed by the different Australasian Parliaments, and on the 2nd March, 1891, the National Australasian Convention commenced its sittings in the Legislative Assembly Chambers, Macquarie-street, Sydney, having been convened at the instance of Mr. James Munro, the Premier of Victoria. There were forty-five Members of the Convention altogether, New South Wales, Victoria, Queensland, South Australia, Tasmania, and Western Australia (which had only recently been placed in possession of the privilege of Responsible Government), each sending seven Delegates, and New Zealand three. At the first meeting of the Convention the seven Delegates from Western Australia were absent, as well as three other Delegates representing Victoria,

Queensland, and New Zealand respectively, but in the course of a few days the whole of Delegates arrived, and the Convention was complete.

Proceedings of the Convention.

The first business transacted by the Convention was the unanimous election of Sir Henry Parkes as President. Mr. F. W. Webb, Clerk of the Legislative Assembly of New South Wales, was appointed Secretary to the Convention, and Sir Samuel Griffiths was elected Vice-President. Mr. J. P. Abbott, Speaker of the New South Wales Legislative Assembly, was subsequently elected Chairman of Committees. Rules of Procedure, similar in the main to those under which the business of Parliament is conducted, were adopted, and arrangements were made for the admission of the public to the debates, and for the publication of an official record of the proceedings.

Resolutions adopted.

A series of resolutions was moved by Sir Henry Parkes, setting forth certain principles necessary to establish and secure an enduring foundation for the structure of a Federal Government, and approving of the framing of a Federal Constitution. These resolutions were discussed by the Convention during nine sittings, part of the time in Committee of the Whole, and after amendment were finally adopted. The resolutions affirmed the following principles :—

1. That the powers and rights of existing Colonies shall remain intact, except as regards such powers as it might be necessary to hand over to the Federal Government.
2. That no alteration shall be made in States without the consent of the Legislatures of such States, as well as of the Federal Parliament.
3. Trade between the federated Colonies to be absolutely free.
4. Power to impose Customs and Excise Duties to be in the Federal Government and Parliament.
5. Military and Naval Defence Forces to be under one command.

6. The Federal Constitution to make provision to enable each State to make amendments in its constitution if necessary for the purposes of Federation.

Federal Constitution.

Further resolutions approved of the framing of a Federal Constitution which should establish a Senate and a House of Representatives—the latter to possess the sole power of originating money bills; also a Federal Supreme Court of Appeal; and an Executive consisting of a Governor-General, with such persons as may be appointed as his advisers.

Adoption of the Constitution.

Three Committees were then chosen among the Delegates—one to consider matters relating to Finance, Taxation, and Trade Regulations; a second to deal with the establishment of a Federal Judiciary; and the third to prepare and submit a Bill for the establishment of a Federal Constitution. On Tuesday, March 31, Sir Samuel Griffith, as Chairman of the Committee on Constitutional Machinery, brought up a draft Constitution Bill, which was fully and carefully considered by the Convention in Committee of the Whole, and was adopted on Thursday, April 9. On the same day the Convention was formally declared to be dissolved, and it now remains for the Colonies individually to adopt or reject the scheme presented to them by the Convention.

PART XIII.

Internal Communication.

FOR many years, settlement was restricted to the narrow belt of land shut in between the Blue Mountains and the sea. Several main roads were formed through this country within a few years after the first settlement of the Colony. These roads connected the infant towns of Parramatta, Liverpool, Windsor, and Penrith with the metropolis, and were constructed entirely by prison labour. The abrupt wall of sandstone rising on the further side of the Nepean barred all access to the interior of the country. As early as the year 1796 George Bass made an attempt to cross the mountain range, and returned after an unsuccessful journey, reporting that it was impossible to find a passage even for a person on foot. In 1813, a protracted season of drought, attended by considerable losses amongst the stock, brought home very clearly to the settlers the conviction that the future of the Colony entirely depended upon the discovery of an extension of grazing land, beyond the narrow limits within which they were then hemmed. In the month of May of the year named, Gregory Blaxland, W. C. Wentworth, and Lieutenant Lawson once more attempted to find a passage across the mountains. After meeting with difficulties which seem astonishing enough to the present generation, who have seen a railway carried over the same track, by which Bathurst may be reached in a few hours, these gentlemen succeeded in opening a way—sometimes by creeping through dense forests, at others by scaling tremendous precipices—to the vast plains lying west of the great Cordillera of Australia. They returned on the 6th June, and shortly afterwards Governor Macquarie sent a party of surveyors, under Mr. Evans, to report

Bass's attempt to cross the mountain range

Blaxland, Wentworth, and Lawson discover a passage.

Construction of the Great Western Road.

on the practicability of making a road, and the report being favourable, the construction of the great western highway was at once commenced, the work being performed by gangs of prisoners. The track thus made formed a continuation of the great Western Road, from Penrith, and it was completed as far as Bathurst by the 21st January, 1815.

Impetus to road-making.

The discovery of the Bathurst Plains, and the completion of the mountain road, gave so great an impetus to settlement that it was found impossible to keep pace in the matter of roads with the demands of the settlers. The Government, therefore, contented itself with maintaining the roads already constructed, and extending them in the direction of the principal centres of settlement. For many years these main roads were the only ones which received attention. This would perhaps have been otherwise had the progress of settlement subsequent to 1850 been similar to that of the years previous to that date. Such, however, was not the case. The gold discovery entirely altered the circumstances of the Colony, and during the period of excitement and change which followed that remarkable event, so many new roads were opened, and so large an increase in traffic occurred, that the general condition of the public highways was by no means good. The Roads Department was formed as far back as 1857, and, although good service was done by the road pioneers before that date, the modern system of roadmaking may be said to have begun with the creation of the department. It was not, however, until 1864 that the whole of the roads, both main and subordinate, received attention at the hands of the State.

The principal main roads of the Colony are:—

Principal main roads.

Northern Road—length, 405 miles, from Morpeth to Maryland, New England.

Western Road—length, 338 miles, from Sydney to Warren through Bathurst, Orange, and many other important townships; thence prolonged to the Darling, at Bourke, by a line 175 miles in length.

Southern Road—length, 385 miles, from Sydney to Albury. This road was, before the construction of the railway, the great highway between Sydney and Melbourne.

South Coast Road—length, 250 miles. This road, after leaving Campbelltown, ascends the coast range, along the top of which it runs as far as Coal Cliff. It then traverses the Illawarra district, parallel to the coast, and passes through the rich lands watered by the Shoalhaven, Clyde, and Moruya, as far as Eden, at the southern limit of the Colony.

None of these roads have now the importance they formerly possessed. The railways of the Colony for the most part follow the direction of the main roads, and attract to themselves nearly all the through traffic. The tendency now is to make the roads act as feeders to the railway, by converging the traffic from outlying districts towards convenient stations along the line.

Importance of main roads less than formerly.

The expenditure by the Government upon the different roads varies considerably, according to their importance. All roads maintained by the Government fall under six classes. On first-class roads the Government expends yearly an amount equal to £50 per mile; on second-class roads, £25 per mile; third-class, £15 per mile; fourth-class, £10 per mile; fifth-class, £7 per mile; and on sixth-class roads, £5 per mile.

Government expenditure on public roads.

The network of roads spread over the face of the Colony is divided, for purposes of maintenance, into road districts and road trusts. There are sixty-two road districts, managed locally by superintendents, who have the greater part of the road communication of the Colony outside the municipal boundaries, under their care. The road trusts number 300, and have the supervision of certain grants for the maintenance of roads in districts chiefly of minor importance. There are, however, certain important roads in the vicinity of the metropolis governed by trusts. The length of roads in charge of superintendents or road engineers is approxi-

Supervision and maintenance of roads.

mately 29,000 miles, while about 3,000 miles are under road trusts. The length of road which has been formed, metalled, and gravelled is not less than 6,500 miles. There are also 10,000 miles of road-way not indeed metalled, but which have been drained, and on which all necessary culverts have been constructed, and 11,000 miles of road wind their way through the forests of the interior, chiefly along the lines marked out by the cart-wheels of the foremost settlers, and form, in dry weather, adequate means of communication for the settlers, although it must be acknowledged that in seasons of rain these roads are not unfrequently impassable. Besides the roads mentioned above, there are 1,500 miles of mountain passes. Many of the passes presented the most formidable difficulties, and their construction reflects great credit upon the engineering skill of the officer, lately deceased, who for so many years designed and supervised the construction and maintenance of the roads and bridges of the Colony.

Length of roads.

Bridges and culverts.

Many of the earliest bridges erected in the Colony were of stone, and are still existing. Those erected in the period following the extension of settlement to the interior were chiefly of timber, and have since been replaced, after a life of about twenty-five years. Nearly all the large bridges of recent erection are of iron or steel, and some of them have been erected under engineering conditions almost unique, owing to the peculiarity of the river flow in some parts of the country. There are altogether 3,200 bridges, covering a length of 25,000 feet, while there are also over 280,000 feet of minor culverts, formed of earthenware piping, from 12 to 24 inches in diameter. Where the traffic has not warranted their construction, or where local circumstances have rendered them unavoidable, punts or ferries have been used instead of bridges. There are 85 punts, 7 of which are propelled by steam, and 78 by hand gear, along wire ropes. The number of boat ferries is 62.

Punts and ferries.

Value of roads and bridges.

The use of roads as the main arteries along which traffic from the metropolis to the interior flows has been superseded by the railways; but the roads remain not only the sole means of communication throughout a large part of the interior, but most valuable feeders to the railway system of the country. No revenue is directly derived from roads, but the indirect advantages to the country have been very great, and after the lands and the railways they form the largest item of national property. It is estimated that £13,154,700 have been expended on roads and bridges since 1857, and the present value to the State, allowing for depreciation, cannot be less than £10,382,000. Their indirect value cannot be calculated, but as an instance of the change brought about by the system of road construction, it may be mentioned that, after the organization of the Roads Department on its present basis, the cost of carriage of goods by road and the time of transit was reduced by more than one-half, as will appear from the following statement:—

Indirect value

Main Roads.	Distance.	Carriage by Road, 1857.		Carriage by Road, 1864.	
		Days of transit.	Cost per ton.	Days of transit.	Cost per ton.
	Miles.		£ s. d.		£ s. d.
Sydney to Goulburn	134	17½	12 5 0	7½	3 15 0
" Bathurst.........	145	23½	15 10 0	11	6 10 0
Newcastle to Murrurundi..	119	21	9 0 0	8	6 10 0

The progress exhibited in these seven years is very great, and it is possible that the cost of carriage on roads was still further reduced before they were superseded in importance by the railways of the Colony. The average cost of carrying 1 ton of goods 1 mile in the year 1864 was about 7½d.; in the year 1872, the first for which the figures are available, the average cost per mile of carriage on railways was 3·61d. per ton, since which year the rates have been as follows:—

Cost of carrying goods by road and rail.

Year	Rate	Year	Rate
1872...........	3·61d.	1880.........	2·32d.
1873...........	3·28d.	1881..........	2·29d.
1874...........	3·00d.	1882...........	2·13d.
1875...........	3·07d.	1883...........	1·96d.
1876...........	2·82d.	1884...........	1·90d.
1877...........	2·68d.	1885...........	1·86d.
1878...........	2·44d.	1886...........	1·81d.
1879...........	2·25d.	1887...........	1·81d.

Saving effected by railways.

The returns, as made out by the Commissioners since 1887, do not show the cost of carriage per ton per mile, but from the reductions that have been made in the rates, the figures must be even lower than those given above. Still, the saving shown in the table is enormous, and although the exact amount of what the saving to the Colony by the extension of the railways to the interior has actually been must remain a matter of speculation, the figures just given may be taken as indicating how large and beneficial an effect railways have upon production, and how greatly they must benefit the general consumer.

Expenditure on roads.

The total expenditure on account of roads of all classes during 1890 was £805,314; this sum, however, includes the expenses of the department, expenditure on punt approaches, and similar works incidental to the road traffic of the country:—

Expenditure for Construction and Maintenance of Roads and Bridges.

Year.	Expenditure by Roads Department.	Expenditure by Trustees.	Total.
	£	£	£
1857 to 1877	4,669,403	704,400	4,373,903
1878	497,033	24,280	521,313
1879	649,774	25,428	675,202
1880	614,709	28,800	643,509
1881	484,567	23,186	507,753
1882	577,212	24,722	601,934
1883	613,847	24,938	638,785
1884	750,584	27,722	778,306
1885	800,962	24,404	825,366
1886	628,379	28,414	656,793
1887	721,994	45,433	767,427
1888	663,928	31,503	695,431
1889	632,398	31,361	663,759
1890	770,814	34,500	805,314
Total...	12,075,609	1,079,091	13,154,700

Municipal roads and streets.

Besides the roads maintained by the Government there existed, at the close of 1890, 6,011 miles of roads and streets belonging, to and maintained by, the municipalities of the Colony. Of these roads, 2,925 miles were regularly formed and metalled, while 3,086 miles were not formed. The value of these roads is estimated at £4,056,843; but this estimate must be looked upon as an approximation only, since the information obtained from the various municipalities is far from complete.

RAILWAYS.

The first attempt to introduce into New South Wales the blessings of railway communication, which has so revolutionised the commerce of the older parts of the world, was made in 1846. On the 26th August of that year a meeting was held in Sydney at which it was decided to survey a line to connect the metropolis with the city of Goulburn. Two years afterwards, on 11th September, 1848, the Sydney Tramroad and Railway Company was formed, with a capital of £100,000, having for its object the construction of railways to Parramatta and Liverpool, with a possible extension, in course of time, to Bathurst and Goulburn.

The Sydney Tramroad and Railway Company.

No time was lost in breaking ground, and on the 3rd July, 1850, the Hon. Mrs. Keith Stewart, daughter of the Governor, Sir Charles Fitzroy, turned the first sod of the first railway constructed in the Australian Colonies.

Railways transferred to State.

The affairs of the Sydney Tramroad and Railway Company did not, however, prosper as the promoters had expected, and it was found necessary to transfer the property of the company to the Government of the Colony. Meanwhile another company had been started in 1853, with the object of constructing a railway from the city of Newcastle to Maitland. It met with no more success than the Sydney company, and shared the same fate. On the Government taking possession of the property of the defunct companies, the works were carried on with more vigour, and on the 26th of September, 1855, the line from Sydney to Parramatta was declared open for public traffic, and the extension to Goulburn was opened on the 27th May, 1869.

The first line from Sydney to Parramatta.

Progress of railway construction.

The progress of railway construction during the twenty years which followed the opening of the first line was very slow, for in 1875 the length of the lines in operation had only reached 437 miles, or at the rate of 21·85 miles per year. Not a single mile of railway was opened during 1865 and 1866; but in 1867 the construction of these great commercial highways received a new impetus, and continued to increase yearly until 1872, when it stood still for another period of two years, during which only 5 miles of railway were thrown open to traffic. In 1875 34 miles were opened, and from the succeeding year till 1889 greater activity prevailed 1,698 miles having been constructed, or a yearly average of 126 miles, but this impetus received a check since then, only 11 miles having been opened. There were, however, 151 miles in course of construction in the middle of 1891. The following table shows the number of miles of line opened in each each year, as well as the total length in operation:—

Length of Railway Line opened for Traffic during each Year.

Year.	Opened during the year.	Total opened.	Year.	Opened during the year.	Total opened
	Miles.	Miles.		Miles.	Miles.
1855	14	14	1874	nil.	403
1856	9	23	1875	34	437
1857	17	40	1876	72	509
1858	15	55	1877	89	598
1859	nil.	55	1878	90	688
1860	15	70	1879	46	734
1861	3	73	1880	115	849
1862	24	97	1881	146	995
1863	27	124	1882	†280	1,275
1864	19	143	1883	52	1,327
1865	nil.	143	1884	298	1,625
1866	nil.	143	1885	114	1,739
1867	61	204	1886	157	1,896
1868	43	247	1887	‡152	2,048
1869	71	318	1888	78	2,126
1870	21	339	*1889	45	2,171
1871	19	358	*1890	11	2,182
1872	40	398	*1891	nil.	2,182
1873	5	403			

* Year ended June 30.

† Inclusive of Campbelltown-Camden line. ‡ Inclusive of Kogarah-Sans Souci line.

Extension of railway facilities

The progress of the accommodation afforded by the State Railways of the Colony can be fairly gauged by comparing the number of persons at different periods to each mile of line open for traffic, and the number of train miles per inhabitants. Thus in 1878, there were 977 persons to each mile of line, but by the end of the year 1891 the work of construction was so much in excess of the increase of population that the proportion per mile had fallen to 496 persons, so that the facilities afforded by the railways are now nearly twice as great as in the year first named. The increase in the number of train miles per inhabitant was very rapid from 1878 to 1884, rising from 4·04 to 7·25. During the three years following a gradual decline in the rate took place, falling as low as 6·44 in 1887; but since then there has been a very satisfactory and regular increase, the rate for the year ending June, 1891, being the highest yet attained. The following statement illustrates the extenison of railway facilities during each year since 1878:—

Population to each mile of Railway and train miles per inhabitants on Government Lines.

Year.	Population to each mile of line.	Number of train miles run.	Number of train miles run per head of Population.
1878	977	2,655,176	4·04
1879	967	2,932,463	4·25
1880	881	3,239,462	4·45
1881	786	3,923,929	5·13
1882	643	4,851,157	6·07
1883	653	5,937,261	7·08
1884	559	6,403,041	7·25
1885	548	6,638,399	7·16
1886	524	6,479,265	6·68
1887	501	6,472,107	6·44
*1888	483	6,689,313	6·56
*1889	484	7,641,769	7·27
*1890	496	8,008,826	7·40
*1891	514	8,410,421	7·50

* Year ended June 30.

Two private lines of railway, 45 and 36 miles in length respectively, were in operation during 1890, connecting the important

Private lines. towns of Moama and Deniliquin, and Silverton and Broken Hill. The first-named line virtually forms an extension of the Victorian railway system from Melbourne to Echuca. Some facts relating to the traffic of these lines will be found in another place. The following figures relate only to lines under Government control.

Capital expended. The capital expended on all lines at the close of June, 1891, amounted to £31,768,617. The amounts expended on lines opened during each year from the commencement of the railway system will be found in the following table :—

Capital expended on Lines open to Traffic.

Year.	Capital expended on lines open.	Year.	Capital expended on lines open.
	£		£
1855	515,347	1874	6,844,546
1856	683,217	1875	7,245,379
1857	1,023,838	1876	7,990,601
1858	1,231,867	1877	8,883,177
1859	1,278,416	1878	9,784,645
1860	1,422,672	1879	10,406,495
1861	1,536,032	1880	11,778,819
1862	1,907,807	1881	13,301,597
1863	2,466,950	1882	15,843,616
1864	2,631,790	1883	16,905,014
1865	2,746,373	1884	20,080,138
1866	2,786,094	1885	21,831,276
1867	3,282,320	1886	24,071,454
1868	4,060,950	1887	26,532,122
1869	4,681,329	*1888	27,722,748
1870	5,566,092	*1889	29,839,167
1871	5,887,258	*1890	30,555,123
1872	6,388,727	*1891	31,768,617
1873	6,739,918		

* Year ended June 30.

The Colony of New South Wales stands in a good position among the Australasian Colonies in regard to railway development, as will be seen from the following table:— Length of railway lines.

Length of Lines open for Traffic in Australasian Colonies—31st December, 1890.

	Lines Open.	
	Government.	Private.
	Miles.	Miles.
New South Wales	2,182	81
Victoria	2,688	...
Queensland	2,142	...
*South Australia	1,756	18
Western Australia	326	198
Tasmania	351	48
New Zealand	1,842	114
Total	10,950	858

* Includes 146 miles of Railway in Northern Territory.

The railway system of the Colony is divided into three distinct branches, each representing a system of its own. The southern system, including the principal line in the Colony, branches at Junee, and places the important district of Riverina, as far as the town of Hay in one direction, and Jerilderie in another, in direct communication with Sydney—from which they are distant 454 and 412 miles respectively. From several other points of the line branches connecting other important districts with the metropolis have been opened for traffic, or are in course of construction. At Cootamundra, a line has been laid down, which now reaches Gundagai, whilst from Murrumburrah a line has been constructed which connects Blayney on the western line with the southern and western systems of New South Wales Railways. This practically enables direct railway communication to be made between Melbourne and Bourke, the capital of Central Australia; and the branch line has been found of much benefit in allowing the direct shipment of stock from the pasture grounds to the Victorian markets. Nearer Sydney the important town of Goulburn will be the centre of a system of branch lines, one of which, that from Goulburn to Cooma, is already built, and brings Railway systems of Colony—Southern lines.

the rich pastoral district of Monaro in direct communication with Sydney. A proposal is under consideration for extending this line as far as the Victorian Border. It is also proposed to connect Goulburn with the township of Crookwell, the centre of a large agricultural district 25 miles distant. Further south the construction of a branch line from Cootamundra to Temora will shortly be commenced, while a branch from Culcairn to Corowa, on the Murray, is now in progress.

Brisbane, Sydney, Melbourne, and Adelaide connected by rail.

The southern main line is the most important of the railway lines in the Colony, as it passes through the richest and most thickly populated districts, and places the four great capitals of Australia—Brisbane, Sydney, Melbourne, and Adelaide—in direct communication with each other. It was not until 1883 that this line was actually open for traffic, the railway bridge across the Murray River, which flows between Wodonga, the Victorian terminus, and Albury, the terminus of the southern line of New South Wales, having been completed in that year. The traffic, both of passengers and goods, on the southern system generally, is very extensive, and arrangements for the regular carriage of mails between the two great cities enable letters to be delivered in less than twenty hours. The time occupied by the express trains on the journey is only eighteen hours, and the ordinary passenger trains running daily cover the distance (576 miles) between Sydney and Melbourne in twenty-four hours and a half. Sleeping cars are attached to these trains, on the New South Wales side, and the comfort of travellers is assured by the introduction of the most modern improvements in the construction and fitting up of the railway carriages. Since the completion of the railway from Melbourne to Adelaide, a distance of 508½ miles, European mails are landed at the latter port and forwarded overland to all parts of Victoria, New South Wales, and Queensland. The time occupied in transit between Adelaide and Sydney is 41 hours, and from Sydney to Brisbane, 28 hours; or 69 hours between Adelaide and Brisbane.

Rapid transit of mails.

Western system.

The western system of railways extends from Sydney in the direction of the Blue Mountains, of which it reaches the upper levels a little above Emu Plains, by a system of zig-zag lines which enables the locomotive to drag its heavy freight up the abrupt eastern slope of the mountains. The line runs along the top of the range, until it descends into the valley below Mount Clarence, by another and more important zig-zag, the construction of which is a triumph of engineering skill. In its course between these two zig-zags the line passes through magnificent mountain scenery of a character peculiar to this part of the world, and none the less remarkable. Leaving the mountains, the Western Railway, after throwing out a branch from Wallerawang to Mudgee, enters the Bathurst Plains, and connects the rich agricultural lands of the Bathurst, Orange, and Wellington districts with the metropolis. Beyond Dubbo it enters the pastoral country, and reaches the Darling at Bourke, 503 miles from Sydney. At Orange a branch line, 22 miles in length, connects that town with Molong. Further up, at Nyngan, 377 miles from Sydney, a line has been commenced to connect the important mining district of Cobar with Sydney, affording at the same time rapid and sure means of communication with the pastoral country, of which Cobar is also the centre. This line, it is expected, will eventually be continued as far as Wilcannia, on the Darling, whence it may be extended to the silver-fields of Silverton and Broken Hill. The western railway system also includes a short line from Blacktown to the Hawkesbury, *viâ* the towns of Windsor and Richmond.

Projected branch lines.

Northern system.

The northern system originally had its terminus at Newcastle, but a connecting line between Homebush and Waratah has been constructed, which makes Sydney the head of the whole of the railway systems of the Colony. The Hawkesbury River has been crossed by an iron bridge, 2,896 feet long, in seven spans, the iron superstructure of which cost £327,000. This connecting line allows direct communication between Adelaide, Melbourne, Sydney, and Brisbane, a distance from end to end of 1,808 miles, and has been found of great value to those requiring quick transit, and for the carriage of postal matter. It facilitates, moreover,

Hawkesbury River Bridge.

the active business life of the colonies, and will be of national importance should at any time strategic movements require to be made in connection with military operations.

The northern line runs *viâ* Newcastle and the great coal centres, through the rich agricultural district of the Hunter Valley, to the important part of the Colony known as New England, passing through some of the largest inland towns in New South Wales, such as Maitland, until lately the fourth town in the Colony in point of population, being surpassed only by the city of Newcastle and the town of Parramatta before Broken Hill attained its present development. The country traversed by this line north of Newcastle is extremely fertile. As the line ascends further north it passes through a rich pastoral and agricultural territory, and some important townships are reached, viz., Tamworth, Armidale, Glen Innes, and Tenterfield, and eleven miles beyond the last-mentioned township, the line crosses the border at Wallangarra or Jennings, where a junction is effected with the Queensland Railways.

Projected branch lines.

The northern system also comprises a branch from Werris Creek to Narrabri, which it has been proposed to extend as far as Moree, in the north-west, and the Darling in the west, thus placing the Namoi and Gwydir pastoral districts in direct communication with the ports of Newcastle and Sydney. The construction of a branch from Muswellbrook to Cassilis is also contemplated. In the New England District a line has been long projected, which would connect the town of Glen Innes with that of Inverell, on one side, and with the city of Grafton, on the Clarence, on the other; an alternative line is now being surveyed to connect the Clarence district with Armidale, but both this route and the one proposed from Glen Innes to Grafton present physical difficulties of such a magnitude that it is doubtful if either line will be carried out, at all events, for some time to come. A portion of the North Coast Railway, from the Tweed River to Lismore, on the Richmond, is now in course of construction.

Circular Quay extension.

The question of the extension, through the heart of the metropolis, of the railway system—which at present has its terminus at some little distance from the business centre of the city—to the Circular Quay is again under consideration, the Government having appointed a Royal Commission to inquire into the respective merits of the many schemes that have from time to time been proposed. A short line has been constructed, branching off the main Northern line at Hornsby, 21 miles from Sydney, to Pearce's Corner, on the heights of St. Leonards; this line is now being extended from the latter place to the North Shore of Port Jackson, which, when finished, will connect the Northern districts of the Colony with the harbor. Proposals have been made from time to time to bridge the harbor, or tunnel under it, and thus allow direct communication by rail between the suburbs on the north and the city on the south shore.

Illawarra Line.

Besides the lines and branches included in the three systems above described, another line, entirely independent of them, has been constructed, connecting the metropolis with the coastal district of Illawarra, which is rich alike in coal and the produce of agriculture. The present terminus of this line is at the thriving town of Kiama; but a continuation of the line is now being constructed to Nowra, whence it is proposed to take it eventually to Jervis Bay, closely following the coast line. A proposal has also been made for the construction of a line from the port of Eden at Twofold Bay, in the south of the Colony, to the township of Bega, in the centre of a rich agricultural district; but this is at present in abeyance.

Growth of traffic.

The contrast between the present condition of the New South Wales railways and their humble beginning in 1855 is a remarkable one. In 1856, the first year which can be fairly taken for purposes of comparison, the number of passenger journeys on the railways was only 350,724, whilst in the year ended June 30, 1891, the number was 19,037,760, or nearly 53 times greater; but the tonnage of goods carried in each of these years represents a very much larger increase, having grown from 2,469 tons to

3,802,849, or over 1,540 times greater than in the first full year of railway operations. In the earlier portion of the period of thirty-seven years, which the above figures illustrate, it would seem that the larger part of the railway earnings was obtained from the passenger traffic, and this was no doubt due to the fact that the first railways were almost entirely suburban. It was not until the line crossed the mountains and opened up the far interior that the proportions changed, and the goods traffic became the principal source of revenue of the railways. This change began to take place in 1867, in which year the construction of railways, after being for two years at a standstill, received a sudden impetus, 61 miles of line having been opened in the year named, as against 19 miles only in the previous period of three years. From 1867 till 1877 the proportion of earnings from goods traffic rapidly increased, reaching in the latter year 66·7 per cent. of the total earnings. Since then, owing to the enormous increase in the suburban passenger traffic, the proportion of earnings from goods has decreased to 60·4 in 1890, as against 39·6 obtained from passenger traffic.

Goods principal source of revenue.

Earnings in different year compared.

The comparison between the earnings of the period previous to 1871—when the net result every year represented only a small portion of the interest due on the capital expended in the construction of the lines—and the subsequent period affords matter for satisfaction. The figures for 1886 and 1887 show a falling off from those of fourteen previous years; but it should be borne in mind in comparing these two years with the excellent results exhibited during the period from 1874 to 1884, when an average of considerably over 4 per cent. was realized, that the fall in receipts is due in a great measure to the previous years of drought, and also to the uncertainty attaching to the land laws which had recently been materially altered.

During the years 1884 and 1885 the last section of the main western line, extending over a distance of 112 miles as far as Bourke, was opened, and the line branching off from Wallerawang was completed as far as Mudgee, 63 miles being opened. On the

South-Western Railway the branch line, Narrandera to Jerilderie, covering a distance of 65 miles, was opened for traffic. All of these extensions run through very sparsely settled districts, and this was the case with regard to nearly the whole of the other 172 miles opened during the two years mentioned. This total of 412 miles opened for traffic in unproductive country caused a serious falling off in the proportion of receipts to expenditure during the period ending June, 1888, the net revenue yielding less than 3 per cent. on the total expenditure. Since then the returns have steadily improved, rising in the year ending June, 1891 to 3·6 per cent. In the Railway Report of 1891 a return is given, comparing the net results of lines which are not at present paying interest, for the two years 1887 and 1890, and from the progress which the latter year shows over the former there is every probability that in the near future the lines mentioned will earn sufficient to pay the interest on their cost. The fact that railways have not returned a profit should occasion no surprise, as the statistics of the railway returns in all the parts of the world show that few lines, except perhaps suburban ones, return anything like a profit during the first few years after their opening. In England a period of seven years has been allowed by good authorities for a line to develop traffic; and if such is the fact in more densely populated countries, whose resources are more developed than is the case in New South Wales, there is every reason to be satisfied with the fact that the lines of this colony have yielded so good a return as they have. And there is good cause to hope that under the present administration of the railways the deficiency will soon be met, as the returns for the year ended June 30, 1891, show that the interest on cost of construction was covered all but 0·29 per cent.

Period required to develop traffic.

A glance at the table of net earnings and interest on capital expended upon railways, which will be found on page 360, will show that during the period from 1870 to 1876, in which the length of new lines yearly constructed was very small, being only 191 miles during the whole period of seven years, or about 27½ miles per year, the railway profits show a constant and regular increase from 1·817 to 4·428 per cent. In 1877 and 1878 170 miles of railway were constructed, and the profits immediately show a decline to 3·741 and 3·341 per cent. respectively. From 1880 to 1884 the railways were extended chiefly to centres already populous and prosperous, viz., Riverina and New England, and the central districts of Goulburn, Wellington, and Dubbo; and as these were years of remarkable prosperity, the railway profits suffered less than usual from the considerable extension, which included the construction of the expensive connecting link joining the New South Wales Railways with those of Victoria, at the River Murray. From 1885 to 1890 the extensions on the main lines were for the most part through pastoral country, such as the continuation of the Western line to Bourke, of the Northern line to Wallangarra, and the further extensions of the lines in the Goulburn district to the rich pastoral lands of Monaro, while several branch lines were constructed tapping important agricultural and dairy-farming districts, notably the lines Cootamundra-Gundagai, Murrumburrah-Blayney, and Sydney-Kiama. In some cases the value of the branch lines will not be felt until the entire system, of which they form part, is completed, or until they become trunk lines. For instance, in the case of the Goulburn-Cooma line, a proposal is under consideration for continuing this line to the Victorian border, with a branch line to Eden, Twofold Bay. It is expected that the Gippsland line will be extended from Bairnsdale to the border, and that by the junction of these two lines an alternative route to Melbourne will be obtained. In that case, no doubt, the Eastern part of Gippsland would find its natural port at Eden. A large sum of money has been expended on each section of the line from Homebush to the Hawkesbury, and from the opposite shore of the river to Waratah; but not until the completion of the bridge over the Hawkesbury River, which was accomplished in May, 1889, could the line be expected to return the interest on the money expended upon it.

Extensions reduce general returns.

Alternative route to Melbourne.

Expensive new lines result in an increase of percentage of working expenses to the gross earnings, as these lines have to be kept in full working order and repair whilst actually returning in gross earnings little over the cost of maintenance. The small returns on expensive incompleted branches further tend to diminish greatly the profits of a railway system taken as a whole; but such is the history of railway construction in all parts of the world, and New South Wales is no exception to the general rule.

Scheme for the construction of new railways.

The Railway Commissioners in their Annual Report for 1891 suggest a plan for paying for new lines from the sale of lands. They recommend that the Crown Lands for a distance of 10 miles each side of proposed railways should be set aside for sale, and half the proceeds of the land sold to be credited to the Railway Capital; and where the land required for railway construction has passed into the hands of private individuals that the land-owners should combine and convey the necessary land free of cost to the Government, it being considered that the owners would be fully remunerated for the gift of the land by the enhanced value of their property through direct railway communication being established with the other parts of the Colony By the adoption of this system it is believed that railways in light undulating country could be constructed at a moderate cost, and yield a fair return on capital from the commencement, especially what are known as "Pioneer Railways," which could be constructed at an average of about £1,750 per mile, exclusive of bridges.

The Betterment system.

The Betterment system as applied to railways was first introduced in the construction of the Culcairn to Corowa Railway. No special Act has been passed for the general establishment of this principle, but by a proviso in a clause of the Public Works Act, the Government were empowered to apply the principle to all railways constructed subsequently to the date of the passing of the Act. In estimating the enhanced value of the land adjoining the Culcairn to Corowa Railway line, now in course of construction, the stations were assumed to be 10 miles apart, the Betterment area having a 5 mile radius from each station, and the land in the vicinity of each station being considered to have an enhanced value of 25 per cent., graduating to 5 per cent.

at the limit of the radius. In the case of the extension of the railway along the Southern Coast it is found that the enhanced value does not reach so high a percentage, owing to the facilities which exist for the transport of produce, &c., by water.

Average cost per mile.

The following table shows the cost of construction of the various branches of the railway system of the Colony to the middle of the year 1891. The average cost for the whole of the lines is calculated to be £12,457 per mile, including all charges, except for rolling-stock, machinery, and workshops, a figure, which, considering the character of some parts of the country through which the lines have been carried, and the cost of labour, which is considerably greater in Australia than in most other countries, is by no means a high one.

Cost of Construction of Railway Lines to 30th June, 1891.

Lines opened for Traffic.	Length in Miles.	Total Cost.	Cost per Mile.
		£	£
Darling Harbour Branch	1	330,681	330,681
Sydney to Granville	13	1,460,310	112,331
Haslem's Creek Branch	½	6,459	12,918
Granville to Wodonga	374½	4,595,879	12,272
Junee to Hay	167	944,983	5,658
Narrandera to Jerilderie	65	409,601	6,301
Granville to Bourke	490	5,219,999	10,653
Wallerawang to Mudgee	85	950,890	11,187
Blacktown to Richmond	16	174,501	10,906
Goulburn to Cooma	127½	1,402,180	10,997
Cootamundra to Gundagai	34	231,252	6,801
Orange to Molong	22	269,327	12,242
Murrumburrah to Blayney	106	1,076,856	10,159
Sydney to Kiama	70	1,908,213	27,260
Homebush to Waratah	93½	2,404,526	25,717
Newcastle to Wallangarra	391	4,829,776	12,352
Werris Creek to Narrabri	97	561,255	5,786
Bullock Island Branch	1½	83,227	55,485
Morpeth Branch	4	60,814	15,203
Hornsby and St. Leonards	11	210,919	19,174
Campbelltown to Camden } Tram lines.	7½	38,667	5,156
Kogarah to Sans Souci } Tram lines.	5	12,111	2,422
	2,182	27,182,426	12,457

The amount expended on rolling-stock to the period named was £3,675,297; for machinery, £271,426; workshops, £630,539; and furniture, £8,929, or £4,586,191 in all. This makes the total cost of all lines open for traffic, £31,768,617, or an average on all charges of £14,559 per mile.

In considering these figures in detail it is interesting to note the comparative low cost per mile of the extensions through the pastoral country from Junee to Hay, and from Werris Creek to Narrabri, which average only £5,658 and £5,786 per mile respectively, or less than half the general average cost of other lines. The Campbelltown-Camden and the Kogarah-Sans Souci lines were constructed cheaply for tram-lines. The cost of the light lines, which will shortly be in course of construction through a country of similar formation, should not reach even the figures just stated, being estimated, as previously mentioned, to cost only £1,750 per mile, exclusive of bridges.

Lines in pastoral country less costly.

The cost of railway construction in some of the principal countries of the world, for which figures are available, is given hereunder. The figures include the whole expense of equipping the lines for traffic, and are brought down to the latest dates available:—

Cost in other countries.

Countries.	Cost per Mile open for Traffic.
	£
United Kingdom	43,955
Belgium	27,802
France	26,944
Germany	20,537
Russia in Europe	20,000
India	13,202
Canada	11,551
Cape Colony	9,217
New South Wales	14,559
Victoria	13,917
New Zealand	7,617
Queensland	6,420
South Australia	6,527
Tasmania	8,269

EARNINGS AND WORKING EXPENSES.

The gross amount of revenue derived from all sources during the year ended 30th June, 1891, was £2,974,421, a larger sum than was obtained in any previous year. The cost of working the railways reached £1,831,371, and the net earnings were £1,143,050,

Gross earnings and working expenses.

or 38·4 per cent. of the total earnings. The following table gives the gross earnings and total working expenses with the proportion per cent. of the expenditure to the receipts.

Gross Earnings and Working Expenses, and Percentage of Working Expenses to Gross Earnings.

Year.	Gross Earnings.	Working Expenses.	Percentage of working expenses to gross earnings.	Year.	Gross Earnings.	Working Expenses.	Percentage of working expenses to gross earnings.
	£	£	per cent.		£	£	per cent.
1855	9,249	5,959	64·43	1874	536,575	257,706	48·03
1856	32,283	21,788	67·49	1875	614,648	296,174	48·18
1857	43,387	31,338	72·23	1876	693,225	339,406	48·96
1858	62,309	43,928	70·56	1877	815,920	418,965	51·35
1859	61,760	47,598	77·07	1878	902,989	536,988	59·47
1860	62,269	50,427	80·98	1879	952,366	604,721	63·49
1861	75,004	61,187	81·58	1880	1,161,017	647,719	55·79
1862	103,871	68,725	66·16	1881	1,444,226	738,334	51·12
1863	123,941	96,867	78·16	1882	1,698,863	934,635	55·02
1864	147,653	103,715	70·24	1883	1,931,464	1,177,788	60·97
1865	166,032	108,926	65·60	1864	2,086,237	1,301,259	62·37
1866	168,535	106,230	63·64	1885	2,174,368	1,458,153	67·06
1867	189,072	117,324	62·08	1886	2,160,070	1,492,992	69·12
1868	224,359	144,201	64·29	1887	2,208,294	1,457,760	66·02
1869	264,975	176,362	66·57	*1888	2,295,124	1,530,551	66·69
1870	307,142	206,003	67·08	*1889	2,538,477	1,634,602	64·39
1871	355,322	197,065	55·46	*1890	2,633,086	1,665,835	63·26
1872	424,989	207,918	48·92	*1891	2,974,421	1,831,371	61·57
1873	484,236	238,035	49·16				

* Year ended 30th June, 1890.

Working expenses.

It will be seen from the following table that a larger proportion of revenue is now absorbed by working expenses than was formerly the case. In 1880, the expense of working per train mile was 46·24d., while in the year ended with June, 1891, the expense was 52·26d. per mile, or 6d. more. An advance has taken place in cost of locomotive power of over 2d. per train mile, while the increase in the cost of repairs of carriages and waggons added a little more than another 2d. An additional expense of very nearly the same amount was due to traffic charges, caused principally by the extension of suburban traffic.

Distribution of Working Expenses per Train Mile.

	1882.	1883.	1884.	1885.	1886.	1887	1888.	1889.	1890.	1891.
	d	d	d	d	d	d	d	d	d	d
Maintenance of Way	12·96	13·88	13·77	15·71	16·02	14·73	15·39	13·87	13·24	12·75
Locomotive Power	15·56	15·44	16·10	15·62	16·58	16·44	16·73	16·45	15·95	17·80
Repairs—Carriages, Waggons, &c.	2·30	2·27	2·99	2·65	3·58	3·10	4·59	4·66	4·75	4·47
Traffic Charges......	13·76	14·23	14·12	14·92	15·95	16·13	15·07	13·68	13·64	15·04
Compensation, Personal...	0·16	0·12	0·11	0·26	0·24	0·45	0·97	0·25	0·32	0·50
General Expenses	1·50	1·67	1·68	3·56	2·93	3·20	2·16	2·43	2·01	1·70
	46·24	47·61	48·77	52·72	55·30	54·05	54·91	51·34	49·91	52·26

For the last four years the returns are made out for the twelve months ended on June 30 of each year.

Net revenue.

The net revenue for the year which expired on the 30th June, 1891, was £1,143,050, while the total amount of capital expended on lines in operation to the same period was £31,768,617. The net return on the capital expended equalled 3·598 per cent., which is the most satisfactory return obtained since 1884, and, as will hereafter appear, only 0·29 per cent. below the average interest payable on all outstanding loans of the Public Debt.

Net Earnings, and Interest on Capital expended on Railways.

Year.	Net Earnings.	Interest on Capital.	Year.	Net Earnings.	Interest on Capital.
	£	per cent.		£	per cent.
1855	3,290	·638	1874	278,872	4·074
1856	10,495	1·536	1875	318,474	4·396
1857	12,050	1·176	1876	353,819	4·426
1858	18,381	1·492	1877	396,935	4·466
1859	14,162	1·107	1878	366,001	3·741
1860	11,841	·832	1879	347,645	3·241
1861	13,817	·899	1880	513,298	4·353
1862	35,146	1·842	1881	705,892	5·307
1863	27,073	1·097	1882	764,228	5·135
1864	43,938	1·669	1883	753,676	4·484
1865	57,106	2·079	1884	784,978	4·201
1866	62,305	2·236	1885	716,215	3·370
1867	71,748	2·185	1886	667,078	2·991
1868	80,158	1·973	1887	750,534	2·965
1869	88,613	1·892	1888	764,573	2·852
1870	101,139	1·817	1889	903,875	3·144
1871	158,257	2·688	1890	967,251	3·176
1872	217,071	3·397	1891	1,143,050	3·598
1873	240,201	3·653			

NOTE.—Since 1887 the accounts have been made up to the 30th June in each year.

Points of comparison between the railways of a large and thinly inhabited country such as New South Wales and the countries of the Old World are difficult to obtain. The following table, however, illustrates the population and area in square miles of territory per mile of line open in the principal countries of the world, compiled from the latest returns. It will be seen that New South Wales comes fairly well out of the comparison :— Comparison with other countries.

Length of Railway in various Countries, with Population and Area per Mile of Line.

Countries.	Length of Railway.	Population per Miles of Line.	Area per Mile of Line.
*Australasia :—			
New South Wales	2,263	496	137
Victoria	2,471	467	36
South Australia	1,774	183	312
Queensland	2,142	180	509
Western Australia	505	96	2,099
Tasmania	399	362	66
New Zealand	1,956	320	53
Argentine Republic	3,635	825	319
Austria-Hungary	15,267	2,481	16
Belgium	2,762	1,999	4
Brazil	4,625	3,027	696
Canada, Dominion of	12,628	402	270
Chili	1,649	1,533	176
Denmark	1,217	1,617	12
France	21,899	1,745	9
Germany	24,270	1,931	9
Great Britain and Ireland	19,943	1,896	6
Greece	371	4,634	67
India (British)	16,095	13,037	54
Italy	7,830	3,635	14
Japan	534	74,171	276
Mexico	3,388	3,391	219
Netherlands	1,616	2,483	8
Portugal	1,188	3,625	29
Roumania	1,460	3,543	34
Russia (in Europe)	17,363	5,291	120
Spain	5,929	2,969	33
Sweden and Norway	5,644	1,194	52
Switzerland	1,869	1,569	8
Turkey (in Europe)	865	5,538	74
United States of America	154,276	398	19

* Australasia, 1890.

PASSENGER TRAFFIC.

Journeys per head of population.

The number of journeys made by each person in the Colony now averages 16·97 per annum, as against 5·63 in 1878. The increase has been exceedingly rapid as well as fairly uniform, as will be seen from the following table:—

Year.	Number of Journeys.	Year.	Number of Journeys.
1878	5·63	1885	14·57
1879	6·25	1886	15·35
1880	7·47	1887	14·38
1881	9·03	*1888	14·87
1882	11·14	*1889	15·30
1883	12·26	*1890	15·78
1884	12·74	*1891	16·97

* Year ended 30th June.

Journeys per head in different Countries.

The figures just given include journeys of season-ticket holders; excluding this traffic, the number of journeys per head would be about 11·13, a number larger than the average of any of the adjacent colonies, Victoria excepted. The average number of journeys performed by inhabitants of the United Kingdom is 19·0, which largely exceeds that of any other population. With this exception, railway travelling is more common in Victoria and New South Wales than in any other country. The average of some of the more important places are:—Belgium, 9·3; France, 5·5; Germany, 5·1; United States, 5·4; Austria, 1·2; Russia, 0·4; South Australia, 10·4; Queensland, 4·5. The total number of persons travelling, including season ticket-holders, and the revenue

Number of passengers carried.

received, are shown in the next table, which should be read in connection with that just given:—

Year.	Number of Passenger journeys.	Receipts.	Year.	Number of Passenger journeys.	Receipts.
		£			£
1855	98,846	9,093	1874	1,085,561	188,595
1856	350,724	29,526	1875	1,288,225	205,941
1857	329,019	34,970	1876	1,727,730	233,870
1858	376,492	45,858	1877	2,957,144	271,588
1859	425,877	46,502	1878	3,706,733	306,308
1860	551,044	45,428	1879	4,317,864	319,950
1861	595,591	49,637	1880	5,440,138	390,149
1862	642,431	62,096	1881	6,907,312	486,675
1863	627,164	71,297	1882	8,984,313	587,825
1864	693,174	81,487	1883	10,272,037	661,751
1865	751,587	92,984	1884	11,253,109	745,665
1866	668,330	85,636	1885	13,506,346	830,904
1867	616,375	87,564	1886	14,881,604	849,253
1868	714,563	99,408	1887	14,451,303	850,499
1869	759,635	109,427	1888	15,174,115	918,975
1870	776,707	117,854	1889	16,086,223	1,025,601
1871	759,062	129,496	1890	17,071,945	1,059,791
1872	753,910	164,862	1891	19,037,760	1,177,037
1873	875,602	178,216			

NOTE.—Since 1887 the accounts have been made up to the 30th June in each year.

The traffic on the suburban lines, which include only distances within 20 miles of Sydney and Newcastle, Liverpool and Morpeth included, has enormously increased of late years. The following are the particulars for the last three years:— Suburban traffic.

Return of Suburban Traffic.

Year.	*1889.	*1890.	*1891.
Number of passengers	8,086,908	8,594,942	9,384,425
" workmen's journeys	1,796,520	1,990,368	2,422,644
" Season ticket holders' journeys	3,460,320	3,936,180	4,127,192
Total passenger journeys	13,343,748	14,521,490	15,934,261
Number of miles travelled	77,323,971	83,216,224	89,270,546
Average mileage per passenger	5·79	5·73	5·61
Amount received from passengers	£205,383	£233,465	£252,271
Average receipts per mile, per passenger	0·64d.	0·67d.	0·68d.

* Year ending 30th June.

Receipts per head of population.

The average receipts from passenger traffic per head of population have very rapidly advanced, and for 1891 stood at 20s. 11·8d., as against 9s. 3·7d. in 1878. This is not due, as might be supposed, to the increased distance travelled by passengers, so much as to the fact that the railway mileage has increased at a greater rate than the population, enabling the public to indulge in a larger measure of railway tavelling, in accordance with the well established rule that the more facilities for travelling are extended, the greater will the traffic be.

Receipts from Passenger Traffic per head of Population.

Year.	Amount per head.	Year.	Amount per head.
	s. d.		s. d.
1878	9 3·76	1885	17 11·06
1879	9 3·18	1886	17 6·24
1880	10 8·50	1887	16 11·1
1881	12 9·31	*1888	18 0·16
1882	14 8·67	*1889	19 6·18
1883	15 9·50	*1890	19 7·11
1884	16 10·65	*1891	20 11·80

* Year ended 30th June.

GOODS TRAFFIC.

Analysis of the goods traffic.

The weight of goods carried per head of population in New South Wales compares favourably with that of many countries where railways have been long established. The average tonnage from 1877 was :—

Tonnage of Merchandise carried per head of Population.

Year.	Tons.	Year.	Tons.
1878	2·47	1885	3·53
1879	2·49	1886	3·32
1880	2·35	1887	3·22
1881	2·66	*1888	3·33
1882	3·28	*1889	3·22
1883	3·42	*1890	3·50
1884	3·54	*1891	3·39

* Year ended 30th June.

The largest amount of tonnage per inhabitant is in Scotland, where it averages 9·5; the lowest important European country is Italy, with only 0·4 tons per head. The relative position of New South Wales will be seen from the next table, the figures inserted being the average of five years:—

Tonnage of merchandise compared with other countries.

Tonnage of Merchandise moved per head of Population in the Principal Countries of the World.

	Tons.		Tons.
Scotland	9·5	Australasia	3·3
England and Wales	8·4	New South Wales	3·4
United States	7·6	Victoria	3·7
Belgium	6·5	Queensland	2·3
Germany	5·3	South Australia	4·1
Canada	3·1	Western Australia	1·3
France	2·5	Tasmania	1·0
Ireland, Japan, British India	0·8	New Zealand	3·4
Spain, Italy, Russia	0·4 to 0·6		

The absolute tonnage of goods carried in each year on New South Wales railways and the earnings therefrom are given in the following table:—

Tonnage of goods carried.

Tonnage of Goods and Earnings of Traffic.

Year.	Tonnage of Goods.	Earnings.	Year.	Tonnage of Goods.	Earnings.
		£			£
1855	140	156	1874	1,070,938	347,980
1856	2,469	2,757	1875	1,171,354	408,707
1857	20,847	8,417	1876	1,244,131	459,355
1858	33,385	16,451	1877	1,430,041	544,332
1859	43,020	15,258	1878	1,625,886	596,681
1860	55,394	16,841	1879	1,720,815	632,416
1861	101,130	25,367	1880	1,712,971	770,868
1862	205,139	41,775	1881	2,033,850	955,551
1863	218,535	52,644	1882	2,619,427	1,111,038
1864	379,661	66,167	1883	2,864,566	1,269,713
1865	416,707	73,048	1884	3,124,425	1,340,572
1866	500,937	82,890	1885	3,273,004	1,343,464
1867	517,022	101,508	1886	3,218,582	1,310,817
1868	596,514	124,951	1887	3,339,253	1,357,796
1869	714,113	155,548	1888	3,399,772	1,376,149
1870	766,523	189,288	1889	3,485,839	1,512,876
1871	741,986	225,826	1890	3,788,950	1,573,295
1872	925,260	260,127	1891	3,802,849	1,797,384
1873	923,788	306,020			

NOTE.—Since 1887 the accounts have been made up to the 30th June in each year.

Receipts per head.

The receipts per head of population from goods traffic steadily increased till 1884, after which year the amount fell off till 1888; since then a very satisfactory advance has taken place, the amount per head for the year ending June, 1891, £1 12s. 0·52d., being the highest yet obtained. The receipts during each year since 1878 are shown herewith :—

Receipts from Goods Traffic per head of Population.

Year.	Amount.	Year.	Amount.
	£ s. d.		£ s. d.
1878	0 18 1·70	1885	1 8 11·72
1879	0 18 3·76	1886	1 7 0·61
1880	1 1 1·89	1887	1 7 0·20
1881	1 4 11·77	*1888	1 6 11·69
1882	1 7 9·92	*1889	1 8 9·44
1883	1 10 3·57	*1890	1 9 1·03
1884	1 10 4·31	*1891	1 12 0·52

* Year ended 30th June.

The following table gives the percentage of earnings from the two sources of Railway Revenue. It will be observed that in the years 1865–66 the earnings from passenger traffic largely exceeded those from goods, but after those years the proportion declined, reaching the minimum in 1877. This falling off was almost entirely due to the considerable extension of the main lines through pastoral country, thinly populated, but well stocked with sheep and cattle, and consequently furnishing the railway with large quantities of produce for carriage to the sea-board. Since 1877, however, the percentage of receipts from passengers has gradually advanced, and for the year 1891 this traffic contributed 39·57 per cent. of the total revenue, figures which compare very favourably with those obtained on the English lines from the same source—44 per cent.:—

Percentages of Earnings from Passenger and Goods Traffic to Total Earnings.

Year.	Percentage of Passenger Earnings to Total.	Percentage of Goods Earnings to Total.	Year.	Percentage of Passenger Earnings to Total.	Percentage of Goods Earnings to Total.
1865	56·0	44·0	1879	33·5	66·4
1866	50·8	49·2	1880	33·6	66·4
1867	46·3	53·7	1881	33·8	66·2
1868	44·3	55·7	1882	34·6	65·4
1869	48·4	51·6	1883	34·3	65·7
1870	38·4	61·6	1884	35·7	64·3
1871	36·4	63·6	1885	38·2	61·8
1872	38·8	61·2	1886	39·3	60·7
1873	36·8	63·2	1887	38·5	61·5
1874	35·2	64·8	1888*	40·1	59·9
1875	33·5	66·5	1889*	40·4	59·6
1876	33·7	66·3	1890*	40·2	59·8
1877	33·3	66·7	1891*	39·6	60·4
1878	33·9	66·1			

* Year ended 30th June.

Lines open, under construction, and authorised.

At the end of 1890 the total length of lines in operation in the Colony was 2,182 miles. Several new lines have been recommended by the Parliamentary Standing Committee on Public Works, and sanctioned by the Legislature. Of these the following are now in course of construction:—Culcairn to Corowa, a length of 47 miles 39 chains; Kiama to Nowra, an extension of the South Coast Railway, 22 miles 33 chains; and Nyngan to Cobar, 81 miles 25 chains; St. Leonards extension to Milson's Point, 2 miles 66 chains, making 154 miles 13 chains altogether of new lines actually in progress. Other works sanctioned are railway from Marrickville to the Burwood Road; from Grafton to the Tweed; and from Cootamundra to Temora.

Rolling stock.

The rolling stock of the New South Wales railways on the 30th June, 1891, consisted of 439 engines, 1,023 passenger cars, and 9,940 goods vehicles, making a total of 11,402 stock. This was an increase of 636 goods stock over the number at the end of the previous twelve months, but a decrease of 41 passenger carriages. The average daily number of engines at work during the year was 328¼, and the total engine miles executed was 12,118,682, giving an annual average mileage per engine of 36,909 miles. This showed an increase of 16·841 per cent. in the mileage per engine employed during the year, as compared with the work of the previous year.

Cost of railways.

The cost of the lines open for traffic, as already stated, was £31,768,617, to meet which £27,734,581 has been realized by the issue of debentures of the nominal value of £28,983,967, the balance having been paid out of the general revenue of the country. Debentures of the value of £1,139,175 have been finally paid off, leaving £27,844,792 still outstanding on the 30th June, 1891. The amount of interest payable on that date was £1,102,001.

Outstanding debt.

Wages paid.

During the year which closed with the end of June, 1891, the wages paid by the Railway Department amounted to £1,279,953, as against £1,199,796 in the previous year. Of this sum the Maintenance Branch took £453,016, and the Locomotive Branch £522,008, while the Traffic Branch absorbed £304,929. Additions and improvements to stations, buildings, siding accommodation, &c., and rolling stock during the year cost £574,039, which sum was charged to capital account. Compensation for personal injury was paid to the amount of £11,165, and for damage to and loss of goods, £3,642.

Number of employees.

There were altogether 10,942 persons employed by the Railway Department during the year ending 30th June, 1891, of which number 1,444 comprised the salaried staff, and 9,498 were on wages. For the previous year the total number was 11,827, of whom 1,305 were on salary, and 10,522 on wages.

PRIVATE RAILWAY LINES.

In the Colony of New South Wales the established policy has hitherto been to keep the railways under State management and control, and this policy has been departed from in two instances only, with the exception of short lines to connect coal-mines with the main railways, &c. The Parliament granted permission to a company to construct a line from Deniliquin, in the centre of the Riverina district, to Moama, on the Murray, where it meets the railway system of Victoria. A considerable proportion of the wool and other produce of Riverina reaches the Melbourne market by this route. The line is 45 miles in length, and was constructed under a special Act of Parliament, assented to on the 3rd March, 1874. The land required was granted by the New South Wales Government, right being reserved for the purchase of the line at any time after twenty-one years from the passing of the Act. The capital of the Company is £125,000, of which £100,000 has been called up, while £46,000 was raised by debentures. The dividends paid during 1887 and 1888 were at the rate of 10 per cent., but more recently averaged only 8 per cent. During the year 1888 a line, 35 miles 54 chains in length, was laid down from the Barrier silver mines, Silverton, and Broken Hill to the South Australian Border. The line, since its inception, has had large support; the dividends paid have amounted to 50 per cent. of the capital subscribed. The following table shows the operations of these lines during the past year:—

Deniliquin to Moama line.

Silverton and Broken Hill line.

Name of Line.	Date of Opening.	Length of Line.	Total Expended on Construction.	Passengers Carried.	Goods Carried.	Train Miles Run.	Rolling Stock.		
							Locomotives.	Passenger Carriages.	Goods Carriages & Vans.
		m. c.	£	No.	Tons.		No.	No.	No.
Deniliquin-Moama..	4 July, 1876	45 0	162,672	16,588	28,023	61,285	4	6	62
Silverton	1 Jan., 1888	35 54	227,055	57,770	314,262	129,855	10	15	450

CITY TRAFFIC, TRAMWAYS, ETC.

Within the Metropolis of Sydney the public traffic, with the exception of the tramway system, is controlled by four Transit Commissioners, comprising the Mayor of Sydney, the Inspector-

General of Police, a representative elected by the Aldermen of Suburban Municipalities, and one by the holders of licenses under the Commissioners. The tramways, like the railways, are the property of the Government, and are under the control of the Commissioners for Railways. There are now three distinct systems of tramways in operation, consisting of the Metropolitan lines, 33½ miles long; the North Shore cable tramway, 1½ miles; and the Newcastle to Plattsburg line, 7½ miles, giving a total length of 42½ miles, including the extension of the Leichhardt line to Five Dock and the Waverley line to the Cemetery. The Campbelltown and Camden line, 7½ miles; and the Kogarah and Sandringham line, 5 miles, formerly classed as Tramways, are now included under the head of Railways.

Tramways.

The Metropolitan tramways may be fairly regarded as street railways, and they are worked by locomotives of a special construction. Proposals for the substitution of cables or electric power for the steam motors have been considered, though no definite decision has been arrived at. A cable tramway was inaugurated at North Sydney some years ago, which is now proving a success, returning 3·67 per cent. on the capital expenditure for the year, June, 1891. The electric system is now being tried on a short line joining the Waverley and Randwick tram-lines, and is working satisfactorily.

Interest on capital.

The net return on Tramway capital has varied greatly from year to year. The favourable results of the first three years encouraged the belief that the metropolitan tramways would prove a source of increase to the general revenue of the Colony. These anticipations were, however, not realized, but should the progress of the two years ending June, 1891, be maintained, the returns will shortly equal those of the favourable years 1881-82. The following Table gives the Revenue, Expenditure, and Capital invested on the Metropolitan Tramways, exclusive of the North Shore Cable Tramway:—

Metropolitan Tramways—Revenue, Expenditure, Capital Invested.

Year.	Length of Line.	Number of Passenger fares collected.	Car Mileage.	Total Earnings.	Working Expenses.	Earnings per Car Mile.	Working cost per Car Mile.	Per centage of working cost of gross earnings.	Net Earnings.	Capital invested on Lines open.	Interest on Capital.
				£	£				£	£	
1879*......	1½	443,341	13,270	4,416	2,278	79·87	41·19	51·59	2,138	22,269	33·00
1880	4	2,066,897	84,074	18,980	13,444	54·18	38·38	70·83	5,536	60,218	12·34
1881	9½	7,090,125	296,906	62,549	52,107	50·56	42·12	83·31	10,442	169,450	6·16
1882	22	15,269,100	670,649	126,202	103,136	45·16	36·91	81·72	23,066	412,561	6·80
1883	25	25,684,285	1,076,096	190,699	178,877	42·53	39·89	93·80	11,822	544,105	2·22
1884	27½	30,202,303	1,242,491	219,942	215,167	42·48	41·56	97·83	4,775	643,111	0·76
1885	27½	†39,594,753	1,220,500	223,340	207,995	43·91	40·90	93·13	15,345	708,109	2·17
1886	27½	52,977,578	1,222,943	226,367	201,737	44·42	39·59	89·12	24,630	742,113	3·32
1887	29½	50,108,256	1,220,026	214,125	201,468	42·12	39·63	94·08	12,657	731,582	1·76
1888‡......	29½	51,563,197	1,246,543	221,060	204,227	42·56	39·32	92·38	16,833	742,555	2·27
1889‡......	29½	52,810,026	1,336,386	225,833	206,092	40·49	36·95	91·25	19,741	771,255	2·56
1890‡......	30½	57,463,650	1,474,646	249,508	207,517	40·60	36·46	83·17	41,991	790,555	5·31
1891‡......	33½	62,676,636	1,553,048	270,365	221,505	41·78	34·23	81·92	48,860	857,455	5·74

* The line was opened for three and a half months only in 1879, and for part of this period was worked with horsepower. † Up to the year 1885, 3d. cash fares and 2d. tickets were counted as single fares; from 1886 inclusive all tickets issued were at 1d. values, and cash fares paid are in this return calculated at the same rate. ‡ Year ending 30th June

Fare per mile.

The fares paid on the tramways average about 1d. per mile, the lines being divided into sections of about 1 and 2 miles. The number of persons using the tram-cars has not been ascertained with any exactness, as the tickets collected give only a partial indication of the number travelling. Cash fares in lieu of tickets are allowed, although this system does not largely prevail, as an extra fee is charged when money is tendered.

Cost of construction.

The following table shows the cost of Construction of the City and Suburban Tramways to 30th June, 1891 :—

	Length in miles	Total Cost.	Cost per mile.
Railway Station to Bridge-street	1¾	93,445	53,397
Liverpool-street to Randwick and Coogee	5¼	110,740	21,093
Darlinghurst Junction to Waverley and Woollahra	4	52,909	13,227
Waverley to Bondi Beach..................................	1¾	25,409	14,519
Waverley to Randwick	1½	11,039	7,359
Crown-street Junction to Cleveland-street	¾	16,069	21,425
Railway Station to Glebe and Forest Lodge	2¼	38,021	16,898
Newtown, Glebe Junction to Dulwich Hill	4¼	57,972	13,640
Forest Lodge Junction to Leichhardt..................	5¼	54,264	10,453
Railway Station Junction to Botany	6¾	90,270	13,373
	33½	548,138	16,362

The Tramways

In the course of the year ended on June 30, 1891, two sections were opened, Leichhardt to Five Dock, 2 miles 39 chains, and

Waverley to the Cemetery, 60 chains, making a total length of 42½ miles opened in the Colony. The City and Suburban lines covered a length of 33½ miles; the gross revenue from which for the year was £270,365, while the expenses amounted to £221,505, which left a balance of £48,860 towards paying interest on the capital. The cost of the city and suburban sections was £857,455, so that the net return gave 5·74 per cent. upon the capital invested, as against 5·31 in the preceding year, and 2·56 for the year ending in June, 1889. The number of passenger fares collected was 62,676,636, and the cars ran 1,553,048 miles.

The revenue of the North Shore cable line was £10,333, and the expenses £7,603. The net profit therefore was £2,730, or 3·67 per cent. upon £74,343, which was the total cost of the line and its equipment—an increase of 2·12 per cent. upon the previous year. The number of fares collected was 2,465,280, and 67,687 car miles were run. North Shore Cable line.

On the Newcastle to Plattsburg tramway line the gross revenue was £12,152, and the working expenses £10,571, so that the profit for the year came to £1,581. The cost of construction and equipment was £72,414, so that the net return was 2·18 per cent. upon the capital investod, a decrease of ·35 per cent. upon the previous year. 2,908,611 fares were collected, and 109,343 car-miles were run during the year. Newcastle to Plattsburg Tramway.

The gross revenue of the Electric Tramway, Waverley to Randwick, was £575, and the working expenses £1,796, showing a deficiency for the eight months in operation of £1,221. However, now that the line is in a satisfactory state no doubt the revenue will increase.

In the following table are given the revenue, expenditure, and capital invested on all State tramways since their inception in 1879:—

State Tramways.—Revenue, Expenditure, and Capital Invested.

Year.	Lines open for Traffic.		Total Capital Expended.	General Total of Passengers' Tickets.	Value of Fares received.	Total Earnings.	Expenditure for Working Expenses.	Net Earnings over Working Expenses.
	Length.	Capital Expended.						
	Miles.	£	£	No.	£	£	£	£
1879	1½	22,061	22,061	443,341	4,416	4,416	2,278	2,139
1880	4½	60,218	61,901	2,086,897	18,968	18,980	13,444	5,536
1881	11¼	181,659	220,318	7,090,125	61,921	62,549	52,107	10,442
1882	29½	447,939	458,145	15,296,238	127,124	128,354	120,181	8,174
1883	32½	579,439	648,125	25,713,433	190,209	193,929	183,218	10,711
1884	35	683,179	789,499	30,231,382	218,885	223,454	215,086	8,368
1885	35	748,506	890,723	39,620,614	220,332	227,144	207,898	19,246
1886	36½	854,260	985,602	*53,973,311	230,374	234,143	207,635	26,507
1887	51	917,995	1,023,635	52,159,808	225,764	229,772	211,722	18,050
1888	†43½	907,987	1,014,664	55,668,800	241,838	241,838	217,629	24,209
‡1889	§38½	909,595	1,016,928	55,510,860	243,563	243,563	221,835	21,728
‡1890	39½	933,614	1,020,808	61,763,761	262,835	268,962	224,073	44,889
‡1891	42½	1,004,212	1,288,454	68,050,527	292,499	292,850	239,679	53,171

* The excessive increase is due to the substitution of penny tickets for those of greater value in use in previous years.
† Camden-Campbelltown line now placed under Railways.
‡ Year ending 30th June.
§ Kogarah and Sans Souci line now placed under Railways.

The amounts expended on rolling stock, machinery, workshops, and furniture, for the Metropolitan Tramways, were £239,102, £12,893, £55,209, and £2,113 respectively, or £309,317 in all. This makes the total cost for all City and Suburban Lines £857,455, or an average on all charges of £25,983 per mile. The cost of the Cable Tramway at North Shore to same date was £74,343, and the Newcastle to Plattsburg £72,414, giving a total expended on the whole Tramway system of £1,004,212, or an average of £23,628 per mile opened. Total cost of construction.

During the year ended on June, 1891, the total amount of wages paid by the Tramway Department amounted to £160,206, as against £147,327 in the previous year. Of this sum £28,072 was paid to the Maintenance Branch, £92,687 to the Locomotive Branch, and the Traffic Branch absorbed £39,447. Wages paid.

The number of men employed was 1,339, as against 1,110 in the previous year. The salaried staff was 42, and 1,297 were on wages. Taking railways and tramways together, the number of persons employed was 12,281, of whom 1,486 were on the salaried staff, and 10,795 were on wages. To the latter the sum of £1,440,159 was paid as wages during the year, being at the rate of £117 5s. 4d. per man employed. Number of employees.

PRIVATE TRAMWAYS.

There are two tramways under private control within the Metropolitan area—one branching from the Illawarra Line at Rockdale and running down to Lady Robinson's Beach, a distance of one mile; it is chiefly used by excursionists visiting the shores of Botany Bay. The other line passes through the township of Parramatta. The line commences at the Park Gates, continuing as far as the Newington Wharf at Duck River, a distance of three miles, and there connects with the Parramatta River steamers conveying passengers and goods to and from Sydney. Private tramways.

The following table gives the particulars supplied for line :—

Name of Line.	Date of opening.	Length of line.	Total expended on construction.	Passengers carried.	Goods carried.	Rolling-stock: Loco-motives.	Passenger carriages.	Goods
		Miles.	£	No.	Tons.	No.	No.	N
Rockdale to Lady Robinson's Beach	1885	1	15,000	181,695	*Nil.*	2	4	*N*
Parramatta Tramway ...	1883	3	...	...	...	2	4	

North Sydney Tramway. There is a private line in construction at North Sydney conne ing the cable tram terminus on the heights of St. Leonards with village of Gordon. On this line a magnificent suspension brid is being built, which will be the only one of its kind in the colo It is designed in three spans—one of 500 ft., and two end spa each of 150 ft., and the altitude will be 180 ft. above wat level. The construction of this line is expected to give impetus to a locality which, although long settled, has progress but little for lack of speedy communication with the metropolis.

The Balmain Municipal Council were granted authority 1886 to construct tramways within the borough, but so far ha not availed themselves of this privilege.

RAILWAY ACCIDENTS.

The railways of the Colony have been as free from accidents of serious character as the lines of most other countries. In ord to obtain a common basis of comparison it is usual to find t proportion which the number of persons killed or injured bears the total passengers carried. There is, however, no necessa connection between the two, for it is obvious that accidents m occur on lines chiefly devoted to goods traffic, and a mo reasonable basis would be the accidents to passengers only compared with the number of passengers carried. The data from which such a comparison could be made are wanting for most countries; the following figures, therefore, show the number of all descriptions, including not only passengers and employés, but trespassers, killed or injured on the lines of the most important countries, compared with the total number of passengers carried, compiled from various authorities, and up to the latest available dates:—

Railway Accidents.

Countries.	Average per million passengers carried.	
	Killed.	Injured.
Germany	1·65	4·26
Austria-Hungary	4·71	10·67
Belgium	2·32	13·39
Denmark	1·54	7·35
France	1·28	3·25
Italy	2·66	25·73
Norway	0·80	1·33
Holland	2·22	1·90
Roumania	11·00	27·00
Russia	12·05	18·92
New Zealand	2·52	4·30
United Kingdom	1·70	6·12
Portugal	3·43	9·25
Average, Europe	2·60	7·73
" United States	1·51	6·10
" Canada*	17·50	66·60
" India	6·00	10·36
" New South Wales*	2·66	5·90
" Victoria*	1·46	5·65
" South Australia*	1·40	3·04
" New Zealand	2·20	25·30

* Average of series of years.

It will be seen that New South Wales stands on a level with the average of the principal European countries. If, however, the more legitimate comparison be made of the proportion of casualties amongst passengers only, fewer countries are available for reference. These are given in the following table:— Colony's average satisfactory.

Passengers Killed or Injured.

Years over which figures extend.	Countries.	Average per Million Passeng[ers]	
		Killed.	Injured.
1885-89	United Kingdom	0·04	[illegible]
1887	Russia	0·50	[illegible]
1885-9	Belgium	0·11	1·31
1885-8	France	0·15	[illegible]
1890	Canada	3·05	12·65
1888-89	Germany	0·09	3·62
1886-91	New South Wales	0·32	3·70
1885-90	Victoria	0·14	4·42
1889-90	South Australia	0·20	[illegible]
1886	New Zealand	0·88	[illegible]

The foregoing statements show that the Australian lines are safe as those of most other countries, the percentage killed bei a little higher than that of the United Kingdom. This mode comparison is, however, not a perfect one, as the question of t distance travelled by each passenger is an important element the risk run, and is omitted from consideration. If this we made a factor of the comparative statement it would probably found that the risk of each traveller by rail would show l variation in the different countries than would seem to be t case from the figures just given.

Classification of casualties.

The persons meeting with accidents on railway lines may grouped under three heads—passengers, servants of the railwa and trespassers; and the accidents themselves may be classifi into those arising from causes beyond the control of the pers injured, and those due to misconduct or want of caution. Adopti these classifications the accidents during the year ended on June 30, 1891, were:—

Accidents arising.	Passengers.		Railway Employés		Trespassers, &c.		Total.	
	Killed.	Injured.	Killed.	Injured.	Killed.	Injured.	Killed.	Injured.
From causes beyond their control	...	20	1	18	...	...	1	38
Through misconduct or want of caution.	7	22	31	96	21	14	59	132
Total.....	7	42	32	114	21	14	60	170

It will be noticed that of the 60 persons killed, 21 were trespassers, or persons who had no business to be on the railway at all. Of the remaining fatal cases 7 were passengers, 4 of whom lost their lives through leaving or entering a train in motion, 2 were run over, and the remaining case was that of a man who fell between the train and platform. Of the persons injured 42 were passengers, more than half of whom received injury through their own misconduct or want of caution; 114 railway employés were injured, and in no less than 96 of these cases they were themselves to blame. Nine of the trespassers who met with accidents were children.

Railway accidents.

The returns of the railways of the United Kingdom for the year 1890 show a slight decrease in the number of fatalities. Accidents to trains, rolling-stock, and permanent way caused the death of 30 persons, and injury to 643, as compared with 92 killed and 1,133 injured in 1889. There were 31 collisions between passenger trains, 70 between passenger trains and goods trains; and 29 between goods trains. 100 passengers were killed and 865 were injured by various other accidents, including those resulting from their own misconduct and want of caution. There were 77 suicides. Accidents to railway employés, caused by the travelling of trains, resulted in the death of 499 persons, and injury to 3,122. Of persons crossing railways and trespassing on them, there were 459 killed, and 238 injured. The total : of persons killed, from all causes, was 1,076, exactly th number as in the previous year. The total number inju 4,721, or a decrease of 115.

Tramway accidents.

No statement can be made of the number of persons inj the tramways of the city compared with the total nur persons carried, as the latter is not definitely known. A of the accidents which occurred during the year which e the 30th June last shows them to have been 65 in nur which 4 were fatal, and 61 were cases of injury. There fatal and 23 non-fatal accidents to passengers. Four serv the Department suffered injury. Thirty-six accidents in tion with trams occurred to persons who were not passe of which were fatal, and 34 non-fatal. Eighteen of the ca arose from persons entering or leaving a tram in motion, accidents occurred to children.

Omnibus traffic.

Besides the tramways the citizens of Sydney are well p with other means of travelling within the city and su limits, as there are numerous omnibus and cab proprietari the head of these stands the Sydney Tramway and O Company. No tramways are maintained by this compan name would imply, but lines of omnibuses have been est by it in all the principal routes of traffic from the cit suburbs. The plant of this Company consists of 1,118 h which 1,051 are in work, the remainder, 67, being held in Their vehicles consist of 157 omnibuses, 28 carriages, and 4 They have 151 drivers constantly at work, and as m 186 other employees, including clerks, mechanics, grooms, men, &c. There are also public vehicles belonging to pri dividuals, or small associations, plying between the ci some of the more distant suburbs, making a total of 263 om in all.

Cabs and vans.

The number of cabs, carriages, and waggonettes registe licensed by the Transit Commissioners under the Municipal amounts to 1,313, in addition to which there are 559 vans a vehicles; and the public interest is secured against exaggerated demands on the part of licensed cabmen, and other drivers of public vehicles, by a system of fares fixed on a scale liberal to the licensee, whilst not too high for the public to fairly pay. The drivers are placed under the direct control of the Transit Commissioners, who have power to obtain redress from the owners of the vehicles, should any just complaints be made against them. The following shows the number of vehicles of each class licensed during the year 1890 and the number of registered drivers :—

Public vehicles.

Description of Vehicle.	No. of Vehicles.	License Fees.	No. of Drivers, &c.	License Fees.
		£		£
Omnibuses	263	1,292	*529	241
Waggonettes	27	93		
Carriages	11	33	1,487	721
Cabs	1,275	1,853		
Drays and vans	559	778	553	138
Total	2,135	4,049	2,569	1,100

* Includes 32 conductors.

POSTS AND TELEGRAPHS.

Postal and telegraphic communication.

In the matter of postal and telegraphic communication the Colony of New South Wales is liberally provided. Not only is the intercolonial telegraphic system as perfect as can be desired, but the metropolis is in direct communication with Europe and the outer world by means of the cables connecting with the various Asiatic continental telegraph lines.

Submarine cable.

A submarine cable also connects the Colony with New Zealand, and has its Australian terminus within sight of the spot where Captain Cook landed on the shores of Botany Bay, and within a stone's throw of the monument erected to the memory of La Pérouse—the unfortunate and gallant emulator of the great English navigator—and the tomb of Père Le Receveur, the botanist attached to his staff.

History of the Postal Department.

The history of the Postal Department of New South Wales is interesting as affording a striking illustration of the manner in which very small beginnings have led to great results. For the first twenty-three years of the Colony's existence there were neither regular post-offices nor means of postal communication.

First post-office.

The first post-office was established by Governor Macquarie in the year 1810, Mr. Isaac Nichols being appointed Postmaster. The office was in High-street (now known as George-street), at the residence of Mr. Nichols, who was, "in consideration of the trouble and expense attendant upon this duty," allowed to charge on delivery to parties addressed, 8d. for every English or foreign letter of whatever weight, and for every parcel weighing not more than 20 lbs., 1s. 6d.; but exceeding that weight, 3s. The charge on Colonial letters was 4d., irrespective of weight; and soldiers' letters, or those addressed to their wives, were charged 1d. Very little improvement in regard to postal matters took place for some years.

First Postal Act.

In 1825 an Act was passed by Sir Thomas Brisbane, with the advice of the Council, "to regulate the postage of letters in New South Wales," giving power for the establishment of post-offices, and to fix the rates of postage. A proclamation was subsequently issued, fixing the rates of postage and the salaries and allowances of the postmasters; and at the same time persons were invited to tender for the conveyance of mails between Sydney and Parramatta, Windsor and Liverpool, and between Liverpool and Campbelltown, and from Parramatta to Emu Plains, and thence to Bathurst. It was, however, not until 1828 that the provisions of the Act were put into full force.

Early postage rates.

The rates of postage appear to have depended upon the distance and the difficulty of transmission. The lowest single inland rate was 3d., and the highest 12d., the postage on a letter increasing according to its weight, which was fixed for a single letter at ¼-ounce. Letters between New South Wales and Van Diemen's Land were charged 3d. each (ship rate), and newspapers 1d. Other ship letters were charged 4d. single rate, and 6d. for any weight in excess.

Franking.

The privilege of franking was allowed to the Governor and a number of the chief public officials, and letters to and from convicts passed free under certain regulations. In-

1828 the total amount of salaries paid to the country postmasters was £34 7s. 9d., and the establishment in Sydney consisted of one principal postmaster, one clerk, and one letter-carrier. A letter-carrier was subsequently appointed for Parramatta, and he was authorized to charge the public 1d. on every letter delivered by him, which was his only remuneration. In 1831 a two-penny post was established in Sydney; and in 1835, under Sir Richard Bourke, the Act of 1825 was repealed, and another Act was passed, which fixed the charge on a single letter at 4d. for 15 miles, 5d. for 20 miles, 6d. for 30 miles, and so on up to 1s. for 300 miles. In 1837 a post-office was established in Melbourne, which was then of course a part of New South Wales. Stamps were introduced in the same year in the shape of stamped covers or envelopes, which are believed to have been the first postage stamps ever issued.

Sir Richard Bourke's Postal Act.

Stamped covers.

The Sydney establishment had grown in the year 1838 until it consisted of one postmaster-general, one accountant, six clerks, six letter-carriers, and one office-keeper, or fifteen persons in all. The revenue for that year was £8,390, and the expenditure was £10,357; there were as many as forty post-offices throughout the Colony, which then included what are now known as Victoria and Queensland, besides which, as New Zealand was not a separate Colony until 1841, the only post-office she had—at Korraika—was paid through the New South Wales Government. An overland mail to Adelaide was established in 1847, the postage on a single letter being 1s. 6d. The Postal Act was amended again in 1849, during the government of Sir Charles Fitzroy, when the postage on town letters was fixed at 1d. and the inland letters 2d., while the postage on ship letters was 3d., in addition to the inland rate. The use of postage stamps in the present form was authorized, and the privilege of franking was abolished, petitions to the Queen, the Governor, and the Executive and Legislative Councils being the only things allowed to pass free through the post.

Growth of the Sydney Post Office.

Reduction of postal rates.

Postage stamps.

Progress of the Department.

From the time of the discovery of gold in the year 1851 t history of the post-office has been one of progress and impro ment. The Postmaster-General was originally a non-politi officer, as the Registrar-General and the Auditor-General are present. In the year 1855—the first for which an annual rep was laid before Parliament—there were in the Colony altogetl 155 post-offices. The head office was in George-street, on the sa site as the present edifice, but the structure was small and inc venient, notwithstanding its doric columns and pediment in fro There were no electric telegraphs in the Colony at that time, a the arrivals of vessels at the Heads were signalled to the Obser tory by means of flags and semaphores. It was in Septemb 1855, that the first railway was opened in New South Wales, a prior to that time the Southern and Western mails used to le the General Post Office in old-fashioned mail coaches every eveni During that year the total number of miles travelled by the pos contractors, by coach and on horseback, was 1,023,255 miles. T number of letters posted was 2,114,179, of which 617,041 described as "foreign," or, in other words, were addressed to pla beyond the Colony. The number of newspapers was 2,100,9 of which 1,281,613 were inland, and 819,376 were "foreig Book parcels and packets were not reckoned separately, but w counted as letters. Ten petitions to the Governor or the Coun were conveyed free during the year. The revenue of the Depa ment for 1855 was £24,902, and the expenditure was £60,2 while the staff numbered 223 persons in all, of whom 56 w attached to the office in Sydney. The annual report states, wi something like pride, that the communication with Victoria w not less than three times a week.

Railways utilised for postal purposes.

Revenue in 1855.

Iron pillar-receivers.

The first iron pillar letter-receivers in Sydney were erected 1856. During the same year 22 miles of railway were utili for postal purposes, and 16½ miles were added in the followi year. The number of letters delivered in Sydney in 1856 w 1,336,032, and 1,481,416 in the country, being an average of ab 10½ to every person in the community. There were 86,9

Improved ocean mail service.

Equally marvellous progress has been made in regard to the means of postal communication with the United Kingdom and the continents of Europe and America. Instead of the unsatisfactory ocean mail service of 1857, which nominally brought monthly mails, with news 58 days old, there are now four great lines of ocean steam-ships, which bring mails *via* the Suez Canal at least once a week, the time occupied in the conveyance of the mails averaging 34 to 35 days. In addition, there is another mail service *via* San Francisco, which averages 40 days in transit, and arrives and departs monthly. Regular steam communication with England was first established in 1852. Prior to that time the Colony has to depend upon the irregular arrival and despatch of sailing vessels, but in that year the steamships "Australia," "Chusan," and "Great Britain" were despatched from England, making the voyage in 60 days, causing a strong desire in the minds of the Colonists for a more frequent and steady system of communication with the Old World. The outbreak of the Crimean War in 1854 hindered for a while the accomplishment of this object, but in 1856 a line of steamers was again laid on, and the service was carried on by the Peninsular and Oriental Company and the Royal Mail Company for some years, without giving so much satisfaction to the public as might have been expected.

First mail steamer.

The Panama line.

As far back as 1854 a proposal was made for the establishment of a line of mail packets *via* Panama, and negotiations on the subject were carried on for several years between the Government of the United Kingdom and those of New South Wales and New Zealand. The result was that in 1866 the line was started, and continued in operation until the end of 1868, when it was terminated through the failure of the company by which it had been carried out. In the following year this Colony, in conjunction with New Zealand, inaugurated a mail service *via* San Francisco, which, with a few interruptions and under various conditions, has been continued up to the present time. The contract expired in November, 1890, and has not been renewed, although the service is still maintained, without any subsidy as far as New South Wales is concerned.

San Francisco route.

Mail service *via* Suez.

The establishment of a mail route *via* America had the effect of stimulating the steamship owners who were engaged in the service *via* Suez, and from that time there was a marked improvement in the steamers laid on, as well as in the punctuality and speed with which the mails were delivered. The Peninsular and Oriental Company have carried mails for the colonies almost from the inception of the ocean steam service until now, with very few interruptions. Towards the end of 1878 the Orient Company commenced carrying mails between Australia and the United Kingdom, and has continued to do so ever since. More recently the

French and German steamers.

fine steamers of the Messageries Maritimes of France and the North German Lloyd's have entered the service, so that there are now one or two mails received and despatched every week, and a voyage to Europe, which was formerly a formidable undertaking, involving great loss of time and much discomfort, is regarded as a mere pleasure trip to fill up a holiday.

New Post-office building.

In the year 1865 the office of Postmaster-General was made a political one, at first without, and subsequently with, a seat in the Cabinet. The old Post-office building in George-street was found so small and inconvenient that it was resolved to build a larger and more commodious edifice on the same site, and in 1863 the business of the department was removed to a temporary wooden building in Wynyard-square. It was not until 1873 that the new building was partly finished so that the officers could remove from the crowded and ill-ventilated structure in Wynyard-square, where they had carried on their business under great disadvantages and difficulties, to the present palatial structure, which is in every respect a credit to the Colony. The head quarters of the Electric Telegraph Department, the Money Order Office, and the Post-office Savings Bank are in the same building, so that the Postmaster-General has around him all the various branches over which he presides. The following return shows the operations of the Post-office in five-year periods from 1855 to 1885, and annually since that date to the end of 1890 :—

Number of Officers, Employés, Income, Expenditure, &c., of the New South Wales Post Office.

Year.	Number of—			Extent of Postal Lines.				Miles actually travelled.	Cost of conveyance of mails, Foreign and Inland.	Income.	Approximate expenditure.
	Post Offices.	Receiving Offices.	Persons employed.	Railway & Tramway.	Coach.	Horse.	Total.				
									£	£	£
1855	155	8	223	*	*	*	*	1,023,255	45,412	24,902	60,221
1860	289	*	289	60½	1,757½	6,413	8,231	1,461,518	44,303	45,613	71,391
1865	435	*	513	140¾	2,528	9,323	11,991¾	2,521,212	49,840	70,985	83,659
1870	562	*	690	339	3,865	10,038	14,242	3,062,458	48,649	84,441	86,722
1875	752	7	967	435	5,407	11,829	17,671	3,787,757	138,912	107,761	196,368
1880	927	119	1,536	891	8,717	12,819	22,427	5,246,373	174,238	194,084	268,128
1885	1,115	202	2,155	1,797		13,150	26,683	6,621,996	226,105	316,172	375,965
1886	1,157	217	2,307			12,606	27,094	6,891,200	233,723	330,591	396,710
1887	1,167	263	2,363			12,135	27,514	7,015,600	264,886	342,094	426,567
1888		288	2,501			11,530	28,160	7,144,500	248,403	368,956	415,392
1889		305	2,650			11,541	28,718	7,299,400	212,725	396,594	[illegible]

Letters, Newspapers, &c., passing through the Post Office of New South Wales

Year.	Number of Letters.		Number of Newspapers.		Packets & Book Parcels.		Total.			
	Beyond the Colony.	Inland and town	Beyond the Colony.	Inland.	Beyond the Colony	Inland.	Letters.	Newspapers.	Packets, &c.	Postal Cards.
1876	1,853,400	12,614,500	1,508,300	5,408,900	109,500	304,400	14,466,900	6,917,200	413,900	109,664
1877	1,979,500	14,529,500	1,652,000	6,733,000	135,000	263,600	16,509,000	8,385,000	398,600	109,080
1878	2,220,600	15,939,300	1,657,600	7,811,600	133,100	403,700	18,159,900	9,469,200	536,800	123,720
1879	2,442,700	16,964,600	2,020,000	9,447,100	136,300	459,200	19,407,300	11,467,100	595,500	155,920
1880	2,776,000	18,956,500	2,381,200	11,409,800	146,600	565,000	21,732,500	13,791,800	711,600	153,360
1881	3,159,400	23,196,200	2,726,400	13,801,500	180,500	670,800	26,355,600	16,527,900	851,300	178,560
1882	3,589,200	25,737,300	2,720,600	15,361,700	218,600	1,044,200	29,326,500	18,082,300	1,262,800	222,800
1883	4,168,100	31,258,300	3,014,500	16,562,800	269,700	1,379,200	35,426,400	19,577,300	1,648,900	259,400
1884	4,947,200	37,289,800	3,689,600	21,373,900	316,200	2,705,900	42,237,000	25,063,500	3,022,100	296,300
1885	5,328,200	34,023,000	3,987,900	21,579,500	552,600	2,894,200	39,351,200	25,567,400	3,446,800	341,000
1886	5,582,700	37,267,200	4,276,300	*25,256,100	865,800	3,983,000	42,849,900	*29,532,400	4,848,800	348,790
1887	5,624,000	39,221,900	4,744,400	*29,437,200	980,800	4,549,000	44,845,900	*34,181,600	5,530,700	442,100
1888	6,202,800	42,783,200	5,255,000	28,500,400	1,041,600	5,560,300	48,986,000	33,755,400	6,601,900	[illegible]
1889	6,346,700	47,624,600	5,599,000	30,931,800	1,305,000	6,564,400	53,971,[illegible]	36,530,800	[illegible]	[illegible]
1890	8,100,[illegible]	[illegible]	6,949,[illegible]	[illegible]	[illegible]	6,725,300	[illegible]	40,597,20[illegible]	[illegible]	[illegible]

The charge on letters between the Australasian Colonies and the United Kingdom, which had for a long period been at the rate of 6d. per half-ounce *via* Italy, and 4d. by the long sea route, was reduced in 1891 to 2½d. By an arrangement made at the Postal Congress held at Vienna in the middle of the year, New South Wales, as well as the rest of the colonies of Australasia, entered the Universal Postal Union on the 1st October, 1891. The effect of this will be to extend the reduced rate to all countries embraced in the Union. A common scale of postage on newspapers has been adopted by New South Wales, Victoria, and South Australia, and it is considered probable that before long the remaining colonies of the group will join in the arrangement. This agreement provides that newspapers to the United Kingdom shall be subject to the charge of 1d., irrespective of weight, and to all places beyond Australasia the same rate shall be charged for every four ounces, with an additional half-penny for every two ounces beyond that weight.

Postage rates.

Compared with the other provinces of Australasia and with the United Kingdom, New South Wales occupies a favourable position as regards the number of letters and newspapers per head of population, as may be seen from the following table :—

Country.	Number per head of population, 1890.	
	Letters and postcards.	Newspapers and packets.
New South Wales	52	45
Victoria	56	27
Queensland	38	35
South Australia	52	33
Western Australia	56	52
Tasmania	36	41
New Zealand	37	25
Australasia	49	34
United Kingdom	49	16
England and Wales	55	17
Scotland	40	14
Ireland	22	8

MONEY ORDERS AND SAVINGS BANKS.

Money order system.

The money order system was brought into operation in thi Colony in January, 1863, when nineteen offices were opened– the head office in Sydney, and eighteen branch offices in variou parts of the Colony. In June of the same year the operation o the system was extended to the United Kingdom, and all th Australasian Colonies with the exception of Tasmania, and th number of offices in the Colony was increased to forty-seven The Colony of Tasmania came into the arrangement in 1865, an the Department has continued steadily to progress. In 189 there were 548 Money Order Offices in the Colony, thirty-thre new offices having been established during the year. Detail respecting the business transacted by the Department will b found in the chapter devoted to Finance and Public Wealth.

Post-office Savings Banks.

The Post-office Savings Bank, which is also under the contr of the Postmaster-General, was established in the year 1871 a the General Post Office, Sydney, with branches at the princip country towns. The growth of this branch of the service ha fully kept pace with those already mentioned. In 1890 ther were 396 Post-office Savings Banks in various parts of th Colony—an increase of twenty-four over the number in th previous year. During the year 32,372 new accounts wer opened, and 25,348 accounts were closed. The number c accounts remaining open at the close of the year was 83,31' The number of deposits received was 223,428, and the amour was £1,198,294, being an increase of 7,024 in the number, an of £82,431 in the amount, as compared with the business of th previous year. The sum of £63,225 was added to depositor accounts for interest. The balance to the credit of depositors the end of the year was £1,875,905. The average amount each deposit was £5 7s. 3½d., and the average balance at the cred of each depositor was £22 10s. 5d. Further information respecting the Post-office Savings Banks will be found in the chapter on Finance and Public Wealth.

TELEGRAPHS.

Electric telegraphs.

The electric telegraph was first opened to the public of New South Wales on 26th January, 1858, when the line from Sydney to Liverpool, 22 miles in length, was instituted. From this small beginning the system has increased until in 1890 there were 628 stations in the Colony, and 23,598 miles of wire in actual use. The following table gives a view of the business of the Electric Telegraph Department, from 1877 to 1890:—

Electric Telegraphs.

Year.	No. of Stations.	No. of Telegrams.	Total Receipts.	Revenue received.	No. of miles of Wire.	Cost of construction.
			£	£		£
1877	190	1,001,884	96,358	65,645	9,761	343,973
1878	236	1,132,287	98,125	76,227	11,760	413,258
1879	273	1,175,218	103,033	80,490	12,426	437,120
1880	289	1,319,537	123,172	84,110	13,188	462,226
1881	318	1,607,206	125,336	98,665	14,278	492,211
1882	345	1,965,931	153,555	120,266	15,901	536,400
1883	368	2,107,288	165,276	134,643	17,272	564,316
1884	394	2,334,052	176,261	146,386	18,681	601,460
1885	404	2,625,992	191,192	155,074	19,864	641,669
1886	425	2,661,126	184,053	158,128	20,797	666,028
1887	434	2,876,504	187,858	164,511	21,444	684,600
1888	460	3,410,407	213,869	185,965	22,219	704,912
1889	485	3,433,562	213,776	186,862	22,606	713,663
1890	628	3,592,519	222,307	193,707	23,598	743,698

At the close of 1890 there were 11,231 miles of line open, and 266 under construction.

The number of telegrams received and desdatched during the year amounted to 3,592,519, or rather over 3¼ per head for every individual of the population.

Construction in various countries.

The state of telegraphic construction in the principal countries of the world at the latest available dates is given herewith. The figures are interesting, though the circumstances of Australasia and the older countries are so dissimilar as to make comparison between them more curious than valuable :—

Length of Telegraph Lines in various Countries.

Country.	Length in Miles—		Country.	Length in Miles—	
	Of Lines.	Of Wires.		Of Lines.	Of Wires.
Australasia	43,142	83,683	India, British.. ...	33,462	96,654
Argentine Republic	19,000	28,550	Italy	21,020	73,592
Austro-Hungary ..	37,085	110,661	Japan	6,596	......
Belgium.............	4,013	19,139	Mexico	27,861	46,000
Brazil.................	6,700	11,556	Netherlands	3,186	11,176
Canada	29,439	62,020	Portugal	3,191	7,420
Cape Colony	4,640	11,791	Russia................	74,276	171,663
Chili	13,730	......	Spain	14,710	33,552
Denmark	2,748	7,514	Sweden & Norway	10,049	22,840
France	59,915	181,598	Switzerland	4,418	16,768
Germany	58,048	206,209	Turkey ,............	15,000	28,000
Great Britain and Ireland...........	31,440	190,027	United States of America	178,754	647,697
Greece	4,382	5,082			

PART XIV.

Defence.

NEW South Wales was garrisoned with British troops from the time of its foundation as a colony until the year 1870. For part of the years 1870 and 1871 the Colony was without regular troops, its defence being entirely in the hands of the volunteer force. In 1871 a local regular defence force was enrolled, comprising one battery of artillery and two companies of foot, the latter, however, were disbanded in the following year. The permanent artillery was strengthened by a second battery in 1876, and by a third in 1877. To supplement the Imperial troops in Australia a volunteer force was enrolled in 1854, Great Britain being then at war with Russia. The Act authorizing the establishment of the force was 18 Vic. No. 8. The original strength of this corps was one troop of cavalry, one battery of artillery, and six companies of foot, but with the termination of the Crimean war this force practically ceased to exist. A few years later, in 1860, the volunteer movement was revived, and a second force enrolled, consisting of one troop of mounted rifles, three batteries of artillery—two stationed at Sydney, and one at Newcastle—and twenty companies of infantry, fourteen of which were recruited from Sydney and its suburbs, and six from the country districts. The total strength of all arms was about 1,700 men. In 1868 the force was reorganized under the Volunteer Regulation Act, passed towards the close of the previous year. In 1873 a further reorganization of the volunteer troops of the Colony took place upon a plan drawn up by Sir William Jervois, and in 1885 an additional force of reserves was enrolled.

Imperial garrison.

Volunteer movement.

Land forces of the Colony.

The land forces of the Colony comprise three distinct branches, the Permanent or Regular Military Force, Volunteers or partially paid Force, and Reserves. The Permanent Force consists of artillery and submarine miners. The mounted infantry was disbanded in July, 1890. The Volunteers consist of artillery, engineers, submarine miners, infantry, mounted infantry, cavalry, naval brigade, and naval artillery; while the Reserves, which are purely volunteer corps, comprise infantry only at present.

Permanent Artillery.

The Permanent Force comprises a general staff of 10 commissioned and 14 non-commissioned officers, and 18 commissioned officers of artillery, 43 non-commissioned and 430 rank and file. There are also 2 commissioned officers in the submarine miners, 1 non-commissioned officer, and 20 rank and file, the whole force thus numbering 538, the permanent mounted infantry which consisted of one major, one captain, two sergeants, and 27 rank and file, having been disbanded in July, 1890. The rates of pay exclusive of allowances of the regular artillery, apart from the permanent staff, were for the year 1890:—Colonel, £730; lieutenant-colonel, £450; majors, £383; captains, £290; lieutenants, £215; brigade-surgeon, £415; staff-surgeon, £365; sergeants from 4s. to 10s. per diem; corporals, 3s. 4d. per diem; bombardiers, 3s. 2d. per diem; trumpeters, 2s. 3d. per diem; master gunners, 7s. to 10s. per diem; gunners, 2s. 3d. per diem; the permanent mounted infantry and submarine miners are paid on the same scale as the artillery, and the total cost was £73,680. The artillery man the batteries guarding the harbours of Sydney, Botany Bay, and Newcastle, mount guard at the vice-regal residence, and perform such other duties as usually appertain to a garrison. The troops are a fine body of men; the minimum height at which recruits are accepted is 5ft. 6in.

Volunteer Force.

The Act authorizing the establishment of a volunteer force was assented to on the 24th July, 1854, and the Act continued in operation with various modifications until 1878, when the land forces of the Colony were remodelled; and further alterations took place in 1888. The volunteer force was retained, but a system of payment was introduced in lieu of the indirect remuneration by a land grant of 50 acres for five years continuous efficiency, which obtained previous to 1878. The ages at which recruits for the volunteer force are taken are between 18 and 40 years. The volunteer force of the Colony consists of five arms in addition to the permanent staff, and the total strength of the force is 8,747 men of all ranks. The staff numbers 130, of whom 62 belong to the permanent and 3 to the honorary staff, 7 are medical officers, and 58 belong to the Medical Staff Corps.

The artillery consists of 518 men of all ranks, of whom 30 are commissioned and 73 non-commissioned officers, with 412 privates, besides which there are 1 commissioned and 2 non-commissioned officers on the permanent staff. It is distributed in four districts the strength of each being:— Artillery.

Sydney	352
Newcastle	59
Wollongong	56
Bulli	51
	518

The engineers are located in Sydney, and number 113 men of all ranks, viz., 7 commissioned officers, 21 non-commissioned officers and buglers, and 85 sappers. The submarine miners are also located in Sydney; they comprise 9 commissioned officers, 14 non-commissioned officers and buglers, 1 non-commissioned officer on the permanent staff, and 86 privates, or 110 of all ranks. Engineers and submarine miners.

The infantry forces are distributed over five districts, the strength of each district being— Infantry.

Sydney	710
Western	641
Northern	669
Southern	302
South-western	297
	2,619

This arm comprises 125 commissioned officers, 313 non-missioned officers, 4 commissioned and 8 non-commissioned of on the permanent staff, and 2,169 privates and buglers.

The mounted infantry were only established in 1888. They number 18 commissioned officers, 40 non-commissioned off 1 commissioned and 2 non-commissioned officers on the perma staff, and 243 privates, and are distributed as follows :—

Western District	105
Northern District	99
Southern District	100
	304

Cavalry.

The cavalry provide their own horses and equipment, uniform and arms being provided by the Government. are equipped as ordinary light cavalry. The force consis 20 commissioned officers and 46 non-commissioned officers, be 1 commissioned and 2 non-commissioned officers on the perma staff, and 283 privates. It is distributed through four district

Sydney	32
Southern District	99
Western District	53
Northern District	168
	352

Volunteer reserves.

Besides the Volunteer force described above, there are the rer of an unpaid Volunteer reserve, with a strength of 101 men ranks. They consist of 5 commissioned and 6 non-commiss officers and 85 privates, besides 3 commissioned and 2 commissioned officers on the permanent staff. They are all stati in Sydney, with the exception of one commissioned and one commissioned officer of the permanent staff, in the Nor District. The reserves have been nearly all merged int partially paid force, or rifle companies; they are provided arms and equipment, and each company is granted an allow for incidental expenses.

Efficiency—how secured.

To rank as an efficient, every volunteer must serve for nine continuously in camp, and for two detached days, together certain specified half-days and night drills, during the year. The artillery are required to attend 11 out of 16 half-day parades, including shot practice. The engineers must attend, in addition to the continuous training, 9 out of 14 half-day parades, and 9 night drills; the submarine miners, 15 out of 22 half-day parades, and the infantry, 9 out of 13 half-day parades, and a course of musketry. Pay is granted to all ranks according to a sliding scale. Gunners, sappers, and privates receive 10s. for each day of continuous training, and a like sum for each detached day's parade; for a half-day parade 5s. is paid, and for a night parade 2s. In addition to these sums, every volunteer passing through the musketry course, and qualifying as a marksman, is granted 15s.; if as a first-class shot, 10s.; and if as a second-class shot, 5s.; with a bonus of £2 if he qualifies at the end of the year as an efficient.

In 1888 a system of rifle companies was established, and at the end of 1891 there were 97 companies, comprising 4,500 men, distributed through the Colony as follows:— Rifle Companies.

	Companies.	Men.
Metropolitan, Western, and Southern Districts ...	65	2,904
Northern District	32	1,596
Total	97	4,500

New South Wales has no navy of its own, with the exception of the corvette "Wolverene," 16 sixty-pounder muzzle-loading rifled guns, and two small torpedo steam-launches, the "Acheron" and the "Avernus," the defence of its coast being in the hands of the British ships on the Australian station, and of the Australian Auxiliary Squadron. The naval forces of the colony comprise 633 men of all ranks, 119 being officers and petty officers, with 514 A.B.'s. Naval Forces.

The Naval Brigade was first enrolled in 1863. It was originally intended to operate chiefly for coastal defence, but hitherto it has been employed mostly as a light artillery land force. Quite recently it has been occasionally put to its proper use by being Naval Brigade.

drilled in naval manœuvres on board the "Wolverene" du short cruises at sea. The force consists of 20 commissi officers, 24 petty officers, 15 midshipmen and cadets, 3 gun instructors, and 276 A.B.s. Of these men 282 are statione Sydney and 56 at Newcastle.

Naval Artillery Volunteers.

There is another arm of the Naval service known as the N Artillery Volunteers. Its duty is to man and work any gun available for this service, or serve as field artillery if other se be not available. The Government supply arms and unifo and allowed in 1890 a subvention of £2,022 for military ins tion and ordinary expenses incidental to the working of su corps. The strength is 276 men of all ranks, including 18 offi 1 warrant officer, 28 petty officers, 200 A.B.'s, and 26 in band.

In connection with the Naval Defence Forces there are 3 staff officers, 11 officers and men in charge of the "Wolver and 5 in charge of the two torpedo-boats.

Total Defence Forces.

The total defence forces of the Colony number 9,918 officers men, distributed as follows:—

Regular Military Force:—	
General Staff	24
Artillery	491
Submarine Miners	23
	538
Volunteer Force:—	
Permanent Staff	62
Medical Staff Corps	65
Honorary Staff	3
Cavalry	352
Artillery	518
Engineers	113
Submarine Miners	110
Mounted Infantry	304
Infantry	2,619
Reserves	101
Rifle Companies	4,500
	8,747

Naval Forces:—	
Naval Defence Force Staff	3
H.M.C.S. "Wolverene"	11
Naval Brigade	338
Naval Artillery Volunteers	276
Torpedo Boats—"Acheron" and "Avernus"	5
	633
Grand Total	9,918

The expenditure by the State during 1890 on defence works and the Permanent and Volunteer Military forces, amounted to £228,043, and was distributed as follows:— Expenditure on Defence.

	£
General Staff	6,496
Military Instructors	924
Artillery Force	58,142
Permanent Submarine Miners	4,509
Permanent Mounted Infantry	3,609
Works of Defence	2,394
Volunteer Force	118,382
Naval Brigade	5,797
Naval Artillery Volunteers	2,022
Training Ship "Wolverene"	2,346
Torpedo Defence	1,254
Ordnance and Barrack Department	22,168
Total	£228,043

Whatever opinion may be entertained of the present condition of the defences of the Colony there can be no doubt that a very large sum of money has been expended upon them. The details cannot now be ascertained respecting the earlier defences of the harbour of Port Jackson, such as Fort Phillip, where the Observatory now stands, Fort Macquarie, and Fort Denison, which, with the batteries at Dawes' Point, Kirribilli, and Mrs. Macquarie's Chair were thought to render Sydney almost impregnable some forty years ago, when the ponderous artillery now in use had not been invented. The returns of expenditure for military, naval, and defence purposes since the year 1860 are, however, available, and are appended hereto. It will be observed that during the thirty-one years no less than £2,838,738 was expended from the Consolidated Revenue, or an average of £91,500 per annum, for these services :—

Year.	Military Expenditure (including Buildings and Works of Defence).	Naval Expenditure.	Total.	Year.	Military Expenditure (including Buildings and Works of Defence).	Naval Expenditure.	Total.
	£	£	£		£	£	£
1860	30,134	......	30,134	1877	84,130	6,497	90,627
1861	36,635	......	36,635	1878	68,716	7,327	76,043
1862	39,703	......	39,703	1879	95,720	8,589	104,309
1863	38,294	1,943	40,237	1880	94,631	6,945	101,576
1864	17,483	919	18,402	1881	96,079	7,165	103,244
1865	19,635	2,050	21,685	1882	94,468	17,696	112,164
1866	17,576	3,944	21,520	1883	124,701	26,880	151,581
1867	20,500	3,655	24,155	1884	160,367	15,627	175,994
1868	32,334	3,660	35,994	1885	101,840	22,451	*124,291
1869	29,148	4,009	33,157	1886	239,727	25,753	265,480
1870	27,525	3,837	31,362	1887	284,471	30,397	314,868
1871	17,896	4,416	22,312	1888	149,246	20,797	170,043
1872	32,966	4,427	37,393	1889	196,201	10,974	207,175
1873	30,842	5,116	35,958	1890	216,624	11,419	228,043
1874	61,366	5,482	66,848				
1875	61,153	5,441	66,594	Total.	2,566,005	272,733	2,838,738
1876	45,894	5,317	51,211				

* Does not include £121,630 Australian Contingent to the Soudan.

Loan money expended on defence.

In addition to the sums paid out of current revenue a large amount of loan money has been expended in the erection of fortifications, which, it is expected, will serve for the protection of future as well as the present generation of colonists. The details of this expenditure are as follow :—

Loan Expenditure on Fortifications, &c.

Previous to 1871............. ... £181,164

Year	£	Year	£
1871............. ...	43,601	1882..................	39,757
1872..................	24,466	1883	24,819
1873..................	35,134	1884..................	4,683
1874............. ...	22	1885...........	54,729
1875..................	368	1886......	61,814
1876.................	4,506	1887..................	8,350
1877......	3,735	1888..................	22,296
1878..........	33,227	1889	56,440
1879..................	21,270	1890..................	46,962
1880..................	14,582		
1881..................	22,640	Total	£704,585

Another source of expenditure to the Colony is that of the Naval Station in Port Jackson. An arrangement was made with the Imperial authorities by which the Government of the Colony undertook to give up Garden Island for the purposes of a naval station, and to erect thereon the requisite buildings; also to provide certain other accommodation required for the use of the war-vessels in the harbour. In consideration of this, it was agreed on the other side, that Sydney should be the head-quarters of the Australian fleet, and also that the Imperial Government should give up all their claim upon certain lands and buildings owned by them in the Colony. These included, among others, the Paddington Barracks, the Domain and Botanic Gardens, and the old Commissariat Stores, as well as other valuable properties. In carrying out the works at Garden Island and Kirribilli Point the following expenditure has been incurred:— Naval Station in Port Jackson.

Loan Expenditure on Naval Stations.

Year.	Amount.
	£
1885	642
1886	33,928
1887	15,431
1888	52,013
1889	15,574
1890	42,409
Total	159,997

It thus appears that the total amount spent by the Colony of New South Wales, for defence purposes, since the beginning of the year 1860, to the end of 1890, was £3,863,221, or an average of about £125,000 per annum. The items which make up this amount may be recapitulated thus:— Total expenditure for defence purposes.

Expenditure on Military, Works of Defence, &c.

	£
From Consolidated Revenue	2,838,738
From Loans—For Harbour Defences	704,586
From Loans—For Naval Station, Port Jackson	159,997
Value of Land alienated in virtue of Volunteer Land Orders, computed at £1 per acre	159,900
Grand Total	3,863,221

Under the provisions of the "Australasian Naval Force Act," which was assented to on 20th December, 1887, all the colonies have entered into an agreement with the British Government f the payment of a *pro rata* subsidy for the maintenance of Australian Auxiliary Squadron. The total subvention to be pa by all the colonies amounts to £91,000, of which New Sou Wales will contribute about £27,000. The fleet consists of fi fast cruisers, and two torpedo gunboats, as represented by tl "Archer" (improved type) and "Rattlesnake" classes of tl British navy; of these, three cruisers and one gun-boat w always be kept in commission, the remainder being held in reser in Australasian ports, but ready for commission whenever circu stances may require their use. The agreement is for a peri of ten years, and shall then, or at the end of any subseque year, be terminable, provided two years' notice has been give The vessels have been built by the British Government, b the Australasian Colonies will pay the interest on their prin cost at the rate of 5 per cent., provided such payment does n exceed £35,000. The colonies are also to pay the actual char for maintenance as mentioned above. On the termination of tl agreement these vessels will remain the property of the Imper Government. The strength of the fleet already in Australi waters will be maintained. The vessels specified in the agreeme between Great Britain and the Colonies are to be in addition these. The Australasian squadron is commanded by the Admi on the Australian station, whose headquarters are in Sydn where a residence is provided for him by the Colony. squadron, particulars of which will be found on page 406, arri in Port Jackson on 5th September, 1891.

Fortifications.

Extensive fortifications have been erected at various importa points on the coast. Sydney has two lines of defence, and is deem almost impregnable; Botany Bay forming the southern defence Sydney is strongly fortified, as also is Newcastle, the great port of the Colony.

The following is a list both of the Imperial war-vessels now the Australasian station under Rear-Admiral Lord Charles Sco and of the vessels of the Australian auxiliary squadron :—

Imperial War Vessels on Station.

Name.	Class.	Material of hull.	Displacement.	Indicated horse-power.	Draught of water extreme.	Length.	Beam.	Armour.	Armament.		Speed.	Coal endurance.	
									Guns.	Torpedo tubes.		Coal that can be carried in bunkers.	Distance that can be steamed at 10 knots' speed.
			tons.		ft. in.	ft. in.	ft. in.				knots.	tons.	knots.
Orlando	Twin-screw cruiser, 1st class, armoured.	Steel	5,600	8,500	24 2	300 0	56 0	Armoured belt at water-line, 10 in.; armoured deck, 2 in.; conning tower, 12 in.	2 9·2-in. 22-ton B.L.R. 10 6-in. 5-ton B.L.R. 16 Q.F. Hotchkiss, 7 M., 2 L.	2	18·5	900	7,000
Curaçoa	Screw cruiser, 3rd class.	Steel and iron sheathed with wood.	2,380	2,540	18 10	225 0	44 6	....	4 6-in. 5-ton B.L.R. 8 5-in. 2-ton B.L.R. 1 Q.F. Hotchkiss 9 M., 2 L.	2	13·0	470	3,800
Cordelia......	Screw cruiser, 3rd class.	do ..	2,380	2,420	18 8	225 0	44 6	....	10 6-in. 4½-ton B.L.R. 10 M., 2 L.	2	13·0	470	3,800
Rapid	Screw cruiser, 3rd class.	Composite.	1,420	1,400	15 9	200 0	38 0	....	2 6-in. 4-ton B.L.R., 10 5-in. 38-cwt. B.L.R., 4 M., 1 L.	....	13·1	425	6,000
Royalist......	Screw cruiser, 3rd class.	do ..	1,420	1,510	15 9	200 0	38 0	....	2 6-in. 4-ton B.L.R., 10 5-in. 38-cwt. B.L.R., 4 M., 1 L.	....	13·1	425	6,000
Lizard	Screw gun-boat, 1st class.	do ..	715	1,000	13 6	165 0	29 0	....	6 4-in. 25-cwt. B.L.R., 4 M.	....	12·7	105	2,500
Goldfinch	Screw gun-boat, 1st class.	do ..	805	1,200	12 8	165 0	30 0	....	6 4-in. 26-cwt. B.L.R., 2 Q.F. Hotchkiss, 2 M.	....	13·0	105	..
Ringdove	Screw gun-boat, 1st class.	do ..	805	1,200	12 8	165 0	30 0	....	6 4-in. 26-cwt. B.L.R., 2 Q.F. Hotchkiss, 2 M.	....	13·0	105	..
Dart*	Screw yacht..	do ..	470	200	12 11	133 0	25 2	....	2 L.	....	8·8	64	....

* Surveying service. M.L.R., Muzzle-loading rifled guns; Q.F., Quick-firing guns; M., Machine guns; L., Light guns under 15 cwt.; B.L.R., Breech-loading rifled guns.

Australian Auxiliary Squadron.

Name.	Class.	Material of hull.	Displacement.	Indicated horse-power.	Draught of water extreme.	Length.	Beam.	Armour.	Armament.		Speed.	Coal endurance.	
									Guns.	Torpedo tubes.		Coal that can be carried in bunkers.	Distance that can be steamed at 10 knots' speed.
			tons.		ft. in.	ft. in.	ft. in.				knots.	tons.	knots.
Katoomba....	Screw cruiser, 3rd class.	Steel	2,575	7,500	16 6	265 0	41 0	Deck armour over machinery space, 2 in. and 1 in.; conning tower, 3 in.	8 4·7 Q.F. guns, 8 3-pr. Q.F. guns, 1 7-pr. M.L.R. gun (boat and field), 4·45 in. 5 barrel Nordenfeldt.	4	16·5	300	6,000
Ringarooma ..	Screw cruiser, 3rd class.	do ..	2,575	7,500	16 6	265 0	41 0	do ..	do ..	4	16·5	300	6,000
Mildura......	Screw cruiser, 3rd class.	do ..	2,575	7,500	16 6	265 0	41 0	do ..	do ..	4	16·5	300	6,000
Wallaroo	Screw cruiser, 3rd class.	do ..	2,575	7,500	16 6	265 0	41 0	do ..	do ..	4	16·5	300	6,000
Tauranga	Screw cruiser, 3rd class.	do ..	2,575	7,500	16 6	265 0	41 0	do ..	do ..	4	16·5	300	6,000
Boomerang ..	Torpedo gun-boat.	do ..	735	4,500	10 6	230 0	27 0	Conning tower, 1 in.	2 4·7 in. Q.F. guns, 4 3-pr. Q.F. guns.	5	*18·75	160	2,500
Karrakatta ..	Torpedo gun-boat	do ..	735	4,500	10 6	230 0	27 0	do ..	do ..	5	*18·75	160	2,500

* This speed can be increased until, under favourable conditions, for a short period, a maximum of 21 knots can be obtained. Q.F.—Quick-firing guns.

however populous, is compelled to take advantage of them, is only by consent of a majority of the prospective ratepay a new municipality can be formed. By the Act of 1867 con districts, with an area of not more than 9 square miles population of not less than 1,000, may be incorporated as bo and districts of not more than 50 square miles, with a po of not less than 500, may be formed into municipal distric the present time the Colony contains 157 incorporated dist which 65 are boroughs, and 92 municipal districts, the Sydney being styled a municipality. The area incor embraces only 2,315 square miles, equal to 0·75 per cent., of the total area of the Colony. The population of New Wales on the 5th April, 1891, was 1,134,207, or 3·65 to the mile; in the municipalities there was a population of about 6 or an average density of 297 persons per square mile, or 205 tin of the rest of the Colony. The estimated value of land, hou other permanent improvements in the Colony may be mately stated at £316,376,000; of this sum £134,010,00 per cent., was in the incorporate districts, and £182,366, 58 per cent., in the other districts. Of course the value c Crown lands is not included in this estimate.

Number of Municipalities.

Powers of Municipalities.

The powers and privileges conferred upon municipali extensive. In addition to maintaining the thoroughfares, porations are entitled to construct sewerage, water supply, works, and to levy the necessary rates in connection the to make and enforce by-laws for the maintenance of publi and the abatement of nuisances; to establish free public l and free infant schools; and to see the material and sanit dition generally of the residents properly attended to. Un Municipalities Act of 1867 assessors are appointed every y all municipal property is valued, and the councils are em to raise revenue by rates on the value so found, not ex 1s. in the £ for ordinary purposes, and not exceeding th amount for special purposes. The amount of rate is ca upon nine-tenths of the fair average rental of all buildi cultivated lands, or lands which are, or have been, let for pastoral, mining, or other purposes, whether such land or buildings be actually in occupation or not, and upon 5 per cent. of the capital value of the fee-simple of all unimproved land. In the City of Sydney the Act directs that valuers shall be appointed from time to time to assess all ratable property within the city, and on the value of such assessment a city rate not exceeding 2s. in the £ may be levied. During the year 1890 the city rate was levied at the amount of 1s. 6d. in the £. The ordinary rate of 1s. in the £ was levied in all the suburban and country municipalities, except only Cobar, where it was 9d., and Condobolin, 6d. There were 68 municipalities where lighting rates were imposed, in most cases of 3d. to 6d. in the £. The Boroughs of Moss Vale, Young, and Tamworth are lit by electricity, the charge being 3d., 5d., and 6d. in the £ respectively. In only 18 municipalities is there a water rate, generally of 1s. in the £, though in some places the charge is by measurement. Other special rates, mostly for street-watering, are charged by some of the suburban boroughs.

The following table shows the present conditions of the Municipalities of New South Wales :—

Capital, value, and assessment of Boroughs and Municipalities, 1890.

Boroughs and Municipal Districts.	Capital Value of		Total Amount of Ordinary Rates Assessed.	Fair Average Annual Value of	
	Buildings and Cultivated Land only.	All Ratable Property—Improved and Unimproved.		Buildings and Cultivated Land only.	All Ratable Property—Improved and Unimproved.
City of Sydney	51,237,600	51,237,600	184,806	2,710,488	2,710,488
Suburbs	37,720,524	47,987,210	143,652	2,627,767	3,141,101
Total, Metropolitan	88,958,124	99,224,810	328,458	5,338,255	5,851,589
Country	29,584,162	34,784,948	113,814	2,245,175	2,505,214
Total, N.S. Wales..	118,542,286	134,009,758	442,272	7,583,430	8,356,803

Out of the total capital value of property in all municipalities for 1890, the sum of £118,542,286 represents the capital value

Capital value of all ratable property.

of improved lands, that is, of lands upon which been erected, or which are cultivated, or have been and other purposes; and £15,467,472, is the v proved lands, classed as such for municipal purpose value is made up of the actual rental of improved la cent. of the capital value of unimproved lands.

Metropolitan Water and Sewerage Rate.

No mention has been made of the rates charged i suburbs of Sydney under the Metropolitan Water Act, since these are levied by the Board constitu Act mentioned and not by the municipalities. Th by the Board for water are, 10s. per annum on pre at £20 and under, and 6d. for every £ in the ass £300. Over £300 a sliding scale comes into fo also supplied by measure at 1s. 6d. per 1,000 ga rate is shortly to be reduced to 1s. per 1,000 gallon

Rates under Country Towns Water and Sewerage Act of 1880.

Municipalities which have availed themselves of of the Country Towns Water and Sewerage Act empowered, under clause 13 of the said Act, to exceeding a maximum of 5 per cent. on the assessed and tenements in addition to the ordinary municip maximum rate is at present levied in eleven munici of which the ratepayers are under a total contribu three of 2s. 3d.; and in two of 2s. 4d. in the £ on the of their properties.

Endowment.

In order to aid municipalities in the difficulti their inception, the Act of 1867 provides for end granted for a period of fifteen years. In eac five years after incorporation, every municipali to a sum equal to, but not exceeding, the whole a raised by rates or assessments and subscription the past year. In each of the next succeeding sum equal to, but not exceeding, one moiety; and next succeeding five years a sum equal to one-fourth so paid. After the expiry of these fifteen years

which municipalities may demand from the Government ceases. The flourishing state of the revenue during many years enabled the Government to grant aid to municipalities beyond what the law directed, and during some years an endowment equal to the assessment was paid to them.

Value of ratable property.

The value of property assessed for municipal purposes during 1890 was returned by the various local authorities at £134,009,758; but this amount somewhat understates the actual capital value, as much of the unimproved land, especially in suburban and country districts, is returned at far below its real worth. Taking all municipalities, this understating amounts to, at least, 10 per cent., so that the actual value of property within incorporated districts is not less than £147,410,733. If, however, the nominal values as returned by the municipal authorities themselves are taken, the capital and annual value of property in all districts during the past nine years were as follow:—

Annual and Capital Value of Property in Boroughs and Municipalities.

Year.	City of Sydney.	Suburbs of Sydney.	Country Municipalities.	Total.
	£	£	£	£
1882—Annual value	1,655,952	1,314,919	1,064,560	4,035,431
Capital value	29,807,140	19,749,107	11,697,199	61,253,446
1883—Annual value	1,838,642	1,449,947	1,266,502	4,555,091
Capital value	36,772,840	20,676,070	14,425,195	71,874,105
1884—Annual value	1,979,772	1,690,109	1,524,218	5,194,099
Capital value	39,595,440	23,046,854	17,661,067	80,303,361
1885—Annual value	2,035,235	1,935,884	1,713,578	5,684,697
Capital value	40,704,700	29,410,787	21,828,805	91,944,292
1886—Annual value	2,096,476	2,289,685	1,727,951	6,114,112
Capital value	41,929,520	32,960,620	21,657,828	96,547,968
1887—Annual value	2,131,026	2,501,904	1,895,591	6,528,521
Capital value	42,529,525	36,644,629	26,699,331	105,904,168
1888—Annual value	2,228,817	2,987,061	2,149,566	7,365,444
Capital value	44,576,340	45,635,138	30,073,617	120,285,095
1889—Annual value	2,276,362	3,110,825	2,405,163	7,792,350
Capital value	45,527,240	48,208,834	33,475,972	127,212,046
1890—Annual value	2,710,488	3,141,101	2,505,214	8,356,803
Capital value	51,237,600	47,987,210	34,784,948	134,009,758

Increase in eight years.

The increase shown in this table is very considerable. Fro[m] 1882 to 1890 the annual value has risen from £4,035,431 t[o] £8,356,803, or at the rate of 9·49 per cent. per annum, while th[e] capital value has advanced from £61,253,446 to £134,009,758, o[r] at the rate of 10·28 per cent. per annum. Part of this increase i[s] due to an additional number of districts incorporated; but whe[n] an allowance is made for these it will still be found that the pro[-]gress is very satisfactory.

The amount of increase during the past eight years will b[e] found in the following table:—

Municipalities.	Increased annual value during eight years.			
	Total.	Per cent.	Total.	
	£		£	
City of Sydney	1,054,536	63·68	21,430,460	71·[illegible]
Suburbs of Sydney........	1,826,182	135·33	28,238,103	14[illegible]
Country Municipalities..	1,440,654	138·88	23,087,749	197·[illegible]
Total...............	4,321,372	107·08	72,756,312	

Position of Sydney amongst cities of the Empire.

The growth of the city and suburbs has been marvellous, an[d] Sydney now stands as the second city of the British Empire, a[s] estimated by the annual value of its ratable property, Melbourn[e] ranking third. The annual value of property in Sydney an[d] suburbs, covering an area of 78,529 acres in 1889, was £5,387,18[7] and in 1890, £5,851,589; the annual value of Melbourne an[d] suburbs during 1889 was £5,649,662, and for 1890 it is returne[d] at £5,798,530. The following are the annual values of th[e] principal British cities for 1889:—

London (Metropolitan Board of Works)...	£31,033,786	Leeds..........................	£1,213,6[illegible]
Glasgow.....................	3,401,790	Sheffield	1,087,03[illegible]
Liverpool	3,301,879	Bradford	1,006,83[illegible]
Manchester and Salford	3,179,337	Bristol	1,005,39[illegible]
Birmingham..............	1,772,855	Nottingham	907,15[illegible]
		Newcastle-on-Tyne.......	

Capital value of each municipality.

The capital value of ratable property in all boroughs and mun[i-]cipal districts for 1890 is shown in the following table:—

Capital Value of Ratable Property in Boroughs and Municipal Districts during 1890.

Boroughs and Municipal Districts.	Total Capital Value of Ratable Property.	Boroughs and Municipal Districts.	Total Capital Value of Ratable Property.
METROPOLITAN—	£	COUNTRY—	£
Sydney	51,237,600	Adamstown	220,996
SUBURBS—		Albury	474,370
Alexandria	950,000	Armidale	305,550
Ashfield	2,500,000	Ballina	92,970
Balmain	3,290,005	Balranald	95,336
Botany	438,980	Bathurst	735,710
Botany North	386,200	Bega	283,291
Burwood	1,357,700	Berry	487,571
Camperdown	694,587	Bingara	44,650
Canterbury	800,000	Blayney	97,454
Concord	439,395	Bourke	450,000
Darlington	302,700	Bowral	311,709
Drummoyne	302,600	Broken Hill†	865,580
Enfield	305,800	Broughton Vale	140,000
Five Dock	300,000	Burrowa	132,257
Glebe	2,118,850	Camden	149,676
Hunter's Hill	699,889	Campbelltown	199,220
Hurstville	1,012,073	Carcoar	43,322
Kogarah	700,000	Carrington	284,749
Leichhardt	2,150,000	Casino	181,209
Macdonald Town	457,470	Cobar	126,930
Manly	1,210,121	Condobolin	30,644
Marrickville	1,914,454	Cooma	182,813
Newtown	2,227,787	Coonamble	211,871
Paddington	2,386,962	Cootamundra	212,524
Petersham	1,657,493	Cowra	169,475
Randwick	2,346,400	Cudgegong	513,739
Redfern	2,250,000	Deniliquin	232,858
Rockdale	838,340	Dubbo	392,842
St. Peters	530,000	Dundas	349,664
Strathfield	808,632	Forbes	220,670
Sydney, North*	5,093,000	Gerringong	211,500
Waterloo	1,442,840	Glen Innes	325,149
Waverley	2,250,000	Gosford	81,545
Willoughby	1,344,945	Goulburn	930,000
Woollahra	2,480,000	Grafton	613,650
		Granville	660,274
Total, Suburbs	47,987,210	Grenfell	103,175
Total, Sydney	51,237,600	Greta	152,243
		Gulgong	78,153
Total, Metropolitan	99,224,810	Gundagai	119,100

NOTE.—The Municipalities of Bombala, Cudal, Moree, and Quirindi were proclaimed, and that of Kiama separated into Kiama and East Kiama towards the end of 1890.

* Formed by the union of the Boroughs of St. Leonards, East St. Leonards, and Victoria.

† The silver-mines within this municipality, the capital value of which may be estimated at £12,000,000, are not liable to taxation under the terms of the Municipal Act.

Country—continued.	£	Country—continued.
Gunnedah	76,482	Port Macquarie
Hamilton	572,431	Prospect & Sherwood
Hay	382,628	Queanbeyan
Hill End	27,298	Raymond Terrace
Hillston	95,806	Richmond
Illawarra Central	995,500	Ryde
Illawarra North	203,658	Scone
Inverell	280,567	Shellharbour
Jerilderie	120,000	Shoalhaven, Central
Junee	148,448	Silverton
Katoomba	208,860	Singleton
Kempsey	282,000	Singleton, South
Kiama & Kiama East	559,000	Smithfield & eld
Lambton	205,092	St. Mary's
Lambton, New	231,196	Stockton
Lismore	499,304	Tamworth
Lithgow	371,417	Taree
Liverpool	562,180	Tenterfield
Maclean	66,538	Tumut
Maitland, East	360,000	Ulladulla
Maitland, West	1,047,204	Ulmarra
Merewether	246,636	Uralla
Mittagong	170,785	Wagga Wagga
Molong	141,250	Walcha
Morpeth	115,775	Wallsend
Moss Vale	220,900	Waratah
Mudgee	318,000	Wellington
Murrumburrah	80,270	Wentworth
Murrurundi	111,538	Wickham
Muswellbrook	101,225	Wilcannia
Narrabri	116,260	Windsor
Narrandera	138,000	Wingham
Newcastle	2,327,655	Wollongong
Nowra	182,000	Yass
Numba	79,500	Young
Orange	498,711	
Orange, East	200,883	Total, Country
Parkes	186,000	Total, Metropolitan
Parramatta	1,692,000	
Penrith	403,540	Total, Metropolitan and Country
Plattsburg	259,600	

Municipal Revenue.

The total revenue collected by all the Municipalties of Colony during the year 1890 amounted to £784,052, inclu the State endowment of £154,736, exclusive of the proceeds of l raised during the year to the amount of £143,586. The chief h of revenue were as follows:—

Percentage of Municipal Revenue derived from various sources.

Incorporated Districts.	General Rates.	Other Rates.	Endowment.	Other Revenue.
	per cent.	per cent.	per cent.	per cent.
Sydney—City	79·55	....	....	20·45
Sydney—Suburbs ...	47·74	14·36	21·83	16·07
Country	35·23	13·95	31·24	19·58
Total—Colony	51·26	10·44	19·73	18·57

Gross revenue of Municipalities.

It will be seen from a previous table that the gross revenue of all municipalities, not including the State Endowment, is £629,316; if to this be added the revenue of the Metropolitan Water and Sewerage Board, the total will reach £857,106. This may be taken as the whole burthen of local taxation, and is equivalent to about 25s. per head of the population residing within the limits of incorporated districts, and to 10·26 per cent. of the total annual value of ratable property.

Expenditure.

The total expenditure during 1890 by the various municipalities amounted to £935,967, which is £151,915 in excess of the receipts from ordinary sources, the excess being accounted for by expenditure from loans raised during the year, or remaining over from previous years. The municipal expenditure may be grouped under the following heads:—

	£
Salaries and office expenses	60,672
Improvement works	510,593
Lighting	76,695
Water (Country)..	21,076
Interest on loans..	84,765
Sinking funds, Repayment of Loans	41,924
Miscellaneous charges	*140,242
Total........................	£935,967

* Includes interests on overdrafts.

The cost of administration shown above, viz., £60,672, amounts to 6·48 per cent. of the disbursements; the expenditure on public works and improvements to 54·55 per cent.; on lighting to 8·20 per cent.; on water supply (in country municipalities only) to 2·25 per cent.; on interest on loans to 9·06 per cent.; on Sinking Funds for repayment of loans to 4·48 per cent. of the total disbursements; while the remaining 14·98 per cent. are made up by miscellaneous items.

Expenditure of the Municipality of Sydney.

The expenditure of the Municipality of Sydney reached in 1890 the sum of £193,008, which may be distributed as under:

	£
Salaries and office expenses	8,861
Improvement works	100,056
Lighting	12,329
Interest on loans	32,450
Interest on overdraft	151
Loans, Streets, and Town Hall Sinking Funds	15,350
Miscellaneous charges	23,811
Total	£193,008

The expenses of administration only amount to 4·59 per cent. of the whole disbursements, improvement works absorb 51·84 per cent., lighting 6·39 per cent., interest 16·81 per cent., sinking funds 7·95 per cent., and other charges 12·42 per cent. of the total expenditure.

Suburban expenditure.

The expenditure of the suburban boroughs and municipalities for the year was £362,624, which may be subdivided under the following heads:—

	£
Salaries and office expenses	22,524
Public works	201,343
Lighting	32,375
Interest on loans	31,695
Repayment of loans	11,770
Miscellaneous	62,917
Total	£362,624

The office expenses amounted to 6·21 per cent. of the total r of these municipalities, and will appear by no means unrea when the smallness of some of the districts and the diff attending the inception of municipalities are borne in mind large proportion of 55·52 per cent. was expended upon works; lighting claiming in addition 8·93 per cent.; and ment of loans 3·25 per cent. of the total expenditure. T interest upon loans 8·74 per cent. was required, the ren proportion of 17·35 per cent. being devoted to miscel services. The expenditure of the country municipalities Colony for the year 1890 was £380,335, which, divided un same headings as given for suburban municipalities, would as follows:—

Country municipal expenditure.

	£
Salaries and office expenses	29,287
Public works	209,194
Lighting and water supply	53,067
Interest on loans	20,620
Repayment of loans	14,804
Miscellaneous	53,363
Total	£380,335

The salaries and office expenses form a charge of 7· cent. upon the total receipts during the year, which is consi larger than in the suburban municipalities. The greater of the country boroughs and municipal districts are large and small in population and revenue, and the propor expenses required to defray salaries and other charges is na larger than in the case of the smaller and more populous d surrounding the metropolis. The proportion of expenditur various heads is as follows:—

Salaries and office expenses	7·71	per cent.
Public works	55·00	,,
Lighting and water supply	13·95	,,
Interest on loans	5·42	,,
Repayment of loans	3·89	,,
Miscellaneous	14·03	,,

The receipts of the municipalities of the Colony from loans amounted to £143,586 during the year 1890; while the sum paid off existing loans, or towards sinking funds for the extinguishing of loans, was £41,924. The total indebtedness at the close of the year, exclusive of the expenditure, in construction and maintenance of sewers, was £1,751,296, and towards meeting this amount there was a sum at the credit of the sinking funds amounting to £123,093, so that the net liability was £1,628,203. The sum quoted above was owing during only part of the year, so that the total interest paid amounted to only £84,765, the rate of interest varying from 4 to 9 per cent.; the average rate being approximately 4·89 per cent. The total debt per head of population living in municipalities amounts to £2 10s. 5d., and if allowance be made for sinking funds £2 6s. 10d., while the yearly charge for interest is 2s. 6d. per head. These sums, viewed apart from the resources of the municipalities, are by no means formidable; but, taken in connection with their general assets, the local debts of municipalities will appear insignificant. The following are the liabilities of the City of Sydney:—

Municipal loans.

Indebtedness per head.

City loans.

	£	£
Debentures (interminable)		100,000
Loans on Debentures (terminable at fixed dates)—		
Cattle Sale-yards Fund	35,000	
Town Hall Loan Fund	275,000	
Streets Loan Fund	300,000	
		610,000
Total		£710,000

Payment of these latter sums on maturity is, by Act of Parliament, in each case peremptorily provided for by the institution of sinking funds. The amount paid into the sinking funds during 1890 was £10,350.

Assets of city of Sydney.

Against this debt of £710,000 there exist assets approxi amounting to £2,658,282, distributed as follows :—

	£
Value of made roads, &c.	816,000
Town Hall	[illegible]
Markets and land	630,000
Other buildings	120,000
Cattle Sale-yards	120,000
Wharves	416,000
Sinking Funds	90,282
City Fund (reserve account)	75,000
Cattle Sale Yard Fund (fixed deposit)	[illegible]
Town Hall Loan Fund (fixed deposit)	50,000
Total	£2,658,282

And if to this sum be added the present value of future allowing twenty years' purchase amounting to £3,270,00 assets of the City Corporation amount to about £5,928,1 that the indebtedness of the city of Sydney amounts to only per cent. of the available assets.

Assets of other municipalities.

The liability of the other incorporated districts of the amounted to £1,041,296, or slightly more than four tim ordinary rates of the year. Against this they have assets ar ing approximately to £3,972,146, distributed as follows :—

	£
Value of made roads and streets	3,207,843
Sewerage works	69,811
Buildings	455,660
Accrued sinking funds	32,811
Other municipal property	206,021
Total	£3,972,146

The assets, other than roads, streets, sewerage, and buildings, chiefly of sinking funds, outstanding rates, plant, and materi construction and maintenance of works within municipaliti

The present value of future rates at twenty years' pu amounts to £4,768,000, which, added to the sum stated would make the total assets of these municipalities reach th of £8,740,146. The total municipal debt of the incorp districts outside the boundaries of the city of Sydney therefore appear to be only 11·91 per cent. of the available

The length of streets and lanes within the boundaries of the city of Sydney is 115 miles, and nearly all the roadways are formed, kerbed, and bordered by pavements of asphalt, tarred stone, flagging, or other suitable material, while 315,055 square yards of carriage-way have been laid with wood blocks. The value to the city of these streets is hardly less than £810,000. Throughout the suburbs the extent of roads and streets is 1,360 miles, of which 775 miles are regularly formed, and the approximate value of these roadways, with culverts, bridges, and similar works, may be set down at £1,671,258. In the other municipalities of the Colony there are 2,035 miles of made roads, and 2,502 miles of unformed roads, in all 4,537 miles, the value of these improvements being about £1,536,585. Streets and roads.

Municipal councils are authorized by law to undertake the construction of water, sewerage, or gas works, in addition to the work usually carried on by them. To regulate the construction, maintenance, and management of these works, various enactments have been passed. Municipal works.

As early as 1850 authority was given the City Corporation by the Legislative Council for the construction of water and sewerage works, and in accordance with such authority a system of water supply from the Lachlan, Bunnerong, and Botany Swamps was adopted. This scheme involved the interception of the water, from the stream draining these swamps, at a point near the shore of Botany Bay, and pumping it to Crown-street Reservoir, 132 feet above the level of the sea; thence a portion was raised to Paddington, 280 feet over sea-level, and a further portion to Woollahra, 320 feet over sea-level. The cost of the water supply works as carried out by the City Corporation, including 301 miles of reticulation pipes, was £1,719,565. These works have now been superseded by the Nepean scheme, recommended by the Royal Commission on Water Supply, and carried out by Mr. E. O. Moriarty, M.I.C.E. The works in connection with this scheme Water supply. Nepean scheme.

have been conceived on a scale of magnitude commensurat the growth to which Sydney will ultimately attain. The of supply is the united waters of the Nepean, Cataract, ar deaux, mountain streams draining an area of 354 square mil by the abundant rain which falls along the coast district v Wollongong. The water is intercepted at a height of 4: above the level of the sea, and flows through a series of cond partly tunnel, partly open canals, and in places wroug aqueducts—to Prospect Reservoir, a distance of 40 miles fr farthest source of supply. Here an impounding reservoir ha constructed capable of holding 11,000 million gallons, of nearly 7,000 million will be available for supply, the rem being intended as a settling area. The top water at P Reservoir is 195 feet over high water in Sydney Harbour. Prospect the water is led through open conduits for a furth tance of 4¾ miles, whence it is taken to Crown-street Reser distance of 16 miles, in iron pipes. The conduits above P Reservoir have a capacity of 150 million gallons per day, a 10 miles below this reservoir the capacity of the canals and equals a maximum of 50 million gallons, while for the l miles the water flows through 48-inch and 42-inch cast-iron having a capacity of 17·5 million gallons daily. In this work are:—

Prospect Reservoir.

Capacity of conduits.

Tunnels	11⅝ mil
Open canals	33¼ "
Wrought-iron pipes, 8ft., 7ft. 6in., and 6ft. diameter	5⅝ "
Cast-iron pipes, 48in. and 42in. diameter	11¼ "
Water surface of reservoir	1⅝ "
Total	63¼ mil

All the works in connection with this magnificent schem completed with the exception of Prospect Reservoir. The connection with this work is 1¾ miles long, and 80 feet d the centre, and contains 2,316,500 cubic yards of earthwork; been already raised sufficiently high to enable the canals l towards Sydney to be supplied. A second line of pipes between the Potts' Hill and the Crown-street reservoirs is now being laid. By a recent Act the management of the whole of the Metropolitan Water Supply, including both the Botany and the Nepean works, as well as the reticulation and supply of Sydney, has been placed in the hands of a board called the Metropolitan Water Supply and Sewerage Board, three members of which, including the chairman, are appointed by the Government, and four elected by the municipalities interested. The revenue received by the Board during 1890 was £145,990, and the expenditure £147,310, of which £20,546 was for maintenance, £14,242 for management, 109,100 for interest on loans, and £3,422 depreciation account. The net loss on the year's transactions was £1,320, but against this there were rates in arrear to the amount of £26,759. The amount expended on construction of Water Supply Works to the end of the year 1890 was £3,203,597. The cost of all works to the close of 1890, including purchase of land, maintenance, and supervision, was £3,203,597. The number of houses and persons supplied with water in the metropolitan district is 71,501 and 343,204 respectively; the average consumption is 8,486,034 gallons daily, or at the rate of 118 gallons per house and 24·70 gallons per person, the total supply for the year being 3,097,402,486 gallons. Cost of works.

The Country Water Supply and Sewerage Act was passed in 1880. Under the provisions of this measure municipalities outside the county of Cumberland are entitled to construct, or have constructed for them by the Government, works for water supply and sewerage, provided the construction of the same be approved by the Governor-in-Council, and the municipalities agree to pay back the original cost of the works, with interest at the rate of 4 per cent. per annum. The Government pays for the certified cost of the works, and the municipalities pay the Government by instalments extending over a period of sixty years. Under the operations of this Act eleven water supply works have been carried Country water supply. Conditions of loans for water works.

Works constructed.

out by the Government and three by municipal councils. The works completed by the Government to the end of 1890 were:—

Town.	Cost.	Town.	Cost.
Albury	£43,760	Hunter River District	£366,865
Bathurst	51,514	Lismore	7,685
Bourke	14,120	Orange	28,273
Balranald	6,361	Wagga Wagga	37,998
Deniliquin	17,622	Wentworth	9,508
Goulburn	54,956		

Water works at Hay, Forbes, and Wilcannia were carried out by the municipalities themselves, and the cost was advanced by the State, but the Parramatta water works were constructed by the municipality without any assistance. During 1890 there was expended on account of the Country Towns' Water Supply a total sum of £25,028, subdivided as follows:—

Town.	Cost.	Town.	Cost.
Orange	£7,870	Balranald	£391
Manly	7,549	Other towns	2,899
Hunter River District	3,992		
Richmond	1,736	Total	£25,028
Goulburn	601		

These various amounts were contributed by the Government towards the cost of maintenance and extension of the works completed in the above mentioned municipalities, and for the construction of new works.

Sewerage.

Under the same Act which authorized the construction of the Sydney water supply, the sewerage works were also undertaken. The original sewerage works of Sydney were begun in 1854, and at the close of [illegible] 70·27 miles of old city sewers were in existence. In [illegible] an entirely new scheme of sewerage of a very comprehensive character was begun. This system will drain the whole of the northern and southern slopes of the city and suburbs, discharging the sewerage of the former into the ocean between Bondi and South Head, and of the latter at a sewerage farm on the shores of Botany Bay. Up to the end of [illegible] the Board had constructed [illegible] miles of new sewers, and [illegible] miles of storm-water drains, making together with the old city sewers a grand total of [illegible] miles of sewers and drains. During [illegible] the revenue of the Board was £[illegible], chiefly from

The persons qualified to vote at municipal elections nu approximately 140,375, thus distributed :—

	Municipal voters.
Sydney	22,000
Suburbs	54,600
Other municipalities	63,766
Total	140,375

Number of electors.

The number of electors entitled to vote for Parliament is 305, so that the proportion of municipal to parliamentary vote 45·95 per 100, and to the total population 12·38 per 100. In ing the twenty-four representatives of the city, there are 1 aldermen in the Colony, and the average number of muni electors per alderman is thus 107. Of the 140,375 electors tioned above, 79,360 are entitled to only one vote, 39,619 entitled to two, 12,158 to three, and 9,238 to the maximu four.

Local option.

In connection with local self-government by means of municipal system, occurs the only instance in which the prin of what is known as local option has been put into operatio the Colony. For many years there was a strong agitatio favour of local option, or the right of the inhabitants of district to control the liquor traffic in that district, and on sev occasions attempts were made to legislate upon the subject wit success. In the year 1882, however, an instalment of the prin was included in the Licensing Act then passed, which, with amendment made in the following year, is still in force. T measures provide that in every municipality, or ward of a m cipality, a local option vote shall be taken every three year the election for aldermen, in which the ratepayers are require vote either Yes or No on two questions: (1) Whether any publicans' licenses shall be granted during the coming three y in the municipality or ward in question; and (2) whether removals of publicans' licenses shall be allowed within the s

Carried out at municipal elections.

period. A majority of over eleven-twentieths of the votes polled is required to make the vote operative in the negative. The advocates of local option are not content with this partial adoption of the principle; they urge its extension to every electorate in the Colony, all persons on the electoral roll to have the right to vote. They further propose to place it in the power of a majority of the electors to say whether licensed public-houses should be suffered to exist at all. The extreme advocates of local option even contend that women should have the right to vote upon this question as well as men, and that public-houses should be abolished without compensation to the occupants or owners.

Extension of local government.

It is proposed by a measure now before Parliament to extend the system of local government over the remaining portions of the Colony. This is on all sides deemed a very necessary step, as under the present system there is no certainty that the expenditure of the Government on purely local works is at all times equitable. Leaving out of consideration the expenditure on works of national importance, the Government during the past thirty-one years expended no less than £20,977,644 on works of a purely local character, not including school buildings. Of this sum £13,849,407 was expended in the country districts, and £7,128,237 in the metropolis, The division of the Colony into local government districts will not necessarily be followed by an entire stoppage of the direct expenditure in works of merely local interest by the central Government, but the larger portion of the works now undertaken by Government will be left to the local authorities, who, having to directly provide part of the expenditure, will probably see that it is laid out to the best advantage. Adopting the two divisions of metropolis and country, already mentioned, the expenditure in each since 1860 is given below. As regards the metropolitan expenditure, nearly half the total—viz., £3,427,465—was expended on water supply and sewerage works, which are sources of revenue. In the country districts the amount expended on similar works was only £712,336:—

Expenditure by Government for local purposes.

Amounts expended on Local Public Works in the Count Districts and Metropolis.

Year.	Country districts.		Metropolis.			
	Expenditure.	Rate per head.	Expenditure.	Rate per head.		
	£	£ s. d.	£	£ s. d.	£	
1860	65,881	0 5 4	21,240	0 4 5	87,101	
1861	103,250	0 8 0	34,709	0 7 1	137,959	
1862	118,131	0 8 11	40,612	0 8 5	158,743	
1863	94,825	0 6 11	15,842	0 3 3	110,667	
1864	133,591	0 9 4	17,352	0 3 6	150,943	
1865	109,835	0 7 5	12,168	0 2 4	122,003	
1866	92,796	0 6 0	9,963	0 1 9	102,759	
1867	137,405	0 8 7	37,621	0 6 4	175,026	
1868	163,819	0 9 11	33,701	0 5 5	197,520	
1869	190,810	0 11 1	21,460	0 3 4	212,270	
1870	124,540	0 7 0	32,347	0 4 10	156,887	
1871	169,239	0 9 4	18,009	0 2 7	187,248	
1872	129,003	0 6 9	40,524	0 5 8	169,527	
1873	230,385	0 11 7	51,056	0 6 10	281,441	
1874	265,003	0 13 0	48,211	0 6 3	313,214	
1875	375,819	0 17 9	47,781	0 6 0	423,600	
1876	415,025	0 19 0	68,710	0 8 2	483,735	
1877	497,184	1 2 0	60,141	0 6 10	557,325	
1878	643,912	1 7 4	86,373	0 9 2	730,285	
1879	794,983	1 12 5	165,856	0 16 6	960,839	
1880	793,966	1 11 0	201,734	0 18 7	995,700	
1881	583,471	1 1 10	357,182	1 10 10	940,653	
1882	704,892	1 5 5	702,696	2 17 8	1,407,588	
1883	758,052	1 6 1	931,615	3 12 7	1,689,667	
1884	940,858	1 10 8	669,209	2 9 5	1,610,067	
1885	981,951	1 10 7	704,636	2 9 5	1,636,587	1
1886	868,923	1 6 0	767,906	2 11 1	1,636,829	1
1887	784,941	1 2 9	556,660	1 15 2	1,341,601	
1888	904,477	1 5 9	344,414	1 0 8	1,248,891	
1889	798,383	1 2 4	583,786	1 13 2	1,382,169	
1890	874,077	1 3 10	444,723	1 4 0	1,318,800	

Public parks and recreation reserves.

It has always been the policy of the State to provide th dents of incorporated towns with parks and reserves for recreation, and the City of Sydney contains within its boun an extent of parks, squares, and public gardens larger exist in most of the great cities of the world without even to area. They cover altogether 776 acres, or 2 cent. of the whole of the city proper. In addition to reserves, the inhabitants of Sydney have the use of 780 formerly reserved for the water supply of the city, but now known as the Centennial Park. This magnificent recreation ground has been cleared and planted, and is laid out with walks and drives, so that it is likely to become a favourite resort with the citizens. The suburban municipalities are also well provided for, as they contain 2,205 acres of public parks and reserves, dedicated to, or purchased for, the people by the Government, or 2·9 per cent. of their aggregate area.

The National Park.

In addition to these reserves, the Government dedicated to the people, in December, 1879, a large area of land, situated within easy distance of the metropolis. This estate, now known as the National Park, with the additions subsequently made in 1880 and 1883, contains a total area of 36,320 acres, surrounding the picturesque bay of Port Hacking, and extending in a southerly direction towards the mountainous district of Illawarra. It is covered with magnificent virgin forests, the scenery is charming, and its beauties attract thousands of visitors.

Temporary and permanent commons.

In the country districts, reserves extending often over one million acres, have been proclaimed as temporary commons, whilst considerable areas have been from time to time dedicated as permanent commons attached to inland townships, which are otherwise well provided with parks and reserves within their boundaries.

PART XVI.

Agricultural Production.

Soils adapted to the produce of many climes.

THERE is found in the Colony of New South Wales sc a variety of soils and climate that almost any kind o whether specially the produce of temperate, and even cold cli or of sub-tropical regions may be grown. The nature of the soil greatly, according to the geological formation, in different p the Colony; but, except in the inaccessible or rugged porti the mountain chains, and the more arid regions of the western districts, the soil is almost everywhere suscepti cultivation. The area absolutely unfit for occupation of an has been roughly estimated at less than 5,000,000 acres, may be said that the greater part of the area adapted for settl is also in some form or another capable of being cultivated. question of the success of agricultural operations in New Wales is, however, altogether independent of the mere fitn the soil for cultivation. So far, experience has shown th irregular rainfall and a want of uniformity in the seasons, are the chief characteristics of the climate of a large part interior, are a great drawback to the success of agricu settlements.

Rich soil of coastal valleys.

Owing to the confined nature of their basins the portion valleys of the coastal rivers adapted for agriculture is li but nowhere could there be found richer soil than along the reaches of these rivers. The brush lands of the Tweed, Rich Clarence, Macleay, and Manning are proverbial for the richn their soil, and the sandy alluvial formations of the Hunter a Hawkesbury valleys have been cultivated for nearly a hu years without rest, being enriched periodically by fluvial inundations. The valleys of the southern rivers of the coast district are not less rich, and along the banks of the Shoalhaven, Clyde, Tuross, and other streams are found unmistakable evidence of thriving industry.

Variety of climate.

The variety of climate experienced in a region extending through 8 degrees of latitude, from 29 degrees to 37 degrees south, of necessity causes a corresponding variety in the kinds of produce which may be successfully grown.

Principal crops grown in the coast districts.

Maize is grown in almost every part of the coastal region, along the river valleys, especially north of Sydney, and yields an abundant return. Sugar-cane is cultivated only on the northern rivers, very little being raised southward of the Clarence. Wheat is grown in the Hunter valley to some extent, but not in the country further north. In the southern district, although the little wheat raised shows a comparatively high return, the extent of land cropped is too small to enable a reliable inference to be drawn as to the true capabilities of this rich district. The climate of the northern coast is particularly favourable to the growth of semi-tropical products, especially sugar-cane, coffee, and tobacco, and in the Hunter valley the vine finds a natural home.

Soil suitable for fruit-trees.

The soil of the coastal region is almost everywhere suitable to the growth of fruit-trees, both semi-tropical and European. Oranges, lemons, shaddocks, and other varieties of this class, thrive well on all parts of the north coast, and nowhere better than in the Wianamatta formations about Parramatta, and in the valleys of the Hawkesbury, Nepean, and Parramatta Rivers.

Suitability of table-land for European cereals.

On the high plateau of the Great Dividing Range a variety of soil is met with, and there is much rich agricultural country, especially suited for the cultivation of wheat, barley, oats, and other agricultural products of cold and temperate regions. Notwithstanding the drawbacks in the shape of uncertain seasons and variable rainfall the results obtained in the cultivation of cereal crops in the rich soils of the Monaro, Tumut, Batl Wellington, Mudgee, and New England districts, on the mou plateaux, are certainly encouraging.

Alluvial deposits.

In the western division of the Colony the alluvial dep extending along the course of the great rivers which carr drainage of the larger portion of the Colony of New South \ to the waters of the Murray, have formed a soil of excellent qu and the cereals which form the more considerable items i sustenance of mankind might be grown in immense quan were the rainfall more abundant and regular. Attempts have made on small patches of country here and there to tes agricultural qualities of the soil, with the result that in yea abundant and regular rains the crops have been magnificent in times of drought the returns have been as scanty as in fa able seasons they have been plentiful. Notwithstanding this back, the cultivation of cereals in the Murray and Murrumb valleys is greatly on the increase, and in no other part of South Wales can there be noticed a greater advance in agricul settlement, except perhaps in the Richmond and Clarence dis bordering the north coast of the Colony. It may be confid asserted with regard to Riverina, that wherever it may be practicable to conserve water, or to establish an intelligent sy of irrigation, the soil will repay with a bountiful harvest the la of the agriculturist. Over what area systematic irrigation m carried on has not yet been ascertained, though possibly this not prove to be very considerable, owing to the comparat small volume of the rivers whence the water must be obta and the irregularity of their flow. The physical formatic New South Wales has been described elsewhere. It will been noticed that it differs greatly from any other country v artificial irrigation has been practised on a large scale, and th absence of mountain ranges capped with perpetual snow, for natural and inexhaustible reservoirs, is a marked peculiari the country.

Practicability of irrigation.

CULTIVATION.

The area of New South Wales under cultivation during 1890 amounted to 1,241,419 acres. This, however, includes 388,715 acres of artificially sown grasses, so that the area under crop, properly so called, was 852,704 acres:— Area under cultivation.

Year ended 31st March.	Total number of acres in cultivation, including grass lands.	Per Inhabitant.
	acres.	acres.
1877	513,840	0·84
1878	546,556	0·85
1879	613,642	0·91
1880	635,641	0·89
1881	710,337	0·93
1882	645,068	0·81
1883	733,582	0·88
1884	789,082	0·89
1885	852,017	0·92
1886	868,093	0·90
1887	977,664	0·97
1888	1,048,305	1·01
1889	999,298	0·94
1890	1,164,475	1·06
1891	1,241,419	1·01

Only 0·43 per cent. of the total area of New South Wales is actually devoted to the growth of agricultural produce, and if the small extent of land upon which permanent artificial grasses have been sown for dairy farming purposes be added to the area under Extent of agricultural cultivation.

crops, this proportion only reaches 0·62 per cent. of t area of New South Wales, and does not represent mu than one acre per head of its population.

An impression appears to prevail that in this count chased lands are used by the settlers for agricultural p whilst leased lands only are used for grazing, but such is being the case, as the very great majority of selectors graziers in a small way of business, and agricultural settleme and simple, are confined to very limited areas in the alluvi of the lower valleys of the coastal rivers and around two centres in the middle division of the table-land. Comp the area of alienated rural lands, the proportion of area cu throughout New South Wales is only 2·07 per cent.

Proportion of cultivated to alienated land.

The proportion of land cultivated by the land-owner selves is 660,745 acres, or 77·5 per cent. of the total are crops, there being only 191,959 acres or 22·5 per cent. cu by tenant occupiers, including Crown tenants. If the are permanent grasses be added, the proportion of cultivated lands would be somewhat higher, as a considerable portio dairy farms in the southern coast are held on lease fr original proprietors.

Electorates adjacent to the Metropolis.

In the electorates immediately adjacent to the met comprising, besides the city electorates, those of St. Le Canterbury, Parramatta, and Central Cumberland, the tot cultivated amounts to 20,403 acres or 12·14 per cent. of the rural lands alienated, which covers 168,116 acres. The part of this area is devoted to the cultivation of a va orchard produce, the orange, lemon, and various kinds o fruit being grown in great quantities, whilst market-garde a fairly extensive area in the immediate vicinity of the met Including 13,774 acres laid down in permanent artificial 4,957 acres lying fallow, and 7,114 acres cleared for futu vation, the total area, at present used or intended for agricultural operations covers 46,248 acres in this district. The total number of persons employed in agricultural and dairy pursuits is stated at 5,703, of whom 344 are females.

In the whole of the Central Coast Division, embracing the electorates of Morpeth, East and West Maitland, the Hunter, he Wollombi, the Hawkesbury, the Nepean, Patrick's Plains, Durham, Gloucester, Northumberland, and Newcastle, the total area under crop is 72,299 acres, or 3·67 per cent. of the alienated rural lands. The proportion of land cultivated by tenant occupiers amount to 31,427 acres, or 43·5 of the total area under crop in the whole district, but in the districts of East Maitland, Morpeth, and West Maitland, the proportion of land cultivated by tenants is much higher—between 66 and 52 per cent. of the whole area cultivated. In the electorates of Durham, Patrick's Plains, and Hunter the proportion decreases to 48·7, 44·0, and 40·9 per cent. respectively, whilst in those of Gloucester and Northumberland it is reduced to 40·1, and 29·6 per cent. respectively.

Maize, potatoes, and other crops are raised in the rich alluvial soil of the Hawkesbury Valley, included in the electorates of Hawkesbury, Nepean, and Wollombi, where the leasing of land, for farming purposes has attained a large proportion, 10,892 acres, or 35·5 per cent. of the area under crop being cultivated by tenant farmers. In the Nepean electorate 43·5 per cent., in that of the Hawkesbury 35·4 per cent., and in that of Wollombi 29·9 per cent., of the area cultivated is worked by leaseholders.

The Hunter River District.

The district embraced within the basin of the river Hunter is, as regards settlement, divided into two very distinct portions, the lower part being occupied by a mining and agricultural population, and the upper portion forming one of the most prosperous pastoral districts of New South Wales. In the Lower Hunter nearly 8 per cent. of the alienated land is under cultivation, this proportion reaching 65·8 per cent., in West Maitland, maize, lucerne, potatoes, and grape-vines being the principal crops grown.

The area at present under crop is only 38·6 per cent. of t devoted to agriculture and prepared for future operations, wh aggregates about 187,226 acres, including 14,592 acres under p manent grasses, 39,757 in fallow, and 60,578 cleared and rea for the plough. The number of persons reported as engaged agricultural pursuits (including dairy farming in the district) 10,735, of whom 2,532 are females.

South coast districts.

The south coast districts are principally devoted to the industry dairy farming, and it is from Camden, Shoalhaven, Kiama, Illawar and Eden, that the metropolis derives most of the dairy prod which it requires for the daily consumption of its populati The area under cultivation, in the strict sense of the term, t is, irrespective of that laid down in permanent artificial gras is only 40,997 acres, or 3·02 per cent. of the total area of ali ated lands. Except in the electorates of Eden and Camd tenant farmers occupy a larger area than that which is cultiva by the landowners themselves, the proportion of land cultiva by tenants to the total area under crop being 60·1, 55·1, and 4 per cent. respectively in the electorates of Kiama, Shoalhaven, a Illawarra. In the electorate of Camden tenant farmers cultiv 40·7 per cent. of the total area under crop in the district. I probable if the total area occupied for agricultural and dairy p poses, which covers 227,488 acres, or 16·8 per cent. of the a alienated in the whole district, is considered, that the percent of tenant holdings would be found still higher. Dairy prod forms the basis of the industry of this portion of New So Wales; and besides grasses the principal crops grown are ma and potatoes, which generally give excellent average returns. T area laid down in permanent artificial grasses in the district 172,251 acres; 14,240 acres are lying fallow, and 92,436 ac are reported as cleared and ready for ploughing, so that a to area of 319,924 acres may be considered as devoted to agricultu and dairy operations, which employ 13,612 hands, of whom 4,5 are females

The north-coast districts, comprising the electorates of the Hastings and Manning, the Macleay, Grafton, Clarence, and the Richmond, altogether contain 122,276 acres of land under crop, or 7·20 per cent. of the area alienated, which is computed at 1,698,043 acres. The proportion of the area farmed by tenant occupiers and the proprietors themselves is as follows:—Area cultivated by owners, equal 80,012 acres, or 65·4 per cent.; area cultivated by tenants, 42,264 acres, or 34·6 per cent. In the electorates of the Macleay and Grafton the proportion of area cultivated by tenants is greater, reaching 46·8 and 39·3 per cent.; but on the Hastings and Manning, the Clarence, and the Richmond, this proportion only attains 30·4, 30·3, and 27·8 per cent. of the total area cultivated. The proportion of land cultivated to that alienated is 7·20 per cent. for the whole district, but this does not include the area laid down in grasses for dairy purposes in the Richmond and the Macleay districts; including 81,077 acres of grasses, 25,030 acres of fallow land, and 61,036 acres prepared for cultivation, the total area devoted to agricultural or dairy purposes in the north-coast district amounts to 289,419 acres, or 17·0 per cent. of the area alienated. The dairy industry is rapidly assuming large proportions in the two electorates just mentioned, but the principal crops raised are maize and sugar, the latter being the chief industry of the more northerly-situated electorates of the Richmond and the Clarence Rivers, with some acres in that of the Macleay. The number of persons employed in agricultural occupations, including dairy farming, is 10,377 of whom 1,828 are females.

North coast districts.

The agricultural future of the north-coast districts certainly looks very bright, as there is no scarcity of land suited to the purpose of the farmer, and the climate is favourable to the growth of all the natural productions of sub-tropical and temperate zones. The lack of means of transport has been the principal drawback to the progress of agricultural settlement in this district, but now that the question of providing railway communication throughout its extent is receiving the attention of Parliament, and that large

Districts favourable for farming.

areas of country lately held under pastoral lease have been th open to free selection, it may be safely predicted that the pro of the districts in the coming years will be very rapid.

The central table-land.

Passing on to the table-land and looking at the state agriculture, it will be seen that in the Central portion, incl the electorates of East and West Macquarie, Hartley, O the Upper Hunter, Mudgee, Wellington, Molong, and Carcoa area under crop amounted to 166,518 acres, or 3·74 per cen the area alienated, which is computed at 4,447,538 acres. and West Macquarie and Orange, are the leading agricul electorates of the group. In these the proportion of land vated to the area alienated is 7·16, 9·14, and 10·14 per respectively; the decrease observable in these proportions, compared to former years is due to the fact that, owing to favorable circumstances, and the occurrence of excessive rai the wheat-sowing season, unusually large areas were allow lie fallow. In the surrounding electorates the proportion decr until in the Upper Hunter the minimum of 0·63 per cen reached. The proportion of land cultivated by the landow for the whole district equals 74 per cent., the remaining 2 cent. being worked by tenant farmers, but this proportion do no means represent the state of agricultural occupation in electorate. In East and West Macquarie 25,572 acres, or 6 cent. out of a total of 38,650 acres under crops this season cultivated by tenant farmers, almost the whole of it being wheat, whilst the reverse proportion is the rule in the electorates. Wheat is the staple crop of this district. The area allowed to lie fallow in this district last year was 66 that laid down in artificial grasses, 28,420, and the area cl and prepared for future farming operations is returned at 25 acres, the total area devoted to this branch of rural industry 515,370 acres, representing 11·6 per cent. of the area alien Upon this area 12,602 persons, including 3,849 females employed in farming and dairy pursuits.

In the Southern division of the table-land, embracing the electorates of Goulburn, Argyle, Boorowa, Yass Plains, Queanbeyan, Braidwood, Monaro, Tumut, Young, and Gundagai, the area cultivated amounts to 141,326 acres or 2·3 per cent. of the alienated area, computed at 6,157,360 acres. The conditions of agricultural occupation differ very much from those which obtain in the coast electorates and also in the older settled portion of the central table-land. Cultivation is carried on here and there in a desultory sort of fashion as an addition to grazing, which is by far the more important of the two occupations. Except perhaps in the districts of Tumut, Yass Plains, and Gundagai, where a considerable area is devoted to the growth of wheat and maize, the cultivation of the soil is a secondary consideration. Within the last few years tobacco culture made very great strides in the districts mentioned; but an excessive production of leaf, prepared in an inferior manner and difficult of sale, is causing a shrinking of this industry; many growers, particularly Chinese, have abandoned its cultivation for that of maize, and in some instances have taken to raising vegetables for the metropolitan market. The proportion of land cultivated by tenant occupiers is only 17·4 per cent., 82·6 per cent. of the land under crop being cultivated by the landowners themselves. The total area upon which agriculture and dairy farming are carried on, including that prepared for future operations, is 499,340 acres, of which 141,326 were under crop last season, 52,337 acres were allowed to lie fallow, 38,332 acres were laid down in grasses, and 267,345 acres were cleared and prepared for future agricultural operations. The number of persons employed in agricultural and dairy occupations was 12,090, of whom 4,451 were female hands. Wheat, oats, barley, maize, potatoes, and tobacco are the principal crops raised in this district.

Southern table-land.

In the northern portion of the table-land a similar state of affairs exists, but the proportion of land under crop to the total area alienated is still further reduced, there being only 56,625 acres, or 1·82 per cent. cultivated out of 3,118,453 acres alienated

Northern table-land.

in this division, which embraces the Electorates of Tenter Glen Innes, Inverell, New England, and Tamworth. Pr tenancy of land is reduced to much smaller proportions th the case in the districts in which agriculture is carried on pendently of grazing, as only 4,868 acres, or 8·6 per cer the area under crops is cultivated by tenant occupiers. addition to the area under crops last season, 25,847 acres allowed to lie fallow, 13,806 acres were laid down in gr and 76,326 acres had been cleared and prepared for agricu so that a total area of 172,604 acres may be considered as de to this branch of an industry which gave employment to persons, of whom 1,573 were females. Wheat and oats and are the principal crops raised in this district.

The Western Slopes.

The districts situated on the Western slopes of the Great ing Range are almost essentially devoted to pastoral pursuit little need be said on the subject of agriculture; in the C Division, nevertheless, that industry shows signs of develop in the electorates of the Bogan, Forbes, and Grenfell, princ on the banks of the river Lachlan, and the immediate vicin the towns of Forbes, Grenfell, and Parkes. The area culti in this district covers in all 33,624 acres, mostly held as y the original selectors, although 2,316 acres are reported as cultivated by tenants. There were also 1,860 acres laid in grasses, 8,952 acres fallow, and 71,728 acres cleared prepared for ploughing at a future time; the total area de to agriculture being, therefore, 116,164 acres, upon which persons, including 936 females, found employment last se In the Northern Division, including the electorates of Gunn the Namoi, and the Gwydir, the progress of agriculture i rapid, being confined to that portion of the district of Gun adjoining that of Tamworth, and a few patches along the of the rivers in the immediate vicinity of townships and v settlements. The total area cultivated in this extensive reg 8,607 acres, of which 7,912 are worked by the proprietors o soil, and 695 by tenant farmers. There are also 1,441

In addition to the area under crops in the Western Districts were also 3,254 acres of fallow land, 143 acres laid dow grasses, and 8,521 acres cleared and prepared for ploughing future period, the total area devoted to or intended for ag tural requirements being 19,764 acres. Although the area crops is small, most of the cultivated land being used for m gardens and orchards, the number of persons employed is paratively large, there being 1,134 persons, of whom 296 females, engaged in agricultural pursuits.

New South Wales a pastoral country.

It will be readily understood from the above analysis that South Wales is essentially a pastoral country, and that, wit exception of a few districts where agriculture has taken a the cultivation of the soil is quite secondary to stock-bree This circumstance is by no means due to the lack of good nor may it even be ascribed to the defects of the climate New South Wales possesses land, the capabilities of whic producing any kind of agricultural produce are unsurpa and its climate is certainly superior to that of other parts Australian Continent where the cultivation of cereals has carried on for years past. Taken as a whole the yield of cro New South Wales is larger than that obtained in any other tinental colony, but, on the other hand, communication with metropolitan market is much more difficult. Agriculture ca be developed unless access to the markets be rendered both and cheap, and to secure this desirable end in a country so and with so small a population as New South Wales, is a mat time and expenditure. Under existing circumstances stock ing is an occupation the results of which are far more remuner whilst entailing considerably less physical labour and per inconvenience; but as population increases and there remain more land to be taken up for grazing purposes, agricultural suits must be resorted to under the pressure of an ever-incre demand. As it is, however, the area devoted to agricu or cleared and prepared for the future extension of this ind is evidently increasing, affording permanent employment to proportion of the working population of New South Wales; the area actually under crops varies, owing to a variety of circumstances, but there is a steady increase in the surface cleared in view of its extension. In April, 1891, the area reported under crops was 852,704 acres, in addition to which 280,839 acres were lying fallow, 388,715 acres were laid down in grasses, and 1,166,228 acres cleared and prepared for future cultivation, of which by far the greater proportion—viz., 613,419 acres—were situated in the Southern Division of the Colony, 393,713 acres being cleared in the East Central Division, 150,575 acres in the Northern, and only 8,521 acres in the Western Plains. The total number of persons reported as employed in agricultural and dairy farming pursuits last season was 82,213, of whom 23,252 were females.

The importance of agriculture is clearly recognized by the State, and much is to be expected from the labours of the newly-created Department of Agriculture in directing the efforts of individuals in the proper channels, acquainting the farmers with the results of scientific investigations in this branch of industry, and applying the experience gained in other lands to the economical developments of the natural resources of the soil of New South Wales. The Department of Agriculture was formed at the beginning of the year 1890 and placed under the administration of the Secretary for Mines, whose title was altered to that of Secretary for Mines and Agriculture. The question of providing technical agricultural education, and establishing a college and model farms in various parts of the country, immediately engaged the attention of the Director, and a site suitable for a central establishment was selected at Ham Common, near the town of Richmond, in the Hawkesbury district, where an area of about 4,000 acres was resumed for the purpose. Department of Agriculture.

The principal crops at present grown in the Colony are wheat, maize, oats, barley, potatoes, sugar-cane, tobacco, grapes, oranges, and other fruits. The quantities produced in the year ended March–April, and the value of each crop is given in the following statement, the values being the average for the whole Colony at the time the harvest was gathered. Quantities and value of produce.

Principal Crops cultivated.	Area.	Produce.	Value.
Cereals :—	acres.	Bushels.	£
Wheat	333,233	3,649,216	820,073
Maize	191,152	5,713,205	833,176
Barley	4,937	81,383	9,156
Oats	14,102	256,659	24,596
Other grain	923	11,546	2,596
Hay :—		Tons.	
Wheat	83,827	118,020	406,060
Oats	70,463	71,305	320,873
Barley	938	1,179	5,895
Lucerne and grass	20,014	41,536	155,876
Straw	....	22,006	44,912
Green food for cattle	37,473	....	168,629
Potatoes	19,406	52,971	171,571
Sugar-cane	20,446*	277,252	210,249
		Cwt.	
Tobacco	1,148	10,592	19,772
		Gals.	
Grapes for wine and brandy	3,896	848,885	147,382
		Tons.	
,, table use	4,148†	3,355	62,627
		No. of Cases.	
Oranges	11,288‡	770,800	240,875
Market garden produce	5,098	....	192,597
Orchard produce	22,355§	....	213,934
Minor crops	7,857	....	78,570
Permanent artificial grasses	388,715	....	....
Total	1,241,419	....	4,131,421

NOTE.—The values given are those at the places where the produce was grown.

* Including 12,102 acres unproductive. † Including 2,076 acres vines as yet unproductive. ‡ Including 2,551 acres oranges not yet bearing. § Including 6,274 acres fruit-trees at present unproductive.

The results of the season 1890–1 can scarcely be considered as satisfactory, especially when compared with those of the previous seasons. The value of the agricultural produce of New South Wales for each year since 1880 is given below; the figures for the last three years have been corrected, as the value of certain kinds of produce had been slightly over-estimated :—

Year.	Value.	Year.	Value.
	£		£
1880	2,930,794	1886	3,943,645
1881	4,194,346	1887	4,151,692
1882	3,304,891	1888	3,296,759
1883	3,806,182	1889	4,459,861
1884	2,836,697	1890	4,136,887
1885	3,375,882		

WHEAT.

In the early days of settlement the Hawkesbury River Valley and the country adjacent to the towns of Parramatta, Liverpool, Penrith, Camden, and Maitland were the centres of considerable wheat growing. Unskilful farming, and the consequent exhaustion of the soil, with the attendant evils of rust, smut, and other diseases, caused these districts to be abandoned little by little as wheat country, and on the discovery of the Bathurst Plains their importance at once ceased. The districts of Bathurst, Goulburn, Gundagai, Tumut, Young, Monaro, and New England were each in turn occupied by agriculturists, and the suitability of their soil and climate, as well as that of the whole of the mountain plateau, for the growth of this cereal became definitely established. Principal centres of cultivation.

The cultivation of this grain during the past thirty years has been very irregular. For some years prior to 1867 the area of land under crop remained almost the same from year to year, being little more than 125,000 acres. In 1867, however, the wheat area had increased to 175,000 acres, and at that acreage it remained practically unaltered for twelve years. Then, again, more land was laid under wheat, and in 1878–9 the area had increased to 233,252 acres. Since then the area of land under this cereal has been greatly extended, and during the year 1887–8 there were Cultivation very irregular.

reaped 389,390 acres, an area larger than in any]
and an increase of 51,660 acres, or 15·29 per cent.
under this grain crop in 1887. During 1888–9 t
wheat for grain fell to 304,803 acres, and owing t
of the season much of this area was not reaped, as
the crop would not pay the farmers to harvest it.
duction of the wheat fields of the Colony amo
Average yield. 1,450,503 bushels, equal to an average of 4·75 bu
which was the smallest return ever experienced i
Wales. But the prospects of the season 1889–9
farmers to increase the area under wheat for grain,
reaching 419,758 acres, and the production 6,57
which is the largest crop ever harvested in New
though the average yield of 15·65 bushels per acre
exceeded in the past; 333,233 acres were cropped
1890–91, the yield from which was 3,649,216 bus
10·95 bushels to the acre. The average yield durin
the period, which extends from the date of the pass
Crown Lands Act to the season which ended on 31s
was 13·22 bushels, the lowest yield being 4·75 bu
in 1888–9, the most bountiful, 17·37 bushels per
during 1886–7. During the first ten years of the
from 1862 to 1871, the yield per acre appears to h
paratively a small one, having averaged only 10·70 b
followed a period of fair seasons, extending over se
when the average fluctuated between a minimum o
obtained in the season of 1885–6, and a maximum
season 1886–7, averaging 14·63 bushels per acre
period, 1871–2 to 1887–8.

Season of 1891–2. The prospects of the coming season, 1891–2
encouraging, and it is expected that a larger area
under cultivation than in the previous year. The
rainy weather gives promise of a magnificent spr
trary to usual Australian experience, fears are exp
excessive rainfall, extending far into the season, n
coming crops. Such wet seasons as those of the l
are almost as abnormal as the extreme drought of

farmer has most to fear from drought, and the experience of the past shows the necessity of conserving, wherever possible, the water which rain-clouds supply in so irregular a fashion. The influence of the rainfall, however, can hardly be shown by means of figures. There are too many considerations affecting the value of rain to admit of this being done. The period of the year at which rain falls, the quantity falling at any one time, and evaporation, are elements of as much importance as the total rainfall. **Influence of rainfall.**

The following statement shows the state of wheat cultivation since the year 1862:— **Cultivation of wheat.**

Area under Wheat—Yield per Acre.

Year ended 31 March.	Area of crop.	Bushels.	Yield per acre.
	Acres.		Bushels.
1862	123,468	1,606,034	13·01
1863	108,136	1,054,954	9·75
1864	103,242	808,919	7·78
1865	104,568	1,246,458	11·92
1866	131,653	1,013,863	7·69
1867	175,033	2,226,027	12·72
1868	149,142	1,433,807	9·61
1869	164,206	1,887,065	10·88
1870	189,452	3,200,959	16·89
1871	147,997	999,595	6·75
1872	154,030	2,229,642	14·48
1873	177,551	2,898,463	16·32
1874	169,330	2,238,414	13·43
1875	166,911	2,148,394	12·87
1876	133,609	1,958,640	14·66
1877	145,608	2,391,979	16·43
1878	176,686	2,445,507	13·84
1879	233,252	3,439,326	14·74
1880	233,368	3,613,286	15·48
1881	253,137	3,717,355	14·69
1882	221,887	3,405,966	15·35
1883	247,361	4,042,356	16·35
1884	289,757	4,345,437	15·00
1885	275,225	4,271,394	15·52
1886	264,867	2,733,133	10·45
1887	337,730	5,868,844	17·37
1888	389,390	4,695,849	12·06
1889	304,808	1,450,503	4·75
1890	419,758	6,570,335	15·65
1891	333,233	3,649,216	10·95
Average yield for thirty years			13·22

Average yield for twenty-five years.

Dividing the quarter century ending April, 1891, into quennial periods, the means were :—

Quinquennial period.	Average per acre.
1867-1871	11·37 bushels.
1872-1876	14·35 ,,
1877-1881	13·06 ,,
1882-1886	14·53 ,,
1887-1891	12·15 ,,

Various districts compared.

The increased yield of the period since 1873 is partly due proved farming; but, at the same time, it must not be lost si that the occurrence of rust, smut, and other forms of disease in has been less frequent and less general of recent years. Gr according to the proportion of land under wheat during 188 1890 to the total area, the districts stand as follows :—

District	Proportion of land under wheat to wh area of district.	
	1889-90. Acres.	189 A
Young	1 in 30	1 i
Gundagai	33	
Bathurst	51	
Orange, Molong, and Carcoar	52	
Murray Valley	114	
Yass and Boorowa	152	
Tamworth	156	
Murrumbidgee	172	
Mudgee	184	
Goulburn	214	
Tumut	465	
Monaro	522	
Wellington and Bogan	527	
Hunter Valley	641	1
Glen Innes, Inverell, and Tenterfield	707	
Forbes and Grenfell	710	
New England	741	1,
Namoi and Gwydir Valleys	4,222	5,

Area of wheat cultivation in districts.

The area of land under wheat in the remaining districts c Colony is so small as not to be worth taking into consider and is therefore neglected in the ensuing comparisons. Owi the alteration of the boundaries of the electoral districts in comparison by electorates is not possible beyond that year. Taking, therefore, the ten years which have since elapsed, the total area under wheat in each district was:—

Area under Wheat, in Acres.

Districts.	1881-2.	1882-3.	1883-4.	1884-5.	1885-6.	1886-7.	1887-8.	1888-9.	1889-90	1890-91
Goulburn ..	8,636	9,598	9,452	9,239	5,661	7,787	9,126	3,505	7,700	4,902
Yass	10,808	12,552	15,732	14,824	12,701	16,824	17,596	10,745	15,751	10,472
Wellington and the Bogan.	8,321	10,463	12,722	12,709	11,153	20,170	17,722	16,445	19,901	17,190
Monaro	9,832	10,253	10,917	10,922	7,072	9,892	13,466	6,880	10,876	7,384
Murray Valley	38,928	38,705	45,498	45,792	50,097	54,240	74,080	64,548	70,729	63,428
Orange	37,429	45,045	52,294	47,890	45,564	59,721	55,033	41,157	62,936	43,375
Gundagai ..	9,150	12,004	15,390	15,412	18,438	20,108	24,253	20,998	30,572	24,071
Forbes	5,215	5,858	9,226	8,156	7,775	11,558	12,545	7,068	14,204	10,613
Murrumbidgee	5,638	4,357	13,142	11,799	19,793	26,204	46,309	45,354	62,663	61,349
Tamworth ..	10,600	11,750	14,275	12,644	12,826	16,543	16,179	9,787	15,768	16,076
New England	6,294	7,687	7,836	7,496	6,201	7,047	8,186	3,524	6,159	3,440
Namoi and Gwydir Valleys.	3,180	3,226	3,436	3,617	4,114	5,485	5,960	4,209	4,068	2,879
North Coast..	471	547	581	503	270	218	283	302	237	60
Glen Innes..	7,428	8,771	8,321	9,465	8,241	8,789	10,401	6,152	8,927	7,578
Young	13,316	16,750	21,964	18,978	21,562	28,609	34,119	31,801	42,918	35,801
Hunter River Valley.	9,012	8,068	8,288	7,750	6,499	8,326	8,235	5,479	7,704	4,836
Bathurst....	28,824	25,573	21,456	20,269	12,858	18,817	18,889	10,736	21,276	14,627
Mudgee	8,298	9,851	12,163	11,586	10,125	12,749	11,511	11,706	12,383	7,236
Tumut......	2,860	3,283	3,696	2,926	2,185	2,739	3,406	2,720	3,144	2,701
South Coast.	282	369	364	261	141	138	152	164	159	118
Hawkesb'y & Nepean.	2,239	2,274	2,763	2,797	1,383	1,597	1,351	1,273	1,417	992
Western Districts.	115	214	230	159	220	166	561	312	310	321

The foregoing figures are instructive, as they throw considerable light upon the history of wheat cultivation and agricultural settlement in New South Wales. Although the interval under examination is a short one, extending over a period of ten years only, great changes are shown to have taken place in parts of the country hitherto devoted mainly to pastoral occupation. It is also interesting to note that agriculture is gaining ground in those districts where the greater number of the huge freehold estates, accumulated by pastoralists under the auction sales and improvement clauses of the Land Act of 1861, are situated. It is in the valleys of the Murray, the Murrumbidgee, and the Lachlan that

Agriculture gaining ground.

Increase of agriculture in Riverine District.

the struggle between squatter and selector has been fierce where the most remarkable increase of agricultural settlement as regards wheat-growing and agriculture generally is n(hibited. The following statement, showing the total area c cultivated in the districts abutting on the three great rivers mentioned, in the years ended March 1882 and 1891 respe(will serve to illustrate this point:—

Districts.	Total Area under Cultivati	
	In 1882.	In 18
	Acres.	Ac
The Murray Valley	55,763	107,
The Murrumbidgee	13,645	94,
Forbes and Grenfell	12,429	[illegible]
Gundagai	13,295	21,
Yass Plains and Boorowa	16,194	18,
Young	21,132	47,
Total	131,858	319,

Murrumbidgee district.

By far the greater proportional increase is exhibited in t of the Murrumbidgee electoral district, where the total area cultivation has increased fully seven times in nine years; w an average the figures for the other districts show an i of nearly 53 per cent. It is also worthy of remark that th under cultivation in these districts represents 26 per cent. total area tilled in New South Wales, including that laid d permanent grasses.

As regards the cultivation of wheat for grain only, it seen that in most of the above-mentioned districts it has tal largest share of the total increased area placed under cult during this short period of nine years. In the Murrumbid area under this crop has increased to nearly eleven times was in 1882; in that of Young it has grown from 13,316 a 35,801 acres; in that of Gundagai, from 9,150 acres to acres; and in the Murray River Valley, from 38,928 acres to acres; whilst in the other districts it has increased in pro to that of the general cultivation. Reverting to the exam of the whole of the principal wheat-growing districts of New

Wales, the average yield per acre for the period of nine years under notice will be seen below:—

Average yield per acre

Wheat.—Average Yield per Acre, in Bushels.

Districts.	1882-3.	1883-4.	1884-5.	1885-6.	1886-7.	1887-8.	1888-9.	1889-90.	1890-1.	Mean.
Goulburn	17·3	13·8	17·1	9·5	18·9	10·7	5·1	14·5	11·1	13·5
Yass	17·5	14·2	17·0	11·1	17·7	11·5	4·2	14·3	9·3	13·4
Wellington & Bogan	16·2	14·1	17·2	6·4	16·2	12·9	2·6	18·7	9·6	11·4
Monaro	16·8	14·9	16·6	11·4	17·0	15·9	8·1	15·6	12·5	14·8
Murray Valley	12·3	13·6	9·6	12·1	14·4	10·2	7·7	10·9	11·0	11·3
Orange	17·9	16·7	15·7	9·9	18·3	11·8	3·8	18·9	9·1	13·8
Gundagai	18·2	15·8	18·4	11·4	20·2	12·6	5·6	18·6	11·1	14·5
Forbes	11·3	15·1	13·4	7·9	20·5	11·8	4·1	22·5	10·2	14·0
Murrumbidgee	14·5	14·4	14·4	5·0	19·9	11·1	3·4	18·1	11·0	11·9
Tamworth	18·6	16·0	16·3	10·1	14·7	15·1	4·0	7·7	11·3	12·7
New England	21·1	19·3	20·1	15·4	17·1	16·7	10 1	14·0	12·3	17·1
Namoi and Gwydir	22·7	15·7	15·9	8·7	18·9	18·3	2·6	9·5	12·0	12·8
North Coast	21·0	22·2	16·2	16·6	18·9	21·3	19·6	15·1	20·9	19·2
Glen Innes	20·8	19·6	20·5	19·2	18·8	17·8	5·9	12·6	16·0	16·6
Young	16·7	13·4	17·5	9·9	19·2	11·0	3·5	18·4	10·4	13·1
Hunter River Valley	8·0	15·4	15·6	8·4	16·8	12·9	3·7	12·7-	9·5	12·0
Bathurst	15·2	11·9	14·3	8·2	16·4	12·2	1·7	14·7	10·4	12·7
Mudgee	21·9	14·1	18·1	6·3	19·0	12·9	0·5	18·7	8·3	13·2
Tumut	20·5	19·0	23·6	14·2	20·0	14·3	13·4	15·2	15·7	17·5
South Coast	20·5	22·6	23 0	17·1	14·6	17·4	15 5	18·2	20·4	19·7
Hawkesbury and Nepean.	13·3	13·9	13·2	12·8	16·3	12·0	8·8	8·0	9·8	12 /
Western District	7·4	10·8	9·4	5·5	12·6	9·0	0·8	10·7	13·2	5·7
Average for whole Colony.	16·2	14·9	15·5	10·4	17·3	12·1	4·7	15·6	11·0	13 0

Effect of drought.

The disastrous effects of the drought of 1888 are plainly illustrated in the foregoing table. With the exception of the Coast districts, which are liable to suffer rather from excess of moisture than otherwise, all the wheat-growing centres were affected, and those that in ordinary seasons would yield the best returns were among the greatest sufferers. The effects of this unexampled season were indeed so ruinous that in the Mudgee and Bathurst districts the farmers did not gather in sufficient grain for the next season's sowing. The Government was appealed to, and in consideration of the prevailing distress, orders were given to supply the farmers with sufficient wheat for the next year's operations. In this way some 50,000 bushels of wheat, imported chiefly from New Zealand, were supplied under certain regulations as to recouping the Government for their expen

Average yield of districts compared.

Comparing now the returns of the various districts, but l aside the North and South Coast districts, where the area wheat is too small to afford a reliable test of their wheat-gr capabilities, it will be seen that Tumut, New Englanc Glen Innes, have given the largest as well as the mos sistent yield during the whole period. This is what migh been anticipated. The situation of these districts on the plateau of the main range dividing the coastal region of the from the Great Western Plains, places them under conditi to climate and rainfall similar to those which obtain richest wheat-growing countries of Europe and America.

Monaro, Gundagai, Orange, Goulburn, and Mudgee, follow in the order named, as regards yield per acre, which in eac may be considered fairly good. Forbes, Yass, Young, Bat and Tamworth also yield a fair average crop. The scale se decreases in the other districts of the Colony, which, wi exception of Bathurst and the Hunter Valley, are situated confines of the lower slope of the main range, and the great of the interior.

Decrease in yield as descent is made to plains.

It may be stated as a general law that those districts si on the higher table-lands of the main Dividing Range are th adapted to the cultivation of wheat, and that the average decreases in an almost constant ratio as a descent is made to the plains, where the average falls as low as in similar tions in South Australia and Victoria. Bathurst is the exception to this general rule, but as it is in the district in the greater quantity of wheat is grown, as compared wi total area, the reason of its small average annual yield m sought apart from the circumstances of its geographical sit It may be that the constant succession of crops has injur productiveness of the soil, and brought about a decreased y the district where cultivation has been most continuous.

Rainfall in wheat centres.

The average rainfall over some of the most important growing centres during the year 1890 will be found together with the average since 1882. In the abunda timely rainfall of 1889 will be found the immediate cause of the fine harvest which was almost everywhere experienced in that year. A copious rainfall does not, however, necessarily ensure a correspondingly good harvest; if it were so the results of the season 1890–91 should have been much better than they actually were. The remarks made in a previous paragraph, explaining the apparent decline of agriculture in the Central Districts, hitherto considered as the great wheat region of New South Wales, may be said to apply with equal force to the rest of the country, with, perhaps, the exception of the Murray and Murrumbidgee Valleys. Incessant winter rains, extending far into the spring, prevented the farmers from sowing as much land as they might have wished, forcing them to allow a considerable percentage of their wheat area to lie fallow. From the reduced area a better harvest might have been expected had not a recurrence of the heavy rains taken place about the harvest time, completely spoiling the crop in some districts and reducing the yield almost throughout the country. The rainfall though much above the average was by no means excessive, but the beneficial effects of the rain were rendered nugatory by its untimely occurrence.

District.	1890. Inches.	1882-90. Inches.	District.	1890. Inches.	1882-90. Inches.
Goulburn	34·3	24·4	Tamworth	41·9	26·8
Yass	36·1	25·9	New England	52·9	30·9
Wellington	32·9	23·0	Bathurst	34·4	24·3
Monaro	32·1	25·5	Mudgee	38·5	25·8
Murray	23·7	20·8	Glen Innes	49·8	32·1
Orange and Carcoar	36·1	25·5	Young	33·1	25·6
Gundagai	37·4	23·9	Hunter Valley	47·2	28·2
Forbes	33·4	20·3	Tumut	37·2	31·1
Murrumbidgee	27·4	18·9			

Average yield of New South Wales compared with other colonies.

If the average production of wheat per acre in New South Wales be compared with that of the other colonies of the Australasian group, it will be found that this Colony occupies a very satisfactory place. Its average is greater than that of any other portion of continental Australia, although somewhat less than the Tasmanian yield, and considerably below that of New Zealand. The following table shows the average produce of each Australasian Colony since 1874.

Average Yield of Wheat in Bushels per Acre in Australasia for the Years ended 31st March, 1875–91.

	1875.	1876.	1877.	1878.	1879.	1880.	1881.	1882.	1883.	1884.	1885.	1886.	1887.	1888.	1889.	1890.	1891.	Mean.
New South Wales	12·87	14·66	16·43	13·84	14·74	15·48	14·69	15·35	16 35	15·00	15·52	10·45	17 87	12·06	4·76	15·65	10·95	13·89
Victoria	14·57	15·49	13·15	12·41	8·76	13·29	9·95	9·40	9·03	14·10	9·52	8·99	11·49	10·81	7·10	9·75	11·13	11·11
Queensland	..	..	..	10·63	13·56	8·11	20·40	8·41	13·89	4·34	16·17	5·11	3·12	22·10	0·89	15·88	20·02	11·62
South Australia	11·75	11·95	5·40	7·76	7·15	9·78	9·96	4·57	4·21	7·94	7·53	7·53	7·53	9·75	3·85	7·91	5·62	7·66
Western Australia	12·00	11·00	12·00	11·00	9·97	14·94	14·94	7·00	11·00	13·00	13·00	11·50	12·25	9·80	10·50	14·00	13·75	11·86
Tasmania	18 51	16·38	19·30	18·12	16·10	23·22	14·99	18·88	20·27	17·74	19·30	17·32	17·91	16·67	20·16	15·42	16·80	18·40
New Zealand	28·15	31·54	28·63	26·30	22·04	28·10	25·07	22·69	26·28	26·02	25·43	24·40	24·89	26·37	24·22	25·15	18·99	25·60

Compared with the majority of European countries, the yield of wheat must appear inconsiderable, both in regard to the total quantity obtained and the produce per acre. The return from some of the chief wheat-growing countries is given as follows:— Comparison with other countries.

Wheat-growing Countries.	Average produce of wheat per acre.
	Bushels.
Denmark	31·1
United Kingdom	26·9
Norway	25·1
Belgium	21·5
Holland	21·5
Manitoba	20·3
Germany	18·8
France	16·9
Austria	16·4
British Columbia	15·0
Ontario	14·1
Hungary	13·6
Italy	12·1
United States	11·7
Quebec, Nova Scotia, and New Brunswick	9·9
Russia in Europe	4·6
New South Wales (since 1875)	14·1
Australasia	14·2

The price of wheat is subject to constant fluctuations as the following table, giving the average rates ruling in the Sydney market in the months of February and March of each year, since 1864, will show. These figures exhibit clearly the tendency to a gradual reduction in the value of that cereal, the rate for 1890 being the lowest of the series. As New South Wales has never grown sufficient wheat for home consumption, the price of wheat in Sydney is generally governed by the rates obtained in the neighbouring Australian markets, where a surplus is produced. This, again, is now determined by the figures realized in London, which is usually equal to that ruling in Adelaide, plus freight and charges. The prices in the following table are for an imperial bushel, and, being for new wheat, are slightly below the average of the year. Price of wheat.

Wholesale Prices of Milling Wheat in the Sydney market during the months of February and March, 1864-91.

Year.	February.	March.
	per bushel. £ s. d.	per bushel. £ s. d.
1864	0 7 0	0 7 6
1865	0 9 6	0 9 7½
1866	0 8 4½	0 8 0
1867	0 4 3	0 4 4
1868	0 5 9	0 5 9
1869	0 4 9	0 4 10
1870	0 5 0	0 5 1½
1871	0 5 7½	0 5 9
1872	0 5 0½	0 5 3
1873	0 5 1	0 5 8½
1874	0 6 9	0 6 1½
1875	0 4 7½	0 4 6
1876	0 5 1½	0 5 6
1877	0 6 1½	0 6 6
1878	0 6 1½	0 5 7½
1879	0 5 0	0 4 9½
1880	0 4 8	0 4 9
1881	0 4 1	0 4 3
1882	0 5 5	0 5 6
1883	0 5 1½	0 5 2
1884	0 4 3	0 4 3
1885	0 3 10½	0 3 7½
1886	0 4 3½	0 4 5
1887	0 3 10	0 3 11
1888	0 3 6	0 3 6½
1889	0 4 9	0 4 9
1890	0 3 6	0 3 6
1891	0 3 7½	0 3 10

WHEAT CROP OF THE WORLD.

The importance of Australasia in the wheat markets of the world is not great, since out of a total production of about 2,194 million bushels raised in 1890 only about 33 million bushels, or 1·05 per cent., were Australasian. The following statement, based on the returns of the U.S. Department of Agriculture, shows the approximate crop of the world for the year named:—

Wheat production of the World.

Countries.	Yield.
	bushels.
United States	399,262,000
Canada	39,231,000
Argentine States and Chili	60,271,000
Austria	51,441,000
Hungary	165,345,000
France	338,902,000
Germany	94,899,000
Great Britain and Ireland	78,306,000
Italy	126,641,000
Roumania	63,954,000
Russia and Poland	220,082,000
Spain	70,143,000
Turkey	37,135,000
Other European Countries	69,330,000
India	235,346,000
Other Asiatic Countries	72,206,000
Africa	38,915,000
*Australasia	32,840,000
Other countries	
Total	2,194,249,000

* Yield 1890-91.

CONSUMPTION AND PRODUCTION OF BREADSTUFFS.

The production of wheat still remains considerably below the consumption of the Colony. The accompanying table has been prepared with a view to illustrate the state of the Colony in this respect, and shows the total consumption of wheat, the home production, and the net deficiency for twenty-nine years.

Production of wheat not equal to demand.

Apparent Consumption and Production of Breadstuffs in New South Wales.

Year.	*Apparent consumption.	†Available home production.	Net deficiency.	†Apparent consumption of wheat per head.	†Home production per head.
	Bushels.	Bushels.	Bushels.	Bushels.	Bushels.
1862	2,333,614	1,458,715	874,899	6·4	4·0
1863	1,867,639	912,234	955,405	5·0	2·4
1864	2,590,623	667,729	1,922,894	6·7	1·7
1865	2,487,146	1,072,727	1,414,419	6·1	2·6
1866	2,706,766	775,307	1,931,459	6·5	1·8
1867	3,188,730	2,023,832	1,164,898	7·3	4·6
1868	2,449,400	1,214,233	1,235,167	5·4	2·7
1869	2,894,180	1,635,998	1,258,182	6·1	3·5
1870	4,258,515	2,992,978	1,265,537	8·7	6·1
1871	2,503,487	796,055	1,707,432	4·9	1·5
1872	3,198,375	1,998,956	1,199,419	6·1	3·8
1873	4,064,706	2,680,177	1,384,529	7·5	4·9
1874	3,388,065	2,019,784	1,368,281	6·0	3·6
1875	3,856,142	1,964,678	1,891,464	6·6	3·4
1876	3,647,938	1,755,235	1,892,703	6·0	2·9
1877	3,624,066	2,134,070	1,489,996	5·8	3·4
1878	4,271,220	2,125,332	2,145,888	6·5	3·2
1879	4,763,341	3,116,015	1,647,326	6·9	4·5
1880	5,149,867	3,245,422	1,904,445	7·1	4·5
1881	4,267,446	3,390,710	876,736	5·6	4·4
1882	5,289,216	3,043,525	2,245,691	6·7	3·8
1883	5,023,468	3,618,475	1,404,993	6·1	4·4
1884	5,737,260	3,893,146	1,844,114	6·7	4·5
1885	6,520,784	3,808,908	2,711,876	7·3	4·3
1886	5,893,766	2,218,383	3,675,383	6·3	2·4
1887	7,809,642	5,306,682	2,502,960	8·1	5·5
1888	7,909,104	4,186,298	3,722,806	7·8	4·1
1889	6,524,438	1,444,000	5,080,438	5·9	1·3
1890	7,916,391	6,049,010	1,867,381	7·2	5·5

* No account is taken of the quantity added to or taken from stocks as the case may

† Exclusive of wheat required for seed.

In this table a higher figure is given for the available production of 1889 than in previous ones. It is thought t much more gloomy view of the harvest was taken in districts than was justified by the actual results. What believed to be the right figures have therefore been ins Taking the above table as it stands a false idea would pro be formed if the result of any one year were separately com with that of any other, as it frequently happens that the sactions of one year affect the trade of the following year very large extent.

Consumption in different years compared.

Nevertheless the average yearly consumption, calculated over a series of years, may be ascertained from those figures with some degree of accuracy, and will be found to amount to 6·4 bushels per head of the mean population during a period of twenty-eight years, and 6·5 bushels per head if only the last twelve years are taken into consideration.

From the following table, in which account is taken of the position of the market at the end of each year and of the quantity by which the stock on hand was either increased or diminished during the year, the true average yearly consumption per head is ascertained to amount to 6·4 bushels, a result identical with that obtained by the former method. The true average consumption will however be found to alter very little from one year to the other, and to maintain itself at a figure closely approximating the general average of the period. The amount of home production for the year 1887, given in the table on page 458, is more than stated below. It is believed that about one million bushels were injured by rain, and therefore did not enter into consumption.

Consumption of Breadstuffs in New South Wales.

Year.	Stocks at end of year.	Stocks increased or diminished during year.	Local production in excess of seed.	Net import of flour and grain.	Total consumption.	For food only per head.
	Bushels.	Bushels.	Bushels.	Bushels.	Bushels.	Bushels.
1877	310,000	......	....	....	....	....
1878	305,000	*5,000	2,125,000	2,146,000	4,276,000	6·50
1879	605,000	300,000	3,116,000	1,647,000	4,463,000	6·46
1880	1,000,000	395,000	3,245,000	1,904,000	4,754,000	6·55
1881	350,000	*650,000	3,391,000	877,000	4,918,000	6·46
1882	490,000	140,000	3,044,000	2,246,000	5,150,000	6·47
1883	300,000	*190,000	3,618,000	1,405,000	5,213,000	6·24
1884	310,000	10,000	3,893,000	1,844,000	5,727,000	6·50
1885	750,000	440,000	3,809,000	2,712,000	6,081,000	6·53
1886	320,000	*430,000	2,218,000	3,675,000	6,323,000	6·45
1887	470,000	150,000	4,300,000	2,503,000	6,653,000	6·56
1888	1,240,000	770,000	4,186,000	3,723,000	7,139,000	6·70
1889	590,000	*650,000	1,440,000	5,100,000	7,190,000	6·49
1890	800,000	210,000	6,049,000	1,877,000	7,716,000	7·00

* Decrease during year.

Referring to the table on the previous page, showing the relation between the apparent consumption and the home production of breadstuffs, it will be seen that during the first half of the period

Average yearly production.

covered by the table the production was slightly more l consumption, the deficiency being about 48 per cent. I half of the series the home production had somewh so that the deficiency was scarcely more than 42 per

It will be seen from the table last given, as well preceding one, that New South Wales is still far re the position of being able to supply the wheat requ food of its inhabitants. From the following summ would seem that in this respect the country is little be it was at the earliest period covered by the figures :—

Period for which an average has been taken.	Consumption of wheat per head.	Home produce per head.
Years.	Bushels per annum.	Bushels per annum.
1862–66	6·1	2·5
1867–71	6·5	3·7
1872–76	6·4	3·7
1877–81	6·4	4·0
1882–86	6·6	3·9
1887–91	7·1	3·9

In the above figures the production and consump have been estimated. With this allowance the defici last four years was 3·2 bushels per head, equivale cent. of the whole consumption. Taking for grant consumption of wheat will not be more than 6·4 bush during 1892, the probable requirements for the c exclusive of seed, will be 7,700,000 bushels, to obta a crop be reaped averaging, say, 13·22 bushels per ac the mean production of New South Wales for the years, the breadth of land to be sown would need to acres, or 56 per cent. more than the grain-producing past season.

The average consumption of wheat in New S as shown above amounts to 6·4 bushels per head; a is higher than that of most countries whose r been available for reference; the excess over that of Kingdom being 0·5 bushels per head. The consump what is used for all purposes except seed, a fact wh borne in mind, as the quantity of flour used for the manufacture of biscuits and other articles, as well as for other than food purposes, is not inconsiderable. The following is the average consumption for the principal countries:—

Average consumption.

	Consumption per Head. (Bushels.)
United Kingdom	5·9
France	8·1
Germany	3·0
Russia	2·1
Austria	2·9
Italy	5·4
Spain and Portugal	6·4
Belgium and Holland	5·0
Scandinavia	1·4
Turkey	6·1
United States	5·4
Canada	6·6
Australasia	6·6

That of the Australasian Colonies will be found below:—

New South Wales	6·50
Victoria	6·28
South Australia	6·50
Queensland	6·09
Tasmania	6·70
New Zealand	7·56

The consumption of Victoria has been estimated from the quantity of flour made, less the net imports, as stated in the Victorian Year Book. The crop returns would give for the past five years an average consumption of 5·2 bushels. It will therefore be seen that there is no correspondence between the two sets of figures.

Importation of breadstuffs.

The relative proportions of flour and wheat imported have changed very considerably during the last twenty-five years, as will be seen hereunder:—

Average yearly Import of Flour and Wheat.

Period.	Flour in equivalent of wheat.	Wheat.
	Bushels.	Bushels.
1862–66	1,066,892	801,765
1867–71	905,540	750,705
1872–76	1,012,110	838,388
1877–81	1,529,140	545,914
1882–86	2,484,045	613,180
1887–91	3,191,375	1,250,502

Decline in quantity of wheat imported.

These figures would seem to warrant the supposition that the mill-power of the Colony is deficient, but this is only a partial

view of the case. A comparison between the importation of f
and the total home consumption gives an entirely different re
as will be seen from the next table. The figures in each case
the yearly averages for the different periods:—

Comparison between amount of Flour Imported and Mad
in the Colony.

Period.	Total consumption of flour in equivalent of wheat. — Yearly average.	Flour imported for home consumption in equivalent of wheat. — Yearly average.	Flour manufactured in the Colony in equivalent of wheat. — Yearly average.	Percentage of manufactur[illegible] the Colony to consumpti[illegible] — Yearly ave[illegible]
	Bushels.	Bushels.	Bushels.	
1862–66	2,397,159	644,206	1,752,952	73·1
1867–71	3,058,863	610,430	2,448,433	80·[illegible]
1872–76	3,631,045	804,692	2,826,353	77·[illegible]
1877–81	4,415,189	1,170,719	3,244,470	73·[illegible]
1882–86	5,692,898	1,835,218	3,857,680	67·[illegible]
1887–90	7,384,445	2,203,582	5,380,863	72·[illegible]

Mill-power and consumption.

It will be seen from this table that though the mill-power of Colony, or rather the manufacture of flour, has hardly kept with the increase in consumption, the actual quantity of manufactured yearly has increased from an average of 1,752 bushels to 5,380,863 bushels.

The change in the character of the imports noted above, th the substitution of flour for grain, is attributable to a chan the markets whence the supply is drawn, Victoria having large extent superseded South Australia. The prominenc Victoria as an exporter of breadstuffs to New South Wales from 1878, and the excess of flour over wheat exported by Colony is very pronounced. South Australia, whence the supply of New South Wales was formerly drawn, and from w large quantities are still obtained, has, since the competitio Victoria became formidable to her, greatly diminished the portion of wheat to flour, so that latterly the quantity of S Australian wheat sent to this Colony has been comparati insignificant. Of late years New Zealand has become an impor factor in the grain market, and the general failure of the cr 1888–9 throughout continental Australia operated greatly in f of that Colony, whose crop was as bountiful as that of the rest of Australasia was scanty.

Export of breadstuffs.

The export of breadstuffs from New South Wales represents for the most part a re-export of foreign produce, Queensland being the chief buyer. In the year 1881 the export, which had previously been small, suddenly increased threefold. And though showing a decline during the succeeding years it still retains respectable proportions, the average during the last five years being about 23 per cent. of the total quantity imported.

Wheat grown for hay.

Wheat is also grown in considerable quantities for hay and dry fodder for cattle, and the area under cultivation is steadily increasing, although the produce is still short of the requirements of the country. The whole of the wheat grown for hay in the Colony is consumed locally. The following statement shows the extent of land under wheat for hay, with the yearly produce, during fourteen years:—

Area under Wheat for Hay, and Yield.

Year ended 31 March.	Acres.	Produce in tons.	Average per acre	Year ended 31 March.	Acres.	Produce in tons.	Average per acre.
1877	17,115	21,297	1·24	1885	86,564	87,328	1·01
1878	29,640	29,137	0·98	1886	105,122	74,606	0·71
1879	22,888	31,320	1·36	1887	74,070	109,851	1·48
1880	25,281	32,943	1·30	1888	60,340	70,392	1·16
1881	41,137	44,037	1·07	1889	102,838	42,041	0·41
1882	39,428	42,378	1·07	1890	82,880	140,348	1·69
1883	42,592	43,997	1·03	1891	83,827	96,014	1·15
1884	49,348	55,119	1·12				

Cultivation of wheat for hay increasing.

From the foregoing figures it will be seen that the cultivation of wheat for hay is increasing at a much greater ratio than for grain, the area so cultivated having reached in 1888–89 nearly five times that cultivated for the same purpose in 1877; since then the area devoted to hay was not so large, the seasons being generally so propitious that a greater proportion of the total area sown with wheat was allowed to come to grain than in former years. Long series of dry years may in some measure account for the increased area devoted to hay, but the steady demand for hay and chaff, wheaten as well as oaten, and the large import of this produce, fully justify an extensio cultivation. There still exists a considerable difference b the demand for hay and the supply from within the Col there were 54,779 tons of hay and chaff imported in 1889, pally for consumption in the Metropolitan district, and tons in 1890; but this difference is well within the capa the colony to produce, and the time is not far distant whe South Wales will become independent of Victoria for the of this commodity. South Australia will probably continu ever, to supply for some years to come the growing wants Barrier, Broken Hill, and Silverton districts.

The total area under wheat in 1890, both for grain and f was 417,060 acres, producing 3,649,216 bushels of grain, tons straw, and 96,014 tons of hay, the value of all k produce being £1,272,145.

MAIZE.

Principal centre of cultivation.

The cultivation of maize in this Colony is almost as im as that of wheat, and forms the staple industry in the valley coastal rivers, which are peculiarly adapted, both by soil a climate, for the growth of this cereal. On the table-land cultivation is attended with fair results, but as the land i elevation so does the average produce per acre proporti decrease. Attempts have been made to grow maize in the w division of the Colony, but success has only been met witl special conditions of natural or artificial irrigation, for th demands a considerable amount of moisture, and thrives b the moist climates of the coast than anywhere else in the c Although the area under maize is much less than that wheat cultivation, the gross yield obtained, measured in b is frequently as large as, and in some seasons greatly e that of wheat.

Distribution of production.

The following statement shows the distribution of th duction of maize in the Colony during the seven years ended with March, 1891, as well as the average yield ol in each district :—

districts of the Colony as regards its high and well average yield of wheat and other grain crops; a circ attributable to the general excellence of the soil, and t abundant and regular supply of rain with which the d favoured. The relative position of the districts of th where maize is principally grown is as follows:—

Maize-growing in various districts.

Districts.	Average per acre for the period 1884-1890.	Maximum average per acre for any one year.	Mini per (
	Bushels.	Bushels.	
North Coast	35·1	43·0	
Tumut	37·1	45·3	
South Coast	32·8	36·9	
Hawkesbury and Nepean	27·7	34·7	
Hunter River	27·1	33·0	
Glen Innes	21·7	24·9	
Tamworth and New England	18·7	23·0	
Mudgee	19·1	26·7	
Other districts, where maize is not grown in large quantities	17·4	21·8	

Increase in area devoted to maize.

The area under maize cultivation was increased fro acres in the year 1862 to 191,152 in 1891, and was there than trebled in twenty-nine years. Considered in the li general advance of settlement, particularly in those distri this cereal may be successfully cultivated, there is nothin able in the progress thus exhibited, especially as there is land in New South Wales fit for maize cultivation. T nevertheless, worthy of notice, that in the year 1888 an area of 24,705 acres was laid down with maize for grain greater increase than was shown during any of the previo eight years, with the exception of the year 1879, when 25, were added to the area under maize; last year the are an increase of 17,316 acres, or very nearly ten per c than the acreage of the previous year.

State of maize cultivation.

The following table shows the state of maize cultivati Colony during the period referred to—1862 to 1891 inc

Maize—Area under Crop, and Yield.

Year ended 31 March.	Area under crop.	Yield.	Average per acre.	Year ended 31 March.	Area under crop.	Yield.	Average per acre.
	Acres.	Bushels.	Bushels		Acres.	Bushels.	Bushels
1862	57,959	1,727,434	29·8	1878	105,510	3,551,806	33·6
1863	75,991	2,559,258	33·6	1879	130,582	4,420,580	33·8
1864	95,689	2,925,950	30·5	1880	135,034	4,761,856	35·2
1865	101,584	3,114,212	30·6	1881	127,196	4,518,897	35·5
1866	113,443	2,759,904	24·3	1882	117,478	4,330,956	36·9
1867	119,519	3,878,064	32·4	1883	118,180	4,057,635	34·3
1868	115,522	3,132,505	27·1	1884	123,634	4,538,604	36·7
1869	120,807	3,777,405	31·2	1885	115,600	3,389,505	29·3
1870	128,041	4,880,805	38·1	1886	132,709	4,336,163	32·6
1871	107,178	2,340,654	21·8	1887	146,957	3,825,146	26·0
1872	119,956	4,015,973	33·4	1888	171,662	4,953,125	28·8
1873	116,745	3,984,958	34·1	1889	166,101	4,910,404	29·5
1874	116,648	4,128,865	35·3	1890	173,836	5,354,827	30·8
1875	118,436	3,618,436	30·5	1891	191,152	5,713,205	29·9
1876	117,582	3,410,517	29·0				
1877	116,364	3,879,537	33·3	Mean for 30 years			31·6

The production per acre, as may be gathered from the foregoing figures, is a somewhat variable item, ranging from a minimum of 21·8 bushels, which was obtained in the year 1871, to a maximum of 38·1 in 1870. It is evident that the quantity of maize now grown in New South Wales is not only sufficient to meet the local demand, but also to supply the Southern colonies, to which the surplus might be exported. The present Sydney price of 2s. per bushel is higher than the amount the farmers realised on crops which, although excellent in some districts, were but indifferent in others, and at such rates maize can scarcely be considered a remunerative crop. Matters would have been worse had a maximum yield of 38 bushels per acre, such as that of 1870, been attained, as about seven and a quarter million bushels of this grain would have been thrown on a market which does not appear to be able to absorb much more than 5,000,000 bushels per season. The future of this branch of

Average produce per acre.

agricultural industry, in the present circumstances of th
seems therefore very limited, as, with the exception of
the Southern colonies, New South Wales is surrounded in
hemisphere by maize-producing countries, and even the E
markets offer little inducements to exporters. In some
maize is used as food for swine, but as there are only
swine in the Colony the demand for this purpose cannot
great. As the quantity of maize now grown is large
normal season than the consumption, it is not probable t
branch of farming can be profitably expanded unless it be
the requirements which would result from an extension c
breeding, or some similar industry.

Maize is not only cultivated as a grain crop, but a smal
sown for green food for cattle, chiefly on dairy farms.
the area thus cultivated was 4,161 acres, the greater par
Camden and south coast districts, and the electorate of the
The total area cultivated with maize in 1891 was 195,313

OATS.

Principal centres of oat cultivation.

This cereal is cultivated as a grain crop, principally in th
growing districts of the Colony; and as it is essentially a
of cold climates it thrives best in those parts of the coun
a winter of some severity. Bathurst, Carcoar, Orange,
and New England are the principal centres of oat cultiva
the latter district yields the best crops. The average
Colony for 1890–91 is 18·20, which is a good deal less t
average of the previous year. The Northern Tableland a
20·50 bushels, Tamworth heading the list with 22·50.
southern coast districts the average was 21·16, and th
western slopes yielded at the rate of 20·36 bushels to the

No oats are grown in the northern portion of the coastal
for the purpose of a grain crop. In the southern coast
the area under oats for grain is very limited, but that un
for hay or green food is not inconsiderable. The followi
illustrates the state of the cultivation of this crop since 18

Area in cultivation.

Oats.—Area under Crop, and Yield.

Year ended 31 March.	Area.	Production.	Average per acre.	Year ended 31 March.	Area.	Production.	Average per acre.
	Acres.	Bushels.	Bushels.		Acres	Bushels.	Bushels.
1862	7,224	152,426	21·1	1877	21,828	461,916	21·2
1863	9,968	201,415	20·2	1878	18,580	358,853	19·3
1864	13,022	213,924	16·4	1879	22,129	447,912	20·2
1865	14,098	189,524	13·4	1880	23,883	516,937	21·6
1866	10,939	116,005	10·6	1881	17,922	356,121	19·9
1867	14,914	304,028	20·4	1882	16,347	356,566	21·8
1868	13,142	156,965	11·9	1883	24,817	617,465	24·9
1869	12,129	164,687	13·6	1884	17,810	376,635	21·1
1870	17,301	400,766	23·2	1885	19,472	425,920	21·9
1871	10,683	119,365	11·2	1886	14,117	279,107	19·8
1872	13,795	280,887	20·3	1887	23,947	600,892	25·1
1873	13,586	270,967	19·9	1888	19,393	394,762	20·3
1874	16,524	322,449	19·5	1889	7,984	109,931	13·8
1875	17,973	293,135	16·3	1890	22,358	543,330	24·3
1876	18,855	352,966	18·7	1891	14,102	256,659	18·2

Cultivation of oats for grain.

It will be seen that the cultivation of oats for grain has been very irregularly pursued during the period embraced by this table, rising rapidly during the earlier years and remaining practically stationary since 1877. The market for oats is chiefly in the metropolitan district, and the demand depends largely upon the price of maize, and the fluctuation in the area devoted to the cultivation of this cereal for grain is very largely due to the uncertainty of sale.

Average yield per acre.

The average production of oats for the period 1862–91 was 19·7 bushels per acre, the minimum obtained in any year being 10·6 bushels in the season 1865-66, and the maximum 25·1 bushels in that of 1886–87. Compared with the other continental Colonies, New South Wales holds, in regard to average yield, the second rank, Victoria coming first, but both these colonies are surpassed by Tasmania and New Zealand. The climate of those two colonies is much more adapted for the successful cultivation of this grain, the average produce of New Zealand in particular being very nearly equal per acre to that of the United Kingdom, and on a par with the best oat-producing countries of the Old World.

Average yield of oats per acre in N.S. Wales and other colonies.

In the following table figures will be found giving the average produce per acre in each of the Australasian Colonies during seventeen years, the records for Queensland alone being incomplete.

Average Production of Oats in Bushels per Acre in the Australasian Colonies.

Colonies.	1874.	1875.	1876.	1877.	1878.	1879.	1880.	1881.	1882.	1883.	1884.	1885.	1886.	1887.	1888.	1889.	1890.	1891.	Mean.
New South Wales......	18·71	16·31	18·72	21·16	19·31	20·24	21·64	19·87	21·81	24·88	21·15	21·87	19·77	25·08	20·35	13·77	24·30	18·20	20·40
Victoria	15·09	18·46	21·92	10·91	19·39	17·60	24·00	17·62	24·57	26·17	25·07	23·40	21·72	22·91	22·92	14·20	23·87	22·26	21·20
*South Australia	10·61	14·61	16·00	10·65	11·96	12·01	15·02	11·50	10·06	11·13	14·65	12·20	12·20	12·20	12·20	5·65	12·76	9·32	12·00
Queensland	..	..	..	..	10·11	9·65	24·74	17·94	12·74	16·58	8·90	15·17	4·84	10·41	24·26	5·65	19·41	21·82	14·44
Western Australia......	19·22	16·00	15·00	15·00	14·00	18·02	19·00	19·00	10·00	15·03	17·00	18·00	14·50	16·00	15·13	[illegible]	20·00	19·50	16·88
Tasmania..............	20·98	26·82	25·40	24·21	22·32	24·82	28·01	22·13	28·44	27·34	27·30	28·65	26·82	[illegible]	18·20	27·97	28·60	25·04	25·54
New Zealand	29·81	35·22	37·70	31·24	31·08	30·11	36·53	32·05	28·45	32·89	35·11	34·84	26·11	[illegible]	31·24	[illegible]	32·09	28·73	31·93

* No returns were collected from 1886 to 1889.

The average yield in the principal countries of the world where oats are extensively grown is as follows:—

Average yield in principal countries.

Principal oat-growing countries.	Average produce of oats per acre.
	Bushels.
Holland	42·1
Belgium	41·8
Norway	39·7
United Kingdom	37·7
Denmark	32·3
France	26·0
United States of America	26·0
Germany	21·9
Austria	20·9
Hungary	20·2
Italy	19·3
Russia	12·3
Cape of Good Hope	8·1
New South Wales	20·5

Cultivation of oats neglected.

The cultivation of oats as a staple agricultural crop has been much neglected in New South Wales, though the return has not been unsatisfactory. It is possible that in the near future this grain will receive greater attention, especially as the deficiency between the production and the consumption is very considerable. The elevated districts of Monaro, Argyle, Bathurst, and New England, in preference to other parts of the Colony, contain vast areas of land where the cultivation of oats could be carried on with remunerative results.

Oats as a fattening food

In connection with this subject it may not be generally known that the relative nourishment of oats exceeds that of either maize or wheat, weight for weight. If 100 be taken as the value of oats for fattening purposes, the respective values of equal weights of the other cereals are:—

Oats	100
Wheat	70
Maize	62

And for equal measures:—

Oats	100
Wheat	131
Maize	107

The production of this grain is far from satisfying the w the Colony, and the importation is, therefore, very large, 1,5 bushels of the estimated value of £152,302, having been in from abroad in the year 1890. New Zealand is the p source of supply, the quantity obtained from that colony i being 1,315,009 bushels. Much yet remains to be done the Colony can be independent of outside assistance in re the supply of oats, as, for some years past the average q produced was only 25 per cent. of the amount consumed, an would thus be an ample market within New South Wales produce of 62,000 acres more than is usually reaped.

Supply from New Zealand.

In parts of the Colony where the climate is not suita maturing the grain, a large area is sown for hay. The area oats for this purpose has increased from 28,109 acres in 1 126,488 acres in 1887, being over four and a half times a in the latter as in the former year. In 1888 the area und for hay had fallen to 86,451 acres, and it was slightly lo 1889. In 1890, however, there was an increase to 103,12 but last year the area had fallen to 70,463. Oaten hay is n demand, and sells readily at remunerative prices; and, as t less expense and lighter labour attached to this form of culti the system of growing oats for hay is consequently m favour with the farmers of New South Wales than the tion of the grain. The area under the two crops s each other in the following relation in the year 1890-91

Oaten hay in demand.

Oats for hay and green food.

Area under oats for grain	14,102 acre
Area under oats for hay	70,463 ,,
Total	84,565 acre

The area harvested for grain was only 16·7 per cent. total area sown with oats. The following statement sh cultivation of oaten hay since 1877, and the yield per acre.

Cultivation of Oats for Hay.

Year ended March.	Area.	Produce.	
		Total.	Per acre.
	acres.	tons.	tons.
1877	77,212	98,901	1·28
1878	79,333	87,660	1·10
1879	61,684	75,138	1·21
1880	67,877	84,915	1·25
1881	68,758	77,811	1·13
1882	86,068	100,773	1·17
1883	112,477	140,979	1·25
1884	107,451	113,899	1·06
1885	121,922	149,489	1·22
1886	96,946	72,484	0·75
1887	126,488	182,921	1·44
1888	86.451	96,126	1·11
1889	85,439	40,753	0·47
1890	103,120	156,920	1·52
1891	70,463	71,305	1·01

In addition to the area cultivated for grain and hay, a small extent of land is yearly sown for green food; last season 2,491 acres of oat lands were so used. The total area under oats during the year ending 31st March, 1891, was therefore 87,056 acres in all.

BARLEY.

The cultivation of barley is very limited, the total area under grain in 1890 being only 5,440 acres,—less than it was twenty-six years ago, but decreased to 4,937 acres in 1891. The following table illustrates the state of barley cultivation since the year 1862. It will be seen that the production of 1889 was less than in any year of the series, 1863 alone excepted, but in 1891 the production amounted to 81,383 bushels.

Cultivation of Barley for Grain.

Year ended 31 March.	Area under barley for grain.	Production.	Year ended 31 March.	Area under barley for grain.	B
	Acres.	Bushels.		Acres.	
1862	3,924	41,054	1877	5,662	
1863	2,538	30,636	1878	5,055	
1864	4,093	67,009	1879	6,152	
1865	4,724	60,355	1880	6,130	
1866	5,844	58,370	1881	6,056	
1867	6,211	91,741	1882	6,496	
1868	5,140	62,392	1883	6,473	
1869	6,397	94,715	1884	5,081	
1870	9,152	148,617	1885	7,035	
1871	4,650	47,701	1886	5,297	
1872	3,462	55,284	1887	6,079	
1873	3,727	70,708	1888	4,402	
1874	3,559	66,225	1889	3,318	
1875	3,984	69,053	1890	5,440	
1876	4,817	98,756	1891	4,937	

Barley grown in the Murray Valley.

Nearly one-fourth of the whole acreage under barley found in the central table-land, and a large proportion is pro the western slopes and table-land of the Southern Divisio electorate having the largest area of barley for grain is th Hunter, and Tamworth also had a large area. Very littl is cultivated in the northern part of New South Wales, it might be grown successfully in the New England distri

Average production.

The average production per acre during the season 1890 16·48 bushels per acre, or equal to 3·31 per cent. below the for the previous ten years, which amounted to 19·79 bushe retrograde condition of this industry is due to the sn uncertain demand for the grain within the Colony.

Quantity of barley imported.

In 1890 the quantity of barley imported to make deficiency of home production amounted to 48,190 bushel at £6,723, principally obtained from New Zealand and It would therefore require a very little effort on the pa farmers to bring the production of this grain up to the the consumption.

Barley or green food for cattle.

An area very nearly equal to that cultivated for grain i said down for hay, and for the purpose of providing gree for cattle. During last season the figures were 4,937 acres of barley for grain; 3,225 acres of barley for hay and green food, the total area cultivated being 8,164 acres.

PRODUCTION AND CONSUMPTION OF GRAIN.

The total consumption of grain of all kinds in New South Wales, calculated on the basis of the last ten years, amounts to 13·5 bushels per head of population, whilst the produce of the Colony is only 9·6 bushels. The deficiency in the production of wheat amounts to 38·7 per cent., barley, 33·3 per cent., and oats, 72·1 per cent. There is, however, an excess in the production of maize over the local consumption, amounting to 3·1 per cent., which reduces the total average deficiency in the production of the principal grain crops to 35 per cent. There is no apparent reason why the local production of grain should not equal the local demand; on the contrary, the resources of the Colony are such that under normal conditions the supply of grain should largely exceed the requirements, and an increasing excess of production become yearly available for export, either as grain or meat.

N.S.W. yield greater than other colonies.

The experience of past years distinctly shows that in the matter of soil, climate, and other natural conditions, New South Wales is, on the whole, better favoured, and consequently her average yield per acre of wheat, maize, and barley, is greater than that of any other continental Australian province, Victoria not excepted. Extending the field of comparison, the production of cereals is found to reach an average which places New South Wales on a level with countries usually considered as rich agricultural states. It is better than the average yield of the United States, of Italy, and Hungary; and, in some respects, almost on a level with that of Germany, Austria, and France. The area adapted for cereal growing is very considerable, and with a better knowledge of the capabilities of the various kinds of soils and well devised means of water storage, there should be practically no limit to the production of grain.

MINOR GRAIN CROPS.

The minor grain crops harvested are rye, millet, sorgh imphee. Little can be said on this subject except that, a case of other cereals, the suitability of the soil for their pr is an established fact. There is, however, so little dem these kinds of grain that their cultivation in New South very limited.

Rye. The area under rye for grain in 1890 covered 672 a produce from which was 9,126 bushels, or at the rate bushels to the acre. There were also 516 acres of rye s green food.

Millet. Millet was only cultivated over an area of 672 acres, which were harvested for grain, the remaining 421 acres b green for cattle. The greater part of the crop of mi obtained in the Hunter River valley. The average produ the Colony amounted to 9·63 bushels per acre.

Sorghum and imphee. The cultivation of sorghum and imphee for grain ap have been abandoned, but the area sown in 1890 for gre for cattle amounted to 8,267 acres, chiefly within the dairy districts of Kiama, Illawarra, and Shoalhaven.

SOWN GRASSES, AS FOOD FOR CATTLE.

The area sown under green food and grasses for cattle stantly increasing in the Colony, and in the course of the ye there were under artificial grasses 388,715 acres, an inc 171,312 acres over the area so cultivated in the previous y

Lucerne. Lucerne and other permanent grasses are laid down pri in the Hunter districts, and the south coast, 172,251 acre thus cultivated in the South Coast districts alone. The of sowing permanent grasses is also extending to th coast districts, and in 1890 there were 46,503 acres under the Richmond district. It is, however, in those portions Colony where dairy farming is principally carried on t practice of laying down permanent grasses is most general

POTATOES.

Area under potatoes.

The cultivation of the potato has shown little improvement for many years past. In regard to acreage under crop, the area planted last year was the largest recorded, with the exception of that of 1888, though the crops have frequently been equalled or exceeded. At present the Colony has to make up by importation from the other colonies, a considerable deficiency, which in 1890 amounted to 50,200 tons, or 50 per cent. of the total consumption for the year, and in 1891 to 39,500 tons. The total yield during the same season amounted to 52,791 tons. The following table illustrates the state of the cultivation of potatoes during each year since 1862:—

Total production and yield per acre.

Area under Potatoes, and Yield.

Year ended 31 March.	Acres.	Tons.	Year ended 31 March.	Acres.	Tons.
1862	10,040	30,942	1877	14,171	42,939
1863	9,284	24,167	1878	13,862	34,957
1864	11,618	32,141	1879	16,724	53,590
1865	14,398	52,061	1880	19,271	62,228
1866	15,210	31,367	1881	19,095	52,112
1867	18,810	43,870	1882	15,943	44,323
1868	15,440	33,482	1883	14,462	43,461
1869	16,391	30,768	1884	14,953	36,977
1870	17,132	54,200	1885	12,417	31,335
1871	13,927	34,118	1886	15,166	38,695
1872	14,770	44,758	1887	17,322	45,803
1873	15,124	45,112	1888	20,915	61,455
1874	14,212	42,281	1889	15,419	36,839
1875	13,604	38,564	1890	17,551	50,096
1876	13,805	41,203	1891	19,406	52,791

Principal centres of cultivation.

The centres of potato-growing at present are Orange, Carcoar, Argyle, and New England. Its cultivation is, however, very widely distributed throughout the Colony, but in many places formerly well-known for its production, it has been largely displaced by maize and other cereals.

TOBACCO.

Soil and climate of New South Wales suited for tobacco.

Both the soil and climate of the Colony of are well fitted for the growth of the tobacco however, demands for its proper cultivation spe the part of the growers, and for this reason cultivated as would otherwise be the case. In first shown on the subsequent table, there we under cultivation, producing 15,315 cwt. of lea following years, however, the area had largely in the agricultural districts of Argyle and the Hu Since then the growth of tobacco seems to entirely abandoned in the districts where it w but has spread to other parts of the Colony; th Macquarie, and Gundagai electorates being n centres of production. Nearly one-half of all in the Colony in 1890 was obtained in those

Chinese principal cultivators.

cultivation is chiefly in the hands of Chine agriculturists apparently possessing the neces proper cultivation and preparation of the leaf.

Area and production.

From the year 1881 the area devoted to tobacco very largely increased, and it is a not the quantity of locally grown leaf used now proportion of the total quantity manufacture In the year 1889 there was a large increase in tobacco, the area being more than four times th a corresponding increase in the yield of leaf. As not compare favorably with the American, it coul profitably, and the consequence was that a large leaf remained upon the farmers' hands, especiall the Tumut, and the quantity that was sold realis tory figures. The natural result was that many o since abandoned the cultivation of tobacco in favo Last year there was a great falling off in the area the yield therefrom. The following table shows t industry during the last twenty-nine years:—

Cultivation of Tobacco.

Year ended 31 March.	Area.	Production.	Year ended 31 March.	Area.	Production.
	Acres.	Cwt.		Acres.	Cwt.
1863	896	15,315	1878	399	3,049
1864	534	4,851	1879	835	7,932
1865	807	4,036	1880	592	6,221
1866	1,499	7,469	1881	1,791	19,469
1867	1,326	2,478	1882	1,625	18,311
1868	627	6,085	1883	1,815	17,540
1869	875	7,925	1884	1,785	20,006
1870	366	3,192	1885	1,046	9,914
1871	225	700	1886	1,603	22,947
1872	567	4,475	1887	1,203	13,642
1873	440	2,751	1888	2,371	23,465
1874	199	1,261	1889	4,833	55,478
1875	539	6,069	1890	3,239	27,724
1876	491	4,098	1891	1,148	10,592
1877	333	2,440			

Over production of tobacco.

The total consumption of manufactured tobacco and cigars during 1890 was 3,028,962 lb., of which 1,915,040 lb. were made in the Colony out of 569,420 lb. of American leaf and 1,345,620 lb. locally grown. The production for 1891 is equal to 1,186,304 lb., and allowing one-third for damage and waste, there will still remain 790,800 lb., a quantity little more than half the probable requirements. As the production of previous years was larger than the local requirements, stocks of leaf have accumulated, so that there is in all likelihood amply sufficient leaf for the current season, and prices have declined. The prospects of the crop of the year 1891-92, however, are not favorable, as blight has affected many districts, causing much land to be withdrawn from cultivation. Under these circumstances the area cropped has naturally diminished.

SUGAR-CANE.

Introduction of the sugar-cane in New South Wales.

The first agricultural returns in which mention is made cultivation of the sugar-cane and the production of sugar i South Wales only date from 1863. In that year 2 acr returned as having produced 280 lb. of sugar, and it will strange that out of this quantity 220 lb. were stated to be t duce of one acre of cane, grown in the northern part of the of Bathurst, while the remaining 60 lb. were produced on th of the Macleay River. The district last mentioned may sidered as the principal seat of this industry, during its stages. Cane cultivation, however, soon extended to the ward, and in a very few years the richest portions of th valleys of the Clarence, Richmond, Tweed, and Brunswic occupied by settlers engaged in the planting and growing (Mills were erected in the chief centres of cane cultivation, ar growing and sugar manufacturing are now the principal a established industries of the north-eastern portions of the C

Northern rivers suit sugar-cane.

The soil and climate of the valleys of the northern river most respects well adapted to the successful cultivation sugar-cane. Occasional spring frosts, however, cause consi damage, and it was the risk of failure from this cause led the settlers on the Macleay to seek a warmer climate north, free from the danger arising from frost. In this th be said to have succeeded, though in the Clarence, Ric and Tweed valleys, frosts are not altogether unknown.

Progress of sugar-growing.

The following table shows the progress of this industry the last thirteen years. The figures relating to the area placed under cane are obtainable for earlier dates, but the of tons produced cannot be ascertained prior to 1876. Th cane not being an annual crop, the area under cultivation l divided, as far as practicable, into productive and non-pro the former representing the number of acres upon whi was cut during the season, and the latter the area over ı was unfit for the mill, or allowed to stand for another year

Area in Production of Sugar-cane.

Progress of sugar-growing.

Year.	Area.		Total.	Production in tons of cane.
	Productive.	Non-productive.		
	Acres.	Acres.	Acres.	
1863	....	....	2	....
1864	....	....	22	....
1865	....	....	141	....
1866	....	....	116	....
1867	....	....	647	....
1868	....	....	2,584	....
1869	....	....	3,917	....
1870	1,475	2,607	4,082	....
1871	1,995	2,399	4,394	....
1872	3,470	2,001	5,471	....
1873	3,565	3,105	6,670	....
1874	4,087	4,453	8,540	....
1875	3,654	2,800	6,454	....
1876	3,524	3,231	6,755	99,430
1877	3,331	3,735	7,066	99,978
1878	2,949	4,489	7,438	104,192
1879	3,675	4,102	7,777	126,119
1880	4,465	6,506	10,971	121,616
1881	4,983	7,184	12,167	128,752
1882	6,362	7,176	13,538	169,192
1883	7,583	7,401	14,984	204,547
1884	6,997	10,520	17,517	105,328
1885	9,583	6,835	16,418	239,347
1886	5,915	9,202	15,117	167,959
1887	8,380	6,907	15,287	273,928
1888	4,997	10,284	15,281	110,218
1889	7,348	11,382	18,730	168,862
1890	8,344	12,102	20,446	277,252

Increase of area under crop.

The figures contained in the above table show the gradual progress of the sugar-growing industry, from the small beginnings of 1863. From the starting point of this cultivation until 1884 there is no break in the yearly increase of land put u During the four succeeding years, however, there was a t retrogress, and the area cultivated in 1888 was less by 2 than in 1884, or 12·7 per cent.; an increase took pla and 1890, and the area under cane reached 20,446 ac last mentioned year. The low price of sugar and the state of the markets of the world a few years ago, sugar manufacturers to correspondingly reduce the pr for the canes, and so caused the abandonment of this by the small farmers, who found in the growth of variable results for their labour. Sugar-cane is gener the second year of its growth, the fields being replanted have given crops for three or four seasons at most, a planting of cane has been conducted at irregular inter chanced that seasons of large production have been followe crops in the immediately succeeding year. This will acco alternately large and small areas of productive cane years, which the preceding table shows. From plan full bearing the weight of cane cut varies from 25 t while the price paid ranges from 11s. to 13s. per ton, i to the cost of cutting, so that the annual yield is from £10 per acre planted.

Low price of sugar.

Principal centres of sugar-cane cultivation.

The Richmond River electorate is now the principal sugar-cane cultivation, and in 1890 there were 623 holdi which areas, varying from 2 to 714 acres in extent, wer to this culture. The total area so planted was 12,35 over three-fifths of the whole area under cane in the Co yield obtained from 5,003 acres of productive cane an 149,968 tons, showing an average of 29·97 tons per acre

On the Clarence River, in the electoral districts of G the Clarence, there were, in 1890, 446 holdings, on w was grown, the aggregate area under this crop being 7, As in the Richmond River district, the majority of farmer sugar-cane in addition to other crops, and only a few entirely devoted to its cultivation. Some planters have areas of from 25 to 100 acres in extent under cane, but their number is very limited. The yield in the Clarence and Grafton electorates was 124,899 tons, or an average of 38·44 tons per acre, cut on an area of 3,249 acres.

In the Macleay River district the area devoted to sugar-cane is now insignificant, only 232 acres having been returned in 1890 as under crop, of which 91 acres were productive. Total crop of sugar.

The estates on which sugar-cane is grown number 1,082, and the whole crop of sugar-cane during the last season amounted to 277,252 tons, obtained from 8,344 acres, showing an average production of 33·23 tons per acre, which is 7·86 tons above the average of the former ten years. On the estates belonging to the Colonial Sugar-refining Company, the conduct of the business of the plantation has been entrusted to practical men, and no money spared to obtain the most approved and complete plant for the manufacture of sugar. This company's mills on the Richmond River are among the most complete in any part of the world, and the sugar manufactured is equal to the best Mauritius and West Indian samples. The quantity of sugar consumed in the Colony during the past two years amounted to 92,567 tons, of which 32,064 tons were the product of the local plantations, the area cut in these years being 15,692 acres. The yield of sugar per ton of course varies with the density of the juice, but in ordinary seasons this may be set down at somewhat over 9 per cent.

VINES AND WINE PRODUCTION.

In every part of the Colony, excepting the essentially subtropical portion, and the higher parts of the mountain ranges, grape vines thrive well, and bear large crops of succulent fruit, equal in size, appearance, and flavour, to the most renowned products of France, the Rhinelands, and Spain; yet the vine-growing and wine manufacturing industries are still in their infancy in this Colony, although their prospects are as hopeful as could be desired. With a demand which the present production hardly satisfies, and the opening up of a market in England, where New South Wales in common with other Australian wines Markets for Australian wine.

have obtained due appreciation, the future of vine-growi fairly assured. The depreciation which French and otl wines have suffered, both in quantity and in quality, ow scourge of the phylloxera, is an additional reason fo growers of New South Wales looking forward to a future for their industry. How small the present pro Australia is compared with the total of the world w from the following table:—

Production of Wine in the principal wine-growing co of the world.

Country.	Production in million gallons.	Country.	I mi
Australia	3	Roumania	
Austria	92	Russia	
Algeria	72	Servia	
Cape Colony	5	Spain	
France	795	Switzerland	
Greece	46	Turkey and Cyprus	
Hungary	185	United States	
Italy	798		
Portugal	132	Total	

Vine planted in early days.

The vine was planted in the early days of the colo New South Wales, but it was not until the year 1828 growing and wine-making may be said to have been fa lished. In that year Mr. Busby returned from Euro large collection of cuttings from the most celebrated vi France, Spain, the Rhine valley, and other parts of the of Europe, and planted, on his estate at Kirkton in tl River district, a vineyard which has been the nursery c cipal vineyards of the Colony. Some years afterwards tl planted in the Murray valley, and in other districts, and w flourish so luxuriantly that the manufacture of win considerable attention. For a time, however, the prosp industry seemed very poor, and production diminished co owing, partly, to the want of a market, and partly to th the wine-makers, many of whom were not vignerons b possessed only a limited knowledge of the manufactu and produced at first an article of inferior and unsaleable quality. But in the principal vineyards of the Murray and the Hunter neither pains nor money was spared to introduce skilled labour and put up presses, vats, and other manufacturing appliances of the most approved pattern.

New South Wales wines at the Bordeaux Exhibition in 1882.

The results of this intelligent treatment became apparent, when prizes were awarded to the New South Wales wines at the Paris Exhibition of 1878, followed by an unbroken series of successes at the Exhibitions of Philadelphia, Sydney, Melbourne, and Amsterdam, and latterly at the Indian and Colonial Exhibition in London. But nowhere was the general excellence of the wines of New South Wales more fully recognized than at the Bordeaux Exhibition of 1882. There, in the principal centre of the wine trade of the world, the wines of New South Wales were classed by the most competent judges in the category of "Grands vins," and their value fully appreciated and established. The following statement shows the progress of the wine industry since 1862:—

Progress of vine-growing.

Area under Grape Vines and Production of Wine.

Year ended 31 March.	Total area under vines.	Area under vines for wine-making only.	Production.	Average per acre.	Year ended 31 March.	Total area under vines.	Area under vines for wine-making only.	Production.	Average per acre.
	Acres.	Acres.	Gallons.	Gallons.		Acres.	Acres.	Gallons.	Gallons.
1862	1,130	562	85,328	151·83	1878	4,183	3,027	708,431	234·04
1863	1,460	795	144,888	182·25	1879	4,237	3,024	684,733	226·43
1864	1,641	880	136,976	155·65	1880	4,266	3,091	733,576	237·33
1865	1,849	945	161,299	170·69	1881	4,724	2,907	602,007	200·99
1866	2,126	1,243	168,123	135·25	1882	4,027	2,597	513,688	197·80
1867	2,281	1,358	242,183	178·33	1883	4,448	2,629	543,596	206·76
1868	2,532	1,483	285,283	192·37	1884	4,378	2,660	589,604	221·65
1869	3,117	1,917	412,587	215·22	1885	4,584	2,405	442,612	184·04
1870	3,907	2,039	460,321	225·75	1886	5,247	2,876	555,470	193·13
1871	4,504	2,371	342,674	144·53	1887	5,840	3,131	601,897	192·23
1872	4,152	2,466	413,321	167·61	1888	6,745	3,292	666,382	202·42
1873	4,090	2,568	451,450	175·80	1889	7,072	3,596	805,813	224·71
1874	4,547	3,183	578,985	181·90	1890	7,867	3,603	688,685	191·14
1875	4,306	3,077	684,256	222·37	1891	8,044	3,896	842,181	216·17
1876	4,459	3,163	831,749	262·96					
1877	4,457	3,217	799,709	248·59	Mean for 30 years......				205·10

Increase of wine industry.

The above figures show that the wine industry has con increased during the thirty years under examination, area planted being now nearly seven times what it wa beginning of the period. The average yield per acre advanced; but this latter is probably due to the fact th earlier period the proportion of young vines not in ful was greater than is at present the case. The years 18 and 1880 were the best of the series, the average p having in 1876 reached the large figure of 262·96 gallons The yield of wine last season is 7·86 per cent. below th of the previous ten years. In the Hunter River District was damaged by the heavy rains which fell when the gr nearly ripe and ready for gathering, causing a very gre the vignerons. The vintage in the Murray River va however, very successful. The total number of wine gr 1890 was 2,486, and the average area of each vineyard acres.

Number of growers.

The phylloxera vastatrix.

The "phylloxera vastatrix," which has caused some d the vineyards of the neighbouring colony of Victoria, nec stringent legislative measures, has also appeared in some of the Camden and Seven Hills districts, but, so far, causing any great ravages. A commission was appoin time ago to report on the appearance of the disease, and means of preventing its spread. The prohibition of the tion of vine-cuttings from abroad has been in force for so and the destruction of infested vineyards has been ca under the direction of the commission.

Cultivation of table grapes.

The industry is not restricted to the cultivation for wine-making purposes; on the contrary, a con area is devoted to the cultivation of table grapes, pr in the neighbourhood of Sydney, and in the dis Ryde, Parramatta, and other portions of Central Cum The area so cultivated in 1890 amounted to 2,072 ac ducing 3,355 tons of grapes, or at the rate of 1·6 tons of fruit per acre. There were also 2,076 acres of vines yet in an unproductive state.

ORANGE-GROWING.

First orangeries near Parramatta.

The cultivation of the orange has become one of the principal industries of the districts surrounding the metropolis. The first orange groves were planted near the town of Parramatta, and soon spread to the neighbouring districts of Ryde, Pennant Hills, Lane Cove, the whole of Central Cumberland, the Hawkesbury and Nepean valleys, and the mountain slopes of the Kurrajong district. The production of oranges has already attained such proportions that the growers are obliged to seek markets abroad for the disposal of their produce, as the demand, both in New South Wales and the adjacent colonies, is in some seasons exceeded by the supply. Efforts have been made of late to open up a market in England, as the fruit can be delivered in London at a time when the supply of oranges from Spain and other countries of the northern hemisphere has ceased.

State of orange growing in 1879.

The statistics relative to this branch of the agricultural industry are only available from the year 1879, when the area under oranges and lemons was 4,287 acres, which last year had increased to 11,288 acres, of which 8,737 were productive. The yield from that area amounted to 11,562,000 dozen oranges and lemons, or rather more than 1,320 dozen per acre. It is usually estimated that over 3,000 dozen per acre can be obtained in an average season from fair-sized trees in full bearing; it is therefore probable that the figures for 1890 included the return from a considerable number of young trees. The following shows the state of the industry in each year since 1879. The number of orangeries during 1890–91 was 2,848, the average area being about 4 acres.

Area of Orangeries.

Year ended 31 March.	Area of Orangeries.	Year ended 31 March.	Area of O
	Acres.		A
1879	4,287	1886	7,
1880	5,106	1887	7,
1881	5,939	1888	8,
1882	6,301	1889	10,
1883	6,716	1890	9,
1884	7,268	1891	11,
1885	6,911		

ORCHARDS AND GARDENS.

During the last ten years there has been very little in the area under gardens and orchards. The cultivati varieties of fruit besides oranges and grapes appears t gressing, instead of sharing in the progress observable all other branches of agriculture. Yet the Colony annually very large quantities of imported fruit, whicl successfully grown within its own limits. Leaving o sideration the large importation of tropical fruit from Caledonia, and Queensland, some of which might be cu the sub-tropical portion of New South Wales, the imp other fruit is very considerable. Thus in 1890, Tasman land, South Australia, Victoria, New Zealand, and t States, supplied New South Wales with green fruit to t £146,827, while other green fruit, mostly the produce subtropical countries, was imported to the amount o The importation of dried and candied fruit during the s amounted to £111,121, and that of nuts to £10,386. Wales is therefore dependent on the outside world, to of £344,600 for fruit, most of which could be adv cultivated within its own territory.

Large quantity of fruit imported.

Number of orchards.

The number of orchards during 1890-91 was 8,868, a 22,355 acres, of which 16,081 acres were productive, were not yet in bearing.

With regard to the figures representing the area of the orangeries and orchards, it should be understood that in many instances part of a holding is devoted to the growth of oranges and lemons, and part to the cultivation of other fruits, so that it is difficult sometimes to tell under which head the holding should be classed. It is believed that the area under oranges and lemons in 1890 was quite equal to that of the previous year, though the figures of 1889 and 1891 appear unduly large owing to the inclusion of areas which were in 1890 classed as orchards. Orangeries and Orchards.

AGRICULTURAL IMPLEMENTS.

A census of agricultural machines and other implements used in farming and allied pursuits was taken in 1891; they were divided into three classes—agricultural, pastoral, and dairy implements—showing the following as the number of the principal kinds in each class used throughout the Colony:— Agricultural implements.

	Number.		Number.
Agricultural Implements.		*Agricultural Implements.*	
Boilers—Steam	627	Extractors—Tree & Stump	460
No. of Horse-power	6,272	Food-preparing Apparatus	152
Carts and Waggons	63,254	Grinders—Bark	169
Crushers—Clod	531	Harrows—Zig-zag	24,258
,, Corn	2,138	,, Chain	2,162
Cultivators—Horse-power	723	,, Disc	2,437
Cutters—Bark	101	Hoes & Grubbers—Horse-pr.	787
,, Horse-pr.—Chaff	3,557	Huskers—Corn	1,596
,, Hand-pr. ,,	7,571	Incubators	304
,, Steam ,,	385	Mills—Bone	46
,, Travelling	54	,, Cider	16
Cutters and Slicers	111	,, Flour	76
Diggers—Potato	71	,, Horse-power	27
Distributors—Manure	7	,, Grape	81
Drills—Seed	150	,, Malt	24
Elevators or Stackers	49	,, Oil-cake	51

Agricultural Implements, &c.—continued.

	Number.		Number.
Agricultural Implements.		*Agricultural Implements.*	
Mowers—Hay	3,015	Seed Sowers — Broadcast—Hand-power	328
Ploughs—Single Furrow	38,675	Seed Sowers — Broadcast—Horse-power	408
,, Double ,,	6,378	Spraying Machines	139
,, Three ,,	707	Steam-engines—	
,, Four ,,	74	Fixed	649
,, Six ,,	154	No. of Horse-power	5,355
,, Above six ,,	35	Portable	767
,, Potato ,,	82	No. of Horse-power	3,723
,, Steam ,,	4	Traction	96
,, Stump-jumping	37	No. of Horse-power	222
,, Subsoil	68	Steam Cultivating Machinery—	
,, Sulky or Riding	265	Cultivators or Scarifiers	97
,, Vineyard	254	Harrows	46
Planters—Corn	515	Strippers	2,888
,, Potato	38	Threshing and Finishing Machines—	
Presses—Ensilage	63	Hand-power	1,483
,, Hay and Straw	763	Horse-power	435
,, Horse-power	27	Steam	145
,, Steam	3	Vats—Wine	2,979
,, Wine	311	Water-lifters — Chain or Bucket	449
Pulpers and Graters—Root	54	Wind-mills	728
Pumps—Hand-power	4,036	Winnowers—Hand-power	3,018
,, Horse-power	329	,, Horse-power	72
,, Californian	168	*Dairy Implements.*	
,, Steam	591	Churns—Horse-power	152
,, Irrigation	212	,, Handpower	11,907
Rakes—Horse-power—Hay	3,234	,, Steam	260
Reapers—Side delivery	585	Coolers and Refrigerators—Milk	621
Reapers and Mowers	1,993		
Reapers and Binders	1,740		
Rollers—Field	6,291		
Scarifiers or Scufflers	7,473		
Screens—Grain	262		

of the principal industries. The total capacity of these silos is stated at 344,585 cubic feet, or an average of 3,250 cubic feet per silo, the weight of ensilage fodder preserved last year being given as 5,132 tons, or 48·4 tons per silo :—

Division.	Number of Silos.	Capacity in cubic feet.	Tons of Ensilage made.
Northern Division.			
Coast	4	2,965	27
Table-land	2	2,760	15
Western Slopes	4	5,150	199
Totals, Northern Division	10	10,875	241
East Central Division.			
Coast	3	1,752	93
Metropolis and Environs	1	2,400	60
Table-land	10	21,704	1,600
Western Slopes	6	2,560	158
Totals, East Central Division	20	28,416	1,911
Southern Division.			
Coast	44	139,982	2,220
Table-land	17	13,374	194
Western Slopes	10	146,642	350
Totals, Southern Division	71	299,998	2,764
Western Division	5	5,296	216

IRRIGATION.

Little has been done in New South Wales with regard to irrigation. Isolated efforts in that direction are generally reported as having met with success, but no general scheme of water conservation and distribution has yet been developed. Such an enterprise would be so vast, the area to be benefited is so great, and the interests to be served are so conflicting, that no private organisation could successfully cope with the subject, which must, therefore, be left to the care of the Government of the country. The Water Conservation Branch attached to the Department of

Mines is at present engaged in the work of obtaining sufficient hydrographical data to form the basis of a comprehensive scheme of irrigation, and the country is being traversed in all directions to ascertain the contour of its surface.

The following table gives the area irrigated by private enterprise in each division of New South Wales, and the kind and number of implements and machinery in use for the purpose. The larger areas irrigated are situated in the Riverina district and the country watered by the Murray, Murrumbidgee, and the Lachlan rivers, where 13,173 acres are irrigated out of a total of 23,106 acres for the whole of New South Wales, throughout which irrigation operations necessitate the aggregate power of 212 pumps, 728 windmills, and 449 water-lifting implements :—

Electorate.	Area Irrigated.	Implements and Machinery.		
		Irrigation Pumps.	Water Lifters, Chain and Bucket.	Windmills.
Northern Division.	acres.			
Coast	369	7	6	29
Table-land	900	10	26	21
Western Slopes	994	9	84	77
Totals, Northern Division...	2,263	26	116	127
East Central Division.				
Coast	297	14	5	48
Metropolis and Environs	178	11	1	46
Table-land	4,011	33	11	84
Western Slopes	4,958	18	50	68
Totals, East Central Division	9,444	76	67	246
Southern Division.				
Coast	513	13	3	40
Table-land	535	22	12	50
Western Slopes	8,215	23	33	113
Totals, Southern Division...	9,263	58	48	203
Western Division.				
Western Slopes	2,136	52	218	152

PART XVII.

Settlement.

Various system of land alienation.

THE systems adopted for the settlement of an indus lation on the lands of New South Wales have b and have differed widely according to the various sta Colony's progress and development. In the first perioc ment land was alienated by grants, orders, and dedic power of disposing of the Crown lands resting solely Governor. In this way grants, frequently of exten were made in favour of naval and military officers and free immigrants. Regulations for the sale of lands allotments were promulgated on the 1st of August, 1831 the principle of sale by auction was introduced, the mini of country lands being then fixed at 5s. per acre. This was raised to 12s. per acre in the year 1839, and two y wards it was increased to 20s. in the district of Port I minimum price of 12s. per acre being resumed for Colony in the following year. It was again increased 20s. per acre, with liberty to select at the upset pri portions offered and not bid for, or when the deposit wa The principle of selection appears therefore for the fi that date in the land legislation of New South Wales, t to portions of land already measured for sale at aucti system lasted until the abrogation of the Order in Oc the introduction of new legislation by the Parliamen South Wales. The following data show the progre alienations at various epochs up to the date upon whi of 1861 became law:—

Area alienated under Surveyor-General Oxley previous to 1st January, 1828	1,
Total area of land alienated as per return and Government map, 1837	4,
Total area of land alienated in all forms previous to 1861	7,

The conditions of colonization greatly altered under the powerful attraction of the gold-fields, and after the first excitment of the rush for gold had died out the question of land settlement had to be dealt with in an entirely new spirit, to meet the wants of a class of immigrants of a different type to those contemplated by former enactments, the result being the passing of the Crown Lands Act of 1861, under the leadership of Sir John Robertson. Before this Act became law the conditions of settlement rendered it difficult for men of small means to establish themselves with fair chances of success. The new measure aimed at facilitating the settlement of an industrial agricultural population, side by side with the pastoral tenants, and, with this view the Act introduced a principle entirely new to the land legislation of the Colony, namely, that of free selection, in limited areas, *before survey*. To this privilege was attached the condition of *bonâ fide* residence, and the land was to be sold at a fixed price, payable by instalments, or partly remaining at interest. The principle of unconditional sales was, however, maintained, and during the twenty-three years the Act of 1861 was in operation there were sold 23,470,140 acres conditionally, and 15,572,001 acres by auction, improvement purchase, or otherwise without conditions; the total area alienated being 39,042,141 acres. In a very large number of cases the land selected, or purchased, reverted to the State, so that the absolute area sold, or in process of sale, when the Act of 1884 came into force, amounted to only 32,819,023 acres, besides 7,338,539 acres alienated previously to 1861.

Crown Lands Act of 1861.

The occupation for pastoral purposes of the waste lands of New South Wales was at first allowed under a system of yearly licenses. Under the old squatting regulations any person was at liberty to apply for such a license to occupy runs the extent of which was only limited by the boundaries of the surrounding stations, the licensing fee being fixed at £10 per year for a section of 25 square miles, or 16,000 acres in extent, £2 10s. per annum being charged for every five additional square miles.

Pastoral Occupation.

The Imperial Act of the 9th March, 1847, which rendered ful for the Queen, by any Order in Council, to make and such regulations as should seem meet for the sale and tion of the waste lands, was immediately followed by introducing an entirely different system in the legislation pastoral occupation of lands in New South Wales. Hithe tenure had been a yearly one, and the fee was paid on the of land occupied by the squatter. For this system was su a fixity of tenure of the leases, and the license was cal upon the stock-carrying capacity of the runs. Under the tions promulgated in 1847 the country was divided parts—the settled, the intermediate, and the unsettled For the latter division the term of the pastoral leases was a period of fourteen years; in the intermediate division was reduced to eight years, and in the settled districts the tenure was retained. The licensing fee was charged at the £10 for 4,000 sheep, or a proportional number of cattle— was the minimum at which the stock carrying capabilities could be assessed—and £2 10s. was charged for every add 1,000 sheep or the proportion of cattle which the run wa mated to carry. In the settled districts lands were let for p purposes only, in sections of not less than 1 square mile i the annual rental for each section being fixed at 10s. The l of alienated lands were permitted to depasture their stock Crown lands adjoining their holdings free of charge, this perm however, constituting only a commonage right. The Occu Act of 1861, which abolished the Orders in Council, inaug a new system, which limited the tenure of pastoral leases years in the unsettled, and intermediate or second-class districts, leaving the whole of the pastoral leases open operations of the free selectors. The evils resulting fro system led Parliament to adopt in 1884 the measure at pre force, the provisions of which, with regard to pastoral occu are described further on.

Occupation Act of 1861.

CROWN LANDS ACTS OF 1884 AND 1889.

Free selection before survey.

The Act of 1861 was, after many amendments, finally superseded by that of 1884, with the supplementary enactment of 1889. Though differing widely from the former Act in many important particulars these measures maintain the principle of free selection before survey, but with one essential difference. Under the original Act the whole area of the Crown lands of the Colony was thrown open to free selection, and the lands held under pastoral leases were not exempted from the operation of the law. Thus were created considerable difficulties between the two principal classes of settlers—the squatters and the selectors. While maintaining the principle of selection before survey, the aim of the Acts of 1884 and 1889 was to give fixity of tenure to the pastoral lessees and obtain a larger rental from the public lands, at the same time restricting the area sold unconditionally. The Act of 1884 became law on the 1st January, 1885, and that of 1889 came into operation on the 1st of December of that year.

Territorial divisions.

Under these measures the whole Colony is subdivided into three natural divisions, each of which is further subdivided into various land districts, one or more such districts forming local divisions, the administration of which is entrusted to a Local Land Board, composed of a chairman and not more than two assessors. In each land district resides a land agent, whose duty is to receive all applications for land, in accordance with certain regulations having the force of law. The decisions of the Local Land Boards may be appealed against to the Land Court. The composition of the Land Court involved one of the principal innovations introduced in the land legislation of the Colony by the Act of 1889; by its constitution and powers it is intended to free the administration of the law from political

2 I

Land Court.

interference. This Court is composed of a Preside members appointed by the Executive, whose decision of administration have the force of judgments of t Court; but whenever questions of law become case may be submitted to the Supreme Court, eith written request of the parties interested, or by the acting of its own accord. The judgments given on are final and conclusive. The conditions of alienation, occupation of Crown lands differ in each of the th above named.

EASTERN DIVISION.

Boundaries and area.

The eastern division has an area of 60,452,000 includes a broad belt of land comprised between the s a line nearly parallel thereto. This line starts from way between the small settlements of Bonshaw and the Dumaresq River, on the northern frontier, and te Howlong on the river Murray, and thus embraces district of the Colony, as well as the northern and sou lands. In this division lie all the original centres of and the markets of the Colony are more readily acc than to the other districts. In it, moreover, is to be of the best agricultural land of the Colony. For th the conditions for the purchase and occupation of the C are more restricted than is the case in the central divisions; nevertheless, every person above the age

Conditional purchases.

upon any part of the Crown lands not speciall from purchase, select an area from 40 to 640 acres together with a conditional lease of contiguous l cannot exceed thrice the area of the conditional pur price demanded by the State is a uniform one of £1 per acre being deposited on making the application, a paid by instalments of 1s. per acre per year, together w of 4 per cent. on the unpaid balance. The instalmen the end of the third year, though the whole of the be paid in one sum at the selector's option, when the instalments fall due. The selector is required to reside for a term of five years, and, within two years from the date of occupation, to fence the boundaries of his conditionally purchased land with a substantial fence, and maintain the same in good order and condition. Upon application to the Land Board, however, the selector may be allowed to substitute other improvements of a permanent and substantial nature in lieu of fencing. On the completion of his term of continuous residence the selector is at liberty to conditionally purchase additional areas contiguous to his original purchase, in extent from 40 to 640 acres, and may, if he has also a conditional leasehold, purchase the whole of the area of the said leasehold, and, in the case of additional purchases, the conditions as to residence are not required, though that of fencing remains unaltered. Any person over 16 years of age may select, and married women, judicially separated from their husbands, are also allowed to select in their own right. Minors taking up lands adjoining the parents' selection may fulfil the conditions of residence under the parental roof. Condition of fencing and bona fide residence.

Conditional leaseholds.—The conditional leasehold, in conjunction with a selection, may be held for a period of fifteen years, at a yearly rental fixed by the Local Land Board, subject to the approval of the Minister, and under conditions of fencing within two years of the date of the confirmation of the application, the one fence, however, being allowed to enclose both the conditional purchase and the lease. Limit of tenure of conditional leasehold

Conditional leases may at any time during their currency be converted into additional conditional purchases, and the term of residence on both the original purchase and the lease together need not exceed a period of five years from date of application. Leases converted into purchases.

Non-residential conditional purchases.—Land may be selected free from conditions as to residence, but the terms under which land may be thus taken up are more stringent than when the purchase is a residential one. In the first place, the ar·a is Limit of area.

limited to a maximum of 320 acres, and no additional cor purchase may be made except for such additional areas, together with that of the original purchase, do not exc maximum, and no conditional lease may be granted. The must be fenced in within twelve months after survey, tl of fencing not being included in that of the permanent i ments, which must be made within five years after survey extent of £1 per acre. Moreover, the price demanded State has been fixed at £2 per acre, the deposits and sub instalments being likewise double the sum required to be the case of ordinary conditional purchases. Lastly, no perso 21 years of age may select under this clause, and no person already taken up a non-residential selection, may be perm make any other conditional purchase whatsoever under thi

Conditions of fencing and improvements.

Price per acre.

Special areas may also be reserved from the operation ordinary conditional purchase clauses of the Act, and thrown open to selection under different terms as to paym with or without the condition of residence. But, in such areas, the price of the land cannot be less than £1 10s. p if the selector elect to fulfil the condition of residence, non- purchasers being charged double the price demanded fo former, and the maximum area of one such purchase at 320 acres.

Price and limit of area.

CENTRAL DIVISION.

Boundaries and area.

The central division of the Colony embraces an area of 55, acres, extending from north to south between the western the eastern division and a line starting from a point on th intyre River, where it is crossed by the 149° of east lon and following this river and the Darling to the junction o Creek; thence along that creek to the Bogan River, and a the river Lachlan, between the townships of Euabalong an dobolin, along the Lachlan to Balranald, and thence to the j of the Edward River with the Murray, on the frontier of V

The central division thus embraces the upper basin of the Darling River in the northern part of the Colony, and portions of those of the Lachlan, the Murrumbidgee, and the other affluents of the Murray in the south. This territory has, hitherto, been mainly given over to pastoral occupation; but there is every warrant for supposing that agricultural and pastoral pursuits could successfully be carried on, side by side, over a considerable part of it.

Conditional purchases and leases.—In this division land may be conditionally purchased under the same terms as to residence, fencing improvements, price, and mode of payment as required in the eastern division; but the limit of an individual selection has been fixed at 2,560 acres, with a corresponding increase of the conditional lease to three times that area. The acreage which may be purchased without residence, as well as the conditions in regard thereto, are the same for the central as for the eastern division.

Limit of area, and other conditions.

In *special areas* the maximum extent of a selection has been fixed at 640 acres in the central division.

Western Division.

The western division comprises the whole of the land situated between the western limit of the central division and the South Australian border. It embraces an area of 79,970,000 acres, watered entirely by the Darling River. This part of New South Wales is essentially devoted to pastoral pursuits. Water conservation, irrigation, and occupation, may in time counteract climatic conditions and irregular rainfall, and make agriculture possible over this large area, as its soil is adapted to the growth of any kind of crop. But legislation in regard to occupation and settlement of the district is based upon the assumption that for many years there will be little inducement for agricultural settlement. Therefore, conditional purchases, except in special areas, are not allowed. Pastoral settlement, in this division, is encouraged in the form of homestead leases.

Limits and area.

Pastoral leases.—Under the Act of 1884, the squatters hitherto held runs under leases which did not exempt from the operation of the free selection system, were i surrender their leases to the Crown, and submit to the su of the unalienated portion of their runs into two equal p one part was returned to the Crown lessee, under an in lease, for a fixed term of years, according to the geo division in which the run was situated, while the r portion was leased under annual occupation licenses, r from year to year, remaining open for selection under t stead lease clause. The Crown Lands Act of 1889 interfere with these provisions, but the tenure of pastor in the western division only, was fixed at twenty-one y rental determined upon an assessment made for seven ye reassessment made every seventh year of the lease's curr term of twenty-one years being susceptible of extensi further period of seven years if the land has been impr satisfactory manner. In the central division the term of leases extends to ten years, and in the eastern divisio years only; in each case the rent is determined by assess no minimum is fixed in any division. Under the Act the Minister for Lands claimed the power of definitely f rental of Crown Leases at a rate other than appraised Land Boards. This claim gave rise to contentions and d which were met by the passing of a short measure, know "Crown Rents Act of 1890." By the terms of this such case may be referred to the Land Court who de upon this appeal the proper rate at which rental should b paid by the applicant under the Crown Lands Act of 18 the commencement of the lease, and the proper rate pay reappraisement or other alterations are made in pursu the Acts of 1884 and 1889. In the central division e sion of five years may be granted to the holder of a pasto

Pastoral tenure of land.

Upon the expiration of a pastoral lease the lands c therein may be re-let, or may be subdivided and let by

Expiration of pastoral lease.

or tender, as a pastoral lease, or may be resumed by the Government, and all improvements on the land at the expiration of the lease become the property of the Crown, without compensation.

Occupation licenses.—Besides the leases for a fixed period thus granted to run-holders of half the unalienated portions of their runs, licenses may be granted to occupy resumed areas or vacant lands. In this case the application for such occupation license must be made at the time of applying for the pastoral lease, and a deposit made at the rate of £2 per section of 640 acres, part of which sum may be refunded when the license fee is fixed by the Minister, after appraisement. These occupation licenses are granted only for a term of one year, and do not exempt the land from the operations of other clauses of the Land Act.

Deposit and term.

Homestead leases.—In the western division, homestead leases with a currency of fifteen years may be granted within the resumed areas or vacant lands. The portion which may be taken up under this clause cannot be less than 2,560 acres, nor more than 10,240 acres. These leases are granted upon application at the Lands Office, and on payment of a deposit equal to 1d. per acre of the area applied for. The applicant must reside upon his lease for a period of at least six consecutive months during each of the first five years of his lease. During the first two years of occupation the lessee must enclose the whole of the lease, with a fence according to a prescribed design; but the Land Board may grant an exemption from fencing any natural or other boundary under certain circumstances, provided other substantial improvements are erected in lieu thereof. On the expiration of the term of fifteen years, above mentioned, an extension of seven years may be granted, if it appears to the Land Board that the carrying capacity of the land has been improved, or that the conditions imposed by the Act have been satisfactorily fulfilled and the land benefited. At the end of the final term the homestead lease may be again leased as such by auction or tender, but the out-going tenant is not entitled to compensation for

Condition of occupation and fencing.

Term of lease.

improvements. Persons who obtain homestead leases ■ ever, required to pay for existing improvements on the lan leased, at a valuation made under the direction of the Local Board. Holders of pastoral leases are not permitted to hold stead leases, neither can any person hold, or cause to be ■ his behalf, more than one such lease.

Minister may proclaim scrub lands.

Limit of area and terms of tenure.

Scrub leases.—Besides pastoral and homestead leases, leases are granted under the Act for special purposes. O recommendation of the Local Land Board the Minister declare* any Crown lands wholly or partly covered with ■ noxious undergrowth, to be scrub land, and such may be leas a term not exceeding twenty-one years, and in areas not ■ 10,240 acres, and not less than 640 acres to any person, ■ to rental fixed by assessment. Every holder of a scrub ■ required to commence destroying the scrub within three ■ after the commencement of the lease, and take all such ■ this object as the Local Land Board may from time to time ■

Leasing of snow lands.

Leases of inferior lands.

Lands covered with snow during part of the year may be in areas not less than 1,280 acres, and not exceeding 10,240 for a term of seven years, with a right of extension for years more, subject to an annual rental determined by the Board. Lands which, in consequence of their inferior charac isolated position, may not have been held under tenure, o been abandoned, may be leased by auction or tender for a not exceeding twenty years.

Leases for the protection of artesian wells.

Upon application by the holder of a pastoral lease for perm to bore or search for water upon the land held under an occu license, an area not exceeding 10,240 acres in one block resumed area may be temporarily exempted from sale or and in the event of artesian water in sufficient quantity discovered, the said area may be held under a fixed lea term of which may not exceed the currency of the pastoral

Annual leases are also granted for pastoral purposes in areas not exceeding 1,920 acres for any Crown lands, by auction or tender, at a minimum upset annual rental of £2 for every section of 640 acres. Annual leases.

Residential leases may also be granted for periods not exceeding fifteen years, of areas not exceeding 10 acres of Crown lands within gold and mineral fields to holders of miners' rights and licenses, for the purpose of *bonâ fide* residence, upon such terms as may be prescribed as to rent, erection of fences, and buildings.

In addition to the various forms of alienation and occupation of the Crown lands described above, land may be sold in the three divisions of the Colony under the following provisions :—

Auction sales.—Crown lands, not exceeding 200,000 acres in the aggregate for the whole Colony in any one year, may be sold by auction. The upset price for such land is notified by the Minister, and is fixed by law at not less than £8 per acre for town lands, £2 10s. for suburban lands, and £1 for other lands. A deposit equal to 25 per cent. of the purchase money is required, and the balance must be paid within three months after the sale. Sales by auction.

Purchases on gold-fields.—On gold-fields any person in duly authorized occupation under the Mining Act may purchase the portion so occupied, without competition, in virtue of the improvements made on the land, at a price to be fixed by the Land Board, being not less than at the rate of £8 per acre for town lands, and £2 10s. for suburban or other lands, or £2 10s. for any area less than 1 acre ; but the maximum which may be so purchased is one quarter of an acre for town lands, and 1 acre for other lands. Gold-field purchases.

Special sales, without competition, in the case of rescission of water frontages, reclamation of land by proprietors of adjoining lands, and in other special cases, may also be made under conditions which are at the discretion of the Minister for Lands in the metropolitan district, and of the Local Land Boards in the other districts. The Act also provides for special leases on the shores of the sea, lakes, harbours or rivers, as well as for cutting and removing timber from Crown lands. Special sales.

LAND REVENUE.

Revenue received since 1861.

Since the year 1862, when the Lands Alienation came into force, there has been received into the Natio from the proceeds of lands alienated the following am

Description of Land Alienated.
Lands alienated before the 1st January, 1862 (approximate)
Lands sold in fee-simple, from 1st January, 1862, to 31st December, 1889 ....
Deposits, interest, and balance of purchase money on lands sold conditionally from 1st January, 1862, to 31st December, 1889 ....
Total amount paid into the National Treasury ..

Amount due to the State.

At the close of 1889 there remained due to t account of unpaid balances on land conditionally pur of about £13,224,311; so that the total amount of sal to the end of 1889 was £44,120,267 in all. Duri period the area of land disposed of by sales was 33,8 the average rate per acre for lands of all kinds sold w about £1 6s.

Number of selections.

From the returns published by the Department would appear that from 1862 to the close of 1890 the of individual selections applied for was 227,794, cove area of 29,873,628 acres, of which at the close of 189 157,062 still in existence, covering an area of 20,4 Of the total number of selections applied for, 18,90 cent., have become absolute freeholds, 138,156, or 60 still in process of alienation, and 70,732, or 31·7 pe been either declared void, forfeited, disallowed or under the provisions of the various Land Acts. It is to ascertain exactly the proportion which the actua distinct rural holdings bears to that of individual sele is evident that the numerous portions taken up as ad ditional purchases greatly reduce the number of hol the gradual absorption of a very large number of sele

Increase in area of holdings.

past ten years, and this tendency is visible during nearly period over which the records extend, as may be seen accompanying table. In 1887 and 1888 the average are considerably. This may be easily accounted for, as a res stoppage of the auction sales of Crown lands, which w the main features of the land policy inaugurated in 18 tendency to increase was again observable in 1889 and 1 bably from an augmentation in the number of large sel consolidated holdings in the central district of the Colo quent upon the extension of the maximum areas of la may be taken up by individual selectors under the pro the Crown Lands Acts at present in force. The decrease o in 1891 is misleading, as it is evident that under the co clauses of the Census Act particulars were obtained fro siderable number of small holders who, in previous ye to furnish any returns.

Average Area of Holdings.

Year ended 31 March.	Average size of holding.	Year ended 31 March.	Aver[illegible]
	Acres.		Ac[illegible]
1876	315	1884	8[illegible]
1877	459	1885	8[illegible]
1878	481	1886	[illegible]
1879	564	1887	8[illegible]
1880	560	1888	7[illegible]
1881	691	1889	[illegible]
1882	703	1890	[illegible]
1883	772	1891	[illegible]

Facilities afforded by Act of 1861.

The increase shown between the first and last yea above series amounts to 508 acres, so that the average holdings is now 160·1 per cent. larger than in 18 result is, in a certain measure, due to the facilities a pastoral occupiers by the improvement clause of the Cro Act of 1861, and its subsequent amendments, which them to purchase at the rate of £1, and subsequently a per acre, in sections from 40 acres to 640 acres, areas w had improved to the extent of £1 per acre. But it i table also, and in a large degree, to the vast areas of Cro

Comparative increase of holdings.

Comparing the number of existing rural holdings sizes, a greater number of which have been returned owing to the operation of the Census Act, with those 1879, when the particulars were first recorded, it will that those under 15 acres have increased 77 per cent. ; 15 to 200 acres have scarcely advanced. Between 20 acres the number of holdings shows an increase of less in number ; those from 400 to 1,000 acres increased 39·1 from 1,000 to 2,000 acres the increase was 97 per c 2,000 to 10,000 acres it was 112 per cent. ; while in class of holdings, from 10,000 acres upwards, the increase has been over 100 per cent. during the ten years. The table shows the number of holdings in various classes in of the period named :—

Holdings of Various Sizes.

Acreage.	1879.	1880.	1881.	1882.	1883.	1884.	1885.	1886.	1887.	[illegible]
Under 15 acres	4,974	5,550	5,188	5,124	5,124	5,409	[illegible]	[illegible]	[illegible]	[illegible]
15 to 200	[illegible]	20,845	[illegible]	[illegible]	20,161	[illegible]	21,167	[illegible]	[illegible]	[illegible]
200 to 400..............	5,199	[illegible]	5,733	5,760	[illegible]	[illegible]	[illegible]	[illegible]	[illegible]	[illegible]
400 to 1,000	[illegible]	[illegible]	[illegible]	[illegible]	[illegible]	[illegible]	6,817	[illegible]	[illegible]	[illegible]
1,000 to 2,000	1,212	1,467	1,470	[illegible]	[illegible]	[illegible]	[illegible]	[illegible]	[illegible]	[illegible]
2,000 to 10,000	940	1,225	1,176	[illegible]	[illegible]	1,412	[illegible]	[illegible]	[illegible]	[illegible]
10,000 and upwards....	[illegible]	414	[illegible]	[illegible]	[illegible]	[illegible]	[illegible]	[illegible]	[illegible]	[illegible]
Total............	[illegible]	[illegible]	[illegible]	[illegible]	[illegible]	43 079	[illegible]	[illegible]	[illegible]	[illegible]

Holdings in vicinity of towns

The holdings under 15 acres in extent are, generally the vicinity of towns, and consist mainly of gardens and the increase of 21 per cent. is what would be expected from the increased demand for their produce population. The least satisfactory feature in the table that the number of holdings of moderate size remains same. In 1879 the total holdings having an area from acres, amounted to 27,501, and in 1889 to only 29,212, very slight advance. On the other hand, the large have increased to a remarkable degree, so that, at the close of the year 1890 there were 11,944 holdings of 400 acres and upwards in extent, compared with 7,443 in 1879, or an increase of 60·5 per cent. in number in that short period. The area of holdings, as returned by occupiers, in each year since 1879, is given below :—

Year.	Under 200 acres.	From 200 to 1,000 acres.	From 1,000 to 10,000 acres.	Upwards of 10,000 acres.	Total Area of Holdings.
1879	1,890,293	4,950,938	5,692,576	10,187,796	22,721,603
1880	1,821,700	4,732,507	7,126,309	14,084,802	27,765,318
1881	1,816,674	4,811,634	6,990,311	14,073,589	27,692,208
1882	1,800,881	5,217,109	7,605,536	16,090,823	30,714,349
1883	1,811,483	5,586,273	8,131,955	17,823,287	33,352,998
1884	1,898,803	5,905,810	8,198,178	19,032,713	35,035,504
1885	1,903,360	6,018,570	8,340,872	21,346,794	37,609,596
1886	1,848,141	6,152,331	8,817,814	19,907,883	36,726,169
1887	1,984,940	6,181,374	9,480,412	19,170,765	36,817,491
1888	1,948,345	6,242,597	10,258,966	20,972,187	39,422,095
1889	2,105,555	6,352,325	10,417,449	22,167,300	41,042,629
1890	2,024,565	6,499,625	11,785,471	20,847,216	41,156,877

Enclosed land.

The area of unenclosed land in 1876 amounted to nearly two-fifths of the whole area of the holdings; but, in the beginning of 1890 the proportion had fallen to considerably less than one-fifteenth, the area unenclosed at that period being only 3,299,740 acres out of a total of 41,156,877 acres occupied. This result is due partly to the operation of legislation, and partly to the saving of labour which fencing enables occupiers to effect.

Present state of settlement.

The foregoing remarks naturally lead to an examination of the statistics which indicate the present state of the settlement of the alienated land in New South Wales. For this purpose it will be necessary to extend this inquiry successively to the various parts of the Colony, and to follow, as much as possible, the order in which they were opened up, following the march of colonization, in each of the four zones of settlement into which New South Wales may be said to be geographically divided, viz., the coast, t land, the western slope of the great dividing range, western plains. Each zone, having its own special offers to the settler different natural resources under climatological conditions. Proceeding from the metro centre, settlement extended first along the coast, the central and more readily accessible parts of the tableland, afterwards the course of the great inland rivers tow southern and western parts of the Colony, thence to plains of the west, spreading slowly across the River D the confines of the territory. Nature, assisted by legisla tributed to shape settlement into its present form, the course of events, however, being at times interrupted b rushes of population to points scattered over the surfa country, even to its remotest extremities.

Metropolitan Electorates excepted.

The electorates which are embraced within the are metropolis and its suburbs are necessarily outside the this examination, as it is not intended to inquire intc th condition of urban settlement; but it may be stated, nev that as regards the subdivision and the distribution of la perty in the city and suburbs of Sydney there is n difference between this and other much older communiti figures given below refer only to rural settlement in the el immediately surrounding the metropolis, where the first to colonize were made, extending but little beyond its limits.

Districts adjacent to the Metropolis.

It will be seen from the following tables that there these districts four distinct classes of holders of alienated (1) Those who occupy their own freehold; (2) persons c holdings which they rent from the freeholders; (3) o land who rent from other private owners lands which t in addition to their own freeholds; and (4) persons addition to their freehold lease from the Crown areas devote themselves to the depasturing of stock.

whole division being only 37 acres for holding. T table, in addition to the average area of holdings in e in the district, also shows to what purpose the land put, from which it will be seen that agricultu especially in the cultivation of market garden pr oranges and other fruit, is carried on in 1,835 holdin are occupied for stock-raising, and 2,119 for resi pleasure grounds attached; in 2 cases a search probably for coal, is proceeding on the holdings. In 13 persons, occupying small Crown leases, are includ

Metropolis and Environs.

	Average Area of Rural Holdings.	Land used. Agriculture.	Grazing.
	Acres.	No.	No.
Metropolis	9	145	27
St. Leonards	35	199	19
Canterbury	16	151	192
Parramatta	6	20	......
Central Cumberland ...	58	1,320	306
Average	37	1,835	544

Progress of colonisation.

Colonisation, which commenced in the metrop advanced thence towards the west, and the allu the Hawkesbury and Nepean valleys were rapidly covered with prosperous farms. The progress of s deflected to the northward by the high range of abr in the west which was so long a barrier to its expa direction. The lower portion of the valley of the abounding with natural resources, mineral as well a soon attracted colonists, and at the present time mo is concentrated in this district than in any other South Wales outside the metropolitan area. The f indicates the actual state of rural settlement:—

Hunter and Morpeth. In the electorates of Durham, Northumberland, and Patrick's Plains the proporti occupied by the owners decreases from a maximum cent. in Durham, to a minimum of 55·2 per cent. in of the total area alienated. That held by the tenan consequently increases from 26·6 to 44·8 per cent. number of occupiers is returned at 6,180 for the whc of these 3,396 occupy their own freeholds, 1,948 are t rent various areas in addition to their own land, an together, with their freeholds, a certain area of Crov lease. A considerable proportion of the holdings in occupy large areas, particularly in the rural electorates, area being 319 acres per holding, with a minimum of the urban district of West Maitland, and a maximu acres in that of Gloucester, in which a considerable po original grant of 1,000,000 acres to the Australian A Company is situated. Patrick's Plains comes next wit per holding, the area being sensibly reduced in the other the Hawkesbury, the Nepean, and Morpeth, not e average area of 111, 141, and 118 acres per holding r as seen in the following Table, which also shows the which the land thus held is devoted.

Number of occupiers.

East Central Division.

Electorates.	Average area of Holdings.	Agri-culture.	Grazing.	Mi
	Acres.	No.	No.	N
Gloucester	1,015	355	219	....
Durham	418	420	219	....
Newcastle	197	18	9	
Morpeth	118	362	52	....
Northumberland	218	83	124	1
Maitland, East	171	104	105	1
Maitland, West	14	52	......	....
The Hunter	227	347	194	
Patrick's Plains	696	314	335	
Wollombi	195	646	122	
The Hawkesbury	111	838	3	....
The Nepean	141	417	186	
Totals and Average	319	3,966	1,568	[illegible]

The above figures include 63 Crown Leases occupied principally by miners. The great majority of rural landholders, 3,966 in number, follow agricultural pursuits, purely pastoral occupations being carried on where the estates of large area are situated—1,568 occupiers using their land for that purpose—whilst in the smaller areas 672 holdings are attached to residences or used as pleasure grounds, whilst 37 occupiers, principally Crown lessees, hold their land under the mining clauses or other special leasing clauses of the various Land Acts.

In the earlier portion of the present century colonization took a southerly direction from the metropolis, and settlement extended rapidly along the lower valleys of the rivers of the South Coast, where again the best of the lands were alienated in grants of large areas to a few families; the nature of the country and a more intelligent apprehension of true colonization resulted in the subdivision of these originally large estates into numerous and comparatively small holdings, at present cultivated by a fairly prosperous tenantry. This is especially the case in the electorates of Kiama and Illawarra, where the average area of holdings is 121 and 116 acres respectively. The average area of estates in the electorate of Eden, owing to its greater distance from the metropolis, and perhaps also to the mountainous character of a considerable portion of its area, reaches 411 acres, and in Shoalhaven the proportion is reduced to 209 acres; but in Camden where a number of the original grants are still held by the grantees or their descendants, an exceedingly small portion of their area being either cultivated or put to any use other than grazing a few head of stock, the average is increased to 262 acres per holding—that of the district, as shown in the table below, being only 255 acres. The land is principally devoted to agriculture, and especially to dairy farming; most of the occupiers following also pastoral pursuits; it is therefore difficult to discriminate between the number of agriculturists and that of graziers, and the figures below should be read conjointly. It would therefore appear that 4,520 occupiers used their

The South Coast

land for these combined purposes, whilst in 775 cases the land was attached to residence; and 38 holdings were occupied by miners, the majority of whom were Crown lessees :—

South Coast.

Electorates.	Average area of Holding.	Agriculture.	Grazing.	Mining.	Residential Areas.
	acres.	No.	No.	No.	No.
Camden	262	341	1,048	7	336
Kiama	121	477	63	......	76
Illawarra	116	365	110	12	102
Shoalhaven	209	884	17	17	171
Eden	411	538	677	2	90
Average and Totals...	255	2,605	1,915	38	775

South Coast Districts.

In the South Coast districts alienated rural lands are occupied in the manner illustrated in the following table :—

South Coast.

Electorates.	Occupiers of Freehold Land.	Occupiers of Rented Land.	Occupiers of Partly Freehold and partly Rented Land.	Occupiers of Freehold and Crown Land.	Total.	Area—Freehold.	Area—Rented.	Total.
	No.	No.	No.	No.	No.	Acres.	Acres.	Acres.
Camden	939	544	215	32	1,730	293,707	159,855	453,562
Kiama	205	316	88	7	616	32,223	42,408	74,631
Illawarra	244	253	85	7	589	40,642	27,896	68,538
Shoalhaven	499	446	92	32	1,069	164,587	58,609	223,196
Eden	878	182	148	95	1,303	453,564	82,565	536,129
	2,765	1,741	628	173	5,307	984,723	371,333	1,356,056

The area of alienated land is shown to cover 1,356,056 acres, or 26·7 per cent., of the total area, 5,077,120 acres, of this portion of New South Wales; the quantity of land occupied by the proprietors themselves being 984,723 acres, or 72·6 per cent., and that leased to tenant occupiers being 371,333 acres or 27·4 per cent. of the area alienated. In the Kiama electorate, out of a total of 74,631 acres alienated, 32,223 acres only, or 43·2 per cent., are occupied by the proprietors of the land; whilst 42,408 acres, or 56·8 per cent. are held by tenant occupiers. In that of Illawarra 27,896 acres, or 40·7 per cent., are occupied by the owners of the soil, and 40,642, or 59·3 per cent., by tenant farmers. In the district of Shoalhaven some 58,609 acres, or 26·3 per cent., of a total area alienated, amounting to 223,196 acres, are held under tenancy, and 164,587 acres are occupied by the owners of the land, whilst in the southern district of Eden only a small area, representing 15·4 per cent. of the total quantity alienated, is occupied by tenants. There are altogether in these electorates 2,765 occupiers of their own freeholds, 1,741 tenants, 628 landholders, occupying both leased and freehold lands, and 173 occupiers of Crown leases in addition to their freehold—a total of 5,307 occupiers, whose aggregate estate would cover 1,356,056 acres, or 255 acres per holding. Although the settlement of the Colony extended from Central Cumberland, the Hunter, and Illawarra inland towards the Central Tableland, the examination of its present state along the Northern Coast will here take precedence, in order that a clear insight into the development of the colonisation of New South Wales in its four great natural divisions may be obtained. Area alienated.

In the Northern Coast Districts the occupation of the country has extended rapidly of late years along the banks of the fine rivers which empty into the Pacific Ocean. Figures regarding this district will be found below:— North Coast Districts.

North Coast.

Electorates.	Occupiers of Freehold Land.	Occupiers of Rented Land.	Occupiers of Partly Freehold and partly Rented Land.	Occupiers of Freehold and Crown Land.	Total.	Area—Freehold.	Area—Rented.	Total area alienated.
	No.	No.	No.	No.	No.	Acres.	Acres.	Acres.
Richmond	1,569	422	91	153	2,235	677,478	52,178	729,656
Clarence	502	236	52	8	798	90,696	17,898	108,594
Grafton	513	224	75	100	912	255,005	29,975	284,980
Macleay	667	406	123	84	1,280	189,998	48,604	238,602
Hastings & Manning	1,026	328	99	116	1,569	276,212	59,999	336,211
Totals	4,277	1,616	440	461	6,794	1,489,389	208,654	1,698,043

Satisfactory settlement.

Of all the districts of New South Wales the Northern Coast electorates exhibit the best and most satisfactory results as regards the settlement of the Crown lands. Nowhere else has the great object of the Act of 1861—to settle an industrious farming population on the soil—been better fulfilled. The total number of land-holders is 6,794, of whom only 1,616 are tenants, whilst 4,277 occupy their own freeholds, 440 work both their own land and additional areas rented from private owners, and 461 occupy areas of Crown lands together with their freeholds. The total area alienated in this rich part of the Colony amounts to 1,698,043 acres, or only 20·3 per cent. of the total extent of the district, which covers some 8,352,640 acres; and the average area of holdings is 249 acres, ranging from 136 acres in the Clarence to 326 in the Richmond. The proportion of leasehold lands to the area alienated is comparatively small, there being only 208,654 acres so held, or 12·3 per cent. of the total alienated area; whilst 1,489,389 acres are in the occupancy of the owners of the land themselves.

In the districts of the Richmond and Grafton the area leased by private persons forms only 7·2 and 10·5 per cent. respectively of the area alienated; and the maximum is reached in the Clarence, where 16·5 per cent. of the settled rural lands is occupied by tenants. Including 22 occupiers of Crown leases the majority of landholders, viz., 4,336, were engaged principally in agriculture and dairy-farming pursuits; maize and sugar-cane growing being also staple industries. In addition, 2,078 returned themselves as graziers, 8 as miners (probably resident on Crown leases), and there were 394 holdings, attached to residences or used for pleasure-grounds, &c., as seen below :—

North Coast.

Electorates.	Average area per Holding.	Land used for			
		Agriculture.	Grazing.	Mining.	Pleasure-grounds, residences, &c.
	Acres.	No.	No.	No.	No.
Richmond	326	1,132	990	...	117
Clarence	136	691	93	...	16
Grafton	313	653	158	...	101
Macleay	186	980	253	8	49
Hastings and Manning	214	880	584	...	111
Average and totals	249	4,336	2,078	8	394

From the above a pretty clear idea may be obtained of the present state of the rural settlement in the valleys of the coastal rivers of New South Wales, and in all that part of the Colony which extends from the sea to the first slopes of the Great Dividing Range. Geographical features and climate are the main elements in determining the occupation of the soil, irrespective of administrative boundaries. In this part of New South Wales the settlement of the public lands has proceeded in a way very different to that of the tableland which extends from north to south across the Colony, and divides the rich agricultural valleys of the coastal rivers and their broken mountainous watershed from the immense plains of the western district.

Slow progress of cultivation.

It would be erroneous to imagine, however, because the coastal region is better fitted for the purpose of the agriculturist, the dairyman and the fruit-grower, that the lands at present alienated are solely devoted to those industries; the agricultural development of New South Wales proceeds very gradually, and even in the districts referred to only a small proportion of the settled area is under cultivation.

Central Tableland.

After the difficulties raised by nature between the coast and the interior had been overcome, the pioneers of colonization penetrated to the central tableland, and thence extended to the south and the north, afterwards gradually overrunning the whole of the great western interior. At first they followed the course of the great rivers, and occupied, little by little, all the available land until, at the present time, only very inferior country remains untenanted.

The central tableland, comprising the electorates grouped around the cities of Bathurst and Orange was the first settled, and the occupation of the alienated lands, at the present time, is illustrated by the figures given in the following table:—

Central Tableland.

Electorate.	Occupiers of				Total.	Area—Freehold.	Area rented.	Total.
	Freehold land.	Rented land.	Partly Freehold and partly rented.	Freehold and Crown land.				
	No.	No.	No.	No.	No.	acres.	acres.	acres.
Hartley	399	66	32	124	621	144,419	28,758	173,177
Upper Hunter ...	678	71	75	389	1,213	1,389,558	83,253	1,472,811
Mudgee	719	234	72	266	1,291	422,138	76,897	499,035
Macquarie, East..	381	172	54	180	787	193,043	106,289	299,332
Macquarie, West.	134	219	37	100	490	121,594	66,805	188,399
Orange	391	133	38	38	600	191,164	45,299	236,463
Carcoar	575	106	64	312	1,057	573,238	117,254	690,492
Molong	526	104	46	157	833	490,849	66,327	557,176
Wellington..... ...	263	57	26	248	594	302,883	27,770	330,653
Totals	4,006	1,162	444	1,814	7,486	3,828,886	618,652	4,447,538

The number of holders of rural lands in this part of New South Wales is 7,486, of whom 4,066 occupy their own freeholds, 1,162 are private tenants, and 444 hold land both as free and lease holders, while 1,814 persons occupy areas of Crown Lands, generally for grazing purposes, in addition to their own freeholds. The area alienated is 4,447,538 acres, representing 37·5 per cent. of the whole area of these districts, which is computed at 11,860,480 acres. The proportion of land occupied by the landowners themselves is 86·1 per cent., or 3,828,886 acres; whilst 618,652 acres are leased to tenant occupiers. In the agricultural electorates of East and West Macquarie the proportion of land leased is considerable, 173,094 acres out of 487,731 acres alienated in these electorates, or 35·5 per cent. are held by tenants; in that of Orange 45,299 acres, or 19·2 per cent. of that area alienated, are held in the same manner. The proportion gradually diminishes from 16·6 per cent. in Hartley, to 8·4 per cent. in Wellington, and 5·7 per cent. in the Upper Hunter, where the country is less thickly settled, and is occupied principally for grazing purposes. In the latter electoral districts are situated some of the finest freehold estates of New South Wales, the land having remained in the hands of the original grantees or their descendants, who consolidated their holdings by taking advantage on a large scale of the auction sale and improvement clauses of the Land Act of 1861. Area alienated.

The average area of holdings in this division is 594 acres, ranging from a maximum of 1,214 acres in the Upper Hunter, owing to the cause just mentioned, to a minimum of 279 acres in Hartley, probably due to the number of selections of medium areas, taken up on the mountain heights along the Western line of railway. In Wellington, Carcoar, and Molong, where grazing occupies much larger areas than does the cultivation of the soil, the average rises to 557, 653, and 669 acres respectively. The holdings are used for agricultural pursuits in a great many cases, but as grazing is generally combined with agriculture it becomes a matter of difficulty to separate leaseholders into the two distinct classes of agriculturists and of graziers; both indus- Size of holdings.

tries combined are carried on upon 6,900 holdings out of 7,634, the latter including 148 Crown leases. Sixty-seven holdings are reported as occupied for mining purposes, and there are 667 residential holdings, the greater number being situated in the district of Hartley, where there are to be found 198 such estates out of a total of 622 rural properties; most of these holdings, situated on the Blue Mountains, are occupied in the summer as health resorts by visitors from the metropolis. The table below shows the average areas of holdings and the purposes for which the land is used in the districts referred to:—

Central Table-land.

Electorates.	Average area of Holdings.	Land used for			
		Agriculture.	Grazing.	Mining.	Residential Areas.
	acres.	No.	No.	No.	No.
Hartley	279	119	295	10	198
Upper Hunter	1,214	214	884	3	117
Mudgee	386	548	614	6	144
Macquarie, East	380	388	344	7	71
Macquarie, West	384	326	168	2	10
Orange	394	494	90	......	8
Carcoar	653	480	587	25	28
Molong	669	548	272	4	16
Wellington	557	319	201	10	75
Average	594	3,436	3,464	67	667

Southern table-land.

The conditions of settlement in the southern table-land do not greatly differ from those which obtain in the central districts, the principal feature being the greater proportion of holdings occupied by their proprietors—a class of small graziers who devote little attention to agriculture, and who in the majority of instances, have not yet complied entirely with the conditions necessary before they can become possessed of their holdings from the hands of the Crown. The following will illustrate the state of settlement in the various electorates which compose this portion of the Colony:—

Southern Table-land.

Electorate.	Occupiers of Freehold Land.	Occupiers of Rented Lands (Private.)	Occupiers of Partly Freehold and partly Private Leases.	Occupiers of Freehold and Crown Lands.	Total.	Area—Freehold.	Area—Rented.	Total.
	No.	No.	No.	No.	No.	acres.	acres.	acres.
Argyle	650	185	128	200	1,226	602,647	188,830	791,477
Goulburn..........	62	32	1	....	95	2,014	1,033	3,047
Braidwood	324	92	38	84	538	218,830	40,509	259,339
Queanbeyan	302	82	54	168	606	497,728	89,356	587,084
Monaro	590	77	75	342	1,084	1,177,314	54,716	1,232,030
Yass Plains......	450	93	61	258	862	675,752	114,847	790,599
Boorowa	228	34	20	221	503	451,627	23,872	475,499
Young	664	84	28	170	946	845,328	44,020	889,348
Gundagai..........	388	100	54	80	622	716,330	95,508	811,838
Tumut..........	410	176	43	92	721	281,965	35,134	317,099
Totals ..	4,068	958	502	1,675	7,203	5,469,535	687,825	6,157,360

Thus the land alienated in this part of New South Wales comprises 6,157,360 acres, or 45·6 per cent. of the whole of its area, which contains over 13,491,200 acres. Of these only 687,825 acres, or 11·2 per cent. of the settled lands, are held in tenancy, whilst 5,469,535 acres, or 88·8 per cent., are occupied by the land-owners themselves. Here, as in all other electorates, tenant holdings are more numerous, and cover a greater area, in the agricultural electorates than in those where grazing farms are the rule, and cultivation the exception. In Goulburn, Argyle, Braidwood, and Yass Plains the proportion of alienated holdings occupied by tenants ranges from 33·9 down to 14·5 per cent.; whilst in the more western electorate of Young this proportion is reduced to 5 per cent. In the whole of this group of electorates the total number of occupiers is 7,203, of whom 4,068 occupy their own freeholds, 958 are tenants, 502 occupy both descriptions of alienated lands, while 1,675 occupy areas of Crown Lands in addition to their freeholds. The conditions of settlement, in which pastoral occupation is the leading feature, must necessarily affect greatly the average extent of rural holdings, and in this division, it will be found, to attain fairly high proportions, Area alienated.

855 acres being the average throughout, with a maximum of 1,305 acres in Gundagai, and a minimum of 32 acres in the urban electorate of Goulburn. In the districts of Yass Plains, Young, Boorowa, and Queanbeyan, the average varies only between 917 and 969 acres; whilst in the electorates of Tumut and and Braidwood it is reduced to 482 and 440 acres respectively. These averages are given in the following table, which also shows the purpose for which land is used in this district, grazing being reported as the principal occupation on 3,646 holdings, and agriculture on 2,626, while 965 holdings are used for residential purposes, and 30 are in the occupation of miners; the figures below include 64 occupiers of Crown Leases.

Southern Table-land.

Electorate.	Average area of Holdings.	Land used for			
		Agriculture.	Grazing.	Mining.	Pleasure Grounds, Residential, &c.
	acres.	No.	No.	No.	No.
Argyle	645	830	357	3	28
Goulburn	32	35	26	...	34
Braidwood	482	66	238	9	252
Queanbeyan	969	142	402	...	65
Monaro	1,136	99	877	2	121
Yass Plains	917	280	487	...	97
Boorowa	945	115	334	5	49
Young	940	438	443	3	66
Gundagai	1,305	320	184	4	119
Tumut	440	301	298	4	122
Average and totals	855	2,626	3,646	30	965

Northern tableland

In the northern tableland the disproportion between freeholders and tenants is very strongly marked, the latter forming a a very small minority of the occupiers of alienated lands, owing to the same causes which operate both in the south and in the centre of this great section of New South Wales. It is evident that the object of the Land Act of 1861 to create a class of independent settlers has been fairly successful, notwithstanding the fact that the number of actual occupiers is small compared to that of the individual selectors who since the year 1861 have applied for conditional purchases. The following figures illustrate the state of settlement in the part of the country in question:—

Northern Table-land.

Electorate.	Occupiers of					Area—Freehold.	Area—Rented.	Total.
	Freehold Land.	Rented Land.	Partly Freehold and partly Rented Land.	Freehold and Crown Land.	Total.			
	No.	No.	No.	No.	No.	acres.	acres.	acres.
Inverell	337	64	39	76	516	397,118	29,262	426,380
New England	607	92	59	418	1,176	1,066,736	134,663	1,201,399
Glen Innes	291	21	25	115	452	391,714	20,951	412,665
Tenterfield	332	32	15	81	460	139,036	6,362	145,398
Tamworth	505	81	59	223	868	894.441	38,170	932,611
Totals......	2,072	290	197	913	3,472	2,889,045	229,408	3,118,453

The total area alienated in these electorates is 3,118,453 acres, or 23·4 per cent. of its whole extent of 13,333,120 acres. The total number of occupiers of rural settled lands is 3,472, of whom 2,072 live on their freeholds; whilst only 290 are tenants, 197 holding both free and leasehold land, and 913 occupying Crown Lands in addition to their freeholds. The proportion of the area occupied by private tenants is 229,408 acres, or 7·4 per cent. of the whole extent of alienated land; whilst 92·6 per cent., representing 2,889,045 acres, is occupied by the landowners themselves. The land is used for both agricultural and pastoral purposes, and as these industries are generally carried on conjointly, it is practically impossible to divide occupiers into the two distinct classes of agriculturists and of graziers. Nevertheless, out of a number of 3,125 landholders who follow these occupations, 1350 are returned as Area alienat agriculturists and 1,775 as graziers, whilst 343 are resident landowners, and on 231 holdings mining operations are carried on, principally in the tin-mining districts of Inverell and Tenterfield, where the miners appear to have availed themselves of the provisions of the Land Acts in their favour to a large extent. The average area of holdings in this district varies between 316 acres per holding in Tenterfield and 1,074 and 1,022 acres in those of Tamworth and New England where large freehold estates are situated; in Glen Innes the average reached 913 acres, and in Inverell 826 acres, the general average of the district being 898 acres.

Northern Tableland.

Electorates.	Average Area of Holdings.	Land used for			
		Agriculture.	Grazing.	Mining.	Residences.
	acres.	No.	No.	No.	No.
Inverell	826	296	188	84	36
New England	1,022	324	709	47	140
Glen Innes	913	163	260	17	23
Tenterfield	316	244	162	78	52
Tamworth	1,074	323	456	5	92
Average and totals	898	1,350	1,775	231	343

The districts situated on the western slopes of the Great Dividing Range mark the transition between the agricultural settlements of the coast and tableland, and the purely pastoral settlements of the great west; the extent of arable land is very considerable, but little is devoted to cultivation, as it is more economical, in the present stage of occupation of the soil, to use the land for grazing purposes, the great distance to the markets being the principal obstacle to a rapid extension of agriculture on the tableland.

It will be noticed that the proportion of land alienated considerably diminishes as these districts are reached, except in those parts where the excellence of the land for grazing purposes, and even for agriculture, impelled the pastoral tenants of the Crown some years ago to secure their holdings from the incursions of the free selector, whom the Act ostensibly intended to favour, by means of systematic alienations under the auction sale and improvement clauses of the Land Act of 1861. In the south-western districts, which are traversed by the principal permanent rivers of western New South Wales, the land has been alienated wholesale, and immense areas of freehold land are in the hands of a very small number of landholders; while in the north-western districts the freehold estates are neither so numerous nor of so enormous an extent as those of the south. The state of settlement of the alienated lands in the electorates situated in the southern part of the western slope of the Great Dividing Range may be gathered from the following figures:— Decrease of alienation in the West.

South-Western Slope.

Electorates.	Occupiers of					Area—Freehold.	Area—Rented.	Total.
	Freehold land.	Rented land.	Partly Freehold and partly Rented land.	Freehold and Crown land.	Total.			
	No.	No.	No.	No.	No.	acres.	acres.	acres.
Hume............	600	80	50	135	865	1,834,932	98,414	1,933,346
Albury	257	36	29	3	325	170,313	12,028	182,341
Murray	338	46	52	94	530	3,348,218	60,094	3,408,312
Murrumbidgee	915	135	93	446	1,589	4,634,158	205,072	4,839,230
Totals......	2,110	297	224	678	3,309	9,987,621	375,608	10,363,229

The total area of this district, commonly called Riverina, is computed at 18,438,518 acres, of which 10,363,229 acres are now alienated, or about 56·2 per cent. of the whole area. In some of Riverina district.

2 L

the electorates, however, a great portion of the land has been parted with; thus, in the Murray, 71·7 per cent., or 3,408,312 acres, are alienated, out of a total of 4,753,920 acres; whilst in Albury little land is left excepting reserves. In the electorate of Hume 1,933,346 acres, or 62·2 per cent. of the area of the district, viz., 3,109,200 acres, are alienated; whilst in that of the Murrumbidgee, which is one of the most extensive electorates in New South Wales, containing 10,392,438 acres, 46·6 per cent. of the area is alienated into the hands of 1,589 occupiers, 1,064 of whom devote their land to purely pastoral purposes. Only a small proportion of this land is held by tenants, the total area so occupied being only 375,608 acres, out of a total of 10,363,229 acres alienated, the remaining 9,987,621 acres being in the occupation of the proprietors themselves.

Grazing in Riverina.

The land is used principally for grazing purposes throughout Riverina, although cultivation is extending with great rapidity in the parts of the districts which have easy access to railway or river carriage. Crops are raised on 1,049 holdings, whilst 2,093 occupiers are engaged in pastoral pursuits, which are also carried on conjointly with agriculture in the previously-mentioned holdings; there are also 190 residential holdings. The above figures include 23 Crown leases. As may be presumed, the average area of holdings must be high in districts where the operations of the auction and improvement clauses of the Crown Lands Act of 1861 were extensively applied for the purpose of consolidating holdings and preventing the land from falling into the hands of the free selectors, whom the great pastoral lessees did not look upon as desirable neighbours. Such was the case in these localities, the land having been bought up wholesale, the pastoralists being greatly helped by the various banking corporations, their joint operations resulting in the alienation of immense areas of the best pastoral land the Colony possesses. Notwithstanding, however, the hostility of the Crown lessees, numerous selections were made, upon which agriculture is now spreading, whilst, with but a few exceptions, the huge pastoral estates of Riverina are entirely given up to the rearing of stock, sheep-breeding being practically their only industry. The average area of holdings for the whole district is 3,132 acres, but in the electorate of the Murray it reaches more than twice this area, viz., 6,431 acres; in the Murrumbidgee the average is 3,045 acres per holding, and in the Hume 2,235 acres; whilst in that of Albury, where the selections were comparatively more numerous, it is only 561 acres, exhibiting thus a healthier state of settlement.

The electorates situated in the Central portion of the Colony on the western slope of the dividing range exhibit somewhat similar results, although the alienation of Crown Lands was not carried on to the same extent as was the case in the south, as an examination of the following table will show:—

Central Western Slopes.

Electorate.	Occupiers of				Total.	Area freehold.	Area rented.	Total.
	Freehold land.	Rented land.	Partly freehold and partly rented.	Freehold and Crown land.				
	No.	No.	No.	No.	No.	Acres.	Acres.	Acres.
Bogan	396	106	44	718	1,266	1,901,646	450,792	2,352,428
Forbes	273	22	15	458	768	606,689	68,552	675,241
Grenfell	386	20	17	436	859	1,162,861	62,517	1,225,378
Totals	1,055	150	76	1,612	2,893	3,671,196	581,861	4,253,057

The total area alienated amounts to 4,253,057 acres, or 21·9 per cent. of the total area of the district, which is estimated at 19,434,660 acres. The greater area alienated is in the electorate of the Bogan, where there are 2,352,428 acres held by settlers. This is, however, but 25·2 per cent. of the total area of this large district, which contains 9,345,700 acres, whilst in Grenfell 1,225,378 acres, or 33·9 per cent. of the whole area of 3,616,640 acres have been parted with by the State. In Forbes only 10·4 per cent. of the area of the electorate is yet alienated, representing 675,241 acres out of a total of 6,472,320 acres. The land is almost entirely devoted to pastoral pursuits, although in

Central Western Slopes.

the eastern portion of this district, and in the vicinity of the towns of Dubbo, Forbes, and Grenfell, agriculture is rapidly spreading. There are, however, only 465 holdings upon which crops are raised, 1,912 being purely pastoral, and 557 residential holdings, whilst in 46 cases mining is carried on; the above figures account for 87 Crown leases in addition to the 2,893 holdings alienated from the State. Although the area held by tenants is proportionately larger than is the case further south, there are only 581,861 acres so held, the proprietors still occupying 3,671,196 acres out of the 4,253,057 acres of alienated land the district contains.

As a result of the small number of settlers in so extensive a district, the average area of holdings is necessarily fairly large, although it does not attain to such proportion as in the south, the average of this division being 1,470 acres, with a maximum of 1,858 acres in the Bogan, a minimum of 879 acres in Forbes and an area of 1,426 acres per holding in Grenfell.

In the northern position of the western slope of the Dividing Range, the distribution of settlement closely resembles that met with in the division just examined, as the following table shows:—

Electorate.	Occupiers of				Total.	Area freehold.	Area rented.	Total.
	Freehold land.	Rented land.	Partly freehold and partly rented.	Freehold and Crown land.				
	No.	No.	No.	No.	No.	Acres.	Acres.	Acres.
Gunnedah..............	233	35	20	153	441	1,484,056	48,252	[illegible]
Gwydir................	227	34	20	280	561	1,435,065	227,214	[illegible]
Namoi	231	42	17	306	596	856,497	135,325	[illegible]
Totals	691	111	57	739	1,598	3,775,618	410,791	[illegible]

The area alienated is 4,186,409 acres, or 24·8 per cent. of the total area which is 16,890,384 acres, the highest proportion of alienated land being in Gunnedah where 1,532,308 acres or 58·3 per cent. of the total area of electorate, calculated at 2,626,560 acres, have been bought from the Crown, the greater portion by the pastoralists, who have succeeded in preventing the settlement of an agricultural class over the best portion of the famed Liverpool Plains.

There are also 1,662,279 acres alienated in the Gwydir out of 7,253,120 acres, or 22·9 per cent. of this total, whilst in the extensive district of the Namoi, out of 7,010,704 acres, 991,822 acres, or 14·2 per cent. only, are as yet alienated. The competition between pastoralists and selectors was not so keen in the north-western districts as it was in the central, and more particularly in the south-western division, presumably because the land, though equally good in quality, was too distant from the markets, besides, the country becomes more exposed to extreme climatic influences in the northern parts. The average area of holdings throughout the district, though higher than in the central western district, is not so large as in those of the south-west; it reaches 2,620 acres, with a maximum of 3,475 acres in Gunnedah, owing to causes explained above, and a minimum of 1,664 in the Namoi, the Gwydir having an average of 2,963 acres per holding. These districts, with the exception of their eastern portion, abutting on the boundary of the tableland of New England, are entirely devoted to the depasturing of stock, 1,319 holdings being occupied for grazing, and only 207 for agricultural purposes, conjointly with stock-rearing, 96 being residential holdings. The above figures include 24 small Crown leases. Tenant occupiers are not numerous, only 111 being returned as renting some 410,791 acres of land, principally for grazing purposes, the remaining 3,775,618 acres, out of a total of 4,186,409 acres alienated, being still occupied by the proprietors themselves.

In the extreme west of the Colony settlement is making but slow progress. With the exception of the great mining centre of Broken Hill, situated on the boundary of the neighbouring colony of South Australia, around which a large population has settled within the last few years, the whole of this vast portion of the domain of New South Wales is given up to the depasturing of stock. Sheep-breeding is practically the only industry, the general character of the country militating against the successful rearing of cattle. The present state of settlement is illustrated by the figures given below :—

Western Plains.

Electorates.	Occupiers of—				Total.	Area, Freehold.	Area, Rented.	Total Area Alienated.
	Freehold Land.	Rented Land.	Partly Freehold and partly Rented Land.	Freehold and Crown Land.				
	No.	No.	No	No.	No.	acres.	acres.	acres.
Balranald	137	24	10	257	428	1,994,157	161,[illegible]	[illegible]
Wentworth ..	49	7	1	64	121	221,078	8,[illegible]	[illegible]
Wilcannia	35	4	1	20	60	27,602	6,[illegible]	[illegible]
Bourke	107	47	4	162	320	648,157	345,[illegible]	[illegible]
Sturt	253	12	....	37	302	25,108	405	[illegible]
Totals....	581	94	16	540	1,231	2,916,102	521,942	[illegible]

The proportion of land alienated is only 4 per cent. of the total area of this district, being an aggregate of 3,438,044 acres out of 85,824,598 acres, which it is estimated to contain. Of this area 2,916,102 acres are in the occupancy of the landowners, only 521,942 acres being held under lease, this kind of tenure being principally met with in the electorate of Bourke, where nearly 35 per cent. of the total area alienated appears to be so held, probably from the fact that some large pastoral estates containing a considerable area of alienated lands are held under lease from the original Crown lessees. The total number of holdings exclusive of Crown leases, containing no alienated lands, which are more numerous in this than in any other division of New

South Wales, is 1,231, of which 581 are freeholds, 94 rented properties, 16 partly freehold and partly leasehold, and 540 freeholds to which considerable areas of Crown lands are attached. Owing to this small number of estates, the average area alienated is very large—viz., 2,793 acres for the whole division, closely approaching in some electorates the average noted in the Riverina district; similar causes having produced like effects in the electorate of Balranald, for example, where the average attains 5,036 acres per holding; in Bourke the average reaches 3,106 acres, and in Wentworth 1,895 acres; but in Sturt the number of small holdings around the silver mines of the Barrier reduces the average to only 84 acres per holding; whilst in Wilcannia the alienated holdings are few in number, and average 564 acres. The land is used purely for pastoral purposes, except in the vicinity of townships, where market-gardening and fruit-growing is carried on, principally by Chinese.

Aggregation of holdings.

It will be seen from an analysis of the figures that settlement in New South Wales has hitherto tended towards the concentration into comparatively few hands of the lands alienated to a large number of individual selectors, and that in the great majority of cases the owner of the land is also the occupier. Tenancy, as understood in older settled communities, has made comparatively little progress, 88·55 per cent. of the land alienated being yet in the occupancy of the proprietors themselves, over an area of 36,445,122 acres, whilst only 4,711,755 acres, or 11·45 per cent., is held under lease from the freeholders.

Size of holdings.

The following table shows the subdivision of the alienated estate of New South Wales, according to size of holdings and the relation that the area held under private lease bears to the total alienated in each category. It will be seen that the proportion of land leased is greatest in areas below 200 acres, and gradually decreases as the area of holdings increases, which in reality means that tenancy is more the rule in the agricultural than in the pastoral districts of the Colony in proportion to the area settled and occupied :—

Subdivision of Alienated Lands.

Size of Holdings.	Occupiers of				Land Used for				Total Number of Holdings.	Area—Freehold.	Area—Leasehold.	Total.	Percentage of Land in the various sizes of Holdings.	Percentage to Total Area of the Colony Alienated.	
	Freehold Land.	Rented Land.	Partly Freehold and Rented Lands.	Freehold and Crown Lands.	Agriculture.	Grazing.	Mining.	Residential Areas, &c.						Freehold.	Rented.
										acres.	acres.	acres.	per cent.	per cent.	per cent.
1 to 30 acres..	7,349	3,328	461	116	4,580	1,355	32	5,287	11,254	62,883	40,783	103,616	0·25	0·15	0·10
31 to 400 ,, ..	16,043	5,289	1,729	3,701	15,352	9,742	56	1,612	26,702	3,232,998	771,564	4,004,562	9·73	7·85	1·87
401 to 1,000 ,, ..	3,294	463	632	2,517	1,482	5,239	21	164	6,906	3,851,730	564,282	4,416,012	10·73	9·36	1·37
1,001 to 10,000 ,, ..	1,692	241	475	1,974	414	3,916	30	22	4,382	10,111,678	1,673,793	11,785,471	28· 3	24·57	4·07
Upwards of 10,000....	73	13	37	533	15	641	..	..	656	19,185,833	1,661,383	20,847,216	50·66	46·62	4·04
Totals......	28,451	9,334	3,334	8,841	21,843	20,893	139	7,085	49,960	36,445,122	4,711,755	41,156,877	100·00	88·55	11·45

The above figures strikingly illustrate the present condition of colonisation in New South Wales, and their meaning should not be lost on those who watch with attention and interest the progress of settlement in this country. The percentage of land in holdings less than 30 acres in area is only 0·25 per cent. of the total area of land alienated in the Colony, and represents an aggregate of 103,616 acres out of a total of 41,156,877 acres; this small acreage is held by 11,254 persons, giving each holding an average of 9·21 acres. Holdings between 31 and 4,000 acres in extent number 26,762 with an aggregate area of 4,004,562 acres or 9·73 per cent. of the area alienated in the Colony, and an average therefore of 149·6 acres per holding. In areas between 401 and 1,000 acres are to be found 6,906 estates, the numbers decreasing rapidly as the areas increase, aggregating in all 4,416,012 acres of 10·73 per cent. of the area alienated, giving each an average of 639·4 acres. The tendency just noted becomes still more marked in the holdings between 1,001 and 10,000 acres in extent, their number being only 4,382, whilst they aggregate 11,785,471 acres or 28·63 per cent. of the total area alienated in the state, an average of 2689·5 acres per holding. The climax is reached however in the holdings of more than 10,000 acres in extent; of these there are but 656 aggregating 20,847,216 acres or 50·66 per cent. of the whole area alienated by the Crown, each averaging an area of 31,774 acres.

Some remarks as to the relative state of agriculture and settlement on the alienated rural lands of New South Wales could not fail to be of interest, especially when read with the preceding figures. The table on next page deals with this question and the figures carry with them their own explanation :—

Settlement and Cultivation.

Size of Holding.	Number	Aggregate area alienated in each series.	Proportion to total area of Colony.	Area cultivated in each series.	Proportion cultivated to aggregate area alienated.	Proportion cultivated to total area of Colony.
1 to 30 acres	11,254	103,616	0·25	36,956	35·67	0·09
31 to 400 „	26,762	4,004,562	9·73	430,549	10·75	1·04
401 to 1000 „	6,906	4,416,012	10·73	185,714	4·21	0·45
1,001 to 10000 „	4,382	11,785,471	28·63	162,579	1·38	0·38
Upwards of 10,000 acres.	656	20,847,216	50·66	31,437	0·15	0·07
Total Proportions.	49,960	41,156,877	100·00	847,235	2·05	2·05

Although the higher proportion of land cultivated in any of these series when compared with the total area alienated in the Colony is found in holdings from 30 to 400 acres, yet when compared with the aggregate area alienated in the series itself it represents only 10·75 per cent. of it, whilst on the smaller holdings less than 30 acres in extent, as much as 35·67 per cent. of the area alienated is under cultivation. The proportion considerably decreases as the higher areas are reached, being reduced to 0·15 per cent. in those over 10,000 acres.

From the above table some interesting information may be gleaned with regard to the proportion of the number of owners of land who still occupy their freeholds, those who reside on rented lands, and those who occupy, in addition to their freeholds, lands rented either from private owners or from the Crown. An idea may also be formed as regards the various purposes to which land is principally devoted, but a better and more comprehensive view of these two phases of settlement will be obtained by an examination of the following table, in which the holdings are divided into a greater number of categories according to their respective size :—

Size of Holdings.	Occupiers of—				Total Number of Occupiers.	Land used for—			
	Freehold Land.	Rented Land.	Partly Freehold and partly Rented Land.	Freehold and Crown Land.		Agriculture.	Grazing.	Mining.	Residential Areas, &c.
acres. 1 to 5....	3,908	1,335	144	67	5,454	1,294	465	15	3,680
6 ,, 15....	2,160	963	193	34	3,350	1,679	459	15	1,197
16 ,, 20....	1,231	1,080	124	15	2,450	1,607	431	2	410
21 ,, 50....	3,077	1,493	172	394	5,136	3,111	1,464	16	545
51 ,, 100....	4,006	1,775	354	703	6,838	4,275	2,113	18	432
101 ,, 200....	4,858	1,256	576	1,039	7,729	4,520	2,820	14	375
201 ,, 300....	2,336	472	358	696	3,862	2,192	1,536	5	161
301 ,, 400....	1,748	298	269	870	3,178	1,254	1,822	3	99
401 ,, 500....	971	162	175	440	1,748	584	1,163	4	63
501 ,, 600....	654	86	147	329	1,216	338	846	5	32
601 ,, 750....	848	161	117	1,206	2,257	290	1,960	4	64
751 ,, 800....	363	42	77	204	686	160	519	1	6
801 ,, 900....	221	39	66	160	486	79	397	2	5
901 ,, 1,000....	242	38	50	178	508	77	415	5	6
1,001 ,, 1,500....	697	106	192	596	1,591	218	1,350	11	12
1,501 ,, 2,000....	318	46	93	340	797	75	715	4	3
2,001 ,, 3,000....	348	46	90	365	849	64	774	9	2
3,001 ,, 4,000....	132	19	40	203	394	25	366	1	2
4,001 ,, 5,000....	73	8	20	130	231	13	216	2	....
5,001 ,, 7,500....	73	5	16	185	279	10	265	2	2
7,501 ,, 10,000....	61	8	24	148	241	9	230	1	1
10,001 ,, 15,000....	39	8	18	155	220	7	213	..	....
15,001 ,, 20,000....	14	2	3	97	116	2	114	..	....
20,001 ,, 30,000....	8	....	7	104	119	4	115	..	....
30,001 ,, 40,000....	2	2	1	62	67	....	67	..	....
40,001 and upwards	10	1	8	115	134	2	132	..	....
General Total..	28,451	9,334	3,334	8,841	49,960	21,848	20,898	139	7,085

From the above it will be seen that the total number of occupiers of freeholds only is 28,451, the proportion to the total number of occupiers being fairly constant in each description of holdings. Absolute tenants to the number of 9,334 are far more numerous in the smaller classes of holdings, and rapidly diminish both in number and proportion as the estates become larger. The same is the case with regard to holders of freehold and rented land, whose number is only 3,334, whilst the reverse obtains in holdings to which Crown lands are attached, their number and proportion increasing with the size of holdings. There are 8,841 such estates the majority of holdings over 1,000 acres in extent being found in that category.

Purposes land used for.

As regards the various purposes for which land is used, it must be understood that no hard and fast rule can be drawn between those holdings which are returned as principally used for agricultural purposes and those devoted to grazing, as both those occupations are carried on conjointly, except in the extreme west of the Colony, where hardly any crops are grown. Still the figures above quoted are interesting, as they show clearly that agriculture is carried on to greater extent on estates below 300 acres in area than in those of greater size, the proportional number of holdings principally occupied for agricultural purposes being greater as the respective areas become smaller. Beyond an area of 500 acres the land becomes more and more used for purely pastoral purposes, the proportion of cultivated estates decreasing as the areas increase; until among those of large areas but few are found upon which any kind of crops are grown.

Both industries, however, are carried on conjointly upon as many as 42,736 holdings, whilst freehold mining estates, principally coal, shale, and tin properties, number 139, the remaining 7,085 holdings being used as residential areas, &c., the greater number, as might be expected, being found in the smaller areas, the proportion decreasing with great rapidity as the area increases, but few estates over 700 acres in extent being attached to residences. It is probable that most estates of large areas reported as used for residential purposes are situated in the vicinity of the Metropolis.

PART XVIII.

Instruction, Science, and Religion.

PRIMARY EDUCATION.

THE history of primary education in New South Wales is naturally divided into four periods. During the first period, which lasted until 1848, the system in force was purely denominational, the Government granting to the heads of religious bodies assistance in proportion to the amount expended by them for educational purposes. No provision was made for the establishment of schools entirely under State control, and considerable dissatisfaction was the result. As early as 1834 attempts were made to modify the system in force, and five years later a grant was made with the object of securing undenominational education for the children of those who preferred it. It was not, however, until 1844 that any definite steps were taken in this direction. In that year a Committee of the Legislative Council reported in favour of the adoption of the Irish National School system, and, in accordance with this recommendation, an Act was passed in 1848 constituting two Boards, to one of which was entrusted the administration of denominational education, and to the other the undenominational, or, as it was called, the National system. This anomaly of two rival Boards existed for eighteen years, until it was abolished by the passing of the Public Schools Act of 1866 This Act provided for two distinct classes of schools, though all schools receiving aid from the State were placed under the control of a Board appointed by the Government, and styled the Council of Education. The Public Schools were entirely administered by this Board, but the denominational schools were

Early system of subsidies.

First grant in aid of undenominational education.

The Public Schools Act of 1866.

partly governed by the various religious bodies by whom they had been founded. Although the system established by the Act of 1866 was essentially one of transition, education nevertheless made considerable progress during the years of its administration. But it was found impossible to maintain this dual system, not only on account of its intrinsic defects but because the principle of granting State aid to religious schools was repugnant to the feelings of the majority of the people.

State aid to denominations abolished.

In 1880 State aid to denominational education was abolished. By an Act passed under the auspices of Sir Henry Parkes, which received the Royal assent on the 16th April, 1880, the entire educational system of the Colony was remodelled. The Act, in the first place, repealed the Education Act of 1866, dissolved the Council of Education, and placed the control of educational matters in the hands of the Minister of Public Instruction. It provides for the establishment and maintenance of Public Schools, to afford primary instruction to all children without sectarian or class distinction; Superior Public Schools, in which additional lessons in the higher branches may be given; Evening Public Schools, with the object of instructing persons who may not have received the advantages of primary education; and High Schools for boys and girls, in which the course of instruction shall be of such a character as to complete the Public School curriculum, or to prepare students for the University. It provides that in all schools under the Act the teaching shall be strictly non-sectarian; but the words "secular instruction" are held to include general religious teaching, as distinguished from dogmatical or polemical theology. The History of England and of Australia are to form part of the course of secular instruction; and it is further provided that four hours during each school day shall be devoted to secular instruction exclusively, but one other hour each day may be set apart for religious instruction, to be given in a separate class-room by the clergyman or religious teacher of any persuasion, to the children of the same persuasion whose parents do not

Minister of Public Instruction.

Primary instruction.

Secondary education.

Secular instruction.

Religious instruction.

object to their receiving such religious instruction. This provision has been taken advantage of to some extent by several of the denominations.

Education compulsory

It is made compulsory upon parents to send their children, between the ages of six and fourteen years, to school for at least seventy days in each half-year, unless just cause of exemption can be shown. Penalties are provided for breaches of this provision. But although education is compulsory, it is not altogether free, for parents are required to pay a weekly fee of three pence per child, but not exceeding one shilling in all for the children of one family. Power is given, however, to the Minister, or the Local Board, to remit the fees where it is shown that the parents are unable to pay. The fees, except in Evening Schools, are not the property of the teacher, but are paid into the Consolidated Revenue Fund. Children attending school are allowed to travel free by rail.

Weekly fee.

Provisional Schools.

Other sections of the Act permit of the establishment of Provisional Schools, and the appointment of itinerant teachers in remote and thinly-populated districts. Provision is also made for the establishment of training schools for teachers. It is enacted that Local Boards shall be appointed, whose duty is to visit and inspect the Public Schools placed under their supervision, to suspend teachers in cases of misconduct not admitting of delay, and to endeavour to induce parents to send their children regularly to school, and to report the names of parents or guardians who refuse or fail to educate their children. It should be observed that parents are not compelled to send their children to the Public Schools; they have full choice in the matter, the State only insisting that a certain standard of education shall be attained.

Local Boards.

Progress of education.

Great as has been the material progress of the Colony, its intellectual advancement has been much more rapid. In the records of the marriage registers signed by marks, a most accurate gauge of educational progress will be found. The earliest official record of marriages was for the year 1857, when out of 5,804 persons married 1,646 or 28·36 per cent. were unable to sign the marriage register. During 1890 the number of such persons was only 426, or 2·70 per cent. of the total number married. A generation has passed away during the period embraced by the following table, and the progress shown thereby cannot fail to be interesting.

Progress of Education in New South Wales, as shown by the Number of Persons signing Marriage Register with Marks.

Year.	Persons married.	Percentage signing with marks.	Number signing with marks.	Year.	Persons married.	Percentage signing with marks.	Number signing with marks.
1857	5,804	28·36	1,646	1874	8,686	11·96	1,039
1858	5,984	20·86	1,248	1875	9,210	12·26	1,129
1859	6,590	26·86	1,770	1876	9,260	10·47	970
1F60	5,890	26·46	1,559	1877	9,988	9·76	975
1861	6,444	24·60	1,585	1878	10,634	8·10	863
1862	6,652	25·01	1,664	1879	10,782	7·58	818
1863	6,628	22·69	1,504	1860	11,144	6·66	743
1864	6,960	22·70	1,580	1881	12,568	6·94	872
1865	7,156	22·06	1,579	1882	13,896	5·63	782
1866	6,924	21·63	1,498	1883	14,810	6·10	903
1867	6,852	18·84	1,291	1884	14,964	5·23	783
1868	7,472	20·14	1,505	1885	15,236	4·74	723
1869	7,598	19·19	1,458	1886	15,622	3·98	622
1870	7,696	18·23	1,403	1887	15,180	3·50	531
1871	7,906	16·96	1,341	1888	15,688	3·74	587
1872	7,850	13·62	1,069	1889	15,060	3·35	504
1873	8,768	14·26	1,252	1890	15,572	2·70	426

Marvellous progress of education.

The progress exhibited in the above table is marvellous. The residuum of population not yet educated is already very small, and, moreover, of the 426 persons using marks a large proportion were not born in New South Wales, but arrived in this Colony too late in life to avail themselves of its educational system. The proportion of persons using marks is somewhat higher in this Colony and Queensland than in any other member of the group. This is in no sense due to the superiority of the educational system of those colonies, but rather to the number of immigrants attracted thither, amongst whom there will always be found many persons unable to write.

Illiteracy in other Colonies.

Figures respecting all the colonies are not available, but as regards those that have furnished returns in the year 1890 the degree of illiteracy, as disclosed by the marriage registers, was :—

	Percentage signing with marks.
New South Wales	2·70
Victoria	1·52
Queensland	3·28
South Australia	2·28
New Zealand	1·78

Children instructed in former years.

Only an imperfect comparison can be made as to the number of children under instruction during past years, as the number in actual attendance cannot be distinguished from the number enrolled. The following table, however, gives the number of schools, both public and private, and enrolled scholars for over fifty years, and though it cannot be taken as absolutely correct, it may be relied on as fairly indicative of the educational progress of the Colony. Victoria, it should be remembered, was separated in 1851, and Queensland in 1861 :—

Progress of Education in New South Wales.

Year.	Population of the Colony.	No. of schools.	Children enrolled.	Proportion of population enrolled.
				per cent.
1836	77,096	85	3,391	4·40
1841	149,669	209	9,632	6·44
1846	196,704	394	19,033	9·68
1851	197,168	423	21,120	10·71
1856	286,873	565	29,426	10·26
1861	357,978	849	37,874	10·58
1866	428,813	1,155	59,594	13·90
1871	517,758	1,450	77,889	15·04
1876	614,181	1,629	131,620	21·43
1881	778,690	2,066	166,536	21·40
1886	989,340	2,833	220,724	22·31
1890	1,121,860	3,134	240,270	21·42

The number of children given in the preceding table as enrolled in the various schools exceeds, in almost every case, the actual school attendance, as the gross enrolment for the year is given, and not the mean for each quarter. The latter information cannot be obtained except for recent years, but the figures as they stand give a basis of comparison, which is not without value.

Enrolment of children.

The following table shows the gross enrolment of distinct children during the ten years which closed with 1890, as well as the quarterly enrolments, in all the schools of the Colony. The last column may be taken as giving the nearest approximation to the number of children actually under tuition in State and private schools :—

Year.	Schools.	Teachers.	Scholars.		
			Gross enrolment.	Mean quarterly enrolment.	Percentage of children of School age attending School.
1881	2,066	3,772	166,536	145,936	85·67
1882	2,161	4,154	188,507	156,768	92·41
1883	2,315	4,543	189,983	164,270	88·12
1884	2,535	4,860	202,519	174,544	89·49
1885	2,666	5,267	210,743	183,873	86·67
1886	2,833	5,659	220,724	192,010	89·12
1887	2,925	5,714	226,669	197,712	87·91
1888	2,964	5,870	229,043	201,083	87·06
1889	3,087	5,998	235,000	206,326	86·79
1890	3,120	6,574	237,853	212,969	89·54

Number of children of school age.

The number of children of school age—that is to say, from five to fifteen years—during 1890 was 286,000, and of this number 238,988, excluding 1,282 attending the University and colleges, were receiving instruction in the schools of the Colony. Of these 195,241 were on the rolls of the State schools, and the remainder were distributed among the various private and denominational schools, reformatories, and charitable institutions, while 47,012 were either receiving no instruction, or were being taught at home. No reliable estimate of the number of children under home tuition can be made, neither is it possible to determine the number of those who have ceased to attend school before reaching their fifteenth year, but it is very probable that considerable numbers are to be found in both classes. The total known enrolment at private schools was 42,612, and the average attendance, 34,378.

Owing to the sparseness of the population in nearly all the country districts of the Colony, the compulsory clauses of the Instruction Act cannot be strictly enforced. Nevertheless, the number of children growing up in absolute ignorance is by no means great, and, though the proportion of such children cannot be even approximately determined, there is sufficient evidence to warrant the conclusion that it is steadily decreasing. At the census periods of 1861, 1871, and 1881, the proportions of children from 5 to 10 years who could read and write were in every ten thousand as follows:— Compulsory clauses not strictly enforced.

	1861.	1871.	1881.
Read and write	2,355	3,470	4,413
Read only	3,289	2,752	1,982
Unable to read	4,356	3,778	3,605

Taking the children from 10 to 15 years, the comparison is still more satisfactory:—

	1861.	1871.	1881.
Read and write	6,769	7,666	8,804
Read only	1,854	1,292	614
Unable to read	1,377	1,042	582

The steady decrease in the proportion of illiterate children from 1861 to 1871, and from 1871 to 1881, is plainly visible from the above tables, and there can be little doubt that this satisfactory decrease has since continued. Progress of education amongst children.

PUBLIC INSTRUCTION—STATE SCHOOLS.

When the present Public Instruction Act came into operation, on the 30th April, 1880, the Council of Education ceased to exist, and handed over to the new administration the schools, until then under its control. At the date mentioned, there were maintained, or subsidized by the Government, 1,220 schools, attended by 101,534 scholars, thus distributed:— Schools when present Act came into force.

	No. of Schools.	No. of Pupils.
Public	705	68,823
Provisional	313	8,312
Half-time	97	1,683
Denominational	105	22,716
	1,220	101,534

At the close of 1882 the connection of the denominational schools with the State ceased, and the subsequent year is marked, as was to have been expected, by a considerable falling off in the number of children who were receiving their education at the expense of the State. The check only operated for a short period, as the year 1884 showed a recovery of more than the ground lost.

Enrolment since passing the Act.

This will be seen by the following table which shows the enrolment and attendance of children at State supported schools only :—

Year.	Gross enrolment of distinct children.	Quarterly enrolment.	Average attendance.
1881	146,106	125,506	82,890
1882	166,611	134,872	90,944
1883	155,918	130,205	88,546
1884	167,134	139,159	95,215
1885	173,440	146,570	100,462
1886	179,990	153,244	105,538
1887	184,060	157,262	106,408
1888	186,692	160,919	112,220
1889	191,215	164,701	114,569
1890	195,241	170,357	116,665

In the gross enrolment for 1890, 21,867 of the children were under the age of 6 years, 160,488 between 6 and 14, and 12,886 over 14 years of age.

Increase in enrolment.

Since the withdrawal of aid from denominational schools the increase in the average quarterly enrolment at State schools has been 30·84 per cent., the increase in each year being :—

1884 .... 6·88 per cent.
1885 .... 5·32 ,,
1886 .... 4·55 ,,
1887 .... 2·62 ,,
1888 .... 2·32 ,,
1889 .... 2·35 ,,
1890 .... 3·43 ,,

The number of schools under the direct control of the Department, during 1890, was 2,423, thus classified :— Number of schools.

High Schools	5
Public Schools—mixed	1,551
„ Two departments	53
„ Three departments	76
Provisional Schools	333
Half-time Schools	289
House-to-house Schools	95
Evening Schools	21
Total	2,423

The following table gives the number of State schools in each of the Australasian Colonies, together with the number of scholars in average attendance :— State Schools in Australasian Colonies.

State Schools, 1890.

Colony.	Number of Schools.	Number of Teachers.	Number of Scholars. [Average Attendance.]	Average attendance of Pupils per School.
New South Wales	2,423	4,181	116,665	48
Victoria	2,170	4,223	133,768	62
Queensland	621	1,539	40,836	66
South Australia	551	1,067	27,552	50
Western Australia	82	129	2,535	31
Tasmania	240	469	8,898	37
New Zealand	1,200	2,978	94,632	79
Australasia	7,287	14,083	424,886	58

The teachers in New South Wales during the year numbered 4,181, viz., 2,087 males, and 2,094 females. Number of Teachers.

	Males.	Females.	Total.
In charge of departments	1,533	901	2,434
Assistants	133	385	518
Pupil-teachers	393	714	1,107
Others	28	94	122
Total	2,087	2,094	4,181

The average number of pupils on the basis of the mean quarterly enrolment per teacher was, therefore, 40·75, and the average attendance per teacher, 27·90, while the average quarterly enrolment of children per school was 70·31.

Public School curriculum.

The curriculum of the public schools of New South Wales provides merely for imparting to children a sound course of primary education, and the elements of those sciences which form the basis of higher courses of education, scientific or technical. The State provides separately the necessary facilities for acquiring technical knowledge, under a system of training recently introduced, about which more will be said further on. The Kindergarten system has been introduced into some of the schools, and about 2,000 children are receiving this kind of instruction.

Training of Teachers.

The staff of male and female Public School teachers is trained in the normal schools of the Colony—the Fort-street training school for male teachers, and the Hurlstone training school for female teachers. These establishments are under the strictest supervision, and improvements are made every year in order to keep pace with the most modern systems of training. Admission is obtainable to these schools by examination, and the students are almost exclusively recruited from the ranks of both sexes of the pupil-teachers. These pupil-teachers are selected with great care, as they are required to undergo severe examinations, and must also satisfy the department as to their physical aptitude and the soundness of their constitutions, in view of the arduous nature of the duties they are called upon to perform.

Teachers and their emoluments.

During the year 1890 the number of teachers in the service of the Department of Public Instruction was, as already stated, 4,181. The teachers obtain promotion only after passing a series of examinations, which are so framed as to efficiently test their progress in general capacity. There are ten classes of male teachers in charge of schools or departments, their emoluments ranging from £128 to £500 per annum including residence; unclassified teachers in charge of Provisional Schools receive from £72 to £96; assistant teachers are paid at rates varying from £50 to £250; and pupil-teachers from £42 to £72 per annum. Female teachers in charge of schools or departments are paid from £218 to £326 per annum, including value of residence; assistant teacher's salaries vary from £114 to £168; and pupil teachers receive from £24 to £48 per annum.

The local supervision of the Public Schools of the Colony is placed in the hands of School Boards appointed in the various districts of the Colony, under the provisions of the Public Instruction Act. These boards are supposed to exercise a general oversight in regard to the Public Schools in their districts, but cannot interfere with the internal discipline or management of the schools, which remain under the direct control of the Minister of Public Instruction, and the inspectors and other officers of his department. Public School Boards.

The average cost per child in average attendance at the Public Schools has greatly varied, as will be seen by the following table, which gives the averages for the ten years, 1881 to 1890, inclusive. Average cost of education per scholar.

Cost of Education per Head.

Year.	For school premises.	For the maintenance of schools.	For administration, including the amount paid as retiring allowances.	Total.
	£ s. d.	£ s. d.	£ s. d.	£ s. d.
1881	1 4 9¾	3 15 3	0 14 3¾	5 14 4½
1882	2 10 2¾	3 15 1¾	0 10 8¼	6 16 0¾
1883	4 8 3¾	4 2 0¼	0 15 3½	9 5 7½
1884	3 3 11	4 4 2¾	0 14 5¾	8 2 7½
1885	1 15 5¼	4 3 7	0 13 1¼	6 12 1½
1886	1 9 4½	4 1 6	0 13 1½	6 4 0
1887	1 2 6½	4 3 7½	0 11 3½	5 17 5½
1888	0 15 1	4 1 7¾	0 9 8½	5 6 5
1889	0 19 1½	4 2 6¼	0 9 3¼	5 10 11
1890	1 5 9½	4 5 3	0 9 8½	6 0 9

In the Public Schools of New South Wales the cost per child was until 1888 higher than in the other Australian Colonies; the figures for 1890, however, show this Colony has now reduced its expenditure per child below that of Victoria, though it is still a little in excess of the other provinces. The following figures do not include cost of buildings:— Cost per child in other colonies.

	Total cost per child in average attendance.
New South Wales	£4 14 11¼
Victoria	5 3 5
Queensland	4 1 10¼
South Australia	3 16 8½
Western Australia	4 1 3¼
New Zealand	3 14 10
Tasmania	3 8 9¼

The total cost per child in average attendance at the Schools under the control of the London School Board, in 1890, was £3 8s. 3d., and the net cost £2 1s. 8d., but no useful purpose is to be gained by comparing England and Australia in regard to cost of education, and in considering the expense incurred by the State in past years it should be borne in mind that a considerable outlay was needed to build the necessary school-houses after the Act of 1880 became law. Under this Act the expenses contingent upon the necessity of obtaining efficient results, in a country so sparsely populated as New South Wales, were unavoidably great. School-houses had to be built, teachers required training, and the whole machinery for providing schools and teachers had to be started in so many parts of the country where there were none but denominational schools, and frequently no educational establishments at all. To these initial expenses was due, in a great measure, the relatively high cost of public education in the earlier years shown in the table on page 551. A great reduction is observable since 1885, and it may be expected that the cost will not at any time greatly exceed the present figures, as the schoolhouses have been built with due regard to the increase in the number of scholars which must be expected in a young, prosperous, and growing colony. It may be added that most of the school-buildings are of such a character as would do credit to the most advanced countries in the world, the greatest care being taken to have them replete with all the improvements which the experience of centuries has suggested in older communities. It should, however, be mentioned here, that the last report of the Minister for Public Instruction states that the expenditure on school-buildings during the past seven years has been insufficient, and that a further large outlay will be required shortly in order to keep pace with the ever increasing demand for accommodation.

Expenses incidental to starting present Act.

Comparative cost of education.

When comparing the average cost of education per child in attendance in New South Wales with that of its neighbour, Victoria, the results for 1890 must appear very satisfactory, especially when it is borne in mind that the smaller extent of the territory of the latter colony, and the greater travelling facilities, which a railway system proportionately much larger offers, must necessarily reduce the cost of education. In South Australia and Western Australia settlement is confined to certain districts in which the population is more compact, whilst the whole of the territory of New South Wales, if we except the extreme west, may be regarded as everywhere settled, at least to such an extent as to necessitate the extension of the Public School system throughout the greater part of the Colony. But the spread of public instruction is considered so pre-eminently important an object that the Legislature has at all times expressed its readiness to make every sacrifice, and spare no expense to render efficacious the system of national education which it adopted in 1880.

The following table will show the total amount expended by the State since the year 1881, and the annual amount per head of population provided for the primary education of the children of the Colony :— Amount expended on primary education.

Amount Expended on Education.

Year.	Amount.	Per head of population.	Year.	Amount.	Per head of population.
	£	s. d.		£	s. d.
1881	474,157	12 7	1886	654,411	13 6
1882	618,800	15 6	1887	624,983	12 5
1883	821,853	19 8	1888	597,102	11 6
1884	774,357	17 6	1889	635,509	11 11
1885	663,697	14 4	1890	704,260	12 9

This statement would not be complete if some details were not furnished, showing under what principal heads this expenditure was incurred, and the amount of school fees received during the same period :— Details of expenditure on education.

State Expenditure on Education.

Year.	Number of Schools.	Gross enrolment of distinct Pupils.	On school premises.	On maintenance of Schools, including Administration, &c.	Total.	School Fees.	Net State Expenditure.
			£	£	£	£	£
1881	1,667	146,106	102,903	371,254	474,157	46,347	[illegible]
1882	1,795	166,611	228,401	390,399	618,800	51,312	[illegible]
1883	1,706	155,918*	391,000	430,853	821,853	51,427	[illegible]
1884	1,912	167,134	304,383	469,974	774,357	56,766	[illegible]
1885	2,046	173,440	178,002	485,695	663,697	58,926	604,771
1886	2,170	179,990	155,072	499,339	654,411	63,165	[illegible]
1887	2,236	184,060	119,957	505,026	624,983	63,896	561,087
1888	2,271	186,692	84,575	512,527	597,102	69,554	527,548
1889	2,373	191,215	109,576	525,933	635,509	72,318	[illegible]
1890	2,423	195,241	150,441	553,819	704,260	71,827	[illegible]

* Certified Denominational Schools were discontinued at the close of 1882.

School fees.

It will be seen that the amount directly contributed by parents towards their children's education is but a small proportion of the total cost. In 1890, however, it was considerably larger than in any year, 1889 excepted, since the existing Act came into force, and the rate per head was exceeded only in 1888 and 1889, as may be seen from the following statement:—

Average cost of Education per Child.

Year.	Cost to State per Child of Average Attendance.	Total Cost per Child of Average Attendance.	Amount of Fees received per Child of Average Attendance.
	£ s. d.	£ s. d.	£ s. d.
1881	5 3 2	5 14 4	0 11 2
1882	6 4 10	6 16 1	0 11 3
1883	8 14 0	9 5 7	0 11 7
1884	7 10 9	8 2 8	0 11 11
1885	6 0 5	6 12 1	0 11 8
1886	5 12 0	6 4 0	0 12 0
1887	5 5 5	5 17 5	0 12 0
1888	4 14 0	5 6 5	0 12 5
1889	4 18 4	5 10 11	0 12 7
1890	5 8 5	6 0 9	0 12 4

Free scholars.

The largest number of free scholars during the year 1890 was that for the December quarter, when they amounted to 8,157; or 4,368 boys and 3,789 girls, equal to a percentage of 6·65 of the average attendance for the some quarter.

School savings' banks.

In accordance with a design long contemplated, savings' banks were opened during 1887 in connection with the public schools of the Colony. At the close of 1890 there were 554 banks in operation, as compared with 547 at the close of 1889, and the deposits for the year amounted to £11,192. Of this amount £8,283 was withdrawn for current use, and £2,909 remained to the credit of the depositors. The object aimed at in establishing these banks is to inculcate practically the principles of economics, while yet the minds of the children are susceptible of deep impressions. A systematic training for this purpose is a thing to be desired in every public school, in order to engender habits of thrift amongst school children, to indoctrinate them as to the uses and effects of money that are ulterior to immediate gratifications, and to make them recognize and calculate upon poverty and degradation as the natural results of waste and improvidence.

DENOMINATIONAL AND PRIVATE SCHOOLS.

Attendance increasing.

The attendance at private schools has increased more than two-fold since 1882. This is entirely due to the withdrawal of aid from denominational schools. At the close of the year mentioned there were 124 denominational schools under the control of the Education Department, with 346 teachers, and 29,651 scholars. Many of these schools ceased to exist immediately on the withdrawal of State aid, and the children by whom they were attended were transferred for the most part to the ordinary Public Schools of the Colony. Some of the schools, however, were still maintained, chiefly those connected with the Roman Catholic Church, and thenceforth appear in the returns as private schools. The increase in the number of private schools during 1883 was 97, and the increase in the attendance of children was 12,361, so that, at the lowest computation, 27 denominational schools were immediately closed, and 17,290 children transferred to Public Schools.

Increase in private schools.

The following table gives the particulars respecting private schools from 1881 to 1890 :—

Private Schools.

Year.	Schools.	Teachers.	Scholars.	Year.	Schools.	Teachers.	Scholars.
1881	507	1,129	18,317	1886	047	1,808	38,766
1882	491	1,154	19,746	1887	689	1,873	40,450
1883	588	1,473	32,107	1888	679	1,854	40,164
1884	611	1,601	33,607	1889	700	1,884	41,685
1885	611	1,654	35,967	1890	697	2,393	42,612

Classification of private schools.

Dividing the private schools of the Colony into their respective classes, there were in operation during 1890 :—

Classification of Denominational and Private Schools.

	Schools.	Teachers.	Scholars.
Undenominational	372	1,000	9,789
Church of England	67	212	3,607
Roman Catholic	244	1,112	28,552
Wesleyan Methodist	6	31	390
Presbyterian	4	27	160
Congregational	2	9	46
Lutheran	1	1	43
Primitive Methodists	1	1	25
Total	697	2,393	42,612

Subjects taught.

With regard to the subjects imparted to these 42,612 children, it appears that 17,821 boys and 22,223 girls were learning reading; writing was taught to 17,817 boys and 22,134 girls; and there were 17,034 boys and 21,242 girls receiving instruction in arithmetic, while 3,465 boys and 2,316 girls were students in other mathematics. Geography was taught to 12,826 boys and 16,987 girls; grammar to 12,242 boys and 16,516 girls; and history to 7,176 boys and 9,918 girls. The ancient languages were studied by 2,032 boys and 1,073 girls, while 2,634 boys and 3,475 girls were making themselves acquainted with modern languages. Drawing was taught to 7,111 boys and 10,503 girls, and music was studied by 3,517 boys and 7,450 girls. No less than 16,649 girls were being instructed in needlework.

Roman Catholic Schools.

Not a few of the schools returned as undenominational are religious schools, though no definite form of religious opinions is inculcated therein. Of distinctly religious schools, those of the Roman Catholic Church comprise the great majority, numbering 75·08 per cent. of professedly denominational schools, and 86·99 per cent. of the scholars educated therein. The number of pupils attending these schools was not ascertained for the years preceding 1886. On the withdrawal of State assistance from denominational schools in 1882 there were in operation under the Department of Education, 75 Roman Catholic Schools, attended by 16,595 pupils, while in 1890 there were 244 schools, attended by 28,552 pupils. There were, however, some Roman Catholic Schools prior to 1882 not receiving aid from the State, and, on the other hand, some of the schools which were closed in 1882 have not since been opened. The following are the figures for the five years for which returns are available :—

Roman Catholic Schools.

Year.	Schools.	Teachers.	Scholars on Roll.			Average Attendance.		
			Males.	Females.	Total.	Males.	Females.	Total.
1886	215	896	11,222	13,798	25,020	9,533	11,766	21,279
1887	238	897	12,518	14,474	26,992	10,158	12,108	22,266
1888	247	916	12,535	14,637	27,172	10,010	11,799	21,809
1889	267	996	13,674	14,872	28,546	10,785	11,977	22,762
1890	244	1,112	13,021	15,531	28,552	10,206	12,225	22,431

Church of England Schools.

The Church of England is the only other religious body maintaining schools of importance. During 1890 such schools numbered 67, and were attended by 3,607 pupils. At the end of 1882 there were in existence 42 Church of England Schools, with an enrolment of 11,927 children. The following table shows the state of these schools during the past five years :—

Church of England Schools.

Year.	Schools.	Teachers.	Scholars on Roll.			Average Attendance.		
			Males.	Females.	Total.	Males.	Females.	Total.
1886	56	143	1,794	1,579	3,373	1,662	1,346	3,008
1887	73	167	1,815	1,514	3,329	1,588	1,258	2,846
1888	66	154	1,548	1,552	3,100	1,272	1,242	2,514
1889	47	115	1,353	1,302	2,655	1,065	999	2,064
1890	64	209	1,844	1,763	3,607	1,449	1,410	2,859

HIGHER EDUCATION.

Curriculum of High Schools.

It has already been mentioned that the State has made provision for higher education, by the establishment of High Schools in the metropolis and the principal centres of population. The curriculum of these schools is of such a character as to enable students to complete the course of instruction, the basis of which they acquired in the Public Schools, and, if they so wish, to prepare themselves for the University examinations. Admission to these schools is by examination only. There were at the close of the year 1890 five High Schools for boys and girls, and the gross enrolment for that year was 383 boys and 465 girls, making a total of 848 children. The average attendance was 598 as against 520 for the year 1889. During the year, 93 pupils passed the junior, 20 the senior, and 36 the matriculation examinations at the University.

Scholarships and bursaries.

A system of scholarships and bursaries for boys and girls at State schools has been brought into operation. Twenty of each—ten for each sex—are available for education at State, High, or Grammar Schools, and six bursaries for boys, and four for girls are tenable at the University. The former are awarded half-yearly, and the latter at the March matriculation examinations, after examination, to the most proficient pupils, in cases where the parents are unable to defray the expense of the pupil's education.

Superior Public Schools.

Superior Public Schools, in which the subjects taught embrace, in addition to the ordinary course prescribed for Public Schools, such other subjects as will enable the students to compete at the senior and junior public examinations, are also established. There were 64 of these schools in existence at the end of 1890, with an enrolment of 47,213 pupils.

State-aided schools.

In addition to the various classes of Public Schools already mentioned, there exist several institutions of an educational character which receive an annual subsidy from the Government. The most important of these is the Sydney Grammar School, which is one of the principal schools in the Colony. In 1890, the average quarterly enrolment was 426, and the daily attendance 405. Towards maintaining this school the Colonial Treasury contributed the sum of £3,650, the school fees and other revenue amounting to £6,105.

THE UNIVERSITY.

In the year 1849 Mr. Wentworth presented a petition to the mixed Legislative Council from certain shareholders of a proprietary school, known as Sydney College, praying for the appointment of a select committee of the House "to consider the best means of carrying on the institution so as to afford the youth of the Colony the means of obtaining instruction in the higher branches of literature and science." The committee was appointed, but had, however, somewhat different instructions, and was directed to "consider and report how best to institute an university for the promotion of literature and science, to be endowed at the public expense." The committee, after a few weeks' deliberation, brought up its report, recommending the establishment of an university with a permanent endowment of £5,000 per annum out of the general revenue, and a Bill was brought in by Mr. Wentworth in accordance with the report. The Council was shortly afterwards prorogued, and the measure consequently lapsed for that session. In 1850 the bill, which was based mainly on the charter of University College, London, was reintroduced by Mr. Wentworth, and, after some discussion and a few amendments, was passed, receiving the Royal assent on 1st October of that year. Sydney College

The endowment was given for "defraying the stipends of teachers in literature, science, and art," and for administration purposes; there being no provision made for teaching any other branch. Power was, however, given to examine and to grant degrees after examination in law and medicine as well as in arts. The University was to be strictly undenominational, and the Act expressly prohibited any religious test for admission to studentship or to any office, or for participation in any of its advantages or privileges. Residence was not contemplated otherwise than in affiliated colleges, but authority was given to license tutors and masters of boarding-houses with whom students of the University might live. Constitution of the University.

Senate.

A Senate of sixteen Fellows was constituted by the original Act to govern the University, and they were empowered to elect from among themselves their own Provost and Vice-Provost, which titles were later on changed to those of Chancellor and Vice-Chancellor. The Fellows were, in the first instance, nominated by the Crown, but were to be replaced, as vacancies arose, by the Fellows themselves until there should be 100 graduates holding the degrees of Master in Arts, or Doctors in Law or Medicine. The first Senate commenced their labours at the close of the year 1850, with Mr. Edward Hamilton, M.A., as Provost, and Sir Charles Nicholson, M.D., as Vice-Provost. They shortly established three chairs in Classics, Mathematics, and Chemistry and Experimental Physics, and sent to England for competent professors to fill them; and on the 11th October, 1852, the University was opened with an imposing ceremony, in presence of the Governor and principal officers, and under the presidency of Sir Charles Nicholson, and twenty-four matriculated students were admitted to membership.

Charter.

In 1858 a royal charter was granted, which declares that "the degrees of this University in arts, law, and medicine shall be recognized as academical distinctions of merit, and be entitled to rank, precedence, and consideration in the United Kingdom as fully as if the said degrees had been granted in any university of the United Kingdom."

Amendments of the Act.

Since the passing of the original Act various changes have been made by amending Acts, of which the principal are as follows:—By an Act passed in 1857, those who had taken the degree of B.A. or M.A. received certain privileges in respect of admission to the Bar or to the Roll of Solicitors. In 1861 it was directed that in addition to the ordinary sixteen Fellows there should be not fewer than three nor more than six *ex officio* members of the Senate who should be Professors in such branches of learning as the Senate should by any by-law select; and such Professors and other Public Teachers and examiners and every superior officer declared to be such by the by-laws should be a member of the University, with the same rights and privileges as to the election of new Fellows as persons holding the degrees of M.A., LL.D., and M.D. In 1881 *Ad eundem* degrees, with equal privileges, were authorized to be conferred; and B.A.'s of three years standing were empowered to vote at new elections of Fellows. In 1884 the Senate's powers as regards teaching and degrees were extended by enabling it to give instruction and grant degrees or certificates in all branches of knowledge with the exception of Theology or Divinity, subject to a proviso that no student should be compelled to attend lectures or to pass examinations in Ethics, Metaphysics, or Modern History; and by the same Act it was directed, in accordance with a previous by-law of the Senate, that the benefits and advantages of the University should extend in all respects to women equally with men.

The number of persons entitled to vote at the elections of new Fellows reached 100 in 1872, whereupon the Senate passed by-laws in respect of such elections, and styled the electoral body "Convocation." This body, including the additions made by the several amending Acts, and comprising heads of affiliated colleges, who had been declared to be superior officers of the University under the Act of 1861, now numbers nearly 500. Convocation.

The public endowment of the University stood at £5,000 a year until 1880, when £1,000 was added for assistant lectureships, but in 1877 a bequest of the value of £6,000, and producing about £300 a year, was made by Mrs. Hovell, widow of the explorer of that name, for instruction in Geology and Physical Geography, which, together with fees, enabled the Senate to divide the Chair of Chemistry and Experimental Physics into two, to the first of which Geology and Physical Geography were attached. In 1882 a further vote of £5,000 was made to enable the Senate to establish Schools of Medicine and Engineering, and to give some further help to the original Department of Arts. Medical and Engineering Professors and Lecturers, and Endowment of the University.

Medicine and engineering.

a Professor of Natural History, and some small le Arts were created; but this sum was soon found in the intended purposes, and has been increased to £7,9 of the £1,000 granted in 1880. Allowances have al for apparatus, and a sum of £2,000 per annum has l for Evening Classes in Arts. Principally out of thi a system of Extension Lectures to non-matriculan menced in 1882, first in the metropolis, but spreadin a distance; and it is not improbable that as time means increase these lectures may become a ver feature in the action and influence of the University.

Grose Farm granted to the University.

In 1855 the present site was granted by Governo Fitzroy, by Royal authority, for the erection of su ings, and also to provide land for the prospective ere denominational Colleges. Before this grant was ma of the University had been carried on in the old Syc which, together with its library and even an endo Scholarship bequeathed by Mr. Solomon Levy, was p the Government for the University, and a grant had been made by Parliament in 1853 as a building present site, granted in 1855, comprises about 126 ac known as Grose Farm, to which a further grant of afterwards added for the enlargement of the dom As early as 1854 an Act was passed to aid and p four colleges within the University. Contribution than £10,000, and not more than £20,000, were from the general revenue for building funds, prov equal sum were subscribed by private individuals, year was to be paid annually by the Government stipends of Principals for each College. Just before t been taken to establish a Church of England Colleg and St. John's Roman Catholic College followed i the Presbyterian College of St. Andrew's in 1867. T body, for whom an equal area had been set apart accept it, and in 1873 some 12 acres of the la intended for a site for their college, was resumed by the Crown and dedicated to the Prince Alfred Hospital; and provision was made for the establishment by the University of a Medical School in connection with it and for the joint control of the University Senate and Hospital Board in respect of all appointments of the medical and surgical officers of the Hospital. But while the regulations under which students have access to the Hospital are framed by the Hospital Board, with the Senate alone rests the appointment of Professors and Lecturers in the Medical School. Affiliated Colleges.

The system of Public Examinations, similar in general character and purpose to the middle class examinations of Oxford and Cambridge, was instituted in 1867, and has gradually spread, till last year there were no less than forty-eight local centres other than Sydney; six of which were in the Colony of Queensland; and at the examination held in September of that year there were 1,301 candidates. Of these, 129 presented themselves for the senior, and 1,172 for the junior, examination. 101 senior and 798 junior candidates passed successfully. The University also initiated examinations of articled clerks in 1877, in compliance with a rule of the Supreme Court, and during 1890 there were 66 successful candidates. An examination of candidates for appointment in the Civil Service was instituted at an earlier date; 97 candidates presented themselves at this examination during 1890, and 93 were successful. Public Examinations.

Many donations have been made to the University for the use and reward of students. Among the first was a gift of £1,000 each from Mr. Thomas Barker and from Sir Edward Deas-Thomson, represented by lands which are now of twice that value. Many others followed, and about £42,000 has been presented up to the present date, exclusive of prizes, which have been exhausted by award, and irrespective of increases in value. About £10,000 of this is still in suspense on account of intervening life estates to the widows of testators. Besides the above, a sum of £30,000 Benefactions.

was left by the late Mr. Thomas Fisher for a library, and has been given by the Hon. Sir William Macleay for a Cu of the Natural History Museum, presented by him to the sity, and for which the Government have erected a building. There have also been bequests of property ot money to the estimated value of £51,000 up to the prese

Challis bequest

Above all, the late Mr. John Henry Challis left his r estate, subject to certain annuties. In December, I trustees handed over to the University the major par Australian portion of the estate consisting of £199,362 i ments, and £3,228 cash balance. Under this bequest th have created new Chairs in Law, Modern Literature, Logic and Mental Philosophy, Anatomy, Engineering, and to which they have given the testator's name. The H Challis bequests constitute the only resources of the U for actual education other than the public endowments.

Teaching staff,

The teaching-staff, now that all the Challis Chairs are fi sists of fourteen Professors, twenty-six Lecturers, of wh are Evening Lecturers, and four Demonstrators. The over which Professors preside are Classics, Mathematics, C and Mineralogy, Physics, Geology and Palæontology, Ph Anatomy, Engineering, Modern Literature, Logic, and Philosophy, Biology, Law, and History. The Lecturers Geology and Physical Geography, Classics, Modern Li Mathematics, Architecture, Principles and Practice of M Principles and Practice of Surgery, Midwifery and Di Women, Materia Medica and Therapeutics, Pathology, Jurisprudence and Public Health, Clinical Medicine, Surgery, Psychological Medicine, Ophthalmic Medicine gery, Medical Tutor, Law of Real Property and Equity, Procedure, including Evidence, Law of Wrongs, C Criminal, and Law of Obligations. The Demonstra appointed in Chemistry, Physiology, Anatomy, and Phys

Since its foundation the University of Sydney has conferred 859 degrees of various kinds, the highest number bestowed in any one year being 70, in 1890. Among the present members of the University there are 207 who hold the degree of M.A., 316 B.A., 17 LL.D., 11 B.L., 28 M.D., 34 M.B., 26 Masters of Surgery, 10 B. Sc., and 14 Bachelors of Engineering. The number of students attending lectures increased from 61 in 1877 to 409 matriculated and 447 non-matriculated students in 1890, whilst the number of candidates who attended the public examinations has increased both in the senior and junior divisions, the former having advanced from 63 in 1877 to 129 in 1890, and the latter from 303 to 1,172. Degrees conferred by the University.

Corresponding increases in the number of successful candidates at the public examinations have also taken place, as the following table will show:— Result of examinations.

Number of Students, and Results of Examinations.

Year.	Number of students.		Number of students qualified by matriculation	Public Examinations.			
				Number of Seniors.		Number of Juniors.	
	Attending Lectures.	Attending extension Lectures.		Examined.	Passed.	Examined.	Passed.
1876	58	...	34	53	40	356	212
1877	61	...	23	63	38	303	135
1878	62	...	24	58	41	364	243
1879	83	...	58	76	64	333	247
1880	76	...	64	66	54	381	209
1881	81	...	80	48	36	392	231
1882	97	...	101	57	43	398	240
1883	128	...	85	57	36	473	299
1884	203	...	142	65	48	563	379
1885	206	...	115	84	73	645	440
1886	203	137	122	107	83	858	548
1887	215	329	132	125	87	834	562
1888	250	403	130	141	110	834	538
1889	275	327	210	115	90	1,085	706
1890	409	447	301	129	101	1,172	798

The expenditure of the University prior to 1890 was met out of the revenue accruing from students' fees, the Government aid, and sundry private sources, irrespectively of income for the Revenue of University.

Expenditure of University.

express use or reward of students. The following tabl the yearly state of the finances of the University period from 1876 to 1890:—

Receipts and Expenditure of the University of S

Year.	Receipts.				
	Government aid.		Lecture fees.	Other sources.	Total.
	Endowment.	Grants for apparatus or other special purposes.			
	£	£	£	£	£
1876	5,000	....	403	100	5,503
1877	5,000	....	334	100	5,434
1878	5,000	1,168	324	100	6,592
1879	5,000	114	476	100	5,690
1880	5,000	1,500	457	100	7,057
1881	5,000	1,000	706	100	6,806
1882	10,000	2,964	1,080	100	14,144
1883	12,000	2,343	1,286	120	15,729
1884	12,000	3,500	2,207	170	17,877
1885	12,000	4,500	2,479	385	19,364
1886	12,000	5,500	2,600	323	20,423
1887	12,000	4,918	2,819	308	20,045
1888	12,000	7,099	3,022	385	22,506
1889	12,000	6,800	5,667	807	25,274
1890	13,900	4,734	5,365	293	24,312

School of Medicine.

An extensive addition to the University's magnifice has been made for the use of the School of Medicine. the most complete accommodation for students desiring t profession of medicine and surgery, and the Prince Alfr erected, as before stated, on the University grant, affor necessary means of study. At the commencement 1890 there were 87 undergraduates, of whom 6 wer the Medical School, a very fair number considering that this school was not established until 1883, and then commenced with only four students. A laboratory for the Department of Physics has also been recently erected, and is replete with every means of illustrating the teaching of physical science, and an equally complete laboratory and halls are in course of construction for the Department of Chemistry and its adjuncts. The prospects of the University of Sydney are excellent, and it cannot fail to prosper, and exert a most beneficial influence on the future of Australia. An Act for founding an Affiliated College for Women has been passed, limiting the building endowment, however, to £5,000, but granting £500 a year for a Principal. It will be brought into operation as soon as the necessary funds are collected. The Department of Public Instruction also contemplates the erection of a College for the training of male teachers. The Senate of the University have granted the necessary site, and the Government have submitted plans of a building, to accommodate 51 students, and to cost £37,500, to the Parliamentary Standing Committee on Public Works.

University laboratory.

DENOMINATIONAL HIGH SCHOOLS AND COLLEGES.

All the principal religious bodies provide high schools and colleges where students may be educated according to the precepts of their various beliefs and prepared to compete for University honors, or the various professions which they may adopt. Evidence of the progress of superior denominational education in the Colony may be seen in the magnificent college buildings which surround the city, among which may be cited Newington College, the colleges of the Marist Brothers, and the Jesuit Fathers, at Hunter's Hill and Riverview, the old-established King's School at Parramatta, the North Sydney Church of England Grammar School, the Presbyterian Ladies' College at Croydon, and a host of other first-class establishments erected under the patronage of the various religious bodies.

Denominational Colleges.

TECHNICAL EDUCATION.

Necessity for technical knowledge.

Public attention was so strongly directed in the years which followed the great world exhibition of 1851, to the necessity of providing the artizan classes, and the people generally, with the means of obtaining a scientific knowledge of the various handicrafts, that technical schools sprang up in various parts of England, some being under the direct patronage of the State, while others were founded by the wealthy trade societies, or guilds, of the great English cities. The excellent results following the establishment of these schools could not fail to attract attention in the colonies, where a sound and practical knowledge of the manual arts is of paramount necessity. The foundation of the New South Wales Technical School was due in great measure to the efforts of a few gentlemen connected with the Sydney Mechanics' School of Arts, and as far back as 1873 it was decided to establish a Technical College affiliated to that institution, with the object of improving the scientific knowledge of Australian artizans. In the year 1878, a sum of £2,000 was granted by Parliament towards the organization of a Technical College, and for five years the work of the institution was carried on in connection with the School of Arts. In 1883, however, a board was appointed by the Government to take over its management, and the Technical College became henceforth a State institution. Towards the end of 1889 the Board was dissolved, and the Technical College came under the direct control of the Minister of Public Instruction.

Foundation of Technical College.

Curriculum.

The course of instruction, under the present constitution of the Technical College, comprises classes in agriculture, applied mechanics, arts, architecture, geology, chemistry, commercial economy, mathematics, elocution, pharmacy, physics, and domestic economy, and these classes are subdivided into sub-classes as may be warranted by circumstances.

The college is open to students of each sex, and, during 1890, 383 female students attended for at least one term. The number of individual students in 1890 averaged 2,822 persons. The average enrolment per term was 1,686. Out of 1,538 students who went up for examination, 864, or 56·2 per cent., were successful in obtaining a pass. Number of students.

Branch technical schools have also been established in the suburbs, and in the northern, southern, and western districts of the Colony. In 1890 these country classes had an average of 2,126 students enrolled. Country classes.

Technical workshops have been fitted up in Sydney, where mechanical classes are held, and the teaching is illustrated by all the various tools and apparatus needed for the proper understanding of the different processes of each separate class of work. The Technical College is now fairly established, and its benefits are already being felt and appreciated, whilst the future has every promise of still greater usefulness. A site for the College has been secured by the Government at Ultimo, on which a building suitable for its requirements is now being erected. Technical workshops.

In 1890 the expenditure of the Board of Technical Education amounted to £25,440. In addition to this, the sum of £2,902 was contributed by the students in the shape of fees. The Parliamentary vote for the year was £29,850. The means at the disposal of the board have not been sufficient for the establishment of country branches in every case where application has been made, but lecturers have been appointed to visit from time to time the principal country centres, and deliver lectures in mineralogy, geology, and agriculture. Proposals have also been made for the granting by the State of suitable areas, or reserves, for the purpose of establishing agricultural colleges and experimental farms, and the near future may see an extension of technical education in this direction. Cost of technical education.

REFORMATORIES.

Industrial Schools.

In addition to the purely educational establishments, the State maintains three reformatories or disciplinary institutions, two for girls—the Industrial School at Parramatta, and the Shaftesbury Reformatory, near South Head—and one for boys—the nautical school-ship "Vernon." At the Parramatta institution the total enrolment of girls during the year was 123, and the new admissions, up to the 31st December last were 36, of whom 11 were under and 25 over 14 years of age. The cost of maintaining the school in 1890 amounted to £2,375. The Shaftesbury Reformatory is under the Minister of Justice. It has been in existence over eleven years, and is designed for the reception of young women under sentence, a wise provision, for by this means are avoided the alternatives of sending the offenders to the institution at Parramatta (late at Biloela), where their influence and example might have a baneful effect on more youthful minds, or of consigning them to gaol. The want of a similar institution for criminal youths is much felt. It would indeed prove a boon in many cases, not only to the individuals themselves but to society at large, and might often be the turning point in a career just started on a downward course. The number of inmates at Shaftesbury at the close of 1890 was 42, and the expenditure during the year amounted to £903. On board the "Vernon" 353 boys were dealt with during the year, and the number remaining at the termination of 1890 was 208. Up to the 30th April, 1891, there had been 2,488 boys admitted on board, of whom 2,264 had left. During 1890 28 of the latter had been under conviction, or a percentage of 1·2 for the year, as against a percentage of 1·8, which is the proportion of convictions if the whole male population over 15 years of age be taken. There were at the date just mentioned 430 apprentices from the "Vernon," who remained still under its supervision, in addition

The "Vernon" Training Ship.

to the number on board. The management of the training-ship is excellent, and its cost to the State during 1890 was £6,745. The results obtained in the three above-mentioned establishments have hitherto been of a very successful character, many children having been reclaimed from a depraved life, or rescued from unhappy surroundings, and turned out, after a course of some years' training, useful members of society.

SCIENTIFIC SOCIETIES.

In a young country such as New South Wales, where most of the people are engaged in the development of its material resources, the existence of a leisured class, or one devoted to the pursuit of science, is hardly to be looked for. Nevertheless it is satisfactory to find that the higher aims of science are far from being neglected. As far back as the year 1821, a scientific society under the title of the Philosophical Society of Australasia was founded in Sydney, which, after experiencing many vicissitudes of fortune, was transformed in 1866 into, and afterwards incorporated under the title of, the Royal Society of New South Wales. The society is now in a flourishing condition, counting amongst its members some of the most eminent men in the Colony. Its object is to forward the advancement of science in Australia, and favour original research in all subjects of scientific, artistic, and philosophical interest, which may further the development of the resources of Australia, draw attention to its productions, or illustrate its natural history. The proceedings, published every year, include papers of the greatest interest on important scientific questions, especially those whose solution is of Australian interest. Royal Society.

The study of the botany and natural history of Australia has attracted many enthusiastic students, and the Linnæan Society of New South Wales was also established for the special purpose of furthering the advancement of these particular sciences. The society is housed in a commodious building at Elizabeth Bay, one Linnæan Society.

of the most beautiful spots near the city, and already possesses a library and museum. The society has been liberally endowed by the Hon. William Macleay, who, not content with being one of its most munificent supporters, is also an indefatigable worker in the field of science. The society's proceedings are published at regular intervals, and contain many valuable papers, together with excellent illustrations of objects of natural history.

Geographical Society.

In 1883 a third scientific society was formed in Sydney under the name of the Geographical Society of Australasia, with the view of promoting geographical research in a part of the world where much remains to be discovered. Branches of this society have been established in the cities of Melbourne, Brisbane, and Adelaide, and there is no lack of interest displayed in their proceedings. Among the first tasks undertaken by this Society was the despatch of an expedition to New Guinea, for which purpose aid was obtained from the various Colonial Governments. The expedition sailed from Sydney on the 10th June, 1885, and resulted in the acquisition of some useful geographical and scientific knowledge of the island, the discovery of a large affluent of the Fly River being, perhaps, the most important achievement of the expedition.

Aid received by scientific societies.

The scientific societies just mentioned depend for support on private contributions, though, except in the case of the Linnæan Society, the Government grants them small sums annually in proportion to the income received from subscriptions, and has hitherto allowed their "Proceedings and Transactions" to be printed free of charge at the Government Printing Office.

Sydney Observatory.

Among the other institutions of a scientific and educational character which the Colony so liberally supports the Sydney Observatory is not the least important. Situated in a commanding position, it is admirably fitted for the purpose it is intended to serve. The present building was erected in 1856 at the instance of Sir William Denison, then Governor of the Colony, who took a great interest in scientific pursuits. The Government Astronomer has under him a complete staff of assistants, and during the year 1890 a sum of £4,985 was expended in connection with the institution. Meteorological observations have received special attention, as befits so important a subject in a country whose prosperity depends so much upon climate. When the present Astronomer took office in 1870, there were in the Colony only six stations, and observations on the climate, rainfall, and other meteorological phenomena were necessarily very limited in character. At the end of 1890 the number of stations had been increased to 1,088. Rain gauges have also been established at most of the sheep and cattle stations of the interior, with a result which is highly satisfactory. The light thrown on the true characteristics of the climate, especially of that part of the Colony remote from the sea coast, has tended to remove the notion long current as to its unfitness for agricultural as well as pastoral settlement.

The Australian Museum, which is the oldest institution of the kind in Australia, occupies a conspicuous site in the centre of Sydney, facing one of the principal parks. The collections contain carefully selected specimens of the principal objects of natural history found in kindred establishments, and also a most complete collection of zoological specimens of distinctly Australian character. The popularity of the institution is evinced by the increasing number of persons by whom it is visited. The Museum is open to the public every day except Monday. On Sundays the visitors are very numerous. The number of visitors during 1890 was 123,724, the daily average being 688 on Sundays, and 331 on week days. The expenses in connection with the institution amounted to £7,389, of which £2,097 was expended on account of purchase, collection, and carriage of specimens. Australian Museum.

Free Public Library.

The Free Public Library was established on the 1st of October, 1869, when the building and books of the Australian Subscription Library were purchased by the Government. The books thus acquired formed the nucleus of the present library. The number of volumes originally purchased was about 16,000, and on the 31st December, 1890, they had increased to 86,284, including those in the lending branch, or lent to country libraries. The lending branch was established in 1877, to meet a growing public want, and, under the present system any person may, on the recommendation of a clergyman, magistrate, or other responsible person, obtain under certain simple regulations, the loan of any of the works on the shelves, free of charge.

Loan of books to country libraries.

The scope of this institution was further extended by the introduction of a system by which country libraries and Mechanics' Institutes may obtain on loan works of a select kind, which in many instances would be too expensive for them to purchase on account of the slender funds at their disposal. Under this system, boxes are made up containing from 60 to 100 books, and forwarded to the country libraries on application, to be returned, or exchanged within four months. This system was initiated in August, 1883, and has been carried on successfully ever since. In the course of 1890, 137 boxes, containing 10,070 volumes, were forwarded to 77 institutions, some of them at considerable distances from the metropolis. The distance which these books were carried amounted to 47,737 miles, being on an average 348 miles for each box, an enormous distance, partly accounted for by the fact that some places to which books are sent were most readily accessible through other colonies. All the charges in connection with the despatch and return of books, insurance, &c., are defrayed by the State, and the system in vogue in New South Wales is the most liberal of its kind in existence.

Reference Library.

The reference department of the Free Public Library contains 61,284 volumes, and the lending branch 20,735. The country libraries were, on the 31st December, 1890, in possession of 4,265 volumes, lent under the system above mentioned, the total number of books and pamphlets, the property of this institution, being 86,284, classified as under:—

Books in Free Public Library.

Synopsis of Classification.	Reference Department	Lending Branch.	Country Libraries.	Total.
Natural Philosophy, Science and the Arts	6,980	3,243	808	11,031
History, Chronology, Antiquities, and Mythology	5,630	2,826	946	9,402
Biography and Correspondence	4,041	3,383	1,118	8,542
Geography, Topography, Voyages and Travels, &c.	5,775	3,110	768	9,653
Periodical and Serial Literature	16,537	......	......	16,537
Jurisprudence	3,227	748	75	4,050
Theology, Moral and Mental Philosophy, and Education	3,547	1,223	110	4,880
Poetry and drama	2,072	718	105	2,895
Miscellaneous Literature and Collected Works	4,653	*4,886	335	9,874
Works of Reference and Philology	4,135	......	......	4,135
Duplicates and unbound volumes	1,604	......	......	1,604
Pamphlets	3,083	......	......	3,083
Books for the Blind	.....	598	......	598
Total Number of Volumes	61,284	20,735	4,265	86,284

* Including 2,245 volumes of Fiction.

The popularity of the Free Public Library is clearly proved by the number of persons availing themselves of the privileges which it affords. The increase has been very regular, as will be seen in the following statement showing the number of visitors to the library, rising from 59,786, in 1870, to 155,822, in 1890, 53,543 of whom were visitors at the lending branch. These figures show a considerable increase on those of the previous year, though they are still below the results of 1886. This is no doubt owing to the interruptions caused through the additions and alterations to the building, which now being complete have caused the increased attendance noticed during the year 1890. Popularity of Library.

Attendance of visitors.

Year	Visitors
1870	59,786
1871	60,165
1872	48,817
1873	76,659
1874 (eleven months)	57,962
1875	66,900
1876	72,724
1877 (Lending Branch first opened)	124,688*
1878	117,047
1879 (Exhibition open)	152,036
1880	134,462
1881	136,272
1882 (eleven months)	133,731
1883	155,431
1884 (eleven months)	161,877
1885	165,715
1886	168,685
1887	139,203*
1888	149,425
1889	132,983
1890	156,822

* Reference Library closed for three months, for moving.

Number of readers

Although the lending branch contains but 20,735 volumes, the total number used during the year was not less than 64,457, and the number of persons availing themselves of the privilege of borrowing was 4,651, so that on an average each book was taken a little over three times, and each person to whom a permit was granted used nearly fourteen volumes during the year. As usual, a large portion of the works read was from fiction, each of the 2,245 novels in the branch having been used about eight times during the year. The number of volumes of each class taken out was as follows :—

Classification of Books used.

Synopsis of Classification.	No. of volumes used.
Natural Philosophy, Science, and Arts	6,865
History, Chronology, Antiquities, and Mythology	6,464
Biography and Correspondence	7,029
Geography, Travels, &c.	9,886
Jurisprudence	1,257
Mental and Moral Philosophy	2,251
Poetry and Drama	1,969
Miscellaneous Literature	10,753
Prose Fiction	17,983
Total	64,457

During 1886 and 1887 considerable extensions were made to the premises of the Free Public Library, which had become much too small for the accommodation of the public, and the proper housing of the books. It was at length decided to pull down the old building in Macquarie-street, and a contract was made about the middle of 1887 for rebuilding a large portion of the Library at a cost of £10,455. This work was progressing throughout the year 1889, and the new building was opened to the public in April, 1890. The Sydney Free Public Library is now one of the most convenient in Australia.

The institution forms a separate department, under the control of the Minister of Public Instruction, and its cost to the State, during 1890, was, in addition to the amount for building:— Cost of maintaining library

Salaries, &c.	£6,040
Buildings and Repairs	2,310
Books	2,332
Total	£10,682

Besides the Free Public Library of Sydney there are smaller libraries established in the principal population centres throughout the Colony. These libraries may be broadly classed under two heads—Schools of Arts—receiving an annual subvention in proportion to the amount of monetary support accorded by the public; and Free Libraries established in connection with Municipalities. The former class are far the more numerous. Under the provisions of the Municipalities Act of 1867 any municipality may establish and maintain a Free Library, and, where such is done, the Council of the Municipality is entitled, for the purchase of books, the sum of £200 if the library is available for the use of a population of 1,000 or to £100 where the population to whom the library would be accessible reaches 300 persons. The number of volumes in the various public libraries, excluding the Free Public Library, is estimated at about 240,000. Schools of Art and Municipal Libraries.

of animal and vegetable products. The popularity of this institution may be gathered from the fact that 94,111 persons visited it during 1890, the Sunday average being 689, and the week day 187. The cost to the State amounted to £3,390, distributed as follows:—

	£
For maintenance	1,133
For specimens, models, &c.	1,236
For salaries	1,021
Total	£3,390

RELIGION.

In the eyes of the State all religions are equal in New South Wales, but during the early days of the Colony such was not the case. New South Wales was originally essentially a Crown Colony, and the Church establishment, as it existed in England, was naturally transplanted to these shores. Ecclesiastical monopoly nevertheless only continued for a short time, and the countenance and support of the State were eventually extended, during the governorship of Sir Richard Bourke, to the principal religious bodies which then existed—the Anglicans, Roman Catholics, Presbyterians, and Wesleyan Methodists. To the clergy of each of these denominations the Government granted what has usually been denominated State aid, which continued long after the old political system had passed away and had been replaced by Responsible Government. In 1862, however, an Act was passed limiting future payments to the clergy then actually in receipt of State aid. In the year following the passing of this Act the claims on the Government amounted to £32,372, and were thus distributed :—

Equality of all religions.

State aid to religion.

Church of England	£17,967
Roman Catholic Church	8,748
Presbyterians	2,873
Wesleyan Methodists	2,784

Year by year the sum payable has been lessening, owing chiefly to the deaths of clergymen in receipt of State aid, so that in 1890 the payment by the State was £9,793, distributed as follows:—

Church of England	£5,591
Roman Catholic Church	2,600
Presbyterians	702
Wesleyan Methodists	900

Payments on account of State aid.

The payments to the clergy of different denominations are given for each year since 1863. It will be observed that in several years the amounts paid were less than in succeeding years. This anomaly is due to the temporary stoppage of the stipends of clergymen who were absent from the Colony:—

Amounts paid to the Clergy since the Abolition of State Aid to Religion.

Year.	Church of England.	Roman Catholic Church.	Presbyterian.	Wesleyan Methodist.	Total—All denominations.
	£	£	£	£	£
1863	17,967	8,748	2,873	2,784	32,372
1864	17,519	8,234	2,614	1,179	29,546
1865	14,111	7,430	3,090	1,572	26,203
1870	12,386	6,583	2,180	1,573	22,722
1875	10,725	5,608	1,626	1,372	19,331
1880	7,739	3,892	1,702	1,716	15,049
1885	6,041	3,000	1,052	1,136	11,229
1890	5,591	2,600	702	900	9,793

The number of persons entitled to State aid during 1890 was 58—32 Church of England, 15 Roman Catholics, 5 Presbyterians, and 6 Wesleyan Methodists.

The number of members of each religious body was estimated at the census of 1881, and the relative proportions of each of the larger denominations were found to differ but slightly from those shown by the previous census. Distributing the population on the basis of the census of 1881, the estimated number of adherents to each of the denominations, with the clergy rgeistered for the celebration of marriages, was during 1890 as follows :— Adherents of each religion.

Adherents of each Denomination.

Denomination.	Clergy.	Adherents.	Proportion of adherents to clergy.
Church of England	324	510,440	1,575
Roman Catholic	281	309,900	1,103
Presbyterian	156	108,350	695
Wesleyan, and other Methodist	179	96,270	538
Congregational	62	21,400	345
Baptist	33	11,000	333
Lutheran	4	7,300	1,825
Unitarian	1	1,400	1,400
Hebrews	3	4,950	1,650
Salvation Army	8	4,150	519
Pagans	...	17,000	.....
Others—unspecified	12	29,700	2,475
Total	1,063	1,121,860	1,056

The number of persons attending Divine Service on Sundays averaged 314,979 for the year 1890. This number represents the attendance of adults only; if school children were included the number would be about 436,900. When the sparseness of the population in some parts of the country is considered the church attendance will appear very large, and though apparently less than found in the colony of Victoria, is proportionately much greater than in England. The number of attendants on Divine Service in 1889 was returned at 312,221; for 1888 the number was 310,859; for 1885 it was 250,041, and for 1881 it was 221,031, so that there has been a gradual increase, fairly keeping pace with the population. The relative numbers of each denomination in attendance have remained very much the same for several years past. In 1881 the Church of England had the largest attendance, but from 1884 the Church of Rome has taken the lead. Church attendance.

The figures showing the attendance at Divine Service on Sundays for each of the principal denominations are given hereunder. Sunday school children are not included :—

Attendance at Divine Service.

Denomination.	Number of distinct persons attending Sunday services.
Church of England	80,754
Roman Catholic	92,166
Presbyterian	32,453
Wesleyan Methodist	61,847
Other Methodists	10,470
Congregationalist	13,004
Baptist	4,610
Salvation Army	15,508
Other denominations	4,167
Total	314,979

Church of England.

The Church of England is the largest religious denomination in the Colony, whether judged by the number of professed adherents, the number of clergy, or the number of buildings used for divine service. During the year 1890 there were 643 churches belonging to this denomination and 132 school-houses and 759 public buildings and dwellings used for public worship, accommodating 121,035 persons; the attendance of distinct persons counting only adults was 80,754. The number of clergy registered under Acts 19 Vic. Nos. 30 and 34, for the celebration of marriages, was 324. The Church of England in the colony is governed by a metropolitan who is also primate of Australia and Tasmania, and five other Bishops whose sees are Bathurst, Goulburn, Newcastle, Grafton and Armidale, and Riverina.

Roman Catholic Church.

The Roman Catholic Church is presided over by the Cardinal Archbishop of Sydney, assisted by a Coadjutor Bishop under whom are the suffragan bishops of Bathurst, Goulburn, Grafton, Maitland, Armidale, and Wilcannia, the whole colony forming an ecclesiastical province. There are 281 priests licensed to celebrate marriages. The number of Roman Catholic Churches properly so called was 438; besides these there were 54 school-houses and 912 public buildings or dwellings used for Divine Service. The accommodation afforded by the churches amounted to about 104,902 sittings and the attendance on Sundays averaged 92,166.

Presbyterian Church.

The various branches of the Presbyterian Church in the colony have 324 churches and 354 schools used for public worship; there were also 44 public buildings or dwellings occasionally used for the same purpose in 1890. The number of ministers was 156, of whom 143 were connected with the Presbyterian Church of New South Wales, 12 with the Synod of Eastern Australia, and 1 with the Presbyterian Church of Scotland. The accommodation provided in churches was 39,375 sittings, and the attendance numbered about 32,153, not including Sunday-school children.

Wesleyan Methodists.

The Wesleyan Methodist communion is divided into eight districts. Throughout the colony there are 387 churches and 433 other preaching places with sittings, in the former to the number of 60,469, and in the latter 24,580, in all 85,049. The denomination owns also 58 school buildings and 81 parsonages, and has in its service 135 regular clergy and 452 local preachers. The number of church members is said to be 7,978, of whom 1,110 are communicants, and the attendance of adherents at Divine Service is not less than 61,847, not including children.

The Primitive Methodists and United Methodists have 92 churches, and 38 other buildings, and 32 clergy; the accommodation provided will seat 16,870 persons, the attendance at Divine Service is about 10,005.

Congregationalists.

The Congregational Church has 66 churches as well as 44 public buildings or dwellings used for worship; the sittings provided will accommodate 20,713 persons. The clergy licensed to celebrate marriages number 62 and the attendance at Divine Service on Sundays averages about 13,004.

Baptists.

The various Baptist Churches in the colony have 33 licensed ministers with 36 churches and 29 school-houses or other buildings devoted to public worship; the Sunday attendance averages 4,610 persons, but there is sitting accommodation for 8,532.

Salvation Army.

The Salvation Army has only 8 officers licensed to celebrate marriages, but has 215 buildings used for service, accommodating 51,491 persons. The number of adherents or soldiers attending Sunday service is stated by the authorities to be 15,508.

Other Denominations.

Besides those above enumerated there are other distinct religious bodies, for the most part Protestant denominations, with clergy licensed by the State to celebrate marriages. The number of clergy ministering to these was 21; the churches, school-houses, and public buildings used for Divine Service numbered 92 and the attendance on Sundays was about 4,632 persons.

The number of registered ministers belonging to all faiths was 1,063, and the churches numbered 2,125, in addition to which there were 651 school-houses and 2,374 dwellings or public buildings used for public worship. The accommodation provided would seat about 457,181 persons. The average attendance was 314,979.

Sunday-schools.

Nearly all the religious bodies maintain Sunday-schools. The attendance of children at these schools shows a considerable increase during the past three years. Some part of this increase is merely apparent, and is due to the greater completeness in the returns, but no small portion of the improved attendance results from the extension of school accommodation in various parts of the country. The attendance of children at the Sunday-schools of the leading denominations, with the number of schools and teachers during 1890, was :— Sunday-school maintained by all denominations.

Sunday-schools of each Denomination.

Denomination.	No. of schools.	Number of teachers.			Average number of scholars.		
		Male.	Female.	Total.	Male.	Female.	Total.
Church of England...	552	1,198	2,543	3,741	16,187	20,698	36,885
Roman Catholic	445	410	1,246	1,656	10,719	14,451	25,170
Presbyterian	228	539	882	1,421	6,001	7,388	13,389
Wesleyan Methodist	321	1,300	1,424	2,724	9,976	11,478	21,454
Other Methodists.....	94	546	457	1,003	3,786	4,148	7,934
Congregational	70	382	436	818	3,539	4,170	7,709
Baptist	26	128	128	256	1,011	1,145	2,156
Salvation Army	67	89	128	217	2,580	3,141	5,721
Other denominations	37	98	85	183	721	746	1,467
Total	1,840	4,690	7,329	12,019	54,520	67,365	121,885

The attendance given above is extremely high, amounting as it does to nearly 50 per cent. of the total children between the ages of 7 and 15 years, at which ages children generally attend Sunday-schools. The number of Sunday-schools and teachers, and the attendance during each of the past ten years, were :— Attendance at Sunday-schools.

Sunday-school Teachers and Children.

Year.	Number of schools.	Number of teachers.	Average attendance.		
			Male.	Female.	Total.
1881	1,405	9,289	34,950	40,722	75,672
1882	1,318	9,190	34,393	41,334	75,727
1883	1,441	9,793	35,205	42,610	77,815
1884	1,461	9,426	35,883	43,202	79,085
1885	1,513	9,986	37,991	46,531	84,522
1886	1,596	10,759	47,307	56,354	103,661
1887	1,614	10,749	48,333	58,999	107,332
1888	1,724	11,267	50,556	61,735	112,291
1889	1,832	11,568	52,778	63,896	116,674
1890	1,840	12,019	54,520	67,365	121,885

PART XIX.

Finance and Public Wealth.

THE Public Revenue of New South Wales largely exceeds that of any other Australian Colony. The total amount raised by each colony during 1890, as well as the revenue per inhabitant, was as follows :—

Colony.	Total Revenue.	Revenue per head of population.
	£	£ s. d.
New South Wales	9,498,620	8 12 5
*Victoria	8,519,159	7 12 8
Queensland	3,260,308	8 7 10
South Australia	2,557,772	7 18 9
Western Australia	414,314	8 15 6
Tasmania	758,100	5 5 11
New Zealand	4,208,029	6 15 5
Total	29,216,302	7 16 1

*Year ending 30 June, 1890.

Revenue for 1825.

Reliable information respecting the revenue and expenditure of New South Wales is not obtainable earlier than 1825, in which year the public receipts amounted to £71,682, and the expenditure to £93,020. Sixty-five years afterwards, at the close of 1890, the revenue had increased more than one hundred and thirty fold, though the population had, during the same interval, increased only about thirty-three fold. From 1825 to 1840,—a date memorable in the annals of the Colony as that in which transportation ceased,—the advance in the revenue was very rapid. In that year the public receipts amounted to £683,112, a sum not again reached until 1853, two years after the discovery of gold. From 1853 to 1859 the revenue made great strides, and amounted to £1,522,668 for the year last mentioned. On the 1st December, 1859, the separation of Queensland took place, and consequently a falling off in the revenue occurred in the following year, the amount collected being £1,308,925. Since 1860 the income of the Colony has increased in a fairly regular manner, as may be seen from the following statement :—

Steady increase in revenue.

Revenue of New South Wales.

Year.	Amount.	Year.	Amount.
	£		£
1861	1,421,831	1876	5,037,661
1862	1,557,639	1877	5,751,878
1863	1,534,187	1878	4,991,919
1864	1,661,805	1879	4,481,665
1865	1,899,468	1880	4,911,990
1866	2,012,079	1881	6,714,327
1867	2,012,042	1882	7,418,536
1868	2,107,157	1883	6,470,341
1869	2,202,970	1884	7,117,592
1870	2,102,697	1885	7,587,368
1871	2,238,900	1886	7,594,300
1872	2,812,011	1887	8,582,811
1873	3,330,913	1888	8,886,360
1874	3,514,314	1889	9,063,397
1875	4,126,303	1890	9,498,620

Classification of revenue.

The revenue is usually classified under four heads, Taxation, Land Revenue, Services (including revenue from railways, tramways, posts, telegraphs, and fees of various kinds), and Mis-

Total receipts. cellaneous. The receipts under each class since 1871 are shown below; the totals will be found in the preceding tables.

Classification of Revenue.

Year.	Taxation.	Land Revenue.	Services.	Miscellaneous.
	£	£	£	£
1871	1,063,204	497,978	561,679	116,039
1872	1,200,203	840,453	659,770	111,585
1873	1,364,806	1,137,914	728,875	99,318
1874	1,200,489	1,426,166	770,895	116,764
1875	1,122,002	2,020,629	858,497	125,175
1876	1,161,406	2,773,003	965,327	137,925
1877	1,233,132	3,236,277	1,119,532	162,937
1878	1,309,718	2,325,704	1,183,582	172,915
1879	1,272,721	1,632,024	1,328,302	248,618
1880	1,417,294	1,646,436	1,594,082	254,178
1881	1,770,849	2,820,988	1,945,076	177,414
1882	1,903,412	2,914,394	2,363,085	237,645
1883	1,891,708	1,656,069	2,666,731	255,833
1884	2,152,854	1,753,344	2,942,643	268,751
1885	2,252,651	1,876,452	3,168,463	289,802
1886	2,611,835	1,643,954	3,089,235	249,276
1887	2,664,548	2,378,995	3,245,907	293,361
1888	2,681,883	2,268,253	3,664,100	272,124
1889	2,677,169	2,137,563	3,924,955	323,710
1890	2,748,339	2,243,039	4,174,938	332,304

Refunds. The amounts given above, as well as those in the other tables referring to revenue, represent the gross receipts. In every year refunds are made, so that the figures just quoted are somewhat too high, but the amount of the refunds is now much less than formerly.

Though a revenue of £9,498,620 is derived from a population of little more than 1,121,000 the people of New South Wales are very lightly taxed, the amount falling upon each person in the community for the last nineteen years averaging only £2 5s. 6d., of which amount the bulk is obtained indirectly through the Customs House:— Taxation very light.

Taxation per Head.

Year.	Amount of taxation per head.	Year.	Amount of taxation per head.
	£ s. d.		£ s. d.
1872	2 5 7	1883	2 5 2
1873	2 10 2	1884	2 8 9
1874	2 2 6	1885	2 8 7
1875	1 18 5	1886	2 13 6
1876	1 18 5	1887	2 13 0
1877	1 19 3	1888	2 11 9
1878	1 19 10	1889	2 10 2
1879	1 16 10	1890	2 9 10
1880	1 19 1	Average for 19 years	£2 5 6
1881	2 6 3		
1882	2 7 8		

The decrease per head in the years following 1873 was due to the falling off of the customs revenue consequent on the reduction of the number of dutiable articles which the Government were able to effect by reason of an overflowing treasury, and through the accidental lapsing of the stamp duties from an oversight. In 1881 the stamp duties were reimposed, and contributed in that year about 5s. per inhabitant. In 1886 the customs duties were increased, which accounts for the large advance shown that year. There was a slight decrease during 1887, arising from the repeal of the tariff of the previous year, which took effect on the 1st October, and a still further decline in 1888, 1889, and 1890, due to the same cause. Increased revenue per head.

Revenue from taxation.

It has been estimated that the total annual income of the inhabitants of the Colony is approximately £62,950,000. The revenue derived from taxation in 1890 was, as shown below, £2,748,339, equivalent, therefore, to a tax of 4·36 per cent. on the income of each person in the community. Dividing the revenue derived from taxation into the four main divisions of Customs, Excise, Stamps, and Licenses, the amount received under each head during the year 1890 was :—

Revenue from Taxation, 1890.

	£	£
CUSTOMS :—		
Spirits	823,418	
Wine	46,141	
Ale and beer	71,597	
Tobacco and cigars	245,326	
Tea	106,928	
Coffee and chicory	10,833	
Sugar and molasses	145,117	
Opium	16,990	
Rice	15,959	
Dried fruits	57,302	
Other specific duties	339,947	
Bonded warehouses	8,694	
Rent of goods in Queen's warehouse	69	
Total, Customs	....	1,888,321
EXCISE :—		
Ale, beer and porter	120,245	
Duty on spirits distilled in the Colony	23,174	
Duty on tobacco, cigars, and cigarettes	121,094	
Tobacco factory license fees	1,374	
Total, Excise	....	265,887
STAMPS	... .	460,975
LICENSES :—		
Wholesale spirit dealers	8,520	
Auctioneers	5,142	
Retail and fermented spirituous liquors	101,496	
Billiard and bagatelle licenses	9,698	
Distillers and rectifiers	99	
Hawkers and pedlers	2,415	
Pawnbrokers	690	
Colonial wine, cider, and perry licenses	1,428	
Licenses under the Gunpowder Act of 1876	758	
Licenses to sell tobacco, cigars, and cigarettes	2,375	
All other licenses	535	
Total, Licenses	....	133,156
Total, Taxation	....	£2,748,339

Under the heads of Trade and Commerce will be found some particulars of the revenue from Customs as well as that obtained from Excise. The cost of collecting revenue by the Customs Department averages about three per cent., a very moderate sum, when the large area of the Colony and the length of its frontiers are considered. The cost in 1890 was 2·9 per cent. against 3·7 for Victoria, 3·6 for South Australia, and 4·7 for Western Australia. The expenditure per cent. for New Zealand was the lowest of all the Colonies, being only 2·4 per cent., while that of Tasmania was but 2·6 per cent., the small cost no doubt being accounted for by the absence of Border collections. Revenue from Customs and Excise.

Stamp Duties during 1890 yielded a revenue of £460,975, or about 8s. 4d. per head, while the cost of collection was very trifling, amounting to £4,711, or a little over one per cent. of the amount received. Stamp Duties.

In addition to the above, a duty is levied on the value of estates of deceased persons, and on settlements of property taking effect after the death of the testator. Probate Duty.

The sale of fermented and spirituous liquors is regulated by Acts 45 Victoria No. 14, and 46 Victoria No. 24. Under the provisions of these Acts five descriptions of licenses are authorized :— Sale of liquors. Licenses.

(a) Publicans' licenses, for which an annual fee of £30 is payable.

(b) Packet licenses—1st class, for vessels over 1,000 tons, £15; 2nd class, from 250 to 1,000 tons, £10; and 3rd class, for vessels of under 250 tons, with a license fee of £3.

(c) Colonial wine licenses, annual fee, £3.

(d) Booth or stand licenses, fee £2; and

(e) Brewers' or spirit merchants' licenses, fee £30 if within, and £20 if outside, the boundaries of the city of Sydney.

There are also billiard and bagatelle licenses, auctioneers' licenses, a license for the sale of tobacco and cigars, and various other licenses, from which an amount of revenue is derived.

Revenue from publicans' licenses.

The revenue received during 1890 from the various licenses amounted to £133,156, of which £101,496 was from publicans and similar retailers, £1,428, from colonial wine sellers, and £8,520 from brewers and wholesale spirit merchants. The following licenses were issued during 1890:—

Publicans	3,428
Colonial wine	475
Distillers	1
Brewers	76
Spirit merchants	297
Total	4,277

Besides the above, there were 57 licenses for the distillation of brandy, 11 for scientific distillation, and 8 apothecaries' distilling licenses. There were 853 holders of publicans' licenses in the metropolitan district, and 2,575 in the remainder of the Colony; in the former case representing 1 licensed house to every 434 residents, while in the latter the proportion is 1 to every 284 residents. During the past thirteen years the number of licensed houses has increased from 3,312 to 3,428, although, as will be seen from the subsequent table, in proportion to population there has been a large decrease. There has been an absolute decrease in the number of houses since 1881, attributable to the operations of the Licensing Act, which came into force in that year. By this Act the granting of licenses was taken out of the hands of the ordinary Bench of Magistrates and entrusted to a Licensing Court, comprising magistrates specially appointed. The alteration in the composition of the Licensing Court led to a stricter scrutiny of applicants, and a consequent decrease in the number of licenses granted. The Act has also operated to decrease the number of hotels, by requiring a specified number of rooms for the accommodation of travellers, and in cases where insufficient accommodation was afforded, not a few hotel-keepers found it better to give up their licenses than to comply with the provisions of the Act.

Amended Licensing Act.

Licensed Public-houses.

Year.	Number of Licensed Houses.			Number of Residents in District to each House.		
	Metropolitan.	Extra-Metropolitan.	Total.	Metropolitan.	Extra-Metropolitan.	Total.
1878 ...	871	2,441	3,312	221	196	203
1879 ...	879	2,409	3,288	237	208	216
1880 ...	883	2,464	3,347	249	212	222
1881 ...	852	2,584	3,436	271	207	223
1882 ...	940	2,123	3,063	259	261	261
1883 ...	923	2,151	3,074	278	270	273
1884 ...	824	2,320	3,144	328	264	281
1885 ...	823	2,356	3,179	346	273	292
1886 ...	840	2,391	3,231	358	280	300
1887 ...	846	2,424	3,270	374	284	317
1888 ...	858	2,510	3,368	389	279	306
1889 ...	856	2,549	3,405	411	280	313
1890 ...	853	2,575	3,428	434	284	321

REVENUE FROM PUBLIC LANDS.

The income derived from the Public lands of the Colony has varied very considerably during the past twenty years, the lowest amount received being in 1871, when the revenue was only £497,978, or, at the rate of 19s. 7d. per head, while the greatest sum was obtained in 1877, when the receipts amounted to £3,236,277, or at the rate of £5 2s. 11d. per head of the population. Other periods also show great variation, due in the years prior to 1884 to the fluctuation in the amount of land sold at auction, but since the year last-named the Land Revenue has been more steady. The revenue from the public estate, compared with population, will gradually decline, as the amount available (Revenue from Public lands.)

for sale or lease is a diminishing quantity, while the population is steadily increasing. The revenue for 1890 amounted to £2,243,039, grouped under the following heads :—

	£
SALES :—	
Auction sales	169,664
Improved purchases, &c.	41,827
Deposits on conditional purchases	204,306
Instalments on conditional purchases (inclusive of interest)	649,924
Balances on conditional purchases	91,177
Miscellaneous purchases	13,896
Total, Land sales	£1,170,794
Interest on land conditionally purchased (under Act of 1861)	£104,864
PASTORAL OCCUPATION :—	
Pastoral leases (runs) 15 years	362,049
Conditional leases	138,699
Annual leases	27,060
Occupation licenses	191,045
Homestead leases, 15 years	41,463
Quit rents	545
Scrub leases	28
Total, Pastoral occupation	£760,889
MINING OCCUPATION :—	£
Mineral leases	36,380
Mineral licenses	2,380
Leases of auriferous lands	13,128
Miners' rights	7,537
Business licenses	3,146
Residential leases	224
Total, Mining occupation	£62,794
MISCELLANEOUS LAND RECEIPTS :—	
Licenses to cut timber, &c.	14,717
Fees on transfer of runs	1,041
Fees on preparation and enrolment of title-deeds	4,623
Survey fees (under Act of 1889)	103,106
All other receipts	20,211
Total, Miscellaneous Land receipts	£143,698
Total, Land revenue	£2,243,039

Falling off in land revenue.

A very great falling off in the land revenue will be observed from 1883 to 1886. This was due in the first instance to the stoppage of auction sales in 1883, and secondly, to the difficulties encountered in bringing the Crown Lands Act of 1884 into operation. These difficulties were overcome in 1887, and the land revenue may now be said to be in a normal condition.

The total income derived from land since 1872 is given below, while the amount per head of population will be found on page 607 :— Land revenue

Year.	Land Revenue.	Year.	Land Revenue.
	£		£
1872	840,453	1882	2,914,394
1873	1,137,914	1883	1,656,069
1874	1,426,166	1884	1,753,344
1875	2,020,629	1885	1,876,452
1876	2,773,003	1886	1,643,954
1877	3,236,277	1887	2,378,995
1878	2,325,704	1888	2,268,253
1879	1,632,024	1889	2,137,563
1880	1,646,436	1890	2,243,039
1881	2,820,988		

The revenue derived from the Crown lands may be conveniently divided into two main classes—receipts from sales, and from pastoral, mining, or other occupation. The amounts received under each head were as follows :— Revenue derived from sales and occupation.

Year.	Sales.	Occupation.	Year.	Sales.	Occupation.
	£	£		£	£
1872	436,483	403,970	1882	2,455,041	459,353
1873	845,410	292,504	1883	1,269,469	386,600
1874	1,163,572	262,594	1884	1,363,483	389,861
1875	1,760,570	260,059	1885	1,314,357	562,095
1876	2,513,404	259,599	1886	1,206,438	437,516
1877	2,967,857	268,420	1887	1,221,776	1,157,219
1878	2,076,004	249,700	1888	1,212,283	1,055,970
1879	1,386,637	245,337	1889	1,149,171	988,392
1880	1,382,026	264,410	1890	1,275,658	967,381
1881	2,483,338	337,650			

Practice of treating proceeds of sales as revenue.

The practice of treating money derived from the sale of Crown lands as revenue obtains in all the Australian Colonies, and the money so raised forms a substantial item of their annual income. In New South Wales the sums realized from this source have been in certain years so considerable as to leave a large surplus when all charges upon the public revenue were defrayed. The revenue derived from the sale of lands may be grouped under three heads:—*(a)* Auction sales and selections after auction; *(b)* Improvement and other purchases; and *(c)* Conditional sales.

Auction sales.

The proceeds of land sold at auction at one time formed the largest item of public income, as the following table, covering a period of twenty years, will show:—

Year.	Auction sales.	Selections after auction.	Total.
	£	£	£
1871	92,994	24,530	117,524
1872	89,129	89,588	178,717
1873	300,229	104,496	404,725
1874	553,973	106,042	660,015
1875	1,019,053	102,440	1,121,493
1876	1,561,243	98,280	1,659,523
1877	1,967,057	166,730	2,133,787
1878	1,061,670	124,197	1,185,867
1879	698,981	66	699,047
1880	437,964	42,495	480,459
1881	566,404	351,885	918,289
1882	707,594	417,715	1,125,309
1883	179,403	37,480	216,883
1884	95,772	767	96,539
1885	116,014	....	116,014
1886	111,083	....	111,083
1887	172,553	....	172,553
1888	207,052	....	207,052
1889	160,695	....	160,695
1890	169,664	....	169,664

It will be observed that the alienation of the public estate by means of auction sales and unconditional selections after auction attained its highest point during the years 1875 to 1878. A temporary lull took place in the two following years, but in 1881 and 1882 the auction sales of Crown lands reached nearly the same proportions as before. It was not until it had become evident that the indiscriminate sale of the public estate was threatening to endanger the vital interests of the country that this form of alienation was stopped. In 1883, auction sales were almost completely suspended, the receipts therefrom immediately falling from £1,125,309 in 1882 to £96,539 in 1884, £207,052 in 1888, and £169,664 in 1890. Large alienations at auction.

The fact had forced itself upon the attention of the authorities that this wholesale alienation of Crown lands was not due to the demand created by the normal progress of settlement, but was the outcome of an unhealthy rivalry between the two principal classes of settlers—the pastoral tenants, and the free selectors. Besides this, the estate of the country was being parted with without any conditions as to improvements or settlement, and as the great object of land sales was to promote settlement, it was deemed advisable by the Government to temporarily suspend land sales by auction, and ultimately it was decided to sell only a limited area (200,000 acres) during any one year. Limitation of auction sales.

Another portion of the land revenue is obtained from the sales, without competition, to the legal occupiers, of Crown lands improved to the value of £1 per acre. To this form of alienation may be added purchases of land made by right of pre-emption on a fixed proportion of the total area held under lease in certain cases. Improvement and pre-emptive purchases.

Revenue from improvement purchases and pre-emptive sales.

From these sources (improvement purchases and pre-emptive sales) the following amounts were received into the Colonial Treasury since the year 1877 :—

Year.	Improvement Purchases.	Pre-emptive Right Sales.	Total.
	£	£	£
1877	133,357	77,263	210,620
1878	239,944	20,046	259,990
1879	156,471	4,743	161,214
1880	245,094	5,799	250,893
1881	494,262	2,908	497,170
1882	179,949	1,041	180,990
1883	116,558	1,345	117,903
1884	305,455	4,450	309,905
1885	413,935	29	413,964
1886	260,526	....	260,526
1887	166,117	....	166,117
1888	86,913	....	86,913
1889	43,202	....	43,202
1890	41,827	....	41,827

Revenue from conditional sales.

Conditional sales formed the main feature of the Land Act of 1861. From 1862, when these sales commenced, to end of 1890, the area of land applied for amounted to 29,873,628 acres, or equal to 15·25 per cent. of the total area of the Colony. According to figures furnished by the Lands Department the total receipts in respect of such land were :—

For deposit	£6,522,490
Balance and instalments of purchase money...	5,583,057
Interest	3,057,613
Total	£15,163,160

The following table shows the gross amounts received during each of the fifteen years ending with 1890, as well as the total since this class of sales was first permitted. The figures are derived from returns furnished by the Lands Department, and differ from others given in this volume which were furnished by the Treasury; the discrepancy, however, is too slight to be of consequence. Total receipts from conditional sales.

Year.	Amounts received.				Total, according to Lands Office.
	Deposits.	Balances.	Instalments.	Interest under Act of 1861.	
	£	£	£	£	£
1862 to 1875	2,063,414	301,980	....	383,929	2,769,323
1876	496,053	68,834	.. ..	99,329	664,216
1877	424,954	71,853	....	126,657	623,464
1878	398,729	47,060	23,775	160,581	630,145
1879	232,285	37,031	87,131	171,148	527,595
1880	293,113	41,849	113,603	204,634	653,199
1881	592,966	92,009	129,547	253,357	1,067,879
1882	621,617	109,667	129,921	287,527	1,148,732
1883	424,968	58,314	137,277	310,676	931,235
1884	381,550	61,466	183,081	326,184	952,281
1885	121,437	68,139	440,286	151,658	781,520
1886	112,892	74,504	514,162	129,978	831,536
1887	92,203	96,562	562,019	123,091	873,875
1888	92,910	100,827	578,187	113,620	885,544
1889	82,540	105,761	607,206	110,380	905,886
1890	70,859	90,827	650,180	104,864	916,730
Total	6,522,490	1,426,683	4,136,374	3,057,613	15,163,160

The figures in the foregoing table represent the gross amounts paid, but in the case of the deposits large sums were received which were afterwards refunded, as the ground applied for was not open to selection. The area set down as sold conditionally is on this account also greatly overstated, and, moreover, includes the area Large sums refunded.

of selections which became forfeited for non-fulfilment of conditions, or on other grounds. The actual area sold conditionally up to the close of 1890 was 20,404,540 acres, and the area for which title deeds have been issued was 1,924,422, leaving a balance of 18,480,118 acres on which the conditions remain unfulfilled. The amount due to the Treasury on conditional purchases was, at the end of 1890, £13,224,311.

The refunds of deposits paid on land conditionally selected have reached considerable amounts in some years, as will be seen from the following statement:—

Year.	Amount of refunds.	Year.	Amount of refunds.
	£		£
1880	28,256	1886	69,094
1881	72,475	1887	41,986
1882	92,804	1888	35,319
1883	132,092	1889	30,602
1884	134,932	1890	36,512
1885	83,868		

Revenue from pastoral occupation.

Another portion of the annual land revenue of the Colony is derived from rents for pastoral occupation, and mineral and other leases. During 1886 the revenue obtained from this source amounted to only £374,920, as the rents were collected according to the old assessment, but it was estimated that more than £500,000 was due at the close of the year for rents accumulating during the previous eighteen months. By an Act of the Legislature, assented to on the 13th July, 1887, the arrears of rent were made payable over a period of two years, with interest at the rate of 5 per cent. During 1887 the rents were paid on the basis of the new tenure, and a large increase is therefore observable under the head of pastoral leases and occupation licenses. The following table gives the annual revenue from pastoral occupation for the eleven years, 1880-90:—

Annual Revenue from Pastoral Occupation.

Head of Revenue.	1880.	1881.	1882.	1883.	1884.	1885.	1886.	1887.	1888.	1889.	1890.
	£	£	£	£	£	£	£	£	£	£	£
Pastoral leases	165,952	221,149	343,333	273,486	268,155	140,436	131,893	644,279	526,447	512,481	362,049
Annual and special leases	55,743	63,968	65,417	66,167	60,694	15,872	17,914	17,648	22,554	26,474	27,088
Conditional and auction leases	......	......	......	......	......	37,592	59,558	67,974	87,896	101,416	138,699
Occupation licenses	......	......	......	......	......	294,686	153,493	329,010	252,121	214,166	191,045
Homestead leases	......	......	......	......	......	15,801	10,660	20,167	27,266	35,888	41,463
Quit rents	930	886	494	477	507	202	1,402	456	906	566	545
Total	222,625	286,003	409,244	340,130	329,356	504,589	374,920	1,079,534	917,190	890,991	760,889

Revenue from mining Leases.

The revenue derived from mining occupation has not been large, though somewhat higher since 1884 than previous to that year, a circumstance due chiefly to the increased attention paid to silver-mining. The following table gives the revenue under this head for the last eleven years :—

Year.	Amount.	Year.	Amount.
	£		£
1880	20,251	1886	31,242
1881	20,283	1887	43,961
1882	20,246	1888	95,347
1883	17,748	1889	53,384
1884	28,060	1890	62,794
1885	31,415		

REVENUE FROM RAILWAYS AND OTHER SERVICES.

Revenue from services.

The revenue derived from services rendered now exceeds that from either taxation or land,—the respective proportion under each head for 1887, 1888, 1889, and 1890 being :—

	1887	1888	1889	1890
	per cent.	per cent.	per cent.	per cent.
Services	37·8	41·2	43·3	44·0
Taxation	31·0	30·2	29·5	28·9
Land	27·7	25·5	23·6	23·6
Miscellaneous	3·5	3·1	3·6	3·5

Government is owner of railways, &c.

The Government of New South Wales is the owner of all the railways constructed in the Colony, with the exception of the line between Moama and Dmiliquin, and that from Broken Hill to the South Australian border, the former 45 miles long and the latter about 36 miles. It owns, also, the entire telegraphic and telephonic system of the Colony, as well as the Post Office. From these, and some other minor sources, the revenue, classed under the head of Services, was obtained. The total amount received for Services during the year 1890, under the different heads, was :—

Revenue from Services during 1890.

	£	£
Railway and tramway receipts	....	3,013,921
Post Office :—		
Postage	427,119	
Telegraph receipts	178,735	
Telephone receipts	7,282	
Commission on money orders	16,758	
		629,894
Mint receipts	....	13,208
Fees for escort and conveyance of gold	....	505
Pilotage, harbour and light rates, and fees	....	54,609
Registration of brands	....	1,394
Public School fees	....	71,827
Metropolitan Water Rates	....	158,151
Country Towns Water Rates	....	5,523
Metropolitan Sewerage Rates	....	74,368
Rabbits account assessment	....	49,764
Fees of office :—		
Certificates of naturalization	95	
Registrar-General	35,481	
Prothonotary of Supreme Court	7,795	
Master in Equity	3,233	
Curator of Intestate Estates	4,503	
In Bankruptcy and Insolvency	5,002	
Sheriff	1,957	
District Courts	8,717	
Courts of Petty Sessions	9,847	
Shipping Masters	2,649	
Other fees	22,494	
		101,773
Total receipts from Services	£	4,174,937

The total revenue derived from Services during each year since 1871 will be found in the following table, and the amount per head of population will also be found in a subsequent table :— Total revenue from services.

Year.	Revenue from Services.	Year.	Revenue from Services.
	£		£
1871	561,679	1881	1,945,076
1872	659,770	1882	2,363,085
1873	728,875	1883	2,666,731
1874	770,895	1884	2,942,643
1875	858,497	1885	3,108,463
1876	965,327	1886	3,089,235
1877	1,119,532	1887	3,245,907
1878	1,183,582	1888	3,664,100
1879	1,328,302	1889	3,924,955
1880	1,594,082	1890	4,174,937

There was an increase during every year of the above series, 1886 excepted, both in the total amount received and the rate per head. The falling off in 1886 is due to a decline in the amount received from the railways, which was in that year £103,552 less than in 1885. The total revenue derived from the railways, properly so called, for the year ending June, 1891, was £2,974,421, against which sum there was a charge of £1,831,371 for working expenses alone, leaving the net earnings £1,143,050. The amount of money invested in the railways of the Colony upon lines open for traffic on June 30th, 1891, was £31,768,617, and the net earnings given above represent a return of 3·6 per cent. The net income earned expressed as a per centage of capital, shows a satisfactory increase since 1888, but is still much below the figures of all years from 1871 to 1884. The actual result realized in any given year is not however to be taken as the sole index of the value of the railways of the Colony. The full value of a work cannot be judged until it is completed, and the railways are essentially an incomplete work, for each year sees an extension of the lines in operation and a further investment of capital, which the proved resources of the country amply justify, though it would be impossible to expect that the advantage to be derived therefrom can be realised until after the lapse of many years.

Railway—earnings and expenditure.

The questions of railway and tramway earnings and expenditure are dealt with exhaustively in another part of this volume; it will not therefore be needful to discuss these matters at length in this chapter.

Revenue from Posts and Telegraphs.

The receipts from the Post and Telegraph services of the Colony have increased substantially year by year, but so also has the expenditure. Although the sum of £629,894 was obtained during 1890 from this source, the expenditure amounted to £648,993, showing a loss on the year's transactions of £19,099, in addition to the amount of interest payable on the debt incurred for these works. These services are carried on, as far as possible, on commercial principles, nevertheless the desire of the Government to extend the facilities of both the post and telegraph to every part of the Colony has led to an expenditure each year in excess of the receipts. It is satisfactory, however, to find that the loss is steadily decreasing. In 1888 it was £53,462, and in 1889 it was £30,194, as against the £19,099 shown above. It is quite possible that the principle of affording the benefit of postal and telegraphic communication to every district of New South Wales would be adhered to even if the system ultimately failed to become self-supporting; but the time cannot be far distant when the revenue derived will more than meet the expenses.

Revenue and Expenditure.

Postal and Telegraphic Services.

Year.	Revenue.	Expenditure.	Year.	Revenue.	Expenditure.
	£	£		£	£
1877	224,449	311,614	1884	442,964	542,182
1878	226,405	351,642	1885	472,564	570,999
1879	259,170	383,391	1886	486,218	610,651
1880	286,134	396,301	1887	524,298	634,077
1881	330,414	421,594	1888	562,909	616,371
1882	358,525	446,658	1889	597,988	628,182
1883	403,794	504,055	1890	629,894	648,993

Receipts from Miscellaneous Services.

The miscellaneous receipts under the head of Services comprise fees of office, which amounted to £101,773 in 1890; public school fees, £71,827; pilotage and harbour fees, £54,609; mint and escort receipts, £13,713; registration of brands, £1,394; Metropolitan water rates, amounting to £158,151; and country towns water rates, £5,523; Rabbit Account Assessment, £49,764; the total being £456,754. The revenue derived from the services above mentioned is merely nominal, as the cost of the service performed generally far exceeds the revenue. The amount received during each year, from 1871 to 1890, was:—

Year.	Miscellaneous Services.	Year.	Miscellaneous Services.
	£		£
1871	81,534	1881	154,978
1872	88,929	1882	176,466
1873	86,803	1883	181,809
1874	88,334	1884	197,666
1875	95,825	1885	203,209
1876	96,053	1886	213,879
1877	95,136	1887	201,274
1878	96,892	1888	341,911
1879	92,234	1889	451,832
1880	118,384	1890	456,754

Miscellaneous items of revenue

The revenue derived from other sources besides Taxation, Lands, and Services, amounted to only £332,304 in 1890, made up chiefly by rents, fines, and forfeitures, and a variety of miscellaneous receipts:—

	£
Rents of Government Property other than land	59,720
Fines and forfeitures	15,806
Interest on bank deposits	95,932
Other receipts	160,844

Revenue per head of the population.

The total revenue of the Colony amounted in 1890 to £8 12s. 5d. per head, which, though nominally a very large sum compared with the revenue of other countries, falls short of the highest amount received in any year, viz., £9 5s. 10d., in 1882, by 13s. 5d. Under the present system of taxation it is anticipated that the revenue will average about £8 10s. per head; and though an increase may be expected in the gross sum obtained under each branch of revenue it is scarcely probable that the amount received per head will advance beyond the rate of 1890, especially as the increase in land revenue will not be proportionate to the increase in population.

Revenue per head from various sources.

The amounts received per head of population under each sub-division during the years 1871–1890 were :—

Taxation and Revenue per Head.

Year.	Taxation.	Land Revenue.	Services.	Miscellaneous.	Total Receipts.
	£ s. d.	£ s. d.	£ s. d.	£ s. d.	£ s. d.
1871	2 1 10	0 19 7	1 2 1	0 4 7	4 8 1
1872	2 5 7	1 11 11	1 5 1	0 4 2	5 6 9
1873	2 10 2	2 1 9	1 6 9	0 3 8	6 2 4
1874	2 2 6	2 10 6	1 7 4	0 4 2	6 4 6
1875	1 18 5	3 9 2	1 9 4	0 4 3	7 1 2
1876	1 18 5	4 11 9	1 11 11	0 4 7	8 6 8
1877	1 19 3	5 2 11	1 15 7	0 5 2	9 2 11
1878	1 19 10	3 10 8	1 16 0	0 5 3	7 11 9
1879	1 16 10	2 7 3	1 18 6	0 7 2	6 9 9
1880	1 19 1	2 5 4	2 3 11	0 7 1	6 15 5
1881	2 6 3	3 13 10	2 10 10	0 4 7	8 15 6
1882	2 7 8	3 13 0	2 19 3	0 5 11	9 5 10
1883	2 5 2	1 19 7	3 3 8	0 6 1	7 14 4
1884	2 8 9	1 19 8	3 6 8	0 6 1	8 1 2
1885	2 8 7	2 0 6	3 8 4	0 6 3	8 3 8
1886	2 13 6	1 13 11	3 3 9	0 5 2	7 16 8
1887	2 13 0	2 7 4	3 4 7	0 5 10	8 10 10
1888	2 11 9	2 3 9	3 10 9	0 5 3	8 11 6
1889	2 10 2	2 0 1	3 13 7	0 6 0	8 9 10
1890	2 9 11	2 0 9	3 15 10	0 5 11	8 12 5

PUBLIC EXPENDITURE.

Expenditure per head of the population.

The expenditure of the Colony, exclusive of loans, during the ten years which closed with 1890, amounted on an average to £8 16s. 4d. per head—the amount for the five years 1883 to 1887 considerably exceeding this average. During 1890 the gross expenditure amounted to £9,553,562, of which sum £8,629,708 was expended on account of services rightly chargeable to the year itself, whilst the balance, amounting to £923,854, was for the service of 1889 and previous years. The liabilities outstanding at the close of 1890 for the services of that year cannot be stated with any exactitude, but it is probable they amount to a sum equal to that paid on account of the services of previous years.

Expenditure under various heads in 1879 and 1889.

The percentage of expenditure has been grouped under six heads, as shown below, with the object of comparing the present expenditure with that of ten years ago. The proportion falling under each head of service during the years 1880 and 1890 respectively, was :—

Expenditure on Services.	1880.	1890.
	per cent.	per cent.
Railways and Tramways	15·08	21·33
Post and Telegraphs	7·13	6·79
Public debt charge	12·88	19·84
Immigration	·78	·06
Public Instruction	6·93	7·55
Other services and Public works	57·20	44·43

Increase in expenditure, to what traceable.

It will be seen that there has been a material advance in the percentage of revenue expended on railway and tramway services. The proportion expended on education has also increased, while the payments on account of the Public Debt are more than 50 per cent. greater than in 1880. This charge is less serious than at first sight appears, as a large part of the debt charges are recouped by the earnings of works constructed out of the loan funds. The absolute amount expended during each of the past twelve years was :—

Public Expenditure, exclusive of Expenditure from Loans, during each year from 1879 to 1890.

Year.	Railways and Tramways.	Post and Telegraphs.	Public Instruction.	Immigration.	Interest on Debt and Extinction of Loan.	Other Services and Public Works.	Total Expenditure less advances.
	£	£	£	£	£	£	£
1879	809,245	383,391	387,786	82,123	584,339	3,592,267	5,839,151
1880	838,559	396,301	385,567	43,522	715,994	3,180,136	5,560,079
1881	786,269	421,594	552,363	45,966	719,752	3,257,739	[illegible]
1882	[illegible]	446,658	665,901	[illegible]	969,198	3,188,427	6,348,205
1883	1,439,327	504,055	879,120	1 2,319	927,905	3,932,287	7,795,013
1884	1,585,603	542,182	817,767	120,038	1,047,322	4,298,927	8,411,839
1885	1,729,894	[illegible]	751,335	52,050	1,300,184	4,157,672	8,562,134
1886	1,710,495	610,651	741,121	35,397	1,579,689	4,400,294	9,077,647
1887	[illegible]	634,077	728,003	32,251	1,692,421	4,453,724	9,216,192
1888	1,824,291	616,371	682,225	7,854	1,745,695	3,902,415	8,778,851
1889	1,782,530	[illegible]	697,224	8,073	1,805,770	4,328,492	[illegible]
1890	[illegible]	648,993	721,248	5,916	1,895,656	4,224,581	9,533,562

Increase of public expenditure.

In a country advancing so rapidly in population as New South Wales the value of figures, such as are given in the preceding table, is apt to be misunderstood, for, though the absolute increase in expenditure from 1878 to 1890 amounted to 88 per cent., the population likewise increased 67 per cent. Nor must the fact be overlooked that much of what is now expended out of current revenue is for the advantage of future years, and for the development of the resources of the country; and that the expenditure on certain services is incurred in order to obtain additional revenue. But even when such allowances are made it will be found there has been no slight advance, especially in some years since 1882, as will be seen from the table here given of the expenditure per head under the several groups:—

Expenditure per Head, exclusive of Expenditure from Loans.

Year.	Railways and Tramways.	Post and Telegraphs.	Public Instruction.	Immigration.	Interest on Debt. &c.	Other Services and Public Works.	Total Expenditure less advances.
	£ s. d.	s. d.	s. d.	s. d.	s. d.	£ s. d.	£ s. d.
1878	1 1 3	10 8	11 8	2 11	17 10	4 10 0	7 14 4
1879	1 3 5	11 1	11 2	2 4	16 11	5 4 0	8 9 1
1880	1 3 1	10 11	10 7	1 2	19 9	4 7 8	7 13 2
1881	1 0 7	11 0	14 5	1 2	18 10	4 5 2	7 11 2
1882	1 5 10	11 2	16 8	1 2	24 3	3 19 7	7 19 9
1883	1 14 4	12 0	21 0	2 8	22 2	4 13 10	9 6 9
1884	1 15 11	12 3	18 6	2 8	23 8	4 17 4	9 0 6
1885	1 17 4	12 4	16 2	1 2	28 0	4 9 8	9 4 8
1886	1 15 3	12 8	15 4	0 8	32 7	4 10 9	9 7 4
1887	1 13 9	12 8	14 6	0 8	33 8	4 8 3	9 3 5
1888	1 15 3	11 11	13 2	0 2	33 8	3 15 4	8 9 6
1889	1 13 5	11 9	13 1	0 2	33 10	4 1 2	8 13 5
1890	1 16 11	11 9	13 2	0 1	34 5	3 17 1	8 13 5

Increase of expenditure on railways and tramways.

The expenditure on interest on public debt shows the largest increase during the period comprised in this table, amounting to 16s. 7d. per head, while railways and tramways have increased by 15s. 8d. The length of railway line in operation in 1878 was only 688 miles, while in 1890 the mileage had increased to 2,182, involving a proportionately large outlay for maintenance and working expenses. The tramway system, which was inaugurated in 1879, involved an expenditure of about 3s. per head in 1890. This service is now yielding a very satisfactory return on capital expended. Public Instruction costs 1s. 6d. more than in

1878, while other Services and Public Works show a decrease of 12s. 11d. per head; Post and Telegraphs cost more by 1s. 1d. per head.

Increase of expenditure on education.

The expenditure per head on account of Public Instruction was a trifle over the figures for 1889, but was 7s. 10d. less than in 1883. The Public Instruction Act of 1880, abolishing State aid to denominational education, necessarily involved an increased expenditure from Public Revenue to supply the place of schools closed under the Act. The greatest activity was, therefore, displayed, especially during the year 1883, immediately following the closing of the denominational schools, both in the building and equipment of public schools, hence the increased expenditure per head noticeable in the table given above. Since 1883 the expenditure rapidly declined, and has now almost reached the normal average.

The increase in the expenditure for 1890 over 1878 upon Post and Telegraphs represents really an advance in the average business transacted by each member of the community, and is accompanied by a corresponding increase in the receipts from this service.

Expenditure on other Services and Public Works.

The expenditure upon other services and public works during 1890 was considerably less per head than in 1878, and was also below that of the intervening years except 1888. The large surplus which the Government had at its disposal during the period immediately following 1877, encouraged a profuse expenditure on public works, which, under other circumstances, might not have been undertaken; hence the large increase during the years in which the surplus was available. The absence of a law placing the responsibility of local works upon the persons actually concerned has necessitated the expenditure, out of the public funds, of large sums upon works only locally important, and, therefore, not strictly chargeable to the public revenue. The District Government Bill now before Parliament proposes to remedy this state of things, and a decrease in the expenditure upon public works may be anticipated.

Expenditure for other services.

Under the head of "Other Services" are included Civil Administration, Defence, Administration of Lands, Mining, and Law. The expenditure per head has been fairly uniform from year to year, averaging £2 19s. 7d. per head for the last ten years.

Accumulated surplus revenue at the close of each year.

The accounts of the Treasury are closed on the 31st December in each year, so that the amounts of expenditure given in the preceding tables refer to the payments made during the currency of any year, irrespective of the date at which the liability occurred or was authorized. Thus payments during 1873 included liabilities as old as 1868; while some payments in 1878 were on account of 1873 and each of the intermediate years. Similar payments occur in every year, so that the figures relating to expenditure can only be taken as a partial presentation of the financial case of the country. The following figures are self-explanatory and cover the last eighteen years; they show the actual as well as the apparent expenditure during this period :—

Year.	Expenditure for Services of each year irrespective of date of payment.*	Expenditure during each year.		
		For Services of that and previous years.	Out of accumulated surplus.	Total, less advances.
	£	£	£	£
1873	2,568,605	2,333,166	....	2,333,166
1874	2,965,464	2,939,227	....	2,939,227
1875	3,378,896	3,346,324	....	3,346,324
1876	3 872,064	3,769,213	....	3,769,213
1877	5,369,833	4,551,652	....	4,551,652
1878	5,079,397	5,100,326	....	5,100,326
1879	4,976,649	5,255,034	584,117	5,839,151
1880	4,977,481	5,228,792	331,287	5,560,079
1881	5,264,448	5,376,160	407,523	5,783,683
1882	6,330,936	5,824,245	523,960	6,348,205
1883	6,901,525	7,062,948	732,065	7,795,013
1884	7,658,129	7,813,414	598,425	8,411,839
1885	9,308,059	8,320,523	241,611	8,562,134
1886	8,536,411	9,005,178	72,469	9,077,647
1887	8,799,156	9,202,377	13,815	9,216,192
1888	8,617,223	8,758,640	20,211	8,778,851
1889	9,106,273	9,244,578	5,693	9,250,271
1890	8,629,708	9,549,885	3,677	9,553,562

* Liabilities outstanding at the close of 1890 for that and previous years are not included.

During the fourteen years which elapsed from 1872 to 1885, New South Wales presented the spectacle, then almost unique in these colonies, of a government with a large surplus of revenue at its disposal. The amount standing to the credit of the Consolidated Fund at the close of each year from 1872 to 1885, was:— Surplus revenue.

Year.	Accumulated surplus.	Year.	Accumulated surplus.
	£		£
1872	132,238	1879	1,341,619
1873	925,069	1880	1,440,228
1874	825,605	1881	2,927,435
1875	1,110,992	1882	3,888,753
1876	1,945,807	1883	2,511,016
1877	2,351,074	1884	1,229,338
1878	1,922,784	1885	2,900

The figures given above represent the amounts standing to the credit of the current account of the Consolidated Revenue. The actual surplus differed somewhat from these amounts, by reason of temporary advances made to loan or other funds out of accumulated surplus. The gross credit balance at the close of 1878 was £3,872,784. The years 1881 and 1882 also yielded surpluses to the extent of £1,441,338 and £1,086,308 in each year as named, making a total surplus of £6,400,430. For the services of 1878 and previous years the sum of £1,377,321 was expended, while in 1879, 1880, 1883, and 1884 the income was exceeded by £1,306,267, thus reducing the surplus to £3,716,842, at the close of 1884. Specific appropriations were made by Parliament out of this sum to the extent of £3,419,174, and £119,993 was written off; thus leaving a balance retained for expenditure at the close of 1884 of £177,675, the difference Advances made from surplus.

between the amount just stated and that shown in the preceding table having been temporarily advanced to revenue from various sources.

Proposals for meeting deficit.

The state of things depicted above was entirely changed during 1886. The disbursements from 1883 to 1886 were nominally more than the income, chiefly through the large appropriations of the surpluses of former years. Thus the year 1885 closed with a sum of £2,900 to the credit of the Revenue Fund, while 1887 opened with a nominal deficit of £1,286,581, and 1888 with a deficit of £2,179,580. In his financial statement, made on the 10th April, 1889, the Treasurer gave the amount of the deficit on the 31st March previous as £2,608,237. It was resolved to treat this deficit as a matter quite apart from the ordinary finances of the year, and the Government were authorised to raise Treasury Bills to the amount of £2,600,000, to meet which a sum of £150,000 was to be set aside every year out of revenue; £2,523,884 was raised, and £150,000 has been paid off, thus leaving the balance £2,373,884 to be provided for.

PUBLIC DEBT.

Loans.

In 1842 a loan of £49,500 was issued for the purposes of immigration, having a currency of two years, and bearing interest at the rate of 5¼d. per day, or 8 per cent. per annum for every £100 of stock. Several loans for similar purposes were raised during the period 1843–50, but were met out of revenue within a few years of the date of raising. In 1851, however, a sum of £79,600 was borrowed, also for immigration purposes, £15,800 only of which was paid out of the general revenue, the remainder being met by a fresh loan; and though no loans raised prior to 1854 remain outstanding, the loan of 1851 must be taken as the actual commencement of the Public Debt of New South Wales. From 1854, the commencement of the existing Public Debt

Account, to the 31st December, 1890, the total sum authorised to be raised by loans was £74,006,518, and the amount of stock sold was £53,450,803, the gross sum realized being £52,065,826, and the net proceeds £51,471,206. The amount authorised, but not yet raised, is £20,555,715. Debentures to the value of £1,801,170 have been redeemed absolutely, and £3,224,300 have been renewed. Thus at the close of 1890 the total public debt was £48,425,333, and the amount of each class of stock was as follows:—

Description of Stock.	Amount outstanding.		Interest thereon.
Debentures :—	£	£	£
Overdue, or unpresented, which have ceased to bear interest...	7,860		
Still bearing interest..............	14,827,100		
		14,834,960	659,589
Permanent Funded Stock	.. ..	530,189	21,208
Inscribed Stock	....	30,686,300	1,109,952
Treasury Bills.........................	....	2,373,884	94,955
Total Public Debt	....	48,425,333	1,885,704

The Inscribed Stocks Act, was passed in March, 1883, and during the course of the same year, two Loans were floated under the new conditions, the amounts of stock issued in each case being £3,000,000. The total amount of Inscribed Stocks issued to the 31st December, 1890, was £29,500,000, and the amount of Debenture Stock converted into the new scrip was £1,186,300, making a total of £30,686,300 Inscribed. This kind of stock has found much more favor in the London market than the old form of Debenture, and although the charges of negotiation to the

Inscribed stock.

Government are greater than prevailed under the former system, the extra outlay has its compensation in the convenience afforded in dealing with the stock. All the Colonies with the exception of Western Australia now issue their loans as Inscribed Stock.

Stock at each rate of interest.

The following table shows the total amount of stock under each rate of interest. The stock bearing 6 per cent. represents the loans raised by the Municipalities of Sydney and Darlington for Sewerage Works, now taken over by the State. With the exception of Municipal Loans to the amount of £58,000, and £2,700 Permanent Stock, all the Loans bearing 5 per cent. interest, will mature in or before 1902; there were, however, also £7,860, overdue 5 per cent. Debentures outstanding at the close of 1890, which have ceased to bear interest.

Interest—per cent.	Amount of Stock.	Percentage of Total Debt.
	£	
6	123,000	0·25
5	6,412,360	13·24
4	18,389,973	37·98
3½	23,500,000	48·53
Total...........	48,425,333	100·00

Debt payable in London.

The greater part of the outstanding Public Debt, amounting to £43,472,000, was raised and is repayable in London, the balance, £4,953,333, including £2,373,884 Treasury Bills, is redeemable in the Colony.

The date of repayment extends from 1891 to 1933, the sums repayable in the different years varying considerably in amount, the largest sum in any one year being £16,500,000 for 1924. The following table shows the due dates and amount repayable in each year :—

Year when due.	Amount of Stock.	Year when due.	Amount of Stock.
1891	256,500	1903	1,901,500
1892	1,782,300	1904	58,000
1893	40,000	1905	2,300
1895	832,000	1906	224,900
1896	977,400	1908	1,450,000
1897	65,800	1909	1,799,500
1898	177,200	1910	2,863,700
1899	197,700	1912	60,000
1900	857,100	1918	7,000,000
1901	404,900	1924	16,500,000
1902	459,000	1933	7,186,300

The foregoing table accounts for £45,096,100, besides this there are outstanding £414,600 of debentures being paid off by annual drawings extending to the year 1897, £532,889 interminable and £7,860 overdue debentures not bearing interest, and Treasury Bills to the amount of £2,373,884.

The specific purposes for which loans were raised were formerly stated in the Acts authorising them, and the proceeds could only be applied in the terms of such Acts. This practice was found inconvenient, and on the 23rd April, 1879, the Loan Fund Amalgamation Act was passed ; the Act provided that the proceeds of loans should be placed under one general account, and the measure has resulted in a considerable saving in interest, as it is now possible to keep the balance to the credit of Loans

Account much lower than formerly. The following statement shows the expenditure of Loan Funds to December 31, 1890, distributed under the principal heads of service :—

Services.	Amount.
	£
Railways	31,219,662
Tramways	1,351,344
Electric Telegraphs	735,493
Harbours and Rivers	2,796,764
Roads and Bridges	625,955
Water Supply—	
Sydney and Suburbs	2,871,976
Country Districts	465,896
Sewerage—Sydney and Suburbs	1,236,816
Fortifications and Warlike Stores	864,582
Immigration	569,930
Municipal Works taken over—	
Water Supply—Sydney	85,000
Sewerage Works—Sydney, Darlington, and Redfern	161,000
Other Public Works and Services	1,427,922
Total Services	£44,412,340
To cover deficiency of Revenue	2,373,884
Total Expenditure	£46,786,224

Reproductive services.

Of the total amount £44,412,340, shown in the above statements, £39,703,002 have been expended on directly reproductive works yielding or capable of yielding revenue towards meeting the charges for interest. The amounts expended on the various reproductive services to the 31st December, 1890, were as follows :—

Service.	Amount.
	£
Railways	31,219,662
Tramways	1,351,345
Electric Telegraphs	735,493
Water Supply	3,422,872
Sewerage	1,397,816
Docks and Wharves	1,575,814
£	39,703,002

Works for the development of the Colony.

Besides the amounts shown in the foregoing table the sum of £3,224,972 has been spent on other works of a permanent nature, such as roads and bridges, improvements to harbours and rivers, lighthouses, schools, and public buildings; these, though not directly productive, have been undertaken for the development of the resources of the Colony, and for facilitating settlement. The balance of the £44,412,340, viz., £1,484,366 was expended on unproductive services—the chief items being £864,582 for fortifications and warlike stores, and £569,930 for immigration, but as this latter amount was spent to encourage settlement, it is a moot point whether it might not with some propriety be classed amongst productive services. These figures, of course, refer to the external debt; the Treasury Bills already alluded to, and now included in the public debt, were raised to meet a deficiency in the revenue of 1886 and previous years.

Interest on Public Debt.

The amount paid during 1890 for interest on the public debt and extinction thereof was £1,895,656. If allowance be made for £38,000 paid during the year in redemption of the loan 31 Vic., No. 11, and the interest on the unexpended balance of loans deposited in banks, which amounted to £95,932 the expense of the public debt will be reduced to £1,761,724, which sum represents approximately the charge which fell upon the general revenue during the year. The net revenue, in 1890, from works constructed out of loan funds was £1,310,604. So that the deficiency of interest to be made good from other sources was £451,120. The net revenue from the public works of the country is entirely comprised in that derived from Railways, Tramways, and Water Supply and Sewerage; docks and wharves, although in the same category, do not at present yield a net revenue. The Water and Sewerage Works of the Metropolitan area are not yet completed, but the latter service in 1890, yielded a surplus of £14,773 above the amount required to be expended on maintenance, management, and interest on capital expenditure. When, however, these undertakings are completed, and the railways are in full operation, the sum available to meet interest and other charges on the public debt, should leave little to be made good from the general revenue of the Colony.

Expenditure from loans and public debt.

The following statement shows the Public Debt, the actual expenditure on Public Works, &c., and rate per head of population, during each year 1879-1890:—

Public Debt and Loan Expenditure.

Year.	Public debt at close of year.				Actual expenditure on public works and services.							
					At the close of each year.				During each year.			
	Amount.	Per inhabitant.			Amount.	Per inhabitant.			Amount.	Per inhabitant.		
	£.	£	s.	d.	£	£	s.	d.	£	£	s.	d.
1879 ...	14,937,419	21	12	6	15,102,213	21	17	4	1,271,705	1	16	10
1880 ...	14,903,919	20	1	9	16,770,851	22	12	1	1,668,638	2	5	8
1881 ...	16,924,019	21	13	1	19,168,219	24	10	7	2,397,368	3	2	8
1882 ..	18,721,219	22	19	5	22,000,978	26	19	11	2,832,759	3	10	11
1883 ...	21,632,459	25	2	4	25,266,689	29	6	8	3,265,711	3	15	10
1884 ...	30,101,959	33	5	3	28,941,395	31	19	7	3,674,706	4	3	2
1885 ...	35,564,259	37	9	1	32,837,540	34	11	7	3,896,145	4	4	0
1886 ...	41,034,250	41	9	6	36,603,896	37	0	0	3,766,356	3	17	8
1887 ...	40,995,350	40	3	7	38,568,915	37	16	0	1,965,019	1	19	1
1888 ...	44,185,149	42	0	9	40,645,222	38	13	4	2,076,307	2	0	1
1889 ...	46,892,449	43	6	11	42,271,122	39	1	6	1,625,900	1	10	6
1890 ...	48,425,333	43	3	4	44,412,340	39	11	9	2,141,218	1	18	10

In several years of the foregoing series the amount of money expended exceed the loans raised, and in those years advances were made to loan funds from Consolidated Revenue or other funds. Included in the outstanding Public Debt at the close of 1890 are Treasury Bills to the amount of £2,373,884, and Municipal Loans assumed by the State to the amount of £246,000, the former is a liability that was only brought into account in 1890, though chargeable to 1886 and previous years; the Municipal Loans, which were expended on local Water and Sewerage Works, taken over by the Government, are debited to the years 1888 and 1889, when the State relieved the local bodies of those works by placing them under the Board of Water Supply and Sewerage.

The net increase in the public debt during the eleven years ended December 31, 1890, was £33,487,914, involving an increase in the annual charge for interest of £1,197,223. During the same period the indebtedness per head advanced from £21 12s. 6d. to £43 3s. 4d., and the charge per head for interest, not including payments in reduction of debt, from 19s. 5d. to £1 13s. 7d.

Increase of the public debt.

Owing to the large surplus revenue available during the early part of the period embraced in the foregoing table the amount of public debt was less than the sum actually expended on account of loans, as advances were made in anticipation of loans authorized to be floated in the London market. The advances in some years reached considerable sums. This was noticeable in 1882, when the total of such advances, being the difference between the amount expended and that raised, was not less than £4,614,989. In 1885, however, the balance of surplus revenue available for advances disappeared, and the loans raised have, therefore, since that year exceeded the expenditure chargeable to loan votes. It appears, from the latest Treasury statement, that the balance to the credit of the General Loans Account at the close of 1890 was £1,349,017, and that of the Old Loans was £132,326, making a total of £1,481,343.

Advances from surplus revenue.

Balance to credit General Loans Account.

Taking the actual expenditure from loan votes as a measure of the increase of the Colony's indebtedness, it will be seen that during the years 1879–90 the total expenditure increased more than 194 per cent., while the population has only increased 58 per cent.—the expenditure per head in 1879 amounting to £21 7s. 4d., while eleven years later it had advanced to £39 11s. 9d., a rate of increase averaging 5·52 per cent. per annum. In few countries would this rate of increase be justifiable, but as regards New South Wales, its immense resources are still in a state of partial development, so that the expenditure need give no cause for uneasiness to the creditors of the Colony. The total expenditure exclusive of the amount spent in redemption of loans during the twelve years covered by the foregoing table amounted to £30,581,832, of which £22,440,292 was for railways and tramways, £305,120 for

Increase of loan expenditure and public debt.

telegraphs, and £3,179,610 for water supply, £1,197,816 for sewerage, and £1,871,140 for Harbours and Rivers. The remaining expenditure, amounting to £1,587,854, was incurred mainly for works and buildings necessary for the development of the resources of the Colony, or incidental to its progress. During the same period the amount spent on renewal of loans was £2,106,200.

Cost of public works charged to general revenue.

It has been a practice of long standing to charge the cost of constructing public works, other than those of national importance or built equally for the requirements of the future as of to-day, to the general revenue of the Colony. This practice is rarely departed from, and the amount of loans spent on works which do not come within such definition is comparatively trifling. The subsequent table gives the amount of the public debt at the close of each year since 1869. It will be seen that the increase in the indebtedness for the ten years ending 1879 was small, averaging less than £539,000 per annum; hence it is that, when in the latter years, much greater activity was manifest in the construction of public works, the average increase was at the rate of nearly £3,045,000 per annum, though the mean yearly increase spread over the period of the last twenty-one years was only £1,851,400:—

Public debt, 1869-89.

No loan was actually floated since the July loan of 1889 to the 31st December, 1890. The increase shown in the following table for the latter year is due to the floating debt of 1886 and previous years being charged to 1890, and not, as might have been done, to the year to which it was properly due.

Year.	Public Debt.	Year.	Public Debt.
	£		£
1869	9,546,030	1880	14,903,919
1870	9,681,130	1881	16,924,019
1871	10,614,330	1882	18,721,219
1872	10,773,230	1883	21,632,459
1873	10,842,415	1884	30,101,959
1874	10,516,371	1885	35,564,259
1875	11,470,637	1886	41,034,280
1876	11,759,519	1887	40,995,350
1877	11,724,419	1888	44,100,149
1878	11,688,119	1889	46,646,449
1879	14,937,419	1890	48,425,333

The present amount of the public debt is undoubtedly large; but no portion of it is due to war charges, and very little to works of an entirely unproductive character, so that the burden on the resources of the country is more apparent than real. The assets of the Colony amount to considerably more than four times the liabilities, and for the most part comprise securities which could readily be converted into money. At a moderate computation the public estate of New South Wales is estimated to be worth, £173,000,000, according to the details given on page 630.

Present amount of public debt.

Estimated value of the public estate.

The following table gives particulars of loans floated since 1875, and from it may be seen the great improvement which has taken place in the credit of the Colony:—

Loans floated since 1875.

Date of Issue.	Currency.	Nominal Interest per cent.	Amount of Loan.	Net proceeds, less charges and accrued interest.		Actual interest per cent. paid by Government.
				Amount.	Average amount per cent.	
	Years.		£	£		£ s. d.
1875	30	4	1,000,000	874,219	87·42	4 11 6
1876	30	4	901,500	813,412	90·23	4 8 8
1879	30	4	3,249,500	3,178,374	97·81	4 1 9
1881	30	4	2,050,000	2,106,430	102·36	3 17 9
1882	30	4	2,000,000	2,024,540	101·23	3 19 0
1883	50	4	3,000,000	2,966,522	98·88	4 0 11
1883	50	4	3,000,000	2,917,367	97·24	4 2 3
1884	40	3½	5,500,000	5,063,349	92·06	3 15 8
1885	40	3½	5,500,000	4,947,339	89·95	3 17 10
1886	38	3½	5,500,000	5,076,685	92·30	3 15 4
1888	30	3½	3,500,000	3,509,995	100·29	3 9 10
1889	30	3½	3,500,000	3,495,585	99·87	3 10 1

The nominal rate of loans prior to 1875 was 5 per cent., but in the year mentioned a loan of £1,000,000 was issued at 4 per cent., although at a heavy discount. The three subsequent 4 per cent. loans were floated more successfully; that raised in 1881 carrying a premium of 2·36 per cent. after charges and accrued interest had been allowed for. The actual interest payable on this loan by the Government was £3 17s. 9d. per cent., as against £4 11s. 6d. for the issue of 1875. The loan of 1881 was the most successful floated at 4 per cent.; the three subsequent ones realising less satisfactory prices. The increase in the currency to 50 years without doubt largely accounts for the fall in the selling price, as the credit of the Colony was steadily rising.

Amount of Loans floated 3½ per cent.

In 1884 the nominal rate of interest was fixed at 3½ per cent., at which rate loans to the amount of £23,500,000 have been floated. The £3,500,000 loan placed on the market in April, 1888, was the most successful yet floated. The average rate, after all incidental charges were paid, was £102 0s. 8½d. A similar loan was floated in July, 1889, realising £100 14s. 11¾d. The 1888 loan carried six months' interest, and that of 1889 three months, reducing the former to £100 5s. 8½d., and the latter to £99 17s. 5½d., or a balance in favour of the former issue of 8s. 3¼d. per cent.

Recent Loans of Australian Colonies.

The following statement shows the terms on which the principal colonies were able to borrow in the London market during the last two years, the computations allowing for the repayment of the various loans at par on maturity:—

Australasian Loans, 1889 and 1890, shewing Net Interest to Investors.

Colony.	Date of Negotiation.	Nominal rate of Interest.	Amount.	Currency of Loan.	Average rate per cent. at which sold.	Net amount as accrued Interest.	Net Interest per cent. to Investors
	1889.	per cent	£	years.	£ s. d.	£ s. d.	£ s. d.
New South Wales..	July ..	3½	3,500,000	30	102 8 0¾	99 17 5½	3 10 2
Victoria	Jan. ..	3½	3,000,000	35	103 5 11½	102 14 10	3 7 3
South Australia..	Jan. ..	3½	1,317,800	40	100 1 10	99 4 6	3 10 9
Western Australia	July ..	4	100,000	45	108 15 8	108 1 11	3 12 2
Tasmania........	April ..	3½	1,000,000	30 to 50	98 5 6½	97 13 6	3 12 3
New Zealand	October	3½	2,700,000	50	96 16 8	95 10 2	3 13 10
	1890.						
Queensland	March..	3½	2,264,784	34½	97 16 7	96 7 4	3 13 8
Victoria	April ..	3½	4,000,000	34	101 10 4½	100 2 4	3 9 11

The extent to which the credit of the Colony has advanced in the eyes of the British capitalist since the year 1870 will be seen from the following figures. The first column shows the average interest computed on the nominal amount of loans outstanding at the end of each year under review; the other column shows the interest on the amount actually realised:—

Year.	Average Interest on nominal Amount of Loan.	Interest on Amount actually realised.
1870	4·82	5·07
1875	4·87	5·12
1880	4·61	4·84
1885	4·19	4·35
1890	3·89	4·05

The selling price of a loan is not perhaps the most exact test which may be applied to ascertain the credit of a country in the London markets. There are many causes which may combine to influence adversely the price obtained by tender, and it will be evident that in some of the instances given in the table on page 624 the selling price of loans was influenced by circumstances entirely apart from the credit of the colonies concerned. A truer gauge of credit will be found in the selling price and interest yielded to investors by representative stock at a given date. The following table shows the interest returned by the stock of different colonies in June, 1891, due allowance being made in each

Selling price of Colonial stock.

case for accrued interest, and for repayment of loans at par at maturity. Similar figures for the same month of 1868 and 1878 have been added :—

Country.	1868.	1878.	1891.
	£ s. d.	£ s. d.	£ s. d.
New South Wales	5 0 0	3 16 3	3 12 2¼
Victoria	4 17 6	4 2 6	3 12 2
Queensland	5 6 3	4 5 0	3 16 11¼
South Australia	5 2 6	4 2 6	3 16 2
Tasmania	5 8 9	4 12 6	3 19 8
New Zealand	5 1 3	4 15 0	3 17 10
Canada	5 12 6	4 9 0	3 12 0
Cape of Good Hope	5 1 3	4 11 3	3 13 0
Natal	5 11 3	4 11 3	3 12 0¼
India	3 13 9	3 10 6	3 8 0

Improvement of Colonial credit.

The improvement in the credit of all the colonies is obvious, and at the rates given New South Wales could borrow £100 to-day at the same cost as £72 could be obtained twenty-three years previously. In June, 1891, British consols were selling at a rate which would yield £2 15s. 8d. per cent. interest; Canadian and Indian stock were also selling at slightly better rates than New South Wales. This is certainly anomalous, as there is nothing in the history of these last mentioned countries, or in the nature of their resources, to warrant even the slight preference shown to their stock above that of New South Wales or Victoria.

These remarks apply to the London market when in a normal state; early in 1891, however, all Australasian stock fell off in selling value, and three of the colonies—Victoria, South Australia, and Queensland—ventured to test the London market, and failed to float their loans to the full amount required. The depreciation which Australasian and other colonial stocks suffered was not due to any sudden want of faith in the resources of the colonies, but to the general stringency which the Argentine crisis generated, and which is likely to continue to operate adversely to these colonies until the British investor has clearly brought under his notice the solid security which they have to offer. In September, 1891, a 3½ per cent. New South Wales Loan of £4,500,000 was offered to British investors, at a minimum of £95; the loan was just covered at an average of £95 0s. 5½d.

Under the Inscribed Stock Act of 1883 the loans of the Colony are now negotiated by the Bank of England, although the first two loans, amounting to £6,000,000, floated under the new conditions were negotiated by the Bank of New South Wales and inscribed by the Bank of England. The particulars of these loans are shown in the following table:—

Total Sales of Inscribed Stock negotiated in London by the Bank of New South Wales and Bank of England.

Currency, in years.	Date from which interest accrued.	Gross proceeds.	Average rate per cent. at which sold.			Charges.				Net proceeds.
						Brokers' and Bank commission.	Discount on balance of scrip, paid up in full.	Stamp duty and Petty expenses.	Total.	
		£	£	s.	d.	£	£	£	£	£
50	July 1883	3,001,067	100	0	8½	12,235	1,495	19,015	32,745	2,968,322
50	Jan. 1884	3,018,791	100	12	6¼	12,494	8,065	19,065	39,624	2,979,167
40	Oct. 1884	5,152,386	93	13	7	41,230	9,573	34,934	85,737	5,066,649
40	Oct. 1885	5,042,041	91	13	5	41,156	18,391	35,155	94,702	4,947,339
40	July 1886	5,247,692	95	8	3	41,213	14,443	35,143	90,799	5,156,893
30	March 1888	3,626,341	103	12	2	26,229	6,341	22,526	55,096	3,571,245
30	June 1889	3,584,105	102	8	0¾	26,167	9,141	22,587	57,895	3,526,210

Cost of inscription.

The first and second loans in the table just given were for £3,000,000 stock, and the next three for £5,500,000, while the loans of 1888 and 1889 were each £3,500,000 stock. The cost of inscription paid to the Bank of England for the first two loans in the table was £600 per million in addition to the charges mentioned. The charges on these loans, inclusive of the cost of inscription, amounted to 1·16 and 1·38 respectively on the capital value, and 1·15 and 1·37 per cent. on the gross proceeds.

Charges on loans.

The charges incidental to the floating of the last five loans shewn, which were negotiated by the Bank of England, amounted to 1·56, 1·72, 1·65, 1·57, and 1·65 per cent. respectively upon the capital value, but on the gross amount raised the percentage for each loan was 1·66, 1·88, 1·73, 1·52, and 1·61 per cent.

Conversion of debentures.

Debentures to the amount of £2,000,000, issued in July, 1882, were afterwards authorised to be converted into Inscribed Stock at the option of the holders, a privilege which was availed of to the extent of £1,186,300 only. The total amount of inscribed stock is therefore, as previously stated, £30,686,300.

Relation between loans and imports and exports.

It will be seen from the remarks on page 673 that New South Wales has been since 1851 an exporter of gold, as it produces a much larger quantity than is required for purposes of currency; the loans raised in England, therefore, do not come to the Colony as coin, but as merchandise, and form the greater portion of the excess of imports over exports, which is so marked a feature in the trade of these colonies. The following table shows the trade of the Colony for twenty years, and the loan expenditure on public works during each year. Making allowance for the imperfection of the trade returns, the earnings of foreign investments in the Colony, and the expenditure of colonists living abroad, it is evident how close the connection is between the loan expenditure and the excess, or otherwise, of the imports:—

Imports, Exports, and Expenditure from Loans.

Year.	Imports.	Exports.	Excess of Imports.	Excess of Exports.	Loans Expenditure on Public Works.
	£	£	£	£	£
1870	7,757,281	7,990,038	....	232,757	621,913
1871	10,933,503	11,259,909	....	326,401	488,727
1872	9,567,843	10,476,654	....	908,811	422,026
1873	10,959,864	12,618,755	....	1,658,891	272,124
1874	11,645,420	12,398,518	....	753,098	529,411
1875	13,735,133	13,797,397	....	62,264	1,149,153
1876	13,800,505	13,061,412	739,093	....	707,511
1877	14,852,778	13,457,900	1,394,878	....	995,353
1878	15,104,645	13,134,405	1,970,240	....	815,268
1879	14,503,826	13,131,931	1,371,895	....	1,271,705
1880	14,176,063	15,682,802	....	1,506,739	1,668,638
1881	17,587,012	16,307,805	1,279,207	....	2,397,368
1882	21,467,899	17,677,355	3,790,544	....	2,832,750
1883	21,522,841	20,262,273	1,260,568	....	3,265,711
1884	23,160,916	18,577,290	4,583,626	....	3,674,706
1885	23,737,461	16,750,107	6,987,354	....	3,896,145
1886	21,313,127	15,717,937	5,595,190	....	3,766,356
1887	19,171,317	18,521,750	649,567	....	1,965,019
1888	21,229,277	20,920,130	309,147	....	1,991,307
1889	22,863,057	23,294,934	....	431,877	1,464,900
1890	22,615,004	22,045,937	567,067	....	2,141,219

Loan money spent on public works.

The expenditure of loan money on public works, from the beginning of 1870 to the close of 1890, was £36,337,319, and the amount of interest paid on the public debt during that period was approximately £19,727,300, leaving the net amount of British capital imported into the Colony at £16,610,019. The excess of imports during the series of years covered by the foregoing table amounts to £24,619,538, or £8,009,519 more than the net proceeds of the loans which reached New South Wales. This excess is spread over twenty-one years, and equals about £381,400 per annum. The sum last mentioned represents the difference between the amount of British capital sent to the Colony for private investment, and the earnings of such capital invested in the country. From the circumstances of the case it is impossible to make an exact estimate of the amount of British and other capital which is sent to this country for investment, but data are not wanting from which a somewhat close approximation may be

made for each of the past six years. It will be seen from the following statement that the flow of money from abroad for investment in New South Wales has been greatly reduced since 1886. The very large excess of imports over exports which has marked the operations of the neighbouring Colony of Victoria would warrant the assumption that the investment of foreign capital in Australia still continues, but that for the present its course has been diverted from New South Wales. In the following table the money received on deposit by banks in London, and transmitted to the Colony is included with investments by private persons.

Investments of British and other Capital in New South Wales.

Year.	Amount.	Year.	Amount.
	£		£
1885	6,800,000	1888	3,260,000
1886	6,030,000	1889	1,460,000
1887	3,650,000	1890	3,720,000

PUBLIC WEALTH.

Valuation of public and private wealth.

At the beginning of the year 1891 the estimated value of the public and private wealth of the Colony was £586,700,000, or about £523 per head of population. The public and municipal estate is valued at £179,295,000, or about £160 per head, while the personal and private wealth of the Colony amounts to £407,405,000, or £363 per head. The public wealth of New South Wales consists of railways, telegraphs, waterworks, sewerage, and other public works, unsold lands, the latter mostly leased to pastoralists, and yielding revenue in the shape of rent. The value of each class was :—

	£
Railways, tramways, telegraphs, waterworks, sewerage, and other revenue yielding works	44,958,000
Public works and buildings, not yielding revenue, or only indirectly	20,313,000
Unsold Crown lands, and balances due on lands sold conditionally	107,024,000
Total value of public property or estate	£172,295,000

Estimated value of public works.

The present value of the Government railways and tramways of the Colony has been taken at the moderate estimate of £39,975,000, the expenditure on lines open and under construction to June, 1891, having been about £33,057,500. The balance of the amount represents the value of Crown lands used for railways, and not specially paid for, and the increased value of railway property during the thirty-five years which have elapsed since the lines were first opened for traffic. The present value of roads and bridges formed chiefly out of general revenue has been taken at £10,382,000, which is the estimate of the Engineer-in-Chief for Roads and Bridges. Harbour works, including wharves and dredging plant, are valued at £3,592,000, water supply and sewerage £4,240,000, electric telegraphs £743,700; other public works £6,338,300, making the total value of public works constructed from loans and revenue, £65,271,000.

Estimated value of the public estate.

The value of the public estate appears in the estimate given in previous table as £107,624,000. Of this sum £13,224,000 represents the amount due to the Crown by conditional purchasers, while the remainder, £94,400,000, is the value of the unsold estate. The total area unalienated at the commencement of the year 1891 was 151,124,000 acres, and of this nearly 148,122,200 acres were leased at a rental of £814,850, the remaining portion of 3,001,800 acres represents unoccupied lands and reserves for public purposes. The value set down for the unsold Crown lands, otherwise than those leased for mining, is about 12s. 6d. per acre, which is certainly by no means extravagant.

Estimated value of municipal works.

The value of municipal works is £6,400,000, this, with the sums already given, making the total value of public and municipal property £179,295,000. Against the wealth, however, must be set the amount of the public debt, £48,425,333, and that of the municipalities £1,751,296 in all, £50,176,629 or 28 per cent. of the total, thus leaving a surplus of about £129,118,400 on the public estate alone, without considering the value of private property.

PRIVATE WEALTH.

Private property in the Colony is estimated at the value of £407,405,000, comprised as follows :—

Land	£173,352,000
Houses, and permanent improvements	120,800,000
Live stock	35,187,000
Personal property, including household furniture	14,637,000
Machinery and implements of trade	9,723,000
Coin and bullion	9,726,000
Merchandise	14,730,000
Shipping owned in the Colony	1,910,000
Mines, including Plant	18,340,000
	£407,405,000

The gross value of the land in the Colony is £186,576,000, but allowance must be made for the amount owing by selectors on conditional purchases to the amount of £13,224,000, which has been included in Public Wealth ; the net value is therefore estimated to be £173,352,000 as shown above.

Large amount of private wealth.

The Private Wealth as shown on the foregoing statement is certainly very large, but may be roughly verified by taking the amount of money left by persons dying during the past five years. Thus the total amount sworn to of property claimed under probate and letters of administration during this period was £26,369,571. The number of deaths during the same period was 71,489, so that the average value of the property left by each person dying was about £369. It is well known that property for probate purposes is not estimated at its full value ; assuming the real value is 10 per cent. above the probate, the total wealth of the Colony, as estimated by this means, on the population of 1890 would be £455,500,000.

Lands and buildings within municipal boundaries.

The value of all lands and buildings assessed for municipal purposes is £134,009,758, the annual value being £8,356,803, or

6·24 per cent. on the nominal capital value. It is well understood, however, that the capital value of unimproved lands is generally greatly understated for municipal purposes, and the annual value per cent. of all property is, in reality, not so high as given above; nevertheless, for the purpose of the foregoing estimate, the value of property within municipalities is taken as substantially the same as that returned by the municipal authorities.

The area of land outside municipalities, which is in private hands, amounts to about 43,276,500 acres. On this area the number of houses was, in 1890, about 108,000, valued at £11,880,000, while the value of the land itself was £105,204,600—exclusive of the amount owing by selectors on their conditional purchases. In making this estimate the lands of the Colony have been classified into various grades having regard to their situation and capability of production, and valued accordingly. The mineral lands are worth, at a moderate computation, £18,340,000. The permanent improvements effected in the purchased lands of the Colony and on the holdings of pastoral tenants have been valued by the Inspector of Stock at £72,982,100. The Census Act provided for a valuation of lands and improvements, and from the returns obtained it would appear that the value of improvements effected, as returned by the landholders, was £44,920,400, or 61 per cent. of Mr. Bruce's estimate, and the figures have been accepted. Lan outside municipalities.

The estimated value of personal property and furniture is set down at £14,637,000, which is not more than 16 per cent. of the value of the houses; this may, perhaps, be considered too low when it is borne in mind that it is usual in England to estimate the value of furniture alone at half the value of the houses furnished. Personal property and furniture.

Merchandise represents the value of the goods and stocks of all kinds, whether in store or shops, or at the place of production, and amounts in value to £14,730,000. Merchandise.

The following is a summary of the total wealth as well as of the value per head of population :—

	Total.	Value per head.
	£	£
Public estate	172,895,000	154
Municipal property	6,400,000	6
Private property	407,405,000	363
Total wealth	586,700,000	523

Increase in value of estates of deceased persons.

The value of the estates in which wills were proved in the Colony, or for which letters of administration were granted, has increased very rapidly; but, unfortunately, the records are not perfect prior to the year 1881 :—

Value of Property for which Probate or Letters of Administration were granted.

Year.	No. of Probates and administrations—will annexed.	Amount sworn to.	No. of Letters of Administration.	Amount sworn to.	Total No. of Estates.	Total Amount sworn to.
		£		£		£
1881	671	2,011,305	526	307,818	1,197	2,319,123
1882	810	3,586,554	589	581,528	1,399	4,168,082
1883	862	3,528,602	613	588,029	1,475	4,116,631
1884	933	3,642,709	648	605,543	1,581	4,248,252
1885	961	3,721,805	659	601,542	1,620	4,323,347
1886	1,026	4,726,918	706	768,628	1,732	5,495,546
1887	961	3,621,874	665	641,426	1,626	4,263,300
1888	998	3,652,963	667	638,295	1,665	4,291,258
1889	1,115	4,317,734	682	473,611	1,797	4,791,345
1890	1,131	6,605,545	680	922,577	1,811	7,528,122

Average value o estates.

Two things are plainly noticeable from this table, especially if it be viewed in connection with the subsequent one, viz.,—that the proportionate number of persons leaving property shows a general tendency to increase faster than the population, whilst the average value of estates is also increasing. As regards the latter, the figures are somewhat peculiar owing to the occurrence at irregular intervals of the deaths of very wealthy men, which amongst so comparatively few deaths considerably affect the average.

Value of Property left by Persons Deceased.

Year.	Number of Wills proved or administrations granted.	Number of deaths.	Percentage of Persons dying who left property.	Average value of Estates left by persons with property.
				£
1866	426	7,361	5·08	1,487
1867	387	8,631	4·48	1,782
1868	437	7,225	6·05	1,412
1869	462	6,691	6·90	1,513
1870	428	6,556	6·53	1,461
1871	475	6,407	7·41	1,283
1872	522	7,468	6·99	1,280
1873	637	7,611	8·37	1,398
1874	685	8,652	7·92	1,776
1875	908	10,771	8·43	*
1876	926	11,193	8·27	*
1877	1,001	9,869	10·14	*
1878	1,087	10,763	10·10	*
1879	1,051	10,200	10·30	*
1880	1,173	11,231	10·44	*
1881	1,197	11,536	10·38	1,938
1882	1,399	12,816	10·92	2,979
1883	1,475	12,249	12·04	2,791
1884	1,581	14,220	12·94	2,687
1885	1,620	15,282	10·60	2,669
1886	1,732	14,587	11·87	3,173
1887	1,626	13,448	12·09	2,683
1888	1,665	14,408	11·56	2,577
1889	1,797	14,829	12·12	2,666
1890	1,811	14,217	12·74	4,157

* Cannot be accurately given, probate duties not in force.

Probates an index of wealth.

In former issues of this work the question was discussed whether the value of estates for which probates or letters of administration were granted could be taken as a basis from which the wealth of the whole community could be determined. Tables were given showing the results for periods of five years; that from 1885 to 1889 showed an average of £319 per inhabitant, which with allowance for undervaluings seemed to indicate approximately the wealth of the community as ascertained by valuing the various elements of which it is composed. Nevertheless the increase of late years seemed so extraordinary as to warrant a suspicion of the correctness of the system of valuation, and though the figures were recorded, it was expressly stated that they were given with diffidence and should be used with caution. The necessity of so using any probate returns is made much stronger when the returns for 1890 are added to those of the four previous years. The sum for which probate was granted in 1890 was £7,528,122 as against £4,791,345 in the previous year, an extraordinary increase due chiefly to some unusually large estates, one of which was valued at £1,255,937.

Value of estates. Taking the five years 1886–90 the average value of estates was £3,055, or £369 per inhabitant, as compared with £2,744 and £319 for the five years which closed with 1889. Such extraordinary variations give ample reason for viewing with distrust conclusions based on the probate returns. It has been urged that these returns are useful in determining the amount of wealth belonging to persons residing in a country as distinguished from the wealth which is in the country itself. Such a theory is based on a defective knowledge of the conditions under which probates are granted. So far as this Colony is concerned the probates show, if anything, about the amount of property within the Colony which belongs to the estates of persons whose wills have been proved, quite irrespective of the place where such persons may have resided at the time of their death,—and should correspond with the value obtained by estimating separately all the elements cf wealth. The following table shows the number and value of estates on which stamp duties were actually paid during the years 1887–90 :—

Classification of Estates on which duties were paid, 1887–90 :—

Estates.	1887.		1888.		1889.		1890.	
	Number.	Value.	Number.	Value.	Number.	Value.	Number.	Value.
		£		£		£		£
Under the value of £5,000.........	1,513	1,095,260	1,503	1,092,885	1,572	1,143,005	1,525	1,269,025
,, ,, £12,500.........	59	487,160	71	578,055	76	610,040	59	461,380
,, ,, £25,000.........	25	444,605	33	632,685	21	379,995	34	636,425
,, ,, £50,000.........	10	362,035	18	627,260	16	588,765	11	412,350
Over ,, £50,000.........	13	1,280,765	12	1,380,550	15	1,566,090	17	3,669,605
Total	1,620	3,669,825	1,637	4,311,435	1,700	4,287,895	1,646	6,448,785

Number of estates.

Though the values of estates as declared for probate purposes may not be taken as giving an indication of the absolute wealth of New South Wales, the number of estates gives some indication of the distribution of that wealth. It will be seen that during the year 1890 stamp duties were paid in 1,646 estates, to the value of £6,448,785, being an average of £3,918 for each estate. The total number of persons who died during the year was 14,217, or at the rate of 12·90 to every 1,000 of the mean population. Presuming that wealth is distributed among the living in the same preportion as it was among those on whose estates stamp duties were paid in relation to the total number of the dead, there would have been, at the end of 1890, 118,217 persons with estates under £5,000, 4,574 with property between £5,000 and £12,500, 2,636 who were worth £12,500 to £25,000, 853 whose wealth was between £25,000 and £50,000, and 1,318 who enjoyed estates valued at over 50,000. This would leave about 994,300 people whose effects were, so to speak, of little or no value, consisting mainly of personal property—chiefly furniture—which is rarely made the subject of formal bequest. Of these unpropertied persons the great bulk consisted of women and children. Thus the number of male persons below 21, and therefore incapable of making a bequest, was 294,900, and of women and children, 518,200, or together 813,100. These, deducted from the number given above, 994,300, would leave, 181,100, being the adult males who do not possess property, compared with 137,600 who are so fortunate. In determining these figures, the fact that not a few women hold property has not been taken into consideration, but if every allowance had been made on this score no appreciable difference would be made in the conclusion just arrived at. Though the property of the Colony may be said to have accumulated into the hands of about one-ninth of the population, a more correct idea of the distribution of wealth will be gained from the statement that of every hundred adult males 41 have property to the value of £100, which, restricted as it may be deemed, is a considerably wider distribution than is found in older countries.

INCOME.

The income of persons living or holding property in New South Wales was estimated in 1890 to be £62,950,000, or at the rate of £57 per head of mean population. The income is derived from the following sources:— Total income.

	£
Pastoral pursuits	13,400,000
Dairy farming	1,400,000
Agricultural and forestry	5,650,000
Mining	4,450,000
Manufacturing pursuits	5,700,000
Professional	2,700,000
Commercial, trade, &c.	8,000,000
Distribution of food and drink and domestic pursuits	4,680,000
Construction	5,870,000
Transport	1,900,000
State employés	1,620,000
Rents derived from houses and land not used for agriculture, pastoral, or mining	6,120,000
Miscellaneous pursuits	1,560,000
Total	£62,950,000

The earnings derived from what are usually termed productive pursuits—pastoral, dairy farming, agriculture, mining, and manufactures—amount to £30,600,000, or 48·6 per cent. of the total earnings of the community. The income of the wage-earners, including females, amounts to £28,550,000, distributed approximately as follows:— Productive pursuits.

Income of Wage-earners.	£
Pastoral and farming	7,720,000
Mines and quarries	3,200,000
Works and manufactories	4,600,000
Transport	1,900,000
Attendance and food distribution	3,530,000
Mechanics and unskilled labourers	5,490,000
Miscellaneous	2,110,000
Total	£28,550,000

The above estimate represents the income of 385,000 persons, of whom 319,000 were males and 66,000 females. The earnings of the former were £25,730,000 and of the latter £2,820,000, the average per head being £80 13s. 2d. and £42 14s. 7d. respectively. The income derived by persons residing abroad who hold property, or have investments in this country, is at present more a matter of speculation than of exact computation. The amount of such income is undoubtedly large, as there has been for many years a constant influx of capital, chiefly from Great Britain and Victoria, for investment in New South Wales. The earnings of this capital has now reached a considerable sum, and there is ample evidence to warrant the supposition that the income of non-residents amounts to not less than £3,500,000 per year.

Income of various countries.

Compared with the older countries the income stated in the foregoing table to be enjoyed by persons living in New South Wales will appear very considerable, but not more so than the high rate of wages and the natural wealth of the Colony would lead one to expect. The following table, extracted from Mulhall's Dictionary of Statistics, gives the rate for the principal countries of Europe and for the United States and Canada:—

Income per Head of Population in Various Countries.

Country.	Total Income.	Income per head.
	Million £	£
United Kingdom	1,285	33·7
England	1,084	37·9
Scotland	128	31·2
Ireland	73	15·3
France	1,046	27·8
Germany	1,076	22·2
Russia	975	11·5
Austria	616	15·5
Italy	363	12·2
Spain	293	16·5
Portugal	55	12·1
Belgium	167	28·0
Holland	102	22·6
Denmark	66	32·5
Sweden and Norway	145	21·3
Switzerland	55	19·0
United States	2,358	39·0
Canada	130	26·0
New South Wales	63	57·0

CURRENCY.

Coins of United Kingdom current.

The coins circulating in Australasia are those of the United Kingdom. Gold is the standard, the silver and copper current are more properly tokens than coins. Gold coins are legal tender to any amount, silver for an amount not exceeding forty shillings, and bronze for one shilling. The standard weight and fineness of each coin are given below. The least current weight of a sovereign is 122·5 Imperial grains, and of a half-sovereign 61·125 grains :—

Standard weight of coins.

Coins in circulation.

Denomination of Coin.		Standard Weight.	Standard Fineness.
		Imperial grains.	
Gold.....	Sovereign..........	123·27447	Eleven-twelfths fine gold, one-twelfth alloy, or decimal fineness ·91666.
	Half-sovereign....	61·63723	
Silver ...	Crown..............	436·36363	Thirty-seven-fortieths fine silver, three-fortieths alloy, or decimal fineness ·925.
	Double Florin.....	349·09090	
	Half-crown	218·18181	
	Florin	174·54545	
	Shilling............	87·27272	
	Sixpence...........	43·63636	
	Threepence	21·81818	
Bronze...	Penny.............	145·83333	Mixed metal, copper, tin, and zinc.
	Halfpenny	87·50000	

Gold coins are the only ones struck at the Sydney Mint, though silver and bronze of English coinage are also issued. The weight of gold sent for coinage from the first opening of the Mint on the 14th May, 1855, to the end of 1890, was 17,918,033 oz., valued at £67,519,827; of this quantity New South Wales produced only 7,416,345 oz., of the value of £28,241,832, the amount from each colony being :—

Weight of gold minted.

Gold received for Coinage at the Sydney Mint to end of 1890.

Colony where gold was produced.	Weight.	Value.
	oz.	£
New South Wales	7,416,345	28,241,832
Queensland	6,564,596	23,550,045
New Zealand	2,165,501	8,556,566
Victoria	1,441,649	5,919,432
Tasmania	11,805	44,817
South Australia	61,914	221,289
Other countries	17,533	60,682
Old coin	238,600	925,164
Total..............................	17,918,033	67,519,827

New South Wales and Queensland gold coined at Sydney.

The greater part of the gold won in New South Wales and Queensland, and also part of the produce of New Zealand and South Australia, comes to Sydney for coinage; but by far the larger portion of the gold of the colonies last-mentioned, as well as of the other colonies of the group, goes to Melbourne. The total value of gold raised in Australasia to the end of 1890 amounted to £341,906,358, £67,519,827 equivalent to 19·75 per cent. of which passed through the Mint of this Colony. The value of gold coin and bullion issued up to the end of 1890, was £67,375,044 of which £64,526,000 worth of gold was converted into coin, the value of sovereigns and half-sovereigns being:—

Gold Coin issued by the Sydney Mint.

Year.	Sovereigns.	Half-sovereigns.	Total.
	£	£	£
1855 to 1877	39,248,500	1,963,500	41,212,000
1878	1,259,000	63,000	1,322,000
1879	1,366,000	47,000	1,413,000
1880	1,459,000	40,000	1,499,000
1881	1,360,000	31,000	1,391,000
1882	1,298,000	26,000	1,324,000
1883	1,108,000	110,000	1,218,000
1884	1,595,000	....	1,595,000
1885	1,486,000	....	1,486,000
1886	1,667,000	41,000	1,708,000
1887	2,002,000	67,000	2,069,000
1888	2,187,000	....	2,187,000
1889	3,262,000	32,000	3,294,000
1890	2,808,000	....	2,808,000
Total	62,105,500	2,420,500	64,526,000

Bronze and silver coin issued by Mint.

Bronze coin was first issued from the Mint in 1868, and silver coin in 1879. The respective value of each to the close of the year 1890 being:—Bronze, £34,020; silver, £396,350. The amount of each particular currency issued in each year is shown in the following table:—

Sydney Mint—Silver and Bronze coin issued.

Year.	Silver Coin.						Bronze Coin.
	Half-crowns.	Florins.	Shillings.	Six-pences.	Three-pences.	Total.	
	£	£	£	£	£	£	£
1868 to 1875	......	......	......	......	......	......	15,185
1876	......	......	......	......	......	......	1,045
1877	......	......	......	......	......	......	770
1878	......	......	......	......	......	......	735
1879	17,000	15,972	12,000	3,681	4,647	53,300	910
1880	11,300	6,428	11,900	2,219	3,153	35,000	545
1881	14,600	10,600	12,000	3,600	2,700	43,500	710
1882	12,100	11,300	13,800	1,300	4,000	42,500	1,950
1883	11,200	9,300	13,000	2,400	3,700	39,600	1,375
1884	15,000	11,800	11,300	4,300	3,800	46,200	1,765
1885	11,100	7,200	12,450	5,550	7,600	43,900	2,485
1886	2,600	200	5,500	1,450	7,650	17,400	1,095
1887	2,375	700	1,850	500	690	6,115	800
1888	1,425	900	3,250	3,100	2,610	11,285	1,630
1889	7,800	4,000	3,900	2,700	3,975	22,375	1,560
1890	*7,500	†8,600	9,200	4,500	5,375	35,175	1,460
Total... £	114,000	87,000	110,150	35,300	49,900	396,350	34,020

* Includes £100 in Crowns. † Includes £100 in double florins.

The amount of silver coin withdrawn from circulation from 1873, when the Mint first received worn coin, until 1890, was of the nominal value of £117,979. The actual weight after smelting was 373,452 oz., and the corresponding weight of new coinage Silver coin withdrawn.

would be 429,015 oz. The loss while the coins were in circulation was therefore 55,562 oz., the average loss being 12·95 per cent.

Coin held by banks.

The amount of coin held by the banks, and in circulation, was larger during 1890 than in any previous year, though, as compared with the population, the total has not varied greatly for some years, as will be seen from the following table:—

Coin in Circulation and in Banks, with Average per Head of Population at close of year.

Year.	Coin in Banks.	Average per head.	Coin in private hands.	Average per head.	Total in Banks and in private hands.	Average per head.
	£	£ s. d.	£	£ s. d.	£	£ s. d.
1880	3,637,568	4 17 3	2,605,370	3 9 8	6,242,938	8 6 11
1881	2,885,890	3 13 10	3,104,397	3 19 7	5,990,287	7 13 5
1882	2,672,799	3 5 7	3,128,415	3 16 9	5,801,214	7 2 4
1883	2,861,980	3 6 5	2,989,137	3 9 5	5,851,117	6 15 10
1884	3,863,873	4 5 4	2,988,744	3 6 0	6,852,617	7 11 4
1885	4,069,840	4 5 8	3,250,082	3 8 5	7,319,922	7 14 1
1886	4,439,742	4 9 9	3,361,904	3 7 11	7,801,646	7 17 8
1887	5,108,996	5 0 2	3,745,980	3 13 5	8,854,976	8 13 7
1888	5,061,000	4 16 3	3,936,000	3 14 11	8,997,000	8 11 2
1889	5,161,011	4 15 5	3,874,058	3 11 8	9,035,069	8 7 1
1890	5,810,568	5 3 7	3,915,260	3 9 9	9,725,828	8 13 4

Stock of gold and silver.

The stock of gold and silver in private hands, in relation to the population, showed a slight decrease during 1890 compared with the previous year; there is evidently a tendency to reduce the quantity of coin needed for the ordinary business of exchange. The spread of the banking system is generally attended with a diminution of

Amount of currency.

the amount of coin required for the use of business, and the decrease in the supply of coin per head points to the extension of banking facilities. The quantity of coin in the colony both reserved in banks and in circulation amounts to about £8 13s. 4d. per head, a larger sum than in any other country except France; if, however, a comparison be made of the quantity of currency, apart from bank reserves, but including paper money, New South Wales is exceeded by France, Belgium, the Netherlands, and the United States. The following table shows the total amount of circulation and the average per inhabitant in some of the principal countries. The extraordinary variations in the requirements arise from the diverse modes of transacting business which obtain, and the poverty of some of the countries enumerated:—

Amount of Coin and Paper circulation of various countries.

Country.	Active Currency.			Per Inhabitant.		
	Coin.	Paper.	Total.			
	£	£	£	£	s.	d.
Great Britain	96,000,000	39,000,000	135,000,000	3	10	8
France	227,000,000	115,000,000	342,000,000	8	16	5
Germany	108,000,000	71,000,000	179,000,000	3	13	8
Russia	20,000,000	123,000,000	143,000,000	1	11	1
Austria	5,500,000	76,000,000	81,500,000	2	0	8
Italy	19,000,000	57,000,000	76,000,000	2	10	2
Spain	33,500,000	30,000,000	63,500,000	3	12	2
Holland	7,400,000	17,000,000	24,400,000	5	6	1
Belgium	17,600,000	15,000,000	32,600,000	5	6	10
Switzerland	2,100,000	6,000,000	8,000,000	2	14	0
United States	193,700,000	208,000,000	401,700,000	6	8	4
Canada	2,600,000	6,000,000	8,600,000	1	15	8
India	168,000,000	12,000,000	180,000,000	0	17	2
Cape Colony	5,400,000	1,000,000	6,400,000	4	0	7
Australia, New South Wales	3,915,000	1,685,000	5,600,000	4	19	10

BANKING.

Capital and profits of banks

The nominal capital of banks trading in New South Wales is £13,929,326, but much of this capital is not exclusively used in the Colony. It has been found impossible to determine the proportion of the whole capital required for the business of the Colony; the figures relating to capital in the ensuing tables, therefore, refer to the nominal capital paid up. The last half-yearly dividend and bonus paid by the banks during 1890 amounted to £894,186, or at an average rate of about 12⅘ per cent. per annum, the rates varying from 5 to 25 per cent. The capital and profits of banks operating in this Colony during 1890 will be found below:—

Banks operating in New South Wales.	Capital paid up at end of 1890.	Rate per Annum of last Dividend and Bonus.	Amount of Reserved Profits at the time of declaring last half-yearly Dividend.
	£	℔ cent.	£
New South Wales	1,250,000	17½	960,000
Commercial	600,000	25	810,604
Australasia	1,600,000	14	815,043
Union of Australia	1,500,000	14	1,120,379
Australian Joint Stock	682,254	15	445,306
London Chartered of Australia	1,000,000	8	330,980
English, Scottish, and Australian Chartered	900,000	10	341,127
Commercial of Australia	1,200,000	17½	1,025,182
City	280,000	12½	185,600
*Mercantile of Sydney	316,532	6	28,696
Federal of Australia	400,000	9	141,294
Queensland National	800,000	12	501,171
New Zealand	825,000	7	96,348
National of Australasia	1,000,000	15	701,090
New Oriental	600,540	6	197,711
South Australia	800,000	6	131,451
North Queensland	175,000	5	665
Totals	13,929,326	12·84	7,832,047

* Amalgamated since the beginning of 1891 with the Commercial Bank of Australia.

Magnitude of banking operations.

The magnitude of the operations of the banking institutions of the Colony may be gathered from the subsequent tables. In the year 1872 the total assets amounted to £13,094,187, while the liabilities were £9,672,266, showing a surplus of £3,421,921, while in 1890 the assets had amounted to £51,679,795, and the liabilities to £36,828,633, the surplus being £14,851,162. During the nineteen years covered by the table the population of the Colony was more than doubled, while the resources of the banks were increased four times.

Increase of resources of banks.

Assets and Liabilities of Banks.

Year.	Assets.	Liabilities.	Surplus Assets.
	£	£	£
1872	13,094,187	9,672,266	3,421,921
1873	14,263,574	10,956,813	3,306,761
1874	16,276,956	12,600,906	3,676,050
1875	18,318,311	14,499,398	3,818,913
1876	19,982,588	16,043,694	3,938,894
1877	21,631,694	17,464,564	4,167,130
1878	22,853,362	18,047,430	4,805,932
1879	23,734,837	18,568,426	5,100,411
1880	24,398,813	19,335,229	5,063,584
1881	26,481,987	21,426,126	5,055,861
1882	30,624,731	24,393,750	6,230,981
1883	32,580,005	25,828,248	6,751,757
1884	35,261,346	27,480,291	7,781,055
1885	37,815,576	29,845,622	7,969,954
1886	39,805,308	30,378,358	9,426,950
1887	42,268,720	31,831,499	10,437,221
1888	44,971,057	33,035,061	11,935,996
1889	48,914,994	34,593,165	14,321,829
1890	51,679,795	36,828,633	14,851,162

The total assets of all banks trading in Australasia at the close of 1890 amounted to £170,371,128, against which there were liabilities to the extent of £117,249,696, so that the surplus provided by the banks out of their own resources was £53,121,432. The Colony showing the largest figures is Victoria, after which comes New South Wales. As regards the last named Colony the amounts shown in the following table differ from those of the preceding one, which were not the assets, &c., at the close of the year as now given, but the average of the whole year:—

Assets compared with liabilities.

Assets and liabilities of Banks in Australasian Colonies for the last quarter of 1890.

Colony.	Assets.	Liabilities.	Excess of Assets.
	£	£	£
New South Wales	52,436,977	37,248,937	15,188,040
Victoria	60,937,955	42,224,084	18,713,871
Queensland	20,906,932	11,183,750	9,723,182
South Australia	11,489,842	7,759,926	3,729,916
Western Australia	1,910,905	1,084,840	826,065
Tasmania	4,919,907	4,511,730	408,177
New Zealand	17,768,610	13,236,429	4,532,181
Total	170,371,128	117,249,696	53,121,432

These figures show the total assets and liabilities, including balances due from one bank to another; as between the banks and the public the actual amounts are:—Assets, £167,182,051; liabilities, £116,683,902. The excess of assets was £50,498,149, which represents £26,571,581 paid-up capital and reserve funds, and £23,926,568 obtained from other sources.

Bank returns no gauge of stability.

The figures just given must be taken with qualifications since the returns for any individual colony do not indicate the stability or otherwise of the banks, as most institutions have branches in the adjoining colonies and in London, and a bank may show, as did the late Oriental Bank Corporation, a large surplus of assets over liabilities in New South Wales and yet be on the brink of insolvency by reason of its operations elsewhere.

Bank deposits.

The amount of money deposited in the various banks of the Colony since 1872 will be found herewith, a distinction between deposits bearing interest and at call being made from 1876. The most striking feature of the table is the rapid advance of interest bearing deposits, which, in 1890, had reached the large sum of £25,114,127, whereas the amount in 1880 was only £12,209,781. The deposits at call amounted to £9,932,310 in 1890, as against £5,683,870 in 1880.

Average Amount of Deposits with Banks of Issue.

Year.	Deposits not bearing Interest.	Deposits bearing Interest.	Total Deposits.
	£	£	£
1872	*	*	8,653,481
1873		*	9,760,661
1874		*	11,369,184
1875		*	13,132,772
1876	5,146,536	9,563,608	14,710,144
1877	5,061,231	10,984,264	16,045,495
1878	4,933,643	11,678,843	16,612,486
1879	4,898,724	12,352,454	17,251,178
1880	5,683,870	12,209,781	17,893,651
1881	7,719,236	11,869,979	19,589,215
1882	8,310,054	13,772,826	22,082,880
1883	7,158,975	16,302,407	23,461,382
1884	7,453,914	17,738,445	25,192,359
1885	8,819,979	18,387,705	27,207,684
1886	8,355,255	18,974,984	27,330,239
1887	8,870,037	20,162,493	29,032,530
1888	10,436,559	20,382,990	30,819,549
1889	9,830,056	22,925,549	32,755,605
1890	9,932,310	25,114,127	35,046,437

* Not distinguished.

There were deposited during the last quarter of 1890 £110,860,143 with the various banks trading in Australasia; of the sum named, £76,887,942—not including deposits in Tasmania—bore interest. The banks of Victoria held £40,292,065 or 36·35 Bank deposits of Australasia.

per cent. of the total deposits; those of New South Wales, £35,460,118, or 32·00 per cent. The large business of the Victorian banks, as compared with those of New South Wales, in this and other respects, is probably due to the extensive interests which capitalists of that Colony have long held in the Southern and Western districts of New South Wales. The following table shows the amount of deposits for the last quarter of 1890. The Tasmanian Banking Returns do not distinguish the two kinds of deposits:—

Total Deposits with Banks of Issue during last quarter of 1890.

Colony.	Deposits bearing Interest.	Deposits not bearing Interest.	Total Deposits.
	£	£	£
New South Wales	25,395,600	10,064,518	35,460,118
Victoria	29,477,948	10,814,117	40,292,065
Queensland	7,190,660	3,175,300	10,365,960
South Australia	5,330,474	1,868,163	7,198,637
Western Australia	562,310	449,165	1,011,475
Tasmania	....	....	4,271,067
New Zealand	8,930,950	3,329,871	12,260,821
Total £	*76,887,942	*29,701,134	110,860,143

* Tasmania not included.

Reserves compared with liabilities.

The proportion of coin and bullion which banking institutions must habitually keep in stock is not fixed by any enactment. Compared with the total liabilities, and with deposits at call and note circulation, the quantity of coin has varied very considerably from year to year, as the following statement shows. The largest per centage was held in 1876, and the least in 1883:—

Yearly Average Coin and Bullion in Banks, compared with Liabilities, and with deposits at call and circulation.

Year.	Per cent. of Metallic Reserves to Liabilities.	Per cent. of Metallic Reserves to deposit at call and note circulation.
1876	18·2	46·5
1877	15·3	42·9
1878	13·0	38·2
1879	13·8	42·4
1880	17·8	49·9
1881	17·1	40·1
1882	12·7	31·0
1883	11·1	32·3
1884	13·2	39·5
1885	14·2	40·0
1886	13·2	40·1
1887	15·5	47·2
1888	16·7	45·6
1889	14·6	44·4
1890	15·4	49·6

Average value of coin reserved.

The quantity of coin in the colony at the close of 1890 has already been stated as £9,725,828, or £8 13s. 4d. per head. Of this amount £5,810,568 was in the hands of the banks, and £3,915,260 in circulation. The value of coin and bullion in banks of issue, at the end of the year, was somewhat in excess of the average amount for the year. The following figures are for the period which has elapsed since 1876:—

Average yearly value of Coin and Bullion in Banks of Issue.

Year.	Coin.	Bullion.	Total.
	£	£	£
1876	2,828,503	87,063	2,915,566
1877	2,586,053	84,415	2,670,468
1878	2,262,526	86,194	2,348,720
1879	2,488,175	83,824	2,571,999
1880	3,373,618	73,651	3,447,269
1881	3,594,914	80,068	3,674,982
1882	3,022,159	74,308	3,096,467
1883	2,798,536	80,018	2,878,554
1884	3,559,859	61,223	3,621,082
1885	4,171,043	62,066	4,233,109
1886	3,958,238	66,243	4,024,481
1887	4,870,315	65,187	4,935,502
1888	5,461,393	59,608	5,521,001
1889	4,997,629	70,528	5,068,157
1890	5,575,068	83,999	5,659,067

Reserves comparatively heavy.

Compared with the total amount of currency, the reserves held by Australasian Banks are proportionately heavier than those of any other country. In New South Wales the bank reserve fully equals the whole of the active circulation both of coin and paper; much the same conditions exist in the neighbouring colonies. The only European country approaching this proportion, is the Netherlands, where the bank reserves equal about 40 per cent. of the active currency of the country. The following table gives the total value of coin and paper currency, both active and reserved in use in the principal countries of the world.

It will be seen that New South Wales has a larger currency per inhabitant than any of the countries mentioned, France alone excepted:—

Total Currency of Banks of Principal Countries.

Country.	Active and Reserved Currency.			Per Inhabitant.		
	Coin.	Paper.	Total.			
	£	£	£	£	s.	d.
Great Britain	124,000,000	39,000,000	163,000,000	4	8	0
France	328,000,000	115,000,000	443,000,000	11	16	0
Germany	167,000,000	71,000,000	238,000,000	5	0	0
Russia	53,000,000	123,000,000	176,000,000	2	2	0
Austria	27,000,000	76,000,000	103,000,000	2	12	0
Italy..................	33,000,000	57,000,000	90,000,000	3	0	0
Spain	43,000,000	30,000,000	73,000,000	4	4	0
Portugal	11,000,000	30,000,000	12,000,000	2	14	0
Scandinavia	8,000,000	13,000,000	21,000,000	2	16	0
Holland	18,000,000	17,000,000	35,000,000	7	14	0
Belgium	22,000,000	15,000,000	37,000,000	6	2	0
Switzerland	6,000,000	6,000,000	12,000,000	4	0	0
United States......	228,000,000	208,000,000	436,000,000	7	0	0
Canada	4,000,000	6,000,000	10,000,000	2	0	0
Japan	28,000,000	26,000,000	54,000,000	1	8	0
China	150,000,000	....	150,000,000	0	10	0
India	180,000,000	12,000,000	192,000,000	1	0	0
Java..................	18,000,000	....	18,000,000	0	18	0
Cape Colony	7,000,000	1,000,000	8,000,000	6	0	0
Egypt	31,000,000	....	31,000,000	6	4	0
Algeria	5,000,000	3,000,000	8,000,000	2	0	0
Cuba	4,000,000	12,000,000	16,000,000	10	0	0
Australia—New South Wales	9,726,000	1,685,000	11,411,000	10	1	3

The advances which the various banks of issue have made to their customers averaged in 1871, £7,593,538, representing £14 19s. per head of the whole population; during 1890 the total had reached £41,623,049, equal to £37 16s. per head; which, whether viewed in connection with banking business outside Australia, or as illustrating the progress of the Colony, cannot but be regarded as extraordinary:— Advances made by Banks.

Amounts Advanced by the Banks to their Customers—Yearly Average.

Year.	Amount of Advances.	Advances per head of Population.	
	£	£	s.
1871	7,593,538	14	19
1872	7,993,223	15	4
1873	9,116,831	16	15
1874	10,074,712	17	17
1875	11,770,185	20	3
1876	12,801,716	21	4
1877	15,354,507	24	8
1878	16,762,111	25	10
1879	17,098,052	24	15
1880	16,661,815	22	17
1881	19,038,386	24	18
1882	23,517,046	29	9
1883	25,894,669	30	18
1884	27,479,142	31	2
1885	30,556,628	32	10
1886	32,527,431	33	11
1887	33,332,179	33	4
1888	35,670,485	34	13
1889	39,956,031	37	9
1890	41,623,049	37	16

Banks trading under act of incorporation are allowed a note circulation equal to the amount of their paid-up capital and the coin and bullion in store. The Banks have in no instance availed themselves to the full extent of their privilege in this regard; indeed, if they were so disposed, such an issue of notes would be impossible, as the currency required for the business of the Colony is scarcely more than the value of gold retained in the vaults of the Banks, and at the same time there is a marked disposition on the part Note circulation of Banks.

of the general public to use gold in preference to notes for their ordinary transactions. The notes current are not a legal tender, a very necessary condition, as in the present state of the law there is nothing to prevent any company or person issuing notes, provided they can be got into circulation. Indeed, it would appear that the issue of paper circulation was contemplated by the Companies Act, since it makes notes a first charge on such in the event of companies being wound up. It will be seen from the following statement that the issue of paper by the Banks has been stationary for about nine years.

Notes and Bills in Circulation not bearing interest, Yearly Average.

Year.	Notes in Circulation.	Bills in Circulation.	Total.	Average per Inhabitant
	£	£	£	£
1871	694,344	42,816	737,160	1·45
1872	789,544	42,916	832,460	1·58
1873	920,620	32,067	952,687	1·73
1874	1,005,639	34,289	1,039,928	1·82
1875	1,080,088	34,811	1,114,899	1·91
1876	1,093,862	33,712	1,127,574	1·87
1877	1,129,279	37,618	1,166,897	1·85
1878	1,167,519	38,621	1,206,140	1·83
1879	1,123,123	41,703	1,164,826	1·69
1880	1,173,663	45,229	1,218,892	1·67
1881	1,390,376	52,687	1,443,063	1·89
1882	1,614,191	57,487	1,671,678	2·09
1883	1,677,146	64,596	1,741,742	2·08
1884	1,644,469	60,443	1,704,912	1·93
1885	1,714,095	55,300	1,769,395	1·91
1886	1,621,090	60,827	1,681,917	1·73
1887	1,526,096	64,146	1,590,242	1·58
1888	1,591,500	84,111	1,675,611	1·62
1889	1,489,153	96,459	1,585,612	1·49
1890	1,503,404	119,938	1,623,342	1·47

Enormous development of banking.

Considering the population of these colonies the banking operations of Australasia have attained enormous development. The following table from Mulhall's Dictionary shows the capital employed in banking, and the amount of deposits in some of the principal countries for the year 1889. The figures regarding Australasia are for 1890 :—

Capital and Deposits in the Banks of Various Countries.

Country.	Million £.			Amount per Inhabitant.
	Paid up Capital and Reserves.	Deposits.	Total.	
				£
United Kingdom	284	626	910	24
France	140	128	268	7
Germany	85	146	231	5
Russia	42	64	106	1
Austria	45	102	147	4
Italy	25	83	108	4
Spain	31	16	47	3
Portugal	6	4	10	2
Belgium	11	19	30	5
Holland	14	6	20	4
Sweden	9	15	24	5
Norway	5	1	6	3
Denmark	2	21	23	12
Switzerland	5	12	17	6
Cape Colony	2	7	9	6
Argentina	12	17	29	8
Uruguay	3	5	8	12
United States	270	760	1,030	16
Canada	13	27	40	8
Australasia	27	111	138	37

The general business transacted by the banks of each Colony is summarized on next page. The reserve of coin consists almost wholly of gold, only about 4 per cent. being in silver. The stock of coin and bullion held by the banks of issue at the end of 1890 was £20,265,308, being less by about £2,479,000 than the amount in the Bank of England at the same date. As the operations of the banks extend to more than one colony it is possible that there is some overlapping in their statements; there are, however, no means by which this supposition may be verified. With the qualifications just mentioned the following table may be taken as showing the assets and liabilities of the banks trading in Australasia during the last quarter of 1890 :—

Assets and liabilities of Australasian Banks.

Bank Returns, Australasia—Averages for the last quarter, 1890.

Colony.	Liabilities.					Assets.						
	Notes in Circulation.	Bills in Circulation.	Balance due to other Banks.	Deposits.	Total Liabilities.	Coin.	Bullion.	Landed Property.	Notes and Bills.	Balances due from other Banks.	Notes and Bills discounted and all other Debts due to the Banks.	Total Assets.
	£	£	£	£	£	£	£	£	£	£	£	£
N. South Wales	1,557,805	127,442	103,572	35,460,118	37,248,937	5,619,111	87,658	1,644,179	287,568	1,738,902	43,009,559	52,436,977
Victoria	1,543,340	142,770	245,909	40,292,065	42,224,084	6,868,323	314,091	1,824,564	231,382	421,849	51,276,841	60,937,955
Queensland	683,897	46,994	86,899	10,365,960	11,183,750	2,051,833	386,556	700,041	42,828	327,581	17,399,093	20,906,932
South Australia ..	480,425	11,247	69,617	7,198,637	7,759,926	1,404,510	15,991	510,785	32,461	273,409	9,252,686	11,489,842
Western Australia	58,939	4,417	10,009	1,011,475	1,084,840	280,374	13,541	92,641	3,245	7,901	1,513,203	1,910,905
Tasmania	161,680	64,173	14,810	4,271,067	4,511,730	*632,226	....	112,313	......	205,290	3,970,078	4,919,907
New Zealand	887,230	53,400	34,978	12,260,821	13,236,429	2,421,580	169,659	513,528	37,007	164,145	14,462,741	17,768,610
Total, Australasia	5,373,316	450,443	565,704	110,860,143	117,249,606	19,277,912	987,396	5,398,051	634,491	3,189,077	140,884,201	170,371,128

* Includes Bullion.

Attracted by the high rate of interest on deposits allowed by the banks in 1887 large sums of British money were forwarded to Australia for investment. This influx was soon felt in the money market, for in the year 1888 the interest declined to an average of 4½ per cent., a rate lower than any prevailing since 1882. In the earlier months of 1889 a slight reaction took place, but towards the end of the year the interest declined to the rate of the previous year, at which point it remained until about July, 1890, when it rose to 5 per cent. for deposits fixed for 12 months.

Rates of Interest.

The interest allowed to depositors by banks of issue during the first seven months of 1890 was 3 per cent. for deposits fixed for three months, 4 per cent. for six months, and 5 per cent. for twelve months, whilst during the last five months of that year it was in every instance 1 per cent. lower. The Savings Bank of New South Wales gave interest at the rate of 4 per cent. on accounts closed during the year, and 5 per cent. on accounts open on the 31st December. The ruling rate during the year for Post Office Banks was 4 per cent. Interest was allowed by the Building and Investment Societies not issuing notes at the rate of 5, 6, and 7½ per cent. for the periods named above. The accompanying table gives the average interest per annum allowed by banks during each year since 1872:—

Average Interest per annum on Money deposited with Banks.

Year.	3 Months.	6 Months.	12 Months.	Year.	3 Months.	6 Months.	12 Months.
	per cent.	per cent.	per cent.		per cent.	per cent.	per cent.
1872	2½	3½	4	1882	2	3	4
1873	2½	3	3½	1883	4	5	6
1874	3	3½	4	1884	3½	4½	5½
1875	3½	4½	5½	1885	3	4	5
1876	3	4	5	1886	3½	4½	5½
1877	3	4	5	1887	3½	4½	5½
1878	3½	4½	5½	1888	2½	3½	4½
1879	4	5	6½	1889	3	4	5
1880	3	4	5	1890	2½	3½	4½
1881	2	2⅔	3⅔				

Rates of Discount.

The following table gives the discount charged by the banks for unexceptional bills. The table covers a period of nineteen years, during which the rates varied from 5½ to 7 per cent. for bills under three months, from 6½ to 8 per cent. for four months, and from 7½ to 9 per cent. for bills with a currency over four months. In the last column of the statement the discount rates of the Bank of England during the same period are given :—

Average Discount Rates per annum in Local Banks.

Year.	Discount on Local Bills.			Bank of England Rate.
	Under 3 Months.	3 to 4 Months.	Over 4 Months.	
	Per cent.	Per cent.	Per cent.	Per cent.
1872	5½	6½	7½	4½
1873	5½	6½	7½	5
1874	7	8	9	3¾
1875	7	8	9	3½
1876	7	8	9	3½
1877	7	8	9	3¾
1878	7	8	9	3½
1879	7	8	9	2 9/10
1880	7	8	9	2 7/10
1881	6	7	8	3½
1882	6	7	8	4½
1883	7	8	9	3½
1884	6½	7½	8½	3¾
1885	6	7	8	3
1886	6½	7½	8½	3¾
1887	6½	7½	8½	3¼
1888	6½	7½	8½	3½
1889	6½	7½	8½	3½
1890	6½	7¼	8¼	4 7/12

Large sums deposited in Banks.

In the next table is given the amount of deposits at the end of each year, from 1871 to 1890, in the Chartered Banks, the Savings Bank of New South Wales, and Post Office banks. The increase has been singularly rapid, not only absolutely, but also as compared with the increase in population. During the nineteen years the deposits increased from £7,989,801 to £40,190,587, the rate per head advancing from £15 8s. 7d. to £35 16s. 6d. The whole of the deposit banks of the Colony are not included in this table ; a very considerable sum is received by building and other societies, which offer a larger interest than the ordinary banks, the Savings or the Post Office Banks. During the last quarter of 1890 the amount of money entrusted to these societies, as far as the returns show, was £3,199,554, so that the total amount of deposits in banks of all descriptions was £43,390,141, equivalent to £38 13s. 6d. per inhabitant. The figures in the ensuing table do not include sums in building and investment societies :— Total deposits in Banks, &c.

Money on Deposit in Banks in New South Wales.

Year.	Banks of Issue.	Savings Banks.	Post Office Banks.	Total.	Amount per head of Population.		
	£	£	£	£	£	s.	d.
1871	7,043,886	931,688	14,227	7,989,801	15	8	7
1872	9,273,067	1,028,758	80,688	10,382,513	19	7	11
1873	10,279,324	1,164,561	206,070	11,649,955	21	0	9
1874	11,884,958	1,275,902	303,113	13,463,973	23	8	5
1875	13,650,892	1,295,797	354,075	15,300,764	25	14	11
1876	14,859,505	1,303,813	400,120	16,563,438	26	19	5
1877	16,325,043	1,355,258	467,453	18,147,754	28	3	10
1878	16,722,453	1,333,017	480,025	18,535,495	27	11	9
1879	17,862,840	1,410,905	511,357	19,784,102	27	17	9
1880	17,883,024	1,489,360	586,496	19,958,880	26	13	8
1881	20,308,017	1,427,202	971,501	22,706,720	29	1	0
1882	22,544,549	1,856,641	1,158,454	25,559,644	31	7	2
1883	23,739,134	1,822,319	1,183,519	26,744,972	31	1	0
1884	26,250,420	1,887,349	1,290,931	29,428,700	32	10	4
1885	26,709,386	2,016,656	1,471,894	30,197,936	31	16	0
1886	28,428,253	2,081,498	1,423,305	31,933,056	32	5	6
1887	29,253,864	2,174,439	1,501,454	32,929,757	32	5	6
1888	31,917,311	2,299,971	1,737,704	35,954,986	34	4	2
1889	33,777,143	2,550,192	1,729,891	38,057,226	35	3	7
1890	35,460,118	2,854,564	1,875,905	40,190,587	35	16	6

During the year 1890 there was an increase in the savings banks, of depositors, to the number of 8,912, and in deposits to the extent of £450,386 ; part of this increase shown is due to interest earned during the year, and part to the extension of the Post Office system, under which there was an addition of over 7,000 depositors, while the total deposits showed an increase of £146,014 over the preceding year. By comparing the figures giving the amount per inhabitant for the different years, the increase will be found Savings Banks.

to be proportionately greater than that of the population. The number of depositors at the close of the last two years and the amount to their credit was :—

Savings Banks.	1889.		1890.	
	Depositors.	Amount.	Depositors.	Amount.
		£		£
Savings Banks	58,626	2,550,192	60,514	2,854,564
Post Office Banks ...	76,288	1,729,891	83,312	1,875,905
Total	134,914	4,280,083	143,826	4,730,469

Savings Bank Deposits.

Of the total deposits in the Savings' Bank, 32,114 were for amounts of £20 and under, averaging £5 1s. 4d. each; 9,854 were sums between £20 and £50, averaging each £32 7s. 2d.; 7,479 were between £50 and £100, averaging each £70 17s. 3d.; 8,626 were between £100 and £200, averaging £129 0s. 7d. each; 2,207 are between £200 and £300, averaging £213 9s. 11d.; and 234 over £300, averaging £1,106 4s. 3d. each. It is hardly to be supposed that these last are individual deposits; they probably included the sums lodged by the various penny banks, hospitals, and other public institutions.

Land and Building Societies.

Besides the chartered banks and those under Government guarantee, as already mentioned, there are banking, land, building and investment companies, which receive money on deposit. Statistics were obtained of the operations of thirty-five of these Companies, and it would appear that they had at the close of 1890 assets to the extent of £7,346,971 against liabilities of £5,107,042, showing a nominal surplus of £2,239,929. Their subscribed capital amounted to £1,832,157 and reserved capital £700,172—in all £2,532,329. The most notable points about these Companies are the large dividends paid, from 6 to 25 per cent., and the large sum for which land figures in their assets. It will appear from the accompanying statement that these Companies held land to the extent of

£3,538,077 at the end of 1890, their other assets, part of which represents lands sold, but not paid for, amounting to £3,808,894:—

Liabilities and Assets of Land, Building, and Investment Companies.

Liabilities.	£	Assets.	£
Bills in circulation	37,309	Coin and bullion	7,794
Balances due to other Banks	350,777	Landed property	3,538,077
Deposits not bearing interest	24,875	Notes and bills of other banks	9,925
Deposits bearing interest..	3,174,679	Balances due from other banks	51,693
Other liabilities	1,519,402	Notes and bills discounted, &c.	3,739,482
Total liabilities ...	£5,107,042	Total assets	£7,346,971

Excess of assets over liabilities	£2,239,929
Capital paid up.......	£1,832,157
Reserved profits	£700,172
Number of Societies making returns	35

Since the foregoing figures were made up no less than ten companies receiving deposits have suspended payment. The liabilities of these companies, from their last statements, appear to have been £2,791,739, and their assets £3,704,852. Some of the companies have since proved to be solvent, their suspension being only temporary, and due to a panic among depositors; but the majority have gone into liquidation. The law with regard to companies receiving money on deposit is extremely lax, and under present conditions it is impossible for the general public, even after scrutinising the sworn returns, to distinguish those that are trading on sound lines from those that are purely speculative. In addition to the registered societies four others not registered have suspended payment. These do not make sworn returns, and their liabilities and assets are not included above.

During the year 1890 the total number of bankruptcy orders made was 1,193, with liabilities amounting to £1,203,685, and assets, £540,726, as shown by the bankrupts' schedules. This amounted to an increase of 131 bankrupts over those of 1889, when the liabilities and assets, as per bankrupts' schedules, were £794,603 and £396,723 respectively. There had been a large increase in the 1889 figures over those of 1888, but this was not

Bankruptcy proceedings.

necessarily caused by a depression of trade. The new Bankruptcy Act came into force at the beginning of 1888, and it is believed that many persons, fearing the stringency of that Act, rushed their estates into the Insolvency Court in 1887, thus causing the liquidations of 1888 to fall considerably below the average of the previous few years. In spite of the increases from 1888 to 1889, and from 1889 to 1890, the number of sequestrations in the latter year is still below that of 1887, and only slightly exceeds that of 1886. The liabilities of 1890, as shown by the schedules, exceed, however, those of 1889, or any previous year, while the assets last year show an increase over those of 1888 and 1889, but are far below those of the four years preceding 1888. It must be borne in mind, however, that the figures in bankrupts' schedules, especially those relating to assets, are to be accepted with caution, and as regards assets, even when stated *bona fide*, they are seldom realised.

Number of Insolvencies and Bankruptcies in New South Wales, and Amount of Liabilities, Assets, &c.

Year.	Number of Insolvencies and Bankruptcies.			Amount of		
	Voluntary.	Compulsory.	Total.	Liabilities as shown in the insolvents' schedules.	Assets as shown in the insolvents' schedules.	Deficiency shown in the insolvents' estates.
				£	£	£
1876	461	41	502	492,847	169,604	323,243
1877	534	54	588	508,352	210,821	297,531
1878	652	64	716	664,736	350,176	314,560
1879	767	96	863	781,334	306,103	475,231
1880	784	50	834	479,864	292,233	187,631
1881	664	60	724	379,290	218,212	161,078
1882	686	48	734	307,084	167,876	139,208
1883	720	65	785	444,594	245,836	198,758
1884	856	62	918	836,165	580,195	255,970
1885	849	80	929	773,212	589,359	183,853
1886	1,116	105	1,221	989,262	733,127	256,135
1887	1,249	102	1,351	1,081,726	788,941	292,785
1888	735	116	851	659,307	459,677	199,630
1889	935	166	1,101	794,603	396,723	397,880
1890	1,079	164	1,243	1,203,685	540,726	662,959

Included in the figures for the last three years are petitions withdrawn and refused, amounting to 28, 39, and 50 respectively, so that the total number of sequestrations during each of the three years was 823, 1,062, and 1,193, respectively.

Money secured by lien on wool

The amount of money advanced on the security of the wool clip and the live stock of the Colony is always very large. Such advances do not necessarily mean a scarcity of money on the part of the borrowers, as the system of liens and mortgages is part of the ordinary method of carrying on the trade of the country. Advances were, however, made more largely during the years of depression, which extended over the period from 1878 to 1882, as will be seen by the following table:—

Preferable Liens on Wool and Mortgages on Live Stock, registered.

Year.	Preferable Liens on Wool.			Mortgages on Live Stock.				
	No. of Liens.	No. of Sheep.	Amount of Liens.	No. of Mortgages.	No. of Sheep.	No. of Horned Cattle.	No. of Horses.	Amount lent.
			£					£
1880	1,479	6,216,741	981,172	901	4,858,265	183,556	401	2,818,967
1881	1,609	5,709,061	904,012	1,275	5,982,994	215,564	9,646	4,628,915
1882	1,289	4,837,667	801,175	1,074	3,865,831	112,441	8,391	3,391,984
1883	1,301	C,349,801	1,026,574	1,077	3,601,890	131,008	7,389	2,486,407
1884	1,379	4,168,185	973,179	1,471	2,696,994	77,241	8,097	1,881,062
1885	1,236	5,263,407	1,327,214	1,481	4,730,232	117 241	10,764	2,968,471
1886	1,187	9,049,194	1,454,184	1,383	4,332,553	79,616	10,349	2,404,823
1887	1,285	9,296,975	1,686,655	1,868	3,964,286	79,812	11,464	2,054,785
1888	1,174	9,800,520	1,288,125	1,998	4,002,148	80,120	12,386	2,003,216
1889	1,169	7,861,233	1,232,065	2,018	4,572,477	100,028	11,894	2,428,704
1890	1,461	9,006,582	1,562,270	2,230	4,962,30?	98,298	12,549	2,159,696

When any sum has been secured, both by a lien on the wool and by a mortgage of the sheep, the amount is included under the head of mortgages only. The above table does not, however, give an

Discharges of advances.

exact statement of the case, as a large portion of the advances made were discharged, as will be seen in the following table :—

Discharges of Mortgages on Live Stock registered.

Year.	Number.	Amount.	Year.	Number.	Amount.
		£			£
1880	232	3,804,475	1886	150	849,742
1881	399	2,781,122	1887	210	1,073,674
1882	258	1,900,443	1888	240	1,160,307
1883	126	600,426	1889	256	1,191,089
1884	306	3,801,352	1890	368	2,512,551
1885	208	1,173,673			

Advances in growing crops.

Other advances on produce are also made, the principal being those on growing crops. Such advances do not ordinarily reach large sums either individually or in their total. In 1888, owing to the drought, farmers were compelled to obtain much heavier advances than usual on such crops as survived the severity of the season ; the advances for 1889 were a little over one third of those of 1888, and those for 1890 show a further reduction. The amount of advances made on crops for ten years was:—

Liens on Growing Crops registered.

Year.	Number.	Amount.	Year.	Number.	Amount.
		£			£
1881	807	42,255	1886	989	70,212
1882	854	40,379	1887	949	67,379
1883	814	50,789	1888	1,006	247,460
1884	888	54,057	1889	1,227	83,748
1885	857	71,153	1890	1,069	75,439

Mortgage transactions have largely increased during the last eleven years. The maximum was reached in 1885, when there were 11,661 mortgages, aggregating £17,445,488, nearly eight millions of which was lent on country lands. In 1890 the number of mortgages registered was 14,580, and the sum advanced £16,631,880. These figures are incomplete, for there were many mortgages not registered; besides, in many instances the amounts lent by the banks are not stated, but simply the words, "valuable consideration," or "cash credit," inserted in the deed. There are two Acts of Parliament under which such transactions are registered. The following table shows the totals, and the numbers registered under each for the last ten years:— Mortgages registered.

Mortgages on Land registered.

Year.	Under Act 7 Vic. No. 16.		Under Act 26 Vic. No. 9.		Total
	Number.	Amount.	Number.	Amount.	
		£		£	£
1880.........	2,995	4,048,952	2,193	3,902,272	7,951,224
1881.........	4,505	5,268,449	2,336	4,155,225	9,423,674
1882.........	4,159	4,924,596	2,605	4,710,855	9,635,451
1883.........	4,088	5,859,472	2,825	5,781,167	11,640,639
1884.........	4,653	5,620,421	3,437	4,447,739	10,068,160
1885.........	7,618	11,360,108	4,043	6,085,380	17,445,488
1886.........	6,933	7,570,210	4,295	5,975,898	13,546,108
1887.........	6,108	5,869,302	4,239	6,930,665	12,799,967
1888.........	7,452	8,765,109	4,274	7,520,914	16,286,023
1889	9,312	7,277,334	4,416	7,256,931	14,534,265
1890.........	9,883	8,072,218	4,697	8,559,662	16,631,880

The amount of mortgages discharged has always been much less than the amount registered. This arises partly from the fact that mortgages are as a rule paid off by instalments, and the discharge is given for the last sum paid, which might happen to bear a very small proportion to the total sum borrowed. The number of mortgages under each Act discharged for the last eleven years is as follows:— Mortgages discharged.

Mortgages discharged.

Year.	Under Act 7 Vic. No. 16.		Under Act 26 Vic. No. 9		Total.
	Number.	Amount.	Number.	Amount.	
		£		£	£
1880	1,860	715,148	1,052	1,945,915	2,661,063
1881.........	2,386	1,926,357	1,501	2,067,140	3,993,497
1882.........	2,051	1,676,224	1,603	2,417,460	4,093,684
1883.........	1,388	1,433,912	1,369	1,833,016	3,266,928
1884.........	2,216	1,957,765	1,696	2,684,470	4,642,235
1885.........	3,473	2,239,075	2,068	3,373,327	5,612,402
1886	2,773	2,515,398	2,082	2,164,254	4,679,652
1887	3,067	2,909,931	2,431	7,520,914	10,430,845
1888........	4,160	4,273,034	2,926	4,179,503	8,452,537
1889........	3,707	2,669,358	2,488	3,300,033	5,969,391
1890..	4,215	2,609,560	2,559	4,230,172	6,839,732

The total amount of liens on wool registered during the eleven years from 1880 to 1890, as shown in the foregoing tables, was £13,279,595; the mortgages on live stock amounted to £30,219,980, and on land, £139,962,879, in all, £183,462,454. During the same period the mortgages discharged were: liens on wool to the full amount in due course, mortgages on live stock, £20,848,854, and on land, £60,641,966, making a gross total of £94,770,415. The sums of money advanced on mortgages of various kinds over that paid off was therefore apparently £88,692,039 in eleven years. As regards the liens, such indebtedness does not exist, for the mortgages over stock and clip are for the most part terminated without being formally discharged. Even in the case of mortgages on real estate the amount outstanding does not represent money actually owing; in very many cases it simply represents the limits within which clients of banks and other loan institutions are entitled to draw, though many of these clients may be in credit while their property is mortgaged and unreleased. Making these allowances, the probable amount of private indebtedness on account of money

Amount of private indebtedness.

advanced on mortgages of various kinds is not less than £35,000,000. The larger portion of this sum represents the engagements incurred by pastoral tenants for the improvement or security of their estates, while a considerable part is due to the purchase of lands in the vicinity of Sydney on credit with payments in redemption extending over a number of years. The weight of this burthen of mortgage will have to be largely reduced before that elasticity will again be found in trade which was visible a few years ago.

Postal business money orders.

The business transacted by the Postal Department in money orders has grown to very large dimensions, for while in 1876 there were issued 18 orders to every hundred persons in the community, in 1890 the number reached 40, the total value advancing from £465,771 to £1,252,305, while the value of orders paid rose from £421,162 to £1,193,954 during the same period. This increase is due mainly to the greater facilities now afforded for the transmission of money by this method, though it is also to some extent attributable to the more general appreciation of the money order system amongst the working classes of the community. The following is a statement of the business transacted since 1876:—

Money Orders issued and paid, and Commission received.

Year.	Issued.		Paid.		Commission.
	Number.	Amount.	Number.	Amount.	
		£		£	£
1876	112,684	465,771	101,492	421,162	4,663
1877	129,120	494,469	120,493	450,477	5,248
1878	142,025	538,800	129,143	487,458	5,772
1879	159,897	582,423	142,201	515,076	6,488
1880	190,606	669,022	168,944	583,340	7,694
1881	220,670	771,978	195,757	675,025	8,799
1882	247,716	883,524	218,334	771,861	10,027
1883	275,592	963,698	239,595	829,770	11,371
1884	305,883	1,068,068	270,678	921,904	12,651
1885	337,856	1,169,569	298,082	997,961	14,243
1886	345,825	1,134,955	309,576	962,336	14,927
1887	360,759	1,131,884	330,594	1,016,297	14,960
1888	388,410	1,215,132	368,081	1,116,433	15,807
1889	400,487	1,188,227	390,414	1,106,066	15,981
1890	442,425	1,252,305	441,845	1,193,954	16,939

Fire risks.

The extent of fire risks held by the Insurance Companies transacting business in the Colony cannot be ascertained exactly. It is not made compulsory upon the Companies to give returns, and in several cases they have abstained from doing so. The following is an account of the amount of risks at the end of 1890, as far as the returns have come to hand:—

	£		£
Sydney and Suburbs	57,148,388	Maitland, West	958,450
Glen Innes	170,430	Newcastle, City	1,000,000
Grafton, North and South	298,687	Tighe's Hill	16,720
Hamilton	60,520	Wagga Wagga	301,628
Lismore	15,000	Windsor	25,000
		Wollongong	250,000

The declared amount of risks held in Sydney and suburbs during the past six years was:—

	£
1885	36,691,000
1886	41,631,582
1887	46,253,370
1888	49,209,395
1889	53,583,000
1890	57,148,388

Increase of risks to population.

The gross increase for the period of five years shown was £20,457,388 or 55·7 per cent. During the same period the population of the metropolitan district increased about 29·9 per cent., from which it would appear that the wealth of Sydney is advancing at a rate much more rapid than the population, though the increase of the latter is abnormally large. Some part of the increase shown may be due to an extension of the facilities offered to insurers, but the amount due to such cause will not be very large.

Fires in metropolis.

The number of fires which occurred in the Metropolitan district during the year was 235, which may be classified as follows, according to the damage done:—

Slight damage	205
Serious damage	12
Total destruction	18
Total	235

Besides these there were 52 chimney fires and 44 false alarms.

Of the premises totally destroyed by fire 12 were insured and 3 not insured, while in 3 cases it was not ascertained whether the properties were insured. Of the other serious fires 11 were insured and 1 uninsured. The information regarding insurance was not obtained in all instances where the loss was slight, but of the property reported to be damaged slightly the loss was insured in 121 cases, uninsured in 29 cases, and 55 insurance unknown. So that it would appear the total number of insurances was 144 as against 33 non-insurances, or 81·36 per cent. of the whole number for which the information is available. The percentage just given must be taken with qualification, for as the premises and the property therein contained frequently belong to different persons, so in order to gauge the extent to which insurance is practised, it would require to be ascertained in how many instances the double insurance was effected, for in the returns above given a property is considered insured if the premises be covered and the contents uninsured, the converse also being the case.

The total number of firemen attached to the brigades in the metropolitan and country districts was as follows, the number of fires attended being also given:— Firemen in metropolitan district.

Name of Station.	Number of actual fires attended.	Average number of men in the brigades.
City Companies—		
Metropolitan Fire Brigades (3 stations)...	235	34
North City	63	12
Paddington Brewery	73	25
Standard Brewery	82	22
Suburban Companies—		
Alexandria	20	22
Ashfield	12	15
Balmain (2 stations)	11	21
Burwood	1	15
Darlington	19	...
Glebe	17	19
Leichhardt	12	17
Manly	6	17
Newtown	21	16
Paddington	22	17

Name of Station.	Number of actual fires attended.	Average number of men in the brigades.
Suburban Companies—*continued.*		
Parramatta No. 1	5	23
Parramatta No. 2	3	23
St. Leonards (2 stations)	2	19
Waterloo	13	19
Waverley	21	17
Woollahra	23	17
Country Companies—		
Albury	6	27
Bathurst	8	20
Bourke	3	7
Broken Hill	28	23
Deniliquin	2	25
Forbes	3	15
Goulburn	1	27
Glen Innes	3	16
Grafton, North	....	15
Do South	1	10
Hamilton	9	20
Hay	2	14
Honeysuckle	14	32
Lambton	3	18
Lismore	1	16
Maitland, West	8	26
Newcastle City	15	20
Newcastle Hose and Reel	12	20
Newcastle Salvage and Ambulance Corps	15	25
Singleton	2	30
Stockton	4	25
Tighe's Hill	4	18
Wagga Wagga	6	22
Wallsend and Plattsburg	2	26
Windsor	1	30
Wollongong	3	15
Total	317	934

LIFE ASSURANCE.

Law relating to Assurance.

The law does not provide for the publishing of sworn returns by Life Assurance Companies, and although valuable and interesting reports are made annually by some companies, it has been found quite impossible to distinguish the progress of assurance in New South Wales, as distinct from the other Colonies. Most of the companies have extended their business beyond the Colony in which their chief office is established; the following figures therefore refer to Australasia generally, though only to those offices whose head-quarters are in the Colonies. The assets of the eleven societies amount to £16,079,136, of which £9,007,310 are invested in mortgage, £2,707,279 in loans on policies and personal security, £1,283,458 in Government securities, £124,909 in shares, £1,717,167 in freehold and leasehold property, and cash, principally at fixed deposit, £723,198, and sundry debts, £515,815. The interest earned during the year amounted to £887,729, being at the rate of 5·81 per cent.; the net increase in the accumulated funds was £1,438,262.

Analysis of assurance business.

On analysing the accounts of these Societies, as published, it is seen that the total number of outstanding policies, and the amount they represent, are not given. With regard to new business it will be found that in 1890 there were 32,011 policies issued, to the value of £9,201,925, or an average amount upon each policy of £287, the highest average for the last ten years. This means an increase of 1,514 policies, amounting to £511,383, over the transactions of the previous year, and an advance in the average value of the policies by £2. Since the end of the year 1880 the Societies in question issued altogether no less than 300,183 new policies, representing an assurance of £83,177,728, but there is nothing in the published accounts to show how many of these policies have lapsed, and how many still remain in force. The new annual premiums, which amount to £296,612, bear an average rate of £3·223 per cent. to the total amount of new assurance.

New policies.

Premiums received.

The amount of premiums received in 1890 was £2,186,791, of which sum £279,624 was income from new premiums, and £1,907,167 was for renewals. The amount just given was £37,707 in excess of the income of the previous year. The total receipts, obtained by adding to the premium income the items "consideration for annuities granted," "interest," and other receipts, came to £3,094,745, as against the sum of £2,966,917 in the year 1889, being an increase of £127,828. The average rate of interest realised by the nine offices from which this could be ascertained, as already stated, was 5·81 per cent.; some of the purely mutual offices, however, realised considerably over 6 per cent.

Claims and surrenders.

Claims and surrenders during the year amounted to £1,087,303, of which sum £715,355 was for claims with bonus additions, £125,572 for endowments and endowment assurances matured, and £246,375 for surrenders, &c. The total amount paid to policy-holders in 1890 was £1,161,644, as against £1,060,494 in 1889. The expenses of the year exceeded those of the previous year by £91,948. This is equivalent to an increase of 8·63 per cent. on the expenditure of 1889, while the increase in the premium income was only 1·75 per cent., and in the gross income 4·31 per cent.

If however, the comparison be made between the years 1881 and 1890, instead of 1889 and 1890, an increase of 116 per cent. is shown in premium income and of 136 per cent. in gross income, while the amount paid for claims and surrenders increased in the same period by no less than 240 per cent.

In 1881 claims and surrenders absorbed 31·42 per cent. of the premium income while in 1890 this ratio had risen to 49·72 per cent. This increase is mainly due to the growth in age of the offices, but partly also to the small proportion of new business permanently retained.

The total income for the ten years was £22,317,496, of which amount £16,779,939 was contributed by policy-holders, and £5,537,557 was from interest and other sources. Of the total income £7,390,101, or 33·11 per cent. was returned to policy-holders, and £3,795,446 or 17·01 per cent. was absorbed by expenses, while £11,131,919, or 49·88 per cent. has been saved, and added to the funds of the Societies to meet future liabilities.

MOVEMENTS OF GOLD.

Since the discovery of gold in the year 1851 large quantities of that metal—in the form of coin as well as bullion—have been exported from the Australasian Colonies every year. The returns for Western Australia were not officially kept prior to 1885, and therefore are not available, but the amount of gold imported and exported from each of the other Colonies, calculated for five-year periods from the year 1851 to the end of 1890, is given herewith. The tables also show the amount by which the exports have exceeded the imports in the various Colonies, or *vice versa*, as the case may be, and the average amount of such excess per annum.

Import and export of Gold.

Reference to the figures shows that Victoria was by far the largest exporter of gold, her total during the whole period amounting in value to £243,807,149, while she imported to the value of £34,526,970, the bulk of which came from New Zealand. The excess of exports over imports in the case of Victoria amounted to £209,280,179. The next largest net exporter was New Zealand, whose excess of exports over imports was £42,196,327, her gross export being £49,186,916, the balance being gold imported, chiefly in the shape of coin. The gross export of New South Wales was much larger than that of New Zealand, amounting to £74,869,711, but she had imported to the value of £47,349,491, so that her excess of exported gold came to but £27,520,220. Queensland came next with an excess of gold exported, amounting to £22,738,957. In the case of Tasmania the amount by which the export of gold exceeded the imports was £1,833,909, but the Colony of South Australia imported gold to the value of £268,535 over and above the amount of her total export.

Export of each Colony.

The largest exporters of gold, it will be found, are the largest producers, as Victoria, New Zealand, and Queensland. The other Colonies now produce very little more than suffices to meet their local requirements. The returns of the gold imports and exports for New South Wales, it must be remembered, are swollen by large quantities of Queensland gold, which is simply sent to Sydney to be minted, and then exported in the shape of coin.

Producers the largest exporters.

Value of Gold (Bullion and Specie) Imported and Exported in each of the Australasian Colonies, 1851–88.

Year.	New South Wales.		Victoria.		Queensland.		South Australia.		Tasmania.		New Zealand.	
	Imports.	Exports.	Imports.	Exports.	Imports.	Exports.	Imports.	Exports.	Imports.	Exports.	Imports.	Exports.
	£	£	£	£	£	£	£	£	£	£	£	£
1851-55 ..	2,182,397	5,895,413	2,112,330	35,491,153	....	......	890,673	2,891,155	....	818,228	11,361	50,300
1856-60 ..	1,692,367	6,316,418	2,287,127	55,200,488	....	......	200,389	100,812	....	24,801	158,967	168,809
1861-65 ..	4,542,675	13,075,907	3,798,130	38,610,988	106,175	204,558	548,699	217,495	10,000	820	969,352	9,245,872
1866-70 ..	7,605,362	12,728,780	8,023,685	35,819,924	260,850	1,931,042	363,450	269,021	48,500	17,610	788,578	12,776,875
1871-75 ..	7,221,739	11,679,003	6,804,924	29,135,595	509,645	4,934,840	722,078	216,723	72,201	70,820	1,064,927	9,665,285
1876-80 ..	6,086,401	6,878,131	4,063,913	18,955,874	874,177	5,879,119	900,124	305,170	330,245	490,822	1,247,400	6,862,185
1881-85 ..	6,613,791	7,740,345	3,960,095	18,679,685	916,599	4,545,954	1,118,776	575,470	264,440	819,078	1,081,890	5,209,890
1886-90 ..	11,404,759	10,555,714	3,526,766	11,913,597	1,616,106	9,526,996	800,565	670,323	305,518	623,689	1,748,119	5,207,500
Totals..	47,349,491	74,869,711	34,526,970	243,807,149	4,283,552	27,022,509	5,514,704	5,246,169	1,030,904	2,864,813	6,990,589	49,186,916

NOTE:—Information for Western Australia is only available for the years 1886-90, during which period the value of gold imported and exported was £144,690 and £179,323 respectively.

Excess of Exports over Imports of Gold (Bullion and Specie).

Year.	New South Wales.	Victoria.	Queensland.	South Australia.	Tasmania.	New Zealand.
	£	£	£	£	£	£
1851-55	3,713,016	33,378,823	....	2,000,482	818,228	39,139
1856-60	4,624,051	52,963,311	....	*99,527	24,801	9,842
1861-65	8,533,232	34,817,803	98,383	*331,204	*9,680	8,256,520
1866-70	5,123,418	27,791,239	1,670,192	*64,429	*30,890	12,038,302
1871-75	4,457,264	22,330,671	4,425,195	*565,355	*1,381	8,696,258
1876-80	791,730	14,891,961	5,004,942	*594,954	160,077	5,614,785
1881-85	1,126,554	14,719,540	3,629,355	*543,306	564,632	4,178,060
1886-90	*849,045	8,386,831	7,910,890	*120,242	318,121	3,459,381
Total, excess of exports	27,920,290	209,280,179	22,738,957	*266,535	1,833,909	42,196,227

* Excess of imports.

Neither in the foregoing nor in the following table, except for the last period, are the figures for Western Australia included; the movement of gold in that colony is by no means large; the excess of exports in the five years which closed with 1890 was only £34,643, or at the rate of £6,928 per annum. For the whole of Australasia the excess of exports of gold since 1851 was £303,335,700, distributed in quinquennial periods as shown below:—

Year.	Amount.	Average per annum.
	£	£
1851-55	39,949,688	7,989,938
1856-60	57,522,478	11,504,496
1861-65	51,365,054	10,273,011
1866-70	46,527,832	9,305,566
1871-75	39,306,752	7,861,350
1876-80	25,868,541	5,173,708
1881-85	23,664,776	4,732,955
1886-90	19,130,579	3,826,116
1851-90	303,335,700	7,583,392

PART XX.

Industrial Progress.

Periods of industrial history.

THE industrial history of the colony is naturally divided into eight periods, each with some distinguishing characteristic; the first extending from the beginning of settlement under Captain Phillip in 1788 to the close of Governor Macquarie's term of office in 1821, at a time when the colony had begun to feel the good effects following the discovery of the passage across the Blue Mountains. The second, from 1821 to 1838, when the system of assigning convicts to free settlers came to an end. The third, from 1838 to 1843, when the progress of the country was disturbed by a commercial crisis rendered memorable by the failure of the Bank of Australia. The fourth, from 1843 to 1851, a period of very great depression, summarily terminated by the discovery of gold. The fifth, from 1851 to 1861, an era of rapid growth and great change, ushered in with the intense excitement of the rush for gold and ending with the introduction of the new system of land sales by free selection before survey. The sixth, from 1861 to 1872, a time of transition and recovery from the fever of the golden era, when the golden dreams of the fifties had faded away, and the social and industrial system now existing was evolved out of the heterogeneous elements brought together during the preceding period. The seventh, from 1872 to 1886, during which the public revenue was increased by lavish sales of the public land, and large sums of borrowed money were expended on public works. The eighth began with the year 1886 and is still incomplete. There are everywhere signs of industrial unrest, and of the determination on the part of the labouring classes to take a large share in governing the country, and the near future may bring forth important changes in the laws relating to labour. A satisfactory feature of the times is the recognition by both employers and workmen of the ruinous consequences of strikes; on all sides there seems to be a disposition, when an industrial dispute arises, to accept any settlement short of a sacrifice of vital principles. This is the dearly bought lesson of the great strikes of 1888 and 1890.

A reference to the industrial condition of the first period is desirable as an historical record; but otherwise it has little bearing upon the industrial developments of to-day, which are in no sense the outcome of conditions existing prior to 1838. Lieutenant-Colonel Collins in his "Account of the English Colony in New South Wales," gives the best and most authentic history of the earlier days and details minutely the events which occurred during the thirteen years of his residence in the colony. At first provisions for the support of the colonists were necessarily imported, and as no strenuous efforts were made to obtain supplies from the soil of the country the people long continued to be dependent upon importations from abroad, and some times suffered great privations from scarcity. In 1792, when retail shops were first open for the sale of goods, wages were fixed by Government regulations, as also was the price of bread. Very little wheaten bread was used, flour being sold at the prohibitive price of 9d. per lb. In the statement of prices during 1792, and the two following years, articles of luxury as well as necessity are quoted, but as labourers were paid only 3s. a day the quantity of luxuries sold by the open stores was probably very limited. The following are some of the retail prices:— The first period.

Maize	per lb., 3d.	Bacon......	per lb., 1s. 6d. to 2s.
Rice	,, 3d.	Moist sugar	per lb., 1s. 6d.
Flour..................	,, 9d.	Soap	per lb., 1s.
Cheese......	per lb., 1s. 6d. to 2s.	Butter ...	per lb., 1s. 6d. to 2s.
Potatoes	per lb., 3d.	Eggs.........	per doz., 2s. to 3s.
Salt pork......	per lb., 6d. to 8d.	Spirits ...	per gal., 10s. to 12s.
Salt beef	per lb., 4d.	Porter...	per quart, 1s. to 1s. 3d.

Payments for work were made "by the piece" at prices regulated by the Government, agricultural labourers being paid £4 for clearing and hoeing for corn 1 acre of ground, and timber-getters, for sawing 100 feet, 7s.; for splitting 100 feet, 1s. 6d. to 2s. In 1796 the sum paid for making a pair of boots was 3s. 6d., a coat 6s., a gown 5s.; carpenters received 5s., and field labourers 3s. a day without rations, and these were considered high prices. During the first five years 1,703 acres were cleared, 1,314 acres were brought under cultivation—for wheat 204 acres, for barley 24, and 1,086 for maize. In 1800 the cultivated area had increased to 4,665 acres, and the live stock had greatly increased in numbers. In 1803, with a population of over 6,000, the ruling rates for provisions were:—

	s.	d.		s.	d.
Butter, per lb.	3	0	Mutton, per lb............	2	0
Cheese ,, ...	3	0	Salt beef ,, ...	0	8
Flour ,, ...	0	7	Wheat, per bushel	12	0
Bacon ,, ...	1	6	Fowls, per pair............	10	0
Fresh pork, per lb.	1	3			

Early colonial disasters.

In the first decade of the present century a series of untoward events, among them a disastrous inundation of the Hawkesbury River, caused a general depression and heavy losses. In 1810, owing to the destruction of crops hy the floods, there was great scarcity of provisions, wheat in the latter half of the year rising to £1 3s. 3d. and £1 5s. 9d. per bushel; mutton, beef, and pork, 1s. 6d. per lb.; potatoes, 11s. 6d. to 17s. 6d. per cwt.; fowls, 5s. per pair; eggs, 2s. 6d. per dozen; bread, 5½d. to 6d. per lb.; maize, 5s. 6d. to 7s. per bushel, were quotations for other kinds of produce. The wise management of Governor Macquarie, whose term of office extended from 1810 to 1821, materially increased the prosperity of the Colony. The people, according to the testimony of Captain Wallis, a contemporary, were in a most flourishing condition, abounding in all the necessaries and comforts of life. Wheat was selling at 7s. 6d. a bushel, maize 4s., potatoes 5s. 6d. cwt., fowls 3s. a couple, fresh beef, mutton, and pork, 5d. lb. Of wheat 18,174 acres were grown, with 9,276 acres of maize, and 3,215 of potatoes, and the production of wool amounted to 415 bales. Coin was scarce; the currency mainly consisted of Government paper, Spanish dollars, and copper, the system of barter necessarily prevailing to a very considerable extent. By the term "flourishing condition" Captain Wallis probably meant that the Australian colonist was better off than the British or Irish agriculturist, whose condition at the beginning of the century was not an enviable one.

In the earlier portion of Sir Thomas Brisbane's government the rate of increase of the population was accelerated by the introduction of greater numbers of free immigrants, a considerable proportion of whom were artisans, whose wages in 1823-4 were from 5s. to 7s. a day, the trades most in request being carpenters, stonemasons, bricklayers, blacksmiths, sawyers, coopers, and shoemakers. Provisions of all kinds were plentiful at moderate prices, the ruling rates being:— The second period.

	s. d.		s. d.		s. d.
Butter, per lb. ...	2 3	to	2 10	Fowls, per pair	3 4
Cheese ,, ...	1 3		......	Wheat, per bushel	8 0
Fresh pork, per lb.	0 6	to	0 8	Maize ,, ...	6 0
Fresh beef ,, ...	0 6	to	0 8	Barley ,, ...	5 0
Mutton ,, ...	0 6	to	0 8	Potatoes, per cwt.	8 0
Bread ,, ...	0 3½		......	Eggs, per dozen..............	1 10

The principal articles of manufacture were coarse woollen clothes, cabbage-tree hats, salt, candles, leather, boots, drain pipes, and other earthenware. In 1830 the population had increased to 46,300, and the services of mechanics and artisans of various classes were in brisk demand. In 1831 the wage of a skilled mechanic was £2 per week, and there was a strong demand for most descriptions of labour. The cost of living was moderate, although house-rent was high. In 1832 bread was sold at 7d. to 8d. per 2 lb. loaf, and flour at 14s. to 15s. per cwt. During the years, 1832 to 1835, under the policy of assisted immigration, 7,683 mechanics and artisans arrived, but the working classes, especially those living in Sydney, strongly objected to the policy on account of the great reluctance to leave the town displayed by the new arrivals. A select committee of

Legislative Council, appointed in 1835, after taking much evidence, reported that good mechanics could earn 30s. to 40s. a week, and farm labourers 7s. 6d. to 10s. a week with rations. The rent of a house of two rooms in Sydney was 5s. to 10s. a week, board and lodging for single men was 10s. 6d. per week, and provisions of all kinds were cheap, beef being 2d. per lb., sugar, 2½d. per lb., and tea, 2s. One of the witnesses stated that he paid shipwrights, coopers, and blacksmiths, 7s. to 8s., and sailmakers 6s. a day, adding, "we consider these wages too high, but find it impracticable to reduce them, as rather than take less the men will go out of work, and they can afford to do so, because the wages of three or four days will suffice to maintain them for a week." Another witness said he paid millwrights, blacksmiths, and engine-drivers 42s. a week, and that a good carpenter could earn £3 3s., and a stonemason £3 to £4 a week. All the witnesses were agreed as to the difficulty of inducing labourers to move into the country districts, a difficulty which told so severely against the agricultural and pastoral industries that in 1838 another select committee was appointed, to whom evidence was offered to the effect that the average rate of wages was 7s. a day, or 42s. a week, for mechanics, with a supply about equal to the demand. It was also deposed that masons were paid 6s. to 8s., plasterers and carpenters, 6s. 3d., quarrymen, 6s., blacksmiths, 7s. a day, and that "no mechanic need ever want employment"; and the cost of living was estimated at double the cost in Scotland or the northern parts of England, "but for constancy of employment there was no comparison." In this contemporary evidence, however, the allusions to the difficulty of obtaining good men, and the high wages enjoyed by mechanics, must be accepted with some caution. In a population numbering under 98,000 the demand for good men must have been limited, while the presence of bond labour, and the necessity of finding employment for it must have interfered very seriously with the regularity of the work to be obtained by free men. There was probably in the country districts a demand in excess of the supply of skilled labourers; but a glance at the following table of ruling rates during the period 1823–38 will show that the wages they could earn offered no inducements at all commensurate with the discomforts and dangers, real and imaginary, they expected to encounter :—

Rate of Wages, 1823 to 1838.

Trade.	1823.	1833.	1836.	1838.
	Per day. £ s. d.	Per day. £ s. d.	Per day. £ s. d.	Per day. £ s. d.
Boat-builders	....	0 6 0	0 7 3	0 6 8
Bookbinders	....	0 6 0	0 5 0	....
Blacksmiths	0 6 0	0 7 0	0 6 8	0 7 0
Bricklayers	0 6 0	0 5 0	0 7 3	0 6 6
Cabinetmakers	0 6 0	0 6 0	0 6 4	0 6 0
Carpenters	0 6 0	0 6 0	0 6 4	0 6 6
Caulkers	0 7 6	0 7 6	0 6 9	....
Chair-makers	....	0 6 0	0 6 0	....
Coopers	0 6 0	0 6 0	0 6 6	0 7 6
Engine and boiler makers	....	0 8 2	0 8 2	....
Farriers	....	0 6 6	0 6 5	0 6 6
Ironfounders	....	0 6 3	0 6 3	0 6 3
Joiners	....	0 5 6	0 6 3	0 7 3
Labourers	0 3 0	0 3 0	0 4 6	0 4 6
Locksmiths	....	0 6 6	0 5 9	0 6 0
Millwrights	0 6 6	0 6 6	0 7 3	0 7 3
Nailers	....	0 5 6	0 4 10	0 6 8
Painters	....	0 5 0	0 5 4	....
Plasterers	0 5 6	0 5 6	0 6 6	0 6 3
Plumbers	....	0 6 0	0 5 8	0 6 4
Quarrymen	....	0 5 6	0 5 6	0 4 6
Shoemakers	0 6 0	0 6 0	0 5 10	0 6 0
Stonemasons	0 6 0	0 6 0	0 7 6	0 6 8
Tailors	....	0 5 6	....	0 6 6
Wheelwrights	....	0 5 6	0 6 0	·6 5 6
		Per annum.	Per annum.	Per annum.
Agricultural labourers	....	22 10 0	22 10 0	25 0 0
	Per 1,000.	Per 1,000.	Per 1,000.	Per 1,000.
Brickmakers	0 6 0	0 9 0	0 5 3	0 9 0

In 1838 the system of assignment came to an end, and two years later transportation of convicts from England was abolished, so that the third period may be said to have opened under favourable auspices. Immigration was encouraged by votes of public money, and in five years the population increased nearly 80 per cent., being at the rate of more than 15,000 a year. By the discoveries of Sir Thomas Mitchell and others large areas of land The third period.

were thrown open for occupation, giving to trade of all kinds a powerful impetus, which was strengthened by the amendment of the land laws. In 1839 there was a great increase in wages, an ordinary mechanic being able to earn from 8s. to 12s. a day, but this was coincident with a rise in the price of provisions, so that, in spite of the general demand for all kinds of labour, employment was difficult to obtain where rations were included. Bread was sold at 7d. per 2-lb. loaf; potatoes, 1d. to 2½d. per lb.; meat, 3d. to 5d. per lb.; with a similar increase in the price of other articles of common use. This abnormal condition lasted until 1841, when wages fell to 7s. 6d. or 8s. a day for mechanics, £32 a year for farm labourers, and £14 to £20 a year for female servants. Notwithstanding the increased cost of living the rates just quoted were higher than had been paid at any time since the foundation of the Colony, but they were not long maintained. The abolition of transportation, advantageous though it ultimately proved, had the immediate effect of stopping the expenditure in the Colony of large sums from the British exchequer, and this, with the inflation of 1839 and the following years, induced a severe reaction; prices fell, property depreciated in value, and the Bank of Australia suspended payment, bringing the period to a disastrous close.

The fourth period.

The year 1843 ushered in a period of extreme depression. Employment became scarce and wages very low, while the prices of all kinds of property continued to decline; but at the same time the cost of living was greatly reduced, bread selling at from 2½d. to 3d. the 2-lb. loaf, meat 2d. to 3d. per lb., sugar 2½d. to 3d. per lb.; while dairy produce and vegetables were both plentiful and cheap. The most acute stage of the depression was reached in 1845, when the wages of tradesmen varied from 2s. 6d. to 4s. 6d. a day, and work was not readily obtained even at those rates. About the middle of the period matters brightened up a little, but the improvement was speedily followed by a relapse, the depression growing more and more pronounced, until the discovery of gold in 1851 introduced a new era under brighter conditions. The wages, for each year of the period, of some of the prominent trades, farm labourers and female servants, are given in the following table. For the most part the rates for mechanics represent town wages, the practice in the country districts being for the employer to provide board and lodging and pay wages in proportion, a tradesman earning 33s. a week in town, receiving probably about 15s. a week and board in the country.

Rate of Wages, 1843 to 1851.

Trade or Calling.	1843.	1844.	1845.	1846.	1847.	1848.	1849.	1850.	1851.
	per day.	per day.	per day.	per day.	per day.	per day	per day.	per day.	per day.
Males—	s. d.	s. d.	s. d.	s. d.	s. d.	s. d.	s. d.	s. d.	s. d.
Carpenters	5 0	4 0	4 0	5 2	5 6	5 3	4 9	4 6	6 5
Smiths	5 0	4 0	4 3	5 2	5 6	5 3	4 9	4 6	6 8
Masons	5 0	4 0	4 0	5 2	5 6	5 3	4 9	4 6	7 8
Bricklayers	5 0	4 0	4 0	5 2	5 6	5 3	4 9	4 6	6 8
Wheelwrights	4 6	3 6	3 3	4 8	5 0	5 3	4 9	4 6	6 4
	per ann.	per ann.	per ann.	per ann.	per ann.	per ann.	per ann.	per ann.	per ann.
With Board and Lodging—	£	£	£	£	£	£	£	£	£
Farm labourers	15	16	18	20	22	21	18	18	20
Shepherds	14	14	17	20	23	21	18	18	20
Females—									
Cooks	15	15	18	20	22	21	17	17	20
Housemaids	15	15	15	17	17	17	14	13	16
Laundresses	12	12	15	17	19	18	15	15	16
Nursemaids	10	10	12	15	16	14	9	9	9
General servants	12	12	16	16	18	16	12	14	16
Farm-house servants	10	10	12	16	17	16	12	11	12
Dairy-women	10	10	12	16	17	16	12	11	12

The discovery of gold not only put an end to the depression of the previous period but it effected a revolution in the industrial conditions of the Colony. According to contemporary evidence the supply of labour in many occupations speedily became exhausted, and there were more persons desirous of hiring labourers than there were labourers to be hired. In 1853 the market was bare of many articles, others were scarce, and all were at high prices; bread was selling at 8d. per 2-lb. loaf, flour at £27 per ton, and other necessaries of life in like proportion. Owing to the violence of the changes introduced, trade and commerce were in a very unsatisfactory state, and all productive industries except

The fifth period.

gold-mining were practically suspended for a time, since it was impossible to obtain the assistance necessary for profitably working them. In 1855 there was some slight abatement of the "gold fever," though wages and the price of provisions were still much above the average, but by the end of 1857 the disturbance had ceased to exercise any violent effects. A glance at the following table will show the magnitude of the changes in the labour market during this period. Prominent trades only are given, since, as may well be imagined, many industries ceased entirely until matters again resumed a normal condition:—

Rate of Wages, 1852 to 1857.

Trade or Calling.	1852.	1853.	1854.	1855.	1856.	1857.
	per day. s. d.	per day. s. d.	per day. s. s.	per day. s. s.	per day. s. s.	per day. s. s.
Bricklayers	9 0	15 6	25 to 30	18 to 25	16 to 18	12 to [illegible]
Blacksmiths	9 0	12 9	20 to 25	14 to 16	8 to 13	10 to [illegible]
Carpenters	9 0	12 6	15 to 20	12 to 15	12 to 15	10 to [illegible]
Coopers	....	....	15 to 20	10 to 12	12 to 14	12 to 14
Cabinetmakers	....	....	15 to 20	12 to 15	12 to 15	12 to 14
Farriers	....	....	12 to 15	10 to 12	9 to 12	10 to [illegible]
Plumbers and glaziers	....	....	16 to 20	12 to 15	12 to 15	12 to [illegible]
Joiners	....	....	17 to 20	12 to 15	12 to 14	15
Ironfounders	....	....	16 to 20	14 to 16	12 to 14	11 to [illegible]
Locksmiths	....	....	18 to 22	16 to 18	12 to 15	10 to [illegible]
Quarrymen	....	....	18 to 21	16 to 18	12/6 to 15	14 to [illegible]
Shoemakers	....	....	......	14 to 22	12 to 14	10 to 12
Wheelwrights	9 0	15 0	18 to 20	14 to 16	12 to 14	12 to 14
Plasterers	9 0	16 0	25 to 30	14 to 16	13 to 17	12 to [illegible]
Painters	....	....	13 to 16/8	13 to 14	10 to 12	8 to [illegible]
Stonemasons	9 0	16 0	25 to 30	......	12/6 to 15	12 to [illegible]
	per annum.	per annum.	per annum.	per annum.	per annum.	per annum.
With Board and Lodging—	£	£	£	£	£	£
Cooks	22	24	24	28	25	
Housemaids	16	17	23	22	21	
Laundresses	20	20	28	28	24	
Nursemaids	16	17	18	18	18	
General servants	17	18	28	23	22	
Farm-house servants	14	15	25	23	20	23
Dairy-women	14	15	25	22	20	[illegible]

Port Curtis rush.

Matters had grown comparatively settled when the rush to Port Curtis occurred in 1858, causing a brief revival of the excitement. The "gold fever" had brought to Australia not only young stalwart enterprising men of great endurance, and capable of adapting themselves to almost any conditions of life, but also multitudes of others whose chief idea was that wealth could be acquired almost without exertion. Unable to endure the hardships of a digger's lot, without trade or profession, and capable of only the lightest manual labour, they had mostly drifted back to Sydney, where a large number of unemployed had gathered together when the rush broke out. Joining the unemployed from the mines of Victoria and New South Wales, they rushed in thousands to the new field, 4,000 leaving Sydney alone in the space of a month, while 6,000 went from other parts of Australia. A few weeks sufficed to show that the Port Curtis gold-field could not maintain so many, and in October, 1858, the majority left for Sydney, where they roamed the streets disappointed and unemployed until drawn away by the attractions of other rushes. In the beginning of 1859 prices had fallen considerably, and the rate of wages for skilled labour receded to 10s. or 11s. a day, remaining at that level until the close of the period.

The eight or nine years during the rage of the gold fever exercised a very great economic effect on the condition of the working classes; for had there been no discovery of gold it is not improbable that, with respect to both standard of living and remuneration of labour, the conditions existing prior to 1850 would have long remained without any great change for the better. In those days the standard of labour in England was the practical test of the condition of the working classes in Australia, who were thought well off simply because their earnings enabled them to enjoy comforts beyond the reach of their fellows in England Since the gold era this has been changed, and the standard now made for themselves by Australian workers has no reference to any other country.

Under the provisions of Sir John Robertson's Land Act, which came into operation in 1861, land was thrown open for selection before survey. This new principle had lasting if not immediately apparent effect on the condition of the working classes, giving them opportunities of employment not previously open to them. The sixth period.

Few incidents calling for special comment marked the industrial history of this period, during which the only important variations in the condition of labour arose from the vicissitudes of the seasons, vast areas of the Colony having been visited alternately by droughts and floods. The average wages of the period are given in the following table:—

Rate of Wages, 1862 to 1871.

Trade or Calling.	1862.	1863.	1864.	1865.	1866.
	per day.	per day.	per day.	per day.	per day.
	s. d.	s. d.	s. d.	s. d.	s. d.
Carpenters	10 0	9 0	8 6	8 6	8 6
Blacksmiths	10 0	9 6	9 6	9 6	9 6
Wheelwrights	10 6	9 6	9 6	9 6	9 6
Bricklayers	12 0	10 0	9 6	9 6	9 6
Masons	10 0	10 0	10 0	10 0	10 0
	per week.	per week.	per week.	per week.	per week.
With Board and Lodging—	s. d. s. d.	s. d. s. d.	s. d. s. d.	s. d s. d.	s. d. s. d.
Farm labourers	12 0 to 15 0	12 0 to 14 0	11 0 to 12 0	11 0 to 12 0	11 0 to 12 0
Shepherds	15 0	12 0 „ 14 0	12 0 „ 14 0	12 0 „ 14 0	12 0 „ 14 0
Females—					
Cooks	10 0 to 15 0	10 0 „ 12 0	10 0 „ 12 0	10 0 „ 14 0	10 0 ....
Housemaids	8 0 „ 10 0	8 0 „ 10 0	8 0 „ 10 0	8 0 „ 10 0	8 0 to 10 0
Laundresses	12 0 „ 15 0	10 0 „ 12 0	10 0 „ 12 0	8 0 „ 10 0	10 0 ....
Nursemaids	6 0 „ 10 0	6 0 „ 10 0	6 0 „ 10 0	6 0 „ 10 0	6 0 to 8 0
General servants	10 0	8 0 „ 12 0	8 0 „ 12 0	8 0 „ 10 0	8 0 „ 10 0
Farm-house servants and dairy-women	9 0	7 0 „ 10 0	7 0 „ 10 0	7 0 „ 10 0	8 0 „ 10 0

Trade or Calling.	1867.	1868.	1869.	1870.	1871.
	per day.	per day.	per day.	per day.	per day.
	s. d.	s. d.	s. d.	s. d.	s. d.
Carpenters	8 6	8 6	8 0	8 6	8 6
Blacksmiths	9 6	9 6	9 6	10 0	8 6
Wheelwrights	9 6	9 6	8 6	8 3	8 6
Bricklayers	9 6	9 6	8 6	10 6	9 0
Masons	10 0	10 0	8 6	9 6	8 6
	per week.	per week.	per week.	per week.	per week.
With Board and Lodging—	s. d. s. d.	s. d. s. d.	s d. s. d.	s. d. s. d.	s. d. s. d.
Farm labourers	11 0 to 12 0	11 0 to 12 0	11 6 to 13 0	11 6 to 14 0	10 0 to 11 6
Shepherds	12 0 „ 14 0	12 0 „ 14 0	12 6 „ 14 0	11 6 „ 14 0	10 0 „ 13 6
Females—					
Cooks	10 0 „ 12 0	10 „ 12 0	10 0 „ 12 6	10 0 „ 11 6	11 6 ....
Housemaids	8 0 „ 10 0	10	8 0 „ 10 0	8 0 „ 10 0	8 0 to 10 0
Laundresses	10 0	12	10 0 „ 11 6	10 0 „ 11 6	10 0 „ 11 6
Nursemaids	6 0 to 8 0	8 0 ...	8 0 . .	8 0 ..	8 0 ....
General servants	8 0 „ 10 0	10 0 to 12 0	10 0	10 0 to 11 6	8 0 to 10 0
Farm-house servants and dairy-women	8 0 „ 10 0	10 0	8 0 to 10 0	8 0 „ 10 0	8 0 „ 10 0

The seventh period.

In considering the table just given regard must be paid to the fact that although there was a marked decline in the daily wage received by skilled mechanics, the prices of commodities in general use also steadily fell. About the year 1872 public attention began to be awake to the necessity of pushing on with the construction of railways, roads, and bridges, to open up the interior of the country, and an expansive public works policy involving the expenditure of large sums of borrowed money was accordingly initiated. Coincident with this, and chiefly on the part of graziers desirous of protecting themselves from the incursions of free selectors, there arose a great demand for land, readily responded to by the State, and the public lands were bought up with such eagerness that in the five years 1872-77 the revenue derived from this source increased from £500,000 to nearly £3,000,000, and the public exchequer was overflowing. Wages were high, employment steady, provisions cheap, and numbers of men, for the most part young and energetic, were attracted to the Colony by the alluring prospects held out to them, the annual increment to the population being doubled within a few years. To keep pace with the demand for labour the Government maintained a vigorous immigration policy, and in the ten years which closed with 1885 nearly 49,000 persons were assisted to these shores from the United Kingdom, and were readily absorbed in the general population. In all likelihood during this period industrial conditions would have improved without any lavish expenditure by the Government, but what was probable was made certain by the favourable combination of circumstances alluded to, whose influence was steadily maintained till the termination of the period about the end of 1885. In the following table of average wages for each year of the term the quotations are classified as daily or weekly, according to the ordinary modes of payment:—

RATE of WAGES, 1872 to 1885.

Trade or Calling.	1872.		1873.		1874.		1875.		1876.		1877.		1878.		1879.		1880.		1881.		1882.		1883.		1884.		1885.	
At per day (without board and lodging)—	s.	d.	s.	d.	s.	d.	s.	d.	s.	d.	s.	d.	s.	d.	s.	d.	s.	d.	s.	d.	s.	d.	s.	d.	s.	d.	s.	d.
Carpenters	9	0	10	0	9	0	9	6	10	0	10	8	10	8	10	8	10	0	10	0	11	0	11	0	11	0	11	0
Blacksmiths	9	0	10	0	11	0	10	3	11	0	11	0	10	0	10	0	10	0	9	6	10	0	10	0	10	0	10	0
Bricklayers	9	6	10	0	11	0	11	0	12	0	11	0	11	0	11	0	11	0	11	0	12	6	12	6	12	6	12	6
Masons	9	6	10	0	11	0	11	0	11	0	11	0	10	6	10	6	10	6	10	6	11	6	11	6	11	6	11	6
Plasterers	10	0	10	0	11	0	11	0	12	0	11	6	11	6	11	6	11	6	11	6	12	0	12	0	12	0	12	6
Painters	9	0	9	0	9	0	9	6	9	6	9	6	9	6	9	6	9	6	9	6	11	0	11	0	11	0	11	0
Boiler-makers	9	0	10	0	10	0	10	0	10	0	10	0	10	0	10	0	9	6	9	6	9	6	9	6	9	6	9	6
Labourers and navvies	7	0	7	0	7	0	7	0	7	0	7	0	7	0	8	0	8	0	8	0	8	0	8	0	8	0	8	0
At per week (with board and lodging)—																												
Farm labourers	14	0	13	0	14	0	15	0	15	0	15	0	15	0	15	0	15	0	15	0	17	6	17	6	17	6	17	6
Shepherds (at per 1,000)	14	0	14	0	14	0	15	0	15	0	15	0	14	6	14	6	14	6	14	6	15	0	15	0	15	0	15	0
Brickmakers	...		...		...		...		22	6	22	6	23	9	23	9	23	9	23	9	23	9	23	9	23	9	23	9
Females.	s.	d.	s.	d.	s.	d.	s.	d.	s.	d.	s.	d.	s.	d.	s.	d.	s.	d.	s.	d.	s.	d.	s.	d.	s.	d.	s.	d.
Housemaids	9	0	10	6	10	6	11	0	11	6	11	6	11	6	11	6	11	6	11	6	13	0	13	0	13	0	13	0
Laundresses	10	6	10	6	13	6	14	0	14	6	14	6	14	6	14	0	14	6	14	6	17	6	17	6	17	6	17	6
Nursemaids	7	6	9	0	9	0	10	0	10	6	10	6	10	6	11	6	11	6	11	6	11	6	11	6	11	6	11	6
General servants	10	0	10	6	10	6	12	6	14	0	14	0	14	0	14	0	14	0	14	0	15	0	15	0	15	0	15	0
Cooks	10	6	13	6	13	6	13	6	16	0	16	0	17	6	18	6	18	6	18	6	18	6	18	6	18	6	18	6

The tide of improvement had reached its highest level during the years 1882–1885, and began to recede in 1886, when employment became difficult to obtain and wages began to fall. In 1886–7 work in some of the southern district collieries was suspended by strikes and disputes for nearly twelve months; in 1888 the coal-miners of the northern district were on strike for several months; in 1888 and 1889 the completion of various large public works threw out of employment some 12,000 men—no inconsiderable proportion of the unskilled labour of the country—and large numbers of unemployed were congregated in and around Sydney; in 1890 the maritime and pastoral industries were disturbed by strikes and disputes very hurtful to the community in general, and to the working classes in particular. It will thus be apparent that a period under vastly changed conditions has been entered upon since 1885, but no accurate estimate of the ultimate effect of these changes can as yet be attempted. So far there has been no reduction in the nominal rate of wages in most trades, but for unskilled labour the rates have experienced a decided decline. The eighth period.

For the periods under review in the foregoing pages money wages only have been dealt with, but it is a matter of much greater importance to ascertain the rate of real wages—that is, the purchasing power of wages in comparison with their nominal value. The data for making this comparison on the basis of the price level of common articles of consumption are given in another chapter under the heading of "Cost of Living." Such a comparison must necessarily be defective in some respects, since with changing conditions come other forms of labour, and with higher wages greater consumption, so that in comparing present times with days long past there is danger of weighing what is now important against what was formerly of no consequence; notwithstanding this it gives a more exact notion of the value of wages at different periods than can be obtained in any other way. It also affords the only true standard by which material conditions at different times can be accurately gauged. In the following table are compared the average daily and weekly wages in money, the level of money wages for several descriptions of labour, the level of real wages on the basis of their purchasing power, and the price-level of the principal articles of consumption, for each period since the foundation of the Colony. Purchasing power of wages.

Comparison of Real and Money Wages.

Period.	Average daily wages.	Weekly wages, with board and lodgings.		Level of money wages.			Level of real wages of mechanics.	Price level of principal articles of consumption.
	Mechanics.	Farm and other labourers.	Female servants.	Mechanics.	Farm and other labourers.	Female servants.		
	d. s.	d. s.	d. s.					
Prior to 1821	5 0	6 0	4 0	50	40	31	47	107
1821 ,, 1838	6 0	7 0	5 0	60	47	39	55	109
1838 ,, 1843	8 0	8 4	5 4	80	56	41	72	111
1843 ,, 1851	4 9	8 0	5 9	48	53	44	53	90
1851 ,, 1857	14 0	11 0	8 0	140	73	62	93	151
1861 ,, 1872	8 6	11 4	10 0	85	75	77	81	105
1872 ,, 1886	10 4	15 0	13 0	103	100	100	100	103
Since 1886...	10 0	15 0	13 0	100	100	100	100	100

From this statement the years 1857 to 1861 have been omitted owing to the impossibility of establishing a fair average price either for labour or commodities under the prevailing disorganisation of industrial affairs already described. Wages were high for those at work, but there was great dearth of employment, so that any quotations which could be given would be at best merely nominal. The rate of wages and prices current during the years since 1886 has been taken as the standard of comparison, in relation to which the rates for the other periods have been estimated.

Effects of the transportation system.

Prior to 1821 the transportation system was in full operation, and wage-earners had to compete with bond labour, or with men who, though free, had been so long accustomed to the hard conditions of servitude that a little above a convict ration seemed as much as they could expect to earn; hence the very low level of both real and money wages during the period. Commencing with 1821, whatever be the point of view, the worst series of years is that from 1843 to 1851, the money wages then paid being less than half the present rate, while the real wages were scarcely more satisfactory. This period, which was one of untoward depression, gave place to the stirring times accompanying the discovery of gold, when money wages rose more than 200 per cent., and at one time averaged twice as much as the wages now current. Nevertheless the industrial condition of the period from 1851 to 1857, though so much in advance of anything previously experienced in the Colony, and even of the period which immediately succeeded, was certainly inferior to that which has prevailed since 1871. This may appear strange in view of the high wages which were paid during the gold rush; but the advance then occurring was attended by a considerable if not a commensurate increase in the price of necessaries, while from 1871 onwards the rates of wages and the cost of living have moved in opposite directions, so that the condition of mechanics since the year named has been better than at any period of the Colony's history.

Improved condition of farm labourers.

The improvement in the lot of farm and station labourers a female servants is still more marked. The rise in wages of m hands has, excepting the period 1843-51, been continuous, wh the increase in the pay of females has suffered no interrupti even during the disastrous years preceding the gold discove Coincident with the rise of nominal wages which this tab exhibits, there has been a marked advance in the standard

Improved standard of living.

living of the working population of the Colony, an advance ev more rapid than that of wages. The cheapening of many artic of food and dress which has taken place of late years, without corresponding fall of wages, has enabled the homes of the bulk the population to be made more comfortable. The acquisition comforts begets the desire for further comforts, and it is therefo unlikely that any fall in wages will be assented to which wi necessitate the labouring classes decreasing the standard of livi they now enjoy; on the contrary, it is more than probable t standard will be still further raised. In this connection it ma be pointed out that the evidence of the savings banks of th Colony cannot be taken as conclusive of the prosperity depression of the working population; for if the standard living indulged in be raised more rapidly than the rate of wage it is obvious that the margin out of which savings are made wi be decreased, although the actual condition of the masses may b materially advanced.

MANUFACTORIES.

Manufactories of New South Wales.

Although New South Wales cannot be considered an importan manufacturing country, this source of national wealth has b no means been neglected. During the year 1890 there wer 2,583 manufactories or works of various descriptions, employin altogether a total of 46,135 hands, of whom 41,582 were males, an 4,553 females. These works had machinery in operation developin a total of 24,662 horse-power, and valued at £4,526,821, whil the value of land and buildings was £7,076,219, so that the tota capital employed in works and manufactories was £11,603,04

Besides these there was a number of hands in works too small to be classified with those enumerated. The average value of plant was £1,752 10s.; the average horse-power employed, 9·5; and the hands per factory, very nearly 18. The average number of hands per factory in the metropolis was 25, and in the country about 12½. Compared with the scale on which manufactories are worked in the older countries of the world, these averages will appear very small, but should evoke no surprise when the nature of the works is considered, and the sparseness of the population throughout a large portion of the Colony. The following is a complete list of the works in operation during the year, with the approximate value of plant employed, and land and buildings:—

Manufactories Classified, with the Number of Hands, Power, and Value of Plant employed during the year 1890.

Description of Manufactory or Work.	Number of Works.	Total Hands.	Plant or Machinery.		Value of Land and Buildings.
			Power.	Value.	
Raw Material, the production of Pastoral Pursuits—			Horse-power.	£	£
Boiling-down and glue.	26	273	204	19,715	40,959
Bone-dust and manure.	3	24	76	6,800	2,909
Grease	2	10	9	1,700	2,971
Tanneries	93	897	537	44,874	141,969
Wool-washing and Fell-mongering	32	842	547	67,478	147,836
	156	2,046	1,373	140,567	336,646
Connected with Food and Drink, or the preparation thereof—					
Aerated waters	104	897	407	83,292	150,164
Beer, ale, stout (including Bottling works)..	41	784	656	190,077	660,046
Biscuits....................	6	504	99	48,587	67,013
Butter and cheese (steam)	142	778	762	58,108	146,800
Butter and cheese (hand or other power)	149	785	54		
Coffee and spice	6	249	122	17,880	51,729
Condiments	5	58	6	2,210	11,271
Confectionery	16	359	86	23,450	112,128
Flour.....	74	841	2,022	299,336	296,890
Ice and refrigerating ...	9	195	679	84,500	97,328
Jam and fruit canning.	19	232	133	13,430	65,900

Description of Manufactory or Work.	Number of Works.	Total Hands.	Plant or Machinery. Power.	Plant or Machinery. Value.	Value of Land & Buildings.
Connected with Food and Drink—*continued*.			Horse-power.	£	£
Maizena and oatmeal ...	2	28	30	4,101	7,[illegible]
Meat-curing and preserving	6	320	226	23,430	20,[illegible]
Self-raising flour and baking powder	4	40	10	2,200	6,[illegible]
Sugar (refined)............	1	300	350	....	....
Sugar (raw)	33	1,621	1,356	382,960	[illegible]
Spirits	1	11	33	....	....
Vinegar.....................	3	24	14	6,600	7,[illegible]
	612	7,726	7,045	1,135,158	1,[illegible]
Clothing and Textile Fabrics—					
Boots and shoes	60	2,806	132	32,248	[illegible]
Clothing	21	2,698	3	4,550	[illegible]
Furriers	2	10	......	40	5,[illegible]
Hats and caps	10	74	4	1,250	16,[illegible]
Oilskin clothing	7	257	......	489	12,[illegible]
Umbrellas	1	5	......	....	....
Woollen cloth	4	155	134	20,500	[illegible]
	105	6,005	273	59,077	[illegible]
Building Materials—					
Asphalt and pavement	14	102	88	10,129	20,[illegible]
Bricks	190	2,018	1,447	157,312	[illegible]
Joinery	61	978	590	55,855	[illegible]
Lime	8	125	95	20,200	[illegible]
Modelling and patterns	9	47	......	1,990	10,[illegible]
Marble	38	314	49	6,780	[illegible]
Paint and varnish	3	17	27	8,653	14,[illegible]
Pottery	18	323	193	23,470	[illegible]
Saw-mills	346	3,788	5,735	338,955	[illegible]
	687	7,712	8,224	623,344	1,1[illegible]
Metal Works, Machinery, &c.—					
Agricultural implements ..	17	304	110	16,830	[illegible]
Galvanised iron & plumbing	51	657	35	24,675	114,[illegible]
Iron and brass foundries	75	1,494	715	103,000	[illegible]
Ironworks (other)	31	373	378	23,170	[illegible]
Machinery and engineering	53	1,683	694	226,900	[illegible]
Railway workshops and carriage factories ...	17	4,146	1,260	202,224	84,[illegible]
Smelting, silver, copper, tin, &c.	20	1,222	846	241,571	[illegible]
Tinware	10	86	4	3,010	11,[illegible]
Wire-works	9	170	82	38,050	[illegible]
Works in other metals	11	101	11	5,070	17,[illegible]
	294	10,236	4,135	880,500	[illegible]

Description of Manufactory or Work.	Number of Works.	Total Hands.	Plant or Machinery.		Value of Land and Buildings.
			Power.	Value.	
Ship-building, Repairing, &c.—			Horse-power.	£	£
Dry docks, floating docks, and slips	5	463	302	114,000	280,214
Masts and blocks	1	3	6	....	....
Sails, tarpaulins, &c. ...	14	94	5	2,810	15,759
Ship and boat building, &c.	21	515	36	5,210	34,984
	41	1,075	349	122,020	310,957
Furniture, Bedding, &c.—					
Bedding	5	103	18	2,320	16,757
Curled hair and flock...	4	23	30	1,150	3,500
Furniture.....	72	938	171	18,093	155,299
Mats and Matting	2	42	3	800	11,342
Picture-frames	9	47	......	850	25,572
Window-blinds	8	81	11	1,445	6,007
	100	1,234	233	24,658	218,477
Books, Paper, Printing, and Engraving—					
Account books, &c.	16	665	87	48,125	101,489
Engraving, &c.	7	28	......	680	8,096
Paper	1	65	200	...	...
Paper bags and boxes...	4	61	1	4,000	9,643
Photo - lithography, electro-photo engraving, &c.	3	38	......	1,100	10,428
Printing and lithographic printing	106	3,294	563	368,555	503,826
Printing ink, printer's materials, sealing-wax, &c.	2	15	19	2,625	2,972
Rubber stamps.	2	9	......	1,150	5,957
Type	2	25	......	9,350	2,857
	143	4,200	870	435,585	646,266
Vehicles, harness, and Saddlery.—					
Coaches and waggons...	139	1,486	139	42,712	207,184
Saddlery, saddle-trees, whips, &c.	42	483	9	3,491	66,087
	181	1,969	148	46,203	273,271
Light, Fuel, and Heat—					
Electric light	11	43	224	27,120	38,972
Coke	4	90	51	14,060	10,728
Gas	31	1,098	416	472,526	407,327
Kerosene Oil	3	314	310	115,000	87,000
	49	1,545	1,001	618,706	544,027

Description of Manufactory or Work.	Number of Works.	Total Hands.	Plant or Machinery.		Value of Land an[d] Buildings
			Power.	Value.	
			Horse-power.	£	£
Miscellaneous—					
Bark mills	1	8	12	....	....
Baskets.....................	6	47	......	106	7,8
Brushes	5	39	......	180	7,7
Chaff and crushed corn	49	250	281	13,226	71,7
Chemicals, patent medicines, &c.	6	99	38	11,206	1
Compressed & fancy leather	3	12	2	490	
Cooperage	10	143	26	1,300	
Dye works	8	46	6	1,206	
Electroplating	2	16	8	2,300	
Glass and glass-staining	9	126	26	3,470	
Jewellery	27	170	1	11,025	
Millet brooms	3	29	3	1,073	
Mint	1	42	30	....	.. ..
Packing-cases	3	38	34	2,560	10,6
Philosophical, optical, & surgical instruments	8	67	2	3,450	26,1
Portmanteaus	3	31	2	802	
Poudrette and Ammonia	2	15	20	3,400	
Ropes	9	133	51	12,545	34,4
Soap and candles	27	194	257	27,380	50,0
Tobacco, cigars, &c. ...	9	678	101	67,842	142,2
Others not included above..............	24	204	111	*273,441	*74,32
	215	2,387	1,011	437,003	7
General Total	2,583	46,135	24,662	4,526,821	

* Includes value of single establishments.

Where only one manufactory of a kind is in operation th[e] value of plant, land, and buildings has been so given that th[e] business of no individual shall be disclosed.

Large number of works for treating raw produce.

It will be seen that a large proportion of the establishment[s] included in the foregoing list are connected with the preparatio[n] of food, or raw produce; for, out of a total of 46,135, the hand[s] employed in treating food, or animal and mineral products, advance[d] one stage only towards complete manufacture, with those engage[d] in domestic industries, numbered about 26,000, or over 56 pe[r] cent. There has, however, been fair progress in other direction[s] and, as will be seen from a subsequent table, the growth of th[e] manufacturing power has been in keeping with the general progres[s] observable in other departments of industry. The number of person[s]

Progress of manufactures.

dependent for their livelihood on the manufacturing interest may be estimated at about 184,000, or nearly one-sixth of the whole population of the Colony.

In the following table the gradual progress of the manufacturing industry of the Colony since the year 1878 may be readily traced. It will be noticed that in the short period embraced by the table, the number of hands employed has advanced from 24,741 to 46,135, or over 86 per cent. during thirteen years :—

Hands employed in Works and Factories, 1878–90.

Year.	No. of Hands employed.		
	Male.	Female.	Total.
1878	21,512	3,229	24,741
1879	22,989	2,695	25,684
1880	26,452	1,807	28,259
1881	28,819	2,372	31,191
1882	31,824	2,065	33,889
1883	32,350	2,384	34,734
1884	36,390	2,404	38,794
1885	38,255	3,420	41,677
1886	40,160	3,367	43,527
1887	39,365	3,686	43,051
1888	41,299	4,265	45,564
1889	40,725	4,264	44,989
1890	41,582	4,553	46,135

A marked feature of the progress exhibited is that the number of women employed in factories and works has not increased at an equal rate with the male employés. In 1878, the number of females employed was 3,229, and in 1890, 4,553, showing an increase of 1,324, or 41 per cent., in thirteen years, while those of the opposite sex increased 93 per cent. during the same period. Females employed.

As regards the future, however, a vast field is open for the development of manufactures in New South Wales. Producing, as it does, the raw material of various kinds necessary for supplying the primary wants of civilization, it is evident that the Colony must ere long find a way into some parts of this field. The one great cause which has hitherto operated to prevent the larger development of manufactures is the impossibility of drawing from Future prospect of manufactures.

a population so small and so widely scattered, a fair profit on the capital required to carry them on. Hitherto abundant employment has been found for labour and capital in the primary productive industries, and, these industries continuing to be profitable and population to increase, whenever the prospect of profit presents itself, manufactures, adapted to the conditions as well as to the wants of the country, will naturally establish themselves, affording other profitable investments for capital, and avenues for the employment of labour.

Woollen manufactures.

As a wool-growing country New South Wales is apparently specially adapted for the manufacture of woollen goods, and accordingly that industry was one of the earliest organised in the Colony. The endeavour to promote the local manufacture of woollen goods has so far met with little success. A number of factories have struggled along for some time, but have made no headway, the largest establishments finding it needful to add to their business the making of slop clothing, and by this means are enabled to carry on at a profit. The machinery in none of the mills is of the best kind, and altogether the industry is disappointing.

The following table shows the number of woollen-mills in operation, the number of employés, and the quantity of cloth manufactured :—

Woollen Mills.

Year.	Number of Woollen-mills.	Hands Employed.			Quantity of Woollen Cloth Manufactured.
		Male.	Female.	Total.	Yards.
1881	5	178	157	335	358,000
1882	8	266	119	385	319,225
1883	9	260	112	372	352,000
1884	7	175	137	312	306,090
1885	6	134	189	323	337,750
1886	6	104	78	182	394,786
1887	5	101	71	172	348,000
1888	5	117	60	177	241,000
1889	5	110	62	172	207,880
1890	4	94	61	155	310,000

From these figures it will be noticed that the number of woollen-mills in operation has decreased, and that the four now at work provide employment for 155 persons only. During the years from 1881 to 1885 more than twice this number of hands were employed. The quantity of cloth manufactured is, however, but little short of the produce of 8 mills and 385 hands, in 1882. Number of Woollen Mills decreased.

The progress of the manufacture of boots and shoes has kept pace with the growth of population, as will be perceived from the table below. The improved efficiency of the machinery employed is apparent in the increased output:— Boot Factories.

Boot Factories.

Year.	Number of Factories.	Hands Employed.			Pairs of Boots made.
		Males.	Females.	Total.	
1881	71	1,849	377	2,226	....
1882	62	1,695	341	2,036	....
1883	61	1,748	377	2,125	....
1884	68	1,871	418	2,289	....
1885	65	1,672	433	2,105	....
1886	68	1,856	416	2,272	1,881,210
1887	60	1,837	436	2,273	2,278,612
1888	57	1,618	427	2,045	2,559,980
1889	59	1,955	465	2,420	2,196,815
1890	60	2,262	544	2,806	2,634,254

From the above figures it will be noticed that there is a slight increase in the number of hands, from 2,226 in 1881 to 2,806 in 1890, while the number of establishments has decreased from 71 to 60. This would indicate a tendency for large factories to supersede small works, and drive the latter out of competition in this particular branch of manufacture. The average number of hands employed in each factory has risen from 31·3 in 1881 to 46·7 in 1890. The number of pairs of boots made during the year was 2,634,254, giving an average of 939 per head employed, as compared with 908 in 1889, 1,250 in 1888, and 1,002 in 1887.

What should, in time, form another great staple industry of Australia is undoubtedly the iron trade. Every natural advantage Prospects of iron trade.

possessed by the great iron and machinery producing countries of the world—such as England and Belgium—is also present here. Not only are iron and coal deposited in abundance, and in positions easily accessible and readily worked, but, as pointed out on page 89, the local iron ore is exceedingly rich. Scarcely any progress, however, has been made in iron smelting, and nearly the whole stock of pig and wrought iron required for the local manufactories is imported. The other descriptions of metal works, both for smelting and manufacturing, are in a more forward state. Works for the treatment of metals in 1881 numbered 218, in which were engaged 4,525 persons, while in 1890 the number of works had increased to 277, and the hands employed to 9,932, agricultural implement factories not being included in either year. The decreased number of hands employed in smelting works will be noticed. In 1881 1,517 hands were employed in 14 establishments, while now, though the works number 20, the hands employed are only 1,222. There were in 1881 over 1,000 men employed in the copper smelting works alone. There has been a large increase in the hands employed making or repairing railway motors, carriages, and other appliances, the employes in 1879 numbering 823 and in 1890, 4,146. The bulk of these were employed in the workshops connected with the State railways.

Preparation of raw materials.

As regards the preparation of raw materials, the products of pastoral pursuits, the amount of employment offering has been not a little affected by the seasons, so that, under the heads of boiling-down, fellmongering, tanning, woolwashing, and allied pursuits, the number of hands employed has only varied from 2,122 in 1881 to 2,046 in 1890, while that of the works has fallen from 298 in 1881 to 156 in 1890.

Breweries.

The brewing industry has declined since 1886, when an excise of 4d. per gallon was imposed on the local manufacture. It is open to question, however, whether the falling-off in production is due to this cause, as there is evidence that the depression which marked the trade of the different colonies during the year immediately preceding 1886 brought about a lessened demand for all forms of alcoholic liquors. The net import of ale and beer from abroad during 1890 reached a value of £342,401, not a very large amount considering that £246,135 of it was for beer in bottle, which the colonial breweries have, so far, not attempted to produce on any extensive scale. The following table illustrates the position of the brewing and bottling industry and its progress during the last ten years :— Beer imported.

Breweries.

Year.	Number of Breweries and Bottling Establishments.	Hands Employed.	Quantity manufactured, Ale, Beer, &c.
			Gallons.
1881	50	637	*
1882	56	699	*
1883	59	747	*
1884	60	788	*
1885	70	805	*11,000,000
1886	74	987	*10,000,000
1887	75	804	9,720,000
1888	79	850	9,300,209
1889	76	826	9,515,200
1890	71	793	9,619,554

* Only approximately ascertained.

Tallow being one of the staple products of the country, the manufacture of soap and candles, as might be expected, is firmly established, and capable of fully supplying the local requirements. The quantity of toilet and fancy soap made, is, however, as yet but small, and in quality it is scarcely equal to that imported at lower prices. Common soap of local make is slightly cheaper than the imported article, and being also quite as good, it commands the local market. The quantity manufactured in 1888 was 198,880 cwt. against 143,520 cwt. in 1890, the supply, including imports, being 210,056 cwt. and 162,044 cwt. respectively. The quantity of candles manufactured was 2,796,700 lb. in 1888, and 1,545,920 lb. in 1890, and the supply, including imports, was 7,187,932 lb. and 4,907,325 lb. respectively. The following table shows the progress of the industry during the past ten years, from which it appears that of the 59 factories at work during 1888 only 27 now survive. The quantities stated in the table are Soap and candles.

those returned by the manufacturers, and are given for what [illegible] are worth, but it is believed that the information is little t[illegible] relied on.

Soap and Candle Manufactories.

Year.	Number of Factories.	Hands Employed.	Quantities Manufactured.	
			Soap.	Candles.
			cwt.	lb.
1881	38	232	106,962	....
1882	40	263	112,513	....
1883	38	220	121,794	....
1884	34	204	131,244	....
1885	40	223	138,849	1,[illegible]
1886	46	321	155,430	2,[illegible]
1887	52	367	190,060	2,[illegible]
1888	59	397	198,880	2,7[illegible]
1889	30	250	164,800	2,[illegible]
1890	27	194	143,520	1,545,92[illegible]

Saw-mills. The number of persons employed in the various timber distri[illegible] in saw-mills, &c., has also increased at a good ratio during [illegible] last ten years. The establishments in 1881 numbered 280, [illegible]ploying a total number of 2,382 persons, while in 1890 there [illegible] 346 mills, and the number of hands employed was 3,788. [illegible] value of capital employed in 1890 was £338,955, the horse-po[illegible] 5,735, while the quantity of timber sawn was estimated [illegible] 201,505,000 feet 1-inch thick:—

Saw-mills.

Year.	Number of Saw-mills.	Hands employed.	Year.	Number of Saw-mills.	Hands employed.
1881	280	2,382	1886	323	3,29[illegible]
1882	334	3,013	1887	322	3,26[illegible]
1883	370	3,318	1888	317	3,61[illegible]
1884	376	3,477	1889	325	3,57[illegible]
1885	415	3,783	1890	346	3,78[illegible]

Sugar-growing. The growth of sugar-cane, and the manufacture of sugar th[illegible] from, in the northern districts of the Colony, is now becoming [illegible] important industry, the output having increased from 159,[illegible] cwt. of sugar and 354,402 gallons of molasses in 1881, to 530,[illegible] cwt. of sugar and 1,074,080 gallons of molasses in 1890.

Since 1887 there has been a considerable increase in the breadth of land under this crop, and, in the year just closed, there were 20,446 acres planted with cane, of which 8,344 acres were productive. In 1877 the number of mills was 50, of which 24 used steam-power, whilst 26 were worked by cattle, and the number of workmen employed was 1,065. These increased, in the year 1885, to 83 steam-mills and 19 worked by cattle, whilst the number of men employed, and the quantity of sugar and molasses turned out, correspondingly increased; but since then the fall in the value of sugar has caused many of the smaller establishments to be closed, and the cane grown has been to an increasing extent sold to the large factories, which pay to the growers a price but slightly below that given prior to 1885. Almost everywhere the tendency to concentrate the manufacture of sugar in large central establishments is increasing; in the West Indies and elsewhere small mills are rapidly disappearing to make room for larger establishments, where business is strictly confined to the industrial process of sugar making, the planters attending solely to the cultivation of the cane.

Number of sugar mills.

Tendency to separate sugar-growing and making.

The following table gives the particulars of the sugar industry for the last ten years :—

Sugar Mills.

Year.	Sugar Mills.		Horse-power.		Quantity of Sugar Manufactured.	Quantity of Molasses Manufactured.	*Hands Employed.
	Worked by Steam.	Worked by Cattle.	Steam.	Cattle.			
					cwt.	gallons.	
1881	59	17	1,432	63	159,048	354,402	1,665
1882	70	16	978	49	270,000	560,000	1,039
1883	79	14	2,651	44	280,000	580,000	1,285
1884	86	12	2,855	50	230,000	450,000	2,190
1885	83	19	2,598	32	369,280	635,000	2,634
1886	57	7	2,531	21	275,000	507,000	2,259
1887	57	7	2,210	26	450,000	880,000	2,646
1888	36	......	1,995	......	225,580	241,068	1,640
1889	38	2	3,034	10	380,320	494,145	2,194
1890	31	2	1,344	12	530,660	1,074,060	1,621

* Hands employed at least for six months in the year.

Sugar refineries.

There was only one establishment in the Colony for refining raw sugar in 1890. The quantity of sugar melted in the year was 660,000 cwt., of which 268,000 cwt. was imported, chiefly from Queensland, Java, Victoria, Hong Kong, and South Australia. The remaining 392,000 cwt. was raw sugar produced in the Colony. As the total quantity made at the mills was 530,660 cwt., it would appear that, even allowing for the amount that went into consumption without being refined, a fairly large quantity of sugar was held over to be refined during the present year.

Sugar Refineries.

Year.	Sugar Refineries.	Number of Hands employed.	Quantity of Sugar melted.
			cwt.
1881	2	222	514,400
1882	2	235	470,000
1883	2	214	468,000
1884	2	172	370,000
1885	2	224	384,000
1886	2	214	510,000
1887	1	200	537,900
1888	1	210	550,149
1889	1	230	600,000
1890	1	300	660,000

The numbers given above are only those of the men in constant employment; in addition there are many others employed for longer or shorter periods discharging ships, storing sugar, and other work incidental to the trade.

Colonial Sugar Company.

In New South Wales, almost from the introduction of the sugar-growing industry, the manufacture of sugar has been largely in the hands of the Colonial Sugar Refining Company, whose mills on the Clarence and on the Richmond have been referred to in another part of this work. This company also owns the only sugar refinery in New South Wales, where the produce of their mills in this colony is refined, together with a portion of the output of their factories in Fiji and Queensland. The other establishments, locally known as refineries, whether worked by steam or cattle, are mostly small factories in which sugar of an inferior quality is turned out, which has afterwards to undergo the process of refining.

Tobacco manufactories.

The use of tobacco manufactured in the Colony has, to a very large extent, superseded that of imported tobacco. The amount of cigars and cigarettes made in the Colony is, on the other hand, very small compared with the total quantity of these commodities consumed. The weight of each description of tobacco used in the Colony during 1890 amounted to :—

Tobacco and Cigars.

	Imported Manufactured.	Made in the Colony.	Total.
	lb.	lb.	lb.
Tobacco	787,533	1,892,592	2,680,125
Cigars	250,956	4,120	255,076
Cigarettes	75,433	18,328	93,761

Imported leaf largely used.

A large amount of imported leaf is used in the manufacture of tobacco in the Colony, the proportion during the past year being 569,420 lb. of imported leaf, chiefly American, to 1,345,620 lb. of New South Wales leaf. The quantities of each kind of tobacco made in the Colony, as well as the weight of leaf used in the manufacture, will be found in the following table. The quantity of leaf given does not include stalks and stems, which are taken out in the process of manufacture. The proportion of leaf not used would be about 25 per cent. of the total weight.

Tobacco Factories.

Year	No. of Tobacco Factories.	No. of Cigar and Cigarette Factories.	Hands Employed.		† Tobacco Leaf Used.		Quantity Manufactured.		
			Males.	Females.	Colonial Leaf.	Imported Leaf.	Tobacco.	Cigars.	Cigarettes.
					lb.	lb.	lb.	lb.	lb.
1885	16	9	411	257	1,480,683	688,788	2,133,168	9,402	6,901
1886	17	9	559	144	1,495,191	561,514	2,044,240	7,125	5,340
1887	13	10	506	156	1,611,527	552,217	2,147,418	6,057	10,269
1888	14	9	554	161	1,463,815	610,485	2,062,380	3,624	8,296
1889	10	4	454	167	1,440,244	545,743	1,971,394	5,393	9,200
1890	9	8	506	172	1,345,620	569,420	1,892,592	4,120	18,328

† Stalks and fibre of leaf removed.

The amount of mill-power for grinding and dressing grain is ample for treating the flour consumed in the Colony. As the Colony does not produce sufficient grain for its own requirements, it is not at all probable that there will be any notable increase in the number of flour-mills, as those existing are mostly at work only part of their time. Wind and horse-power, as applied to the dressing of grain, have fallen into disuse, and though some water-mills still exist, there are not so many as formerly, and their number is decreasing. The returns of the millers for the year 1889 showed that the quantity of flour made was 118,691 tons, and 118,396 tons in 1890. It is believed that these figures are wide of the mark, and other sources of information give the quantities which will be found in the following table, and these are believed to approximate closely to the truth :—

Mills for grinding and dressing grain.

Flour made in the Colony.

Flour Manufactured.

Year.	New South Wales Wheat treated.	Imported Wheat treated.	Total Wheat treated.	Total Flour made.
	Bushels.	Bushels.	Bushels.	Tons.
1881	3,400,934	108,096	3,509,030	70,180
1882	3,136,461	629,841	3,766,302	75,326
1883	3,733,171	175,138	3,908,309	78,166
1884	3,983,246	418,434	4,401,680	88,033
1885	3,927,273	497,775	4,425,048	88,501
1886	2,402,057	984,773	3,386,830	67 736
1887	4,460,629	233,535	4,694,164	93,883
1888	3,975,030	1,509,646	5,484,676	114,270
1889	1,442,060	2,605,130	4,135,128	86,150
1890	6,049,000	133,258	6,182,258	123,797

The following are the particulars of the mills in operation in the Colony for the last ten years :—

Mills in Operation, 1890.

Year.	Steam.		Water.		Total.		Hands Employed.
	No.	Horse power.	No.	Horse power.	No.	Horse power.	
1881	148	2,806	9	95	157	2,963	695
1882	156	2,929	7	72	163	3,091	703
1883	145	2,759	9	88	154	2,847	685
1884	153	3,109	8	98	161	3,270	662
1885	152	3,026	7	66	159	3,185	662
1886	128	2,602	5	48	133	2,735	571
1887	122	2,721	5	48	127	2,848	599
1888	107	2,844	3	33	110	2,954	628
1889	101	2,611	2	27	103	2,713	635
1890	97	2,325	5	38	102	2,363	594

In addition to these there were in 1881 one windmill of ten-horse power, and one horse-mill of two-horse power; in 1882 one windmill of ten-horse power, and two horse-mills of fourteen-horse power; and in 1887 one horse-mill of twelve-horse power, the hands employed in all of which are included in the table.

WAGES.

Constant demand for labour.

In New South Wales, as in most other Australian Colonies, the rapid settlement of the country has created a demand for labour of all kinds, which could not be satisfied except by a constant accession of labourers from other countries. This demand, which has been continuous for many years, has resulted in the establishment of a rate of wages much higher than is ordinarily found in older lands. The wave of depression which affected most countries during 1885-8 did not leave this Colony untouched, and the labouring classes shared largely in the general suffering. Although the normal rate of wages sanctioned by the various labour organizations showed no decline, the actual amount which workmen were willing to accept in most trades was below these rates. The slight revival of prosperity which appears to have set in has had a beneficial effect, and the following rates may be taken as now current in the Colony :—

Rates of Wages of various Trades, &c., during 1890.

Metal Workers.

Black-iron workers	9/-	per day of 8 hours.
Blacksmiths	8/- to 9/-	,, 8 ,,
Blacksmiths' strikers	6/- to 8/-	,, 8 ,,
Boiler-makers	9/4 to 10/8	,, 8 ,,
Brass-finishers	9/- to 10/-	,, 8 ,,
Copper-smiths	9/- to 10/-	,, 8 ,,
Corrugated-iron workers.....	9/-	8
Engine-drivers	7/- to 8/-	,, 8 ,,
Engine-fitters	9/4 to 10/8	,, 8 ,,
Furnacemen	7/- to 8/-	,, 8 ,,
Galvanized-iron workers.. ...	9/-	8
Iron-moulders	9/4 to 10/8	,, 8 ,,
Labourers (in iron trades) ...	6/- to 8/-	,, 8 ,,
Millwrights	9/4 to 10/8	,, 8 ,,
Pattern-makers	9/4 to 10/8	,, 8 ,,
Shipbuilders	9/4 to 10/8	,, 8 ,,
Tinsmiths	8/- to 10/-	,, 8 ,,
Turners (iron)	9/4 to 10/8	,, 8 ,,
Wireworkers	6/- to 10/-	,, 9 ,,

Timber Workers.

Carpenters	8/- to 11/-	per day of 8 hours.
Joiners	8/- to 11/-	,, 8 ,,
Sawyers	9/- to 10/-	.. 9 ,,
Wood-carvers	8/-	8 ,,
Wood-turners	8/-	8 ,,

Building Trades (General).

Bricklayers	9/- to 11/-	per day of 8 hours.
Gasfitters	10/-	" 8 "
Labourers (builders)	8/-	8 "
Painters	9/- to 10/-	" 8 "
Plasterers	10/- to 11/-	" 8 "
Plumbers	9/- to 10/-	" 8 "
Stonemasons	9/- to 11/-	" 8 "
Slaters	10/-	8 "

Leather Workers.

Bootmakers—		
Foremen	60/- to 70/-	per week of 50 hours.
Makers (piece)	35/- to 60/-	" 50 "
Finishers (piece)	40/- to 60/-	" 50 "
Clickers	40/- to 55/-	" 50 "
Sole-cutters	40/- to 55/-	" 50 "
Machinists (females)	17/- to 25/-	" 50 "
Improvers	6/- to 8/-	" 50 "
Tiers-off (girls)	2/6 to 7/6	" 50 "
Apprentices (boys)	12/- to 15/-	" 50 "
Curriers	45/-	54 "
Harnessmakers	45/-	54 "
Portmanteau-makers	36/- to 40/-	" 54 "
Saddlers	40/- to 50/-	" 54 "
Tanners	45/-	54 "
Warehousemen	57/6	50 "

Stationery, Printing, &c.

Bookbinders	8/- to 11/-	per day of 8 hours.
Compositors	10/-	" piecework, 1/1 and 1/2 per 1,000; 1/8 per hour overtime.
Engravers (metal)	60/- to 80/-	per week of 54 hours.
" (wood)	50/- to 60/-	" 54 "
Lithographers	10/- to 12/-	per day of 8 hours.
Pressmen	9/- to 10/-	" 8 "
Stationers	10/- to 12/-	" 8 "
Stereotypers	9/- to 10/-	" 8 "
Warehousemen	60/- to 80/-	per week of 48 hours.

Woollen Cloth Manufactory.

				Hours.
Carders and spinners (man)…………	£1 10/- to £2 per week		…..	50
,, ,, (boys)…………	8/- to 14/-	,,	……	50
Weavers (women, on piece)…………	17/- to 30/-	,,	……	50
,, (boys, ,,)… ………	15/- to 20/-	,,	……	50
Picker and winders (women) ………	15/- to 20/-	,,	……	50
,, ,, (girls) …………	8/- to 13/-	,,	……	50
Finishers (men) ………………………	£1 10/- to £2	,,	……	50
,, (boys)………………………	15/-	,,	……	50
Wool-washers (men) ……………… …	£1 15/- to £2 5/-	,,	……	50
,, sorters (men) …………………	£1 15/- to £2 5/-	,,	……	50
,, dyers (men)…………………	£1 15/- to £2 5/-	,,	……	50

Clothiers.

Tailors (order)—cutters …………	£4 to £4 10/-	,,	……	48
,, ,, journeymen (piece)..	£2 7/- to £4	,,	……	48
,, ,, pressers (piece) ……	£3 to £4	,,	……	48
,, ,, tailoresses (piece) …	15/- to 30/-	,,	……	48
,, ,, apprentices (girls)…	2/6 to 12/6	,,	……	48
,, ,, ,, (boys)…	5/- to 20/-	,,	……	48
,, (slop)—cutters (males)………	£3 to £5	,,	……	48
,, ,, foremen (examiners)..	£3 to £4	,,	……	48
,, ,, pressers (piece)………	£2 10/- to £3 10/-	,,	……	48
,, ,, trimmers ……………	£1 10/- to £3 10/-	,,	……	48
,, ,, machinists (males) …	£2 5/- to £4	,,	……	48
,, ,, ,, (females)	15/- to £2	,,	……	48
,, ,, finishers………………	18/- to £2	,,	……	48
,, ,, improvers ……… ……	7/6 to 17/6	,,	……	48
,, ,, apprentices …………	2/6 to 10/-	,,	……	48
,, ,, complete (manual labour) …………	25/- to £2 15/-	,,	……	48
Drapers' assistants ……………………	£2 to £5	,,	……	60
Hatters…………………………………	8/- to 10/- per day		…………	54
Oilskin-makers ……………………	8/-	,,	……	54
Shirt-makers—cutters ………………	£4 to £7	per week	……	48
,, machinists (females)	12/6 to £1 2/6	,,	……	48
,, improvers (females)..	5/- to 12/6	,,	……	48
Dressmakers—cutters and fitters …	£2 to £7	,,	……	48
,, heads of tables ……	£1 5/- to £1 15/-	,,	……	48
,, skirt drapers ………	£1 10/- to £2 10/-	,,	……	48

Clothiers—continued.			Hours.
Dressmakers—bodice hands	13/- to 20/-	per week	48
,, skirt hands	12/- to 18/-	,,	48
,, sleeve hands	12/- to 18/-	,,	48
Milliners—head milliners and sales-women	£2 to £5	,,	48
,, trimmers	10/- to £1 5/-	,,	48
,, improvers	5/- to 10/-	,,	48
,, apprentices	Nil to 2/6	,,	48
Underclothing and White Sewing—cutters	£1 15/- to £2 10/-	,,	48
,, forewomen	£1 to £1 10/-	,,	48
,, machinists	10/- to 20/-	,,	48
,, apprentices	2/6 to 5/-	,,	48
,, home workers	10/- to £1 5/-	,,	48
Food and Drink Supply.			
Bread-bakers—foremen	£3 to £4	,,	48
,, journeymen	£2 10/- to £3	,,	48
,, general hands	£2 to £2 5/-	,,	48
,, apprentices	10/- to £1 5/-	,,	48
,, pastry-cooks	£2 10/- to £3	,,	48
Biscuit-makers—foreman	£3 to £4	,,	48
,, bakers	£2 10/- to £3	,,	48
,, heads of departments	£2 5/- to £2 15/-	,,	48
,, general hands (male)	£1 5/- to £1 15/-	,,	48
,, females	12/- to £1 5/-	,,	48
,, boys	7/6 to 12/6	,,	48
Butchers—slaughtermen	£2 10/- to £3 10/-	,,	60
,, shopmen	30/- to £2 per week (with board)		70
,, boys	15/- to £1 per week (with board and residence)		70
Confectioners—foremen	£3 to £3 10/-	per week	48
,, general hands	25/- to 35/-	,,	48
,, storemen	20/- to 35/-	,,	48
,, apprentices	5/- to 20/-	,,	48
Grocers' assistants	£1 10/- to £2	,,	66
Millers	£4	,,	60
Mill hands	£2 to £2 10/-	,,	60
Fishermen	£1 to £3	,,	...

Food and Drink Supply—continued.

Gardeners, Market.

European	£1 to £2 per week (with board)	
Chinese	16/- to £1	,, ,,

Maritime Pursuits.

Boatswains	£8	per month, 48 hours per week
Coal-trimmers & Deck-hands	£7	,, 48 ,,
Engineers, first	£20	per month, no fixed time specified.
,, second	£16	,, ,,
Firemen	£9	,, 48 hours per week
Lumpers	1/3	per hour, no fixed time specified.
,, constant hands	50/-	per week of 60 hours.
Masters and engineers of harbour boats	55/-	,, 90 ,,
Sailmakers	10/-	per day, 54 hours per week.
Sailors	£7	per month, 48 hours per week
Sea cooks	£4 to £12	,, 48 ,,
Wharf labourers	1/- to 1/6	per hour, 48 hours per week.
Youths on steamers	15/- to 22/-	per week of 48 hours.

Coaching.

'Busmen	36/- to 50/-	per week of 70 hours.
'Bus conductors	15/- to 20/-	,, ,,
Dray and trollymen	40/- for one horse, 2/6 for every additional, 70 hours.	
Drivers (licensed)	20/- with board and lodging, 36/- if without, 70 hours.	
Farriers	8/- to 9/-	per day, 48 hours per week.
Grooms	36/-	per week of 72 hours.

Attendance and Service.

Males.

Barmen	20/- to 40/-	per week, with board and lodging, no fixed time specified.
Butlers	20/- to 30/-	,, ,,
Coachmen	20/-	
Cooks	20/- to 60/-	..
Dairymen	15/- to 20/-	..

Attendance and Service—continued.

	Males.	
Gardeners	20/- to 30/-	per week, with board and lodging, no fixed time specified.
Gardeners' Labourers	15/- to 20/-	,, ,,
Scullery	15/- to 20/-	..
Waiters	20/- to 25/-	..
	Female.	
Barmaids	20/- to 30/-	..
Cooks	25/-	
General Servants	10/- to 18/-	..
Housemaids	12/- to 16/-	..
Laundresses	16/- to 20/-	..
Nursemaids	7/- to 10/-	..
Waitresses	14/- to 20/-	..

Agricultural and Pastoral Pursuits.

Agricultural Labourers	£30 to £50	per annum, no fixed time specified.
Boundary Riders	£40 to £50	,, ,,
Bush Carpenters	£40 to £50	
Cooks (Station)	£30 to £50	,, ,,
Farm Hands	£30 to £50	,, ,,
Fellmongers	7/6	per day, 55 hours per week.
Fencers	£40 to £50	per annum, with board and lodging, no fixed time specified.
Married Couples (wife cook).	£65 to £80	,, ,,
,, ,, (husband cook)	£75 to £100	,, ,,
Shearers	20/- per 100 sheep, no fixed time specified.	
Stockmen	£40 to £60	per annum, with keep, no fixed time specified.
Winegrowers	£70 to £100	,, ,,
Wool-scourers	7/6 per day, or in piecework 1¼d. to 1½d. per lb., no fixed time specified.	
Wool-sorters	20/- per 1,000 fleeces,	,, ,,

Miscellaneous Trades.

			Hours.
Basket-makers—journeymen (piece).	£2 to £2 10/-	per week	48
,, apprentices	7/- to 15/-	,,	48
,, (blind)	15/- to 30/-	,,	48
Bellows-makers	£2 10/-	,,	54

Miscellaneous Trades—continued.			Hours.
Coach-builders—journeymen	8/- to 10/- per day		48
,, body buildess	8/- to 9/- ,,		48
wheelmakers	8/- to 9/- ,,		48
,, painters	8/- to 10/- ,,		48
,, trimmers	8/- to 10/- ,,		48
,, apprentices	6/- to 20/- per week		48
Coopers (generally piece-work)	£2 15/- per week (average earnings)		44
Cordial Factories—foremen	£2 10/- to £3 10/- per week.		60
,, bottlewashers	£1 10/- to £2 ,,		60
bottlers	£1 10/- to £2 ,,		60
wirers	£1 15/-		60
carters	£2 to £3		60
,, storemen	£2 to £2 10/- ,,		54
,, boys	10/- to £1		60
Copper Smelters—overseers	12/- per day		72
,, mechanics	9/- to 11/- per day		48
,, labourers	7/- to 10/- ,,		48
,, smelters	7/- to 12/- ,,		72
Coke Works—overseers	£3 10/- per week		60
,, cokemen (piece)	10/- per day		60
,, machine men	7/- to 8/- per day		60
,, bagmen	6/- ,,		60
,, labourers	7/- to 8/- ,,		60
Electric Lighting—engineers	£4 to £5 per week		54
,, stokers	£2 to £2 10/- per week		54
lamp inspectors	£3 to £3 5/- ,,		54
,, day labourers	1/- per hour		48
,, boys	15/- to 25/- per week		54
Gas Works—stokers	9/- to 11/- per day		56
,, service layers	9/- to 12/- ,,		48
,, inspectors of meters	£3 to £4 per week		48
,, labourers	6/- to 8/- per day		48
,, boys	10/- to 15/- per week		48
,, iron mechanics	10/- to 12/- per day		48
Glue-makers—general hands	£2 to £2 10/- per week		50
,, boys	10/- to 15/- ,,		50
Hair-dressers	£2 to £3 per week		54
Jewellers	8/- to 10/- per day		48
Labourers	6/- to 8/- ,,		48

Miscellaneous Trades—continued.		Hours.
Lime Burners—general hands	7/- to 8/- per day	54
,, labourers	6/- to 7/- ,,	54
Perambulator-makers	7/- to 9/- ,,	48
Photographers	£4 per week	48
,, assistants	30/- to £2 per week	48
Potters	8/- to 10/- per day	48
Quarrymen	10/- per day	48
Soapmakers—stillmen	8/4 per day	48
,, soapmakers	£3 to £4 per week	48
,, candlemakers	6/8 to 10/- per day	48
,, labourers	6/8 to 7/6 ,,	54
,, boys	1/8 to 5/- ,,	48
Sweeps	30/- to 40/- per week.	
Tobacco operatives—twisters	£1 8/- to £2 10/- per week	54
,, plug hands, &c.	£1 5/- to £2 ,, ...	54
pickers and strippers	10/- to 18/- ..	54
plug coverers (females)	15/- to £1 1/- ,, ...	48
Venetian Blind makers	£1 15/- to £2 10/- ,, ...	48
Watchmakers	£2 15/- to £3 15/- ,, ...	48
Furniture, Bedding, &c.—		
Cabinet-makers (piece)	£2 10/- to £3 5/- ,, ...	48
,, (weekly wage)	£2 5/- to £3 ,, ...	48
,, (Chinese)	£1 to £1 15/-	72
French-polishers (piece)	£2 10/- to £3 5/- ,, ...	48
,, ,, (wages)	£2 5/- to £3 ,, ...	48
Machinists	£2 10/- to £3 ,, ...	48
Chair-makers	£2 10/- to £3 ,, ...	48
Engineers	£2 to £3 10/- ,, ...	48
Wire mattress-frame-makers ...	£1 10/- to £1 15/- ,, ...	48
,, makers	£1 5/- .	48
Bedding hands	£1 5/- to £1 15/- ,, ...	48
Upholsterers (piece)	£2 10/- to £3 ,, ...	48
,, (wages)	£2 5/- to £2 15/- ,, ...	48
Carpet-sewers (females)	12/- to 20/-	48
Mattress-makers (females)	15/- to 25/- ,, ...	48
Upholstresses	10/- to 25/- ,, ...	48
Chinese cabinet-makers	30/- per week (with board and lodging) ...	...
Sand-paper men, polishers (Chinese)	20/- to 25/- per week (with board and lodging) ...	...

Miscellaneous Trades—continued.

		Hours.
Brickmakers—		
Moulders (piece)	9/- to 11/- per day	48
Pressers, setters, and burners	7/6 ,,	48
Carters	£2 to £2 10/- per week	48
Day labourers	7/6 per day	48
Boys	15/- to 25/- per week	48
Engine-drivers	£2 to £2 10/- ,,	48

Municipal Employees (City).

Carters	11/6 per day (finding horse)	44
Gangers	8/- to 11/- ,,	44
Labourers	7/- to 8/- ,,	44
Overseers	8/- to 9/- ,,	44
Regulators of street traffic	8/- to 9/- ,,	44
Masons	8/- to 10/- ,,	48
Pipe-layers	8/- ,,	48
Street cleaners	4/2 to 8/- ,,	48
Stone-breakers (piece)	2/6 to 3/- per cubic yard	54
Timekeepers	£1 10/- to £2 per week	48

State Railway Employees.

Blacksmiths	9/- to 12/2 per day	48
,, strikers	7/6 to 8/6 ,,	48
Boilermakers	9/- to 12/2 ,,	48
Brakesmen	£2 2/- per week	55
Brassfinishers	9/- to 11/- per day	48
Carpenters	8/8 to 11/- ,,	48
Carriage-builders	10/- to 11/4 ,,	48
,, trimmers	10/- to 10/8 ,,	48
Cleaners, engine	5/- to 7/- ,,	55
Engine-drivers (locomotive)	11/- to 15/- ,,	55
,, (stationary)	7/6 to 10/- ,,	55
Fettlers	7/6 ,,	48
Firemen	8/- to 10/- ,,	48
Fitters	9/- to 13/- ,,	48
Foremen	£240 to £450 per annum	48
Gangers	9/- per day	48
Guards	9/- to 11/- ,,	55
Labourers	7/- to 7/6 ,,	48
Porters and Signalmen	7/- to 10/- ,,	55
Shunters	8/- to 11/- ,,	55
Station-masters	£150 to £400 per annum, no fixed time specified.	

State Railway Employés—continued.				Hours.
Waggon builders	9/6 to 10/4 per day			48
Watchmen	£2 2/- to £2 5/-per week			55

Mining.

Coal—(Northern mines)—				
,, Miners, piece-work, average	4/2	per ton		48
,, Overmen (underground)	12/- to 15/-	per day		48
,, Deputy overmen	8/6 to 12/-	,,		48
,, Shiftmen	6/6 to 10/-	,,		48
,, Onsetters	6/6 to 10/-	,,		48
,, Bankers off	6/- to 10/-	,,		48
,, Screenmen	6/6 to 8/-	per day		48
,, Engine-drivers	10/- to 12/-	,,		48
,, Enginemen and firemen	7/- to 9/-	,,		48
,, Screen overmen	10/-	,,		48
,, Overmen (overground)	10/- to 12/-	,,		48
,, Plate-layers	9/- to 10/-	,,		48
,, Furnace-men	7/- to 8/-	,,		48
,, Harnessmaker	8/-	,,		48
,, Packers	2/6 to 4/-	,,		48
,, Wheelers	5/- to 7/-	,,		48
,, Water-bailers	3/6 to 8/-	,,		48
,, Horse-drivers	3/6 to 8/-	,,		48
,, Stablemen	7/- to 8/-	,,		48
,, Labourers	6/- to 8/-	,,		48
,, Flatters	4/- to 6/6	,,		48
,, Trappers	2/- to 3/-	,,		48
,, Boys	2/- to 4/-	,,		48
(Southern mines)—				
,, Miners (2/6 to 3/- per ton)	8/- to 9/-	,,		48
Gold	£2 10/- per week			44
Silver-mining, Broken Hill—				
Mechanics and Surface Hands.				
Engineers	10/- to 12/-	per shift of 8 hours.		
Carpenters	10/- to 12/-	,,	,,	
Blacksmiths	10/- to 12/-	,,		
,, strikers	8/4			
Engine-drivers (hoisting)	10/- to 11/-	,,		
Firemen	8/4 to 9/-	,,		
Fitters	10/- to 12/-	,,		
Machine men (shop)	9/- to 10/-	,,		

Mining—continued.

Boilermakers	12/-	per shift of 8 hours.
Riveters	9/- to 10/-	,, ,,
Tinsmiths	10/-	
Saw-millers	8/4 to 10/-	,,
Horse-drivers	8/4	
Labourers (all)	8/4	
Boys	3/- to 7/6	,,
Trappers	10/-	
Flag-wheelers	9/-	
Feeders	10/-	
Charge-wheelers	9/-	
Underground Hands.		
Miners ... (6 hours on Sunday to constitute a shift work)	10/-	
,, (in wet shafts)	10/10	
Brace and plat men	9/-	
Truckers	8/4	
Ore-dressing Hands.		
Shift-washers	10/-	
Head-runners	9/-	
,, feeders	9/-	..
Engine-drivers	10/-	,, ,,

Overtime.—All time worked over eight (8) hours per day to be paid for at the rate of time and a quarter (Sundays not excepted).

		Hours.
Tin	£2 10/- per week	44

An inspection of the preceding table at once reveals the fact that the labouring classes in this community are far in advance of their fellow-workmen in older countries, in other respects, besides the mere question of better wages. In nearly all departments of labour the daily toil is restricted to eight hours, and though there is no statutory recognition of this time as the limit of a man's labour, it is tacitly acknowledged even by the Governments of the various colonies. Labour organizations and trades' unions are particularly strong in the two provinces of New South Wales and Victoria. Every year a day is set apart in these colonies by the Trades and Labour Councils for the public celebration of the foundation of the eight-hour system; and the State countenances the demonstration by making the day a public holiday.

Comparatively high rate of wages.

Eight-hour system generally adopted.

GOVERNMENT EMPLOYEES.

The Government of the Colony is a very considerable factor in the labour market, as it employed no less than 24,709 permanent, and 1,258 temporary officials during 1889, including the police and defence forces, and all persons receiving remuneration from the State. These officials may be conveniently divided into five classes, as in the following summary, which shows the number and salaries of all officers, distinguishing the permanent officers from those temporarily employed :—

Persons employed by the State, 1889.

Departments.	Permanent Officers.	Permanent Salaries.	Temporary Officers.	Temporary Salaries.
		£		£
Commercial	14,996	2,112,064	955	73,020
Educational	4,119	507,584	....	....
Police and Defence	2,226	362,207	....	....
Gaols and Asylums	843	102,741	14	1,224
Persons partly paid by the State	1,200	18,000	....	....
All Others	1,325	380,309	289	43,751
Total	24,709	3,482,905	1,258	118,995

The first division comprises the commercial and revenue yielding departments, the details of which are thus stated :—

Commercial and Revenue-yielding Departments.

Departments.	Permanent Officers.	Permanent Salaries.	Temporary Officers.	Temporary Salaries.
		£		£
Railways	11,091	1,483,000	....	....
Post Offices	2,138	287,712	692	30,288
Lands, survey, sales, &c.	818	162,465	....	....
Water and Sewerage	198	32,000	....	....
Customs	200	49,541	78	11,842
Harbours and Rivers	287	50,660	185	30,890
Marine Board	221	36,975	....	....
Royal Mint	43	9,711	....	....
Total	14,996	2,112,064	955	73,020

The next two clauses—Education, and Police and Defence Forces—have no temporary appointments. The details of those are as follow :—

Education.			Police and Defence.		
Department.	Officers.	Salaries.	Department.	Officers.	Salaries.
		£			£
Public Instruction...	4,042	490,342	Police	1,585	288,452
Sydney University...	77	17,242	Defences.........	641	73,755
Total...........	4,119	507,584	Total...........	2,226	362,207

The fourth division includes gaols and penal establishments, hospitals and asylums for the insane, &c., as well as reformatories and industrial schools. The particulars of these institutions are thus given :—

Gaols and Asylums.

	Permanent Officers.	Permanent Salaries.	Temporary Officers.	Temporary Salaries.
		£		£
Gaols and Penal Establishments.....	457	64,799	9	952
Hospitals and Asylums	358	34,439	2	132
Industrial and Reformatory Schools	28	3,503	3	150
Total	843	102,741	14	1,234

Class 5 consists mainly of country postmasters, who are only partly paid by the State. There were 1,200 of these in round numbers, and they received £18,000 from the Government. The last division includes the Governor, ministers of religion in receipt of State pay, judges, and civil servants not included in the above. There were 1,325 permanent officers in this class, with salaries amounting to £380,309; the temporary appointments amounted to 289, with salaries to the sum of £43,751. As further illustrating the important part played by the State as an employer of labour, it may be mentioned that there are usually 5,500 hands employed in the maintenance of public roads, while at times the number has reached 9,000.

STEAM POWER.

The power used in the Colony for manufacturing, transporti and other purposes is equivalent to 141,300 horse-power, or horse-power for every thousand persons, a rate comparing unfavourably with other countries, as will be seen from subjoined statement computed from Mulhall's Dictionary Statistics :—

Country.	Steam power employed.	Per 1,000 of the population.
	H.p. Thousands.	H.p.
United Kingdom	9,200	250
France	4,520	118
Germany	6,200	130
Russia	2,240	30
Austria	2,150	50
Italy	830	30
Spain	740	40
Belgium	810	140
Holland	340	80
United States	14,400	240
New South Wales	141	129

Value of machinery.

Of the total power employed* in the Colony, by far the grea portion is derived from steam. The amount used in man tories is 24,662 horse-power, or about 17 per cent. of the employed, and the value of plant and machinery worked by power is estimated at £4,526,821. The value of land buildings devoted to works and manufactories may be appr mately set down at £7,076,219, which, with the sum set d for plant, would make the total invested in these industries much as £11,603,040 for plant, land, and buildings.

The services for which steam power is used are shown in following table, from which it will be seen that land and transport absorb 78,900 horse-power, or nearly 56 per cent the total horse-power consumed. The information with regard manufactures and transport is fairly exact, but is only approximate for the other industries :—

Industries employing power.	Horse-power.
Manufactures, &c.	27,200
Land transport	58,709
Water transport	20,200
Agricultural and Pastoral	13,300
Mining	12,300
Other industries	9,600
	141,300

TRADE UNIONS.

The subject of Trade Unionism has been dealt with by legislation in only one instance in this Colony—the Trade Union Act of 1881. This measure commences by enacting that the purpose of any trade union shall not be deemed to be unlawful, so as to render its members liable for conspiracy or otherwise, merely because it is in restraint of trade; nor for such a reason shall any agreement be made void or voidable. It is declared that nothing in the Act shall enable any Court to entertain any legal proceeding in respect to agreements between the members themselves of a trade union with reference to the terms upon which they shall transact business, employ, or be employed, or for the recovery of subscriptions, penalties, or applications of the funds to certain specified purposes. At the same time the Act is not to be deemed to make such agreements unlawful. Neither the Friendly Societies Act nor the Companies Act are to apply to trade unions, nor can they be registered under those Acts. Provision is made, however, for the registration of such trade unions under the present Act, provided always that if one of the purposes of such trade union be unlawful the registration shall be void. The Registrar of Friendly Societies is made registrar of trade unions, and provisions are made for the appointment of trustees, treasurers, &c., for the

Legislation on Trade Unions.

Registration of Trade Unions.

establishment of rules, the preparation of annual returns dissolution or amalgamation, change of name, and other matt

Definition of Trade Unions.

The term "Trade Union" is defined to mean "any combinat whether temporary or permanent, for regulating the relati between workmen and employers, or between workmen and wo men, or between employer and employers, for imposing restric conditions on the conduct of any trade or business, whether s combination would or would not, if this Act had not been pas have been deemed to have been an unlawful combination reason of some one or more of its purposes being in restraint trade." Few of the Trade Unions have complied with the p visions of the Act relative to returns, consequently particulars regard to their membership cannot be given with any accura At the middle of 1890 the number of Societies registered ninety-five.

IMPORTATION OF LABOUR.

Since the cessation of assisted immigration by the State th has been very little labour imported by the capitalists and ma facturers of the Colony; in fact almost all the artisans labourers who have arrived here within the last few years h been those who have left the other Australasian Colonies, in hope of improving their position in New South Wales. question of the importation of labour has not been largely de with by legislation in this Colony. The chief enactment on subject is the Agreements Validating Act, 39 Victoria, No. which provides that agreements made in any place beyond Colony, for a period of service not exceeding two years, shall as binding and effectual as though they had been entered i within the Colony, provided that the contract or agreement sl have been made and subscribed in the presence of some off duly authorised in that behalf by the Governor and Execut Council of New South Wales.

Agreements Validating Act.

PATENTS.

The law relating to the registration of inventions and improvements has been in force since 1855, but it is only within recent years that the provisions of the Act have been used to any great extent. In 1887 the law was amended, and the fees reduced to the nominal sum of £5 for Letters Patent, and £2 for a certificate of provisional protection, which latter may, if application be made within twelve months from its granting, be converted into a patent on the payment of an additional £3. The result has been that the business of the Patent Office has greatly increased. The inventions registered in 1890 were for the most part not local but foreign, and this feature has marked the operations of the Patent Office since its inception. The following is the business transacted since 1855:—

Liberality of the law.

Letters of Registration and Assignments thereof for Inventions or Improvements registered.

Year.	No. of Registrations.			Year.	No. of Registrations.		
	Patents.	Assignments.	Total.		Patents.	Assignments.	Total.
1855	......	......	3	1873	43	6	49
1856	......	......	1	1874	39	21	60
1857	......	......	1	1875	34	16	50
1858	......	......	10	1876	44	18	62
1859	......	......	11	1877	62	27	89
1860	......	......	10	1878	45	19	64
1861	......	......	13	1879	57	16	73
1862	......	......	14	1880	89	23	112
1863	18	4	22	1881	113	13	126
1864	15	2	17	1882	129	21	150
1865	15	5	20	1883	149	24	173
1866	20	5	25	1884	183	29	212
1867	20	4	24	1885	161	27	188
1868	21	2	23	1886	203	31	234
1869	27	5	32	1887	*545	44	589
1870	32	4	36	1888	*742	50	792
1871	27	5	32	1889	*796	84	880
1872	43	5	48	1890	*768	102	870

* Provisional protection and letters patent.

The new law came into force on 31st July, in 1887. The number of certificates of Provisional Protection and Letters

Operations of Act of 1887.

Patent applied for during 1890 was 232 and 536 respect while 102 assignments were registered during the same p The countries from which applications for Patents in New S Wales were received, were as follows:—

Great Britain	145	Canada	
Germany	6	Cape of Good Hope	
France	6	South African Republic	
Belgium	2	New South Wales	[illegible]
New Caledonia	1	New Zealand	[illegible]
Sweden	2	Queensland	[illegible]
Austria	1	South Australia	[illegible]
Portugal	1	Tasmania	[illegible]
United States	43	Victoria	15
Argentine Republic	1	Western Australia	

Making a total of 768 applications, over 41 per cent. of w were made by persons residing in the Colony, though necessarily for inventions perfected in New South Wales.

COPYRIGHT.

The Copyright Act in force in this Colony was passed on May, 1879, and became law on 1st July, 1879. The A divided into four parts, dealing with the following subject Part I. Literary, Dramatic, and Musical Works; Part II. Arts; Part III. Designs; Part IV. Miscellaneous Provisio

Registration of books, &c.

Part I provides for the registration of copyright in book publications, as understood in the widest sense of the term, for every new edition containing any alterations in the ma and also for the registration of playright, or the right of represen or performing dramatic or musical productions, whether previ printed and published or not. The copyright granted in Colony applies only to works first published here, and comme to run on first publication, representation, or performance; no remedy can be obtained or legal proceedings taken for anyt done before registration. The term of protection is 42 years, or the life of the author plus 7 years, whichever is the longer period. Nothing blasphemous, seditious or libellous is entitled to be registered, nor any mere advertisement. Literary works for which registration is sought must be submitted to the Registrar in a complete state as published; but dramatic or musical works may be in manuscript, and will be returned. A best copy of the first and each subsequent edition of every printed "book" published in the Colony must be delivered within two months of publication to the respective Librarians of the Free Public Library and of the Library of the University of Sydney. The penalty for default in delivering Library copies is the forfeiture of the value of the book and a sum not exceeding £10. Library copies must be delivered whether the book is registered or not. Lectures receive protection without being registered, on compliance with the requirements of the Act; but lectures are public property if delivered in any University, Public School, or College, or on any public foundation, or by any individual, by virtue of, or according to any gift, endowment, or foundation. The registration fee is 5s. and the fee for certificate, if one be required, 3s.

Period of copyright.

Part II gives copyright in paintings, drawings, works of sculpture, and engravings, including the design thereof, for 14 years, and in photography and the negatives thereof, for 3 years. The fees to be paid are:—1s. for photographs and chromographic cards, 5s. for other subjects, and 3s. for certificates. Copyright in a work of fine art when not executed under commission does not necessarily either follow the work or remain with the artist, but ceases to exist, unless it has been secured by agreement between the parties at or before the time of the sale of the original. The work must be made in the Colony, and be new and original to entitle it to copyright.

Copyright in paintings, &c.

Part III. Under this part of the Act protection can be obtained for new and original designs, not previously published in the Colony or elsewhere, such designs being for articles of manufacture

Copyright in designs.

and works of art, whether intended for works of utility, ornament, or otherwise. The protection does not extend to the article itself but only to the design thereof; consequently it does not apply to any mechanical action, principle, contrivance, application, or adaptation, or to the material of which the article is composed. The articles which are capable of being registered are divided by the Act into fourteen classes, two years protection being assigned to some, and three years to others. The registration fee is ten shillings, and registered designs must bear a registration mark.

Part IV contains general provisions, and amongst other matters declares copyright to be personal property, assignable at law, and transmissible by bequest, and subject in case of intestacy to the same law of distribution as other personal property.

International copyright.

The Copyright Law of England is comprised chiefly in some fourteen Acts of Parliament, of an unusually obscure and conflicting character, and extensively elaborated by judicial decisions. Under the "International Copyright Act, 1886," 49 & 50 Vic. c. 33, the greater part of this body of law, together with the terms of the Copyright Convention of Berne, is made reciprocally applicable to Great Britain and each of its Dependencies, and to the countries that are parties to the Convention, with their Colonies, namely:—Germany, Spain, France, Great Britain, Häiti, Honduras, Italy, The Netherlands, Sweden and Norway, Switzerland, and Tunis,—previous copyright treaties being for the most part abrogated.

Effect of international copyright.

Under this arrangement, copyright, when registered in the country of origin, is covered by the local laws within that country, and by the Imperial Laws and the convention elsewhere. Thus, in order to secure international and intercolonial protection for a copyright registered in this Colony, it is only necessary to obtain an International Certificate executed by the Registrar and confirmed by the Minister of Justice, and this may be used anywhere within the province of the Union.

The total number of registrations of copyright effected has been :—

	During 1890.	From the passing of the Act in 1879 to 31st December, 1890.
PART I. *Literature* :—		
Printing and publishing right—		
Books	27	305
Periodicals	16	165
Music	....	33
Playright—		
Drama	....	48
Music	1	5
Total	44	556
PART II. *Fine Arts* :—		
Painting	2	4
Drawing	2	35
Sculpture	....	7
Engraving	11	130
Photography	39	553
Total	54	729
PART III. *Designs, &c.*	10	336
Grand Total	108	1,621

PART XXI.

Food Supply and Cost of Living.

THE soil of New South Wales is capable of producing in abundance most of the things necessary for the sustenance of human life, though the production of some of these necessaries has been almost entirely neglected, while others are obtained in quantities insufficient for the wants of the community. Considering the comparatively high rate of wages which prevails, food of all kinds is fairly cheap; and articles of diet, which in other countries are almost within the category of luxuries, are in New South Wales largely consumed even by the poorest classes.

Cost of foods. The cost of providing food and beverages, other than intoxicants, consumed in the Colony during 1890 was £15,873,400. This sum represents the price to the consumer, and covers all charges, except that of cooking and preparing the food for the table. The expenditure on wines, spirits, and beer, amounted to £4,774,100, so that the total expenditure for all foods and beverages was £20,647,500, equal to £18 14s. 9½d. per inhabitant, or 12¼d. daily; excluding intoxicants the yearly expenditure per inhabitant is £14 8s. 1½d., and the average per day 9½d. Compared with the cost of food supply in other countries this sum will not appear considerable, especially when allowance is made for the profusion with which flesh meat is consumed and wasted in this Colony. The following figures are taken from the Dictionary of Statistics, and show the annual expenditure per head of the more important European countries and of the United States:—

Annual expenditure on food, including liquors.

Country.	Per Inhabitant.			Country.	Per Inhabitant.		
	£	s.	d.		£	s.	d.
United Kingdom	14	4	9	Norway	9	15	0
France	12	4	5	Denmark	11	14	0
Germany	10	18	5	Holland	10	8	0
Russia	5	19	7	Belgium	12	3	1
Austria	7	17	4	Switzerland	8	11	7
Italy	6	4	10	Roumania	6	10	0
Spain	8	9	0	Servia	6	10	0
Portugal	7	3	0	United States	9	17	7
Sweden	9	18	11	Canada	8	9	0

The main articles of consumption in the Colony are meat and bread, the retail value of which equals about 39 per cent. of the total expenditure on food. The following is the approximate cost of the main articles which enter into daily consumption:— Retail cost of foods.

Retail value of foods, &c., consumed, 1890.

	£
Bread	2,833,500
Fresh meat	3,350,500
Vegetables and fruits	2,889,100
Milk, butter, cheese, &c.	2,388,800
Other farm produce	635,800
Sugar	1,568,600
Tea, coffee, &c.	725,300
Other foods and beverages	1,481,800
	£15,873,400

The amount of the principal articles of diet annually required by each member of the community is estimated to be as follows:— Principal article of diet require per head.

Flour		260·0 lb.
Rice		10·9 „
Meat	Beef ... 176 lb. Mutton ... 85 „ Pork, &c. 10 „	271·0 „
Potatoes		182·0 „
Sugar		94·8 „
Butter		16·6 „
Cheese		4·3 „
Tea		108·8 oz.
Coffee		8·7 „

For the year 1891 the total demand of the Colony for the above classes of food will be approximately:—

Flour	[illegible]	tons.
Bran	[illegible]	"
Beef	[illegible]	"
Mutton	[illegible]	"
Pork and bacon	[illegible]	"
Potatoes	[illegible]	
Sugar	[illegible]	"
Butter	[illegible]	"
Cheese	[illegible]	"
Tea	[illegible]	lb.
Coffee	[illegible]	"

[illegible]

The production of wheat in the [illegible] is not yet equal to the demands of the population. In 1890 the deficiency of home production was about [illegible] bushles, equal to [illegible] tons of flour, or [illegible] per cent. of the whole requirements. The wheat crop of [illegible] was the largest ever harvested in New South Wales, so that the deficiency to be made good from outside sources was [illegible] small. Based on the average yearly consumption [illegible] bushels per head, the demand for 1891 will be [illegible] bushels [illegible] will be available from the [illegible]

[illegible]

[illegible]

head of sheep; and, though the supply of cattle sufficient to meet the demand was beyond the resources of the Colony, the number of sheep available for market very largely exceeded even the number given above, and, were it not for the preference of beef to mutton, no stock need have been imported for slaughtering.

The swine slaughtered for food in 1890 numbered 108,180, and from these were manufactured 7,429,971 lb. of bacon and hams, the balance being consumed as pork. The quantity of bacon and hams imported for home consumption during the same year was 1,357,673 lb., so that, allowing for export, the total consumption of swine products was 9,761,629 lb. Pork and bacon

The amount of potatoes imported for local consumption during 1890 was 39,523 tons, while the quantity available from the fields of the Colony was only 50,096 tons. The net imports amount, therefore, to 44 per cent. of the total consumption, a result due not so much to the inability of the farmers to grow this crop as to the low prices prevailing for some years in the local markets. Potatoes.

The consumption of sugar in the Colony is enormous, averaging about 95 lb. per head during each year. The fields of the Colony produced during 1890 about 19,617 tons, or 34,238 tons short of the local demand. This large quantity was imported principally from Queensland and the Dutch East Indies. As pointed out in the previous pages relating to agriculture, a large part of the Colony is well adapted to the growth of sugar-cane; but the low price which sugar brought some few years ago, when the market was affected by the bounties given by Germany and France, made the industry unprofitable, and the cultivation of cane was, to some extent, neglected. The considerable rise in the price of sugar during 1889 led to an increase of cultivation over that of the previous year, and this was followed by a further extension in 1890, but the area under cane could still be increased 72 per cent. before the production of sugar would equal the local demand. Sugar.

Butter and cheese.

The year 1890 proved very encouraging to the dairy farmers, and the quantity of butter and cheese manufactured was sufficient to meet local wants, and leave a small balance for export. The amount of butter made during 1890 was 18,534,130 lb. and of cheese 4,796,567 lb., and the excess of exports over imports was butter 281,341 lb., and cheese 76,101 lb.

Tea and coffee.

The quantity of the beverages, tea and coffee, consumed is remarkably large, the average of the first-named being 6 lb. 12 oz. per inhabitant, and of the latter 9 oz. The consumption of tea is universal throughout the colonies, and the four million people in Australasia probably use more of this beverage than the millions who inhabit continental Europe, other than Russia. Though the soil and climate of a part of New South Wales are adapted to the cultivation of tea, no systematic attempt has been made to grow this plant. The coffee berry, especially the Liberian variety, thrives in the north coast district, but it has not yet been cultivated for commercial purposes.

Food consumption in Australasia.

The average quantity of the principal articles of common diet is given herewith for the various Colonies of Australasia. It will be seen that the consumption of wheat varies from 246 lb. in Queensland to 454 lb. in New Zealand, the average consumption being 331 lb. per head. Rice and oatmeal vary greatly in the quantity used, only 13·8 lb. being the consumption of South Australia, as against 32·4 lb. in Western Australia. The use of tea is universal in Australia, the consumption being largest in Western Australia and Queensland—with 171 oz. and 136 oz. respectively. Sugar also enters largely into consumption, the average being 106 lb. per head in Victoria and 95 lb. in New South Wales. Coffee is not a favourite beverage in Australasia, the consumption being not quite one-ninth that of tea. It is used most largely in South Australia, where the annual demand amounts to 21 oz.

Consumption of Foods, 1890.

Article.	New South Wales.	Victoria.	Queensland.	South Australia.	Western Australia.	Tasmania.	New Zealand.	Australasia.
Grain—								
Wheat ....lb.	390	300	246	390	390	362	454	334
Rice & Oatmeal ....lb.	18·9	22·2	22·5	13·8	32·4	16·2	15·9	18·0
Potatoes ....lb.	182	311	242	210	102	509	472	288
Sugar ....lb.	94·8	105	102	96·9	114	96·3	86·7	95·8
Tea .. ..lb.	6·8	7·3	8·5	5·6	10·7	7·2	6·0	7·0
Coffee ....oz.	8·7	17·8	11·2	20·8	21·0	12·2	8·1	13·0
Cheese ....lb.	4·3	...	...	...	...	...	4·5	4·5
Butter ....lb.	16·6	...	...	...	...	...	16·0	16·0
Salt ....lb.	33·7	22·0	46·3	33·0	19·0	36·1	29·6	33·0
Meat—								
Beef ....lb.	176	155	280	...	...	60	90	...
Mutton .. ...lb.	85	96	90	...	...	150	110	...
Pork & Bacon. lb.	10	12	...	...	...	...	...	...

The consumption per head of potatoes in some of the colonies is probably less than the foregoing table shows; thus in the case of Tasmania the returns show a consumption of 509 lb., and in New Zealand 472 lb. It is probable that potatoes are in some years grown in excess of the local requirements, and the market in New South Wales and other continental Colonies not being sufficient to absorb this excess, it remains unconsumed or is given to live stock and poultry; under the circumstances it is impossible to determine the quantity actually entering into the food consumption of the population. Potatoes.

Judged by the standard of food consumed, the population of New South Wales, as well as of all the other colonies of Australasia, must appear remarkably prosperous. Compared with those of other countries, this will most clearly appear from the following table, the particulars given in which, with the exception of those referring to Australasia, have been taken from Mulhall's Dictionary of Statistics:— Quantity of food indicative of prosperity.

Quantity of Food Annually Consumed in principal Countries.

Country.	lb. per Inhabitant. Grain.	Meat.	Sugar.	Butter and Cheese.	Potatoes.	Salt.	Tea and Coffee—Ounces.	Daily Energy—Foot tons.
United Kingdam ...	378	109	75	19	380	40	91	3,739
France	540	77	20	8	570	20	66	[illegible]
Germany	550	64	18	8	1,020	17	78	[illegible]
Russia	635	51	11	5	180	19	6	[illegible]
Austria	460	61	18	7	560	14	28	[illegible]
Italy	400	26	8	4	50	18	20	2,153
Spain	480	71	6	3	20	17	6	[illegible]
Portugal	500	49	12	3	40	17	18	[illegible]
Sweden	560	62	22	11	500	28	112	[illegible]
Norway	440	78	13	14	500	40	144	[illegible]
Denmark	560	64	22	22	410	25	140	4,071
Holland	560	57	35	15	820	20	240	[illegible]
Belgium	590	65	27	15	1,050	...	142	[illegible]
Switzerland	440	62	26	11	140	...	110	[illegible]
Roumania	400	82	4	9	80	...	8	2,414
Servia	400	84	4	9	80	...	8	[illegible]
United States	370	150	53	20	170	39	162	3,415
Canada	400	90	45	22	600	40	72	4,013
New South Wales ...	409	271	95	21	182	34	117	[illegible]

Thermo-dynamic power of foods.

Taking the articles of the foregoing list, with the exception of tea and coffee, and reducing them to a common basis of comparison, it will be found that the amount of thermo-dynamic power, capable of being generated by the food consumed in this Colony is only exceeded by that of Germany, Holland, and Belgium. For purpose of comparison the figures of Dr. Edward Smith, F.R.S., in his well known work on Foods, have been used, and the heat developed has been reduced to the equivalent weight lifted 1 foot high. In estimating the thermo-dynamic effect of food, grain has been reduced to its equivalent in flour, and regard has been paid to the probable nature of the meat consumed. The figures for potatoes are given as they appear in the Dictionary of Statistics, but it is a probable supposition that but a small proportion of the quantity over 400lb set down for any country is required for human consumption, and the figures relating to some of the countries—notably the three just mentioned—are therefore excessive. The substances included in this table are largely supplemented both in America and Europe by other foods, but not more so than in these colonies; and in the table just given will probably be found a just view of the comparative quantity and food-value of the articles of consumption in each of the countries mentioned. The comparison will appear much more strongly in favour of this Colony when the average amount of work which each individual in the community is called upon to perform is taken into consideration. In New South Wales, and indeed in all Australasia, the proportion of women and children engaged in laborious occupations is far smaller than in Europe and America, and the hours of labour of all persons are also less, so that the amount of food-energy required is reduced in proportion.

In Mulhall's Dictionary of Statistics, under the heading of "Diet," is given a measure of the aggregate amount of work performed by persons doing physical and mental labour, and it would appear that the food of an average man, when burnt in the body, should be equal to at least 3,300 foot tons of work daily, that of a woman 2,200, and of a child 1,100 foot tons. For this Colony the average of all persons would be about 2,125 foot tons, whereas, from the table just given, the amount of work which the daily food consumed by each individual in the Colony from the principal foods consumed is equivalent to, is not less than 4,337 foot tons. The quantity of food consumed in New South Wales would therefore appear to be far in excess of the actual requirements of the population, and though the excess may be looked upon as waste, it is none the less evidence of the wealth of the people whose circumstances permit them to indulge in it.

Food consumed in excess of requirements.

The following table gives the annual consumption of tobacco in Australasia and the principal countries of the world. The use of tobacco appears to be more prevalent in Queensland and Western Australia than in any of the other colonies, while the least consumption is in Tasmania and South Australia. Compared with other parts of the world, the average consumption of Australasia will not appear excessive:—

Tobacco.

Average Annual Consumption of Tobacco per Inhabitant in various Countries.

	lb.		lb.
Australasia	2·53	Austria-Hungary	3·77
New South Wales	2·75	Italy	1·34
Victoria	2·61	Spain	1·70
Queensland	3·34	Holland	6·92
South Australia	1·93	Belgium	3·15
Western Australia	3·18	Switzerland	3·24
Tasmania	1·97	Sweden	1·87
New Zealand	2·06	Denmark	3·70
United Kingdom	1·41	Turkey	4·37
France	2·05	United States	4·40
Germany	3·00	Canada	2·11
Russia	1·23	Brazil	4·37

CONSUMPTION OF INTOXICANTS.

Quantity of proof alcohol.

The consumption of wines, spirits, and fermented liquors has been decreasing for some years, as will be seen from the following statement, showing the average consumption of spirit per inhabitant during the past seven years.

	Gallons.		Gallons.
1883	3·52	1887	2·97
1884	3·53	1888	2·88
1885	3·37	1889	2·71
1886	3·23	1890	2·68

These figures represent the amount of alcohol contained in the liquor consumed; the quantities are given in proof spirit as being a measure more easily understood, if less scientific, than that of absolute alcohol.

Decrease of intoxicants consumed.

The satisfactory state of things depicted in the foregoing table is due to a combination of causes. Four of these are most notable: the more stringent provisions of the Licensing Act, the decrease in the proportion of rougher labourers to the general community, the depression of trade, and, lastly, the spread of teetotal principles. It were futile to attempt to determine how these causes have operated individually in decreasing the consumption of intoxicants; but the fact of such a decrease cannot be gainsaid, for the direct evidence given above is corroborated by the decline in the number of arrests.

The volume of spirits consumed in the Colony during 1890 was 33,105 gallons of Colonial rum, and 1,168,841 gallons of imported spirits, in all 1,201,946 gallons, equal to 1·09 gallons per head—a quantity not much more than two-thirds of the consumption during the year 1879, as will appear from the following table:— Spirits consumed.

Consumption of Spirits in Proof Gallons.

Year.	Quantity Consumed.		Year.	Quantity Consumed.	
	Total.	Per Inhabitant.		Total.	Per Inhabitant.
	Gallons.	Gallons.		Gallons.	Gallons.
1879	1,039,687	1·50	1885	1,219,024	1·30
1880	1,011,999	1·38	1886	1,172,140	1·20
1881	1,109,274	1·46	1887	1,136,863	1·11
1882	1,164,115	1·46	1888	1,164,975	1·10
1883	1,214,990	1·45	1889	1,159,380	1·05
1884	1,257,201	1·43	1890	1,201,946	1·09

The quantity of Colonial beer which has been consumed can only be given accurately for the last four years, though approximations have been made for the years 1885 and 1886. It will be seen that the consumption has declined considerably, in spite of the increase in population. The importation of beer during 1890 fell below that of the previous year; all other years show an increase, as will be seen from the following statement:— Beer consumed.

Consumption of Beer, Porter, &c.

Year.	Colonial.	Imported.	Total.	Per Inhabitant.
	gallons.	gallons.	gallons.	gallons.
1885	11,000,000	1,839,500	12,839,500	13·79
1886	10,000,000	2,075,000	12,075,000	12·32
1887	9,720,000	2,126,000	11,846,000	11·69
1888	9,300,000	2,413,000	11,713,000	11·01
1889	9,515,000	2,514,000	12,029,000	10·89
1890	9,504,000	2,207,000	11,711,000	10·63

Falling off in consumption of beer.

The amount of beer drunk in 1885 was approximately 12,839,500 gallons, of which 11,000,000 gallons were the produce of the Colony, representing 85·7 per cent. of the total consumption. In 1890 the quantity had fallen to 11,711,000 gallons, and the proportion, locally made to 81·2 per cent. During the same period the consumption per head had declined from 13·79 gallons to 10·63.

Consumption of wine.

The wine drunk in the Colony is mostly the produce of its own vineyards, but it is nevertheless much less than might have been expected in a country so eminently adapted to wine-growing as New South Wales, and amounts to only about half that drunk in Victoria. The consumption of Australian and European wines for the past eleven years is given in the following table:—

Consumption of Wine.

Year.	Australian.	Foreign.	Total.	Per Inhabitant.
	gallons.	gallons.	gallons.	
1880	705,992	154,190	860,182	1·18
1881	579,630	172,846	752,476	0·99
1882	491,263	186,006	677,269	0·85
1883	500,308	182,613	682,921	0·82
1884	560,447	188,069	748,516	0·85
1885	414,113	193,642	607,755	0·65
1886	531,253	173,995	705,248	0·72
1887	584,179	161,033	745,212	0·73
1888	625,359	180,502	805,861	0·76
1889	747,435	170,526	917,961	0·83
1890	640,205	161,945	802,150	0·73

Expenditure on liquors.

The amount expended upon wines, spirits, and fermented liquors, consumed in the Colony during the year 1890, was about £4,774,100. Of this sum £2,891,800 was the cost of liquors to the retailer, of which £1,187,500 represents duty, excise, and license fees, and £1,704,300 the invoice price of the goods. The cost of working the trade and the profits of the merchants and retailers therefore came to £1,882,300. The expenditure on liquors per inhabitant amounted to £4 6s. 7¾d. during the year, which, though undoubtedly a large sum, amounting, as it does, to 7·6 per cent. of the average income, is nevertheless proportionately smaller than the expenditure of several European countries. The following table gives the rate per inhabitant and the proportion of income devoted to liquors. The figures should, however, be taken with this qualification, that in several of the countries enumerated, liquors are consumed principally with meals in place of tea or coffee, so largely partaken of in English-speaking countries :—

Yearly Amount expended on Liquors in various Countries.

Countries.	Amount per inhabitant. £ s. d.	Percentage of income.
United Kingdom	2 18 0	8·2
France	1 19 0	7·7
Germany	1 14 0	9·4
Russia	1 0 0	9·9
Austria	1 13 0	10·5
Italy	1 5 0	10·7
Spain	1 5 0	9·1
Belgium and Holland	2 0 0	8·5
Denmark	2 10 0	11·1
Scandinavia	1 6 0	7·7
United States	1 10 0	4·2
New South Wales	4 6 8	7·6
Victoria	5 5 0	......

Consumption of liquors in Australasia.

As pointed out in the part of this volume relating to crime, the consumption of intoxicants in this Colony is less than in Victoria and Queensland, and about equal to the average of Australasia.

The following table shows the consumption for all the colo during the year 1890. In the case of South Australia and Weste Australia, whence no returns relating to breweries are obtained the consumption of beer has been assumed to be at the same ra as that of New South Wales. The largest consumption of spir per inhabitant is in Queensland, Western Australia being secon Wine is used most freely in Western Australia, South Austral and Victoria, and beer in the Colony of Victoria. The avera consumption of alcohol in all the colonies amounts to 2·90 gall of proof spirit per inhabitant, ranging from 3·98 gallons in Weste Australia to 1·77 gallons in New Zealand. The total for Victo is 45 per cent. larger than that of New South Wales. The figu relating to the production of beer in Victoria may, however, over-stated, for as no excise duty is levied in that colony it quite possible that the returns furnished by the various brewer are greatly exaggerated.

Consumption of Alcohol in each Colony.

Consumption of Intoxicants in the Australasian Colonies, 189

Colony.	Spirits.		Wine.		Beer, &c.		Equival in Alcohol (proof) per inhabitant
	Total.	Per inhabitant.	Total.	Per inhabitant.	Total.	Per inhabitant.	
	galls.	galls.	galls.	galls.	galls.	galls.	galls.
New South Wales	1,201,946	1·09	802,150	0·73	11,710,986	10·6[illegible]	[illegible]
Victoria...............	1,110,371	0·99	1,559,603	1·39	21,490,556	19·21	[illegible]
Queensland	613,620	1·58	270,508	0·70	3,948,093	10·16	[illegible]
South Australia	169,126	0·53	554,402	1·74	3,385,442	[illegible]	[illegible]
Western Australia	58,025	1·23	216,800	4·00	501,534	10·6[illegible]	[illegible]
Tasmania	92,209	0·64	24,073	0·17	1,329,671	[illegible]	[illegible]
New Zealand	432,882	0·70	115,068	0·19	4,922,577	7·92	1·77
Total and Means....	3,678,179	0·98	3,542,744	0·95	47,288,809	12·65	2·90

Taking Australasia as a whole it compares very favoural with most of the European countries in the quantity of intoxica annually consumed by each inhabitant, as the following statem shows. The figures are reduced to gallons of proof spirit from data given in Mulhall's Dictionary of Statistics, and would look even more favourable to Australasia were the fact of the large preponderance of males over females in these colonies made a feature in the comparison:—

Consumption of Alcohol in various countries—in Proof Gallons.

Country.	Consumption.	Country.	Consumption.
	gallons		gallons.
United Kingdom	3·57	Portugal	3·00
France	5·10	Holland	4·00
Germany	3·08	Belgium	4·00
Russia	2·02	Denmark	5·00
Austria	2·80	Scandinavia	4·36
Italy	3·40	United States	2·65
Spain	2·85	Australasia	2·90

It is popularly supposed that Australian wines and beers are not heavily charged with spirit as compared with the imported articles; this belief is erroneous. Several descriptions of Australian wines have a natural strength of 30 per cent. of proof spirit, while from analyses recently made it would appear that the strength of these wines offered for sale varies from 24 to 37 per cent. of spirit. On the same authority it was stated that imported beers ranged from 13·88 to 15·42 per cent. in the case of English, and from 9·58 to 11·76 per cent. of proof spirit in Lager, while the local manufacture varied according to the make from 11·21 to 15·12, the average being 13·75 per cent. It is generally understood, however, that since the imposition of excise duties on colonial beer in 1887, the strength of the article has been somewhat reduced, and does not average more than 13 per cent. of proof spirit.

Strength of Australian Wines and Beers.

COST OF LIVING.

In the year 1890 an estimate was made of the yearly expenditure of the population of New South Wales, and it was found that while the income amounted to 63 million pounds sterling the

Income and expenditure.

expenditure amounted to £52,131,400, the balance of £10,868,600 representing the savings of the people, and the incomes of absentees. By "savings" is meant that portion of their income, whether realised or not, which was not expended by the people of the country on their necessary maintenance. It will, of course, be understood that no increments to land values have been taken as part of the unrealised income. The expenditure of the year 1890, distributed under various heads, is herewith given, as an indication of the way in which the people of this Colony disburse their income :—

Distribution of Expenditure of the Population of New South Wales, 1890.

	£
Food and non-alcoholic beverages	15,873,400
Fermented and spirituous liquors	4,774,160
Tobacco	1,193,880
Clothing and drapery	8,391,600
Furniture	805,900
Rent or value of buildings used as dwellings	6,726,700
Locomotion	1,705,600
Fuel and light	1,797,300
Personal attendance and service	1,918,000
Medical attendance, medicine, and nursing	1,427,800
Religion, charities, education (not including State expenditure)	716,400
Art and amusement	995,900
Books, newspapers, &c.	765,400
State services, postage, telegrams, succession dues	743,100
Household expenses not included elsewhere	2,814,600
Miscellaneous expenses	1,482,000
	£52,131,400

The expenditure for the year given amounted to £47 6s. 3¼d. per head, or at the rate of 2s. 7d. per day. The daily expenditure may be thus distributed :—

	Pence per day.	Proportion of Expenditure.
Food	9·5	30·4
Clothing	5·0	16·1
Rent	4·0	12·9
Taxes	0·3	0·9
Sundries	12·3	39·7
	31·1	100·0

According to Mulhall the expenditure per head in the leading countries of Europe and in the United States is :—

Annual Expenditure per head in various countries.

Countries.	Expenditure per head.
	£ s. d
United Kingdom	29 14 9
France	23 19 4
Germany	20 3 4
Russia	10 1 11
Austria	14 4 9
Italy	11 11 0
Spain	15 12 6
Portugal	11 5 6
Sweden	20 8 4
Norway	19 0 0
Denmark	28 11 5
Holland	20 17 4
Belgium	25 8 2
Switzerland	18 0 0
United States	32 16 2
Canada	23 6 2
New South Wales	47 6 3

The table just given affords but a partial view of the question of the cost of living; for if the total earnings of the countries above enumerated be considered as an element of comparison, it will be found that few countries approach New South Wales in the small proportion of income absorbed in providing food for the people. The following table, given on the same authority as the preceding, shows that, while the actual cost of food and drink is £18 14s. 9d. in this Colony, as against £14 4s. 9d. in Great Britain, the earnings required to pay for this food are not

Cost of living and earnings.

Cost of food compared with earnings.

larger proportionately than in the countries which show most favourably in the table. The number of working days in the year is assumed to be 300, allowing for thirteen days' sickness and fifty-two Sundays :—

Annual Cost of Food and Beverage.

Country.	Average annual cost of food and beverage.			Ratio of cost of food to earnings.	Day's earnings equal to annual cost of food.
	£	s.	d.	per cent.	days.
United Kingdom	14	4	9	42·2	127
France	12	4	5	44·0	132
Germany	10	18	5	49·1	148
Russia	5	19	7	52·0	156
Austria..........................	7	17	4	50·8	152
Italy	6	4	10	51·2	153
Spain	8	9	0	51·2	154
Portugal	7	3	0	59·1	177
Sweden	9	18	11	45·2	136
Norway	9	15	0	47·6	143
Denmark	11	14	0	36·0	108
Holland	10	8	0	46·0	138
Belgium	12	3	1	43·4	130
Switzerland	8	11	7	45·2	135
United States...........	9	17	7	25·3	76
Canada...........................	8	9	0	32·5	98
Australasia (New South Wales)	18	14	9	32·8	98

The area of New South Wales is so extensive, and the population, except on the sea-board, so scattered, that the determination with any exactness of the average prices of the various commodities consumed is a matter of no little difficulty. No attempt has therefore been made to ascertain the average for the Colony, and in the following pages the prices refer to the Metropolitan markets alone. For the earlier years the authority of contemporary newspapers has been followed where the official records were obscure or silent, but since 1836 these records have been available, and have for the most part been adopted. The following table exhibits the average prices of nine commodities during each year since 1820:— Retail prices of food.

Average Retail Prices of Nine Commodities during each year since 1820.

Year.	Wheat per bushel.		Bread per 2 lb loaf.	Fresh Beef per lb.	Butter per lb.		Cheese per lb.		Sugar per lb.	Tea per lb.		Potatoes per cwt.		Maize per bushel.	
	s.	d.	d.	d.	s.	d.	s.	d.	d.	s.	d.	s.	d.	s.	d.
1820	8	4	5	5½	2	9	1	1	...	...		7	3	5	6
1821	10	3	6	5½	2	8	1	2	...	...		7	3	5	0
1822	8	8	5	5½	2	6	1	3	...	...		5	9	4	9
1823	5	0	3½	5½	2	2	1	2	...	...		6	1	2	6
1824	8	9	5	5½	3	0	1	4	...	...		6	10	4	10
1825	9	5	4½	6	2	2	1	5	...	...		8	4	5	6
1826	7	6	5½	5½	2	4	0	10	...	...		9	0	4	0
1827	7	0	4½	6½	2	3	1	1	...	...		8	0	5	0
1828	10	6	6	5	2	6	1	4	...	...		18	6	9	0
1829	9	4	7	6	1	10	1	1	...	...		12	6	7	9
1830	6	0	4½	3½	1	0	0	11	3½	2	6	8	0	3	10
1831	5	6	4	4½	1	8	0	6	3½	2	6	5	0	3	8
1832	6	0	5	5	2	3	0	7	3½	2	6	5	0	4	7
1833	4	4	4	3½	1	5	0	6	3½	2	6	10	0	2	11
1834	8	9	5	4	1	6	0	6	3½	2	6	14	0	4	4
1835	8	6	4	3½	1	10	0	5	3½	2	6	10	0	4	6
1836	10	0	5½	3	1	9	0	8½	3½	2	6	7	0	6	9
1837	6	9	3	4½	1	9	0	7½	3½	2	6	10	0	4	2
1838	8	0	5	4½	1	6	0	8½	3½	2	6	10	6	3	7
1839	17	4	11½	3	2	6	1	1	3½	2	6	11	0	9	0
1840	10	6	7½	4½	2	0	1	0	3½	2	6	9	6	5	3
1841	7	0	4½	4½	2	6	0	10	3½	2	6	12	0	2	10
1842	7	6	5	3½	2	6	1	1½	3½	2	6	14	6	4	9
1843	4	9	3½	2½	1	9	0	9	3	2	6	10	6	2	9
1844	3	4	2½	2	1	5	0	4½	2½	1	6	4	6	1	5
1845	4	0	2½	2½	1	6	0	6	3	1	6	4	6	2	11
1846	5	0	3½	2¼	1	8	0	6	4	2	3	6	9	4	1
1847	4	9	3½	2	1	2	0	7	4	2	4	5	6	2	1
1848	5	0	3½	2	1	1	0	8	3¾	2	0	6	0	1	8

Year.	Wheat per bushel.		Bread per 2 lb. loaf.	Fresh Beef per lb.	Butter per lb.		Cheese per lb.		Sugar per lb.	Tea per lb.		Pota-toes	
	s.	d.	d.	d.	s.	d.	s.	d.	d.	s.	d.	s.	d.
1849	4	0	2½	1¾	1	2	0	6¼	3¾	1	9	6	2
1850	6	3	4½	1¾	1	3	0	7	3½	1	10	7	6
1851	8	6	5	2¾	1	3	0	7	3½	1	4	6	6
1852	6	3	4½	3	1	3	0	7	3½	1	4	6	0
1853	9	3	6½	3½	1	5¼	0	7¼	3½	1	4	13	6
1854	11	6	7½	4½	2	3	0	9	5	2	6	18	8
1855	14	0	9	6	2	4	1	3	7	2	5	21	4
1856	11	3	7½	3½	1	11	1	2	5½	2	2¼	10	9
1857	7	4	5	3½	2	0	1	0	7½	2	6	14	8
1858	8	4	6	4	2	0	1	0	7	2	6	15	8
1859	10	0	6	4	1	10	1	0	5	2	6	8	0
1860	8	0	6½	4	1	6	1	10	5½	2	3	7	8
1861	6	6	6½	3	1	8	0	9	5½	2	4	7	3
1862	7	0	4½	4½	2	3	0	9	4½	2	0	8	0
1863	6	6	4	4¼	1	6	0	10	4½	2	0	7	6
1864	7	0	5½	4	1	6	0	8	4½	2	0	5	6
1865	9	6	7½	3	1	9	0	9	4½	2	0	8	0
1866	8	4	6½	3	1	3	1	0	4	2	6	6	0
1867	4	3	3½	2½	1	6	0	7½	4	2	0	7	0
1868	5	9	4	3½	1	3	0	9	4	2	0	9	0
1869	4	9	3½	2	1	6	0	6	4	2	0	4	0
1870	5	0	3½	3½	1	3	0	6	4	2	0	5	0
1871	5	7	3½	2½	1	3	0	7½	4	2	3	4	0
1872	5	0	3½	2½	1	0	0	9	4	1	9	5	0
1873	5	1	4	2½	1	3	0	5	4	1	9	3	6
1874	6	9	3½	4	1	7	0	6	4	1	9	4	9
1875	4	7	3	3½	1	3	0	9	4½	1	9	5	6
1876	5	1	3½	5½	1	3	0	7	4	1	9	4	9
1877	6	1	4	4½	1	6	0	6	4	2	0	4	9
1878	6	1	4	4	1	3	0	6	4	1	9	5	10
1879	5	0	3½	4	0	10½	0	6	3½	1	6	6	0
1880	4	8	3	3½	0	10	0	7	4	2	0	4	3
1881	4	1	3½	3½	0	10½	0	6½	3½	2	0	4	0
1882	5	5	4	4½	1	3	0	8	4	2	0	5	6
1883	5	2	3½	4	1	6	1	0	4	2	0	5	0
1884	4	3	3	4½	1	3	0	9	3½	1	6	5	0
1885	3	10	3	4½	1	6	1	3	3	1	9	6	0
1886	4	3	3½	4½	2	0	1	1	3½	1	9	6	9
1887	3	10	3½	4	1	3	0	10½	3½	1	9	5	6
1888	3	6	3	4	1	11	0	8½	3½	1	6	7	0
1889	4	8	3½	3	1	7	0	9	3¼	1	6	9	0
1890	3	7	3	3	1	0	0	6	3¼	1	6	5	6

Variation of price in early years.

The most noteworthy feature of the history of prices Colony—the great range of some of the commodities duri year—is not disclosed by the foregoing table. This varia most noticeable during the early years, and amongst arti local production, and was the result of the almost complet tion of the Colony from the markets of the world. Prior to the discovery of gold, communication by letter with the outside world was at best uncertain, and as late as 1878 the regular mails were made up but once a month. The establishment of telegraphic communication, amongst other results, has had a marked effect on prices, so that except in rare instances, and for goods produced in excess of the demand, the production of Australia no longer determines the prices of goods required for the local markets. Exception must, of course, be made for perishable produce, which is still liable to a great range in price during the course of a single year, as will be shown by some examples hereafter given.

Wheat has exhibited very great variation in value, not only from year to year, but even within the same year. The lowest average for twelve months was in 1844, when the bushel sold for 3s. 4d. In 1888 the average was 3s. 6d., but in 1839 the average was not less than 17s. 4d. In 1828 the price was 10s. 6d., and in 1840 it was also 10s. 6d. In 1854–5–6 the quotations were 11s. 6d., 14s., and 11s. 3d. for those years in their order. Since then the price of the cereal has never averaged more than 10s. per bushel for a period of twelve months, and from 1880 has averaged over 5s. in two years only. As illustrating the range of prices within a year, the case of 1824 may be cited, when wheat varied from 4s. to 13s. 6d. the bushel; in 1828 the prices were from 8s. to 15s.; in the following year, from 7s. 6d. to 16s.; and in 1839, from 8s. 6d. to 25s. The last-mentioned was the highest price at which there is a record of sales having been made. In that same year the 2-lb. loaf was sold at 14d. Price of wheat.

Potatoes have also varied in price from year to year. The lowest average for a whole twelvemonth was 3s. 6d. per cwt. in 1873, and the highest was 21s. 4d. in 1855, shortly after the discovery of gold; and it may not be without interest to note that from 1853 to 1858 the price of potatoes was extraordinarily high. Commencing with the year first named, the averages were 13s., 18s. 6d., 21s. 4d., 10s., 14s. 6d., and 15s. 6d. per cwt. With Price of potatoes.

regard to the variation in a single year, the following exa may be cited :—In 1820, from 4s. 6d. to 10s. per cwt. ; in from 4s. 8d. to 12s. ; in 1829, from 9s. to 26s. ; in 1834 9s. to 19s. ; in 1839, from 7s. to 25s. ; in 1854, from 11s. to in 1856, from 3s. to 11s. ; and in 1888, from 2s. to 24s.

Price of maize. The price of maize has not been subject to the same fluctu as that of wheat, since, being little used except for horse-fee grain is capable of being replaced by other products ; nevert the prices have ranged from 1s. 8d. in 1848 to 10s. in 1854

Price of bread. In the list given at page 747 are included quotations of br per 2 lb. loaf. It will be seen that in most years the price somewhat regularly with that of wheat. There are, how exceptions to this rule, chiefly in the years during which brought an unusually high figure, when the price of bread w found to have been less than might have been expected. lowest price at which bread has been retailed was 2½d. in and the highest was 14d. the 2 lb. loaf, which figure was pa a short time in 1839.

In addition to the nine commodities which are given in 747, the following list of articles largely used may not be wi interest. The information begins with 1836, beyond which it is difficult to determine the exact average :—

Average Retail Prices.

Year.	Bacon per lb.	Eggs per doz.	Rice per lb.	Oat-meal per lb.	Coffee per lb.	Salt per lb.	Beer (Col.) per gall.	Soap per lb.	Starch per lb.	Tobacco per lb. (Col.)
	s. d.	s. d.	d.	s. d.	s. d.	d.	s. d.	d.	s. d.	s. d.
1836......	...	2 2	9	...	...	...	...	4½	...	...
1837......	...	2 6	...	...	1 6	1	1 0	...	...	...
1838......	...	4 0	...	...	...	...	...	...	...	...
1839......	...	3 0	...	...	1 6	...	...	4½	...	...
1840......	0 10	2 9	...	...	1 4	...	...	4½	...	...
1841......	0 11	2 3	...	...	1 4	..	...	4½	...	...
1842......	0 10½	1 11	2	...	1 4	1	1 9	4½	...	...
1843......	0 10	2 0	1½	...	0 10	0½	2 3	...	...	1 4
1844......	0 5½	0 11	1¾	...	0 8½	1¼	1 3	3¾	...	1 6
1845......	0 6½	1 1	3	...	0 7½	1½	1 1	3½	...	1 6

Year.	Bacon per lb.	Eggs per doz.	Rice per lb.	Oat-meal per lb.	Coffee per lb.	Salt per lb.	Beer (Col.) per gall.	Soap per lb.	Starch per lb.	Tobacco per lb. (Col.)	Tobacco per lb. (Imp.)
	s. d.	s. d.	s. d.	s. d.	s. d.	s. d.	s. d.	s. d.	s. d.	s. d.	s. d.
1846	0 9½	1 3	1½	...	0 10	1½	2 0	5	...	1 9	4 6
1847......	0 6½	1 1	3¾	6	1 1	1½	3 4	5	1 0	1 9	4 4
1848... ..	0 9	1 3	3½	6	1 1	1½	3 3	5	1 0	1 9	4 4
1849......	0 8½	1 1	3¾	5¾	1 0	1½	2 8	5½	1 1	2 0	4 7
1850......	0 8½	1 4	4	6	1 2	1¾	2 9	5½	1 0	2 7	4 10
1851......	0 9½	1 8	4	6	1 3	1½	2 6	5½	1 0	3 8	7 9
1852......	1 1	1 6	4	6	1 3	1½	2 6	6	1 0	4 0	8 0
1853......	1 2½	2 3	4½	6	1 3	1½	2 4½	6	1 0	4 0	7 6
1854......	1 4½	2 9	5	7½	1 6	2½	3 6	8	1 6	4 0	5 6
1855....	0 11½	2 8	6	9	1 8	4	4 7	8	1 6	3 0	5 0
1856......	0 10	2 2	5½	7	1 7½	3	3 6	7½	1 1½	2 6½	5 3
1857......	0 9½	1 11	5	7	1 8	2¾	4 0	7	1 0	2 7	5 0
1858......	0 7½	2 3	6	7	1 8	4½	4 3	7	1 5	2 6	5 0
1859......	0 8½	1 10	4½	7	1 8	2½	4 0	6½	1 0	2 6	5 0
1860......	1 0	1 3	5	6	1 6	2½	3 6	7	1 0	2 3	5 0
1861......	0 10	1 6	4	6	1 6	2½	3 6	6	0 10½	2 0	5 6
1862.....	0 10	1 5	3	5	1 5	1½	2 0	4½	0 8	4 6	6 0
1863.....	0 10½	1 7	3	4	1 4	1½	1 6	4	0 7	3 0	7 6
1864......	0 10	1 6	3	4	1 4	1½	2 0	4	0 8	1 6	5 6
1865......	0 9¾	1 6	3	4	1 4	1½	2 0	4	0 8	2 6	5 6
1866......	1 0	1 6	4	4	1 4	1½	2 0	4½	0 7	2 6	5 0
1867......	0 10	1 7	3½	4	1 4	1	1 6	4	0 7	1 9	4 6
1868......	0 9½	1 2	4	4	1 4	1½	2 0	4	0 7	1 9	5 0
1869... ..	0 10	1 3	3	4	1 0	1	1 4	4	0 8	1 0	3 6
1870... ..	0 10½	1 4	3	4	1 2	1	1 4	4	0 7	1 3	3 6
1871	0 9½	1 4	2½	2½	1 0	0½	2 3	3	0 4½	1 0	3 0
1872......	0 9	1 1	3	3	1 1	0¾	1 4	3	0 5	1 4	3 6
1873......	0 9	1 4	2½	2¾	1 2	0½	2 3	3	0 5	2 0	3 6
1874.. ...	0 8¾	1 6	3	3¾	1 4	0½	2 0	2¾	0 6	1 9	3 3
1875......	0 9½	1 6	3	3	1 2	1½	3 0	3	0 5	2 0	3 9
1876......	0 9	1 0	3	3	1 2	1	2 0	2¾	0 5	1 9	3 0
1877	0 8½	1 6	3	3½	1 3	1	2 0	2¾	0 5	2 0	3 6
1878.. ...	0 9	1 3	3	3	1 3	0½	2 0	2	0 5	1 6	3 0
1879......	0 8	1 7	2½	2¼	1 0	0½	2 0	2	0 5	1 6	3 9
1880......	0 7½	1 4	3	3	1 5	0¾	2 0	3	0 5½	2 0	4 0
1881......	0 7½	1 0	3	3	1 5	0¾	2 0	3	0 5½	2 0	4 0
1882	1 0	2 0	3½	4	1 5	1	2 0	2½	0 6	3 0	5 0
1883......	1 0	1 6	3	4	1 9	1	2 0	3	0 7	3 0	6 0
1884	0 10½	1 3	2½	3	1 4	1	2 0	3	0 6	3 0	5 0
1885......	0 10½	1 6	3	3	1 5	0¾	2 0	3	0 6½	3 0	6 0
1886......	0 10½	1 8	3½	2¾	1 6	1	2 0	4	0 6½	4 0	5 6
1887......	0 10	1 9	3	2¾	1 6	1	2 0	3½	0 6½	4 0	5 6
1888......	0 10½	1 8	3	2½	1 6	1	2 0	3½	0 6	4 0	5 6
1889......	0 11	1 8	3	3½	1 6	1	2 0	3½	0 6	4 0	5 6
1890......	0 10½	1 7	3	3	1 6	1	2 0	3½	0 5	4 0	5 6

In the quotations of prices in the foregoing tables the figures given are those charged in the shops throughout the metropolitan district. It is quite possible that produce of all kinds may have been bought at cheaper rates than those stated; but the

Retail prices.

figures will be found to represent the fair average rates, regard to the class of goods consumed. It is of importa take into consideration the quality of the produce con for very considerable changes, in the direction of improv have taken place in this respect. Thus, the ordinary sug used, and obtainable for about 3½d. per lb., is a good white whereas some years ago only the commonest quality of moist was found on the tables of the people. A very material im ment has been effected in the quality of flour, a large prop of the present consumption being roller-made. Salt-butte forms the bulk of the supply, but it is usually of recent while formerly the butter was imported from Great Britai was several months old before reaching the dining table. candles now used are made of stearine, but the time is not when only the common tallow candle was in general use so with many other articles of ordinary consumption. retail prices are those actually paid from day to day, irres of the nominal wholesale rates of the commodities in the S markets.

Improved quality of commodities.

Price-level of commodities.

A consideration of retail prices would not be complete w a statement of the price-level in different years. This c given for foods; but at present the data are hardly suffic establish an exact series of price-levels, taking into conside all the elements of ordinary expenditure. The informat regard to foods is given below, the assumption being that the quantities entering into consumption were the formerly as at the present day. This assumption, howeve some respects erroneous; but there appears to be no other within reach to effect a juster comparison. Sugar, tea, butter, cheese, and potatoes, are now more largely used than prior to 1870; but bread, or other forms in which flour is and meat, are not consumed so largely. However, whe allowance is made on this score, the following table will s found to approximate closely to the truth :—

Price-level of Foods, 1830-90.

Five-year period.	Price-Level—Period 1830-4 = 1,000.	Price-Level—Period 1885-90 = 1,000.
1830-4	1,000	1,156
1835-9	1,116	1,290
1840-4	992	1,147
1845-9	655	757
1850-4	962	1,112
1855-9	1,273	1,472
1860-4	1,053	1,217
1865-9	900	1,040
1870-4	780	902
1875-9	919	1,062
1880-4	867	1,002
1885-90	865	1,000

During the period of sixty years, which this table embraces, there has been a range from 655 or 757 for 1845-9, to 1,273 or 1,472 for 1855-9, equal to over 95 per cent. Comparing the last period of the series with the others it will be seen that only two are marked with lower prices—1845-9 and 1870-4. Little practical good can be gained by comparing the prices of one period with those of another, unless regard is also paid to the earnings of labour, and as means of comparison are afforded in the chapter of this volume dealing with wages, it will be unnecessary to pursue the subject further in this place. Range of Prices.

WHOLESALE PRICES.

The average wholesale prices of the principal kinds of milling produce, feed grains, root crops, and fodder for each month of the year 1890 are given in the following statement. The average for the whole year is also shown, but is given irrespective of the quantities sold in each month. In using the table it would be well if this qualification were borne in mind, as the apparent average obtained by dividing the sum of the prices of each month by twelve may, and in some instances does, differ from the true average obtained by taking into account the total sold at each price. Wholesale prices.

Average Wholesale Current Prices of Milling Produce and Feed Grains, 1890.

Month.	Milling Produce.								Feed Grains.		
	Wheat.		Flour.								
				Australian.							
	New Zealand.	Australian.	New Zealand.	Roller.	Stone.	Oatmeal.	Bran.	Pollard.	Barley.	Oats.	Maize.
	Per bushel.	Per bushel.	Per ton.	Per ton.	Per ton.	Per ton.	Per bushel.	Per bushel.	Per bushel.	Per bushel.	Per bushel.
	s. d.	s. d.	£ s. d.	£ s. d.	£ s. d.	£ s. d.	d.	d.	s. d.	s. d.	s. d.
January	2 11¼	3 5½	9 5 0	10 5 0	9 12 6	12 5 0	7	7¼	3 0	2 1¼	3 7
February	3 3	3 3¼	9 0 0	10 0 0	9 7 6	12 0 0	7	7¾	3 0	2 0½	3 3
March	3 3	3 6	8 17 6	10 0 0	9 5 0	12 0 0	7¼	7½	3 6¼	2 1¼	3 8½
April	3 0¾	3 5¼	8 15 0	10 0 0	9 5 0	12 15 0	8¼	8¼	3 6	2 1¾	3 11
May	3 6	3 6¾	8 17 6	10 0 0	9 2 6	12 15 0	9	9¼	2 11	2 0	3 3¼
June	3 6½	3 6½	8 15 0	10 0 0	9 0 0	12 15 0	7¾	8¼	2 10½	1 11¼	3 6¼
July	3 6	3 8	8 12 6	9 17 6	8 15 0	11 15 0	7¼	7½	2 10¼	1 11	3 7
August	3 6½	3 8	8 12 6	10 0 0	8 17 6	11 15 0	7½	7½	2 7½	1 10¼	3 6
September	3 8	3 9	9 2 6	10 2 6	9 5 0	11 15 0	7¾	7½	2 8	2 0½	3 7¼
October	3 7	3 9	9 2 6	10 0 0	9 0 0	11 15 0	7½	7¼	2 8	2 0	3 9
November	3 9	3 9½	9 2 6	10 0 0	9 1 3	11 15 0	7¼	8¼	2 7¾	1 11	3 9½
December	3 9½	3 9½	9 2 6	9 17 6	9 1 3	10 10 0	7½	8½	2 7½	1 10¼	3 10½
Mean Prices, 1890	3 5½	3 7¼	8 18 9	10 0 3	9 2 9	11 9 7	7½	8	2 11	2 0	3 7½

Average Wholesale Current Prices of Farm Produce for each month, 1890.

Month.	Root Crops. Potatoes. New Zealand.	Root Crops. Potatoes. Tasmania.	Root Crops. Potatoes. New South Wales.	Root Crops. Onions. New Zealand.	Root Crops. Onions. New South Wales.	Root Crops. Turnips.	Root Crops. Carrots.	Fodder. Hay. Oaten or Wheaten.	Fodder. Hay. Lucerne.	Fodder. Straw.	Fodder. Chaff. Oaten.	Fodder. Chaff. Other.	Fodder. Straw Chaff.
	Per ton.	Per ton.	Per ton.	Per ton.	Per ton.	Per ton.	Per ton.	Per ton.	Per ton.	Per ton.	Per ton.	Per ton.	Per ton.
	£ s. d.	£ s. d.	£ s. d.	£ s. d.	£ s. d.	£ s. d.	£ s. d.	£ s. d.	£ s. d.	£ s. d.	£ s. d.	£ s. d.	£ s. d.
January	3 15 0	4 15 0	3 3 8	5 0 0	4 2 6	...	...	4 6 2	2 7 6	2 7 6	5 5 0	4 9 7	2 10 0
February	4 0 0	5 5 0	4 18 4	5 0 0	4 15 7	...	...	3 12 1	3 5 0	2 5 0	5 0 0	4 1 10	2 13 4
March	4 5 0	5 0 0	4 16 0	5 5 0	4 10 0	...	...	4 3 4	4 1 6	2 6 0	4 10 0	4 1 3	2 15 0
April	4 17 6	4 13 9	4 0 0	5 7 6	5 2 6	...	...	4 5 6	4 8 4	2 10 0	5 5 0	4 8 9	3 0 0
May	4 2 6	4 3 4	4 2 6	5 10 0	5 5 0	...	...	3 7 0	3 18 5	2 7 0	4 10 0	4 3 4	3 0 0
June	3 17 6	3 15 6	3 7 6	5 17 6	5 11 10	...	...	3 11 2	4 0 0	2 4 6	4 13 4	4 3 0	3 3 0
July	4 3 4	4 1 8	3 10 0	6 4 2	5 15 7	2 10 0	2 10 0	4 5 0	3 14 7	2 3 0	4 15 0	3 9 2	3 5 7
August	3 13 6	3 7 11	3 0 0	13 0 0	10 16 8	2 10 0	2 10 0	4 15 4	3 10 5	2 5 0	5 5 0	3 12 2	2 16 6
September	3 11 8	3 10 0	2 12 6	10 0 0	9 10 0	2 10 0	2 10 0	3 10 0	3 6 11	2 6 0	5 0 0	3 6 0	2 4 4
October	1 11 10	1 11 10	1 11 10	11 0 0	10 0 0	2 10 0	2 10 0	3 17 6	3 10 0	2 5 0	5 0 0	4 0 0	2 13 0
November	6 1 3	6 1 3	6 1 3	14 0 0	13 5 0	2 10 0	2 10 0	3 11 10	3 19 2	2 5 0	5 0 0	3 10 8	2 10 0
December	5 0 0	5 0 0	5 0 0	...	8 5 0	2 10 0	2 10 0	3 15 0	3 12 8	2 8 4	5 0 0	4 0 0	3 0 0
Mean Prices, 1890	4 1 7	4 5 5	3 17 0	7 16 9	7 5 0	2 10 0	2 10 0	3 18 4	3 12 10	2 6 0	4 18 7	3 18 10	2 15 11

Average Wholesale Current Prices, Farm-yard and Dairy Produce, 1890.

Month.	Butter.		Cheese.	Bacon.		Lard.		Eggs.	Poultry.				Bee Produce.		Pigs.		Milk.
	Dairy.	Factory.		New Zealand.	New South Wales.	Bladder.	Bulk.		Fowls.	Ducks.	Geese.	Turkeys.	Honey.	Wax.	Porkers.	Bacon.	
	Per lb.	Per lb.	Per lb.	Per lb.	Per lb.	Per lb.	Per lb.	Per doz.	Per pair.	Per pair.	Per pair.	Per pair.	Per lb.	Per lb.	Per lb.	Per lb.	Per gallon.
	d.	d.	d.	d.	d.	d.	d.	d.	s. d.	s. d.	s. d.	s. d.	d.	d.	d.	d.	
January	5¾	8	4¼	9	7¼	3½	1½	13½	3 3	3 1	7 2	16 0	3½	10	4¾	3¾	6
February	9	10¼	4¾	9½	7¼	3¾	1¾	18	3 0	2 10	5 2	10 7	3¾	10	4¾	3¾	6
March	8¼	12½	3½	9½	7	4	2	15¼	3 2	3 3	5 8	9 0	3½	10	5	3¾	6
April	9¼	11¾	3½	9	6½	4½	2½	22¼	2 11	3 3	5 11	8 3	3½	10	4¼	3¼	8
May	8¾	10¾	3¾	9	6½	4¼	2¼	21	3 6	3 3	5 6	7 6	3¾	10	4¼	3¼	8
June	10¾	14¾	3¾	9	6¾	3½	2¼	19¼	3 0	3 6	5 6	7 6	3¾	10	4	3½	8
July	10½	14	4	9½	5¾	3¾	2¼	15½	3 1	3 10	5 11	8 0	4	10	4	3¾	8
August	9½	13½	3½	9	6	4	2	14¼	3 1	4 1	6 0	8 0	4	10	4½	3½	8
September	7	9	3¾	9½	5¾	4¼	2	9	3 2	4 0	5 9	8 0	4	10	4¼	3¾	8
October	7	9	3½	9	6½	4	2½	9½	3 2	4 0	5 9	8 0	4	10	5	4	6
November	6	8	4	8	6	4	2	12	3 11	4 2	7 2	11 10	4	10	4½	3¾	6
December	6	8	4	7	5¾	4½	2½	12½	3 0	3 3	7 3	10 0	4	10	4½	4	6
Mean Prices, 1890.	8¼	10¾	4	9	6	4	2	15¼	3 2¼	3 6½	6 0¾	9 4¾	3¾	10	4½	3¾	7

Milling produce, feed grains, and fodder, were on the whole remarkably steady in price during the year. Locally grown wheat ranged from 3s. 3¼d. per bushel in February, when the new crop was already harvested, or ripe for gathering, to 3s. 9½d. at the close of the year, the difference representing the various items of risk, interest, and shrinkage in volume. Quotations are given for New Zealand, as well as locally made flour. This is necessary, as, owing to the annual shortage of the New South Wales wheat crop, a large importation of breadstuffs is necessary, and New Zealand furnishes a market whence supplies may be readily drawn. Barley and oats are for the most part imported, and the prices of those cereals during the year call for little notice. Maize, on the contrary, is almost wholly of local growth. Its price averaged 3s. 7½d. per bushel, which was also the price of wheat, and its range was almost within the same limits. The general steadiness in prices noted above also extended to the various forms of fodder, most of the defect below the average which is observable in some months is due to want of quality in the commodity offered. Root crops, on the other hand, show very great range. Thus, potatoes varied between £1 11s. 10d. per ton and £6 1s. 3d., while onions sold for £4 2s. 6d. in January, as against £13 5s. per ton in November. No quotations are given in some of the columns of the foregoing tables; in the months in which these omissions occur no produce was offered, or a quantity insufficient to merit a quotation. Cereals, &c.

The wholesale prices of farm-yard and dairy produce in the Sydney markets are shown in the preceding table. The figures call for little comment beyond the caution already given in regard to the prices of commodities generally—that the averages are irrespective of the quantities sold. As regards most of the articles in the list, the lower the price the larger the consumption. The exception to this rule is poultry, which is most in demand before the Christmas season, when prices are correspondingly high. Farm and Dairy Produce.

The prices of the items set forth in the tables here given are determined by the local, or at all events the Australasian, demand, wheat, of course, being an exception, its price being fixed by that ruling in the markets of the world. The prices of pastoral and other raw produce, which form so large a proportion of the exports of the Colony, are not sensibly affected by local consumption.

No object is to be gained by showing the monthly variations, so that in the statement only the average for the year is given.

Average Wholesale Current Prices of Pastoral Produce, &c., for year 1890.

Commodity.		Price.
Beef	per 100 lb.	16s. 6d.
Wool—		d. d.
Merino, washed	per lb.	11½ to 15
" scoured	"	14 to 17½
" greasy	"	7½ to 10½
Crossbred, greasy	"	7 to 10
Skirtings, scoured	"	9½ to 14
" greasy	"	5¾ to 9¼
Sheepskins—		d.
Full wool	"	6¼
Medium	"	5
Short	"	3¾
Pelts	"	2¾
Hides—		
Cattle, heavy	"	3¼
" medium	"	2¼
" Others	"	1¾
Horse	each	33d. to 81d.
Leather skins—		
Calves	"	7d. to 29d.
Kangaroo, extra large	per doz.	125d.
" other	"	27d. to 96d.
Fur skins—		s. d. s. d.
Opossum	"	3 0 to 15 0
Platypus	"	2 0 to 7 0
Bear	"	1 3 to 3 0
Hair—		d.
Horse, mane	per lb.	13¼
" tail	"	15
Ox, clean tail	"	12½
" stumps	"	6½
		s. d. s. d.
Bones	per ton	64 6 to 119 6
Horns	per 100	2 9 to 32 3
Hoofs	per ton	42s.
Tallow—		£ s. d.
Mutton	"	20 10 8
Mixed	"	20 0 0
Beef	"	17 16 6
Wattle bark—		
Good	"	7 11 4
Medium	"	6 9 9
Tobacco—		
Good	per lb.	0 0 5
Medium	"	0 0 3

PART XXII.

Population and Vital Statistics.

ONE of the first results of the recent Census has been the re-adjustment of the estimates of population. Prior to the 5th April, 1891, there had been no actual count of the people of New South Wales since 1881, but an approximate return was made up of the estimated population on the 31st December of each year. This was done by taking into account the increase caused by the excess of births over deaths, and arrivals over departures. It is evident that if these data could be ascertained exactly, there would be no difficulty in making an accurate estimate of the population at any time. But although the machinery for the registration of births and deaths ensures a fairly correct return under these heads, it is not so easy to obtain exact particulars respecting the arrivals and departures—especially the latter. The lists of passengers arriving by the sea are usually accurate; but in the case of persons departing, it is found that large numbers go on board steamers at the last moment, without having previously booked their names, and so are not recorded amongst the emigrants

Results of the Census.

from the Colony. It therefore becomes necessary when estimating the population to make allowance for unrecorded departures. The result of the recent Census, however, shows that the allowance made was not sufficient, and that the estimates, for the last few years especially, were in excess of the truth. Consequently, in the present issue the figures have been re-cast, and proper allowance has been made, which will account for whatever discrepancy there may be between the tables now published, and those contained in former issues.

Estimate of population.

The following is an estimate of the population of each of the Australasian Colonies on the 31st December, 1890:—

Population of Australasia.

Colony.	Population.
New South Wales	1,121,860
Victoria	1,133,266
Queensland	392,965
South Australia (with Northern Territory)	320,225
Western Australia	48,626
Tasmania	145,290
New Zealand (exclusive of about 41,500 Maoris)	625,662

In the preceding table due allowance has been made for unrecorded departures, and in the case of Western Australia for unrecorded arrivals which took place in the northern parts of that enormous territory where there did not exist proper official means of keeping account of the adventurers, who, from time to time, attracted by rumours of its vast natural resources, visited that comparatively unknown land. It will be seen that the population of Australasia was estimated at 3,787,894 at the end of 1890, the proportion belonging to each Colony being as follows:—New South Wales, 29·62; Victoria, 29·92; Queensland, 10·38; South Australia, 8·45; Western Australia, 1·28; Tasmania, 3·83; New Zealand, 16·52.

The estimated population of the Colony at the close of each year, from 1861 to 1890, will be found hereunder:— Estimated population of the Colony.

Population of New South Wales.

Year.	Males.	Females.	Total.
1861	201,574	156,404	357,978
1862	204,199	162,522	366,721
1863	207,560	170,152	377,712
1864	213,365	177,499	390,864
1865	223,254	185,893	409,147
1866	235,116	193,697	428,813
1867	243,131	201,578	444,709
1868	254,003	209,185	463,188
1869	263,899	217,549	481,448
1870	272,543	226,116	498,659
1871	282,846	234,912	517,758
1872	292,015	243,204	535,219
1873	301,399	252,434	553,833
1874	312,843	262,100	574,943
1875	323,080	271,217	594,297
1876	333,515	280,666	614,181
1877	350,329	293,378	643,707
1878	365,625	306,263	671,888
1879	386,926	322,533	709,459
1880	409,030	338,920	747,950
1881	429,020	353,060	782,080
1882	447,100	367,900	815,000
1883	473,980	387,330	861,310
1884	498,310	406,670	904,980
1885	523,030	426,540	949,570
1886	543,260	446,080	989,340
1887	558,350	461,980	1,020,330
1888	573,190	477,890	1,051,080
1889	589,010	492,810	1,081,820
1890	609,650	512,210	1,121,860

Net increase.

The following table gives the net increase of male and female population during each year since 1880, after allowing for the number of persons whose departure from the Colony was not formally recorded.

Increase of Population.

Year.	Males.	Females.	Total.
1881	19,990	14,140	34,130
1882	18,080	14,840	32,920
1883	26,880	19,430	46,310
1884	24,330	19,340	43,670
1885	24,720	19,870	44,590
1886	20,230	19,540	39,770
1887	15,090	15,900	30,990
1888	14,840	15,910	30,750
1889	15,820	14,920	30,740
1890	20,640	19,400	40,040

Annual rate of increase—Australasia.

In the following table will be found the rate at which population has increased during each of the last ten years in the various colonies, the average rate for Australasia being 3·39 per cent.

Growth of Population.—Yearly Increase per cent.

	New South Wales.	Victoria.	Queensland.	South Australia.	Western Australia.	Tasmania.	New Zealand.
1881	4·56	2·21	5·36	6·85	3·60	3·20	3·14
1882	4 21	2·24	9·14	2·32	3·07	2·30	3·14
1883	5·68	2·35	15·57	3·56	3·42	2·34	4·23
1884	5·07	2·59	7·47	2·52	4·56	2·76	4·06
1885	4·93	2·61	4·97	0·37	7·41	1·76	2·93
1886	4·19	3·23	4·56	— 0·53	13·53	1·83	2·25
1887	3·13	3·25	5·90	1·29	8 02	3·32	2·24
1888	3·01	4 26	4·03	— 0·55	— 0·45	1·75	0·44
1889	2·92	2·48	3·40	1·40	4·09	2·77	1·98
1890	3·70	2·68	2·35	1·08	6·32	2·25	1·54
Mean of 10 years.	4·14	2·79	6·28	1·83	5·36	2·43	2·60

Minus sign (—) denotes a decrease.

The growth of population in the continent of Australia, and also in the whole of Australasia, from 1860 to the end of last year, is shown in the following table:— Growth of Population.

Population of Australia and Australasia.

Year.	Continent of Australia.	Australasia.
1860	1,054,061	1,221,547
1861	1,076,666	1,265,896
1862	1,118,249	1,334,789
1863	1,168,761	1,424,828
1864	1,231,715	1,497,180
1865	1,293,507	1,579,315
1866	1,345,068	1,646,540
1867	1,389,383	1,706,506
1868	1,442,736	1,770,960
1869	1,495,196	1,834,037
1870	1,549,407	1,898,572
1871	1,601,295	1,970,066
1872	1,645,479	2,027,964
1873	1,696,398	2,096,561
1874	1,752,566	2,196,602
1875	1,804,135	2,283,654
1876	1,855,996	2,360,555
1877	1,926,987	2,451,713
1878	1,981,730	2,524,196
1879	2,049,224	2,625,429
1880	2,116,156	2,715,782
1881	2,204,495	2,822,999
1882	2,285,360	2,922,256
1883	2,402,760	3,064,304
1884	2,500,765	3,187,565
1885	2,592,906	3,296,318
1886	2,677,911	3,396,658
1887	2,768,537	3,506,882
1888	2,855,705	3,599,086
1889	2,931,978	3,691,190
1890	3,016,942	3,788,851

As tested by the voluntary influx of population, the attraction which New South Wales has for many years offered to the settler are most marked, and no test could be more practical. As long as the balance of attraction remained with the other colonies,

Marked advantages of N.S.W. to settlers.

so long did the tide of immigration set to their shores; many years past New South Wales has offered a more sub reward to the settler than any of its neighbours, and the seen in the increased numbers who have come hither.

Excess of Arrivals over Departures in each of the Aust Colonies between the Census of 1881 and 1891 :—

Colony.	Net Increase due to Immigra
New South Wales	165,096
Victoria	116,361
Queensland	102,776
South Australia	23,278
Western Australia	14,106
Continent of Australia	370,061
Tasmania	5,961
New Zealand	7,437
Australasia	383,459

Increase by immigration.

The above table shows that out of a total increase by gration of 383,459 persons, the large proportion of 43 p found a home in New South Wales, as against 30 pe attracted to Victoria, and 24 per cent. to Queensland. total of 165,096 credited to New South Wales are i 34,079 assisted immigrants. During the same period assisted immigrants arrived in Queensland, but as t increase from immigration was only 102,776, it is evide some of the immigrants did not remain in that Colony.

Since 1860, the year following the separation of Queensl arrivals in New South Wales have in every year exceeded th tures. The greatest apparent excess during any one year 1883, when the number of arrivals was greater than the tures by 28,579.

Assisted immigration.

Assisted immigration dates from 1832, and continued to settled policy of the country, with slight interruptions, u practical cessation during 1888. The number of assis migrants arriving in New South Wales from 1860 to th of 1890 will be found herewith.

Assisted Immigrants.

Year.	Adults.			Children under 12 Years.			Total.
	Males.	Females.	Total.	Males.	Females.	Total.	
1860	1,351	1,235	2,586	245	258	503	3,089
1861	794	595	1,389	101	99	200	1,589
1862	1,172	1,047	2,219	214	198	412	2,631
1863	1,966	1,872	3,838	391	404	795	4,633
1864	1,701	1,672	3,373	289	315	604	3,977
1865	1,073	1,214	2,287	213	217	430	2,717
1866	501	543	1,044	92	68	160	1,204
1867	385	435	820	66	58	124	944
1868	183	215	398	41	31	72	470
1869	......	47	47	......	......	......	47
1870	......	......	......	......	......	......	......
1871	28	299	327	15	15	30	357
1872	25	271	296	16	14	30	326
1873	13	119	122	3	5	8	140
1874	427	411	838	109	133	242	1,080
1875	395	324	719	135	119	254	973
1876	642	429	1,071	208	184	392	1,463
1877	2,892	1,627	4,519	743	756	1,499	6,018
1878	2,091	1,754	3,845	699	646	1,345	5,190
1879	1,906	2,141	4,047	840	844	1,684	5,731
1880	1,150	1,195	2,345	414	375	789	3,134
1881	929	1,029	1,958	327	292	619	2,577
1882	1,209	991	2,200	509	524	1,033	3,233
1883	3,370	2,718	6,088	1,154	1,127	2,281	8,369
1884	2,785	2,606	5,391	1,095	1,082	2,177	7,568
1885	1,871	2,211	4,082	736	736	1,472	5,554
1886	1,044	1,905	2,949	572	560	1,132	4,081
1887	131	687	818	286	258	544	1,362
1888	58	190	248	149	131	280	528
1889	44	168	212	104	115	219	431
1890	55	132	187	110	79	189	376
Total...	30,191	30,082	60,273	9,876	9,643	19,519	79,792

The birthplaces of immigrants cannot in all cases be accurately determined, but it is quite clear, from the different census returns, that the great bulk has come from the United Kingdom, as will presently appear. A record, however, has been kept of the native countries of immigrants who were assisted by Government, and of the 79,792 persons enumerated in the foregoing table, 78,071 were British born—37,688 being from England and Wales; 31,823 from Ireland; and 8,560 from Scotland; and the remainder, 1,721, from other countries. Birthplaces of immigrants.

The total number of persons arriving in the Colony by sea, and also the number departing therefrom, during each year from 1880 to 1890, are hereunder notified :—

Arrivals by sea.

Year.	Adults.			*Children.	Total Immigrants.
	Male.	Female	Total.		
1880	26,894	10,499	37,393	5,535	45,870
1881	30,538	10,645	41,183	4,449	50,097
1882	29,102	10,904	40,006	5,100	46,113
1883	40,914	15,852	56,766	7,135	65,837
1884	44,667	17,579	62,246	6,899	71,336
1885	46,570	18,352	64,922	7,885	75,738
1886	45,035	18,334	63,369	5,535	71,996
1887	43,769	15,236	59,005	4,413	67,854
1888	40,473	15,605	56,078	4,435	62,361
1889	39,401	16,888	56,289	4,855	61,151
1890	43,274	19,225	62,499	5,285	67,799

* Sexes no stated by shipping authorities.

Departures by sea.

Year.	Adults.			* Children.	Total Emigrants.
	Male.	Female.	Total.		
1880	16,270	7,054	23,324	2,359	26,559
1881	18,668	7,273	25,941	2,484	29,354
1882	18,672	6,857	25,529	2,512	28,925
1883	23,407	8,739	32,146	3,176	36,724
1884	29,311	10,685	39,996	3,599	44,633
1885	31,060	11,508	42,568	3,707	48,001
1886	34,453	11,841	46,294	2,736	50,913
1887	38,162	12,439	50,601	3,619	56,993
1888	36,535	14,744	51,309	4,070	56,941
1889	32,791	14,277	47,068	3,753	51,762
1890	34,444	15,683	50,127	4,043	54,807

* Sexes not stated by shipping authorities.

BIRTHPLACES OF THE PEOPLE.

Tendency of immigrants to live in large cities.

There is a tendency operating in all new countries for immigrants to locate themselves in and near the large cities. This colony has been no exception to the rule, and it will be seen from subsequent tables that the percentage of British born and foreigners residing in the metropolis is higher than for the rest of the colony, and the native-born correspondingly lower.

Proportion of native-born increasing.

As far back as 1861, when the native-born population amounted to only 45·69 per cent. of the whole colony, the number living in Sydney and its suburbs formed only 42·13 per cent. of the total, while British born colonists, amounting to 46·18 per cent. of the population, constituted 52·93 per cent. of the metropolitan population. No great difference is observable between the proportion of persons attracted to New South Wales from other colonies who remained in Sydney during late years, and those who made the country districts their home. What difference there is favours the supposition that the metropolis has proved more attractive. The non-British population have, as a rule, preferred the country districts to Sydney; but of late years there has been a tendency on the part of certain foreign elements to gravitate towards Sydney; this is especially noticeable amongst Chinese and Hindoos, as well as Syrians and others from the Levant.

Birthplaces of the people.

The following table shows the proportion per cent. of each element of the population at the three periods 1861, 1871, and 1881, to the whole city population, and also the proportion which each bore to the whole community:—

Birthplaces of the People.

Year.	Native Born of New South Wales.		Natives of other Australian Colonies.		Other British-born Subjects.		Foreigners.	
	Per cent. of population, metropolitan.	Per cent. of total population.	Per cent. of population, metropolitan.	Per cent. of total population.	Per cent. of population, metropolitan.	Per cent. of total population.	Per cent. of population, metropolitan.	Per cent. of total population.
1861	42·13	45·69	1·77	1·34	52·93	46·18	3·17	6·79
1871	54·24	58·57	3·07	2·67	40·22	34·85	2·47	3·91
1881	56·87	62·17	6·18	5·95	33·62	27·97	3·33	3·91

Racial composition of people.

The racial composition of the people at the three censuses—of 1861, 1871, and 1881—will be seen from the following table:—

Racial Composition of Population.

Nationality.	1861.	1871.	1881.
	per cent.	per cent.	per cent.
New South Wales	45·69	58·38	61·95
Other Australasian Colonies	1·34	2·67	5·95
Aborigines	...	0·19	0·22
English	23·98	17·33	14·32
Irish	15·63	12·49	9·21
Scotch	5·19	3·98	3·34
Welsh	0·39	0·37	0·41
Other British Subjects	0·99	0·68	0·69
Total, British Subjects	93·21	96·09	96·09
Chinese	3·70	1·43	1·36
German	1·56	1·31	1·00
Other Foreigners	1·53	1·17	1·55
Total, Foreigners	6·79	3·91	3·91

CENTRALIZATION OF POPULATION.

Tendency of population towards cities.

One of the most notable problems in the progress of modern civilization is the tendency, everywhere exhibited in the chief countries of the world, of the population to accumulate in great cities. Not only is this apparent in England, France, and other countries, where the development of manufactures has brought about an entire change in the employment of the people, and has necessarily caused their aggregation in towns, but it is seen also in the United States, the most favoured country for the agricultural labourer.

The conditions of progress in these colonies approximate somewhat to those of the United States, and a comparison between the increase of town population there and in New South Wales is not without interest. The great defect in the comparison arises from the fact that in America there exist many large cities; in New South Wales there is practically only one. The population of the United States for three periods, and the proportion of rural to city population, will be seen below:— Comparison of colonies with America.

Population of the United States.

Year.	Population of the United States.	Population of Cities of United States.	Percentage of whole population in Cities.
1860	31,443,321	5,072,256	16·1
1870	38,558,371	8,071,875	20·7
1880	50,155,783	11,318,547	22·5

The rapid increase of city population shown above has given rise to considerable speculation. It seems an established fact that the movement of population towards the towns in the old countries of the world is a sign of a desire for improvement in the circumstances manifested by the ruder population; for, like every other commodity, labour gravitates to the market where it will obtain the highest price. In America the increase in town population has been derived mainly from abroad; and there seems no reason to suppose that, large as the proportion of urban population has become, it has reached an unhealthy stage. In Australasia, however, the case is different, and it is impossible to believe that healthy progress is consistent with the wonderful growth of the metropolis at the expense of the country. Causes which lead to increase in cities.

In this colony the proportion of town population is even more remarkable than in the United States, as will be seen from the table here given, showing the percentage of population of Sydney and suburbs as compared with New South Wales as a whole:— Urban and rural population.

New South Wales Population.

Year.	Metropolitan.	Country.
	per cent.	per cent.
1861	26·70	73·30
1871	26·73	73·27
1881	30·34	69·66
1890	33·88	66·12

In regard to the neighbouring Colony of Victoria, the figures are:—

Victorian Population.

Year.	Metropolitan.	Country.
	Per cent.	Per cent.
1861	25·89	74·11
1871	28·87	71·13
1881	32·81	67·19
1890	42·76	57·24

Proportion of urban population.

In the table of urban population of the United States on the preceding page, is included all towns exceeding 8,000 inhabitants; nevertheless, the proportion to the whole is much less than in either New South Wales or Victoria. The case of Melbourne is even more marked than that of Sydney; for during the period comprised in the table, the former city increased proportionately more than the latter, as compared with the population of its colony, and its numerical increase has also been greater.

Population of the City and Suburbs of Sydney and Melbourne.

Year.	Sydney.	Melbourne.
1861	95,596	139,860
1871	136,483	206,780
1881	237,300	296,347
1884	277,630	349,166
1885	292,550	368,788
1886	308,270	389,512
1887	324,830	411,400
1888	342,280	434,519
1889	360,670	458,937
1890	380,040	484,630

Extraordinary progress of Sydney and Melbourne.

The progress of these cities has been extraordinary, and has no parallel amongst the cities of the Old World. Even in America the rise of the great cities has been accompanied by a somewhat corresponding increase in the rural population. In these colonies, perhaps for the first time in the history of the world, is seen the spectacle of magnificent cities growing with wonderful rapidity, and embracing within their limits one-third of the population of the territory on which they depend. The chief cities of the other Australian colonies present somewhat similar features to Sydney and Melbourne, but with the exception of Adelaide, which contains nearly two-fifths of the whole population of South Australia, they are not so large in proportion to their rural population as either Sydney or Melbourne.

The population of the chief cities of the Australasian Colonies is given below :— Population of Australasian cities.

City.	Population, 5th April, 1891.
Sydney	386,859
Melbourne	490,902
Adelaide	133,252
Brisbane	101,554
Wellington	33,224
Hobart	34,028
Perth	9,617

Wellington, the capital of New Zealand, is not the most populous city in that colony; Auckland, which was the seat of Government and the capital until 1865, contains a much larger population, the census of 1891 giving a total of 51,287 persons.

Sydney stands alone amongst Australian cities for convenience of position and natural advantages for external and internal trade. Nor has the progress it has made in wealth and population been less than expectation warranted. The growth of population within the municipal boundaries of the city forms an interesting feature in the progress of the colony. In the table given below the population set down for the years previous to 1871 is that ascertained at the date of different census; from 1871 the figures show the estimated population at the close of the year :— Growth of Sydney.

Population of Sydney within its Municipal Boundari

Year.	Persons.	Year.	Persons.	Year.	Persons.	Year.	[illegible]
1828	10,815	1861	56,394	1877	91,008	1884	[illegible]
1833	16,232	1871	77,680	1878	94,228	1885	[illegible]
1836	19,729	1872	79,455	1879	98,824	1886	[illegible]
1841	29,973	1873	81,482	1880	102,160	1887	[illegible]
1846	38,358	1874	83,631	1881	106,580	1888	[illegible]
1851	44,240	1875	85,267	1882	110,110	1889	[illegible]
1856	53,358	1876	87,261	1883	115,850	1890	[illegible]

Growth of metropolitan population.

At the census of 1861 the population of the whole met was 95,596; ten years later it had risen to 136,483; while census of 1881 the number had reached 224,211; and at the 1890 the estimated number of persons in Sydney and its was, as already stated, 380,040. The progress of the popu in the city and suburbs will be found in the following which also includes the country districts, and the whole commencing with the year 1880.

Estimated Population of the Metropolitan and Country Di and New South Wales, on the 31st December of each 1880–90.

Year.	Metropolitan.			Country.	New South Wale		
	City.	Suburbs.	Total.		Males.	Females.	[illegible]
1880	102,160	123,040	225,200	522,750	409,030	[illegible]	
1881	106,580	130,720	237,300	544,780	429,020	[illegible]	
1882	110,110	139,940	250,050	564,950	447,100	367,900	
1883	115,850	147,630	263,480	597,830	473,980	[illegible]	
1884	121,440	156,190	277,630	627,350	498,310	406,670	
1885	122,910	169,640	292,550	657,020	523,030	[illegible]	
1886	124,380	183,890	308,270	681,070	543,260	446,080	
1887	121,160	203,670	324,830	695,500	558,850	[illegible]	[illegible]
1888	118,020	224,260	342,280	708,800	573,190	477,9[illegible]	[illegible]
1889	114,960	245,710	360,670	721,150	589,010	492,810	[illegible]
1890	111,980	268,060	380,040	741,820	609,650	512,210	[illegible]

NOTE.—The figures in this table have been recast since last publication.

The increase of population during the twenty years closed with 1890 has been 170 per cent. for the metropolis, that of the country districts amounted to 97 per cent. The lation of the whole colony has more than doubled itself this period; the total for 1890 showing an increase of 11 cent. on the total for 1871.

The area of the metropolitan district incorporated is nearly 120 square miles, or 76,417 acres, so that the average density of population at the end of the year was 5 persons per acre, some of the more immediate suburbs being almost as densely populated as the city itself. The area of land permanently dedicated for public recreation in the metropolis comprises 3,761 acres (776 acres in the city, and 2,985 in the suburbs; this includes the Centennial Park, the area of which is about 780 acres), equal to nearly one twentieth of the total extent of the district, which must certainly be looked upon as a very liberal provision for the maintenance of public health. This is quite apart from the National Park, an area of 36,320 acres, which is within an hour's journey by train of the city. The area of Melbourne and suburbs is 163,942 acres, or about 256 square miles, and the population at the census of the year 1891 was 491,378; this shows a density of population of 3 persons to the acre. The area taken for Melbourne is an arbitrary one, being the land included within a radius of 10 miles of the centre of the city. An area of 256 square miles around Sydney would include Parramatta, Hunter's Hill, Ryde, and surroundings, and would at the close of 1890 have embraced a population of probably not fewer than 400,000—a number less by 85,000 than the Melbourne metropolitan population. **Area of the metropolis.**

The suburbs of Sydney consist of the following districts, which are here grouped according to locality:—*North-western*—Balmain, Leichhardt, Glebe; *West Central*—Newtown, St. Peters, Camperdown, Macdonaldtown; *East Central*—Redfern, Darlington, Waterloo, Alexandria, Botany; *Eastern*—Paddington, Randwick, Waverley, Woollahra; *Western*—Ashfield, Burwood, Five Dock, Drummoyne, Marrickville, Petersham; *Southern*—Canterbury, Hurstville, Kogarah, Rockdale; and *North Shore*—North Sydney, Manly, Ryde, and Hunter's Hill.

The population of the suburbs has more than doubled itself since the census of 1881. The increase has been general, varying from 92 per cent. in the east central districts of Redfern, **Suburbs of Sydney.**

Waterloo, &c., to 216 per cent. in the western and southern suburbs, which constitute the *electorate* of Canterbury :—

Suburbs.	Population, 1881.	Estimated population, 5th April, 1891.	Increase per cent.
North-western	27,785	57,521	107
West central	15,991	34,701	118
East central	25,664	49,294	92
Eastern	20,220	43,477	115
Western	18,129	50,808	180
Southern	2,033	12,842	532
North Shore	11,010	30,972	181

Municipalities.

The suburbs of Sydney comprise thirty-four distinct municipalities. The population of those in existence at the date of the census of 1881 and at that of 1891, will be found below :—

Population of the various Municipalities.

Municipality.	Population at Census of 1881.	Estimated population 5th April, 1891.	Municipality.	Population at Census of 1881.	Estimated population 5th April, 1891.
Alexandria	3,449	7,486	Macdonaldtown	1,870	5,286
Ashfield	4,087	11,811	Manly	1,327	3,438
Balmain	15,063	24,320	Marrickville	3,501	13,491
Botany	......	2,059	Newtown	8,327	17,884
Botany, North	......	2,392	North Willoughby	1,411	3,318
Burwood	2,472	6,030	North Sydney	7,149	16,836
Camperdown	3,522	6,753	Paddington	9,608	18,414
Canterbury	1,175	2,428	Petersham	3,413	10,374
Concord	......	2,317	Randwick	2,079	6,302
Darlington	2,026	3,418	Redfern	10,868	21,363
Enfield	......	2,054	Rockdale	858	5,161
Five Dock	888	1,250	Ryde	1,673	3,542
The Glebe	10,500	17,085	St. Peter's	2,272	4,846
Hunter's Hill	2,282	3,675	Strathfield	......	2,092
Hurstville	......	3,194	Waterloo	5,762	8,722
Kogarah	......	2,658	Waverley	2,365	8,853
Leichhardt	1,866	17,069	Woollahra	6,168	10,172

Municipalities outside the metropolis.

At the time of the census of 1881 there were only sixty boroughs and municipalities outside the metropolis, but now there are one hundred and twenty-one. The following are their names and the most recent estimates of population :—

Population of Chief Country Municipalities, April, 1890.

Country Municipalities.	Estimated Population.	Country Municipalities.	Estimated Population.	Country Municipalities.	Estimated Population.
Adamstown	6,000	Gundagai	951	Penrith	3,686
Albury	5,452	Gunnedah	1,388	Plattsburg	3,300
Armidale	3,834	Hamilton	4,836	Port Macquarie	962
Ballina	1,488	Hay	2,731	Prospect and	
Balranald	660	Hill End	784	Sherwood	2,067
Bathurst	9,069	Hillston	762	Queanbeyan	1,261
Bega	1,619	Illawarra, Central	2,700	Quirindi	264
Berry	1,609	,, North	2,515	Raymond Terrace	843
Bingara	738	Inverell	2,566	Richmond	1,242
Blayney	1,255	Jerilderie	540	Scone	876
Bombala	1,101	Junee	1,617	Shellharbour	1,596
Bourke	3,256	Katoomba	1,626	Shoalhaven,	
Bowral	2,286	Kempsey	2,145	Central	452
Broken Hill	19,792	Kiama }	4,530	Silverton	1,390
Broughton Vale	600	,, East }		Singleton }	2,603
Burrowa	769	Lambton	3,434	,, South }	
Camden	1,305	,, New	1,548	Smithfield and	
Campbelltown	1,022	Lismore	2,949	Fairfield	1,368
Carcoar	562	Lithgow	3,838	St. Mary's	1,897
Carrington	2,112	Liverpool	4,464	Stockton	2,416
Casino	2,024	Maclean	913	Tamworth	4,603
Cobar	1,191	Maitland, East	2,693	Taree	712
Condobolin	747	,, West	7,214	Tenterfield	2,477
Cooma	1,739	Merewether	4,340	Tumut	1,260
Coonamble	1,155	Mittagong	1,489	Ulladulla	1,629
Cootamundra	2,028	Molong	1,131	Ulmarra	1,601
Cowra	1,555	Moree	1,165	Uralla	651
Cudal	650	Morpeth	1,131	Wagga Wagga	4,589
Cudgegong	2,438	Moss Vale	1,256	Walcha	953
Deniliquin	2,275	Mudgee	2,871	Wallsend	3,642
Dubbo	4,584	Murrumburrah	1,300	Waratah	2,719
Dundas	1,600	Murrurundi	1,252	Wellington	1,562
Forbes	3,028	Musclebrook	1,301	Wentworth	891
Gerringong	1,360	Narrabri	1,982	Wickham	6,586
Glen Innes	2,528	Narrandera	1,687	Wilcannia	1,205
Gosford	679	Newcastle	12,913	Windsor	2,026
Goulburn	10,902	Nowra	1,705	Wingham	494
Grafton	4,447	Numba	1,060	Wollongong	3,043
Granville	4,000	Orange	3,235	Yass	1,853
Grenfell	746	,, East	1,829	Young	2,692
Greta	1,751	Parkes	3,005		
Gulgong	1,289	Parramatta	11,680		

The great bulk of the population dwells along the seaboard. Outside the metropolis the most thickly peopled districts are the fertile valleys of the rivers. Amongst these, in point of population, the Hunter River valley, with large agricultural and mining indus-

Population densest along seaboard.

tries, stands first. The Illawarra district, rich in coal and p comes next; then the maize and sugar-growing country Clarence and the Richmond. The settlement of populatio nally followed the main roads of the Colony, and is now draw great trunk lines of railway, which have almost superseded

NATURALIZATION.

Law relating to aliens.

The law relating to the naturalization of foreigners i South Wales is mainly contained in two statutes. The

Denization Act.

these is the Denization Act of 1828, 9 George IV, No. 6. Act enables the Governor, or Acting Governor, to grant le denization to such foreigners as may arrive in the Colony recommendation to that effect from the Principal Secretary for the Colonies, such letters of denization to entitle the h all the rights, privileges, and advantages in the Colony British-born citizen could claim. The second enactment

Naturalization Act.

upon the question is that known as the Naturalization New South Wales, 39 Victoria, No. 19, which was passed i and assented to in 1876, having been reserved for the pleasure. This Act provides that an alien in New South may hold and acquire real and personal property, but shall qualified for any office nor enjoy either a municipal or parlian franchise; he shall not be qualified to be the owner of a ship, nor have any rights and privileges except such as are ex conferred upon him. After a residence in the Colony of n than five years a foreigner may apply for letters of naturali and the Governor may give or withhold the same as he thin for the public good. Such letters if granted are to be of n until the oath of allegiance has been taken, after which the becomes in every respect entitled to all the privileges which to those who are British by birth. The only case in which n zation is no longer permitted is in regard to the Chinese, was provided for by special legislation, as will be shown he

There were 99 foreigners naturalized in this Colony during the year 1890. Their length of residence in New South Wales ranged from five to thirty-four years. Twenty had been resident more than twenty years in the Colony. Of European races the Germans have availed themselves most largely of the privileges of naturalization, the number of certificates issued to them amounting to nearly one-fourth of the total number granted within the past ten years. The following table shows the native countries of those colonists who obtained certificates of naturalization during each year, from 1881 to 1890:—

Naturalization of Germans.

Naturalization of Foreigners.

Native Countries.	1881.	1882.	1883.	1884.	1885.	1886.	1887.	1888.	1889.	1890.	Total.
France	5	3	4	3	10	8	8	7	9	6	63
Spain	...	...	...	1	...	...	...	1	...	1	3
Portugal	1	1	1	...	...	...	...	3	2	...	8
Switzerland	1	...	4	4	1	3	1	1	3	5	23
Italy	4	3	4	3	4	5	6	6	5	5	45
Germany	34	32	46	44	47	45	48	32	58	34	420
Austria	4	1	3	8	1	5	3	3	6	3	37
Holland	2	...	2	2	1	2	3	1	2	3	18
Belgium	...	...	...	...	...	2	...	...	...	...	2
Denmark	7	5	12	11	7	18	19	10	15	9	113
Norway	8	1	3	6	3	4	5	9	8	3	50
Sweden	7	5	13	8	17	10	13	17	13	18	121
Russia	2	2	2	3	7	6	3	5	5	7	42
Poland	...	...	2	4	4	4	3	5	1	2	25
Greece	1	1	2	1	1	2	3	2	4	...	17
Turkey	...	...	...	...	...	...	...	...	1	...	1
Bulgaria	...	...	...	1	...	...	...	...	...	...	1
Roumania	...	...	...	...	..	...	...	1	1	...	2
China	31	93	301	265	22	5	1	...	...	...	718
Syria	...	...	...	...	...	...	...	3	...	...	3
Penang	...	...	...	...	...	...	1	...	...	...	1
Persia	...	...	1	...	...	...	...	...	...	...	1
Egypt	...	...	...	...	...	...	...	...	1	1	2
America	...	..	4	2	...	...	1	...	3	...	10
United States	...	...	1	...	2	1	...	...	...	1	5
Western Islands	1	...	...	...	1	4	..	...	...	...	6
Corsica	...	...	1	...	...	...	...	...	...	...	1
New Caledonia	...	...	...	...	...	...	1	...	...	...	1
Japan	...	...	...	...	...	...	...	...	...	1	1
Unknown	...	...	...	1	...	...	...	...	...	...	1
Total	108	147	406	367	128	124	119	106	137	99	1,741

Large number of Chinese naturalized.

From this it will be seen that the Chinese have, until late y more than any other nation, evinced a desire to become Br subjects; and the tendency is even more marked in Victoria, w out of 3,621 persons naturalized during the ten years from to 1888, no fewer than 2,939 were born in China, the gre number naturalized in any one year being 1,178 in 1885. result of the Conference held in Sydney in 1888, reference to w is made a few pages further on, has been to place a bar to naturalization of the Chinese as well as to restrict the num arriving in the Colonies. The total number of persons natura in New South Wales from 26th July, 1849, to 31st Decen 1890, was 6,051.

Of those naturalized during 1890, there were 1 blacksmit bakers, 1 boatman, 1 commercial traveller, 3 contractor clergyman, 1 cook, 1 clothier, 1 civil engineer, 1 draper, 1 f grower, 9 carpenters, 13 farmers, 2 grocers, 1 glazier, 1 ge dealer, 1 hairdresser, 12 labourers, 4 miners, 3 gardene medical practitioner, 1 merchant, 1 messenger, 2 furniture dea 4 engineers, 3 master mariners, 1 publican, 3 tobacconist tailor, 1 tanner, 2 selectors, 1 sawyer, 13 sailors, 1 storeke 1 restaurant-keeper, 1 woolscourer, and 1 stationer.

CHINESE POPULATION.

Chinese undesirable as colonists.

The uniformity with which the different colonies have pa laws restricting the immigration of Chinese, and prohibiting t landing, except upon payment of a heavy poll-tax, may be ta as some evidence of the undesirability of the race as colon At the census of 1861 there were in the Colony 12,988 Chin in 1871 the number had fallen to 7,220; rising again in 188 10,205. For many years New South Wales offered little inc ment to the Chinese as a place of settlement, the sup attractiveness of Victoria and other colonies, as gold produ claiming their attention. At the rush to Lambing Flat in 1 however, large numbers of Chinese came across the border established themselves in this Colony, their strength being constantly recruited by fresh arrivals from China; but these Chinese did not remain in the Colony, for at the census of 1871 there were 5,768 less than ten years previously, and it is probable that although the census of 1891 shows only 12,781, in 1889 the number was nearly 15,000. Immigration and emigration of Chinese.

The numbers of Chinese arriving at and departing from New South Wales since 1871 will be found in the following table :—

Year.	Arrivals.	Departures.	Year.	Arrivals.	Departures.
1871	426	441	1881	4,465	929
1872	229	597	1882	1,007	884
1873	406	400	1883	1,936	1,402
1874	863	933	1884	2,191	1,038
1875	625	1,209	1885	2,929	1,726
1876	696	940	1886	3,092	1,883
1877	884	490	1887	4,436	2,773
1878	2,485	1,560	1888	1,848	1,562
1879	1,979	557	1889	7	941
1880	2,942	876	1890	15	637

It will be seen that 1878 and the following years are marked by a large increase in the arrivals from China. The influx appeared in 1881 sufficiently formidable to demand the interference of the Legislature. Accordingly, the "Influx of Chinese Restriction Act" was passed, with the result that the subsequent year was marked by a decrease in the arrivals to the extent of 3,458, since which time there has been a steady increase until 1888, when legislation again stepped in, this time with more stringent regulations, to restrict the numbers arriving on these shores. It would seem, from a comparison of the amount of poll-tax collected (£10 a head until July, 1888, when it was raised to £100) with the recorded arrivals, that a very considerable proportion of the Chinese immigrants were already British subjects, or had availed themselves of the privilege granted by the Act of returning to the Colony after an absence of nine months without paying a second tax. This is evidently so to a large extent, for from the 6th December, 1881, the date of the Act just mentioned, to the 11th Influx of Chinese to New South Wales.

Evasion of poll-tax.

July, 1888, when the present Act became law, 3,178 certi of exemption were issued in this Colony to Chinese, the d the last certificate being the 28th April, 1888, and of this n 1,788 have been received from returned Chinese. No such ficates have been granted since the passing of the "C Restriction and Regulation Act of 1888."

Year.	Chinese arriving.	Chinese paying Poll-tax.
1882	1,007	852
1883	1,936	1,220
1884	2,191	1,074
1885	2,929	1,060
1886	3,092	1,284
1887	4,436	1,798
1888	1,848	462
1889	7	1
1890	15	3

Chinese immigration in Australia increasing.

There has very clearly been an increasing desire durin last few years on the part of the Chinese to migrate to tralia. This of late brought about considerable discussion, culminated in a Conference of delegates from all the co being held in Sydney in 1888. As a result, the Confe prepared a draft bill, which was afterwards submitted to the P ments of the different colonies. The bill provided that stringent regulations should be enforced to check the infl Chinese to these shores; and although it was not deemed adv that their landing should be prohibited altogether, yet it wa sidered necessary that such a limit should be placed to the nu privileged to land as would prove an efficient check to Ch immigration. Before the Conference met, progress had been in the New South Wales Legislature with a bill which was proc with after the Conference adjourned, and became law on the July, 1888. By this measure vessels are prohibited from car to the Colony more than one Chinese passenger to every 300 Chinese landing are to pay a poll-tax of £100, and are not to e in mining, without express authority under the hand and s

Recent legislation against influx.

the Minister of Mines, nor are they permitted to become naturalized. The penalty for a breach of the Act is £500. The Act has already operated to the entire cessation of Chinese immigration.

It is estimated that in the beginning of the year 1890 there were 45,381 Chinese in the Australasian colonies, exclusive of Fiji. When the census of 1881 was taken the total number in the colonies was set down as 43,706, which is 3,727 less than the present estimate. Chinese in the colonies in 1890

Chinese in the Australasian Colonies, 1890.

Colony.	Number.
New South Wales	13,529
Victoria	11,290
Queensland	7,691
South Australia	6,660
New Zealand	4,585
Tasmania	1,000
Western Australia	626
Total	45,381

ABORIGINES.

This name, signifying "from the origin," was given to the earliest known inhabitants of Italy, but is now applied to the original or primitive inhabitants of any country. As the history of the native race in these colonies is so entwined with the progress of the British people in Australia, a few words concerning them may not be out of place. The aborigines of Australia form a distinct race, and it may be presumed that the whole of them throughout the continent sprang from the same stock, although it is remarkable that their languages differ so greatly that tribes within short distances of each other are often quite Aborigines.

unable to understand each other; and in fact almost every community of natives has its own peculiar dialect. It is diffic form a correct estimate of their numbers, and while there is r to believe that some generations ago they were very num there is ample evidence of late years that in many places are decreasing; and they may now be counted by fives where were formerly counted by hundreds. In Tasmania they hav appeared altogether, the last of the tribe in that colony h died in 1876.

Estimate by Governor Phillip.

It is recorded that Governor Phillip estimated the abori population about the close of the last century at one mil the number between Broken Bay and Botany Bay appeari have been about 3,000. It is impossible to say how far this mate was in accordance with fact; for, although at the ti did not probably seem an exaggerated conjecture in the face large a number as 3,000 having been found within the small between the bays above mentioned; yet, considering how sm portion of the territory was then explored by the early set the statement must be accepted as what it professes to be, na an estimate at a time when the data to hand were very lim

Aborigines at census of 1881.

At the census of 1881 the aborigines in Australia were to number 31,700, distributed as follows:—

Aborigines in Australian Colonies, 1881.

Colony.	Males.	Females.	Total
New South Wales	938	705	1,64
Victoria	460	320	78
Queensland	10,719	9,866	20,58
South Australia	3,478	2,868	6,34
Western Australia	1,640	706	2,34
Total	17,235	14,465	31,70

Estimate untrustworthy.

There are various reasons for believing that the above does not include the entire aboriginal population of the col

In New South Wales, for instance, only the "civilized" blacks were enumerated in the returns, and, from reliable information since available, it is certain that the actual number, including those in a wild state, was much higher. The figures for Queensland are in a great measure derived from estimates which are considered by the Registrar-General of that colony to be too low, for in his report on the census he says:—"In the northern parts of the colony the aborigines are comparatively numerous, and some persons resident in the Cook and Palmer districts have supposed that there may be 70,000 in Queensland. This, however, is a very crude estimate, and may be far wide of the truth." In the case of South Australia, the aborigines in the Northern Territory were not included in the returns, and it seems probable that they are as numerous in that colony as in Queensland. The census of Western Australia includes only those aboriginals in the employment of the colonists, and as large portions of this, the greatest in area of all the Australasian colonies, are as yet unexplored, it may be presumed that the number of aborigines enumerated in the census is very far short of the total in the colony. The aboriginal population of the entire Continent may be set down at something like 200,000.

The Maoris.

The original inhabitants of New Zealand, or Maoris, as they are called, are quite a different race. They are gifted with a considerable amount of intelligence, quick at imitation, and brave even to rashness; on the other hand they are avaricious, and ofttimes ferocious. According to the census of 1881 they numbered 44,097. Like the Australian aborigines they appear to be decreasing in number, the census of 1886 enumerating only 41,432, although at that of 1891 the total was 41,523. It is believed, however, that at the time the colonists first landed their number was fully 120,000.

Aborigines decreasing.

According to the most recent enumeration, it is estimated that there were 7,700 aborigines in New South Wales in 1890, as compared with 7,529 in 1889. These totals include half-castes, who last year numbered 2,877, and in 1888, 2,767. The number of full-blood aborigines has therefore increased by 41, while the half-castes have increased by 130, so that the increase on the total was 171. The number of births reported during 1890 was 282 (143 of the children being half-castes), and the deaths 223 (38 half-castes). There are three mission stations under the control of the Board. These establishments, when first formed, were little more than camping grounds for the aborigines, where they worked for their rations, elementary instruction being imparted to the children, but now they have developed into settlements, with greatly improved huts for married couples, and adequate accommodation for teaching, duly qualified instructors having been appointed by the Department of Public Instruction. During the year, 7,849 blankets were forwarded from the Government Stores Department to the various Benches of Magistrates for distribution among the blacks. This bounty has been conceded for many years. At the census of 1881 only 4,673 were enumerated, but the returns for 1890 must not be taken as showing an increase, but as proving that at the previous census the aboriginals passed over as being in a wild state far outnumbered those within the bounds of civilization.

Crimes and misfortunes of native blacks.

It has been the misfortune of the aborigines of Australia, as it was of the Carribee, the North American Indian, and the Hottentot, to be found in the way of European colonization; and the blacks have not seen the white man take possession of their territory without many an attempt, by deeds of cunning and of blood, to stop the invasion and to avenge the injury. It would be easy to gather from the records of British colonization in Australia many instances of horrible crimes committed by the aborigines, who are, in fact, partakers of the worst passions of human nature. But it must not be forgotten that, amongst the people of British origin who settled upon the land formerly occupied by the blacks alone, were many whose crimes against the aborigines at least equalled in atrocity any committed by that unfortunate race. Cunning and ferocity were the natural concomitants of such a struggle; and the remembrance of what cunning and ferocity have done

Oral traditions.

tends to make the colonists slow to recognize any characteristics of an opposite kind in the blacks. There is, however, evidence from their songs and their cherished traditions,* that they are by no means destitute of some qualities in which civilized men glory —such as the power of inventing tragic and sarcastic fiction, the thirst for religious mystery, stoical contempt of pain, and reverence for departed friends and ancestors. The manner in which they have displayed these characteristics presents such a strange mixture of wisdom and folly, of elevating and degrading thoughts, of interesting and of repulsive traditions, of pathetic and grotesque observances, that, in order to account for the apparent contradictions, recourse must be had to the supposition that this race has descended from an ancient and higher civilization, of which they have retained some memorials.

THE CENSUS.

Census of the British Dominions.

On the night of Sunday, April 5, 1891, a census was taken throughout Australasia, as well as the other portions of the British Dominions, which comprise about one-fourth of the surface of the habitable globe, and nearly one-fifth of the population of the world. The object of taking the census, and the necessity thereof will be apparent to every thoughtful mind. The information, which can be obtained only by this means, regarding the numbers of the people; the manner in which they are congregated together in some parts, and separated in others, their industrial pursuits, their educational condition, and other particulars, are matters which require to be known in order to deal effectually with the many social and economic problems that constantly arise in the community. For instance, it is important to know how many bread-winners there are among the people, and how many there are dependent upon them through youth, age, or helplessness, in order to make proper provision to render effectual the efforts of the former, and to ameliorate the condition of the latter class. Besides, the census enables comparison to be made with former

Object of taking the census.

* *Vide* Kamilaroi and other Australian Languages, by Rev. W. Ridley, M.A.

Affords means of comparison.

periods, and shows not only where improvement has take[n] but also the directions in which it is necessary to make in[creased] efforts in the future.

Anti-census prejudice formerly existing.

The prejudice against taking a census, which existed a century and a half ago in England to such an extent as [to pre]vent the authorities from taking one, has now died out, an[d] in Australasia the only idea and desire is to make the cen[sus as] perfect as possible. With this object in view a Confere[nce of] Statisticians was held at Hobart in March, 1890, at which [all the] Australasian Colonies were represented. The whole subje[ct was] exhaustively discussed, and matters of detail were careful[ly con]sidered, the result being that uniformity in regard to [the] principal matters of inquiry was agreed upon, at the sam[e time] leaving it free for any Colony to extend the scope of its in[quiry] in any direction where it should be deemed well to go beyo[nd the] general scheme. It was in accordance with the principle[s] agreed upon that the census of 1891 was taken.

Conference of Statisticians.

Scheme of inquiry.

Census of New South Wales.

So far as New South Wales was concerned the requisi[te in]formation was obtained by means of schedules left at [every] dwelling in the Colony, to be filled up by the occupant or [by the] person charged with the duty of delivering and collectin[g the] schedules. The "Householder's Schedule" had to be fill[ed in] with the name of every person who slept or abode in each [house] on census night, with particulars as to relationship to he[ad of] family, sex, age, social condition, occupation, sickness and infir[mity,] birthplace, religion, and degree of education. Another c[olumn] was devoted to particulars descriptive of the dwelling. It w[as] optional whether the information respecting religion were [given] or not, but all the other items were compulsory. There wa[s also] an agricultural schedule, in which minute information was coll[ected] respecting land, live stock, agricultural produce, machiner[y and] implements, and other matters. Other schedules were us[ed to] gather particulars respecting mills and manufactories, p[rivate] schools, &c.

Householder's Schedule.

Agricultural Schedule.

The immense mass of information collected in these schedules is like metal in the ore—comparatively useless until concentrated, and separated from extraneous matter. It is here that the bulk of the work in connection with census-taking occurs, for every schedule has to be dissected, and every figure classified, tabulated, and arranged. This is a work of time, and although a large staff has been engaged upon it the results have not yet advanced sufficiently to be incorporated to any great extent in the present volume, but will form a rich source of illustration for future issues.

Tabulation of the information.

The following are the figures disclosed by the censuses of 1861, 1871, 1881, and 1891 :—

Population at different censuses.

Population of New South Wales.

Year.	Males.	Females.	Total.
1861	198,488	152,372	350,860
1871	275,551	228,430	503,981
1881	411,149	340,319	751,468
1891	612,697	519,804	1,132,501

DISTRIBUTION OF SEXES.

The relative proportion of males to females in the whole Colony has undergone little change for many years past, as will be seen from the following figures :—

Percentage of Males and Females to whole Population.

Year.	Males.	Females.
1861	56·57	43·43
1871	54·67	45·33
1881	54·86	45·14
1885	55·08	44·92
1886	54·90	45·10
1887	54·72	45·28
1888	54·53	45·47
1889	54·45	45·55
1890	54·34	45·66

Excess of male population.

The excess of male over female population is chiefly at the ages of from 20 to 50 years, and is caused by the large influx of males in the prime of life, from the neighbouring colonies and the British Islands.

MARRIAGES.

Marriage rate declining.

The number of marriages registered in the Colony shows an uninterrupted annual increase from 1875 to 1886; in 1887 and 1889, however, there was a falling off, while during 1890 there were more marriages than in any previous year. The rate per 1,000 of population had been declining during the period from 1883 to 1889, but 1890 presented a slight improvement on the rate of the previous year.

Marriages in New South Wales.

Year.	Marriages registered.	Per 1,000 of mean population.	Year.	Marriages registered.	Per 1,000 of mean Population.
1871	3,953	7·77	1882	6,948	8·70
1872	3,925	7·45	1883	7,405	8·83
1873	4,384	8·05	1884	7,482	8·47
1874	4,343	7·69	1885	7,618	8·22
1875	4,605	7·87	1886	7,811	8·06
1876	4,630	7·66	1887	7,590	7·55
1877	4,994	7·94	1888	7,844	7·57
1878	5,317	8·08	1889	7,530	7·06
1879	5,391	7·80	1890	7,876	7·15
1880	5,572	7·65			
1881	6,284	8·82	Mean for 20 years ...		7·92

Marriages in European countries.

Compared with some European countries the proportion of marriages to the whole population in the Colony appears somewhat less than might be anticipated, but it will be found that the circumstances of the countries where marriages are more largely entered into are entirely dissimilar, and the national habits different from our own. The highest European marriage-rate is found in the dominions of the two great empires, Germany and Austria, as the following table will show. The ratios for Prussia and the rest of Germany, and for Hungary and the other portions of Austria, are given separately. Their mean marriage-rates since 1870 have been declining year by year; and reference to the table will show that the average rate for each during 1881–89 was lower than the average for the twenty years prior to 1881.

Marriages in United Kingdom.

The marriage-rate of the United Kingdom is always much the same as that of the Australasian Colonies, in spite of the comparatively few marriages solemnized in Ireland. The information in the following table is taken from the report of the Registrar-General of England:—

Marriage-rate per Thousand of Mean Population in certain European countries.

Countries.	Mean of 20 years, 1861–80.	1881.	1882.	1883.	1884.	1885.	1886.	1887.	1888.	1889.	Mean of 9 years.
England and Wales	8·2	7·6	7·7	7·7	7·5	7·2	7·0	7·1	7·1	7·3	7·4
Scotland	7·1	7·0	7·0	7·0	6·7	6·5	6·2	6·2	6·3	6·4	6·6
Ireland	4·9	4·3	4·3	4·3	4·5	4·3	4·2	4·4	4·2	4·5	4·3
France	7·9	7·5	7·4	7·5	7·6	7·5	7·4	7·3	7·2	7·1	7·4
Spain	7·2	6·4	6·0	6·3	6·7	...	...	...	..	...	6·4
Switzerland	7·6	6·8	6·8	6·8	6·8	6·9	6·8	7·1	7·0	7·0	6·9
Italy	7·6	8·1	7·9	8·0	8·2	7·9	7·8	7·8	7·8	7·5	7·9
German Empire	8·7	7·5	7·7	7·7	7·8	7·9	7·9	7·8	7·8	8·0	7·8
Prussia	8·6	7·6	7·9	7·9	8·0	8·2	8·1	8·0	8·0	8·2	8·0
Austria	8·6	8·0	8·2	7·9	7·8	7·6	7·8	7·8	7·9	7·5	7·8
Hungary	10·3	10·0	10·3	10·4	10·2	10·0	9·5	9·0	9·2	8·0	9·6
Holland	8·1	7·3	7·2	7·1	7·2	6·9	6·9	7·0	6·9	6·9	7·0
Belgium	7·3	7·1	7·0	6·7	6·7	6·8	6·7	7·1	7·3	7·2	7·0
Denmark	7·7	7·8	7·7	7·7	7·8	7·6	7·1	7·0	7·1	7·1	7·4
Norway	7·2	6·4	6·7	6·6	6·8	6·7	6·5	6·3	6·2	6·2	6·5
Sweden	6·7	6·2	6·4	6·4	6·5	6·6	6·4	6·3	5·9	6·0	6·3

The means for the series of years prior to 1881 are not for the full period of twenty years for all the countries above mentioned

In the case of Ireland the ratio is the average from 1864 to 1880; Spain, 1861 to 1878; Switzerland, 1868 to 1880; Italy, 1863 to 1880; German Empire, 1872 to 1880; Hungary, 1866 to 1880; and Norway, 1871 to 1880. It must be borne in mind that the above are the ratios of *marriages* to population; to ascertain the ratios of *persons* married it is therefore necessary to double the figures in each case.

Circumstances of Australia induce marriages.

But no one of the European countries referred to above is to any great extent similar to the Australasian Colonies in its social customs, or in the prosperity of the great bulk of its people. The nearness of the marriage-rate of the United Kingdom to that of Australasia is accidental, as the circumstances of the two countries are very dissimilar. In the former case there is a large excess of female population, due to the emigration of males, while in these colonies the preponderance is greatly on the side of the males. Besides this, the social condition of the working-classes, in even the least forward of the Australasian Colonies, is much more advanced than in the British Islands; the probabilities are therefore greatly in favour of a higher marriage-rate in these colonies.

Lowest marriage-rate in New Zealand.

The lowest marriage-rate of any of the Colonies is found in New Zealand, and the highest, taking a series of years, in Queensland. The rates during the last ten years, which will be found hereunder, show that the average of the whole colonies has been approximately 7·54.

The Colonies whose rates are above the average are:—

Queensland	8·58
New South Wales	7·98
Victoria	7·74
Tasmania	7·60

Those below the average are:—

South Australia	7·47
Western Australia	6·97
New Zealand	6·43

Mean Marriage Rates of the Australasian Colonies.

Marriage-rate of all Colonies.

Year.	New South Wales.	Victoria.	Queensland.	South Australia.	Western Australia.	Tasmania.	New Zealand.
1881	8·21	6·79	7·71	8·34	6·67	7·34	6·65
1882	8·70	7·09	8·59	8·75	7·04	8·10	7·09
1883	8·83	7·44	8·97	8·53	6·89	9·15	6·86
1884	8·47	7·74	8·98	8·33	7·02	8·00	6·93
1885	8·22	7·73	9·32	7·86	7·37	8·23	6·72
1886	8·06	7·86	8·44	6·36	7·73	7·56	5·99
1887	7·55	7·64	8·40	6·33	7·44	7·03	5·98
1888	7·57	8·48	8·94	6·65	6·90	6·95	6·00
1889	7·06	8·43	8·27	6·56	6·77	6·92	5·95
1890	7·15	8·21	8·22	7·02	5·89	6·67	6·11
Mean...	7·98	7·74	8·58	7·47	6·97	7·60	6·43

The following are the numbers of marriages registered in each of the colonies during the years 1876 to 1890:—

Marriages in each Colony Australasia.

Year.	New South Wales.	Victoria.	Queensland.	South Australia.	Western Australia.	Tasmania.	New Zealand.
1876	4,630	4,949	1,394	1,852	191	746	3,196
1877	4,994	5,103	1,447	2,002	176	831	3,114
1878	5,317	5,092	1,444	2,299	182	866	3,377
1879	5,391	4,986	1,604	2,238	215	804	3,352
1880	5,572	5,286	1,547	2,291	214	840	3,181
1881	6,284	5,896	1,703	2,308	197	856	3,277
1882	6,948	6,309	2,034	2 530	215	969	3,600
1883	7,405	6,771	2,392	2,539	217	1,120	3,612
1884	7,482	7,218	2,661	2,535	230	1,003	3,800
1885	7,618	7,395	2,842	2,447	256	1,054	3,813
1886	7,811	7,737	2,785	1,976	297	985	3,488
1887	7,590	7,768	2,914	1,977	316	939	3,563
1888	7,844	8,946	3,254	2,084	304	951	3,617
1889	7,530	9,203	3,123	2,062	300	967	3,630
1890	7,876	9,187	3,195	2,235	278	954	3,797

Factors influencing marriages.

So far as these colonies are concerned, the factors influencing the marriage-rate are—first, and chiefly, the general prosperity of the community; secondly, the number of marriageable males, and the occupations of the people. Judged by certain standard tests, which are elsewhere described, the prosperity of the people of New South Wales was perhaps greater than that of any of the other colonies during the period from 1880 to 1886; hence the high marriage-rate for that period compared with most of the other colonies. During some of the succeeding years the material condition of the working population of the colony has not been so satisfactory, and the marriage-rate during these years shows a marked decline.

Large number of single men in New South Wales.

The number of single men (bachelors and widowers) of marriageable age was, numerically, larger in New South Wales than in any of the other colonies, but, proportionately to the whole population, larger only than in Victoria, Tasmania, and South Australia during the year 1881. Under similar conditions it would, therefore, be natural to suppose that, were it not for the greater material prosperity of New South Wales, the marriage-rates of the remaining colonies would have been higher than in this Colony. Such, however, was not the case, for, as mentioned above, the rate for New South Wales is exceeded only by Queensland, over a series of years.

Number of persons signing with marks.

The number of persons signing the marriage register with marks has steadily declined for many years past; the proportion of signatures made with marks was, in 1871, 16·96 per cent. of the whole, while in 1890, the percentage had fallen to 2·70, thus showing a satisfactory decrease of illiteracy. The greatest number of persons signing with marks was recorded in the country districts of the Colony, where, in 1871, 18·92 per cent. of the total signatures were so made, as against 13·94 in the city, and 10·98 in the suburbs of Sydney. The proportion of persons unable to write is still much higher in the country than in the metropolis, though it is satisfactory to note the reduction of the percentage from 18·92 in the year mentioned to 3·56 in 1890. Illiteracy greater in country.

Percentage of Marks to Total Signatures of Persons signing Marriage Registers.

Year.	Metropolis.			Country Districts.	New South Wales.
	City of Sydney.	Suburbs.	Total.		
1871	13·94	10·98	13·50	18·92	16·96
1872	11·47	8·22	10·77	15·09	13·62
1873	10·73	8·38	10·26	16·53	14·26
1874	10·12	7·93	8·81	15·85	11·96
1875	10·67	3·28	8·77	14·21	12·26
1876	7·63	3·56	6·54	16·71	10·47
1877	8·30	5·85	7·58	11·10	9·76
1878	7·16	4·59	6·36	9·21	8·10
1879	6·42	4·34	5·70	8·85	7·58
1880	6·58	3·97	5·76	7·31	6·66
1881	5·41	4·24	5·05	8·34	6·94
1882	6·17	3·47	5·19	6·00	5·63
1883	5·00	4·00	4·60	7·28	6·10
1884	3·60	3·12	3·40	6·77	5·23
1885	3·76	2·03	3·34	5·99	4·74
1886	3·63	1·90	2·89	5·00	3·98
1887	2·85	1·23	2·12	4·68	3·50
1888	3·51	1·84	2·75	4·55	3·74
1889	3·09	1·59	2·39	4·13	3·35
1890	1·71	1·52	1·63	3·56	2·70

Illiteracy of women.

The amount of illiteracy, as displayed by inability to write, has for many years been greater amongst females than males. The next table shows that such was the case in every year since 1871, with the exception of the last two years, from which it would appear that women are now quite on a par with men in the acquirement of the rudiments of education. In 1871, the first year shown on the foregoing table, the number of women unable to sign their names, who were married, amounted to nearly one-fifth of the whole, but the proportion fell to 2½ per cent. in 1889.

The following table gives the percentage of males and females signing the marriage registers with marks for every year since 1871.

Year.	Males signing with marks, per cent.	Females signing with marks, per cent.	Year.	Males signing with marks, per cent.	Females signing with marks, per cent.
1871	14	19	1881	5	8
1872	11	15	1882	5	6
1873	12	15	1883	5	6
1874	10	13	1884	4	5
1875	10	13	1885	4	5
1876	9	11	1886	4	4
1877	8	11	1887	3	4
1878	7	8	1888	4	3½
1879	6	8	1889	3½	3
1880	6	7	1890	2¾	2½

Marriages chiefly by clergy.

The greater number of marriages are solemnized by the clergy; nevertheless, the number of persons married by registrars is fairly large, averaging 6·05 per cent. of the whole, during the past twenty years.

Percentage of Marriages by the Clergy and at Registrars' offices.

Year.	Marriages by Clergy.	Marriages at Registrars' offices.	Year.	Marriages by Clergy.	Marriages at Registrars' offices.
1871	94·46	5·54	1883	93·44	6·56
1872	95·13	4·87	1884	92·82	7·18
1873	95·92	4·08	1885	93·30	6·70
1874	95·21	4·79	1886	93·18	6·82
1875	94·56	5·44	1887	93·31	6·69
1876	94·06	5·94	1888	93·49	6·51
1877	93·93	6·07	1889	93·24	6·76
1878	94·19	5·81	1890	93·00	7·00
1879	94·03	5·97			
1880	94·29	5·71	Average for 20 years ...	93·95	6·05
1881	93·76	6·24			
1882	93·75	6·25			

As may naturally be expected, the largest number of marriages were celebrated by the Church of England, the Roman Catholic Church coming next; but the percentage of marriages celebrated by each of these Churches falls short of what might have been anticipated from their strength as shown by the census. This is noticeably the case with the Roman Catholic Church. The adherents of this denomination at the census of 1881 were 27·63 per cent. of the population, whereas the marriages solemnized according to its rites during the year 1890 were only 17·43 per cent. of the whole marriages. To bring the number of Roman Catholic marriages up to the proper proportion they should increase at least 60 per cent. It is plain, therefore, that the adherents of

Church of England and Roman Catholic marriages.

Roman Catholic marriages.

this Church either do not marry within their own communion, or that they do not undertake the responsibilities of marriage to the same extent as other members of the community. The latter supposition is doubtless the correct explanation of the anomaly; for the adherents of the Roman Catholic Church are amongst the poorest in the Colony, and want of means is, perhaps, the chief cause of the comparatively small number of their marriages, though it is undoubtedly true that what are termed "mixed" marriages are numerous.

Marriages by Church of England.

The disparity between the number of marriages solemnized by the clergy of the Church of England and what might be expected from the numerical strength of the denomination is not so great. During the year 1890 there were celebrated 3,126 marriages according to the rites of this Church, being 39·69 per cent. of the total marriages, while the estimated percentage of its adherents was 45·50. A glance at the following table will show that the number of marriages celebrated during 1890 by ministers of other denominations, notably the Presbyterian, Methodist, Congregational, and Baptist, far exceeded their apparent due proportions:—

Proportion of marriages by each denomination.

Marriages in 1890.

Denomination.	No. of Marriages.	Percentage of total Marriages.	Percentage of adherents to total population, census 1881.
Church of England	3,126	39·69	45·50
Roman Catholic	1,373	17·43	27·63
Presbyterian	965	12·25	9·66
Wesleyan and Primitive Methodist	1,054	13·38	8·58
Congregational	540	6·86	1·91
Baptist	118	1·50	0·98
Hebrew	23	0·29	0·44
Other Denominations	126	1·60	5·30
Registrars' Offices	551	7·00	
	7,876	100·00	

Marriages registered in the Colony, 1876–90.

Denomination.	1876.	1877.	1878.	1879.	1880.	1881.	1882.	1883.	1884.	1885.	1886.	1887.	1888.	1889.	1890.
Church of England...	1,759	1,869	2,098	2,182	2,252	2,487	2,768	2,949	2,893	2,990	2,967	3,66	3,34	2,885	3,126
Roman Catholic.......	921	990	1,009	982	1,021	1,171	1,315	1,414	1,448	1,258	1,323	1,21	1,30	1,288	1,373
Presbyterian	761	854	821	722	768	872	955	950	1,009	1,155	1,147	1,60	97	99	965
Wesleyan	487	509	556	605	618	651	704	712	759	739	832	770	85	753	798
Primitive Methodist	101	110	94	111	101	146	134	157	165	193	207	227	256	271	256
Congregational	232	243	291	331	364	433	516	565	484	532	554	536	534	540	540
Baptist	39	70	89	90	93	85	79	101	117	137	120	120	33	67	118
Hebrew..................	14	20	20	22	17	27	22	24	27	27	18	27	32	35	28
German Evangelical	19	20	11	13	9	13	14	10	18	26	17	20	28	28	23
Christians..............	4	3	11	7	9	3	5	3	9	8	31	34	35	28	28
Salvation Army	...	...	...	...	...	...	...	3	3	3	11	10	22	26	41
Other Denominations	18	3	8	4	2	4	2	31	13	40	31	31	17	15	34
Registrars' Offices...	275	303	309	322	318	392	434	486	537	510	533	508	511	509	551
Total......	4,630	4,994	5,317	5,391	5,572	6,284	6,948	7,405	7,482	7,618	7,811	7,590	7,844	7,530	7,876

DIVORCES.

Marriages dissolved.

The Matrimonial Causes Act was assented to on the 3rd of March, 1873. From 1875 to the end of 1890, 359 marriages have been dissolved, the largest number in any year being forty-four, during 1889. The subjoined table shows the number of decrees for dissolution of marriage granted during the period 1875–90 :—

Year.	Decrees for dissolution of marriage.	Year.	Decrees for dissolution of marriage.
1875	9	1884	27
1876	19	1885	23
1877	19	1886	32
1878	11	1887	25
1879	10	1888	28
1880	22	1889	44
1881	15	1890	42
1882	19		
1883	14	Total.........	359

Marriages of divorced persons.

The number of persons divorced in the Colony who married again cannot be ascertained; but during the sixteen years which ended with 1890, eighty men and seventy-nine women, who had been divorced in New South Wales or elsewhere, were re-married. The largest number in any year was in 1890, when twenty-three divorced persons (ten males and thirteen females) married again.

Year.	No. of divorced persons re-married.		Year.	No. of divorced persons re-married.	
	Males.	Females.		Males.	Females.
1875	1	....	1884	6	6
1876	2	1	1885	9	6
1877	1	3	1886	8	8
1878	2	3	1887	4	11
1879	4	2	1888	8	7
1880	....	1	1889	11	6
1881	1	5	1890	10	13
1882	2	2			
1883	11	5	Total......	80	79

BIRTH-RATE PER MARRIAGE.

The average number of children born to a marriage in each colony, with the exception of Western Australia, during the decennial period 1881–1890, is shown below:— Number of children born to a marriage.

Colony.	Average number of children per marriage.
New South Wales	4·86
Victoria	4·31
South Australia	4·82
Western Australia	5·16
Queensland	4·72
Tasmania	4·66
New Zealand	5·36
Average of Australasian Colonies	4·83

Considering the whole of the above-named colonies as representing Australasia, the number of children to each marriage is 4·73. This is higher than in the United Kingdom, as might be expected from the number of married women of child-bearing age who have come to these colonies from other countries. Thus the birth-rate is increased, while the marriage rate has not been affected. The average number of children to a marriage in the United Kingdom is:— Children per marriage in United Kingdom.

England and Wales	4·30
Ireland	5·38
Scotland	4·56

The figures for Ireland are exceptionally high, which is somewhat surprising, as the average age of persons marrying there is much higher than in Australia. The lowest number of children born to a marriage in any of the important European countries is in France, where the average is only 3·04.

BIRTHS.

The mean annual birth-rate of this colony is higher than that of any of the other Australasian colonies with the exception of Queensland, as will be seen from the following decennial table:— Mean annual birth-rate.

Australasia.—Birth-rates per 1,000 of Population

Year.	New South Wales.	Victoria.	Queensland.	South Australia.	Western Australia.	Tasmania
1881	37·90	31·24	37·22	38·69	34·03	34·61
1882	37·20	30·06	35·95	37·49	35·68	33·78
1883	37·32	30·26	37·11	37·53	33·57	34·80
1884	38·44	30·93	36·02	38·62	33·38	36·51
1885	37·79	31·33	37·08	38·71	34·53	36·19
1886	37·43	31·30	38·16	35·95	38·15	35·51
1887	37·06	32·50	38·94	34·38	36·64	35·46
1888	37·20	32·70	39·12	33·35	34·47	34·91
1889	34·97	33·35	38·13	32·80	34·95	34·03
1890	35·36	33·60	39·66	32·54	33·09	33·64
Mean for 10 years	37·07	31·73	37·74	36·02	34·85	34·94

For further comparison the mean annual birth-rates years (1880 to 1889) are given for several European c from which the high rate of New South Wales is st apparent. The information in this table is taken from tl of the Registrar-General of England:—

Births per 1,000 of Population.

United Kingdom	31·32
England and Wales	32·58
Scotland	32·31
Ireland	23·66
France	24·15
Spain	36·70
Switzerland	28·38
Italy	37·14
Germany	36·99
Prussia	37·59
Austria	38·08
Hungary	44·07
Holland	34·46
Belgium	30·22
Denmark	32·19
Norway	30·70
Sweden	29·40

Increase of births.

The births in New South Wales have increased yea since 1865, and now exceed those of any other colo superiority in regard to the number of births rested with until the year 1879, when the births in this Colony excee of its southern neighbour by 94. During each of the last twelve years the excess has been maintained, the greatest being in 1886, when the births registered in New South Wales were more numerous than those registered in Victoria by 5,460. Last year the difference was 1,386 in favour of this Colony.

Number of births in each colony of Australasia.

The number of births registered in each of the colonies for the period 1876–90 is shown in the following table :—

Year.	New South Wales.	Victoria.	Queensland.	South Australia.	Western Australia.	Tasmania.	New Zealand.
1876	23,298	26,769	6,903	8,224	918	3,149	16,168
1877	23,851	26,010	7,169	8,640	912	3,211	16,856
1878	25,328	26,581	7,397	9,282	871	3,502	17,770
1879	26,933	26,839	7,870	9,902	977	3,564	18,070
1880	28,162	26,148	8,196	10,262	933	3,739	19,341
1881	28,993	27,145	8,220	10.708	1,005	3,918	18,732
1882	29,702	26,747	8,518	10,844	1,089	4,043	19,009
1883	31,281	27,541	9,890	11,173	1,058	4,259	19,202
1884	33,946	28,850	10,679	11,847	1,094	4,578	19,846
1885	35,043	29,975	11,672	12,046	1,200	4,637	19,693
1886	36,284	30,824	12,582	11,177	1,466	4,627	19,299
1887	37,236	33,043	13,513	10,831	1,557	4,736	19,135
1888	38,525	34,503	14,247	10,510	1,518	4,777	18,902
1889	37,295	36,359	14,401	10,318	1,594	4,757	18,457
1890	38,960	37,578	15,407	10,384	1,561	4,813	18,278

Sex of children born.

In no year, as far as observation extends, has the number of females born exceeded the males. The numbers of each sex born in New South Wales since 1871 are given below :—

Year.	Males.	Females.	Total.	Year.	Males.	Females.	Total.
1871	10,326	9,817	20,143	1881	14,891	14,102	28,993
1872	10,276	9,974	20,250	1882	15,087	14,615	29,702
1873	10,952	10,492	21,444	1883	16,014	15,267	31,281
1874	11,323	10,855	22,178	1884	17,417	16,529	33,946
1875	11,380	11,148	22,528	1885	17,939	17,104	35,043
1876	11,791	11,507	23,298	1886	18,700	17,584	36,284
1877	12,292	11,559	23,851	1887	18,901	18,335	37,236
1878	13,082	12,246	25,328	1888	19,616	18,909	38,525
1879	13,840	13,093	26,933	1889	19,335	17,960	37,295
1880	14,424	13,738	28,162	1890	19,887	19,073	38,960

Births of males exceed females.

The excess of males born over females during the past twenty years has varied from 2·08 per cent. in 1875 to 7·65 in 1889, the average being 4·72 per cent. The following table shows the proportion of males born to every 100 females:—

Year.	Males born to every 100 females.	Year.	Males born to every 100 females.
1871	105·18	1881	105·89
1872	103·03	1882	106·23
1873	104·38	1883	104·89
1874	104·31	1884	105·37
1875	102·08	1885	104·88
1876	102·47	1886	106·35
1877	106·34	1887	106·09
1878	106·83	1888	106·74
1879	105·71	1889	107·65
1880	105·00	1890	104·27

Births most numerous in spring.

Births are more numerous in spring than in any other portion of the year, and are fewest in the March quarter. This is found to be the case in the other colonies of Australasia as well as in New South Wales. The following table gives the number of births in each quarter of the year since 1877:—

Year.	31 March.	30 June.	30 September.	31 December.
1877	5,620	5,837	6,421	5,973
1878	5,962	6,165	6,976	6,236
1879	6,231	6,591	7,264	6,847
1880	6,590	7,116	7,230	7,238
1881	6,976	6,983	7,514	7,[illegible]
1882	7,195	7,273	7,827	7,407
1883	7,378	7,755	8,006	8,148
1884	8,141	8,443	9,160	8,[illegible]
1885	8,178	8,506	9,656	8,791
1886	8,451	8,976	9,592	9,[illegible]
1887	9,075	9,183	9,890	9,058
1888	9,058	9,651	10,162	9,654
1889	9,125	9,292	9,635	9,[illegible]
1890	9,154	9,667	10,497	9,[illegible]

Birth-rate per thousand.

Separating the Colony into the divisions of city of Sydney, suburbs, and country districts, it will be seen from the following table that the birth-rate per thousand is much higher in the suburbs than in the other divisions. The highest rate reached for the whole Colony was 39·63, in 1871, which was also the year of the greatest birth-rate in the city. The estimated maximum rate for the suburbs was reached in 1886, when the births were 52·58 per thousand of the population. In the country districts the greatest number of births in proportion to the population occurred in 1874, when the rate was 39·72 per thousand.

Annual Birth-rate of New South Wales. Annual birth-rate.

Year.	Births per thousand of the population.				
	Metropolis.			Country Districts.	New South Wales.
	City of Sydney.	Suburbs.	Total.		
1871	38·91	42·62	40·56	39·29	39·68
1872	36·63	37·69	37·12	38·96	38·46
1873	38·09	40·55	39·22	39·44	39·38
1874	37·81	38·57	38·16	39·72	39·29
1875	37·44	37·92	37·67	38·86	38·53
1876	36·37	37·73	38·06	38·74	38·55
1877	38·13	37·18	37·67	38·02	37·92
1878	37·62	38·67	38·15	38·65	38·50
1879	38·48	39·84	39·18	38·92	38·99
1880	37·17	40·61	39·00	38·73	38·61
1881	35·84	40·76	38·54	37·62	37·90
1882	34·65	43·42	39·52	36·17	37·20
1883	33·24	45·44	40·07	36·14	37·82
1884	34·80	50·97	43·88	36·03	38·44
1885	31·81	51·44	44·41	35·47	37·79
1886	31·01	52·58	43·70	34·61	37·43
1887	30·76	49·76	42·39	34·60	37·06
1888	31·46	46·48	41·09	35·35	37·20
1889	30·47	41·68	37·97	33·50	34·97
1890	30·96	38·96	36·53	34·77	35·36
Mean ...	35·18	42·64	39·60	37·18	37·94

The excess of births over deaths has not shown a steady increase year by year, but has fluctuated somewhat, as will be seen from the succeeding table. In the whole Colony, during the twenty years from 1871 to 1890, the least excess was 11,757 in 1875, the highest being 24,742 in the year 1890. In the city of Sydney the least excess was in 1875, viz., 489; the highest in 1887, when the number reached 1,835. The suburbs show a more progressive uniformity than the city. The least excess of births over deaths also occurred in 1875, when it was 1,261; the greatest excess was 6,323, being, as in the case of the city, in the year 1890. In Excess of births over deaths.

the country districts the number ranged from 9,913, in 1876, to 16,804, in 1890.

Excess of Births over Deaths in New South Wales.

Year.	Metropolis.			Country Districts.	New South Wales.
	City of Sydney.	Suburbs.	Total.		
1871	1,397	1,718	3,115	10,621	13,736
1872	1,069	1,521	2,590	10,192	12,782
1873	1,265	1,766	3,031	10,802	13,833
1874	1,044	1,588	2,632	10,894	13,526
1875	489	1,261	1,750	10,007	11,757
1876	819	1,373	2,192	9,913	12,105
1877	1,399	1,925	3,324	10,658	13,982
1878	1,163	2,023	3,186	11,379	14,565
1879	1,448	2,499	3,947	12,786	16,733
1880	995	2,439	3,434	13,497	16,931
1881	1,495	3,065	4,560	12,897	17,457
1882	1,229	3,379	4,608	12,278	16,886
1883	1,523	3,819	5,342	13,690	19,032
1884	1,594	4,352	5,946	13,780	19,726
1885	1,250	4,523	5,773	13,988	19,761
1886	1,610	5,250	6,860	14,837	21,697
1887	1,835	6,039	7,874	15,914	23,788
1888	1,599	5,850	7,449	16,668	24,117
1889	1,431	5,575	7,006	15,493	22,499
1890	1,615	6,323	7,938	16,804	24,742

Net annual increase.

The mean annual increase to the population by reason of the excess of births over deaths amounts to 2·28 per cent. for a period extending over twenty years—that is, going back to immediately before the census of 1871.

Excess in favour of females.

Notwithstanding that the number of males born is considerably larger than that of females, the actual increase of population from the excess of births over deaths is, owing to the greater mortality amongst male children, greatly in favour of the females. During the ten years which closed with 1890, the number of females added to the community by excess of births exceeded the males by 14,883, or 15·28 per cent.

ILLEGITIMACY.

Illegitimacy increasing.

The number of illegitimate births in the city, suburbs, and country districts, will be found in the following table. Taking the whole period over which the tables extend, it will be seen that the percentage has increased throughout the Colony, notably in the city and suburbs of Sydney, the increase in the country districts being very slight, as shown in the table of percentages on page 809. As regards the city proper the increase in illegitimacy has been most marked.

Number of Illegitimate Births.

Year.	Metropolis.			Country Districts.	New South Wales.
	City of Sydney.	Suburbs.	Total.		
1871	206	61	267	515	782
1872	182	66	248	568	816
1873	199	86	285	604	889
1874	241	88	329	606	935
1875	260	85	345	602	947
1876	306	88	394	556	950
1877	305	77	382	607	989
1878	317	108	425	596	1,021
1879	389	117	506	709	1,215
1880	411	150	561	665	1,226
1881	425	167	592	671	1,263
1882	440	161	601	660	1,261
1883	439	237	676	642	1,318
1884	527	259	786	709	1,495
1885	529	316	845	767	1,612
1886	533	372	905	782	1,687
1887	496	377	873	838	1,711
1888	567	482	1,049	909	1,958
1889	618	448	1,066	921	1,987
1890	590	466	1,056	995	2,051

Dividing the years 1871 to 1890 into quinquennial periods, the average number of children born out of wedlock, compared with the total births, and with the legitimate children born during each period, was for the city of Sydney:— Illegitimacy in Sydney.

Quinquennial Period.	Per cent. of total births.	Per cent. of legitimate births.
1871-75	7·13	7·70
1876-80	9·75	10·92
1881-85	12·23	13·96
1886-90	15·26	17·94

Illegitimate births.

The bare statement of these figures is a serious reflection upon the morals of the community. That during the past five years one child in every seven should have been born with the brand of illegitimacy is a startling revelation with regard to social morality. It is also a matter of State concern, as a very large percentage of these unfortunate children become a burden to the country from their birth, and it is from such that the pauper population of the Colony is largely recruited. Happily, as regards the city, the case is not so bad as it appears from the table. Not a few of the women whose children are born out of wedlock in the city really belong to the suburbs or country districts, but to what extent does not appear; possibly the smaller proportion of illegitimate births noticeable in the country districts is due to the fact that women who have fallen come to Sydney to hide their shame. The records of accouchements at the Benevolent Asylum certainly give colour to this supposition, for out of the large number of unmarried women whose confinements took place in that institution it is only reasonable to suppose that the suburbs and country contributed a large quota.

Cause of excess of illegitimacy in the city.

Accouchements in the Benevolent Asylum, Sydney.

Year.	No. of Confinements.	Married.	Unmarried	Year.	No. of Confinements.	Married.	Unmarried
1865	129	50	79	1878	160	38	122
1866	129	51	78	1879	203	45	158
1867	121	44	77	1880	233	51	182
1868	102	46	56	1881	225	50	175
1869	112	40	72	1882	237	45	192
1870	95	29	66	1883	210	33	177
1871	117	54	63	1884	305	84	221
1872	102	37	65	1885	262	55	207
1873	107	27	80	1886	300	71	229
1874	126	36	90	1887	257	76	181
1875	113	30	83	1888	281	70	211
1876	156	38	118	1889	252	48	204
1877	169	41	128	1890	266	35	231

Illegitimacy in the city and suburbs.

Taking the city and suburbs of Sydney together, the rates of illegitimacy during the five-year periods since 1871, are :—

Quinquennial Period.	Per cent. of total births.	Per cent. of Legitimate births
1871-75	5·11	5·41
1876-80	6·21	6·65
1881-85	6·60	7·07
1886-90	7·37	7·96

The rates are much more favourable than those of the city taken separately, and perhaps represent the true state of affairs as regards illegitimacy more accurately than the table already given.

For the country districts the rates are much lower :—

Quinquennial Period.	Per cent. of total births.	Per cent. of Legitimate births.
1871-75	3·72	3·86
1876-80	3·44	3·56
1881-85	3·25	3·36
1886-90	3·67	3·81

Dividing the illegitimate births of the whole Colony into the same periods as given for the city, their proportions, as compared with the total births, and with legitimate births, are :—

Quinquennial Period.	Per cent. of total births.	Per cent. of Legitimate births.
1871-75	4·09	4·27
1876-80	4·22	4·42
1881-85	4·36	4·57
1886-90	4·99	5·25

Colony compares favourably with other countries.

Taken as a whole, the Colony compares favourably with most other countries, though its rate as computed for the ten years 1880–89 is higher than that of any other of the Colonies, with the exception of Victoria, as shown in the following table :

Percentage of Illegitimate Births to Total Births in the Australasian Colonies and United Kingdom.

Country.	Illegitimate births per cent.	Country.	Illegitimate births per cent.
New South Wales	4·49	Tasmania	4·05
Victoria	4·71	New Zealand	2·98
Queensland	4·21	England and Wales..	4·83
South Australia	2·33	Ireland	2·80
Western Australia	4·17	Scotland	8·35

Of the total number of children born in Australasia during the last ten years 4·05 per cent. were illegitimate.

Illegitimacy in Foreign States.

The following figures, taken from Mulhall's Dictionary of Statistics, show the percentage of illegitimate births in various countries:—

Percentage of Illegitimate Births.

Country	Per cent.	Country	Per cent.
Denmark..........................	11·1	Spain	5·5
Sweden	10·2	Portugal	5·6
Norway	8·5	Canada..........................	5·0
Germany..........................	8·7	Switzerland	4·6
France	7·4	Holland	3·5
Belgium	7·1	Russia	3·1
United States..	7·0	Greece	1·6
Italy	6·5		

The rate of illegitimate births in Austria was 13·5 per cent., a ratio much larger than that of any country included in the above table, the excessive number of children born out of wedlock being occasioned by the extraordinary laws formerly enforced by the government of the Austrian Empire, regulating the age before which a man was incapable of contracting a legal marriage.

The rates for all these colonies are smaller than those of England and Scotland, but illegitimacy is increasing here, while it is decreasing in the United Kingdom.

Illegitimate Births—Percentage to Total Births in New South Wales.

Percentage of illegitimacy to total births.

Year.	Metropolis.			Country Districts.	New South Wales.
	City of Sydney.	Suburbs.	Total.		
1871	6·91	2·34	4·78	3·53	3·88
1872	6·32	2·70	4·66	3·80	4·02
1873	6·49	3·11	4·89	3·86	4·14
1874	7·72	3·15	5·56	3·72	4·21
1875	8·22	2·92	5·68	3·65	4·20
1876	9·24	2·87	6·19	3·28	4·07
1877	8·97	2·37	5·75	3·52	4·14
1878	9·09	2·93	5·94	3·28	4·03
1879	10·47	2·82	6·44	3·72	4·51
1880	11·00	3·25	6·71	3·36	4·35
1881	11·36	3·23	6·64	3·34	4·36
1882	11·72	2·74	6·24	3·28	4·24
1883	11·68	3·62	6·59	3·05	4·21
1884	12·76	3·34	6·62	3·21	4·40
1885	13·61	3·77	6·89	3·37	4·60
1886	13·90	4·00	6·89	3·38	4·65
1887	13·13	3·91	6·50	3·52	4·59
1888	15·07	4·85	7·65	3·66	5·08
1889	17·41	4·57	7·99	3·84	5·33
1890	16·79	4·65	7·81	3·91	5·26

TWINS AND TRIPLETS.

During the year 1890 there was one case of triplets. Twins numbered 398 cases, comprising 405 males and 391 females, in all 796 children. The number of children born as triplets and twins forms 2·05 per cent. of the total births.

Triplets and Twins.

District.	Triplets.				Twins.			
	No. of cases.	M.	F.	Total.	No. of cases.	M.	F.	Total.
Sydney...	......	......	.....	......	41	43	39	82
Suburbs..	1	3	......	3	107	114	100	214
Country..	......	......	......	......	250	248	252	500
	1	2	1	3	398	405	391	796

Twins and Triplets born in New South Wales.

Year.	Triplets.				Twins.			
	No. of cases.	M.	F.	Total.	No. of cases.	M.	F.	Total living at Birth.
1881	4	8	4	12	224	219	227	446
1882	......	......	......	......	213	217	208	425
1883	2	3	3	6	287	277	297	574
1884	4	6	6	12	288	277	295	572
1885	2	5	1	6	306	305	307	612
1886	1	......	3	3	330	284	373	657
1887	1	3	......	3	310	294	325	619
1888	1	1	2	3	363	371	355	726
1889	1	2	1	3	329	358	298	656
1890	1	3	......	3	398	405	391	796
	17	31	20	51	3,048	3,007	3,076	6,083

As stated in the foregoing table there were 3,048 cases of twins and 17 cases of triplets during the ten years 1881–90. The total number of confinements recorded in this period was 344,196. It follows, therefore, that one mother in every 113 gave birth to twins, and one mother in every 20,247 was delivered of three children at a birth.

DEATHS.

Mean death-rate.

The number of deaths occurring in the Colony during the last twenty years averaged annually 16·28 per thousand for males, and 13·77 for females, or 15·14 for the whole population. Compared with the death-rates of other countries, especially those of the Old World, this rate is remarkably low. Yet, as will presently appear, it is higher than might be anticipated from the peculiarly healthy climatic conditions which pertain to New South Wales.

The mean decennial death-rate of the Australasian Colonies from 1881 to 1890 varies from 10·45 per thousand, in New Zealand, to 17·27, in Queensland, and averages 14·78, to which the New South Wales rate is the nearest approach. Four colonies are over the mean rate:—Queensland, with 17·27; Western Australia, 16·33; Tasmania, 15·59; Victoria, 15·35; while three are lower,—New South Wales, 14·74; South Australia, 13·73; and New Zealand, 10·45 per thousand.

Mean Death-rate of the Australasian Colonies.

Year.	New South Wales.	Victoria.	Queensland.	South Australia.	Western Australia.	Tasmania.	New Zealand.
1881	15·08	14·16	15·04	14·45	13·95	14·87	11·15
1882	16·05	15·32	18·04	15·41	14·09	15·93	11·22
1883	14·61	14·29	18·01	15·09	17·77	17·34	11·51
1884	16·10	14·48	23·14	15·78	21·57	15·87	10·47
1885	16·48	15·01	19·81	12·92	17·87	15·89	10·71
1886	15·05	15·18	16·91	13·95	20·98	15·17	10·54
1887	13·38	15·74	14·89	13·07	16·52	16·18	10·31
1888	13·91	15·44	15·18	12·52	15·28	14·88	9·46
1889	13·87	17·79	16·24	11·49	13·78	15·01	9·45
1890	12·90	16·10	14·51	12·66	11·45	14·80	9·65
Mean.. ..	14·74	15·35	17·27	13·73	16·33	15·59	10·45

The numbers of deaths registered in each of the Colonies during the years 1876 to 1890 are here given:— Deaths in each Colony of Australasia.

Deaths in each Colony of Australasia.

Year.	New South Wales.	Victoria.	Queensland.	South Australia.	Western Australia	Tasmania.	New Zealand.
1876	11,193	13,561	3,467	3,550	383	1,733	4,904
1877	9,869	12,776	3,373	3,235	433	2,040	4,685
1878	10,763	12,702	4,220	3,749	394	1,700	4,645
1879	10,200	12,120	3,207	3,580	411	1,688	5,563
1880	11,231	11,652	3,017	3,912	382	1,832	5,437
1881	11,536	12,302	3,320	4,012	412	1,733	5,491
1882	12,816	13,634	4,274	4,393	430	1,906	5,701
1883	12,249	13,006	5,041	4,435	560	2,122	6,061
1884	14,220	13,505	6,861	4,788	707	1,990	5,740
1885	15,282	14,364	6,235	3,970	600	2,036	6,081
1886	14,587	14,952	5,575	4,234	806	1,976	6,135
1887	13,448	16,006	5,106	3,944	702	2,161	6,137
1888	14,408	16,287	5,529	3,759	673	2,036	5,708
1889	14,796	19,392	6,132	3,501	611	2,098	5,772
1890	14,218	18,012	5,638	3,923	540	2,118	5,994

Death-rate of males and females compared.

The death-rate of males averages in this Colony 16·28 per thousand, or more than one-sixth higher than that of females. The deaths of both sexes will be seen below :—

Deaths, and Death-rate of New South Wales.

Year.	Males.	Females.	Total.	Death Rate per 1,000 of mean population.		
				Males.	Females.	Total.
1871	3,882	2,525	6,407	13·98	10·95	12·61
1872	4,442	3,026	7,468	15·45	12·66	14·18
1873	4,599	3,012	7,611	15·50	12·15	13·98
1874	5,022	3,630	8,652	16·35	14·11	15·33
1875	6,245	4,526	10,771	19·64	16·97	18·43
1876	6,508	4,685	11,193	19·82	16·98	18·52
1877	5,877	3,992	9,869	17·19	13·91	15·69
1878	6,284	4,479	10,763	17·55	14·94	16·36
1879	6,082	4,118	10,200	16·16	13·10	14·77
1880	6,638	4,593	11,231	16·76	13·94	15·46
1881	6,753	4,783	11,536	16·12	13·82	15·06
1882	7,596	5,220	12,816	17·34	14·48	16·05
1883	7,116	5,133	12,249	15·45	13·54	14·61
1884	8,325	5,895	14,220	17·12	14·85	16·10
1885	8,900	6,382	15,282	17·43	15·32	16·49
1886	8,501	6,086	14,587	15·95	13·95	15·05
1887	7,776	5,672	14,448	14·12	12·49	13·38
1888	8,453	5,955	14,408	14·94	12·67	13·91
1889	8,674	6,122	14,796	14·93	12·61	13·87
1890	8,282	5,936	14,218	13·82	11·81	12·90
Mean for 20 years				16·28	13·77	15·14

Greater mortality amongst males.

The principal cause of the greater mortality amongst males is found in the nature of their occupations, with the accidents and exposure attendant thereon. This is especially marked in the country districts of the Colony, where deaths from accident are extremely numerous, especially among males. Besides this, the greater delicateness of male infants operates to increase the death-rate as compared with that of females. It has been shown elsewhere that the natural increment to the population by births is in the proportion of 104·72 males to 100 females ; but, from the causes alluded to, the net increase of population by excess of births over deaths is largely in favour of females. For the five years, 1886–90, the excess of births over deaths averaged annually for males 26·27 per cent., and for females 29·79 per cent.

The excess of males in the community, with the consequent larger number of male deaths, makes the comparison appear more favourable to female lives than is actually the case. The following table has been computed on the assumption that the males and females in the community are equal in number, as they soon would be if it were not for the excess of males yearly added to the population by immigration. It would appear, however, from the table, that the extra proportion of males born does not counterbalance the extra number of male deaths.

Comparison of male with female deaths.

Male birth in excess.

Male and Female Deaths.

Year.	Male deaths.	Female deaths.	Computed male deaths, if male and female population were equal.	Excess of computed male over female deaths.	Excess of male over female births.
1881	6,753	4,783	5,576	793	789
1882	7,596	5,220	6,251	1,031	472
1883	7,116	5,133	5,835	702	747
1884	8,325	5,895	6,798	903	838
1885	8,900	6,382	7,261	879	835
1886	8,501	6,086	6,957	871	1,116
1887	7,776	5,672	6,410	738	566
1888	8,453	5,955	7,021	1,066	707
1889	8,674	6,122	7,245	1,123	1,375
1890	8,282	5,936	6,943	1,007	841
Total for ten years................				9,113	8,336

The season of the year in which deaths are most numerous is the quarter ending March, but the number of deaths in the December quarter is nearly as great, and for some years has exceeded that of the first quarter. The deaths in 1890, when

Deaths most numerous in March quarter.

compared with the population, present a lower death-rate than is shown for any year since 1871. Taking the last ten years the deaths during each quarter of the year were :—

Deaths during each Quarter of the Year.

Year.	31 March.	30 June.	30 September.	31 December.
1880	2,677	2,621	2,571	3,362
1881	3,169	2,825	2,608	2,934
1882	3,485	3,290	2,911	3,130
1883	3,125	3,081	2,790	3,253
1884	3,699	3,602	3,126	3,793
1885	3,924	3,750	3,586	4,022
1886	3,718	3,720	3,320	3,829
1887	3,980	3,362	2,805	3,301
1888	3,624	3,595	3,387	3,802
1889	4,101	3,728	3,158	3,809
1890	3,652	3,448	3,516	3,602

Favourable death-rate of Colony.

It has been already pointed out that in regard to its death-rate the Colony compares very favourably with the older countries of the world. Taken over a decennial period (1880–89), the average deaths per thousand of mean population in the United Kingdom and several of the leading European countries, are :—

United Kingdom	18·93	Austria	29·55
England and Wales	19·08	Hungary	33·11
Scotland	19·06	Holland	21·27
Ireland	18·16	Belgium	20·48
France	22·01	Denmark	18·75
Spain	31·06	Norway	16·75
Switzerland	21·92	Sweden	17·17
Italy	27·39		
Germany	25·28	Average	22·66
Prussia	24·86		

Contrast this with the mean decennial rates (1880–89) in the Colonies :—

New South Wales	14·74	Tasmania	15·59
Victoria	15·35	New Zealand	10·45
Queensland	17·27		
South Australia	13·73	Average, Australasia	14·78
Western Australia	16·33		

There are many causes operating to increase the European rate, which have not yet affected the colonies. Chief amongst these are the scourges of small-pox and cholera. It is not, therefore, surprising that even the healthiest country of Europe should have a higher annual death-rate than any part of Australasia. Considering the favourable environments of the population in New South Wales, the matter for surprise is not that the difference is so great but that it is not greater. Apart from climatic conditions, which are most favourable here, the social condition of the great body of the people is far superior, and their occupations more healthful than in Europe; and were it not for the pitiable loss of infant life, the death-rate of this Colony would not reach much more than half the European average.

Death-rate lower in Australia than Europe.

For the purpose of comparison, the obvious divisions of city, suburbs, and country districts suggest themselves, and the annual death-rate of each subdivision of the Colony for the years 1871-90 is given in the subjoined table:—

Mortality in the Colony and its subdivisions.

Deaths in New South Wales, per Thousand of Population.

Year.	Metropolis.			Country Districts.	New South Wales.
	City of Sydney.	Suburbs.	Total.		
1871	20·67	14·46	17·92	10·63	12·61
1872	23·03	14·15	19·03	12·37	14·18
1873	22·37	14·63	18·83	12·15	13·98
1874	25·16	16·59	21·16	13·12	15·33
1875	31·65	21·47	26·81	15·23	18·42
1876	28·87	20·79	24·96	16·05	18·52
1877	22·43	15·13	18·82	14·47	15·69
1878	25·06	17·37	21·17	14·44	16·36
1879	23·47	15·83	19·51	12·83	14·77
1880	27·26	19·17	22·97	12·34	15·48
1881	21·52	16·60	18·82	13·46	15·08
1882	23·31	18·45	20·31	14·05	16·05
1883	19·76	18·88	19·27	12·57	14·61
1884	21·37	22·32	21·90	13·54	16·10
1885	21·58	23·67	22·42	13·69	16·48
1886	17·99	22·88	20·87	12·43	15·05
1887	15·82	18·60	17·52	11·48	13·38
1888	18·09	19·14	18·76	11·61	13·91
1889	18·19	17·95	18·03	11·83	13·87
1890	16·74	14·37	15·10	11·79	12·90
Mean	22·22	18·12	20·21	13·00	15·14

Variations in death rates.

The death-rate for the whole Colony varied from 12·61 to 18·52, a range of 5·91 per thousand. In the city, however, the rate varied between 15·82 and 31·65, the range being 15·83 per thousand; in the suburbs the lowest rate was 14·15, and the highest touched 23·67, giving a range of 9·52 per thousand. In the country districts 10·63 was the lowest rate in the twenty years, and 16·05 tho highest, 5·42 being the range.

Maximum, Minimum, and Mean Death-rate.

Districts.	Per 1,000 of mean population.		
	Maximum.	Minimum.	Mean.
City of Sydney	31·65	15·82	22·22
Suburbs	21·47	14·15	18·12
Metropolis (Sydney and Suburbs)	26·81	15·10	20·21
Country Districts	16·05	10·63	13·09
New South Wales	18·52	12·61	15·14

Death-rate of persons over 5 years.

Taking the deaths of persons over 5 years of age, the rates for the metropolitan district and the country are not only more favourable but more equal.

Death-rates of Persons over Five Years of Age.

Districts.	Per 1,000 of mean population.		
	Maximum.	Minimum.	Mean.
City of Sydney	19·70	10·90	14·[illegible]
Suburbs	12·86	7·64	9·77
Metropolis (Sydney and Suburbs)	15·55	9·79	12·[illegible]
Country Districts	11·71	7·97	9·[illegible]
New South Wales	12·78	8·70	10·12

Infant mortality cause of high death-rate in city and suburbs.

The city maximum rate was in 1876, and is the disturbing element in the whole series, otherwise the death-rates are particularly favourable for these ages. Turning to deaths under 5 years, which may be generally termed the ages of infantile life, the chief factor of the excessive death-rate of the city and suburbs will be found.

Death-rates of Children under Five Years of Age.

Districts.	Per 1,000 of mean population.		
	Maximum.	Minimum.	Mean.
City of Sydney	105·64	48·08	69·95
Suburbs	86·99	45·00	66·61
Metropolis (Sydney and Suburbs)	93·32	45·85	68·69
Country Districts	40·37	24·00	32·09
New South Wales	53·64	32·56	43·24

The lesson conveyed by the above table is a very striking one. The minimum death-rate of infants in the Metropolis exceeded the maximum rate of the country by 13 per cent., and the mean rate of the country was only half the metropolitan.

Natural salubrity of the Colony.

When the circumstances of life in the country districts are considered, the distance sick persons are removed from the comforts, and even the necessaries, which sickness demands, the full meaning of the low rate, both for adults and children, will best be understood. No more potent argument could be advanced as to the natural salubrity of the Colony than the statement of the death-rates, as recorded outside the walls of the metropolis.

Death-rate of children lowest in the country.

All satisfaction, however, in regard to the low death-rate is confined to the country districts. As far as Sydney and its suburbs are concerned, there is no cause for congratulation; on the contrary, the rate at which children of tender years drop into the grave forms a pathetic commentary on the civilization of the Colony. Taking the whole period embraced in the table, the death-rates of children under 5 years were 70 per thousand in the city, and 67 per thousand in the suburbs. During the ten years, 1871 to 1880, the suburbs could boast a death-rate of one-third less than the city, but since 1880 the suburban has been the higher of the two. The following quinquennial table has been compiled in order to illustrate the gradual change which has occurred since 1871:—

Comparison of quinquennial periods.

Death-rate of New South Wales in Quinquennial Periods per thousand of population.

Quinquennial records.	Metropolis.			Country Districts.	New South Wales.
	City of Sydney.	Suburbs.	Total.		
		All ages.			
1871-75	24·69	16·46	20·91	12·77	14·99
1876-80	25·41	17·63	21·46	13·96	16·10
1881-85	21·49	20·21	20·77	13·46	15·70
1886-90	17·36	18·26	17·94	11·82	13·80
		Over 5 years.			
1871-75	15·94	8·87	12·72	9·25	10·21
1876-80	16·82	8·97	12·82	9·86	10·73
1881-85	14·76	10·80	12·56	9·50	11·40
1886-90	11·66	10·51	10·93	8·49	9·27
		Under 5 years.			
1871-75	75·45	56·35	66·28	30·55	39·78
1876-80	80·52	74·43	77·45	35·80	46·36
1881-85	67·77	77·20	73·35	35·99	46·63
1886-90	56·45	80·95	58·12	31·68	40·04

Improvement in city death-rate.

A remarkable improvement may be noticed in the death-rate of the city, both for ages over and under 5 years. In the country, during the second quinquennial period, the rate showed an increase, particularly amongst infant lives; but the third period is marked by a slight recovery, which is quite eclipsed by the striking decline in the death-rates of 1886-90. As regards the suburbs the signs are not so assuring, for although a considerable improvement is manifest in 1886-90, the previous five years are much higher than in the two preceding quinquennial periods; and during the last five years the death-rates of persons under five years were considerably higher than in the city or the country. The following tables show the mortality in the city and suburbs of Sydney and in the country districts from

1871 to 1890. In the first will be found the actual number of deaths, and in the second the proportion of children under five years, and of persons over that age, who died, as compared with the whole population :—

Deaths of persons under and over 5 years.

Deaths in New South Wales, 1871-90.

Year.	Children under 5 years.				Persons over 5 years.			
	City.	Suburbs.	Country.	N.S.W.	City.	Suburbs.	Country.	N.S.W.
1871	743	487	1,475	2,705	840	396	2,466	3,702
1872	815	593	1,885	3,203	995	412	2,858	4,265
1873	719	510	1,695	2,924	1,081	487	3,119	4,687
1874	929	672	2,167	3,768	1,148	527	3,209	4,884
1875	1,264	913	2,781	4,958	1,409	734	3,670	5,813
1876	1,024	917	2,730	4,671	1,467	768	4,287	6,522
1877	815	723	2,755	4,293	1,185	598	3,793	5,576
1878	1,022	920	2,942	4,884	1,299	731	3,849	5,879
1879	899	902	2,568	4,369	1,367	746	3,718	5,831
1880	1,293	1,276	2,341	4,910	1,447	904	3,970	6,321
1881	848	1,147	2,894	4,889	1,398	959	4,290	6,647
1882	990	1,355	3,107	5,452	1,535	1,142	4,687	7,364
1883	940	1,455	2,909	5,304	1,293	1,260	4,392	6,945
1884	1,053	1,838	3,337	6,228	1,482	1,553	4,957	7,992
1885	1,043	2,091	3,478	6,612	1,593	1,766	5,311	8,670
1886	919	2,150	3,225	6,294	1,305	1,895	5,093	8,293
1887	770	1,828	3,022	5,620	1,172	1,776	4,880	7,828
1888	913	2,122	3,172	6,207	1,250	1,973	4,978	8,201
1889	961	2,278	3,284	6,523	1,158	1,941	5,174	8,273
1890	723	1,775	3,278	5,776	1,177	1,916	5,349	8,442

Death-rate of persons under 5 years.

Death-rate in New South Wales under Five Years of age per Thousand of Mean Population.

Year.	Children under 5 years.				
	City.	Suburbs.	Metropolis.	Country.	N.S.W.
1871	65·35	47·57	56·93	24·00	32·56
1872	69·26	46·95	58·63	29·58	37·16
1873	59·91	46·02	53·25	25·84	32·97
1874	76·51	59·18	68·14	32·07	41·37
1875	105·64	80·35	93·32	40·37	53·64
1876	86·55	80·71	83·70	38·52	49·66
1877	67·42	61·56	64·54	37·83	44·41
1878	82·08	73·91	78·00	39·77	49·39
1879	69·34	67·13	68·22	33·88	42·75
1880	95·30	86·99	91·45	31·62	45·83
1881	61·79	71·00	66·77	35·21	43·63
1882	70·27	74·93	72·89	36·66	46·61
1883	65·32	73·48	70·05	33·12	43·46
1884	71·49	82·22	77·98	36·98	48·92
1885	69·59	81·50	77·11	37·84	49·86
1886	60·91	74·92	70·09	34·03	45·42
1887	50·50	57·05	54·94	30·82	38·66
1888	59·27	60·60	60·19	31·33	40·92
1889	63·42	61·06	61·74	31·56	41·68
1890	48·08	45·00	45·85	30·83	35·92
Mean......	69·95	66·61	68·69	32·09	43·24

Deaths of Children under One Year of Age.

Year.	Metropolis.						Country Districts.		New South Wales.	
	City of Sydney.		Suburbs.		Total.					
	Deaths under 1.	Per 1,000 births.	Deaths under 1.	Per 1,000 births.	Deaths under 1.	Per 1,000 births.	Deaths under 1.	Per 1,000 births.	Deaths under 1.	Per 1,000 births.
1871	467	156·7	318	122·2	785	140·7	1,027	70·5	1,812	89·9
1872	507	175·1	339	139·1	846	159·2	1,270	85·0	2,116	104·4
1873	487	158·8	341	123·4	828	142·1	1,157	74·0	1,985	92·5
1874	588	188·4	403	144·6	991	167·7	1,437	88·3	2,428	109·4
1875	613	193·8	461	158·5	1,074	175·9	1,621	98·4	2,695	119·6
1876	561	169·4	521	170·3	1,082	169·9	1,547	91·3	2,629	112·8
1877	562	165·3	476	146·6	1,038	156·2	1,747	101·5	2,785	116·7
1878	650	186·5	591	160·8	1,241	173·4	1,885	103·7	3,126	123·4
1879	612	164·7	594	143·2	1,206	153·4	1,680	88·0	2,886	107·1
1880	785	210·1	821	177·7	1,606	192·2	1,594	80·4	3,200	113·6
1881	608	162·5	836	161·6	1,444	162·0	1,897	94·4	3,341	115·2
1882	737	196·3	1,028	174·9	1,765	183·3	2,132	106·2	3,897	131·2
1883	668	177·8	1,012	154·8	1,680	163·2	1,910	90·9	3,590	114·7
1884	769	186·2	1,272	164·2	2,041	171·9	2,244	101·6	4,285	126·2
1885	780	200·7	1,512	180·4	2,292	186·8	2,304	101·1	4,596	131·1
1886	702	183·1	1,573	169·2	2,275	173·3	2,360	101·9	4,635	127·7
1887	573	151·7	1,317	136·6	1,890	140·8	2,055	86·3	3,945	105·9
1888	640	170·1	1,444	145·2	2,084	152·0	2,187	88·1	4,271	110·9
1889	706	198·9	1,595	162·8	2,301	172·4	2,371	99·0	4,672	125·3
1890	545	58·0	1,278	127·6	1,823	155·4	2,249	88·4	4,071	104·5
Mean...............	......	177·6	.....	153·2	....	164·6	......	92·0	......	114·1

The experience of the United Kingdom shows that infant mortality is always higher in large towns than in the country districts. The experience of this Colony is somewhat similar. But, though the conditions of life in England are more favourable in the country districts than in the towns, the same is not necessarily the case here. In sparsely scattered communities, such as the country districts of this Colony mainly comprise, it is frequently impossible to obtain for children of tender years articles which in towns are considered, and rightly so, almost necessaries of life. Were it not, therefore, for the contagions which seem incidental to towns, the death-rate of children might naturally be expected to be, so far as this Colony is concerned, higher in the country than in the city. That such is not the case is evident from the foregoing table. Compared with the other colonies, and England and France, the rates of New South Wales, nevertheless, seem very favourable, as will be seen on reference to the following table, which gives the mean annual rates calculated for a period of ten years:— *Infant mortality greater in towns.*

Death-rates of Children under One Year in the Australasian Colonies, England, and France. *The Colonies compared with England and France.*

Country.	Deaths of children under 1 year per 1,000 births.
New South Wales	119·27
,, ,, Sydney and suburbs	166·11
,, ,, country districts	95·79
Victoria	126·21
,, Melbourne and suburbs	171·73
,, country districts	93·21
Queensland	131·40
South Australia	122·22
Western Australia	122·5
Tasmania	105·73
New Zealand	88·32
England and Wales	142·00
,, London	151·10
Scotland	117·01
France	157·00

Colony compare favourably with other countries.

The general salubrity of the Colony may be taken as well established, and if the deaths of Sydney and suburbs, especially amongst young children, were not relatively more numerous than for the rest of the Colony, New South Wales need not fear comparison with any country.

The high death-rates of Sydney certainly do not arise from natural causes. Seated on the hilly shores of Port Jackson, its situation is all that could be desired, and the configuration of the ground on which it stands is especially adapted to the requirements of a perfect drainage system. What Nature with lavish hand has bestowed, is, however, in danger of being destroyed or polluted; for looking through the causes of death the conclusion is inevitable that no small part of the mortality of Sydney and its suburbs arises primarily, or indirectly, from diseases which sanitary precautions might avert.

Sydney compares well with other capitals.

With the exception of Hobart and Wellington, there is not much difference in the mean annual death-rates of the capitals of the Australasian Colonies. The rates for a single year, however, do not present such uniformity, as will be seen by the following figures for 1890—Melbourne, 19·6; Hobart, 19·3; Perth, 19·2; Brisbane, 18·2; Adelaide, 16·5; Sydney, 15·1; and Wellington, 12·4. Of course the suburbs of the various cities are included in these calculations. Compared with cities in other parts of the world, the result is generally favourable to Australasia. The following table shows the mean death rate of the chief Australasian, European, and American cities :—

Mean Death-rates.

	Annual Death-rate.		Annual Death-rate.
Melbourne	19·6	Adelaide	16·5
Hobart	19·3	Sydney	15·1
Perth	19·2	Wellington	12·4
Brisbane	18·2		

United Kingdom.

	Annual Death-rate.		Annual Death-rate.
Dublin	27·1	Sheffield	21·6
Liverpool	26·7	London	21·1
Cork	26·1	Edinburgh	20·2
Manchester	25·5	Birmingham	19·8
Glasgow	25·3	Portsmouth	19·7
Plymouth	22·3	Bristol	19·6
Newcastle	21·8	Brighton	19·0

Continental Europe.

Madrid	38.3	Berlin	25·6
St. Petersburg	35·2	Paris	24·5
Buda-Pesth	33·1	Amsterdam	24·3
Prague	32·3	Stockholm	23·4
Breslau	31·2	Copenhagen	23·0
Munich	30·7	Venice	22·7
Milan	29·1	Brussels	22·6
Rome	27·3	Rotterdam	22·6
Vienna	26·9	The Hague	22·4
Cologne	26·2	Geneva	21·2
Leipsic	26·1	Christiania	20·6
Hamburg	25·7		

America.

Montreal	27·9	Toronto	21·5
New York	26·2	Baltimore	21·1
Brooklyn	25·6	San Francisco	20·7
Boston	23·5	Philadelphia	20·3
New Orleans	22·7	St. Louis	19·3

This list is fairly representative, and largely as the rate for Sydney is swollen by the deaths of children of tender years, whose lives are often needlessly sacrificed, the comparison is satisfactory.

The following table shows the numbers of deaths at all ages during the year 1890, distinguishing those which occurred in the city and suburbs of Sydney and in the country districts :—

Table showing the Deaths at all ages in Sydney, Suburbs, and Country Districts, for the year ending 31st December, 1890.

	Under 1 year.	1 to 2 years.	2 to 3 years.	3 to 4 years.	4 to 5 years.	5 to 10 years.	10 to 15 years.	15 to 20 years.	20 to 25 years.	25 to 30 years.	30 to 35 years.	35 to 40 years.	40 to 45 years.	45 to 50 years.	50 to 55 years.	55 to 60 years.	60 to 65 years.	65 to 70 years.	70 to 75 years.	75 to 80 years.	80 to 85 years.	85 to 90 years.	90 to 95 years.	95 to 100 years.	100 years and upwards.	Age not specified.	Total.
Males—																											
Sydney	304	56	23	7	12	22	7	27	44	59	68	64	59	85	64	59	59	32	28	20	9	3	2	1	...	...	1,114
Suburbs.........	693	125	61	35	17	84	25	33	60	84	77	76	84	81	73	66	76	83	47	45	16	15	2	...	...	1	1,959
Country.........	1,240	241	139	87	63	181	105	99	157	215	197	207	174	207	274	257	308	231	285	228	151	74	41	10	1	37	5,209
Total	2,237	422	223	129	92	287	137	159	261	358	342	347	317	373	411	382	443	346	360	293	176	92	45	11	1	38	8,282
Females—																											
Sydney	241	51	16	7	6	18	5	25	32	48	45	36	31	31	42	32	20	21	32	18	14	12	2	..	...	1	786
Suburbs.	585	158	45	35	21	55	20	35	74	79	75	52	59	47	56	52	46	65	68	55	26	16	6	2	...	...	1,732
Country........	1,009	230	137	86	46	177	85	91	123	144	137	110	121	90	95	98	118	111	121	133	77	47	17	9	...	6	3,418
Total	1,835	439	198	128	73	250	110	151	229	271	257	198	211	168	193	182	184	197	221	206	117	75	25	11	...	7	5,936
Total, both sexes	4,072	861	421	257	165	537	247	310	490	629	599	545	528	541	604	564	627	543	581	499	293	167	70	22	1	45	14,218

The number of persons of the age of 70 years and upwards who died during the year was 1,633, and of these 978 were males and 655 females. The numbers in the city and suburbs of Sydney, and in the country districts, are given in the foregoing table. There were 1,080 between the ages of 70 and 80 years, 460 between 80 and 90 years, 92 between 90 and 100 years, and 1 centenarian, who died at Inverell, at the age of 102 years.

The next table gives the average age at death of all persons dying in the Colony during the last ten years, together with the average age of those who were over 5 years of age :— Average age at death.

Average Age at Death, Males and Females, from 1881 to 1890.

Year.	Males.		Females.	
	All Ages.	Over 5 years.	All Ages.	Over 5 years.
1881	30·59	48·88	23·52	44·39
1882	30·05	48·17	23·06	43·94
1883	29·38	47·98	22·88	43·35
1884	28·14	46·50	22·53	42·91
1885	29·12	47·49	22·56	42·78
1886	29·22	47·85	23·79	44·04
1887	29·33	46·95	24·31	44·53
1888	29·44	48·11	23·42	44·01
1889	29·32	48·33	23·07	44·83
1890	30·08	47·62	25·46	45·82
Mean of 10 years ...	29·47	47·79	23·46	44·11

CAUSES OF DEATH.

The system of classifying causes of death proposed by the late Dr. William Farr, F.R.S., in conjunction with Dr. Marc d'Espine, which was in vogue in the United Kingdom and in the colonies for over a quarter of a century, has within the last few years been abandoned in favour of one arranged by Dr. William Ogle, Dr. Farr's successor at the General Register Office, London, upon the basis of a mode of classification determined upon by a joint committee appointed by the Royal College of Physicians,

Order 5. *Venereal Diseases.*—Syphilis, 32; gonorrhœa, stricture of urethra, 3.

Order 6. *Septic Diseases.*—Phagedæna, 2; erysipelas, 5; pyæmia, septicæmia, 16; puerperal fever, 14.

Class II.—Parasitic Diseases.

Thrush, 11; hydatid disease, 14; worms, &c., 2.

Class III.—Dietetic Diseases.

Starvation, want of breast milk, 83; intemperance—*(a)* chronic alcoholism, 32; *(b)* delirium tremens, 16; *(c)* opium smoking, 1.

Class IV.—Constitutional Diseases.

Rheumatic fever, rheumatism of heart, 19; rheumatism, 21; gout, 10; rickets, 2; cancer, 152; tabes mesenterica, 76; tubercular meningitis (hydrocephalus), 58; phthisis, 546; other forms of tuberculosis, scrofula, 33; purpura, hæmorrhagic diathesis, 5; anæmia, chlorosis, leucocythæmia, 15; diabetes mellitus, 14; leprosy, 2.

Class V.—Developmental Diseases.

Premature birth, 216; atelectasis, 7; cyanosis, 15; spina bifida, 7; imperforate anus, 4; cleft palate, harelip, 2; other congenital defects, 7; old age, 120.

Class VI.—Local Diseases.

Order 1. *Diseases of the Nervous System.*—Inflammation of the brain or its membranes, 81; apoplexy, 124; softening of the brain, 22; hemiplegia, brain paralysis, 47; paralysis agitans, 2; insanity, general paralysis of the brain, 45; chorea, 3; epilepsy, 45; convulsions, 227; laryngismus stridulus, 6; idiopathic tetanus, 9; paraplegia, diseases of the spinal cord, 33; congestion of the brain, 9; other diseases of the brain, 18.

Order 2. *Diseases of the Organs of Special Sense.*—Otitis, otorrhœa, disease of the ear, 1; epistaxis, disease of the nose, 4; ophthalmia, disease of the eye, 1.

Order 3. *Diseases of the Circulatory System.*—Endocarditis, valvular disease, 67; pericarditis, 6; hypertrophy of heart, 7; angina pectoris, 4; syncope, 27; aneurism, 27; senile gangrene, 3; embolism, thrombosis, 11; phlebitis, 3; varicose veins, 2; heart disease (undefined), 161.

Order 4. *Diseases of the Respiratory Sys*
42; other diseases of larynx and trachea, :
bronchitis, 295; pneumonia, 249; congestio
27; lung disease (undefined), 9.

Order 5. *Diseases of the Digestive Syste*
78; sore throat, quinsy, 3; dyspepsia, 11;
diseases of the stomach, 31; enteritis, 264;
ileus, obstruction of intestine, 20; stricture
4; intussusception, 7; hernia, 11; fistula, 1
gallstones, 4; cirrhosis of liver, 45; hepati
diseases of liver, 25; other diseases of the di

Order 6. *Diseases of the Lymphatic Sy*
Diseases of lymphatic system, 3; diseases
Addison's disease, 1.

Order 7. *Diseases of the Urinary System.*—
disease, 114; uræmia, 23; suppression of urir
1; diseases of bladder and of prostate, 17; ki

Order 8. *Diseases of the Organs of Gen*
diseases of uterus and vagina, 7; pelvic absce
scrotum, &c., 1.

Order 9. *Diseases of Parturition.*—Aborti
convulsions, 11; placenta prævia, flooding,
birth, 18.

Order 10. *Diseases of the Organs of Loc*
arthritis, ostitis, periostitis, 1; curvature of

Order 11. *Diseases of the Integument*
phlegmon, cellulitis, 4; lupus, 1; ulcer, be
phigus, 1.

Class VII.—Viol

Order 1. *Accident or Negligence.*—Frac
gunshot wounds 1; cuts, 3 (tetanus, 1); burn
poison, 3; drowning, 52; suffocation, 12; ot
6; umbilic l hæmorrhage, 1; chloroform—
quent on immersion, 1).

Order 2. *Homicide.*—Murder, 13; manslau

Order 3. *Suicide.*—By shooting, 8; by cut
by drowning, 8; by hanging, 9; otherwise, 4

Order 5. *Violent Deaths not classed.*—Found drowned, 19; injuries (undefined), 1; injuries through falling from a window, 1 (open verdicts).

Class VIII.—Ill-defined and not Specified Causes.

Dropsy, 9; atrophy, debility, inanition, 303; mortification, 2; tumour, 1; other ill-defined and not specified causes, 11.

MALES, 3,073; FEMALES, 2,518. TOTAL, 5,591.

COUNTRY DISTRICTS.

Classification of diseases—Country districts.

Classification of Fatal Diseases, and proportions per cent. of Deaths from each cause in the Country Districts of New South Wales—1889.

Class.	Causes of Death.	Under 5 Years.		Over 5 Years.		Total.	Proportion per cent.
		Male.	Female.	Male.	Female.		
I.	Specific febrile, or zymotic diseases	339	325	261	277	1,202	13·93
II.	Parasitic diseases	15	9	5	15	44	0·51
III.	Dietetic diseases	7	7	75	14	103	1·19
IV.	Constitutional diseases	105	74	524	332	1,035	12·00
V.	Developmental diseases	177	133	420	214	944	10·95
VI.	Local diseases	832	703	1,484	915	3,934	45·60
VII.	Violence	80	61	612	108	861	9·98
VIII.	Ill-defined and not specified causes	215	196	58	35	504	5·84
	All causes	1,770	1,508	3,439	1,910	8,627	100·00

COUNTRY DISTRICTS.

Class I.—Specific Febrile, or Zymotic Diseases.

Order 1. *Miasmatic Diseases.*—Chicken-pox, 1; measles, 3; epidemic rose rash, 2; scarlet fever, 33; influenza, 106; whooping-cough, 169; mumps, 1; diphtheria, 291; cerebro-spinal fever, 2; simple and ill-defined fever, 5; typhoid, enteric fever, 163.

Order 2. *Diarrhœal Diseases.*—Cholera, 32; diarrhœa, 233; dysentery, 61.

Order 3. *Malarial Diseases.*—Remittent fever, 5.

Order 4. *Zoogenous Diseases.*—Splenic fever, 1.

Order 5. *Venereal Diseases.*—Syphilis, 11; gonorrhœa, stricture of urethra, 4.

Order 6. *Septic Diseases.*—Erysipelas, 17; pyæmia, septicæmia, 35; puerperal fever, 27.

Class II.—Parasitic Diseases.

Thrush, 23; hydatid disease, 21.

Class III.—Dietetic Diseases.

Privation, 29; want of breast milk, 14; intemperance—*(a)* chronic alcoholism, 51; *(b)* delirium tremens, 8; *(c)* opium-smoking, 1.

Class IV.—Constitutional Diseases.

Rheumatic fever, rheumatism of heart, 27; rheumatism, 22; gout, 10; rickets, 1; cancer, 240; tabes mesenterica, 94; tubercular meningitis (hydrocephalus), 53; phthisis, 483; other forms of tuberculosis, scrofula, 53; purpura, hæmorrhagic diathesis, 10; anæmia, chlorosis, leucocythæmia, 17; diabetes mellitus, 25.

Class V.—Developmental Diseases.

Premature birth, 247; atelectasis, 14; cyanosis, 24; spina bifida, 7; imperforate anus, 2; cleft palate, harelip, 3; other congenital defects, 14; old age, 633.

Class VI.—Local Diseases.

Order 1. *Diseases of the Nervous System.*—Inflammation of the brain or its membranes, 95; apoplexy, 155; softening of the brain, 22; hemiplegia brain paralysis, 88; insanity, general paralysis of the insane, 52; chorea, 2; epilepsy, 40; convulsions, 390; laryngismus stridulus, 3; idiopathic tetanus, 12; paraplegia, diseases of the spinal cord, 33; congestion of the brain, 14; brain disease (undefined), 17.

Order 2. *Diseases of the Organs of Special Sense.*—Otitis, otorrhœa, disease of the ear, 3; epistaxis, disease of the nose, 3.

Order 3. *Diseases of the Circulatory System.*—Endocarditis, valvular disease, 75; pericarditis, 8; hypertrophy of heart, 5; angina pectoris, 6; syncope, 58; aneurism, 32; senile gangrene, 13; embolism, thrombosis, 5; phlebitis, 1; varicose veins, 2; heart disease (undefined), 374.

Order 4. *Diseases of the Respiratory System.*—Laryngitis, 37; croup, 167; other diseases of larynx and trachea, 2; asthma, emphysema, 55; bronchitis, 483; pneumonia, 432; congestion of the lungs, 72; pleurisy, 55; lung disease (undefined), 16.

Order 5. *Diseases of the Digestive System.*—Stomatitis, 5; dentition, 138; sore throat, quinsy, 16; dyspepsia, 17; hæmatemesis, 7; melæna, 2; diseases of the stomach, 55; enteritis, 230; ulceration of intestines, 7; ileus, obstruction of intestine, 49; stricture, or strangulation of intestine, 3; intussusception, 6; hernia, 13; fistula, 2; peritonitis, 83; ascites, 9; gallstones, 2; cirrhosis of liver, 36; hepatitis, 18; jaundice, 26; other diseases of liver, 49; other diseases of the digestive system, 20.

Order 6. *Diseases of the Lymphatic System and Ductless Glands.*—Diseases of lymphatic system, 4; diseases of spleen, 2; bronchocele, 5; Addison's Disease, 2.

Order 7. *Diseases of the Urinary System.*—Acute nephritis, 36; Bright's disease, 57; uræmia, 14; suppression of urine, 1; calculus, 4; hæmaturia, 2; disease of bladder and of prostate, 27; kidney disease (undefined), 15.

Order 8. *Diseases of the Organs of Generation.*—Ovarian disease, 6; diseases of uterus and vagina, 10; disorders of menstruation, 4; perineal abscess, 1.

Order 9. *Diseases of Parturition.*—Abortion, miscarriage, 9; puerperal mania, 2; puerperal convulsions, 20; placenta prævia, flooding, 4; other accidents of childbirth, 56.

Order 10. *Diseases of the Organs of Locomotion.*—Caries, necrosis, 4; arthritis, ostitis, periostitis, 6; curvature of spine, 3.

Order 11. *Diseases of the Integumentary System.*—Carbuncle, 2; phlegmon, cellulitis, 4; ulcer, bed sores, 1; eczema, 8; other diseases of the integumentary system, 5.

Class VII.—Violence.

Order 1. *Accident or Negligence.*—Fractures and contusions, 285; gunshot wounds, 15; cuts, 6; burns, 59; scalds, 23; sunstroke, 15; lightning, 6; poison, 18; bite of snake or insect, 10; drowning, 267; suffocation, 25; otherwise, 29.

Order 2. *Homicide.*—Murder, 8; manslaughter, 4.

Order 3. *Suicide.*—By shooting, 12; by cutting throat, 11; by poison, 16; by drowning, 11; by hanging, 18; by the explosion of a dynamite cap, 1; undefined, 1.

Order 4. *Execution.*—Judicial hanging, 1.

Order 5. *Violent Deaths not classed.*—Found drowned, 20.

Class VIII.—Ill-defined and not Specified Causes.

Dropsy, 28; atrophy, debility, inanition, 398; mortification, 3; tumour, 5; abscess, 4; hæmorrhage, 5; other ill-defined and not specified causes, 58.

MALES, 5,209; FEMALES, 3,418. TOTAL, 8,627.

Fatality of phthisis.

From the foregoing it will be seen that the number of deaths from phthisis in the Colony during 1890 was greater than from any other disease. The following are the principal causes of death, arranged in order of fatality:—

	Number of deaths.		Number of deaths.
Phthisis	1,029	Intemperance	109
Accidents	972	Insanity	97
Bronchitis	778	Tuberculosis, scrofula	86
Old age	753	Epilepsy	85
Atrophy, debility (infants)	701	Pleurisy	82
Heart disease (exclusive of endocarditis, pericarditis, and aneurism)	682	Dysentery	78
Convulsions	617	Asthma	77
Diarrhœa	496	Ileus, obstruction of the intestines	69
Enteritis	494	Scarlet fever	67
Premature birth	463	Diseases of spinal cord	66
Diphtheria	440	Cholera	65
Cancer	392	Aneurism	59
Typhoid, enteric fever	306	Pyæmia septicæmia	51
Apoplexy	279	Laryngitis	49
Whooping-cough	254	Rheumatic fever and rheumatism of heart	46
Liver diseases	230	Softening of the brain	44
Croup	209	Rheumatism	43
Diseases of the urinary system (exclusive of Bright's disease)	189	Syphilis	43
Childbirth and puerperal fever	183	Diabetes mellitus	39
Inflammation of the brain	176	Found drowned	39
Bright's disease	171	Dropsy	37
Tabes mesenterica	170	Thrush	34
Endocarditis and pericarditis	156	Anæmia chlorosis, leucocythæmia	32
Paralysis	135	Murder and manslaughter	31
Peritonitis	126	Lung disease (undefined)	25
Congestion of the lungs	120	Ulceration of the intestines	24
Suicides	118	Congestion of the brain	23
Want of breast milk	112	Erysipelas	22
Tubercular meningitis (hydrocephalus)	111		

Percentage of Deaths to total Deaths, and Rate of Mortality per Thousand persons living in New South Wales from the several Classes of Diseases.

Causes of Death.	1883.			1884.			1885.			1886.		
	Deaths.	Percentage.	Per 1,000 living.	Deaths.	Percentage.	Per 1,000 living.	Deaths.	Percentage.	Per 1,000 living.	Deaths.	Percentage.	Per 1,000 living.
Specific febrile, or zymotic diseases	1,815	14·82	2·17	2,359	16·59	2·67	2,383	15·59	2·57	2,315	15·87	2·39
Parasitic diseases..........	51	·42	·06	66	·47	·07	89	·58	·10	82	·56	·08
Dietetic diseases	172	1·40	·21	198	1·39	·22	211	1·38	·23	198	1·36	·20
Constitutional diseases	1,517	12·38	1·81	1,680	11·58	1·86	1,837	12·02	1·98	1,960	13·67	2·04
Developmental diseases....	1,232	10·06	1·47	1,270	8·93	1·44	1,326	8·68	1·43	1,285	8·81	1·33
Local diseases	5,496	44·86	6·56	6,343	44·60	7·18	6,951	45·48	7·50	6,482	44·44	6·69
Violence	850	6·94	1·01	990	6·96	1·12	1,106	7·24	1·19	1,083	7·42	1·12
Ill-defined and not specified causes	1,117	9·12	1·33	1,356	9·53	1·53	1,380	9·03	1·49	1,162	7·97	1·20
	12,249	100·00	14·62	14,220	100·00	16·09	15,282	100·00	16·49	14,587	100·00	15·05

Causes of Death.	1887.			1888.			1889.			1890.		
	Deaths.	Percentage.	Per 1,000 living.	Deaths.	Percentage.	Per 1,000 living.	Deaths.	Percentage.	Per 1,000 living.	Deaths.	Percentage.	Per 1,000 living.
Specific febrile, or zymotic diseases	1,979	14·71	1·97	2,143	14·87	2·07	2,497	16·88	2·34	2,022	14·22	1·84
Parasitic diseases..........	61	·46	·06	53	·37	·05	68	·46	·06	71	·50	·08
Dietetic diseases	179	1·33	·17	183	1·27	·18	289	1·96	·27	235	1·65	·21
Constitutional diseases	1,896	14·10	1·89	2,111	14·65	2·04	2,025	13·64	1·89	1,988	13·98	1·80
Developmental diseases	1,128	8·39	1·12	1,195	8·30	1·15	1,277	8·63	1·20	1,322	9·30	1·20
Local diseases	6,110	45·43	6·08	6,542	45·41	6·32	6,615	44·71	6·20	6,567	46·23	5·93
Violence	1,148	8·54	1·14	1,140	7·91	1·07	1,110	7·50	1·04	1,163	8·18	1·06
Ill-defined and not specified causes	948	7·05	·94	1,040	7·22	1·00	922	6·23	·86	830	5·84	·75
	13,448	100·00	13·37	14,408	100·00	13·88	14,796	100·00	13·88	14,218	100·00	12·90

ACCIDENTS.

Accidental deaths.

Accidental deaths are very numerous, especially in the country. The number registered during 1890 was 972, or 214 in the Metropolis and 758 in the country districts. The numbers for 1889 were 247 and 658 respectively. An increase is therefore apparent in the country districts, and a corresponding decrease in the metropolis. The number of accidents in the colony during each of the previous three years has been about 900.

Accidents, 1884–90.

	1884.	1885.	1886.	1887.	1888.	1889.	1890.
Sydney and Suburbs...	208	281	225	211	272	247	214
Country	664	676	637	692	628	658	758
	872	957	862	903	900	905	972

In the following table a more detailed account will be found of the various accidents during the last ten years :—

Accidents, 1881–90.

	Fractures, Contusions.	Gunshot Wounds.	Cuts, &c.	Burns, Scalds.	Sunstroke.	Lightning.	Poison.	Bite of Snake or Insect.	Drowning.	Suffocation.	Otherwise.	All causes. M.	All causes. F.	All causes. Total
1881	394	10	8	92	30	*	32	5	159	35	7	606	166	
1882	351	23	15	96	36	*	38	...	216	29	6	660	150	
1883	310	25	14	85	21	*	44	4	213	35	12	594	169	
1884	403	24	19	95	41	*	42	8	203	29	8	685	187	
1885	448	13	23	121	34	*	41	3	222	42	10	755	202	
1886	357	23	14	114	37	3	12	5	210	60	27	676	192	
1887	352	11	18	93	24	2	16	3	228	129	27	727	176	
1888	396	28	22	133	37	5	15	5	176	42	41	713	187	
1889	417	15	13	101	29	7	24	4	204	54	37	712	192	
1890	394	16	9	103	17	6	21	10	319	37	40	770	202	
Total ...	3,822	188	155	1,033	306	23	285	47	2,150	492	215	6,[illegible]	1,823	8,713

* Included with "Sunstroke" during these years.

The average annual rate of accidents during the ten years 1881 to 1890 has been 94 per 100,000 of the population. This, although much lower than in Queensland, is higher than in the other colonies,

or in any country whose records are available for comparison, as will be seen from the following statement:—

Accidents per 100,000 of population, per annum.

New South Wales	94	Italy	18
Victoria	82	Germany	42
Queensland	137	Prussia	41
South Australia	65	Austria	31
Tasmania	74	Hungary	34
New Zealand	83	Belgium	37
England and Wales	56	Denmark	23
Scotland	62	Norway	56
Ireland	37	Sweden	48
France	34	Russia	20
Spain	21	United States	62
Switzerland	64		

SUICIDES.

Number and modes of suicides

The number of suicides registered during the ten years 1881-90, and the various modes adopted by the suicides for taking life, are:—

Year.	Shooting.		Cut, Stab, &c.		Poison.		Drowning.		Hanging.		Other Modes.		All cases.		
	M.	F.	M.	F.	M.	F.	M.	F.	M.	F.	M.	F.	M.	F.	Total
1881	16	...	10	1	8	2	8	2	22	2	11	1	75	8	83
1882	6	...	10	...	8	5	5	4	11	2	4	...	44	11	55
1883	12	...	10	...	5	1	2	...	14	1	8	1	51	3	54
1884	17	...	12	1	9	6	8	3	14	4	6	1	66	15	81
1885	19	1	18	...	13	5	1	3	26	5	4	...	81	14	95
1886	24	1	12	...	14	6	3	3	23	3	6	...	82	13	95
1887	22	...	14	1	17	11	14	7	26	4	4	1	97	24	121
1888	29	...	18	5	26	19	7	4	16	1	6	1	102	30	132
1889	25	...	20	4	18	11	8	5	15	3	3	...	89	23	112
1890	19	1	16	2	16	12	14	5	25	2	4	2	94	24	118
Total	189	3	140	14	134	78	70	36	192	27	56	7	781	165	946

Suicide by hanging claims the largest number of male victims for the ten years ended 1890, viz., 192; but death by poisoning was most favoured by women. Of the twenty-eight suicides by poison last year, it is stated in five cases that the poison taken was "Rough on Rats." Fourteen suicides selected this poison in 1889, and eighteen in 1888. Four of the suicides selected carbolic acid as a means of procuring death, while six took strychnine, one spirit of salt, one ratsbane, one arsenic, and one laudanum. In nine cases of suicide by poison, the name of the particular poison used was not mentioned.

Proportion of suicides to total deaths.

Number of Suicides and Proportion to Total Deaths.

Year.	Suicides by males.		Suicides by females.		Total Suicides.	
	No.	Per thousand of total deaths of males.	No.	Per thousand of total deaths of females.	No.	Per thousand deaths.
1881	75	11·11	8	1·67	83	7·19
1882	44	5·79	11	2·11	55	4·29
1883	51	7·17	3	·58	54	4·41
1884	66	7·93	15	2·54	81	5·70
1885	81	9·10	14	2·19	95	6·22
1886	82	9·64	13	2·13	95	6·51
1887	97	12·47	24	4·23	121	9·00
1888	102	12·07	30	5·04	132	9·16
1889	89	10·24	23	3·74	112	7·55
1890	94	11·35	24	4·04	118	8·30

Proportion to population.

In proportion to the whole population the yearly number of suicides is very light, and bears favourable comparison with the other colonies of the group. For the sake of clearness the rates in the following table are for every 100,000 of the population :—

Year.	Number of suicides.	Per 100,000 of mean population.
1881	83	10·7
1882	55	6·9
1883	54	6·4
1884	81	9·2
1885	95	10·3
1886	95	9·8
1887	121	12·0
1888	132	12·7
1889	112	10·5
1890	118	10·7
	Mean...........	9·9

Suicides in New South Wales compared with other colonies.

The mean rate of the whole of Australasia was 10·2, which is slightly higher than in New South Wales; in respect to suicide, however, all the colonies, Tasmania alone excepted, compare somewhat unfavourably with Great Britain; deaths by suicide averaging 7·7 per 100,000 of population in England and Wales, and 5·6 in Scotland.

Deaths from Suicide in the Australasian Colonies.

Colony.	Per 100,000 of mean population.
Tasmania	4·7
New Zealand	9·1
South Australia	9·5
New South Wales	9·9
Victoria	11·2
Western Australia	11·6
Queensland	14·1

The above are the mean annual rates from 1880 for each colony, with the exception of Western Australia, for which the rate given is the mean of 1886–89.

EXPECTATION OF LIFE.

The number of deaths at the various ages taken in connection with the numbers of persons living at each period of life, as disclosed by the census, forms the basis of a calculation which gives most interesting information, namely, the length of time that people of any age may expect to live. Not that the exact age to which any given individual will attain can be ascertained; but, by taking a number of persons at a given age, the *average* duration of life beyond that age may be estimated; and it is as certain that some will out-live the period of life set down in the table as it is that some will not survive to reach it. The idea has been very clearly expressed by Babbage, who wrote :—"Nothing is more uncertain than the duration of life when the maxim is applied to the individual, but there are few things less subject to fluctuation than the duration of life in a multitude of individuals." It is on this principle that annuities and life assurances can be made the subject of definite and exact calculations, the final results being found to vary within very narrow limits. The duration of life is a problem upon which vital statistics throw considerable light. Meaning of term.

Theory of expectation of life.

The table here presented is calculated for the three colonies of New South Wales, Victoria, and Queensland taken together, from statistics for the years 1870-81; but before drawing a comparison between the estimates therein contained and the results that have been obtained in other countries, it may be well to explain that the application of the theory of computing the average duration of human life after any given age is founded on two assumptions. "Of these the first is that the experience of the future will accord with that of the past; that is to say, that what ratio soever may have been found to exist in times past between the number surviving and the number dying in a given time, out of a specified number of individuals observed upon, the same ratio will be found to subsist in time to come between the number living and the number dying in the same space of time out of any given number of individuals similarly circumstanced with the others. And the second assumption is, that the individuals, the possibility of whose living and dying in any specified time may be in question, have all the same prospect of longevity with each other."* The phrase "expectation of life" has been taken exception to by some writers, on the ground that it is misleading to the uninitiated. The idea intended to be conveyed is the mean time which a number of persons at any age will live after that age. The late Dr. Farr, F.R.S., favoured the term "after-lifetime" as being a more correct expression, and in his report wrote as follows:—"The after-lifetime of men at the age of 30 is 33 years, by the English Life Table; 33 years is not the precise time probably that any one of that age will live, but the average time that a number of men of that age will live taken one with another. Age + after-lifetime = lifetime. At age 30 this is 30 + 33 = 63, the average age which men now aged 30 will attain. At birth this is 0 + 40 = 40; when lifetime and after-lifetime are the same thing. The lifetime simply, without the addition at a given age, will serve to express in one word what is often improperly called the "expectation of life at birth."

* Tables of Life Contingencies. Peter Gray, F.R.A.S., &c., pp. 36 and 37.

Experience of A.M.P. Society.

In addition to the expectation of life in the three colonies above-mentioned will be found a column showing the H.M. (healthy male) table of the Australian Mutual Provident Society. And while the after-lifetime at each age from 10 to 50 in the latter is higher than in the former, the gradation is much the same in each calculation. That one should give an estimate of greater longevity, after different ages, than the other is but natural, for in computing the table for the different colonies the total numbers of persons living and dying at each period of life are taken into consideration whereas in the case of the H.M. table only selected lives, or such as would be accepted by an insurance society, form the basis of computation. Looking at the two tables, therefore, in their true light, the one is more an index of the correctness of the other than if the figures in both were identical. Dr. Farr calls the Life Table a *biometer*, and speaks of it as of equal importance, in all inquiries connected with human life or sanitary improvements, with the barometer or thermometer and similar instruments employed in physical research; and as being also the key-stone or pivot on which the whole science of life assurance hinges. For even supposing that an insurance society had empirically arrived at an equitable rate of premium for assuring lives, the Mortality or Life Table is still required in order to ascertain the value of such premiums for a prospective term of years, as against the value of the sums assured thereby, so that a statement of assets and liabilities may be periodically prepared. Without such knowledge a division of "profits" would be impossible. In fact the Life Table is absolutely essential for the "solution of all questions depending on the duration of human life."

Length of life in other countries.

By way of comparison several additional columns are here given. They are reprinted from Mulhall's Dictionary of Statistics, and show the expectation of life in England, and in various other countries.

Expectation of Life at Various Ages.

Age.	*New South Wales, Victoria, and Queensland.		H.M. A.M.P. Soc.	England.		Holland.		Belgium.		Sweden.		Saxony.	United States	Age.
	M.	F.		M.	F.	M.	F.	M.	F.	M.	F.			
Birth	46·5	49·6	...	41·9	45·2	31·4	36·4	...	...	41·3	45·6	....	....	Birth.
5 years	53·0	55·4	...	51·5	53·6	48·7	49·2	...	...	49·4	53·0	....	....	5
10 „	49·2	51·7	50·3	48·2	50·3	45·9	46·5	43·8	44·8	46·5	50·0	47·0	48·7	10
15 „	44·9	47·4	46·2	43·9	46·2	...	...	...	...	...	...	....	....	15
20 „	40·8	43·3	42·1	39·9	42·1	38·3	39·2	36·4	37·7	38·6	42·1	39·3	42·2	20
25 „	37·0	39·4	38·4	36·1	38·4	...	...	...	...	...	...	....	....	25
30 „	33·3	35·7	34·7	33·2	34·1	31·8	32·4	30·5	31·9	31·2	34·5	32·1	35·3	30
35 „	29·7	32·3	31·0	28·9	31·1	...	...	...	...	...	...	....	....	35
40 „	26·2	28·9	27·4	26·5	27·5	25·0	26·4	24·8	26·1	24·3	27·2	25·0	28·2	40
45 „	22·9	25·6	23·8	22·3	24·2	...	...	...	...	...	...	....	....	45
50 „	19·8	22·3	20·3	19·9	20·8	18·5	19·7	18·9	20·3	18·0	20·1	18·0	20·9	50
55 „	16·7	18·8	17·0	16·1	17·4	...	...	...	...	...	...	....	....	55
60 „	13·8	15·5	13·8	13·6	14·5	12·8	13·3	12·4	13·9	12·3	13·5	11·7	14·1	60
65 „	11·2	12·5	11·0	10·8	11·5	...	...	...	...	...	...	....	....	65
70 „	8·9	9·7	8·5	8·6	9·1	7·9	8·1	8·1	8·3	7·4	8·0	6·9	8·5	70
75 „	6·9	7·2	6·4	6·5	7·0	...	...	...	...	...	...	....	....	75
80 „	5·4	5·7	4·7	5·2	5·6	4·4	4·5	5·2	5·4	3·9	4·3	3·9	4·4	80
85 „	4·0	4·2	3·5	3·8	4·1	...	...	...	...	...	...	....	....	85
90 „	3·0	3·2	2·4	2·8	3·1	2·4	2·7	2·9	3·1	2·4	2·8	....	....	90

* *Vide* A. F. Burridge in Journal of Institute of Actuaries, vol. xxiv.

From this table it will be seen that the colonies stand very well when compared with other quarters of the globe. The average expectation of life of males and females at infancy, youth, and after the age of 50 years is higher than in any of the countries given.

VACCINATION.

Vaccination returns.

Vaccination is not compulsory in New South Wales, and is resorted to only in times of scare, when an epidemic of small-pox is thought imminent. It is easy to discover, from the returns of the Government vaccinators, the years when the community was threatened by the disease, as at such times the number of persons submitting themselves to vaccination largely increased. The number returned does not include those treated by private medical officers, by whom a large number of persons are vaccinated.

Persons Vaccinated by Government Medical Officers.

Year.	Sydney and Suburbs.	Country.	Total.	Year.	Sydney and Suburbs.	Country.	Total.
1876	2 69	3,276	4,545	1884	630	6,569	7,199
1877	5,308	11,943	17,251	1885	346	1,884	2,230
1878	532	3,038	3,570	1886	452	1,311	1,763
1879	657	4,981	5,638	1887	1,031	2,199	3,230
1880	460	4,699	5,159	1888	1,091	1,095	2,186
1881	8,738	52,501	61,239	1889	728	1,676	2,404
1882	308	1,869	2,249	1890	900	1,212	2,112
1883	296	600	896				

Age of persons vaccinated.

The number and ages of persons vaccinated by the Government vaccinators during 1890 will be found below :—

District.	Under 1 year.	From 1 to 5 years.	From 5 to 10 years.	10 years and upwards.	Total.
Sydney and suburbs	218	298	207	177	900
Country districts	122	456	489	145	1,212
Total	340	754	696	322	2,112

INSANITY.

The number of insane persons under treatment in hospitals is almost a fixed proportion of the total population, viz., 2·78 per thousand. Since 1871 the proportion has varied only 0·07 above, and 0·11 per thousand below, the average stated. The hospitals for insane, under the immediate control of the Government, are five in number—four for ordinary insane, and one, at Parramatta, for criminals. Besides these there are two licensed houses each for a single patient, at Picton.

Number of insane under treatment.

The number of insane persons under treatment on the 31st December, 1890, under official cognizance, was 3,102, distributed as follows:—

Name of Hospital.	No. on Register.		
	Males.	Females.	Total.
Gladesville	533	301	834
Parramatta, free	693	354	1,047
Do. criminal	45	9	54
Callan Park	485	335	820
Newcastle	137	118	255
Cook's River	13	82	95
Licensed Houses, Picton	......	2	2
Total	1,906	1,194	3,102

These figures are 128 in excess of the total for 1889.

Proportion of insane a constant quantity.

The proportion of insane to the whole population, as already pointed out, is almost a constant quantity, as will be seen from the accompanying table, giving the number of persons in hospitals for insane at the close of each year from 1871 to 1890:—

Year ended 31 December.	No. of Insane.	Proportion of Insane to population per 1,000.	Year ended 31 December.	No. of Insane.	Proportion of Insane to population per 1,000.
1871	1,387	2·67	1882	2,307	2·83
1872	1,440	2·69	1883	2,403	2·78
1873	1,526	2·75	1884	2,524	2·79
1874	1,588	2·76	1885	2,643	2·78
1875	1,697	2·85	1886	2,717	2·75
1876	1,743	2·83	1887	2,821	2·76
1877	1,829	2·84	1888	2,898	2·75
1878	1,916	2·85	1889	2,974	2·75
1879	2,011	2·83	1890	3,102	2·77
1880	2,099	2·83			
1881	2,218	2·84		Mean...	2·78

The amount of insanity in New South Wales and in England, compared with their respective populations, is about the same, though there appears to be a tendency in the latter country for the rate to increase. The greatest proportion of lunacy in these colonies is found in Victoria, and the lowest in Tasmania, South Australia, and Queensland.

Amount of insanity in England.

Insanity in the United Kingdom and Australasian Colonies.

Country.	Insane persons per 1,000 of population.	Country.	Insane persons per 1,000 of population.
England	2·88	Queensland	2·44
Scotland	2·91	South Australia	2·47
Ireland	3·16	Western Australia	2·75
New South Wales	2·77	Tasmania	2·03
Victoria	3·25	New Zealand	2·66

The percentage of deaths of insane persons is comparatively light. The following table has been computed on the basis of the average number of patients resident in hospitals for insane:—

Death-rate of the insane.

Year.	Percentage of deaths of average number resident.			Year.	Percentage of deaths of average number resident.		
	Male.	Female.	Total.		Male.	Female.	Total.
1881	6·52	4·21	5·63	1887	6·64	7·03	6·79
1882	6·76	5·61	6·32	1888	7·59	6·32	7·11
1883	9·71	4·98	6·64	1889	7·73	6·44	7·24
1884	8·18	6·22	7·43	1890	7·01	5·74	6·52
1885	7·61	4·97	6·59				
1886	7·54	6·37	7·08	Mean ...	7·53	5·79	6·74

The number of persons admitted to the hospitals has varied a great deal. The effect of the continued commercial depression

Increase of admissions in seasons of depression.

during late years was experienced in the unusual number of idiotic and imbecile children, as well as demented people, found amongst the admissions, whose relatives would willingly have maintained them in more prosperous times.

Admissions to Hospitals for Insane and Proportion to Mean Population.

Year.	Admissions.	Proportion to population per 1,000.	Year.	Admissions.	Proportion to population per 1,000.
1871	340	0·66	1881	494	0·64
1872	303	0·57	1882	473	0·59
1873	342	0·62	1883	476	0·57
1874	330	0·58	1884	493	0·55
1875	356	0·60	1885	567	0·60
1876	360	0·59	1886	567	0·58
1877	457	0·72	1887	532	0·52
1878	424	0·64	1888	587	0·55
1879	440	0·63	1889	550	0·50
1880	476	0·65	1890	611	0·54
				Mean	0·60

Influx of insane from abroad.

There is no law in force in this Colony to prevent the influx of insane persons; and, as a consequence, the splendid hospitals, which the bounty of the Government has established for the treatment of the insane, have been the means of burdening the community with the care of unfortunate persons belonging to other countries, where the treatment meted out to the insane is less generous or less scientific than in New South Wales. Were it not for this influx of insane from outside its boundaries, the rate for this Colony would be much lower than it is at present.

Birth-places of Patients in Hospitals for Insane, 1890.

Country.	No. of Patients.	Percentage of total.	Country.	No. of Patients.	Percentage of total.
New South Wales	1,121	30·64	France	24	0·65
Other British Colonies	143	3·91	Germany	90	2·46
England	870	23·78	China	74	2·02
Ireland	974	26·62	Other Countries and not ascertained	193	5·27
Scotland...........	170	4·65			

In this and the two following tables all the patients received into the hospitals for insane during the whole of the year are enumerated; the number remaining under control on the 31st December is given in a previous table.

The number of persons under restraint, who are natives of this Colony, is only 30·64 per cent. of the total, whilst the native-born element of the total population is at least 64 per cent. Of the British-born patients, England contributes very nearly twice the number that her population in this country would warrant, and Ireland at least thrice the number. Small proportion of Insane born in the Colony.

The ages of the insane are set forth in the following table, which shows that nearly one-half of the whole number (47 per cent.) are between 30 and 50 years of age. The table deals only with patients in hospitals for insane, and gives the percentage for 1890 at each period of life. Ages of Insane.

Ages of Insane.	No. of Patients.	Percentage of all ages.
Under 5 years	6	·16
5 to 10	33	·90
10 ,, 15	50	1·37
15 ,, 20	97	2·65
20 ,, 30	531	14·51
30 ,, 40	833	22·77
40 ,, 50	881	24·08
50 ,, 60	705	19·27
60 ,, 70	346	9·46
70 ,, 80	152	4·15
80 years and upwards	25	·68

Juvenile lunatics are as a rule sent to the Hospital for the Insane at Newcastle, an asylum which is set apart for imbecile and idiotic patients, so that of the 89 mentioned in the foregoing table as being under 15 years of age, 85 were in that institution.

The major portion of the persons under restraint are single; amongst the married, females largely predominate, as also amongst

Condition as regards marriage.

the widowed. The condition as to marriage of patients in hospitals for the insane during 1890 is shown hereunder :—

Condition as to Marriage.	Male.	Female	Total.
Single	1,442	543	1,985
Married	482	623	1,105
Widowed	95	170	265
Unascertained	220	84	304

Intemperance as a cause of insanity.

It is popularly supposed that the principal cause of insanity is intemperance. The experience of this Colony, however, does not bear out this opinion. The amount of insanity directly due to drink, though certainly large, is not so considerable as that due to other causes. As far as the records of the hospitals show, the percentage of persons admitted suffering from insanity traceable to intemperance, is not more than 11·57 per cent. of the total admissions.

Persons insane from drink soon recover.

Persons suffering from mania induced by excess of drink recover comparatively quickly, and at any one time their number in the hospitals for the insane is scarcely more than 5·5 per cent. The most potent cause appears to be hereditary influence. How far this is productive of insanity cannot, however, be exactly determined; for although the Inspector-General of the Insane, a high authority on lunacy, has ascertained that hereditary influence and congenital defect can be credited with only 8·86 per cent. of the total insanity, this percentage gives no idea of the actual amount of hereditary insanity in the Colony. Of the large number of patients the causes of whose insanity is unknown, it is believed that in most instances the insanity is due to hereditary influence, and even in those cases where the primary cause of insanity has been ascertained, there is strong presumption that many of the patients have inherited an insane neurosis.

Insane neurosis.

In the following table will be found the percentages of the various causes of insanity. The calculations are made on the apparent or assigned causes in the cases of all patients admitted into the asylums for the insane :—

Causation of Insanity.

Cause of Insanity.	Percentage of male insanity.	Percentage of female insanity.	Percentage of total insanity.	
Moral :—				
Domestic trouble (including loss of relatives and friends)	·90	8·19	3·72	
Adverse circumstances (including business anxiety and pecuniary difficulties)	3·15	·36	2·07	
Mental anxiety and "worry" (not included under above two heads), and overwork	3·60	3·20	3·45	13·10
Religious excitement	1·80	2·14	1·93	
Love affairs (including seduction)	·68	·36	·55	
Fright and nervous shock	·23	1·78	·83	
Isolation	·68	...	·41	
Nostalgia	·23	...	·14	
Physical :—				
Intemperance in drink	11·49	7·12	9·79	
Do (sexual)	·23	1·78	·83	
Venereal disease	·68	...	·41	
Self-abuse	2·03	...	1·24	
Sunstroke	2·03	·36	1·38	
Accident or injury	1·35	·71	1·10	
Pregnancy	...	·71	·28	
Parturition and the puerperal state	...	6·76	2·64	
Lactation	...	1·07	·41	
Uterine and ovarian disorders	...	·71	·27	
Puberty	1·35	...	·83	
Change of life	...	3·20	1·24	
Fevers	·22	·35	·27	
Privation and overwork	·45	·35	·41	
Phthisis	·22	·35	·28	53·66
Epilepsy	2·93	4·27	3·45	
Disease of skull and brain	3·15	1·42	2·48	
Exophthalmic bronchocele	...	·35	·14	
Old age	3·15	5·34	4·00	
Other bodily diseases and disorders	2·25	5·34	3·45	
Excess of opium	...	·36	·14	
Excess of cocaine	·45	...	·28	
Previous attacks	9·46	7·12	8·55	
Hereditary influence ascertained	6·53	8·54	7·31	
Congenital defect ascertained	2·03	2·85	2·34	
Other ascertained causes	·22	...	·14	
Unknown	38·51	24·91	33·24	33·24

Deaths of insane.

During the year 1890 the deaths of persons afflicted with lunacy numbered 193, viz., 128 males and 65 females. The following are the causes of death, and the number who died from each disease :—

	Males.	Females.	Total.
CEREBRAL DISEASES—			
Apoplexy and paralysis	2	3	5
Epilepsy and convulsions	8	3	11
General paralysis	25	1	26
Maniacal and melancholic exhaustion and decay	7	10	17
Inflamation and other diseases of the brain	20	6	26
THORACIC DISEASES—			
Inflamation of the lungs, pleura and bronchi	10	3	13
Pulmonary consumption	13	12	25
Disease of the heart and bloodvessels ...	8	5	13
ABDOMINAL DISEASES—			
Inflammation and ulceration of stomach, intestines, and peritoneum	1	1	2
Dysentery and diarrhœa	6	5	11
Disease of liver	4	......	4
General debilty and old age	16	15	31
Epithelioma of face	2	......	2
Suicide	2	1	3
Accident	3	......	3
Erysipelas	1	......	1
Total	128	65	193

Lunacy not incompatible with longevity.

Of the above total 14 males and 11 females were over 70 years of age, so that the malady of lunacy is not incompatible with longevity. Four males and three females were over 80 years of age.

The average weekly cost during the year 1890, of maintaining insane patients in the hospitals was about 11s. 11¼d. per week, of which the State paid 10s. 4¼d., the balance being made up by contributions from the estates of the patients themselves, or by their friends. The subjoined table shows the average weekly cost per head, and average private contributions from 1881 to 1890:— Cost of patients.

Average Weekly Cost of Patients in Hospitals for the Insane.

Year.	Cost per head to State.	Contribution per head from private sources.	Total weekly cost per head.
	s. d.	s. d.	s. d.
1881	10 8¼	1 2¼	11 10½
1882	12 0¼	1 2¼	13 2½
1883	11 5¾	1 0¼	12 6
1884	11 0	1 3¼	12 3¼
1885	11 3½	1 4½	12 8
1886	11 1¾	1 5½	12 7¼
1887	10 6	1 5½	11 11½
1888	10 2	1 6¼	11 8¼
1889	11 3¼	1 6½	12 9¾
1890	10 4¼	1 7	11 11¼
Average for 10 years	10 11½	1 4½	12 4

Criminal lunatics are confined at Parramatta. At the end of last year the total in confinement was 54, of whom 45 were males and 9 females, as compared with 51 twelve months before. During 1890 the admissions numbered 11, there were 3 discharged, recovered, 1 died, and 4 were transferred to other hospitals. The offences for which the criminal insane are detained are amongst the blackest in the calendar, as will be seen from the following table, which refers to the number in the institution on the 31st December, 1890:— Criminal insane.

Criminal Insanity.

Crimes committed by the Insane.	Number of insane.		
	Males.	Females.	Total.
Murder	19	3	22
Attempt to murder	......	1	1
Manslaughter	1	......	1
Rape	2	......	2
Indecent assault	2	......	2
Unnatural offence	1	......	1
Cutting and wounding, shooting with intent, &c.	12	3	15
Horse stealing	4	......	4
Assault and battery	1	......	1
False pretences	1	......	1
Vagrancy	2	......	2
Arson and malicious burning	......	1	1
Attempting suicide	......	1	1
Total	45	9	54

PART XXIII.

Social Condition and Charities.

IT will be seen from the foregoing pages that the material prosperity of New South Wales compares favourably with that of any other country, however fortunate may be its lot. But in one particular this Colony, in common with all the provinces of Australasia, differs greatly from other countries, especially those of the Old World. Wealth is widely distributed, and the contrast between rich and poor, which seems so peculiar a phase of old-world civilizations, finds no parallel in these southern lands. That there is poverty in the colonies is undeniable, but no one in Australasia is born to poverty, and that hereditary pauper class, which forms so grave a menace to the freedom of many States, has, therefore, no existence here.

Propertied classes.

It is estimated that in the United Kingdom six persons in every hundred possess property to the amount of £100; whereas in the colonies the proportion is not less than twelve per cent. This bare statement shows the vast difference in the conditions of life in Australasia and in the richest country of Europe. No poor rate is levied in the colonies, nor is such needed; for although it may happen that from time to time the assistance of the State is claimed by, and granted to, able-bodied men who are unable to find employment, that assistance takes the form of wages paid for work specially provided by the State to meet a condition of the labour market which is certainly abnormal.

State assistance to charities.

The chief efforts of the authorities, as regards charity, are directed towards the rescue of the young from criminal companionship and

that the average air space to each dormitory was 7,829 cubic feet. There were 2,306 beds, and the average air space to each patient was a minimum of 1,314 cubic feet; but as the hospitals are rarely filled to the limit of their accommodation, the air space to each patient was as a rule greater than the minimum just stated. During the year 17,041 persons were under treatment as indoor patients. Of this number 1,285 remained from the previous year, and 15,756 were admitted during 1890. There were discharged 14,195 persons, either as cured or relieved, or at their own request, and 191 as past all human assistance, while 1,361 died. The number remaining in hospital at the close of the year was therefore 1,294. The following statement shows the number of admissions, discharges, and deaths for the past twelve years:— Persons under treatment.

Number of Cases treated in Hospitals.

Year.	Total Patients under Treatment.	Number Discharged as Cured, &c.	Deaths.		Number of Patients at the close of Year.
			Number.	Per cent. under treatment.	
1879	7,560	6,021	755	9·98	784
1880	8,315	6,656	847	10·18	812
1881	9,136	7,275	946	10·35	915
1882	8,445	6,855	894	10·58	696
1883	8,245	6,659	796	9·65	790
1884	9,318	7,375	952	10·21	991
1885	12,793	10,449	1,329	10·38	1,015
1886	13,115	10,825	1,249	9·52	1,041
1887	13,438	11,140	1,190	8·85	1,106
1888	15,176	12,569	1,424	9·38	1,233
1889	16,865	13,535	1,477	8·76	1,311
1890	17,041	14,195	1,361	8·00	1,294

The number remaining at the close of the year may be taken as representing the average number resident. It will be seen from the preceding table that the increase has been fairly regular, so that the proportion of the population to be found in hospitals is about the same in each year, and averaged 1·17 per thousand in 1890. The length of time during which patients remain under treatment has not been exactly determined; but as far as the information extends it would appear the average is about 28 days for all Average number of hospital cases.

hospitals. In the Sydney Hospital the average stay of patients during the year 1890 was 24·9 days. It is interesting to note that patients received under orders from the Government, remained in hospital on the average longer than those paying for or contributing towards their own support.

Death rates in hospitals.

The death rate per 100 persons under treatment during the past ten years was 9·40, while the rate for 1890 was 8·00 or 1·40 below the decennial average. The rate for each year will be found in the preceding table. The death rate of hospitals in New South Wales, compared with Europe, is undoubtedly very high. The number of fatal cases is swollen by the inclusion of the deaths of persons already moribund when admitted, and of persons in the last stage of phthisis. It has elsewhere been pointed out that deaths from accidents form a very considerable proportion of the total deaths registered, a circumstance due to the nature of the occupations of the people, and the dangers incidental to pioneering enterprise. A large majority of the accidents that occur, when not immediately fatal, are treated in the hospitals; and, indeed, these institutions, especially in country districts, are for the most part maintained for the treatment of surgical cases. When these circumstances are taken into consideration the cause of the apparent excess of deaths in the hospitals of the Colony will be at once understood.

State expenditure for pauper patients.

The amount expended by the State for the maintenance of sick paupers in the year 1890 was £9,131 8s., which was distributed thus :—Sydney Hospital (including Moorcliff) for the maintenance of pauper patients, £5,413 15s. 6d.; Prince Alfred Hospital, ditto, £3,717 12s. 6d. During the year there were 5,485 applications for admission into the metropolitan hospitals, of which number 2,675 were granted; the other cases received recommendations for admission to the Asylums for the Infirm and Destitute, orders for out-door hospital treatment, or were refused as unfit subjects for State relief; 533 persons were admitted into these hospitals as urgent cases, the remainder were admitted on recommendations from the hospital admission depôt. During the past three years the Sydney Hospital, including the Moorcliff branch for ophthalmic cases, has received from the Government, for the maintenance of sick paupers, £18,350, or an average of £6,116 a year, and the Prince Alfred Hospital, £12,507, or an average of £4,169 a year. These sums are in addition to the £4,000 a year given as a conditional endowment to each of these hospitals, and £400 a year which the Government pays as the rent of Moorcliff. The total sum paid by the Government to the Sydney and Prince Alfred Hospitals during the last three years, exclusive of subsidies for special purposes, was £56,077, or an average of £18,692 a year. The expenses of the Coast Hospital, which are borne entirely by the Government, averaged £12,495 annually for the same period, so that over £31,000 a year is spent by the Government in medical relief in the metropolis, in addition to grants to suburban and country hospitals, payments for attendance of aborigines, expenses attending special outbreaks of disease in country districts, which are met from the general medical vote, and the maintenance in the asylums for the Infirm and Destitute of a large number of chronic and incurable hospital cases. Cost to the State.

No exact information is to hand respecting the outdoor relief afforded by hospitals, this form of charity not being so important as indoor relief; nevertheless, the number of attendances during 1890 was 28,637, and estimating four attendances to each person, there were relieved 7,159 persons. Outdoor relief.

Omitting from consideration the Government establishment at Little Bay, the expenditure in 1890 of all the hospitals of the Colony for purposes other than building, repairs, and out-door relief, was £94,189, representing an average of £83 7s. 1d. per patient resident, or for each bed occupied. This sum is somewhat in excess of the truth, as full deduction cannot be made for out-patients. The average cost per patient treated was £6 2s. 10d. The subscriptions Expenditure on hospitals.

hospitals and asylums, with the exception of asylums for the insane, was £145,892. This sum includes £26,415 to the State Children's Relief Department, £13,961 paid to support the asylum for old men at Liverpool, £8,884 for the asylum for the aged and infirm at Newington, Parramatta River; £23,449 for the two asylums and the cottage homes for married couples at Parramatta, and £4,541 for the Benevolent Asylum, Sydney. In these last-mentioned asylums, the number of wards or dormitories was 174, with a total capacity of 1,536,673 cubic feet, giving an average air space of 8,831 cubic feet to each dormitory. There were 2,730 beds; the average air space to each patient was therefore 563 cubic feet. The number of inmates in each institution will be found in tables on pages 865 and 866, but in addition, considerable aid was extended to the outside poor. Apart from medical advice and medicines, out-door relief consists largely of supplies of provisions. Information is not to hand for the full extent of the relief thus afforded at all institutions, but the goods gratuitously distributed at the Benevolent Asylum, Sydney, during the year 1890 were as follows:—Bread, 99,275 loaves; flour, 58,687 lb.; meat, 8,800 lb.; tea, 6,956 lb.; sugar, 28,144 lb.; sago, 2,470 lb.; rice, 5,250 lb.; oatmeal, 2,812 lb.; arrowroot, 97 lb.; raisins, 576 lb.; and milk, 140 quarts. Boots, blankets, flannel and other drapery goods, formed portion of the bounty distributed; and in addition to this a sum of money was granted in payment of rent allowances, so that many of the needy were assisted by the helping hand of this deserving charity in their own homes.

The Infants' Home, Ashfield; the Hospital for sick children, Glebe; the Institution for the deaf and dumb, and the blind, Newtown, besides other institutions in different parts of the Colony, receive help from the State; but they are maintained principally by private contributions. The management of these, and, indeed, of almost all institutions for the relief of the sick, is in the hands of committees elected by persons subscribing towards their support:—

Number of Persons in various Charitable Institutions, mainly supported by Private Charity, at the end of each year, 1881–90.

Institution.	1881.		1882.		1883.		1884.		1885.		1886.		1887.		1888.		1889.		1890.	
	M.	F.	M.	F.	M.	F.	M.	F.	M.	F.	M.	F.	M.	F.	M.	F.	M.	F.	M.	F.
Industrial Blind Institution, Sydney	...	...	9	...	10	...	20	...	20	...	21	...	22	...	25	...	30	...	31	...
Industrial Home for Blind Women, Petersham	...	...	...	...	...	...	...	...	...	...	...	...	...	14	...	17	...	14	...	15
Consumptives' Home, Picton	...	...	...	...	12	4	12	5	13	4	19	8	22	10	24	8	21	9	20	5
House of the Good Samaritan	...	49	...	56	...	84	...	62	...	64	...	80	...	66	...	58	...	63	...	64
Sydney Female Refuge	...	40	...	47	...	37	...	43	...	44	...	48	...	44	...	39	...	51	...	42
Hospital for Sick Children, Glebe	14	11	16	23	9	12	20	17	21	22	19	15	20	19	20	20	15	16	27	21
*Infants' Home, Ashfield (women)	...	...	...	20	...	12	...	23	...	11	...	19	...	22	...	22	*	*	*	*
Infants' Home, Ashfield (children)	30	17	30	20	20	11	34	20	19	13	20	15	8	15	28	28	59	59	34	28
City Night Refuge, &c.	20	...	20	...	20	...	20	...	19	...	18	...	18	...	18	...	18	...	18	...
Total	64	117	75	166	71	160	106	170	92	158	97	185	90	184	115	192	143	212	130	175

* This Institution now admits children only.

Besides hospitals properly so called, there exist various institutions for the reception of fallen women, for the treatment of the blind, and the deaf and dumb; for destitute women, for casual aid to indigent persons, for the help of discharged prisoners, and for many other purposes which rouse the charity of the people. Exact figures respecting every institution have not been procurable. The foregoing table gives the number of adult persons remaining at the close of 1890 in some of the institutions named, and may be taken as representing the average for the year. The figures for the City Night Refuge and Soup Kitchen show only the number of persons usually retained about the establishment. There were 94,169 meals given during the year ending 30th June, 1890, at the Refuge, and shelter was provided in 33,300 instances, the daily average being 258 meals, and 92 nightly shelters.

Charitable asylums.

City Night Refuge.

The problem of dealing with destitute children and those liable from their environment to become criminal is naturally surrounded with very great difficulty, and its solution was attempted many years ago by the establishment of the orphanages at Parramatta, and the destitute children's asylum at Randwick, as well as the Vernon Training Ship for boys, and the Biloela Reformatory and Industrial School for girls. The system of crowding children in large establishments was rightly considered as open to many grave objections, and in 1880 a scheme of separate treatment was inaugurated. Accordingly an Act was passed by the Legislature, empowering the formation of a Board, to whose charge the destitute or neglected children of the Colony were entrusted. The Board was empowered to take children from the various institutions, and deal with them in certain specified ways.

Destitute children.

During the ten years ending 5th April, 1891, the number of children placed out by the State Children's Relief Board had

State Children's Relief Board.

increased to 3,910. Of these 1,541 were reclaimed by their relatives or friends, or otherwise discharged, and 157 were adopted principally by persons possessing no children of their own. The number under the control of the Board in April, 1891, was 2,369, of whom 1,417 were boys, and 952 girls. Of these 806 boys and 568 girls were boarded-out under payment to persons deemed eligible, at rates varying from 5s. to 10s. per week, the officers of the Board being required to exercise a strict supervision to ensure that the children are not neglected or illtreated. In addition to those boarded-out, 66 boys and 91 girls were adopted, by which arrangement a subsidy to the amount of £1,820 was saved. At the age of 12 years, children, if physically fit, may be apprenticed; and since the Board has had control, 543 boys and 295 girls have been indentured. The majority of the girls are sent to domestic service, and about two-thirds of the boys have been apprenticed to farmers. During the year the number of children boarded-out was 494, and 60 were apprenticed. The number of children remaining in the institutions in April last were distributed as follows:—2 in the depôt, 5 in hospitals, and 116 consigned to cottage-homes for invalids, of which there are 2 at Parramatta, and 6 at Mittagong. Although as many as 775 passed through the Central Home at Paddington during the year, the system in force provides for their speedy removal to the country; and so the average daily number of inmates at that institution was only 7. Of the number under the Board's care 12 boys and 5 girls died during the year. In the annual reports of the State Children's Relief Department much interesting information is given concerning the problem of how to cope successfully with the difficulty of maintaining State children; and, after ten years' experience of the boarding-out system in this Colony, it is claimed that when fairly tested the advantages that may be realised thereby, are much greater than those under the system of aggregating children in asylums.

Supervision of children.

Number of children under control.

The number of children under the control of the Board for each year ending April, since 1881, is shown in the following table:—

Year ending April.	Boys.	Girls.	Total.	Year ending April.	Boys.	Girls.	Total.
1881	24	35	59	1887	1,099	703	1,802
1882	40	63	103	1888	1,202	758	1,960
1883	119	188	307	1889	1,316	857	2,173
1884	232	320	552	1890	1,380	904	2,284
1885	564	462	1,026	1891	1,417	952	2,369
1886	779	587	1,366				

Ages of children.

The ages of children placed out since the inauguration of the Board's operations were:—

Year.		Year.	
Under 1	38	8 and under 9.........	465
1 and under 2	77	9 ,, ,, 10.........	438
2 ,, ,, 3	239	10 ,, ,, 11.........	350
3 ,, ,, 4	322	11 ,, ,, 12.........	300
4 ,, ,, 5	334	Over 12	272
5 ,, ,, 6	324		
6 ,, ,, 7	382	Total	3,910
7 ,, ,, 8	369		

The largest number of children dealt with by the Board have been received from the Benevolent Asylum, Sydney, 2,754 having been transferred up to the end of 1890; from the Randwick Asylum 306, and from the Orphan Schools, Parramatta, 362 children were taken. The orphan schools were closed in September, 1886, and the children who would formerly have been sent to them are now taken charge of by the Board. The remaining children were removed from other public institutions and hospitals; from the Vernon, 218; from the Infants' Home, Ashfield, 66; from Industrial School, Parramatta, 88; from Little Bay Hospital, 26; from Benevolent Asylum, Newcastle, 37; and other institutions, 53; making a total of 3,910 as aforesaid. The gross amount expended by the Government on the State Children's Relief Department during the year was £26,330.

Operations of Board successful.

Judged by the saving to the State effected by the Board, which cannot be placed at less than £15,000 per annum, its operations must be held to be entirely successful. But there are other and higher grounds of gratulation, for not only are the children individually more satisfactorily treated than could be the case in crowded institutions, but the number becoming a charge on the State is now proportionally less than formerly, and the admirable system of relief organized by the Board bids fair to solve the difficult problem of juvenile destitution and juvenile crime. The number of destitute children, including those detained at Biloela (now transferred to Parramatta) and on the Vernon, and in the various asylums, during each of the past fourteen years, was :—

Destitute Children.

Year.	Number.	Year.	Number.
1877	1,573	1884	1,787
1878	1,582	1885	1,868
1879	1,726	1886	1,886
1880	1,742	1887	1,973
1881	1,817	1888	2,091
1882	1,858	1889	2,218
1883	1,861	1890	2,077

The increase of 504 during the period bears but a small proportion of what might have been expected from the large increase in the juvenile population of the Colony.

Reformatories. Three institutions are maintained at the charge of the State for the reformation of children: the Shaftesbury Reformatory, for girls who are in danger of becoming habitual criminals; the Parramatta Industrial School, for girls of more tender years; and the Vernon training-ship, for boys. No reformatory exclusively for criminal boys exists; but the necessity for such an institution has long been recognized by the Government, and there is little doubt that such an establishment will shortly be provided. The Vernon at present fills the double purpose of training-school and reformatory. The number of children in these institutions at the close of each of the last twelve years was :—

Children in Reformatories.

Year.	Vernon.	Biloela (now Parramatta).	Shaftesbury.	Total.
1879	124	115	4	243
1880	148	117	11	276
1881	177	130	19	326
1882	186	130	29	345
1883	213	119	27	359
1884	202	105	25	332
1885	202	106	29	337
1886	205	90	24	319
1887	203	90	26	319
1888	209	93	28	330
1889	227	87	42	356
1890	208	64	32	304

During 1887 the industrial school for girls was removed from Biloela, Cockatoo Island, to the building formerly occupied by the Roman Catholic Orphan School, Parramatta. Industrial School.

The numbers of destitute children in other charitable institutions at the close of each of the last twelve years were as follows :—

Children in Asylums.

Year.	Orphan Schools.	Randwick Asylum.	Benevolent Asylum.	Infants' Home, Ashfield.	State Children's Relief Department.	Total.
1879	574	641	191	77	....	1,483
1880	552	639	177	46	52	1,466
1881	546	671	147	47	80	1,491
1882	442	643	156	50	222	1,513
1883	339	545	161	31	426	1,502
1884	150	352	149	54	750	1,455
1885	108	199	122	32	1,058	1,519
1886	*	254	130	35	1,128	1,547
1887	....	267	101	23	1,263	1,654
1888	....	246	168	56	1,291	1,761
1889	....	216	151	118	1,377	1,862
1890	....	212	161	62	1,338	1,773

* Orphanages closed in this year.

The number of destitute adults wholly or in part supported by the State as inmates of the various asylums of the Colony at the close of the year 1890 was 2,621, of whom 2,039 were men, and Destitute adults.

582 women. The great majority of those in the asylums persons of very advanced years and unable to work. The inm of the Benevolent Asylum, Sydney, however, form an excep to this rule, as a large proportion of them are destitute wo who use the institution as a lying-in hospital. The number of and women in the various institutions with the ratio per 1,00 adult population at the close of each of the past twelve years wa

Adult paupers.

Adults in Benevolent Asylums.

Year.	Males.	Females.	Total.	Per 1,000 of Adult Populati		
				Male.	Female.	Tot
1879	1,044	368	1,412	4·28	2·00	3·
1880	994	382	1,376	3·89	1·99	3·
1881	985	375	1,360	3·65	1·88	2·
1882	980	402	1,382	3·50	1·92	2·
1883	1,282	408	1,690	4·31	1·85	3·
1884	1,363	435	1,798	4·33	1·86	3·
1885	1,366	400	1,766	4·06	1·63	3·
1886	1,504	448	1,952	4·60	1·67	3·
1887	1,719	471	2,190	5·10	1·70	3·
1888	1,820	521	2,341	5·24	1·82	3·
1889	1,912	588	2,500	5·35	2·00	3·
1890	2,039	582	2,621	5·52	1·90	3·

The following is the number of adults remaining in the vari Benevolent Asylums at the close of the years 1879 to 1890 :–

Adults in the various Asylums.

Year.	Sydney (Pitt-street).	Newington.	Liverpool.	Parramatta.			West Maitland.	Newcastle.	Singleton.	To
				George-street.	Mac-quarie-st.	Cottage Homes.				
1879	92	262	756	254	18	...	13	...	17	1,
1880	77	288	707	259	22	...	12	...	11	1,
1881	73	277	724	237	20	...	13	...	16	1,
1882	88	284	733	219	30	...	13	...	15	1,
1883	107	292	724	267	268	...	16	...	16	1,
1884	115	312	724	339	276	...	16	...	16	1,
1885	88	304	710	342	292	...	16	...	14	1,
1886	83	331	741	421	297	...	35	27	17	1,
1887	77	366	767	644	258	...	35	28	15	2,
1888	97	397	778	721	286	...	36	26	...	2,
1889	83	454	801	771	283	39	37	32	...	2,
1890	92	462	789	867	288	42	39	28	14	2,

The Liverpool and Parramatta (2) Asylums are homes for males, and the Newington and Sydney Benevolent Asylums for females.

The Cottage Homes opened at Parramatta in March, 1889, are for old and indigent married couples. The number resident at the end of 1890 was 42.

Adding together the numbers of adults and children in order to show the proportion, as compared with the whole population, of those dependent on the State for support, the ratios per 1,000 for the last twelve years, are found to be as follows:—

Paupers.

Year.	Children.	Adults.	Total.	Per 1,000 of		
				Children under 15 years.	Adult Population.	Total Population.
1879	1,726	1,412	3,138	6·13	3·30	4·42
1880	1,742	1,376	3,118	5·91	3·08	4·16
1881	1,817	1,360	3,177	5·86	2·89	4·06
1882	1,858	1,382	3,240	5·78	2·82	3·98
1883	1,861	1,690	3,551	5·49	3·26	4·12
1884	1,787	1,798	3,585	5·01	3·28	3·96
1885	1,856	1,766	3,622	4·94	3·03	3·81
1886	1,866	1,952	3,818	4·74	3·28	3·86
1887	1,973	2,182	4,155	4·81	3·57	4·07
1888	2,091	2,341	4,432	4·90	3·70	4·21
1889	2,218	2,500	4,718	5·04	3·84	4·36
1890	2,077	2,621	4,698	4·65	3·89	4·20

The increase noticeable during some years is probably due to the defective seasons experienced from time to time throughout the Colony, and the consequent closing of avenues of income which remained open to some of these old people, in more favourable times. The proportion of paupers to the whole population shown in the above table will appear extremely small compared

Increase due to depression.

with that of other countries. The proportion of population in the United Kingdom dependent upon the State for support was, at the beginning of the year 1889 :—

England and Wales	28·16 per thousand.
Scotland	22·30 ,,
Ireland	23·24 ,,
United Kingdom	26·92 ,,

as against 4·2 per thousand in this Colony, a state of things plainly illustrating the happier lot of the people of Australia.

Treatment of insane.

The treatment of the insane has been dealt with under the head of Vital Statistics. The average number of insane persons resident in hospital during the year was 2,960, while the total number under care was 3,659. These numbers include those resident at the Private Asylum. The gross expenditure on hospitals for insane, wholly supported by the State, during 1890, was £88,693; the collections from private sources amounted to £11,668, leaving a net cost to the Government of £77,025—equivalent to a weekly average cost of 10s. 4½d. per patient, and an annual expenditure per head of population of 1s. 5d. The total expenditure by the State on all institutions connected with the care of the insane, inclusive of the cost of maintenance of Government patients at the private asylum, Cook's River, was £96,138, and the total collections amounted to £11,902, so that the actual expenditure during the year was £84,236. The treatment meted out to the insane is that dictated by the greatest humanity, and the hospitals are fitted with all conveniences and appliances which modern science points out as most calculated to mitigate or remove the affliction under which these unfortunates labour.

Aborigines Protection Board.

A Board is in existence for the protection of the Aborigines, the object of which is to ameliorate the condition of the blacks, and to exercise a general guardianship over them. There are also three mission stations for the benefit of the Aborigines. These are Cumeroogunga, on the River Murray; Warrangesda, on the Murrumbidgee; and Breewarrina, on the Darling. The mission stations are under the control of a society called the Aborigines' Protection Association, who are responsible to the Board for their administration. The natives at these settlements are comfortably housed, and are encouraged to devote their energies to agricultural and kindred occupations, and elementary education is imparted to the children. The State expenditure during 1890 by the Board, including medical expenses, &c., was £9,483, and by the Association, £3,139, making a total of £12,622, besides which there were private contributions amounting to £220. The Aborigines are referred to at length in the part dealing with population and vital statistics.

Public and private expenditure in charity.

The total expenditure of the State in connection with all forms of relief and in aid of hospitals and other charitable institutions amounted in 1890 to £244,058; adding to this the amount of private subscriptions, &c., the poor and the unfortunate have benefited during the year to the extent of about £335,000. This sum, though not excessive in proportion to the population, may yet appear large in view of the general wealth of the Colony, which should preclude the necessity of so many seeking assistance; for the present there is no risk that the charitable institutions will encourage the growth of the pauper element, and that free quarters and free food will be made so accessible that those who are disinclined to work will be tempted to live at the public expense.

Material and intellectual progress.

It will have been gathered from the foregoing pages that in its anxiety to foster material progress, the State has not overlooked the care of those whom old age or misfortune has afflicted, nor has that psychical progress been neglected without which material advancement would be incomplete. The solicitude manifested for the spread of education and enlightenment, and the impartial toleration meted out to all forms of belief, leave nothing in these respects to be desired.

Intellectual progress.

The intellectual progress of the people has been even more rapid than their material advancement. Nor has this progress been confined to those sciences which are necessary for ma prosperity. The State, conscious of the value of literatu softening the minds and manners of the people, encourages great liberality the establishment of libraries and reading-r In spite of their busy lives, the colonists of New South Wales done something towards increasing the general wealth of English literature, and with less stirring times—inevitable t building-up of a nation—and the existence of a leisured clas fruits of the care now lavished upon intellectual culture wi found in literature worthy of Australia.

Destiny of Australia.

More truly can it be said of the Australians than of any c people that their destiny is in their own hands. Their count most happily situated. Unlike most other lands it stand danger from no enemies upon its border, nor is it possible tha Government should ever engage in a struggle to subvert liberties of its people. Its colonization in these latter days au a future free from old world strifes and traditional hatreds, thus, happy in its situation and most fortunate in its wealt may await its future in calm confidence.

INDEX.

Sydney: George Stephen Chapman, Acting Government Printer.—1891.